W9-BUT-901

For Reference

Not to be taken from this room

Social
Issues
Primary
Sources
Collection

Human
and Civil Rights

Essential Primary Sources

Social
Issues
Primary
Sources
Collection

Human and Civil Rights

Essential Primary Sources

K. Lee Lerner, Brenda Wilmoth Lerner, and
Adrienne Wilmoth Lerner, Editors

Detroit • New York • San Francisco • New Haven, Conn. • Waterville, Maine • London • Munich

RENFRO LIBRARY
MARS HILL COLLEGE
MARS HILL, N.C. 28754
DISCARD

THOMSON

GALE
™

Human and Civil Rights: Essential Primary Sources

K. Lee Lerner, Brenda Wilmoth Lerner, and Adrienne Wilmoth Lerner, Editors

Project Editors
Dwayne D. Hayes and John McCoy

Editorial
Luann Brennan, Grant Eldridge, Anne Marie Hacht, Joshua Kondek, Andy Malonis, Mark Milne, Rebecca Parks, Mark Springer, Jennifer Stock

Permissions
Margaret Abendroth, Emma Hull, Jackie Jones

Imaging and Multimedia
Dean Dauphinais, Leitha Etheridge-Sims, Lezlie Light, Michael Logusz, Dan Newell, Christine O'Bryan, Kelly A. Quin, Denay Wilding, Robyn Young

Product Design
Pamela A. Galbreath

Composition and Electronic Capture
Evi Seoud

Manufacturing
Rita Wimberley

Product Manager
Carol Nagel

© 2006 by Thomson Gale, a part of The Thomson Corporation.

Thomson and Star Logo are trademarks and Gale is a registered trademark used herein under license.

For more information, contact
Thomson Gale
27500 Drake Rd.
Farmington Hills, MI 48331-3535
Or you can visit our Internet site at
http://www.gale.com

ALL RIGHTS RESERVED
No part of this work covered by the copyright herein may be reproduced or used in any form or by any means—graphic, electronic, or mechanical, including photocopying, recording, taping, Web distribution, or information storage retrieval systems—without the written permission of the publisher.

This publication is a creative work fully protected by all applicable copyright laws, as well as by misappropriation, trade secret, unfair competition, and other applicable laws. The authors and editors of this work have added value to the underlying factual material herein through one or more of the following: unique and original selection, coordination, expression, arrangement, and classification of the information.

For permission to use material from the product, submit your request via the Web at http://www.gale-edit.com/permissions, or you may download our Permissions Request form and submit your request by fax or mail to:

Permissions Department
Thomson Gale
27500 Drake Rd.
Farmington Hills, MI 48331-3535
Permissions Hotline:
248-699-8006 or 800-877-4253, ext. 8006
Fax 248-699-8074 or 800-762-4058

Cover photograph of Civil Rights March on Washington D.C., August 28, 1963 reproduced by permission. © Bettman/Corbis

Since this page cannot legibly accommodate all copyright notices, the acknowledgments constitute an extension of the copyright notice.

While every effort has been made to secure permission to reprint material and to ensure the reliability of the information presented in this publication, Thomson Gale neither guarantees the accuracy of the data contained herein nor assumes any responsibility for errors, omissions or discrepancies. Thomson Gale accepts no payment for listing; and inclusion in the publication of any organization, agency, institution, publication, service, or individual does not imply endorsement of the editors or publisher. Errors brought to the attention of the publisher and verified to the satisfaction of the publisher will be corrected in future editions.

LIBRARY OF CONGRESS CATALOGING-IN-PUBLICATION DATA

Human and civil rights : essential primary sources / K. Lee and Brenda Wilmoth Lerner, editors.
    p. cm. – (Social issues primary sources collection)
  Includes bibliographical references and index.
  ISBN 1-4144-0326-7 (hardcover : alk. paper)
  1. Civil rights–Sources. 2. Human rights–Sources. I. Lerner, K. Lee. II. Lerner, Brenda Wilmoth.

  JC571.H7626 2007
  323–dc22
                          2006020044

This title is also available as an e-book.
ISBN 1-4144-1262-2
Contact your Thomson Gale sales representative for ordering information.

Printed in the United States of America
10 9 8 7 6 5 4 3 2 1

R
323
H918L
2006

FEB 29 2008

Table of Contents

1   DEVELOPMENT OF HUMAN RIGHTS

2 SLAVERY AND GENOCIDE

3 IMPRISONMENT

4   HEALTH AND HOUSING

5   LABOR AND WORKING CONDITIONS

6 CIVIL AND POLITICAL RIGHTS

7   BORDERS, SOVEREIGNTY AND CULTURE

8 EDUCATION AND CHILDHOOD

Advisors and Contributors

While compiling this volume, the editors relied upon the expertise and contributions of the following scholars, journalists, and researchers who served as advisors and/or contributors for *Human and Civil Rights: Essential Primary Sources*:

Annessa Babic, Instructor and Ph.D. Candidate
SUNY at Stony Brook
Stony Brook, NY

Alicia Cafferty
University College
Dublin, Ireland

James Anthony Charles Corbett
Journalist
London, UK

Bryan Davies, J.D.
Ontario, Canada

Sandra Dunavan, M.S.
Saline, Michigan

Larry Gilman, Ph.D.
Sharon, Vermont

Amit Gupta, Ph.D.
Ahmedabad, India

Stacey N. Hannem
Journalist
Quebec, Canada

Alexander Ioffe, Ph.D.
Russian Academy of Sciences
Moscow, Russia

S. Layman, M.A.
Abingdon, MD

Adrienne Wilmoth Lerner (J.D. Candidate)
University of Tennessee College of Law
Knoxville, Tennessee

Pamela V. Michaels, M.A.
Forensic Psychologist
Santa Fe, New Mexico

Caryn Neumann, Ph.D.
Ohio State University
Columbus, Ohio

Mark Phillips, Ph.D.
Abilene Christian University
Abilene, Texas

Nephele Tempest
Los Angeles, California

Melanie Barton Zoltán, M.S.
Amherst, Massachusetts

Human and Civil Rights: Essential Primary Sources is the product of a global group of multi-lingual scholars, researchers, and writers. The editors are grateful to Christine Jeryan, Amy Loerch Strumolo, and Kate Kretschmann for their dedication and skill in copy-editing both text and translations. Their efforts added significant accuracy and readability to this book. The editors also wish to acknowledge and thank Adrienne Wilmoth Lerner and Alicia Cafferty for their tenacious research efforts.

The editors gratefully acknowledge and extend thanks to Peter Gareffa, Carol Nagel, and Ellen McGeagh at Thomson Gale for their faith in the project and for their sound content advice. Special thanks go to the Thomson Gale copyright research and imaging teams for their patience, good advice, and skilled research into sometimes vexing copyright issues. The editors offer profound thanks to project managers Dwayne Hayes and John McCoy. Their clear thoughts, insights and trusted editorial judgment added significantly to the quality of *Human and Civil Rights: Essential Primary Sources*.

Acknowledgements

Copyrighted excerpts in *Human and Civil Rights: Essential Primary Sources* were reproduced from the following periodicals:

Amnesty International, November 6, 1996, for "Nigeria. On the Anniversary of Ken Saro-Wiwa's Execution, Human Rights Organization's Call for Reform," AI Index: AFR 44/26/96. Available at http://web.amnesty.org/library/Index/ENGAFR4402 61996?open&of=ENG-NGA. © Amnesty International Publications, 1 Easton Street, London WC1X ODW, United Kingdom, http://www.amnesty.org. Reproduced by permission.—*Associated Press*, February 8, 2005. Copyright © 2005 Associated Press. All rights reserved. Reproduced by permission.—*Convention Against Torture and Other Cruel, Inhuman or Degrading Treatment or Punishment*, December 10, 1984. Office of the High Commissioner for Human Rights. Copyright © United Nations. The United Nations is the author of the original material. Reproduced by permission.—*The Economist*, December 3, 1998. Copyright © 1998 The Economist Newspaper Ltd. All rights reserved. Reprinted with permission. Further reproduction prohibited. www.economist.com—*The Final Act of the Conference on Security and Cooperation in Europe, August 1, 1975, 14 I.L.M. 1292 (Helsinki Declaration)*, August 1, 1975. Copyright © 1975 United Nations. The United Nations is the author of the original material. Reproduced by permission.—*Frontline*, December, 2003. Copyright © Frontline WGBH, Boston. All rights reserved. Reproduced by permission of WGBH Educational Foundation.—*Geneva Convention Relative to the Treatment of Prisoners of War*, United Nations, October 21, 1950. Copyright © United Nations. The United Nations is the author of the original material. Reproduced by permission.

Human Rights Watch, v. 17, October, 2004; December 16, 2004. © 2004 Human Rights Watch. All reproduced by permission.—*New York Sun*, January 31, 2006. Copyright © 2006 The New York Sun, One SL, LLC. All rights reserved. Reproduced by permission.—*The New York Times*, August 3, 2003. Copyright © 2003 by The New York Times Company. Reproduced by permission.—*New York Times*, January 24, 2001. Copyright © 2001 by The New York Times Company. Reproduced by permission.—*Protocol To Prevent, Suppress and Punish Trafficking in Persons, Especially Women and Children, Supplementing the United Nations Convention Against Transnational Organized Crime*, United Nations, 2000. Copyright © 2000 UNODC. The United Nation is the author of the original material. All rights reserved. Reproduced by permission.—*United Nations Convention on the Rights of the Child*, November 20, 1989. Copyright © United Nations. The United Nations is the author of the original material. Reproduced by permission.—*United Nations Rules for the Protection of Juveniles Deprived of Their Liberty*, G.A. res 45/113, annex, 45 U.N. GAOR Supp. (No 49A) at 205, U.N. Doc. A/45/49 (1990), 1990. Copyright © 1990 United Nations. The United Nations is the author of the original material. Reproduced by permission.—*The Washington Post*, September 8, 2003. Copyright © 2003, The Washington Post. Reprinted with permission.

Copyrighted excerpts in *Human and Civil Rights: Essential Primary Sources* were reproduced from the following books:

International Convention on the Protection of the Rights of All Migrant Workers and Members of Their Families, G.A. res. 45/158/annex, 45 U.N. GAOR

Supp. (No. 49A) at 262, U.N. Doc. A/45/49 (1990). United Nations, 2003. © 2003 United Nations. The United Nations is the author of the original material. Reproduced by permission.—From *Bringing Them Home: Report of the National Inquiry into the Separation of Aboriginal and Torres Strait Islander Children from Their Families.* Australian Human Rights 1997 Human Rights and Equal Opportunity Commission. Reproduced by permission.—From *Pocket World in Figures 2005.* The Economist/Profile Books, 2004. Copyright © The Economist Newspaper Ltd, 1991, 1992, 1993, 1994, 1995, 1996, 1997, 1998, 1999, 2000, 2001, 2002, 2003, 2004. Reproduced by permission.—From "Human Rights Abuses in Shahist Iran," in *Amnesty International Briefing: Iran.* Amnesty International, November 1976. Copyright © 1976 Amnesty International Publications, 1 Easton Street, London WC1X ODW, United Kingdom, http://www.amnesty.org. Reproduced by permission.—From "Attacks on Jews in Arab Countries," in *Major Knesset Debates: 1948-1981.* Edited by Netanel Lorch. Translated by Dorothea Vanson-Shefer. University Press of America, 1993. Copyright © 1993 by The Jerusalem Center for Public Affairs, University Press of America, Inc. All rights reserved. Reproduced by permission.—From "Statement by the AFL-CIO Executive Council on International Human Rights Conference, Bal Harbour, Florida, February 23, 1968," in *AFL-CIO Executive Council Statements and Reports, 1956-1975.* Edited by Gary M. Fink. Greenwood Press, 1977. All rights reserved. Reproduced by permission of Greenwood Publishing Group, Inc., Westport, CT.

From "Human Rights Charter," in *Major Knesset Debates: 1948-1981.* Edited by Netanel Lorch. Translated by Dorothea Vanson-Shefer. University Press of America, 1993. Copyright © 1993 by The Jerusalem Center for Public Affairs, University Press of America, Inc. All rights reserved. Reproduced by permission.—Chinese Human Rights Movement Committee, Beijing. From "Tiananmen Square Declaration of Human Rights," in *The Chinese Human Rights Reader: Documents and Commentary, 1900-2000.* Edited by Stephen C. Angle and Marina Svensson. Armonk, NY: M E Sharpe, 2002. Translation copyright © 2002 by M. E. Sharpe, Inc. All rights reserved. Not for reproduction. Used with permission of M.E. Sharpe, Inc.—Embassy of India. From *The Human Rights Crisis in Kashmir: A Pattern of Impunity.* Human Rights Watch, 1993. Copyright © June 1993 by Human Rights Watch and Physicians for Human Rights. All rights reserved. Reproduced by permission.—Zhinazi (Pseudonym). From "The People's Legal Right to Freedom (1903)," in *The Chinese*

Human Rights Reader: Documents and Commentary, 1900-2000. Edited by Stephen C. Angle and Marina Svensson. M. E. Sharpe, 2001. Armonk, NY: ME: Sharpe, 2002. Translation copyright © 2002 by M. E. Sharpe, Inc. All rights reserved. Not for reproduction. Used with permission of M.E. Sharpe, Inc.—Bradshaw, Robert. From *The Fugitive Years: The True Story of a Compulsive Gambler.* Penguin Books Ltd., 1986. Copyright © Robert Bradshaw, 1986. All rights reserved. Reproduced by permission of Penguin Books Ltd.—Bradshaw, Robert. From *The Fugitive Years: The True Story of a Compulsive Gambler.* Penguin Books, 1986. Copyright © Robert Bradshaw, 1986. All rights reserved. Reproduced by permission of Penguin Books Ltd.—de Weydenthal, J. B. From *RAD Background Report/291 (Poland).* Radio Free Europe/Radio Liberty, 1981. Copyright © 1981, RFE/RL, Inc.. Reprinted with the permission of Radio Free Europe/Radio Liberty, 1201 Connecticut Ave., N.W. Washington DC 20036. www.rferl.org.

El-Saadawi, Nawal. From "A Passion for Solitude," in *Memoirs from the Women's Prison.* Translated from the Arabic by Marilyn Booth. Women's Press, 1986. Copyright © 1986. Reproduced by permission.—Gandhi, Mahatma. From *Speeches and Writings of Mahatma Gandhi.* G. A. Natesan & Co., Madras, 1933. Reproduced by permission of the author's estate.—Garton-Ash, Timothy. From *Granta (Gazza Agonistes).* Granta, 1993. Reproduced by permission of the author.—From a speech, "I Have a Dream," by Rev. Dr. Martin Luther King, Jr., 1963. Copyright © 1963 by Martin Luther King Jr., copyright renewed 1991 Coretta Scott King. Reprinted by arrangement with the Estate of Martin Luther King, Jr., c/o Writers House as agent for the proprietor New York, NY.—Koh, Harold Hongju. From *Economist.* 2003. Copyright © 2003 The Economist Newspaper Ltd. All rights reserved. Reprinted with permission. Further reproduction prohibited. www.economist.com—Lizhi, Fang. From "Open Letter to Deng Xiaoping," in *The Chinese Human Rights Reader: Documents and Commentary, 1900-2000.* Edited by Stephen C. Angle and Marina Svensson. Armonk, NY: M. E. Sharpe, 2002. Translation copyright © 2002 by M. E. Sharpe, Inc. All rights reserved. Not for reproduction. Used with permission of M.E. Sharpe, Inc.—Mandela, Nelson. From *Nelson Mandela: The Struggle in My Life.* International Defense and Aid Fund for Southern Africa, 1978. Reproduced by permission.

Millay, Edna St. Vincent. From "Conscientious Objector," in *Collected Poems.* Harper Solzhenitsyn, Aleksandr. From *The Nobel Lecture on Literature.* Translated from the Russian by Thomas P. Whitney. Harper 1972 by the Nobel Foundation. English translation copyright © 1972 by Thomas P. Whitney. Reprinted by permission of HarperCollins Publishers.—Solzhenitsyn, Alexander. From *One Day in the Life of Ivan Denisovich.* Translated from the Russian by Ralph Parker. E. P. Dutton 1963 by E. P. Dutton 1991 by Penguin USA and Victor Gallancz, Ltd. In the U.S. reproduced by permission of Dutton, a division of Penguin Group (USA), Inc. In the U.K. reproduced by permission of Victor Gollancz, Ltd.—Tambo, Oliver Reginald. From "Appeal for Action to Stop Repression and Trial in South Africa," in *Apartheid and the International Community.* Edited by E.S. Reddy. Namedia Foundation, Sterling Publishers Private Limited, 1991. Reproduced by permission of the editor.—Tvardovsky, Alexander. From an English translation of the poem "By Right of Memory," in *Gulag: A History.* Translated by Anne Applebaum. Doubleday, 2003. Copyright © 2003 by Anne Applebaum, Inc. Used by permission of Doubleday, a division of Random House, Inc and Georges Borchardt, Inc., on behalf of the author. In the United Kingdom by Penguin Group.—Vanzetti, Bartolomeo. From "Bartolomeo Vanzetti Bids Farwell to Dante Sacco on the Eve of His Execution" in *The Letters of Sacco and Vanzetti.* The Viking Press, 1928. Copyright 1928, renewed 1955 by The Viking Press, Inc. Used by permission of Viking Penguin, a division of Penguin Group (USA) Inc.

Photographs and illustrations appearing in *Human and Civil Rights: Essential Primary Sources* were received from the following sources:

A barefoot gypsy child stands amid garbage near a gypsy camp, photograph. AP Images.—A British Passport Office volunteer has his fingerprints scanned, photograph. © Peter MacDiarmid/Reuters/Corbis.—A cell of the old prison of the Pierre-and-Paul fortress 1991, photograph. Photo by Lipnitzki/Roger Viollet/Getty Images.—A courtyard in Theresienstadt, photograph. © Corbis.—A crew of undocumented migrant farm workers, photograph. © Andrew Lichtenstein/Corbis.—A detainee being guided by two US Army MPs at Camp X-Ray in Guantanamo Bay, Cuba, photograph. Peter Muhly/AFP/Getty Images.—A detainee spends time outside his cell at Camp Delta Four in the Guantanamo Bay Naval Station, Cuba, photograph. AP Images.—A draft of President Franklin D. Roosevelt's message to Congress in 1941, photograph. Photo by Herbert Orth//Time Life Pictures/Getty Images.—A Fort Myer Elementary School classroom on September 8, 1954, the day it was desegregated, photograph. © Bettmann/Corbis.—A fourteen-year-old girl working as a spool tender in a Massachusetts cotton mill, photograph. AP Images.—A group of Black protesters during funerals for victims of police repression, photograph. © Bernard Bisson/Corbis SYGMA.—A group of Israeli soldiers reverently take their first look at the Jewish religion's holiest place, the Wailing Wall, photograph. AP Images.—A group of young Afghan girls doing schoolwork in Heart, Afghanistan, November 23, 2001, photograph. © Jacques Langevin/Sygma/Corbis.—A handbill offering a reward for the return of a runaway slave, photograph. © Louie Psihoyos/Corbis.—A Kenyan slum dweller walks on the side of a road, photograph. © Reuters/Corbis.—A little Japanese boy is awaiting the return of his parents, photograph. AP Images.—A man buying theater tickets at a segregated ticket counter, photograph. © Eudora Welty/Corbis.—A man crouches on the ground holding his head in his hands, in front of a crumbling brick building, photograph. © Smailes Alex/Corbis Sygma.

A man looks at the front page of the British tabloid newspaper *The Sun*, carrying a photo showing former Iraqi president Saddam Hussein, photograph. AP Images.—A man protesting China's occupation of Tibet protests in the streets of Paris while holding a Tibetan flag in front of his body, photograph. © J. L. Bulcao/Corbis.—A man walks past an illuminated panel bearing the words of the Universal declaration of Human Rights, photograph. Adrian Dennis/AFP/Getty Images.—A member of a Kremlin-backed youth group called Nashi (Ours) hands out leaflets standing in front of a replica of a Holocaust period Jewish room, photograph. Denis Sinyakov/AFP/Getty Images.—A member of Amnesty International displays a photo of Chinese prisoner of conscience Gao Yu, photograph. Robyn Beck/AFP/Getty Images.—A mob of Iranian demonstrators riots outside of a Beverly Hills, California home, photograph. © Bettmann/Corbis.—A modern Chinese family, photograph. © Liu Liqun/Corbis.—A Pakistani woman holds a placard carrying names of honor killing victims at a rally on Friday, October 8, 2004 in Islamabad, Pakistan, photograph. AP Images—A poem in the Ladies Department of the anti-slavery newspaper *The Liberator*, published by William Lloyd Garrison, photograph. © Bettmann/Corbis.—A poster displayed at the UN Human Rights Conference, photograph. © Vienna Report Agency/Sygma/Corbis—A scene from the Cite Soleil slum and shantytown northwest of Haiti's capital, Port-au-Prince, photograph. © Les Stone/ZUMA/Corbis.—A Slavey Dene woman hangs white fish on wooden beams, photograph. Photo by Raymond K Gehman/National Geographic/Getty Images.—A teenage Kurdish girl stoops as she harvests cotton by hand, photograph. © Reza Webistan/

Corbis.—A Third Liberty Loan Poster by Laurence Harris, photograph. © Swim Ink 2, LLC/Corbis.—A train conductor signaling from the 'Jim Crow' coach, reserved for African Americans, photograph. © Corbis.

A view of photographer Oliviero Toscani's work, photograph. Photo by Gareth Cattermole/Getty Images.—A woman carrying her dying child cries out for help at the Red Cross feeding center, photograph. © Andrew Holbrooke/Corbis.—A worker looks at the camera while he uses a piece of cloth to protect his nose from dust, while his coworkers are seen sewing different parts of t-shirts for the clothing line of Sean P Diddy Combs, Sean John, at the Setisa, photograph. AP Images—A World War I poster "For Every Fighter a Woman Worker" by Adolph Triedler, photograph. © K J Historical/Corbis.—A young girl bonded laborer working in a slate mine in Mandsaur, India, photograph. © Sophie Elbaz/Sygma/Corbis.—A young girl migrant farm worker, photograph. © Bettmann/Corbis.—A young Sudanese refugee cries for his mother at a camp, photograph. © Stephen Morrison/epa/Corbis.—Abernathy, Ralph, Bishop Julian Smith, and Dr. Martin Luther King, Jr., photograph. AP Images.—About 20 people from the Students for a Free Tibet, including Rebecca Nelson, gather in front of Google Inc., photograph. AP Images.—Aerial view of the central prison in Belgrade, photograph. AP Images.—Afghan women approach a voting station, photograph. © Teru Kuwayama/Corbis.—African Americans vote for the first time in Alabama after enactment of the Voting Rights Act, 1966, photograph. © Flip Schulke/Corbis.—American prisoners of war who died during the infamous Bataan Death March are lined up on the ground in the Philippines in April 1942 during World War II, photograph. AP Images.—An 1837 woodcut used to illustrate a broadside of John Greenleaf Whittier's anti-slavery poem "Our Countrymen in Chains," photograph. The Library of Congress—An Australian Aborigine wearing a headpiece and face paint, in Alice Springs, Australia, circa 1930, photograph. © EO Hoppe/Corbis.—An editorial cartoon from Harpers Weekly, May 8, 1875 with the title "No Church Need Apply," photograph. Provided courtesy of HarpWeek.—An eight-year-old child soldier from Chad takes a break to smoke a cigarette, photograph. © Reuters/Corbis.—An emaciated, clearly starving Sudanese boy cries inside a compound run by Doctors Without Borders, photograph. AP Images.—An estimated 5,000 people march outside the Minnesota Capitol Building in protest to the January 22, 1973 Supreme Court ruling on abortion as a result of the Roe vs. Wade case, photograph. AP

Images.—An illustration depicting former runaway slaves, photograph. © Bettmann/Corbis.—An illustration in Harpers Weekly shows disabled women being taught crafts in a class in England circa 1871, photograph. © Corbis.

An illustration of a woman being hanged, during the nineteenth century, original caption The Execution of Mrs. Hibbins, photograph. © Bettmann/Corbis.—An Indian woman collects water from the local well, photograph. © Reuters/Corbis.—Bataan Death March, photograph. © Corbis.—Berkenwald, Ben, photograph. AP Images.—Bodies of dead civilians lie among mangled bicycles, photograph. AP Images.—Bolton, Todd and George Rutherford, photograph. AP Images.—Brooks, Rose and Jesse Meadows, photograph. AP Images.—Cadets at the Negro Training Center examine a map before taking off in a biplane for a training exercise, photograph. © Bettmann/Corbis.—Chinese man hanging from branch labeled "Freedom to All," photograph. Hulton Getty/Liaison Agency.—Clash between young African-Americans and Ku Klux Klan members in Miami after the murder of a 20-year-old, photograph. © J. L. Atlan/Sygma/Corbis.—Close-up shot of a jail cell door, photograph. © H Armstrong Roberts/Corbis.—Coffin, William S., Dr. David E. Swift, and Dr. John D. Maguire, Freedom Riders, photograph by Perry Aycock. AP Images.—Copper slave tags, photograph. © Louie Psihoyos/Corbis.—Copy of the Bill of Rights, 1789, print. National Archives and Records Administration.—Declaration of the Rights of Man and Citizen painting by Jean Jacques Francois LeBarbier, photograph. © The Art Archive/Corbis.—Demonstrators in Trafalgar Square, photograph. © Hulton-Deutsch Collection/Corbis.—Detainee's hold onto a fence at Camp 4 of the maximum security prison Camp Delta at Guantanamo Naval Base, photograph. Mark Wilson/AFP/Getty Images.—Disabled activists on Capitol Hill, photograph. Photo by Terry Ashe/Time Life Pictures/Getty Images.—Display of Red Literature, photograph. © Bettmann/Corbis.—Dreyfus disgraced on cover of Let Petit Journal, photograph. © Leonard de Selva/Corbis.

Du Bois, W.E.B., photograph. Fisk University Library. Reproduced by permission.—Eckford, Elizabeth, an African American teenager, walks towards Central High School in Little Rock, Arkansas, on September 4, 1957, photograph. © Bettmann/Corbis.—Emancipation Proclamation, painting by A. A. Lamb. © A. A. Lamb/Francis G. Mayer/Corbis.—Engraving depicting the United States Slave Trade 1830, photograph. © Corbis.—Engraving of an anti-slavery public meeting, photograph. © Corbis.—Ford, Gerald signs the Final Act of the Conference on Security and Cooperation in Europe, photograph. © Corbis.—Four Indonesian children play on a jungle gym in Jakarta a park, photograph. © Bagus Indahonoepa/Corbis.—Freed slaves waiting for work opportunities, photograph. U.S. Signal Corps, National Archives and Records Administration.—Gandhi, Mahatma, with his two granddaughters Ava and Manu, photograph. © Bettmann/Corbis.—Goddess of Democracy stands before portrait of Mao Zedong in Tiananmen Square, photograph. © Peter Turnley/Corbis.—Gourley, Christi, photograph. AP Images.—Haden, Ablavi, photograph. AP Images.—Hasan, Xaawo Mohammed lies with her newborn in a hospital in Baidoa, Somalia, photograph. © David Turnley/Corbis.—Holy Cross' first two women Air Force ROTC students stand at attention with fellow cadets, photograph. © Bettmann/Corbis.—Honecker, Erich, photograph. AP Images.—Human rights activists sprawl on the main road to the parliament building in Beirut, photograph. © Jamal Saidi/Reuters/Corbis.—Hundreds of people gather around a huge well in Natwarghad, photograph. © Reuters/Corbis.—I'm Counting on You! poster by Leon Helguera, photograph. © K J Historical/Corbis.—Illustration of Don Juan Seducing a Woman, photograph. © Bettmann/Corbis.—Indian female Dalit, photograph. Indranil Mukherjee/AFP/Getty Images.—Insignia of the AFL-CIO, photograph. © Bettmann/Corbis.—Israeli soldiers round up Egyptian prisoners in the area of the Gaza-El Arish crossroad, photograph. AP Images.

Jean, Faubert, a Haitian migrant worker, photograph. © Gideon Mendel/Corbis.—Johnson, Mark and his partner Shaun Johnson cut their wedding cake, photograph. © Colin McPherson/Corbis.—Keller, Helen, reads with her teacher, Anne Sullivan Macy, photograph. © Corbis.—King, Dr. Martin Luther, Jr. (speaking before bank of microphones), Washington D. C., 1963, photograph. © UPI/Corbis-Bettmann.—Kosovar Albanians bury the Seventy-five victims of a massacre, photograph. © Patrick Robert/Sygma/Corbis.—Lama, Dalai meditates while listening to a speech, photograph. © Jayanta Shaw/Reuters/Corbis.—Levi, Primo, photograph. © Gianni Giansanti/Sygma/Corbis.—Li, Yi, photograph. AP Images.—Mandela, Nelson, photograph. © David Turnley/Corbis.—Members of CORE (Committee on Racial Equality) picketing the home of a landlord, photograph. Photo by Herb Scharfman/Time Life Pictures/Getty Images.—Members of the National Association for the Advancement of Colored People picket under the

marquee of the Republic Movie Theatre against race discrimination featured in the movie, The Birth of a Nation, photograph. © Corbis.—Menchu, Rigoberta, photograph. © Reuters/Corbis.—Millay, Edna St. Vincent, photograph. The Library of Congress.—Milosevic, Slobodan, photograph. © Bas Czerwinski/Pool/Reuters/Corbis.—More than 150 children in Trafalgar Square protest teacher dismissal, photograph. © Hulton-Deutsch Collection/Corbis.—Mornod, Jan, photograph. © Sophie Elbaz/Sygma/Corbis.—Mourners surround the coffin of black leader Steve Biko, photograph. AP Images.—Muslim women demonstrate against the French proposal to bar Muslim women from wearing headscarves, photograph. Photo by Pascal Le Segretain/Getty Images.—National Guardsmen called out to quell race riots in Chicago, photograph. Photo by Jun Fujita/Getty Images.—New York City sweat shop full of female workers, interior. © Bettmann/Corbis.—Osburn, C Dixon, photograph. AP Images.—Palestinian Peoples Party activist burn an effigy, photograph. AP Images.—Pamuk, Orhan, photograph by Sophie Bassouls. © Corbis.—Parks, Rosa (riding in front of bus), photograph. © Bettmann/Corbis.—Parks, Rosa, being fingerprinted by police officer, Montgomery, Alabama, photograph. AP Images.—Paul, Alice, photograph. © Bettmann/Corbis.—Pax Sovietica Polish Solidarity Movement Poster, photograph. © Stapleton Collection/Corbis.—People marching in Melbourne, Australia, carrying wreaths in the form of the female symbol, photograph. © Nik Wheeler/Corbis.—People stand beside a portrait of late comfort woman Kim Hak-Sun, photograph. Toru Yamanaka/AFP/Getty Images.

People supporting NATO military operations in the Balkans demonstrate, photograph. Hector Mata/AFP/Getty Images.—Perm 35, the last Russian gulag, prisoners outside in a fenced yard, photograph. © P. Perrin/Corbis Sygma.—Photo of a traditional 1950s family meal, photograph. Photo by George Marx/Retrofile/Getty Images.—Police use tear gas and a water cannon to disperse a demonstration by some 1650 priests, nuns and pacifists protesting against the use of torture by Chile's Secret Police force, photograph. © Bettmann/Corbis.—Portrait of American abolitionist and writer Frederick Douglass, photograph. © Bettmann/Corbis.—Portrait of John Quincy Adams, photograph. © Bettmann/Corbis.—Poster depicts a mother and baby during China's "one-child family" policy to encourage small families and prevent over-population, photograph. © Owen Franken/Corbis.—Poster for D.W. Griffith's The Birth of a Nation, illustration. The Library of Congress.—President Kennedy, handing out pens during ceremony at which he signed bill to assure women of paychecks equal to those of men doing the same work, photograph. © Bettmann/Corbis.—Protesters in central London burn a mock-up of an identity card of Prime Minister Tony Blair, photograph. AP Images.—Protesters on the Berlin Wall near the Brandenburg Gate, photograph. © Robert Maass/Corbis.—Protestors look on as a man pulls up his shirt to show the camera scars on his back he received from torture at the hands of General Augusto Pinochet's Chilean government, Santiago, Chile, circa 1983, photograph. © Greg Smith/Corbis.—Qualls, David and Jules Lobel, photograph. AP Images.—Refugees fleeing from Rwanda's civil war pass corpses lying by the side of a road, photograph. © David Turnley/Corbis.—Remains of a Gulag prison camp, photograph. © Staffan Widstrand/Corbis.—Roman Catholic mission school, photograph. Photo by Art Rickerby/Time Life Pictures/Getty Images.—Roosevelt, Eleanor, photograph. Photo by Jean Manzon/Stringer/Time Life Pictures/Getty Images.—Russian guard searching prisoner, photograph. © David Turnley/Corbis.—Saadawi, Nawal with her husband Sherif Hetata, photograph. © Reuters/Corbis.—Sanitation workers strike, Memphis, Tennessee, 1968, photograph. © Bettmann/Corbis.

Saro-Wiwa, Ken, photograph. Reuters/Archive Photos, Inc.—Scene from D. W. Griffiths 1914 movie *Birth of a Nation*, photograph. AP Images.—Shahzaidi, Nayyar, photograph. © Lynsey Addario/Corbis.—Shaw, Herman, photograph. AP Images.—Sitting Bull with his family, Fort Randall, 1852, photograph. The Granger Collection, New York.—Skulls are seen in Phnom Penh, Cambodia, photograph. AP Images.—Slaves in chains on the island of Zanzibar, off the cost of east Africa, in the nineteenth century; nine black men and boys are standing in a street, wearing metal collars connected to each other by chains, photograph. © Bojan Brecelj/Corbis.—Solzhenitsyn, Alexander, photograph. © Bettmann/Corbis.—Somalians load the bodies of people who died from living in a famine-stricken village, photograph. © David Turnley/Corbis.—St. Patrick's Cathedral at Fifth Avenue between 50th and 51st streets, New York City, circa 1880, photograph. © Corbis.—Supporters of woman's liberation hold banners and stand in front of a sea wall at the Statue of Liberty, photograph. © Bettmann/Corbis.—Teacher directs a special education class for disabled children, photograph. © Richard Nowitz/Corbis.—Ten inmates freed from Illinois death row, photograph. AP Images.—The bodies of people killed by street violence in Bogotá, Colombia, photograph. Photo by Piero Pomponi/Getty Images.—"The Crisis, A Record of the Darker Races," edited by W.E.B. DuBois, cover for November 1910, print.—The fourteenth Dalai Lama as a young boy, photograph. © Bettmann/Corbis.—The inside of a Manhattan ferry boat is jammed with commuters on May 11, 1953, photograph. © Bettmann/Corbis.—The main entrance to Wormwood Scrubs prison in London, photograph. Photo by F. Brooks/Fox Photos/Getty Images.—The title page of a report titled "Negro Slavery, No Evil or The North and the South" published in 1854, photograph. © Corbis.—The Wormwood Scrubs prison in London, photograph. Photo by Dennis Oulds/Central Press/Getty Images.—Third grade student, Adela, right, talks with fifth grader Sanita, photograph. AP Images.—Three Chinese women employed at a Reebok factory in Zongshan, China, 1996. They are wearing face masks and are brushing glue onto sports shoes, photograph. © Michael S Yamashita/Corbis.

Three demonstrators join hands to build strength against the force of water sprayed by riot police in Birmingham, Alabama, during a protest of segregation practices, photograph. © Bettmann/Corbis.—Three police officers in camouflage uniforms dragging an anti-apartheid protestor at a demonstration, photograph. © William Campbell/Sygma/Corbis.—Travelers wait in line to be screened by security personnel at Hartsfield-Jackson Atlanta International Airport, photograph. AP Images.—Trnopolje Detention Camp, (starving Muslim), 1992, Banjaluka, Bosnia-Herzegovina, photograph. AP Images.—Two white employees of a downtown cafe in Nashville, Tennessee, form a human barricade, photograph. AP Images.—Undated composite picture shows people tortured in Iraqi prisons, photograph. © Association of Muslim Scholars in Iraq/Handout/Reuters/Corbis.—Undated photo of a Soviet prison labor site, photograph. AP Images.—Unidentified pathologist and archaeologist examine human remains found in a mass grave near Samawa in the Muthanna Province, photograph. AP Images.—Victims of the Triangle Shirtwaist Company Fire, photograph. © Bettmann/Corbis.—Villagers grieve over the bodies of family members massacred at Vermachak village in Jehanabad district of central Bihar, India in this December 18, 2000 photo, photograph. AP Images.—Washington D.C.'s Black community celebrating the passage of the Thirteenth Amendment, photograph. Photo by MPI/Stringer/Getty Images.—Wiesel, Elie (with fellow inmates, Buchenwald, Germany), photograph. National Archives and Records Administration.—Workers at a Ford plant in River Rouge, Michigan voting, photograph. Photo by

MPI/Getty Images.—Yersin, Isabelle, an MSF (Doctors Without Boarders) medic, helps a potential cholera-victim, Domingo Mucato- busi, photograph. © Corbis.—Young children weave carpets at a Katmandu factory, photograph. © Alison Wright/Corbis.—Young prostitutes stand on a dusty street in the gold mining town of Curionopolis, Brazil, photograph. © Stephanie Maze/Corbis.—Young women in front of a primary school in Acarlar, photograph. AP Images.

Copyrighted excerpts in *Human and Civil Rights: Essential Primary Sources* were reproduced from the following websites or other sources:

"3068 (XXVIII) International Convention on the Suppression and Punishment of the Crime of Apartheid," in *Resolutions Adopted on the Reports of the Third Committee*, United Nations, November 30, 1973. Copyright © 1973 United Nations. The United Nations is the author of the original material. Reproduced by permission.—"Act for the relief of the parents of Theresa Marie Schiavo," *Findlaw*, March 20, 2005. Copyright © 2005 Findlaw, a Thomson business. This Column Originally appeared On Findlaw.com. Reproduced by permission.—*Amnesty International Canada*, October 4, 2004, for "Canada: Stolen Sisters: A Human Rights Response to Discrimination and Violence Against Indigenous Women in Canada," *Indigenous Peoples, AI Index: AMR 20/003/2004*, Available at http://web.amnesty.org/library/index/engamr200032004. © 2004 Amnesty International Publications, 1 Easton Street, London WC1X ODW, United Kingdom, http://www.amnesty.org. Reproduced by permission.—CBS News Online Staff, "Chirac Calls for Ban on Headscarves," *CBC.CA News*, December 17, 2003. Copyright © 2004 Canadian Broadcasting Corporation. All rights reserved. Reproduced by permission.

"Commission on Human Rights," *Documents E/56/Rev. 1 and Document E/84, Paragraph 4, Both as Amended by the Council*, United Nations, June 21, 1946. Copyright © United Nations. The United Nations is the author of the original material. Reproduced by permission.—"EU Policy on the Death Penalty (11249/03 Presse 204) P 83/03," *European Union, The Council*, Brussels, July 14, 2003. Reproduced by permission.—"Framework Convention for the Protection of National Minorities," H(1995)010, *Council of Europe*, Strasbourg, February, 1995. Copyright © Council of Europe 1995. Reproduced by permission.—Joelle Tanguy, "Responding to Complex Humanitarian Crises and Massive Abuses of Human Rights: Reflections On the Legal, Political and Humanitarian Framework," *Speeches & Open Letters*, September 16,

1998. Reproduced by permission of the author.—Larry Siems, "PEN Protests Charges Against Turkish Author Orhan Pamuk," Press Release, www.pen.org, September 2, 2005. Copyright © Pen American Center. All rights reserved. Reproduced by permission.—"Milosevic case Information Sheet (IT-02-54) 'Bosnia and Herzegovina.'" United Nations, April 5, 2005. The United Nations is the author of the original material. Reproduced by permission.—Paul D. Amato, "Benetton Produces, 'We, On Death Row,'" www.nodeathpenalty.org, February, 2000. Reproduced by permission.—"Preamble and Recommendation," Resolution on the Prohibition of Access of Women to Health Care and the Prohibition of Practice by Female Doctors in Afghanistan (1997), World Medical Association, 49th WMA General Assembly, November, 1997. Copyright © World Medical Association. Reproduced by permission.

"Question Of Detainees in US Naval Base in Guantanamo," *E/CN.4/2005/L.94, United Nations, Commission on Human Rights, Sixty-First Session*, April 14, 2005. Copyright © United Nations. The United Nations is the author of the original material. Reproduced by permission.—"Resolution 242," in *United Nations 1382nd Meeting*, November 22, 1967. Copyright © United Nations. The United Nations is the author of the original material. Reproduced by permission.—Rigoberta Menchu Tum, "Acceptance and Nobel Lecture (translation)," December 10, 1992. The Nobel Prize.org, 1992. Copyright © The Nobel Foundation 1992. Reproduced by permission.—"Saudi Arabia, Information Transmitted to the Government and Replies Received," *E/CN.4/1996/35Add.1*, United Nations, January 16, 1996. Copyright © United Nations. The United Nations is the author of the original material. Reproduced by permission.—*The Guardian*, October 25, 2005. Copyright © Guardian Unlimited and Guardian Newspapers Limited, 2005. Reproduced by permission of Guardian News Service, LTD.—"The Menace that wasn't," *Economist.com*, November 11, 2004. Copyright © 2005 The Economist Newspaper and The Economist Group. All rights reserved. Further reproduction prohibited. www.economist.com—"UN Report on Torture and Other Cruel, Inhuman or Degrading Treatment or Punishment," *E/CN.4/1996/35*, United Nations, January 9, 1996. Copyright © 1996 United Nations. The United Nations is the author of the original material. Reproduced by permission.—"Universal Declaration of Human Rights," in *General Assembly of the United Nations, Resolution 217 A (III)*, December 10, 1948. Copyright © 1948 United Nations. The United

Nations is the author of the original material. Reproduced by permission.—Valli Ollendorff, "Fate Did Not Let Me Go (letter)," *www.fatedidnotletmego.org.* August 24, 1942. Copyright © Ollendorff Center for Religious and Human Understanding. All Rights Reserved. Reproduced by permission.—World Medical Association, "World Medical Association Declaration of Helsinki Ethical Principles for Medical Research Involving Human Subjects," *WMA General Assembly Policy,* June, 1964. Reproduced by permission.

About the Set

Essential Primary Source titles are part of a ten-volume set of books in the Social Issues Primary Sources Collection designed to provide primary source documents on leading social issues of the nineteenth, twentieth, and twenty-first centuries. International in scope, each volume is devoted to one topic and contains approximately 150 to 175 documents that will include and discuss speeches, legislation, magazine and newspaper articles, memoirs, letters, interviews, novels, essays, songs, and works of art essential to understanding the complexity of the topic.

Each entry will include standard subheads: key facts about the author; an introduction placing the piece in context; the full or excerpted document; a discussion of the significance of the document and related event; and a listing of further resources (books, periodicals, Web sites, and audio and visual media).

Each volume will contain a topic-specific introduction, topic-specific chronology of major events, an index especially prepared to coordinate with the volume topic, and approximately 150 images.

Volumes are intended to be sold individually or as a set.

THE ESSENTIAL PRIMARY SOURCE SERIES

- Terrorism: Essential Primary Sources
- Medicine, Health, and Bioethics: Essential Primary Sources
- Environmental Issues: Essential Primary Sources
- Crime and Punishment: Essential Primary Sources
- Gender Issues and Sexuality: Essential Primary Sources
- Human and Civil Rights: Essential Primary Sources
- Government, Politics, and Protest: Essential Primary Sources
- Social Policy: Essential Primary Sources
- Immigration and Multiculturalism: Essential Primary Sources
- Family in Society: Essential Primary Sources

Introduction

Human and Civil Rights: Essential Primary Sources provides insight into over two centuries of struggle for human and civil rights and the issues that struggle engenders.

Human rights are universal guarantees of security of person and freedom of conscience for all individuals regardless of nationality, ethnicity, race, religion, or gender. The preamble of the United Nations Universal Declaration of Human Rights of 1948 states: "...recognition of the inherent dignity and of the equal and inalienable rights of all members of the human family is the foundation of freedom, justice and peace in the world... disregard and contempt for human rights have resulted in barbarous acts which have outraged the conscience of mankind, and the advent of a world in which human beings shall enjoy freedom of speech and belief and freedom from fear and want has been proclaimed as the highest aspiration of the common people..."

The resources in *Human and Civil Rights: Essential Primary Sources* provide evidence to support the assertions of the U.N. Declaration and in doing so represent rights as natural rights (e.g. those of life, liberty, pursuit of property) and as expressions of the highest democratic ideals of equality, justice, and political and religious liberty. The resources also provide insight into emerging concepts of rights as related to security and privacy in times of both war and peace.

Universal rights should, by definition, embrace all of humanity and transcend borders and political systems. Alas, they are often subverted or repressed by culture or governments. Accordingly, the primary sources contained in *Human and Civil Rights: Essential Primary Sources* provide a global perspective regarding both success and failure in human and civil rights movements. Although it is beyond the scope of this collection to cover all rights issues, and all facets of those issues, *Human and Civil Rights: Essential Primary Sources* provides a wide-ranging and readable collection of sources designed to stimulate interest and critical thinking, and to highlight the complexity of rights related issues.

The editors sincerely hope that this book helps to foster respect for both the human and civil rights that advance civilization and that ennoble humankind. Moreover, the editors intend that readers gain from the sources and commentary offered an appreciation that the struggle for human and civil rights is an unfinished work in progress.

K. Lee Lerner, Brenda Wilmoth Lerner, & Adrienne Wilmoth Lerner, editors
Paris, France and London, U.K.
June, 2006

About the Entry

The primary source is the centerpiece and main focus of each entry in *Human and Civil Rights: Essential Primary Sources*. In keeping with the philosophy that much of the benefit from using primary sources derives from the reader's own process of inquiry, the contextual material surrounding each entry provides access and ease of use, as well as giving the reader a springboard for delving into the primary source. Rubrics identify each section and enable the reader to navigate entries with ease.

ENTRY STRUCTURE

- Primary Source/Entry Title, Subtitle, Primary Source Type
- Key Facts—essential information about the primary source, including creator, date, source citation, and notes about the creator.
- Introduction—historical background and contributing factors for the primary source.
- Primary Source—in text, text facsimile, or image format; full or excerpted.
- Significance—importance and impact of the primary source related events.
- Further Resources—books, periodicals, websites, and audio and visual material.

NAVIGATING AN ENTRY

Entry elements are numbered and reproduced here, with an explanation of the data contained in these elements explained immediately thereafter according to the corresponding numeral.

Primary Source/Entry Title, Subtitle, Primary Source Type

[1] **Secretary of State's Morning Summary for June 5 and 6, 1989**

[2] For June 5 and 6, 1989

[3] **Government record**

[1] **Primary Source/Entry Title:** The entry title is usually the primary source title. In some cases where long titles must be shortened, or more generalized topic titles are needed for clarity primary source titles are generally depicted as subtitles. Entry titles appear as catchwords at the top outer margin of each page.

[2] **Subtitle:** Some entries contain subtitles.

[3] **Primary Source Type:** The type of primary source is listed just below the title. When assigning source types, great weight was given to how the author of the primary source categorized the source.

Key Facts

[4] **Author:** James A. Baker, III

[5] **Date:** June 5–6, 1989

[6] **Source:** Baker, James. "Secretary of State's Morning Summary for June, 1989" and "Secretary of State's Morning Summary for June 6, 1989." Department of State. Washington, D.C., 1989.

[7] **About the Author:** Texan-born James A. Baker III served as Secretary of State from January 1989 to August 1992 under President George H.W. Bush.

Baker now serves as Chair of the James A. Baker III Institute of Public Policy at Rice University in Houston, Texas.

[4]   **Author, Artist, or Organization:** The name of the author, artist, or organization responsible for the creation of the primary source begins the Key Facts section.

[5]   **Date of Origin:** The date of origin of the primary source appears in this field, and may differ from the date of publication in the source citation below it; for example, speeches are often delivered before they are published.

[6]   **Source Citation:** The source citation is a full bibliographic citation, giving original publication data as well as reprint and/or online availability.

[7]   **About the Author:** A brief bio of the author or originator of the primary source gives birth and death dates and a quick overview of the person's work. This rubric has been customized in some cases. If the primary source is a written document, the term "author" appears; however, if the primary source is a work of art, the term "artist" is used, showing the person's direct relationship to the primary source. For primary sources created by a group, "organization" may have been used instead of "author." Other terms may also be used to describe the creator or originator of the primary source. If an author is anonymous or unknown, a brief "About the Publication" sketch may appear.

Introduction Essay

[8]   **INTRODUCTION**

In June 1989, the world watched as the China's People's Liberation Army (PLA) forcibly removed thousands of demonstrators from Tiananmen Square in Beijing. The circumstances which led to the unprecedented suppression of the protests in June of 1989 actually began in 1985 and 1986. During this time, students and workers began to demonstrate in support of broad democratic reforms in China. These protests originated on university campuses as students opposed the presence of the PLA in the schools. In addition, protesters demonstrated against nuclear testing that occurred in the Xinjiang province. The movement became a pro-democracy demonstration and adopted slogans of "Law, not authoritarianism" and "Long live democracy." As these demonstrations escalated to nationwide protests, members of the Chinese Communist Party (CCP) supported a harsh government response. However, party chairman Hu Yaobang was sympathetic to the reformers and refused to respond with military force. As a result, in 1987, he lost his position as party chairman.

On April 15, 1989, Hu Yaobang died. People began to gather in Tiananmen Square in his remembrance and in support for his political stand. On April 26, however, an editorial appeared in the *People's Daily* newspaper discrediting the gathering of Hu Yaobang's supporters. As a result, the mood shifted from an expression of grief to a political stand for democratic reforms. According to Chinese government figures, the demonstrations that began in Tiananmen Square began to spread to twenty-nine provinces and eighty-four cities. On May 13, students began a hunger strike and by May 17, approximately one million demonstrators had converged on Tiananmen Square. Many of these protesters were students. However, unlike demonstrations in the past, this gathering became a cross-class protest that included students, urban workers, party and government employees, and others. In all, over seven hundred organizations participated.

On May 20, the party leadership, under the control of Deng Xiaoping (1904–1997), declared martial law. Initial attempts on the part of the PLA to dispel the demonstrators failed. By May 30, the protesters erected a ten-meter-high (about 33.5-feet-tall) plaster statue called the "Goddess of Democracy." The statue, inspired partly by the Statue of Liberty, was raised to face the portrait of China's historical Communist Party leader Mao Zedong (1893—1976) hanging in Tiananmen Square. As a result, the Chinese government began to implement a policy of forceful removal and disbursement of the protesters. This policy began on June 1, 1989, by removing the access of foreign journalists to the events. The next day, convoys of tanks and soldiers began to move into central Beijing. By June 3, the military began to use tear gas and rubber bullets to force the demonstrators' eviction of the square. The PLA's tanks entered Tiananmen Square by midnight on June 3, at which time many demonstrators agreed to leave the square. However, the army began to open fire on the protesters in the early morning of June 4.

In a cable written to the U.S. State Department from the American Embassy in Beijing, approximately 10,000 troops surrounded the 3,000 remaining protesters resulting in violent clashes along Changan Boulevard, the main thoroughfare in Tiananmen Square. The military used automatic weapons, tanks, and armored personnel carriers to suppress the demonstration, which until this point had been peaceful. According to reports, the military opened fire on unarmed civilians, to include members of the press. The U.S. Embassy reported that journalists for CBS had been beaten by the PLA and their equipment, especially cameras, had been smashed.

As is customary with all pressing situations overseas, the U.S. Secretary of State, then James A. Baker

III, kept the president, then George H. W. Bush, aware of developments through frequent updates. The following reports, initially labeled "top secret" were excised of still-sensitive material and made available to the American public in 1993.

[8]   **Introduction:** The introduction is a brief essay on the contributing factors and historical context of the primary source. Intended to promote understanding and equip the reader with essential facts to understand the context of the primary source.

To maintain ease of reference to the primary source, spellings of names and places are used in accord with their use in the primary source. According names and places may have different spellings in different articles. Whenever possible, alternative spellings are provided to provide clarity.

To the greatest extent possible, we have attempted to use Arabic names instead of their Latinized versions. Where required for clarity, we have included Latinized names in parentheses after the Arabic version. We could not retain some diacritical marks (e.g. bars over vowels, dots under consonants). Because there is no generally accepted rule or consensus regarding the format of translated Arabic names, we have adopted the straightforward, and we hope sensitive, policy of using names as they are used or cited in their region of origin.

[9] PRIMARY SOURCE

1. China

A. After the bloodbath

Yesterday and this morning troops continued to fire indiscriminately at citizens in the area near Tianamen [*sic*] Square. Citizens tried to block streets and burned armored vehicles and army trucks. Hundreds of military vehicles including at least 34 tanks and numerous armored personnel carriers have been destroyed over the last two days, according to [unidentified source] and press reports.

Secured a university campus where students had captured an armored personnel carrier, and issued a warning that executions of students will begin tonight, according to [unidentified source] units are poised outside several other colleges, and the military said troops will move against the campuses if resistance does not cease. Some students have seized weapons and are vowing to resist. Non-violent protests have occurred in half a dozen other cities. . . .

Press have reported hat more than 1,000 soldiers and police were killed or wounded and that some civilians were killed. Foreign estimates range from hundreds to as many as 2,600 civilians killed and thousands injured. But the severity of the assault on Tianamen Square is clear. Troops shot indiscriminately into crowds of unarmed civilians, including women and children, often with automatic weapons. In one case, students attempting to parlay with troops were gunned down. Foreign journalists report seeing fleeting protesters shot in the back. Enraged protesters burned personnel carriers and killed some security personnel.

Secretary of State's Morning Summary for June 6, 1989, China: Descent into Chaos

In the western edge of the city, according to press reports, elements of the 28th army clashed with the 27th army, which is being blamed for the worst atrocities against civilians during Saturday night's attack on Tiananmen Square. Told [unidentified source] that Chinese troops are out of control.

That at least some of the troops still entering Beijing are arriving without authorization and are intent upon attacking the 27the army. An unconfirmed Hong Kong television broadcast today reported fighting at Nanyuan military airport, where several thousand fresh troops may have arrived today from the Nanjing military region.

The Nanijng commander is believed to be personally loyal to Deng. A security guard in the great hall of the people shot Premier Li Peng in the thigh yesterday, according to press reports. The would-be assassin was immediately killed by security forces. The report, from a reliable Hong Kong newspaper, will gain wide dissemination.

Sporadic gunfire continued in the center of Beijing yesterday, with some civilian casualties, according to press reports. Troops, supported by tanks, have taken up defensive positions near the US embassy.

Strikes and protests are spreading to other cities; martial law has been declared in Chengdu where violent clashes between troops and demonstrators have left at least 300 dead. According to the consulate general, on Monday night an angry mob tried to break into the hotel where the consulate is housed, although looting, rather than attacks on foreigners, was believed to be the purpose.

Unconfirmed accounts suggest that troops are poised outside Shanghai to intervene if ordered, and the city is paralyzed by strikes and roadblocks erected by protesters. Demonstrations have also occurred in Guanghzhou and other cities.

Leaders and army commanders who have ordered or conducted atrocities now feel they are fighting for their lives. They have ringed the Zhongnanhai leadership compound with armored vehicles and troops.

Convoys of limousines like mini-buses, escorted by tanks, left Zhongnanhai Sunday night for a wartime command center in the suburbs, according to unconfirmed press reports.

[9] Primary Source: The majority of primary sources are reproduced as plain text. The primary source may appear excerpted or in full, and may appear as text, text facsimile (photographic reproduction of the original text), image, or graphic display (such as a table, chart, or graph).

The font and leading of the primary sources are distinct from that of the context—to provide a visual clue to the change, as well as to facilitate ease of reading. As needed, the original formatting of the text is preserved in order to more accurately represent the original (screenplays, for example). In order to respect the integrity of the primary sources, content some readers may consider sensitive (for example, the use of slang, ethnic or racial slurs, etc.) is retained when deemed to be integral to understanding the source and the context of its creation.

Primary source images (whether photographs, text facsimiles, or graphic displays) are bordered with a distinctive double rule. Most images have brief captions.

The term "narrative break" appears where there is a significant amount of elided (omitted) material with the text provided (for example, excerpts from a work's first and fifth chapters, selections from a journal article abstract and summary, or dialogue from two acts of a play).

Significance Essay

[10] SIGNIFICANCE

The U.S. Embassy in Beijing reported that relative calm had been restored to the region by June 8, 1989. Human rights organizations assert that approximately 1,000–2,600 people were killed during the protests in Tiananmen Square.

By 1991, the Chinese government had confirmed 2,578 arrests of those involved in participating and organizing the protests. Unlike the gentle handling of the 1985–1986 pro-democracy protests, the CCP leadership enacted sweeping responses to prevent future demonstrations from occurring. In addition to jailing protesters, many of the demonstration's leadership

were exiled. Policy changes also occurred. The CCP intensified the political education of students through programs such as an eight-week university program that teaches party principles. Many schools adopted a state written curriculum that focuses on China's achievements and the perceived excesses of the West.

[10] Significance: The significance discusses the importance and impact of the primary source and the event it describes.

Further Resources

[11] Further Resources: A brief list of resources categorized as Books, Periodicals, Web sites, and Audio and Visual Media provides a stepping stone to further study.

Books

Casserly, Jack. *The Triumph at Tiananmen Square.* Lincoln, Neb.: ASJA Press, 2005.

Periodicals

Mason, T. David., Clements, Jonathan. "Tiananmen Square 13 Years After: The Prospects for Civil Unrest in China." *Asian Affairs: An American Review.* 29 (2002): 159.

Web sites

Guardian Unlimited. "Tiananmen: Ten Years On." 1999. <http:// www.guardian.co.uk/Tiananmen/0,2759,193066, 00.html> (accessed April 30, 2006).

National Security Archive Electronic Briefing Book No.16. "Tiananmen Square, 1989." <http://www.gwu.edu/~nsarchiv/NSAEBB/NSAEBB16/> (accessed April 30, 2006).

SECONDARY SOURCE CITATION FORMATS (HOW TO CITE ARTICLES AND SOURCES)

Alternative forms of citations exist and examples of how to cite articles from this book are provided below:

APA Style

Books: Cridge, Ann Denton. (1870). *Man's Rights, or, How Would You Like It? Comprising Dreams.* Wellesley, Mass.: E.M.F. Denton. Excerpted in K. Lee Lerner and Brenda Wilmoth Lerner, eds. (2006) *Human and Civil Rights: Essential Primary Sources*, Farmington Hills, Mich.: Thomson Gale.

Periodicals: Constable, Pamela. (2003, September 8). Attacks Beset Afghan Girls' Schools. *Washington Post.* Excerpted in K. Lee Lerner and Brenda Wilmoth Lerner, eds. (2006) *Human and Civil*

Rights: Essential Primary Sources, Farmington Hills, Mich.: Thomson Gale.

Web sites: *Yale Law School; The Avalon Project.* "League of Nations. Convention to Suppress the Slave Trade and Slavery. September 25, 1926." Retrieved May 29, 2006 from http://www.yale.edu/lawweb/ avalon/league/lea001.htm. Excerpted in K. Lee Lerner and Brenda Wilmoth Lerner, eds. (2006) *Human and Civil Rights: Essential Primary Sources,* Farmington Hills, Mich.: Thomson Gale.

Chicago Style

Books: Cridge, Ann Denton. *Man's Rights, or, How Would You Like It? Comprising Dreams.* Wellesley, Mass.: E.M.F. Denton, 1870. Excerpted in K. Lee Lerner and Brenda Wilmoth Lerner, eds., *Human and Civil Rights: Essential Primary Sources,* Farmington Hills, Mich.: Thomson Gale, 2006.

Periodicals: Constable, Pamela. "Attacks Beset Afghan Girls' Schools." *Washington Post* (September 8, 2003). Excerpted in K. Lee Lerner and Brenda Wilmoth Lerner, eds., *Human and Civil Rights: Essential Primary Sources,* Farmington Hills, Mich.: Thomson Gale, 2006.

Web sites: *Yale Law School; The Avalon Project.* "League of Nations. Convention to Suppress the Slave Trade and Slavery. September 25, 1926." <http:// www.yale.edu/lawweb/avalon/league/lea001.htm> (accessed May 29, 2006). Excerpted in K. Lee Lerner and Brenda Wilmoth Lerner, eds., *Human and Civil Rights: Essential Primary Sources,* Farmington Hills, Mich.: Thomson Gale, 2006.

MLA Style

Books: Cridge, Ann Denton. *Man's Rights, or, How Would You Like It? Comprising Dreams,* Wellesley, Mass.: E.M.F. Denton, 1870. Excerpted in K. Lee Lerner and Brenda Wilmoth Lerner, eds., *Human and Civil Rights: Essential Primary Sources,* Farmington Hills, Mich.: Thomson Gale, 2006.

Periodicals: Constable, Pamela. "Attacks Beset Afghan Girls' Schools." *Washington Post*, 8 September, 2003. Excerpted in K. Lee Lerner and Brenda Wilmoth Lerner, eds., *Human and Civil Rights: Essential Primary Sources,* Farmington Hills, Mich.: Thomson Gale, 2006.

Web sites: "League of Nations. Convention to Suppress the Slave Trade and Slavery. September 25, 1926." *Yale Law School; The Avalon Project.* 29 May 2006. <http://www.yale.edu/lawweb/avalon/league/lea001. htm>. Excerpted in K. Lee Lerner and Brenda Wilmoth Lerner, eds., *Human and Civil Rights: Essential Primary Sources,* Farmington Hills, Mich.: Thomson Gale, 2006.

Turabian Style

Books: Cridge, Ann Denton. *Man's Rights, or, How Would You Like It? Comprising Dreams* (Wellesley, Mass.: E.M.F. Denton, 1870). Excerpted in K. Lee Lerner and Brenda Wilmoth Lerner, eds., *Human and Civil Rights: Essential Primary Sources* (Farmington Hills, Mich.: Thomson Gale, 2006).

Periodicals: Constable, Pamela. "Attacks Beset Afghan Girls' Schools." *Washington Post* 8 September, 2003. Excerpted in K. Lee Lerner and Brenda Wilmoth Lerner, eds., *Human and Civil Rights: Essential Primary Sources* (Farmington Hills, Mich.: Thomson Gale, 2006).

Web sites: *Yale Law School; The Avalon Project.* "League of Nations. Convention to Suppress the Slave Trade and Slavery. September 25, 1926" available from http://www.yale.edu/lawweb/avalon/league/ lea001.htm; accessed 29 May, 2006. Excerpted in K. Lee Lerner and Brenda Wilmoth Lerner, eds., *Human and Civil Rights: Essential Primary Sources* (Farmington Hills, Mich.: Thomson Gale, 2006).

Using Primary Sources

The definition of what constitutes a primary source is often the subject of scholarly debate and interpretation. Although primary sources come from a wide spectrum of resources, they are united by the fact that they individually provide insight into the historical *milieu* (context and environment) during which they were produced. Primary sources include materials such as newspaper articles, press dispatches, autobiographies, essays, letters, diaries, speeches, song lyrics, posters, works of art—and in the twenty-first century, web logs—that offer direct, first-hand insight or witness to events of their day.

Categories of primary sources include:

- Documents containing firsthand accounts of historic events by witnesses and participants. This category includes diary or journal entries, letters, email, newspaper articles, interviews, memoirs, and testimony in legal proceedings.
- Documents or works representing the official views of both government leaders and leaders of terrorist organizations. These include primary sources such as policy statements, speeches, interviews, press releases, government reports, and legislation.
- Works of art, including (but certainly not limited to) photographs, poems, and songs, including advertisements and reviews of those works that help establish an understanding of the cultural milieu (the cultural environment with regard to attitudes and perceptions of events).
- Secondary sources. In some cases, secondary sources or tertiary sources may be treated as primary sources. In some cases articles and sources are created many years after an event. Ordinarily, a

historical retrospective published after the initial event is not be considered a primary source. If, however, a resource contains statement or recollections of participants or witnesses to the original event, the source may be considered primary with regard to those statements and recollections.

ANALYSIS OF PRIMARY SOURCES

The material collected in this volume is not intended to provide a comprehensive overview of a topic or event. Rather, the primary sources are intended to generate interest and lay a foundation for further inquiry and study.

In order to properly analyze a primary source, readers should remain skeptical and develop probing questions about the source. As in reading a chemistry or algebra textbook, historical documents require readers to analyze them carefully and extract specific information. However, readers must also read "beyond the text" to garner larger clues about the social impact of the primary source.

In addition to providing information about their topics, primary sources may also supply a wealth of insight into their creator's viewpoint. For example, when reading a news article about an outbreak of disease, consider whether the reporter's words also indicate something about his or her origin, bias (an irrational disposition in favor of someone or something), prejudices (an irrational disposition against someone or something), or intended audience.

Students should remember that primary sources often contain information later proven to be false, or contain viewpoints and terms unacceptable to future generations. It is important to view the primary source within the historical and social context existing at its creation. If for example, a newspaper article is written within hours or days of an event, later developments may reveal some assertions in the original article as false or misleading.

TEST NEW CONCLUSIONS AND IDEAS

Whatever opinion or working hypothesis the reader forms, it is critical that they then test that hypothesis against other facts and sources related to the incident. For example, it might be wrong to conclude that factual mistakes are deliberate unless evidence can be produced of a pattern and practice of such mistakes with an intent to promote a false idea.

The difference between sound reasoning and preposterous conspiracy theories (or the birth of urban legends) lies in the willingness to test new ideas against other sources, rather than rest on one piece of evidence such as a single primary source that may contain errors. Sound reasoning requires that arguments and assertions guard against argument fallacies that utilize the following:

- false dilemmas (only two choices are given when in fact there are three or more options)
- arguments from ignorance (*argumentum ad ignorantiam*; because something is not known to be true, it is assumed to be false)
- possibilist fallacies (a favorite among conspiracy theorists who attempt to demonstrate that a factual statement is true or false by establishing the possibility of its truth or falsity. An argument where "it could be" is usually followed by an unearned "therefore, it is.")
- slippery slope arguments or fallacies (a series of increasingly dramatic consequences is drawn from an initial fact or idea)
- begging the question (the truth of the conclusion is assumed by the premises)
- straw man arguments (the arguer mischaracterizes an argument or theory and then attacks the merits of their own false representations)
- appeals to pity or force (the argument attempts to persuade people to agree by sympathy or force)
- prejudicial language (values or moral judgements—good and bad—are attached to certain arguments or facts)
- personal attacks (*ad hominem*; an attack on a person's character or circumstances)
- anecdotal or testimonial evidence (stories that are unsupported by impartial or data that is not reproducible)
- *post hoc* (after the fact) fallacies (because one thing follows another, it is held to cause the other)
- the fallacy of the appeal to authority (the argument rests upon the credentials of a person, not the evidence)

Despite the fact that some primary sources can contain false information or lead readers to false conclusions based on the "facts" presented, they remain an invaluable resource regarding past events. Primary sources allow readers and researchers to come as close as possible to understanding the perceptions and context of events and thus, to more fully appreciate how and why misconceptions occur.

Chronology

So that the events in this volume may be placed in a larger historical context, the following is a general chronology of important historical and social events along with specific events related to the subject of this volume.

1600–1799

1679: The *Habeas Corpus* Act is formally passed by English Parliament.

1689: British Bill of Rights is adopted.

1772: England outlaws slavery.

1773: Boston Tea Party.

1774: First Continental Congress meets in Philadelphia.

1775: British and American forces clash at the battles of Lexington and Concord, igniting the American Revolution.

1775: James Watt invents the steam engine. The invention marks the start of the Industrial Revolution.

1776: Declaration of Independence asserts American colonies' independence from the British Empire and proclaims that "all men are created equal."

1781: The thirteenth state ratifies the Articles of Confederation, creating the United States.

1783: American Revolutionary War ends with the signing of the Treaty of Paris.

1785: The *Daily Universal Register*, later known as *The Times* (London), publishes its first issue.

1786: Britain establishes its first colony in Southeast Asia, beginning an age of European colonial expansion in Asia.

1787: The Constitutional Convention in Philadelphia adopts the United States Constitution.

1787: The "Society for the Abolition of the Slave Trade" is established in Britain.

1789: First nationwide election in the United States.

1789: Citizens of Paris storm the Bastille prison. The event ignites the French Revolution.

1789: Declaration of the Rights of Man is issued in France.

1790: First U.S. census is taken.

1791: The states ratify the Bill of Rights, the first ten amendments to the United States Constitution.

1793: Louis XVI, King of France, is guillotined by revolutionaries.

1793: "Reign of Terror" begins in France. Almost 40,000 people face execution.

1794: The French Republic abolishes slavery.

1796: Edward Jenner administers the first vaccination for smallpox.

1798: Irish tenant farmers rebel against British landowners in the Irish Rebellion of 1798.

1798: The United States enacts the Alien and Sedition Acts making it a federal crime to "write, publish, or utter false or malicious statements" about the United States government.

1800–1849

1800: World population reaches one billion.

1801: Union of Great Britain and Ireland.

1803: Napoleonic Wars begin. Napoleon's army conquers much of Europe before Napoleon is defeated at Waterloo in 1815.

1803: The United States pays France $15 million for the Louisiana Territory extending from the Mississippi River to the Rocky Mountains.

1807: The importation of slaves is outlawed in the United States, but the institution of African slavery continues until 1864.

1812: The North American War of 1812 between the United States and the United Kingdom of Great Britain and Ireland. The war lasted until the beginning of 1815.

1814: The Congress of Vienna redraws the map of Europe after the defeat of Napoleon.

1819: South American colonial revolutions begin when Columbia declares its independence from Spain in 1819.

1820: Temperance movement begins in United States.

1822: American Colonization Society advocates the repatriation of freed African slaves to the Colony of Liberia.

1829: Lambert-Adolphe-Jacques Quetelet (1796–1874), Belgian statistician and astronomer, gives the first statistical breakdown of a national census. He correlates death with age, sex, occupation, and economic status in the Belgian census.

1830: Indian Removal Act forces the removal of Native Americans living in the eastern part of the United States.

1838: More than 15,000 Cherokee Indians are forced to march from Georgia to present-day Oklahoma on the "Trail of Tears."

1838: Samuel Finley Breese Morse (1791–1872) and Alfred Vail (1807–1859) unveil their telegraph system.

1840: John William Draper (1811–1882), American chemist, takes a daguerreotype portrait of his sister, Dorothy. This is the oldest surviving photograph of a person.

1840: Pierre-Charles-Alexandre Louis (1787–1872), French physician, pioneers medical statistics, being the first to systematically compile records of diseases and treatments.

1841: Horace Greeley (1811–1872), American editor and publisher, founds the *New York Tribune*, which eventually becomes the *Herald Tribune* after a merger in 1924.

1842: The first shipment of milk by rail in the United States is successfully accomplished.

1845: The potato famine begins in Ireland. Crop failures and high rents on tenant farms cause a three-year famine. Millions of Irish immigrate to flee starvation.

1846: Mexican War begins as the United States attempts to expand its territory in the Southwest.

1847: John Collins Warren (1778–1856), American surgeon, introduces ether anesthesia for general surgery. It is soon taken up worldwide as an essential part of surgery.

1847: Richard March Hoe (1812–1886), American inventor and manufacturer, patents what proves to be the first successful rotary printing press. He discards the old flatbed press and places the type on a revolving cylinder. This revolutionary system is first used by the *Philadelphia Public Ledger* this same year, and it produces 8,000 sheets per hour printed on one side.

1848: Karl Marx publishes *The Communist Manifesto*.

1848: Delegates at the Seneca Falls Convention on Woman Rights advocate equal property and voting rights for women.

1848: Series of political conflicts and violent revolts erupt in several European nations. The conflicts are collectively known as the Revolution of 1848.

1848: A group of six New York newspapers form an association or news agency to share telegraph costs. It is later called the Associated Press.

1848: The first large-scale department store opens in the United States. The Marble Dry Goods Palace in New York occupies an entire city block.

1849: John Snow (1813–1858), English physician, first states the theory that cholera is a water-borne disease and that it is usually contracted by drinking. During a cholera epidemic in London in 1854, Snow breaks the handle of the Broad Street Pump, thereby shutting down what he considered to be the main public source of the epidemic.

1850–1899

1852: Harriet Beecher Stowe's novel *Uncle Tom's Cabin* is published. It becomes one of the most influential works to stir anti-slavery sentiments.

1854: Crimean War begins between Russia and allied forces of Great Britain, Sardinia, France, and the Ottoman Empire.

1854: Violent conflicts erupt between pro-and anti-slavery settlers in Kansas Territory. The "Bleeding Kansas" violence lasts five years.

1854: Florence Nightingale (1823–1910), English nurse, takes charge of a barracks hospital when the Crimean War breaks out. Through dedication and hard work, she goes on to create a female nursing service and a nursing school at St. Thomas' Hospital (1860). Her compassion and common sense approach to nursing set new standards and create a new era in the history of the sick and wounded.

1854: Cyrus West Field (1819–1892), American financier, forms the New York, Newfoundland and London telegraph Company and proposes to lay a transatlantic telegraph cable.

1856: *Illustrated London News* becomes the first periodical to include regular color plates.

1857: Supreme Court of the United States decision in *Dred Scott v. Sanford* holds that slaves are not citizens and that Congress cannot prohibit slavery in the individual states.

1857: The Indian Mutiny revolt against British colonial rule in India begins.

1859: Charles Robert Darwin (1809–1882), English naturalist, publishes his landmark work *On the Origin of Species by Means of Natural Selection.* This classic of science establishes the mechanism of natural selection of favorable, inherited traits or variations as the mechanism of his theory of evolution.

1860: The United States Congress institutes the U.S. Government Printing Office in Washington, D. C.

1861: The Civil War begins in the United States.

1861: The popular press begins in England with the publication of the *Daily Telegraph.*

1864: U.S. President Abraham Lincoln issues the Emancipation Proclamation, freeing the slaves in Union-occupied lands.

1865: The Civil War ends with the surrender of the secession states. The United States is reunified.

1865: President Lincoln is assassinated by John Wilkes Booth.

1865: The Thirteenth and Fourteenth Amendments to the United States Constitution are ratified. The Thirteenth Amendment outlaws slavery; the Fourteenth Amendment all persons born or naturalized in the United States as United States citizens and extends equal protection under the law.

1867: Britain grants Canada home rule.

1869: The first transcontinental railroad across the United States is completed.

1870: The Franco-Prussian War (1870–1871) begins.

1871: The era of New Imperialism, or "empire for empire's sake," starts a multinational competition for colonies in Africa, Asia, and the Middle East.

1876: Alexander Bell files for a patent for the telephone.

1876: The American Library Association is founded in Philadelphia, Pennsylvania by American librarian, Melvil Dewey (1851–1931), the founder of the decimal system of library classification.

1877: Reconstruction, the period of rebuilding and reunification following the U.S. Civil War, ends.

1884: International conference is held at Washington, D.C., at which Greenwich, England, is chosen as the common prime meridian for the entire world.

1885: Karl Benz invents an automobile in Germany.

1885: Louis Pasteur (1822–1895), French chemist, inoculates a boy, Joseph Meister, against rabies. He had been bitten by a mad dog and the treatment saves his life. This is the first case of Pasteur's use of an attenuated germ on a human being.

1886: Richard von Krafft-Ebing (1840–1902), German neurologist, publishes his landmark case history study of sexual abnormalities, *Psychopathia Sexualis*, and helps found the scientific consideration of human sexuality.

1890: The United States Census Bureau announces that the American frontier is closed.

1890: Herman Hollerith (1860–1929), American inventor, puts his electric sorting and tabulating machines to work on the United States Census. He wins this contract after a trial "run-off" with two other rival systems and his system performs in one year what would have taken eight years of hand tabulating. This marks the beginning of modern data processing.

1892: Ellis Island becomes chief immigration station of the eastern United States.

1893: Panic of 1893 triggers a three-year economic depression in the United States.

1893: Sigmund Freud (1856–1939), Austrian psychiatrist, describes paralysis originating from purely mental conditions and distinguishes it from that of organic origin.

1894: Thomas Alva Edison (1847–1931), American inventor, first displays his peep-show Kinetoscopes in New York. These demonstrations serve to stimulate research on the screen projection of motion pictures as well as entertain.

1896: Landmark Supreme Court of the United States decision, *Plessy v. Ferguson*, upholds racial segregation laws.

1897: Havelock Ellis (1859–1939), English physician, publishes the first of his seven-volume work *Studies in the Psychology of Sex.* This contributes to the more open discussion of human sexuality and supports sex education.

1898: *USS Maine* sinks in harbor in Havana, Cuba; Spanish-American War begins.

1900–1949

1901: Guglielmo Marconi (1874–1937), Italian electrical engineer, successfully sends a radio signal from England to Newfoundland. This is the first transatlantic telegraphic radio transmission and as such, is considered by most as the day radio is invented.

1903: Wright brothers make first successful flight of a controlled, powered airplane that is heavier than air.

1903: *The Great Train Robbery*, the first modern movie, debuts.

1904: Russo-Japanese War (1904–1905): Japan gains territory on the Asian mainland and becomes a world power.

1905: Albert Einstein (1879–1955), German-Swiss-American physicist, submits his first paper on the special theory of relativity titled "Zur Elektrodynamik bewegter Korpen." It states that the speed of light is constant for all conditions and that time is relative or passes at different rates for objects in constant relative motion. This is a fundamentally new and revolutionary way to look at the universe and it soon replaces the old Newtonian system.

1908: A. A. Campbell-Swinton of England first suggests the use of a cathode ray tube as both the transmitter (camera) and receiver. This is the first description of the modern, all-electronic television system.

1914: Assassination of Archduke Franz Ferdinand of Austria-Hungary and his wife Sophie; World War I begins.

1914: Panama Canal is completed.

1914: The beginning of the massacre of 1.5 million Armenians by the Turkish government, later known as the Armenian Genocide.

1915: German U-boats sink the British passenger steamer *RMS Lusitania.*

1916: Easter Rising in Ireland begins fight for Irish independence.

1917: The United States enters World War I, declaring war on Germany.

1917: The Russian Revolution begins as Bolsheviks overthrow the Russian monarchy.

1918: World War I ends.

1918: The Great Flu; nearly twenty million perish during the two-year pandemic.

1918: The Red Terror in Russia: Thousands of political dissidents are tried and imprisoned; Five million die of famine as Communists collectivize agriculture and transform the Soviet economy.

1919: The ratification of the Nineteenth Amendment to the United States constitution gives women the right to vote.

1919: Mahatma Gandhi initiates satyagraha (truth force) campaigns, beginning his nonviolent resistance movement against British rule in India.

1920: Red Scare (1920–1922) in the United States leads to the arrest, trial, and imprisonment of suspected communist, socialist, and anarchist "radicals."

1920: KDKA, a Pittsburgh Westinghouse station, transmits the first commercial radio broadcast.

1922: Twenty-six of Ireland's counties gain independence; the remaining six become Northern Ireland and remain under British rule.

1922: Mussolini forms Fascist government in Italy.

1925: Geneva Protocol, signed by sixteen nations, outlaws the use of poisonous gas as an agent of warfare.

1925: The Scopes Monkey Trial (July 10-25) in Tennessee debates the state's ban on the teaching of evolution.

1927: Charles Lindbergh makes the first solo nonstop transatlantic flight.

1928: Alexander Fleming discovers penicillin.

1929: Black Tuesday. The United States stock market crashes, beginning the Great Depression.

1930: Rubber condoms made of a thin latex are introduced.

1932: Hattie Wyatt Caraway of Arkansas is the first woman elected to the United States Senate.

1932: The Nazi party capture 230 seats in the German Reichstag during national elections.

1932: RCA (Radio Corporation of America) makes experimental television broadcasts from the Empire State Building in New York.

1933: Adolf Hitler named German chancellor.

1933: President Franklin D. Roosevelt announces the New Deal, a plan to revitalize the United States economy and provide relief during the Great Depression. The United States unemployment rate reaches twenty-five percent.

1933: U.S. President Franklin Delano Roosevelt (1882–1945) makes the first of his "fireside chats" to the

American people. He is the first national leader to use the radio medium comfortably and regularly to explain his programs and to garner popular support.

1935: Germany's Nuremburg Laws codify discrimination and denaturalization of the nation's Jews.

1938: Anti-Jewish riots across Germany. The destruction and looting of Jewish-owned businesses is know as *Kristalnacht*, "Night of the Broken Glass."

1938: Hitler marches into Austria; political and geographical union of Germany and Austria proclaimed. Munich Pact—Britain, France, and Italy agree to let Germany partition Czechoslovakia.

1939: The United States declares its neutrality in World War II.

1939: Germany invades Poland. Britain, France, and Russia go to war against Germany.

1939: The Holocaust (Shoah) begins in German-occupied Europe. Jews are removed from their homes and relocated to ghettos or concentration camps. The *Einsatzgruppen*, or mobile killing squads, begin the execution of one million Jews, Poles, Russians, Gypsies, and others.

1939: Television debuts to the public at the World's Fair.

1941: The United States Naval base at Pearl Harbor, Hawaii is bombed by Japanese Air Force. Soon after, the United States enters World War II, declaring war on Germany and Japan.

1941: The first Nazi death camp, Chelmno, opens. Victims, mainly Jews, are executed by carbon monoxide poisoning in specially designed killing vans.

1942: Executive Order 9066 orders the internment of Japanese immigrants and Japanese-American citizens for the duration of World War II.

1942: Enrico Fermi (1901–1954), Italian-American physicist, heads a Manhattan Project team at the University of Chicago that produces the first controlled chain reaction in an atomic pile of uranium and graphite. With this first self-sustaining chain reaction, the atomic age begins.

1943: Penicillin is first used on a large scale by the United States Army in the North African campaigns. Data obtained from these studies show that early expectations for the new drug are correct, and the groundwork is laid for the massive introduction of penicillin into civilian medical practice after the war.

1945: Auschwitz death camp is liberated by allied forces.

1945: World War II and the Holocaust end in Europe.

1945: Trials of Nazi War criminals begin in Nuremberg, Germany.

1945: United Nations is established.

1945: Displaced Persons (DP) camps established throughout Europe to aid Holocaust survivors. In the three years following the end of World War II, many DPs immigrate to Israel and the United States.

1945: United States destroys the Japanese city of Hiroshima with a nuclear fission bomb based on uranium-235. Three days later, a plutonium-based bomb destroys the city of Nagasaki. Japan surrenders on August 14 and World War II ends. This is the first use of nuclear power as a weapon.

1948: Gandhi assassinated in New Delhi.

1948: The Soviet Union blockades Berlin. The United States and Great Britain begin airlift of fuel, food and necessities to West Berlin. The event, the first conflict of the Cold War, became known as the Berlin Airlift (June 26-Sept 30, 1949).

1948: United Nations issues the Universal Declaration of Human Rights.

1948: Israel is established as an independent nation.

1948: American zoologist and student of sexual behavior, Alfred C. Kinsey (1894–1956) first publishes his *Sexual Behavior in the Human Male*.

1949: South Africa codifies apartheid.

1949: The Soviet Union tests their first atomic device.

1950–1999

1950: President Truman commits U.S. troops to aid anti-Communist forces on the Korean Peninsula. The Korean War lasts from 1950–1953.

1951: First successful oral contraceptive drug is introduced. Gregory Pincus (1903–1967), American biologist, discovers a synthetic hormone that renders a woman infertile without altering her capacity for sexual pleasure. It soon is marketed in pill form and effects a social revolution with its ability to divorce the sex act from the consequences of impregnation.

1952: First hydrogen bomb is detonated by the United States on an atoll in the Marshall Islands.

1954: Sen. Joseph R. McCarthy begins hearings of the House Un-American Activities Committee, publicly accusing military officials, politicians, media, and others of Communist involvement.

1954: Landmark decision of the United States Supreme Court, Brown v. Board of Education, ends segregation of schools in the United States.

1955: Emmett Till, age fourteen, is brutally murdered for allegedly whistling at a white woman. The event galvanizes the civil rights movement.

1955: Rosa Parks refuses to give up her seat on a Montgomery, Alabama, bus to a white passenger, defying segregation.

1955: Warsaw Pact solidifies relationship between the Soviet Union and its communist satellite nations in Eastern Europe.

1957: President Eisenhower sends federal troops to Central High School in Little Rock, Arkansas, to enforce integration.

1957: Soviet Union launches the first satellite, Sputnik, into space. The Space Race between the USSR and the United States begins.

1958: Explorer I, first American satellite, is launched.

1960: African-American students in North Carolina begin a sit-in at a segregated Woolworth's lunch counter; the sit-in spread throughout the South.

1961: Soviet Cosmonaut Yuri Gagarin becomes first human in space.

1961: Berlin Wall is built.

1961: Bay of Pigs Invasion: the United States sponsors invasion to overthrow Cuba's socialist government but fails.

1962: Rachel Carson's *Silent Spring* is published; environmental movement begins.

1962: Cuban Missile Crisis occurs.

1963: Rev. Martin Luther King, Jr., delivers his "I Have a Dream" speech at a civil rights march on Washington, D.C.

1963: The United States and the Soviet Union establish a direct telephone link called the "hot line" between the White House and the Kremlin. It is intended to permit the leaders of both countries to speak directly and immediately to each other in times of crisis.

1964: U.S. President Lyndon Johnson announces ambitious social reform programs known as the Great Society.

1964: President Johnson signs the Civil Rights Act of 1964.

1965: March to Selma: state troopers and local police fight a crowd of peaceful civil rights demonstrators, including the Rev. Martin Luther King, Jr., as the group attempted to cross a bridge into the city of Selma.

1965: First United States combat troops arrive in South Vietnam.

1965: Voting Rights Act prohibits discriminatory voting practices in the United States.

1965: Watts Riots: Thirty-five people are killed and 883 injured in six days of riots in Los Angeles.

1966: Betty Friedan and other leaders of the feminist movement found the National Organization for Women (NOW).

1968: Rev. Martin Luther King, Jr., is assassinated in Memphis, Tennessee.

1968: Cesar Chavez leads a national boycott of California table grape growers, which becomes known as "La Causa."

1969: Stonewall Riots in New York City spark the gay rights movement.

1969: The United States successfully lands a manned mission, Apollo 11, on the moon.

1972: Arab terrorists massacre Israeli athletes at Olympic Games in Munich, Germany.

1973: Roe v. Wade: Landmark Supreme Court decision legalizes abortion on demand during the first trimester of pregnancy.

1973: The American Psychiatric Association removes the classification of homosexuality as a mental disorder.

1976: Steve Jobs and Steve Wozniak invent personal computer.

1977: International human rights advocacy group Amnesty International awarded the Noble Peace Prize.

1978: The Camp David Accord ends a three-decade long conflict between Israel and Egypt.

1979: Iran hostage crisis begins when Iranian students storm the United States embassy in Teheran. They hold sixty-six people hostage until 1981, when the hostages are finally released after 444 days in captivity.

1980: President Carter announces that U.S. athletes will boycott Summer Olympics in Moscow to protest Soviet involvement in Afghanistan (Jan. 20).

1981: Urban riots breakout in several British cities, protesting lack of opportunity for minorities and police brutality.

1981: AIDS identified.

1986: U.S. space shuttle Challenger explodes seventy-three seconds after liftoff.

1987: U.S. President Ronald Reagan challenges Soviet leader Mikhail Gorbachev to open Eastern Europe and the Soviet Union to political and economic reform.

1989: Fall of the Berlin Wall.

1989: Tiananmen Square protest in Beijing, China.

1989: The Internet revolution begins with the invention of the World Wide Web.

1991: The Soviet Union dissolves.

1991: Persian Gulf War (January 16-February 28): United States leads "Operation Desert Storm" to push Iraqi occupying forces out of Kuwait.

1992: U.S. and Russian leaders formally declare an end to the Cold War.

1992: L.A. Riots: The acquittal of four white police officers charged with police brutality in the beating of black motorist Rodney King sparks days of widespread rioting in Los Angeles.

1992: WHO (World Health Organization) predicts that by the year 2000, thirty to forty million people will be infected with the AIDS-causing HIV. A Harvard University group argues that the number could reach more than 100 million.

1993: A terrorist bomb explodes in a basement parking garage of the World Trade Center, killing six.

1994: First all-race elections in South Africa; Nelson Mandela elected President.

1998: Gay college student Matthew Shepherd is tortured and murdered.

1999: NATO forces in former Yugoslavia attempt to end mass killings of ethnic Albanians by Serbian forces in Kosovo.

2000–

2001: Terrorist attacks on the World Trade Center in New York and the Pentagon in Washington, DC kill 2,752 people.

2001: Controversial Patriot Act passes in the United States.

2001: United States and coalition forces begin War on Terror by invading Afghanistan (Operation Enduring Freedom), overthrowing the nation's Islamist Taliban regime in December of 2001.

2002: Slobodan Milosevic begins his war crimes trial at the UN International Criminal Tribunal on charges of genocide and crimes against humanity. He is the first head of state to stand trial in an international war-crimes court, but he dies before the trial concludes.

2002: After United States and coalition forces depose Islamist Taliban regime in Afghanistan, girls are allowed to return to school and women's rights are partially restored in areas controlled by the United States and coalition forces.

2003: U.S. space shuttle Columbia breaks apart upon re-entry, killing all seven crew members.

2003: United States and coalition forces invade Iraq.

2003: The United States declares an end to major combat operations in Iraq. As of June 2006, U.S. fighting forces remain engaged in Iraq.

2003: On November 18, the Massachusetts Supreme Judicial court rules that denying same-sex couples marriage rights violates the state constitution, legalizing same-sex marriages.

2004: Islamist terrorist bombing of commuter rail network in Madrid, Spain.

2005: Islamist terrorist bombings in London. Bombs simultaneously detonate on the Underground and city buses.

Development of Human Rights

Human rights are the basic freedoms, liberties, and protections to which all persons are entitled. Human rights are not specific to one government or religion. They do not differ in times of war or peace. Human rights are constant and inalienable rights, possessed by all people. Ideally, governments should promote and protect human rights through systems of law.

Today, human rights include life, liberty, and security of person; the freedom of religion, thought, political expression, movement, assembly, speech, and organization; due process of law, education, employment, health, property ownership, cultural preservation; the right to marry and found a family; and freedom from discrimination, unjust punishment, persecution, tyranny, and oppression.

The modern concept of human rights developed over three centuries. In the seventeenth and eighteenth centuries, the concept of natural rights emerged. Natural rights are not subject to any political, legal, or religious system. They are inalienable rights that humans possess from birth. The Declaration of Independence (1776) perhaps best summarized natural rights: "all men are created equal, that they are endowed by their Creator with certain inalienable rights, that among these are Life, Liberty and the pursuit of Happiness."

The concept of natural rights gained popularity during the American and French Revolutions of the late eighteenth century. Both nations struggled to forge new representative governments that would best promote the natural rights of citizens. Both nations produced contemporaneous statements of rights—France, the Declaration of the Rights of Man and of Citizens, and the United States the Constitution and the Bill of Rights (both included in this chapter).

These documents provide the foundation for the modern concept of human rights. However, the Declaration of the Rights of Man and of Citizens and the Bill of Rights did not extend all natural rights to all persons. Slavery and indentured servitude continued in fledgling United States and neither nation extended full rights to women or indigenous populations.

The concept of human rights as it is now understood emerged in the twentieth century after World War II (1938–1945). Outraged by the horrors of war and the Holocaust, the newly-formed United Nations addressed issues such as torture, warfare against civilians, the treatment of prisoners of war, and the prosecution of war criminals, setting forth new rules for warfare that protected basic rights. In 1948, the member states of the United Nations drafted the United Nations Universal Declaration of Human Rights. Since the adoption of the declaration, the UN, national governments, and independent organizations have worked to advance, promote, and enforce human rights throughout the world.

The fundamental structure of this book is based on the rights enumerated in the United Nations Universal Declaration of Human Rights, which is featured in three articles in this chapter. The major principles of the declaration are the basis of international humanitarian law. Even though the document is non-binding, the Universal Declaration of Human Rights is the best-known and most widely translated modern statement of human rights.

Declaration of the Rights of Man and of the Citizen

The Birth of the French Republic

Declaration

By: National Assembly of France

Date: August 26, 1789

Source: National Assembly of France

About the Author: The National Assembly of France formed on June 17, 1789 when the Estates General decided to change its name as revolutionary sentiments spread. The Assembly is responsible for stating France's revolutionary principles in the Declaration of Man and Citizen as well as writing the first French constitution in 1791.

INTRODUCTION

The Declaration of the Rights of Man and of the Citizen is the founding document of the French republic. A product of the 1789 French Revolution, it reflected a radically new view of human rights.

In June 1789, King Louis XVI responded to widespread anger in France by proposing a charter of rights to the Estates General. Although he granted freedom of the press along with some measure of equality to the citizens, he preserved many of the feudal rights of his nobles. The king offered far too little, far too late. Within days, he was forced to recognize the authority of the National Assembly. For the majority of representatives in the Assembly, the Revolution meant a guarantee of citizens's rights, freedoms, and equality before the law. On August 4, 1789, the Assembly decreed the abolition of the feudal regime by freeing the few remaining serfs and eliminating all special privileges given to the nobility in matters of taxation. It also mandated equality of opportunity in access to official posts. Enlightenment principles were beginning to become law.

On August 26, 1789, the Assembly further emphasized its support of the Enlightenment ideals by passing the Declaration of the Rights of Man and of the Citizen. The French were inspired to issue a document by a draft of a bill of rights that Thomas Jefferson offered to the Assembly. Jefferson, the principle author of the Declaration of Independence, served as U.S. ambassador to France in 1789. The French Declaration closely resembles the American one. Both granted freedom of religion, freedom of the press, and power to the people rather than a sovereign.

The Declaration of Rights of Man and of the Citizen reflects French thought by further mandating equality of taxation and equality before the law.

PRIMARY SOURCE

The representatives of the French people, organized as a National Assembly, believing that the ignorance, neglect, or contempt of the rights of man are the sole cause of public calamities and of the corruption of governments, have determined to set forth in a solemn declaration the natural, unalienable, and sacred rights of man, in order that this declaration, being constantly before all the members of the Social body, shall remind them continually of their rights and duties; in order that the acts of the legislative power, as well as those of the executive power, may be compared at any moment with the objects and purposes of all political institutions and may thus be more respected, and, lastly, in order that the grievances of the citizens, based hereafter upon simple and incontestable principles, shall tend to the maintenance of the constitution and redound to the happiness of all. Therefore the National Assembly recognizes and proclaims, in the presence and under the auspices of the Supreme Being, the following rights of man and of the citizen:

Articles:

1. Men are born and remain free and equal in rights. Social distinctions may be founded only upon the general good.
2. The aim of all political association is the preservation of the natural and imprescriptible rights of man. These rights are liberty, property, security, and resistance to oppression.
3. The principle of all sovereignty resides essentially in the nation. No body nor individual may exercise any authority which does not proceed directly from the nation.
4. Liberty consists in the freedom to do everything which injures no one else; hence the exercise of the natural rights of each man has no limits except those which assure to the other members of the society the enjoyment of the same rights. These limits can only be determined by law.
5. Law can only prohibit such actions as are hurtful to society. Nothing may be prevented which is not forbidden by law, and no one may be forced to do anything not provided for by law.
6. Law is the expression of the general will. Every citizen has a right to participate personally, or through his representative, in its foundation. It must be the same for all, whether it protects or punishes. All citizens, being equal in the eyes of the law, are equally eligible to all dignities and to all public positions and

The painting "Declaration of the Rights of Man and Citizen" by Jean Jacques Francois Le Barbier. It depicts the document of the same name, a manifesto from the early stages of the French Revolution, in the form of two tablets watched over by heavenly beings. © ARCHIVO ICONOGRAFICO, S.A./CORBIS.

occupations, according to their abilities, and without distinction except that of their virtues and talents.

7. No person shall be accused, arrested, or imprisoned except in the cases and according to the forms prescribed by law. Any one soliciting, transmitting, executing, or causing to be executed, any arbitrary order, shall be punished. But any citizen summoned or arrested in virtue of the law shall submit without delay, as resistance constitutes an offense.

8. The law shall provide for such punishments only as are strictly and obviously necessary, and no one shall suffer punishment except it be legally inflicted in virtue of a law passed and promulgated before the commission of the offense.

9. As all persons are held innocent until they shall have been declared guilty, if arrest shall be deemed indispensable, all harshness not essential to the securing of the prisoner's person shall be severely repressed by law.

10. No one shall be disquieted on account of his opinions, including his religious views, provided their manifestation does not disturb the public order established by law.

11. The free communication of ideas and opinions is one of the most precious of the rights of man. Every citizen may, accordingly, speak, write, and print with freedom, but shall be responsible for such abuses of this freedom as shall be defined by law.

12. The security of the rights of man and of the citizen requires public military forces. These forces are, therefore, established for the good of all and not for the personal advantage of those to whom they shall be intrusted.

13. A common contribution is essential for the maintenance of the public forces and for the cost of administration. This should be equitably distributed among all the citizens in proportion to their means.

14. All the citizens have a right to decide, either personally or by their representatives, as to the necessity of the public contribution; to grant this freely; to know to what uses it is put; and to fix the proportion, the mode of assessment and of collection and the duration of the taxes.

15. Society has the right to require of every public agent an account of his administration.

16. A society in which the observance of the law is not assured, nor the separation of powers defined, has no constitution at all.

17. Since property is an inviolable and sacred right, no one shall be deprived thereof except where public necessity, legally determined, shall clearly demand it, and then only on condition that the owner shall have been previously and equitably indemnified.

SIGNIFICANCE

The Declaration of Rights of Man and of the Citizen does much more than simply state the obligations of French citizens. It struck at the divine right of kings, severing the nation from a past based on religion. It is a document of the Age of Reason. The Declaration ended the thousand-year-old mystique of monarchy by demoting the king to the mere executive of the people's will. He was no longer God's choice to rule and a representative of the divine. Instead, the king was a leader who had failed his people. Accordingly, the people's revolt was justified since resistance to oppression is a natural right of men.

The most enduring legacy of the Declaration lies in its assertion that citizens are equal before the law. In 1789, this assertion only applied to men. Revolutionary women such as Olympe de Gouges, author of the 1791 Declaration of the Rights of Woman and the Female Citizen, unsuccessfully sought to extend rights to women. Only in the twentieth century would French men and women gain equal rights and protections. Nevertheless, despite its shortcomings with respect to gender, the Declaration made it possible for all French citizens to eventually receive equal status. It dismantled the hereditary distinctions and privileges that had formed the center of monarchical society. The nature of sovereignty, the class structure of society, and the face of justice had been transformed forever in France.

FURTHER RESOURCES
Books

Barny, Roger. *Le Triomphe du Droit Naturel: La Constitution de la Doctrine Revolutionnaire des Droits De L'Homme*. Paris: Diffusion, 1997.

Dunn, Susan. *Sister Revolutions: French Lightning, American Light*. New York: Faber and Faber, 1999.

Van Kley, Dale, ed. *The French Idea of Freedom: The Old Regime and the Declaration of Rights of 1789*. Stanford: Stanford University Press, 1994.

Bill of Rights

The First Ten Amendments to the U.S. Constitution

Legislation

By: U.S. Congress

Date: December 15, 1791

Source: National Archives and Records Administration

About the Author: Congress is the legislative branch of the U.S. federal government and is responsible for writing the nation's laws. It consists of two branches, the Senate and the House of Representatives. The first Congress under the U.S. Constitution met in New York City in 1789. Drafting what became the Bill of Rights was one of its first priorities.

INTRODUCTION

In 1776, Americans feared excessive power in the hands of rulers, but ten years later they feared excessive power in the hands of the subjects, when Shays' Rebellion illuminated the government's ability under the Articles of Confederation to handle civil disorder.

The Constitutional Convention, led by James Madison, Benjamin Franklin, and others, met at Philadelphia in May 1787 to address concerns about weaknesses in the Articles of Confederation and to write a new constitution. The Federalists favored the creation of a strong national government, while the Anti-Federalists wanted a specific statement of individual rights and freedoms to protect the people from a tyrannical national government.

The Constitution, the basic framework of government in the United States, was ratified by two-thirds of the states (nine of thirteen) on June 21, 1788, and has been amended twenty-seven times since its creation. Congress met on March 4, 1789, to consider 103 amendments from the states, forty-two from groups within the states, and two complete bills of rights offered by New York and Virginia. Congress submitted twelve of these to the states on September 25, 1789. Ten were ratified by December 15, 1791, and these became known as the Bill of Rights. Written primarily by Madison, George Mason, and Thomas Jefferson, they were designed to clarify the basic rights and freedoms of the people, which many Americans argued were insufficiently protected by the language of the Constitution. Initially the Bill of Rights applied only to the federal government, and was superseded by individual state's bills of rights. This allowed southern states, for example, to censor abolitionist literature. In a series of decisions, however, the Supreme Court gradually subverted state laws to the Bill of Rights.

▓ PRIMARY SOURCE

The Preamble to The Bill of Rights

Congress of the United States

begun and held at the City of New-York, on

Wednesday the fourth of March, one thousand seven hundred and eighty nine

THE Conventions of a number of the States, having at the time of their adopting the Constitution, expressed a desire, in order to prevent misconstruction or abuse of its powers, that further declaratory and restrictive clauses should be added: And as extending the ground of public confidence in the Government, will best ensure the beneficent ends of its institution.

RESOLVED by the Senate and House of Representatives of the United States of America, in Congress assembled, two thirds of both Houses concurring, that the following Articles be proposed to the Legislatures of the several States, as amendments to the Constitution of the United States, all, or any of which Articles, when ratified by three fourths of the said Legislatures, to be valid to all intents and purposes, as part of the said Constitution; viz.

ARTICLES in addition to, and Amendment of the Constitution of the United States of America, proposed by Congress, and ratified by the Legislatures of the several States, pursuant to the fifth Article of the original Constitution.

Amendment I

Congress shall make no law respecting an establishment of religion, or prohibiting the free exercise thereof; or abridging the freedom of speech, or of the press; or the right of the people peaceably to assemble, and to petition the government for a redress of grievances.

Amendment II

A well regulated militia, being necessary to the security of a free state, the right of the people to keep and bear arms, shall not be infringed.

Amendment III

No soldier shall, in time of peace be quartered in any house, without the consent of the owner, nor in time of war, but in a manner to be prescribed by law.

Amendment IV

The right of the people to be secure in their persons, houses, papers, and effects, against unreasonable searches and seizures, shall not be violated, and no warrants shall issue, but upon probable cause, supported by oath or affirmation, and particularly describing the place to be searched, and the persons or things to be seized.

Amendment V

No person shall be held to answer for a capital, or otherwise infamous crime, unless on a presentment or indictment of a grand jury, except in cases arising in the land or naval forces, or in the militia, when in actual service in time of war or public danger; nor shall any person be subject for the same offense to be twice put in jeopardy of life or limb; nor shall be compelled in any criminal case to be a witness against himself, nor be deprived of life, liberty, or property,

An original copy of the Bill of Rights drafted March 4, 1789. NATIONAL ARCHIVES AND RECORDS ADMINISTRATION.

without due process of law; nor shall private property be taken for public use, without just compensation.

Amendment VI

In all criminal prosecutions, the accused shall enjoy the right to a speedy and public trial, by an impartial jury of the state and district wherein the crime shall have been committed, which district shall have been previously ascertained by law, and to be informed of the nature and cause of the accusation; to be confronted with the witnesses against him; to have compulsory process for obtaining witnesses in his favor, and to have the assistance of counsel for his defense.

Amendment VII

In suits at common law, where the value in controversy shall exceed twenty dollars, the right of trial by jury shall be preserved, and no fact tried by a jury, shall be otherwise reexamined in any court of the United States, than according to the rules of the common law.

Amendment VIII

Excessive bail shall not be required, nor excessive fines imposed, nor cruel and unusual punishments inflicted.

Amendment IX

The enumeration in the Constitution, of certain rights, shall not be construed to deny or disparage others retained by the people.

Amendment X

The powers not delegated to the United States by the Constitution, nor prohibited by it to the states, are reserved to the states respectively, or to the people.

SIGNIFICANCE

Although the amendments in the Bill of Rights were not part of the original Constitution, they contain many of the rights and freedoms considered fundamental to the American system of government. The Framers believed that the right to free expression without fear of government retribution is the foundation of effective citizen participation in and control of government. Accordingly, the First Amendment protects freedom of speech. The Fifth Amendment, which derives from English law, insures that the government does not use abusive means to secure criminal convictions. The Eighth Amendment, the least debated of all the amendments in the Bill of Rights, uses terms borrowed from England's Bill of Rights of 1689 and inserted into Virginia's Declaration of Rights in 1776. It protects the people from government's power to punish.

Originally drafted as protections against an overreaching federal government, most of the rights embodied in the Bill of Rights have been extended by the U.S. Supreme Court to apply to the state governments as well. Through a principle known as the incorporation doctrine, the court has found in a series of decisions that the due process clause of the Fourteenth Amendment prohibits the states from infringing on virtually all of the major protections of the Bill of Rights.

FURTHER RESOURCES
Books

Amar, Akhil Reed. *The Bill of Rights: Creation and Reconstruction.* New Haven, CT: Yale University Press, 2000.

Levy, Leonard. *Origins of the Bill of the Rights.* Yale Contemporary Law Series. New Haven, CT: Yale University Press, 2001.

Palmer, Kris E. *Constitutional Amendments: 1789 to the Present.* Detroit: Gale Group, 2000.

On the Legal Rights and Responsibilities of the Deaf and Dumb

Book excerpt

By: Harvey P. Peet

Date: 1857

Source: Peet, Harvey P. *On the Legal Rights and Responsibilities of the Deaf and Dumb.* Richmond, Va.: C. H. Wynne's Steam-Powered Press, 1857.

About the Author: Harvey Prindle Peet was an educator who dedicated his professional life to work with deaf individuals. He believed that educational materials for this group were lacking and wrote many books for classroom use. In addition, Peet was a prolific writer on sign language, teaching methods for the deaf, and the merits of instruction in verbal articulation. His writings also addressed the philosophical beliefs and misconceptions of popular culture regarding the deaf population.

INTRODUCTION

Historically, deaf people have been treated as though they were cognitively impaired, particularly if they signed or wrote rather than spoke in order to communicate with the hearing world. This probably stemmed from early theories linking intelligence with spoken language. Since most early learning, as well as the transmission of cultural and traditional knowledge, was accomplished orally, persons who were deaf were excluded from educational opportunities by the prevailing culture. Deaf people had few, if any, civil rights, and were often confined to institutions and asylums for the insane because of the eccentricities of their behavior and speech. In the Middle Ages, it was believed that deaf people were somehow more sinful than the hearing population, since they were unable to hear religious communications. As a result, the deaf were thought to be unable to hold spiritual beliefs or to participate in a sentient way in religious practices.

Fortunately, in the sixteenth century, society's view of the deaf began to change. The Spanish monk

Helen Keller, reading with her teacher, Anne Sullivan Macy. Illness at a young age left Keller deaf and blind, but with the help of her teacher she learned to communicate and became a world famous public figure. © CORBIS.

Pedro Ponce de Leon established the world's first school for the deaf at the monastery of San Salvador near Madrid. He developed methods to teach reading, writing, and speaking to deaf members of nobility in order to prepare them to inherit money and property. Pablo Bonet developed and used a single hand, manual alphabet in order to teach deaf members of the Spanish nobility to read; he also taught them to speak. De Leon's and Bonet's methods laid the foundation for the development of the French and American Sign Languages, the predominant manual languages in contemporary culture.

The work of de Leon and Bonet was broadened and extended during the eighteenth century by Charles Michel de L'Eppe, who founded a public school for deaf students in France in 1771. He also wrote textbooks on teaching deaf students using manual (sign) language. De L'Eppe is credited with writing the first French sign language dictionary.

In the early 1800s, an American theologian named Thomas Gallaudet saw a French Sign Language presentation involving a deaf teacher named Laurent

Clerc. He was so impressed with what he learned that he went to France to study their teaching methods. In 1817, Gallaudet and Clerc returned to America and founded the First American School for the Deaf in Hartford, Connecticut (named the Connecticut Asylum for the Education and Instruction of Deaf and Dumb Persons until 1895). They translated French Sign Language for use with American students.

A substantial number of the early students at the school came from Martha's Vineyard, which had an unusually large deaf population. The deaf population of Martha's Vineyard was a fully recognized part of the Vineyard community, and they had developed a local sign language. They also were pioneers in using simultaneous sign language translation at all spoken public meetings. The children from Martha's Vineyard taught their signs to the School's staff and had a significant impact on the development of American Sign Language (ASL).

▇ PRIMARY SOURCE

The result of this examination of English common law, as the foundation of American law, is, that the Deaf and Dumb have ever possessed the same rights of inheritance as those who are not deaf and dumb: and, like the latter, are restricted in the full enjoyment of such rights only upon proof of the want of the requisite intelligence. This, also, we believe, is the case throughout Europe; the old feudal codes having mostly passed away. As to what would be deemed satisfactory proof of the requisite intelligence, there is evidently room for much diversity of opinion; and different decisions may be given in similar cases, according to the degree of intelligence and freedom from prejudice of the judge or jury. In such cases, indeed, the intelligence of the judge has often more to do with the decision than the intelligence of the Deaf Mute.

We will next consider whether a Deaf Mute can make a valid will. Evidently, a person deprived of the control of his property during his lifetime, cannot consistently be permitted to alienate it from the legal heirs at his death. The Roman law on this point we have already cited. The English law would decide this question according to the actual intelligence manifested. Other European codes, more influenced by the spirit of the Roman law, exact formalities which only Deaf Mutes able to write can comply with. In France, a Deaf Mute able to read and write, is admitted on all hands to be competent to make a valid will, writing, signing and dating it with his own hand, conforming in this to the spirit of the Roman law, and avoiding the ignorant exclusion of Deaf Mutes from birth from the possibility of education. It is required, however, that "the judges should have positive proofs that the Deaf Mute testator had exact notions of the nature and effects of a testament; that reading was in him not merely an operation of the eyes, but also an operation of the understanding, giving a sense to the written characters, and acquiring by them knowledge of the ideas of another; that writing was the manifestation of his own thoughts; that on the whole, the testamentary dispositions were such as showed the effect of an intelligent will—and these proofs are at the charge of the person to whose benefit the will is made."

From this statement, taken from a standard French work, it appears that, whereas in ordinary cases, every person of lawful age is considered competent to make a will till the contrary is proved, a Deaf Mute, on the other hand, is considered incompetent till his competency is proved.

Prioux records a case in which the holograph will of a Deaf Mute, Theresa Charlotte Lange, was, in August, 1838, annulled by the Tribunal of Saint Jean d'Angely, on the ground that, though it was not contested that the will was written by the own hand of the testatrix, yet there was no evidence that she could use writing to express her own ideas, but, on the contrary, evidence that she could only express herself by signs. As this case was an important one, and seems to have been argued at much length, and carefully considered by the court, we will give an abstract of the points in which the judgment was founded:

"The heirs have not denied that the characters which compose the material body of the document purporting to be the testament of Theresa Charlotte Lange were the work of her hand, but maintained that they could not be the work of her intelligence; hence that there was no occasion for a verification of the hand-writing, or for enquiring at whose charge such verification should be."

"No provision of the law places the Deaf Mute in any exceptional case as to the capacity of making a will; he possesses the common rights of other men; and therefore can, like the generality of citizens, bequeath or give away property, provided he complies with the formalities exacted by law."

"If in consequence of his infirmity, he cannot make a will by *acte publique*, he cannot, at least, when he knows how to write, when he can manifest his will in an unequivocal manner, contest his ability to make a holographic or a *mystique* testament; this is a point on which there is now no difficulty."

"To be valid, the holographic testament must be written, dated and signed by the hand of the testator."

"In ordinary language, and in the strict acceptation of the term, it is true that to write may be understood to trace on paper letters or characters, no regard being had to their signification."

"But in the eyes of the law, and in its more extended acceptation, this expression has a very different sense; and it is evident that in a matter of such importance as making a will, to *write* most evidently cannot be understood of the purely mechanical act which consists in copying, instinctively or by imitation, characters that have been placed before one's eyes, and of which the copier does not know the use or meaning; that to know how to write is to be able at once to conceive, collect, arrange one's thoughts, put them in form and express them on paper by means of certain conventional characters; and consequently, it is much more an operation of the mind, a work of the intelligence, than a labor of the hand."

"Whence it follows, that to know how to *write* in the true acceptation of the word, it is indispensable to know the significance of words, to comprehend the relations which they have, the objects and ideas which they represent; that thus to establish that an individual knows or knew how to write, it is not enough to produce a sample of characters placed one after another; this would only prove that he had been habituated to figure letters, or to draw; but it is necessary to prove that he has received, whether in a public institution or by the care of capable persons, the education necessary to attain this result; this is above all true when the question is of a Deaf Mute from birth, who, deprived of two organs, so essential as hearing and speech, whatever natural genius and capacity he might have otherwise, has so many difficulties to overcome in order to develop, or rather to form, to re-temper his intelligence."

"When such a proof becomes necessary, it is without doubt incumbent on the party who would have the benefit of a writing attributed to a Deaf Mute; in this matter the general rule is, the state in which nature has placed the individual afflicted with dumbness and deafness; the exception is, the modification or amelioration wrought in that state: the presumption of law is, that the Deaf Mute is illiterate, and the fact to be proved, that he has been brought out of his ignorance by education—which is consequently to be proved by him who alleges this fact, or claims the exception."

"Therese Charlotte Lange was born deaf and dumb. Nothing offered in evidence shows her to have been, whether in youth or at a more advanced age, placed in an establishment consecrated to the special education of those unfortunate persons afflicted like her with this double and deplorable infirmity. It is alleged, indeed, that on her arrival in France, she was, as well as her sister Rose, also deaf and dumb from birth, received by the Abbé Hardy, then vicar-general of the bishoprick of Saintes, and that this ecclesiastic, devoting himself wholly to the care of their education, had taught them to read and to write; but no proof of this fact is to be found in the documents produced in the case: the only piece which has been adduced in support of these allegations, the *acte* of 19th September, 1789, far from justifying them, seems to prove the contrary."

"In effect it results from this *acte* that one of the ancestors of the plaintiffs had wished at that time to withdraw the demoiselles Rose and Charlotte Lange from under the guardianship of the Vicar Hardy, in order that they should, as he said, re-enter the bosom of their family; and it was only by gestures and signs that Therese Charlotte, particularly, manifested her opposition, and her refusal to adhere to the demand of the Sieur D. F. Desportes. Four witnesses, whose communications with the demoiselles Lange were frequent, were on this occasion called in to assist at this declaration in mimic language, and to interpret the signs by which they made known their resolutions; all these circumstances are such as to give a strong suspicion, in spite of the physical fact (*fait materiel*) of the apposition of the signature of Charlotte Lange at the bottom of the protestation, which was written, as is mentioned in the *acte* itself, by Rose Lange—that signs were the only means she knew to manifest her will or wishes."

"From this epoch to that of her marriage in 1821, nothing is shown which could tend to invalidate this conclusion. If it is alleged that she had a great facility to divine the signs addressed to her, and to make herself understood by means of gestures by those with whom she was habituated to communicate, that fact may prove that by a just compensation, nature had endowed her with a remarkable instinct and penetration, but not destroy the presumptions, weighty, precise and consistent, which result from the other circumstances of the case; because these presumptions are yet farther justified by the fact that she appears to have made no use of writing, which ought, however, to have been one of the easiest and surest means of communicating with her relatives and friends."

"These presumptions, already so strong, become certain proofs when, in the most solemn circumstance of her life, at the epoch of her marriage with the Sieur Hardy in 1821, we see Therese Charlotte, in order to accomplish *Garde des Sceaux* (Keeper of the Seals,) to obtain an authorization to this effect, because of the impossibility in which she found herself to express her consent; and on the other side, obliged to employ an interpreter to transmit to the public officer the consent which she gave as is mentioned in the *acte civile* , (the civil part of the contract of marriage) *by signs*, showing her intelligence by conversation on all sorts of subjects, when it had been so easy for her to avoid all these difficulties by giving her consent in writing, if in fact she knew how to write."

"Hence there can be no doubt that at the epoch of her marriage with the Sieur Hardy, Charlotte Lange, then aged sixty-five years, did not know how to write, and it is difficult to admit that she could have learned since; moreover no proof has been offered on that point."

"It must be concluded, from all these facts, that evidently, if the *acte* called her testament, materially emanated from her, it is not the work of her intelligence, and that, in this point of view, it cannot be valid in the eye of the law."

The testament dated 7th August, 1834, and enregistered 8th August, 1836, was accordingly declared null. The plaintiffs, M. M. Desportes, having offered a *liberality* of 12,000 francs to the defendant and legatee Hardy, the latter acquiesced in the judgment; a fact that induces a suspicion that the decision of the court was not considered altogether conclusive, and that there was some possibility of a different ruling by a higher tribunal; or at least doubt enough to encourage the defendant to prosecute an appeal, if not bought off.

The reader will observe that, in this case, the general intelligence of Therese Charlotte Lange, and her competency to make her wishes distinctly known by signs, were not called in question. The only question was whether she could read and write with sufficient understanding to write her own will, with a full knowledge of its provisions and their effect. In this point of view, we are not prepared to dispute that the decision of the court was correct. It is probable, from the facts shown in the case, that though Therese Charlotte might have had some idea of the meaning of simple sentences, those about her and possessing her confidence, might have placed almost any instrument before her to copy as her own; she would have had to rely on their interpretation in signs for its purport.

We have, however, to object to the reasoning of the judgment before us on one or two points. It is by no means true that a Deaf Mute who has been taught to read and write, however expert he may be, finds writing "the easiest and surest means of communication with his relatives and friends." In most cases, on the contrary, the relatives and friends of an educated Deaf Mute find it much easier to learn to communicate with him by signs, than to suffer the tediousness and other inconveniences of having to write every communication. And there are few Deaf Mutes from birth, however well educated, who do not understand signs skillfully made, more easily and readily than writing.

We may further remark that a Deaf Mute who uses written language so imperfectly that he prefers to express himself by signs, may yet have a fair idea of the meaning of what he reads or copies. Whether this last was the case with Charlotte Lange, the evidence before us does not show.

Under this decision, and others of the same tenor, it seems that, in France, an uneducated or imperfectly educated Deaf Mute cannot make a valid will at all. As it is certain that there are some uneducated, and many partially educated, Deaf Mutes who are perfectly competent to manage their own affairs, and as fully aware of the nature and effects of a testament as illiterate speaking persons generally are, it must be considered as a defect of the law, if they are, by consequence of the formalities exacted, precluded from disposing by will of property perhaps acquired by their own industry.

SIGNIFICANCE

Many of the early students at the First American School for the Deaf were trained to be teachers and ministers and went on to establish new schools. During the remainder of the nineteenth century, schools for the deaf proliferated across the United States. Thomas Gallaudet's son Edward became a teacher of the deaf and established the world's first college for deaf students in 1864. Originally called the Columbia Institute, it was renamed Gallaudet College in 1894, in honor of Thomas Gallaudet, the founder of deaf education in America. In 1986, the name was changed once again, to Gallaudet University.

At an international congress for educators of the deaf held in Milan, Italy, in 1880, a decision was made to discontinue all forms of sign language in deaf education and to mandate that all students be taught to speak and to become proficient at lip-reading. This movement was called Oralism. Gallaudet and the American educators strongly disagreed with this philosophy and felt that oral language should be offered as an educational component, but should not be the predominant teaching method. Gallaudet College continued to use ASL as a primary teaching method.

The National Association for the Deaf (NAD) was founded in 1880, partly in reaction to the rise of Oralism. As the deaf culture began to develop coherence in America, there was growing concern that the tradition and richness of American Sign Language might be lost by the growth of Oralism.

There are a range of cultural and physiological terms associated with deaf culture. The word deaf is a clinical and medical term for profound or complete absence of hearing. To be deafened means to lose one's hearing after having been able to hear for some period of time. People who are profoundly deaf have very little hearing and may only be able to discern a small amount of environmental sound. Those who are hard of hearing have varying abilities to hear sound and language. The term deaf is a cultural, linguistic, and

political one, and it relates to a community that uses ASL as its primary language.

Deaf culture is an expression of enormous pride in the richness and diversity of the deaf population that uses American Sign Language as a primary communication medium. A seminal moment in the development of American deaf culture occurred in 1988 at Gallaudet University, with the Deaf President Now protest movement (DPN). At that time, a new president of the university was to be elected. Among the three top candidates for the position, only one, Dr. Elisabeth Zinser, was a hearing individual. She had the least experience with deaf culture and was the least familiar with ASL. She was elected president by the University's Board of Trustees. Before her election, the school had only had presidents who were unable to hear. For a week after the election, the students refused to attend classes and staged a protest in which they demanded that a deaf president replace Dr. Zinser, and that the board membership be changed to include a fifty-one percent majority of deaf members. Those demands were met, and Gallaudet University increased the visibility of deaf persons around the world.

There is a predominant assumption among the hearing that ASL is an exact replica of spoken English. In fact, ASL is its own language, with a semantic, grammatical, and structural complexity equivalent to that of any spoken language. ASL does not simply finger spell words, it has a wealth of idiomatic gestures that express abstract concepts, phrases, and ideas. Sign languages are culturally based, and vary from country to country. Historically, deaf children have attended residential schools, where much of deaf culture and language are transmitted. Members of deaf culture do not typically view themselves as differently abled or handicapped and often prefer to remain within their own subculture for most social interactions.

FURTHER RESOURCES
Books

Carroll, Cathryn. *Laurent Clerc: The Story of His Early Years*. Washington, D.C.: Kendall Green Publications/ Gallaudet University Press, 1991.

Lane, Harlan, and Francois Grosjean, eds. *Recent Perspectives on American Sign Language*. Hillsdale, N.J.: Lawrence Erlbaum Associates, 1980.

Marschark, Mark, and Patricia Elizabeth Spencer, eds. *Oxford Handbook of Deaf Studies, Language, and Education*. New York: Oxford University Press, 2003.

Meier, Richard P., Kearsey Cormier, and David Quinto-Pozos, eds. *Modality and Structure in Signed and Spoken*

Languages. Cambridge, U.K.: Cambridge University Press, 2002.

Neimark, A. E. *A Deaf Child Listened: Thomas Gallaudet, Pioneer in American Education*. New York: William Morrow, 1983.

Periodicals

Peet, Harvey P. "Analysis of Bonet's Treatise on the Art of Teaching the Dumb to Speak." *American Annals of the Deaf and Dumb* 3 (1851): 200–211.

Peet, Harvey P. "Elements of the Language of Signs." *American Annals of the Deaf and Dumb* 3 (1851): 129–161.

Peet, Harvey P. "Words Not 'Representatives' of Signs, But of Ideas." *American Annals of the Deaf and Dumb* 11 (1859): 1–8.

Pittman, Paula, and Dixie Snow Huefner. "Will the Courts Go Bi-Bi? IDEA 1997, the Courts, and Deaf Education." *Exceptional Children* 67 (Winter 2001): 187–198.

Man's Rights, or, How Would You Like It? Comprising Dreams

Book excerpt

By: Annie Denton Cridge

Date: 1870

Source: Cridge, Ann Denton. *Man's Rights, or, How Would You Like It? Comprising Dreams*. Wellesley, Mass.: E.M.F. Denton, 1870.

About the Author: Annie Denton Cridge was an American spiritualist, writer, and utopian. Part of the spiritualist movement with such luminaries as Victoria Woodhull, the first woman to run for president of the United States, Cridge claimed to have spiritual and psychic powers; her brother, geology professor William Denton, participated in psychometric studies in which Cridge divined extrasensory information from inanimate objects. Her exact date of death is unknown, but she is believed to have died in the mid-1880s.

INTRODUCTION

Mary Shelley's novel *Frankenstein; or, The Modern Prometheus*, published in 1818, reflects a form of utopianism in which man exhibits such control over the natural world that he creates life. At a time in American society when a woman's role was confined to the domestic sphere, Shelley dreamed of an alternate world.

Female science fiction and utopian writers in that era often examined future changes in social convention, morality, and gender equality. Writers such as Mary Griffith, in her 1836 book *Three Hundred Years Hence* used a Rip van Winkle device in which the main character, Edgar Hastings, falls asleep in 1835 to awaken in 2135 to a very different world in which gender equality is the norm. That book, like Annie Cridge's, uses long narrative lectures to describe the changes in society spearheaded by women.

In the 1840s spiritualism, the belief that mediums and trance lecturers could communicate with the dead, swept through upper- and middle-class society, attracting many female adherents. Most mediums and trance lecturers, in fact, were women, and many female spiritualists were also part of the utopian and women's rights movements.

Annie Denton Cridge believed she had psychometric powers—the ability to divine an object's past from contact with it. Cridge, for instance, took part in a series of experiments designed by her brother, geology professor William Denton, and claimed to have extrasensory knowledge about the objects. Spiritualism and utopianism blended together, giving women greater public voices and sparking interest in social organizations outside the norm, such as utopian communities, open marriages, non-Christian belief systems, and gender equality. Cridge published her 1870 novel, *Man's Rights* at the crossroads of spiritualism, utopianism, and the growing women's rights movement in the United States. The novel involves a series of dreams that take place in a society on Mars, and in this excerpt a lecture on "Man's Rights" causes quite a stir in a society where women hold all the power.

▮ PRIMARY SOURCE

But it does seem especially remarkable to me, that, after having penned down at midnight one dream, I should, on returning to my pillow, have found myself in the very spot where my late dream ended; again in that strange city, again looking at the large posters headed,—

"MAN's RIGHTS!!

MR. SAMMIE SMILEY, MR. JOHNNIE SMITH, AND OTHERS,

Will address the meeting on the

RIGHTS OF MAN!"

I was pleased on coming to these words: "Discussion is invited." "I will go," I said, and turned to follow the crowd; but, as by magic, was transferred to one of the large cooking-establishments which I saw in my first dream, and soon recognized it to be the same.

There were the huge machines at work cooking dinner, while in a comfortable rocking-chair sat the same gentleman who had in that same dream showed me over the establishment. He was reading a newspaper. "Ah!" he said, as he looked up from his paper, "glad to see you, madam. You see I have time to read while the dinner is cooking. All goes on well. We supply one-eighth of the city with meals, and everybody is satisfied, nay, more than satisfied: they are delighted with the arrangement; for every poor man is relieved of washing, ironing, and cooking. And yet all this is done at less cost than when every house had its little selfish, dirty kitchen."

"And what is this about 'man's rights'?" I asked. "I see posters all over your city, headed, 'Man's Rights!'"

He smiled as he replied, "Well, Madam, emancipating man from the drudgery of the kitchen has given him leisure for thought; and, in his thinking, he has discovered that he labors under many wrongs, and is deprived of quite as many rights. The idea of men lecturing, men voting, men holding office, etc., excites considerable ridicule; but ridicule proves nothing."

"Are you going to the lecture?" I asked.

"I will go if I have company," he replied; "but it would not look well for me to go alone: besides, I would be afraid to go home so late."

I made no answer; but I thought musingly, "Afraid! afraid of what? of what can these men be afraid? I wonder if there are any wild beasts prowling around this strange city at night. Perhaps there are wolves or mad dogs; but then he is a man, and could carry a revolver and protect himself." But, as by a flash, the truth came to me, and I wondered I had not thought of it before. In this land, *woman* is the natural protector; and so, of course, he was afraid to go without a lady to take care of him.

I had scarcely arrived at this conclusion, when I found myself *en rapport* with every husband in that city. "I would like to go to the lecture on 'men's rights,'" I heard one man say to his wife very timidly.

"I shall go to no such place," replied his wife loftily; "neither will you. 'Man's rights,' indeed!"

"Let us go to the lecture," said another husband to his wife, with a pleasant smile on his face.

"No, no, my dear," replied the lady: "I like you just as you are; and I don't admire womanish men. Nothing is more disgusting than feminine men. We don't want men running to the polls, and electioneering: what would become of the babies at such times?"

Then I looked in on a bevy of young boys ranging in age from sixteen to twenty. How they did laugh at the very mention of "man's rights," as they put on their pretty coats and hats, looking in the mirror, and turning half round to see how their coat-tails looked!

"Man's rights!" said one. "I have all the rights I want."

"So have I," said a young boy of nineteen. "I don't want any more rights."

"We'll have rights enough, I presume, when we get married," said a tall boy of seventeen, as he touched up the flowers in his pretty hat, and perched it carefully on his head.

"Are you all ready?" said a lady, looking into the room. "Come, I want you all to learn your rights to-night. I warrant that after to-night you will want to carry the purse, don the long robes, and send us ladies into the nursery to take care of the babies!"

Hundreds of ladies and gentlemen were on their way to the meeting; and it rejoiced me greatly to find in the hearts of many of the ladies a profound respect for the rights of man, and a sincere desire that man should enjoy every right equally with themselves.

Then I found myself in the lecture-room, which was well filled with ladies and gentlemen, many of whom seemed greatly amused as they whispered and smiled to each other. Very soon three little gentlemen and one rather tall, thin, pale-faced gentleman walked to the platform, and were received with great demonstrations of applause and suppressed laughter. The audience were evidently not accustomed to hear gentlemen lecture.

"How ridiculous those men look!" I heard one elderly lady say. "What does it look like to see a parcel of men pretending to make speeches, in their tawdry pants and fly-away coat-tails, covered with finery and furbelows?"

"They sadly lack the dignity," said another female, "that belongs to ladies and long robes." "They are decidedly out of their sphere," I heard another remark.

The meeting was opened by the tall gentleman being nominated as president, who at once introduced Mr. Sammie Smiley to the audience, remarking that Mr. Sammie Smiley, with whom they were probably all acquainted by reputation, would address the audience on the all-important subject of *Man's Rights*.

"*Sammie Smiley!*" said a young lady contemptuously. "Suppose we should call ourselves *Lizzie* instead of Elizabeth, or *Maggie* instead of Margaret. Their very names lack dignity."

Mr. Sammie Smiley stepped to the front of the platform with remarkable self-possession for one of the gentlemen of that Dreamland. He wore a suit of black silk,—coat, vest, and pants all-alike, bordered with broad black lace. He wore no ornaments, except ear-rings, a plain breastpin, and one or two rings on the fingers. Very good taste, I thought.

"Ladies and gentlemen," he said, "our subject this evening is the *Rights of Man;* but to properly understand this question, it would be well, before considering man's *rights,* to define his *wrongs.*"

"Hear, hear!" applauded the audience.

"Education," he continued, "commences with childhood; and men's wrongs also commence with childhood, inasmuch as they are restricted from healthful physical exercise. The merry, active boy, that would romp and play like his sister, is told that it would be improper for a boy. How often your little son has to be reminded that a *boy* must not do so and so: he must be a dear little gentleman, and not rough and boisterous like a girl.

"He is kept in over-heated rooms; seldom breathes the pure air of heaven; and when he is taken out, how different his dress from that of the girl! Look at his flimsy pants of white muslin; look at his flimsy jacket and paper shoes: and contrast them with the warm cloth dress, the substantial over-garments, and thick shoes of the girl! Think how seldom the boy is permitted to inhale the life-giving, open atmosphere! The girl may romp and play in the snow, climb fences and trees, and thus strengthen every muscle; while the little pale-faced boy presses his nose against the window-pane, and wishes—alas! vainly—that he, too, had been a girl.

"The course of training for our boys causes weakness and disease in after-life, and more than a natural degree of muscular inferiority. The pale faces of boys are a sad contrast to the rosy-cheeked girls in the same family. In our boys is laid, not by Nature, but by ignorance and custom, the foundation for bodily weakness, consequently dependence and mental imbecility: in our girls, muscular strength and their accompaniments, independence and vivacity, both of body and mind. Were boys subject to the same physical training as girls (and no valid reason can be given why they should not be), the result would prove that no natural inferiority exists.

"True education I conceive to be the harmonious development of the whole being, both physical and mental. The natural or physical is before the intellectual. First the stalk, then the ear, and then the full corn in the ear. Through ignorance of these primary truths, many well-intentioned fathers hurry their children to premature graves.

"Why is it that, of all the children born, one-fifth die annually? Can not this large mortality be traced to the present ignorance of *males?* Can it not be traced to their flimsy and imperfect educational training? If men had their rights, were all literary institutions as free to one sex as to the other, our young men would be taught what is of the utmost importance for them to know, but what is kept sedulously from them; viz., a knowledge of mental and physical science.

"Let man be educated as liberally as woman; let him be made to feel the value of a sound mind, and that the brightest ornament to man, as well as woman, is intellect; then, and not until then, will he stand forth in all his beauty.

"We frequently hear that woman's mind is superior to man's; and therefore he ought not to have equal educational facilities. If, as is stated by the opponents of man's rights, men are naturally and necessarily inferior to women, it must follow that they should have superior opportunities for mental culture. If, on the other hand, men are by nature mentally equal to women, no reason can be given why they should not have equal educational facilities."

In the midst of the audience, a beautiful, stately woman rose, and said, that, if it was not out of order, she would like to ask a question: Did not the literature written expressly for men—gentlemen's magazines, gentlemen's fashion-books, etc.,—prove their inferiority? This question caused a laugh, and round after round of applause; but the little gentleman-speaker smilingly replied, that many gentlemen never read the trash prepared for them just as simple reading is prepared for children: but the works written for women to read, they study and digest, feeling that they were as much for them as for women. The lecturer then continued by stating the appreciative estimates of the truths of science and philosophy evinced by men as well as women, which would be the case to a still greater extent as the *opportunities* for culture were increased, when gentlemen's books and their flimsy trash would disappear; that even were man weaker in judgment than woman, it did not follow that he should never use it; and, if women did all the reasoning for man, it would not be surprising if he had lost the power to reason.

"Pretty good, Mr. Sammie Smiley," said a lady near me.

"Smiley can reason pretty well: that is pretty good logic," remarked another. Then applause after applause arose, accompanied by stamping and clapping of hands, while some young folks in the back of the hall crowed like roosters.

It was really very funny; but Mr. Sammie Smiley took no notice of the proceeding. He referred to the exclusion of men from nearly all occupations, from governing States to measuring tape; also that men were paid only one-third of the wages of women, even for the same work, their occupations being mainly restricted to sewing and teaching; while women could do both these, and whatever else they chose. He urged the gentlemen to push their way into the employment and professions of women, and be equal sharers in the rights of humanity.

A wife serving her husband dinner in an example of the traditional gender roles that Cridge reversed in her story *Man's Rights*.
PHOTO BY GEORGE MARX/RETROFILE/GETTY IMAGES.

SIGNIFICANCE

Man's Rights, which used satire to explore social questions, was published just two years after the passage of the Fourteenth Amendment, which gave African American men the right to vote. Women's rights activists such as Elizabeth Cady Stanton and Lucretia Mott had fought for female enfranchisement as well; lecture circuits were filled with female speakers urging audiences to support women's suffrage. Cridge's reversal of gender roles and stereotypes sparked some distinctly antifeminist writing, such as Minnie Finkelstein's 1891 book *The Newest Woman*.

Eighteen years after Cridge's book, Edward Bellamy published *Looking Backward*, another utopian work that used time travel as a device for examining a future in which women's roles changed drastically. Both Bellamy and Cridge depict futures in which technology meets the physical needs of domestic life, eliminating household drudgery. Yet Bellamy's work, unlike Cridge's, depicts a future in which women have their own cabinet-level department in government, work in distinctly different jobs, and live a separate but equal existence.

FURTHER RESOURCES
Books

Bellamy, Edward. *Looking Backward*. Dover Publications, 1996.

Braude, Ann. *Radical Spirits: Spiritualism and Women's Rights in Nineteenth-Century America*. Bloomington: Indiana University Press, 2001.

Clift, Eleanor. *Founding Sisters and the NineteenthAmendment*. New York: Wiley, 2003.

Dubois, Ellen Carol. *Feminism and Suffrage: The Emergence of an Independent Women's Movement in America, 1848–1869*. Ithaca, New York: Cornell University Press, 1999.

Griffith, Mary. *Three Hundred Years Hence*. Gregg Press, 1975.

Shelley, Mary. *Frankenstein; or, the Modern Prometheus*. London: Lackington, Allen & Co., 1818.

The Duties of American Citizenship

Speech

By: Theodore Roosevelt

Date: January 11, 1883

Source: Roosevelt, Theodore. "The Duties of American Citizenship." Buffalo, N.Y.: January 11, 1883.

About the Author: Theodore Roosevelt, Jr., served as a New York State Assemblyman, the Police Commissioner of New York City, Assistant Secretary of the U.S. Navy, and other public offices before volunteering for military service during the Spanish-American War (1898). He helped lead the Rough Riders unit to fame during the war and was elected governor of New York later that year. In 1900 he was elected vice president of the United States, and in 1901 he became the nation's twenty-sixth president after the assassination of President William McKinley. Roosevelt held the office until 1909. As president he supported progressive reforms, such as greater government control over business and the conservation of nature. Dissatisfied with his successor, President Taft, Roosevelt ran unsuccessfully for a third term in 1912 under the banner of the "Bull Moose" Party. Theodore Roosevelt's fifth cousin is Franklin D. Roosevelt, president of the United States from 1933 to 1945.

INTRODUCTION

The 1880s in the United States proved to be a time of rapid economic and personal growth, and it marked the height of the Gilded Age. The Gilded Age ran from approximately 1870 to 1900. The U.S. Civil War ended in 1865, Reconstruction officially ended in 1877, and the Second Industrial Revolution brought new products and residents to the nation. The 1880s saw more than five million immigrants from Europe migrate to the United States, and new technologies like steam made transportation faster. Railroads connected the American West with the east, and farmers were more eager to move westward. The ease of transportation, the promise of lands, cattle, and homes incited the American public to push forward.

As the west expanded, cities boomed with the new waves of immigrants. Encouraging the growth of immigrants came from U.S. industries contracting foreign labor, until 1885 when the Foran Act made the practice illegal. Also, the padrone system flourished. This system used a labor boss who encouraged ethnic groups to come to the United States for work. These individuals would come here and live and work with friends, families, and peoples of the same nationality. Hence, newcomers to the United States could retain a sense of the old world while building a new life in another country. However, even though the rise of new and expanded industries—those of coal, steel, and manufacturing—needed cheap immigrant labor for production, not everyone remained happy about the changing shape of the American social landscape.

The rise in immigration saw traditional immigrant groups become outnumbered. Some of those old-stock groups consisted of British, Irish, Scotch, Scandinavian, and German immigrants. These are also the traditional White Anglo-Saxon immigrants from the colonies and early years of the nation's forming. These older immigrant groups upheld social standards of the middle-class ideal, while the newer groups worked the least desirable jobs. These jobs ranged from agricultural work to steel mills. The middle classes viewed the manufacturing jobs as beneath them and those of uneducated and common men. These tensions, along with the expanding territory of the nation, laid the framework for the intense political and social divisions that lay ahead.

In cities like New York, Boston, and Chicago, the rise of immigrants brought the growth of political machines and changes in voting patterns. These machines rallied working-class and immigrant votes to bring non-middle class, old-stock immigrant candidates into office. In places like New York, which had a higher immigrant population than a native one, this

shift in office holders ignited heated debates among the city's residents. Many upper and middle class citizens felt that the lower classes were bringing down their quality of life, and they believed that these new voters were corrupting society with their lack of morals and education. New York City's Boss Tweed, William Marcy Tweed, is probably the most famous of these political reformers. Through coercion, ethnic affiliations, and corruption, leaders like Tweed helped bring police departments, fire stations, and public services to growing American cities. Tweed died in 1878, but his legacy survived him. More importantly, the growth of political corruption reflects the growing divide between the wealthy and poor in society. John D. Rockefeller and Andrew Carnegie made their fortunes in the oil and steel industries. Men like Carnegie and Rockefeller earned the title of Robber Baron because of their aggressive business practices. They quickly built up their companies by buying out the competition, forcing competitors to go bankrupt with price wars, and obtaining and holding monopolies on the market. These business practices reflected many of the political practices of the day, especially those of the political bosses in urban areas.

Social forces began to react against these political and economic units, and writings of muckraker journalists brought a wide array of issues to light. Muckraker journalists tended to investigate areas of corruption, corporate crime, child labor, and other areas of social contempt. The writings of the muckrakers brought forth the 1890 Sherman Anti-Trust Law. This law banned pacts, agreements, and laws preventing or restricting interstate or foreign trade. As reforms began to take hold, and grassroots organizations developed to reform labor laws, housing codes, and city services, U.S. society grappled with its growing pains. The middle and upper classes viewed the rise in immigration as the problem; they claimed that new immigrants were taking jobs away from Americans, and they felt isolated from local politics. As these social dilemmas worked their way into national politics, senators, writers, and reformers continually focused their works on reforming the state of American society. Theodore Roosevelt, then an assemblyman in New York, captured these social moods by declaring that both the wealthy and the poor were responsible for urban decay, declining morals, and political and economic corruption. His words mirror John Henry Hopkins' 1857 *The American Citizen: His Rights and Duties According to the Spirit of the Constitution of the United States*. This work followed the nineteenth-century belief that citizenship and patriotism were linked through political action, and public speeches like Roosevelt's merely captured

A poster promoting the World War I era Third Liberty Loan, encouraging Americans to show their patriotism by purchasing government bonds. © SWIM INK 2, LLC/CORBIS.

PRIMARY SOURCE

But let me reiterate, that in being virtuous he must not become ineffective, and that he must not excuse himself for shirking his duties by any false plea that he cannot do his duties and retain his self-respect. This is nonsense, he can; and when he urges such a plea it is a mark of mere laziness and self-indulgence. And again, he should beware how he becomes a critic of the actions of others, rather than a doer of deeds himself; and in so far as he does act as a critic (and of course the critic has a great and necessary function) he must beware of indiscriminate censure even more than of indiscriminate praise. The screaming vulgarity of the foolish spread-eagle orator who is continually

yelling defiance at Europe, praising everything American, good and bad, and resenting the introduction of any reform because it has previously been tried successfully abroad, is offensive and contemptible to the last degree; but after all it is scarcely as harmful as the peevish, fretful, sneering, and continual faultfinding of the refined, well-educated man, who is always attacking good and bad alike, who genuinely distrusts America, and in the true spirit of servile colonialism considers us inferior to the people across the water. It may be taken for granted that the man who is always sneering at our public life and our public men is a thoroughly bad citizen, and that what little influence he wields in the community is wielded for evil. The public speaker or the editorial writer who teaches men of education that their proper attitude toward American politics should be one of dislike or indifference is doing all he can to perpetuate and aggravate the very evils of which he is ostensibly complaining. Exactly as it is generally the case that when a man bewails the decadence of our civilization he is himself physically, mentally, and morally a first-class type of the decadent, so it is usually the case that when a man is perpetually sneering at American politicians, whether worthy or unworthy, he himself is a poor citizen and a friend of the very forces of evil against which he professes to contend. Too often these men seem to care less for attacking bad men, than for ruining the characters of good men with whom they disagree on some pubic question; and while their influence against the bad is almost nil, they are sometimes able to weaken the hands of the good by withdrawing from them support to which they are entitled, and they thus count in the sum total of forces that work for evil. They answer to the political prohibitionist, who, in a close contest between a temperance man and a liquor seller diverts enough votes from the former to elect the liquor seller. Occasionally it is necessary to beat a pretty good man, who is not quite good enough, even at the cost of electing a bad one—but it should be thoroughly recognized that this can be necessary only occasionally and indeed, I may say, only in very exceptional cases, and that as a rule where it is done the effect is thoroughly unwholesome in every way, and those taking part in it deserve the severest censure from all honest men.

Moreover, the very need of denouncing evil makes it all the more wicked to weaken the effect of such denunciations by denouncing also the good. It is the duty of all citizens, irrespective of party, to denounce, and, so far as may be, to punish crimes against the public on the part of politicians or officials. But exactly as the public man who commits a crime against the public is one of the worst of criminals, so, close on his heels in the race for iniquitous distinction, comes the man who falsely charges the public servant with outrageous wrongdoing; whether it is done with foul-mouthed and foolish directness in the vulgar and

the sentiment. Reiterating patriotism and activism in politics proved poignant as the United States expanded its borders and continued to grow economically.

violent party organ, or with sarcasm, innuendo, and the half-truths that are worse than lies, in some professed organ of independence. Not only should criticism be honest, but it should be intelligent, in order to be effective. . . .

Criticism should be fearless, but I again reiterate that it should be honest and should be discriminating. When it is sweeping and unintelligent, and directed against good and bad alike, or against the good and bad qualities of any man alike, it is very harmful. It tends steadily to deteriorate the character of our public men; and it tends to produce a very unwholesome spirit among young men of education, and especially among the young men in our colleges.

Against nothing is fearless and specific criticism more urgently needed than against the "spoils system," which is the degradation of American politics. And nothing is more effective in thwarting the purposes of the spoilsmen than the civil service reform. To be sure, practical politicians sneer at it. One of them even went so far as to say that civil-service reform is asking a man irrelevant questions. What more irrelevant question could there be than that of the practical politician who asks the aspirant for his political favor—"Whom did you vote for in the last election?" There is certainly nothing more interesting, from a humorous point of view, than the heads of departments urging changes to be made in their underlings, "on the score of increased efficiency" they say; when as the result of such a change the old incumbent often spends six months teaching the new incumbent how to do the work almost as well as he did himself! Occasionally the civil-service reform has been abused, but not often. Certainly the reform is needed when you contemplate the spectacle of a New York City treasurer who acknowledges his annual fees to be eighty-five thousand dollars, and who pays a deputy one thousand five hundred dollars to do his work—when you note the corruptions in the New York legislature, where one man says he has a horror of the Constitution because it prevents active benevolence, and another says that you should never allow the Constitution to come between friends! All these corruptions and vices are what every good American citizen must fight against.

Finally, the man who wishes to do his duty as a citizen in our country must be imbued through and through with the spirit of Americanism. I am not saying this as a matter of spread-eagle rhetoric: I am saying it quite soberly as a piece of matter-of-fact, common-sense advice, derived from my own experience of others. Of course, the question of Americanism has several sides. If a man is an educated man, he must show his Americanism by not getting misled into following out and trying to apply all the theories of the political thinkers of other countries, such as Germany and France, to our own entirely different conditions. He must not get a fad, for instance, about responsible government; and above all things he must

not, merely because he is intelligent, or a college professor well read in political literature, try to discuss our institutions when he has had no practical knowledge of how they are worked. Again, if he is a wealthy man, a man of means and standing, he must really feel, not merely affect to feel, that no social differences obtain save such as a man can in some way himself make by his own actions. People sometimes ask me if there is not a prejudice against a man of wealth and education in ward politics. I do not think that there is, unless the man in turn shows that he regards the facts of his having wealth and education as giving him a claim to superiority aside from the merit he is able to prove himself to have in actual service. Of course, if he feels that he ought to have a little better treatment than a carpenter, a plumber, or a butcher, who happens to stand beside him, he is going to be thrown out of the race very quickly, and probably quite roughly; and if he starts in to patronize and elaborately condescend to these men he will find that they resent this attitude even more. Do not let him think about the matter at all. Let him go into the political contest with no more thought of such matters than a college boy gives to the social standing of the members of his own and rival teams in a hotly contested football match. As soon as he begins to take an interest in politics (and he will speedily not only get interested for the sake of politics, but also take a good healthy interest in playing the game itself—an interest which is perfectly normal and praise-worthy, and to which only a prig would object), he will begin to work up the organization in the way that will be most effective, and he won't care a rap about who is put to work with him, save in so far as he is a good fellow and an efficient worker. There was one time that a number of men who think as we do here to-night (one of the number being myself) got hold of one of the assembly districts of New York, and ran it in really an ideal way, better than any other assembly district has ever been run before or since by either party. We did it by hard work and good organization; by working practically, and yet by being honest and square in motive and method: especially did we do it by all turning in as straight-out Americans without any regard to distinctions of race origin. Among the many men who did a great deal in organizing our victories was the son of a Presbyterian clergyman, the nephew of a Hebrew rabbi, and two well-known Catholic gentlemen. We also had a Columbia College professor (the stroke-oar of a university crew), a noted retail butcher, and the editor of a local German paper, various brokers, bankers, lawyers, bricklayers and a stone-mason who was particularly useful to us, although on questions of theoretic rather than applied politics he had a decidedly socialistic turn of mind.

Again, questions of race origin, like questions of creed, must not be considered: we wish to do good work, and we are all Americans, pure and simple. In the New York legislature, when it fell to my lot to choose a committee—which I always esteemed my most important duty at Albany—no less than three out of the four men I chose were of Irish birth or parentage; and three abler and more fearless and disinterested men never sat in a legislative body; while among my especial political and personal friends in that body was a gentleman from the southern tier of counties, who was, I incidentally found out, a German by birth, but who was just as straight United States as if his ancestors had come over here in the Mayflower or in Henry Hudson's yacht. Of course, none of these men of Irish or German birth would have been worth their salt had they continued to act after coming here as Irishmen or Germans, or as anything but plain straight-out Americans. We have not any room here for a divided allegiance. A man has got to be an American and nothing else; and he has no business to be mixing us up with questions of foreign politics, British or Irish, German or French, and no business to try to perpetuate their language and customs in the land of complete religious toleration and equality. If, however, he does become honestly and in good faith an American, then he is entitled to stand precisely as all other Americans stand, and it is the height of un-Americanism to discriminate against him in any way because of creed or birthplace. No spirit can be more thoroughly alien to American institutions, than the spirit of the Know-Nothings.

In facing the future and in striving, each according to the measure of his individual capacity, to work out the salvation of our land, we should be neither timid pessimists nor foolish optimists. We should recognize the dangers that exist and that threaten us: we should neither overestimate them nor shrink from them, but steadily fronting them should set to work to overcome and beat them down. Grave perils are yet to be encountered in the stormy course of the Republic—perils from political corruption, perils from individual laziness, indolence and timidity, perils springing from the greed of the unscrupulous rich, and from the anarchic violence of the thriftless and turbulent poor. There is every reason why we should recognize them, but there is no reason why we should fear them or doubt our capacity to overcome them, if only each will, according to the measure of his ability, do his full duty, and endeavor so to live as to deserve the high praise of being called a good American citizen.

SIGNIFICANCE

Dilemmas within American society continued to erupt, soften, and manifest into new social concerns. The 1880s saw Americans continue to fight over political and national boundaries. In 1887, after years of disputes between white society and the Native Americans, the Dawes Act attempted to protect

A World War II era poster calls on citizens and soldiers to do their duty to the United States and not discuss information that might be helpful to America's enemies. © K.J. HISTORICAL/CORBIS.

Native American lands. The act gave Native American homestead lots, but continued white aggression for land ownership; the Oklahoma land rush of 1889 cost Native Americans over half of their land. Land disputes in the 1880s also paved the way for the growth of the Department of Labor, in 1888, and labor unions. The rise of immigrants brought cheap labor, and initially old-stock immigrants sought protections through unions to keep their jobs. But, labor unions quickly changed shape as workers realized that they must unite together, across ethnic boundaries, to give themselves a united front.

Labor unions and the acquisition of land were not initially seen as political activism, but these actions forced new laws and regulations to be enacted. The twentieth century saw the birth of labor laws and restrictions. They limited the hours of children, the workday, and eventually legalized unions. More importantly, the era saw the integration of citizenship ideals and education merge. In 1914, Henry Ford established his Americanism program in his auto plants, and in 1915, the National Education Association adopted curriculum for teaching citizenship advocacy in the classroom. Here, workers were given higher wages, shorter hours, and better benefits while being instructed in courses on civics and living moderate and moral lifestyles. Ford saw this program as a way to integrate the much-needed immigrant worker into American life and culture. Parts of his program filtered into schools and other factories.

American citizenship debates continue into the present era. As of May 2006, proposed legislation circulates in the U.S. Congress concerning immigration restrictions for the United States. The 2006 debate mirrors previous citizenship and immigration discussions because of the 1882 passage of the Chinese Exclusion Act by the U.S. Congress. This act prevented Asian immigrants from coming to the United States because many feared they were taking jobs away from whites. The rise of Chinese (and Asian immigrants) came from the building of the railroads. In 1924, the Immigration Act performed similar restrictions on immigrants, but it placed quotas on entry numbers from the 1890 census. The 2006 debate concerned removing, restricting, and legalizing illegal immigrants. Also, parts of the debate concerned a changing population—one with an emerging majority of Hispanic residents—and fluctuating political identities. Similar to what the 1880s experienced with election results favoring immigrant desires, the same trends occurred in 2006, and old fears that immigrant workers were taking jobs away was again a hot political topic. Questions of what it means to be an American citizen and what a person's role is in society have taken the forefront in early twenty-first century political debates.

FURTHER RESOURCES

Books

Cashman, Sean Dennis. *America in the Gilded Age: From the Death of Lincoln to the Rise of Theodore Roosevelt.* New York: New York University Press, 1993.

O'Leary, Cecilia Elizabeth. *To Die For: The Paradox of American Patriotism.* Princeton, N.J.: Princeton University Press, 1999.

Skowronek, Stephen. *Building A New American State: The Expansion of National Administrative Capacities, 1877–1920.* Cambridge, U.K. and New York: Cambridge University Press, 1984.

Periodicals

Reuben, Julie A. "Beyond Politics: Community Civics and the Redefinition of Citizenship in the Progressive Era." *History Education Quarterly* 37, 4 (Winter 1997): 399–420.

The Communist Manifesto

Book excerpt

By: Karl Marx and Friedrich Engels

Date: 1848

Source: Marx, Karl, and Friedrich Engels. *The Communist Manifesto.* 1848.

About the Author: Karl Marx (1818–1883) and Friedrich Engels (1820–1895) are the German-born founders of modern international communism. Both men wrote *The Communist Manifesto*, but Engels generally edited and translated Marx's writings. They attacked the state as the instrument of oppression.

INTRODUCTION

The Communist Manifesto grew out of criticism of early industrial society. Socialists condemned economic inequalities and attacked the capitalist system that permitted the exploitation of workers. Karl Marx and Friedrich Engels explored the sociology of poverty and the social structures that allowed a concentration of power and wealth in the hands of relatively few individuals.

Marx and Engels were the most prominent of the nineteenth century socialists. These German-born theorists believed that the social problems of the nineteenth century were the inevitable results of a capitalist economy. They argued that capitalism divided people into two main classes, each with its own economic interests and social status: the capitalists, who owned industrial machinery and factories (the means of production), and the proletariat, consisting of wage workers who had only their own labor to sell. Intense competition between capitalists trying to make a profit resulted in ruthless exploitation of the working class. To make matters worse, according to Marx and Engels, the state and its coercive institutions, such as police forces and courts of law, were agencies of the capitalist ruling class. The function of the state was to maintain capitalists in power and enable them to continue their exploitation of the working class.

Marx developed these views fully in *Capital: Critique of Political Economy*, a long, theoretical work that was published in three volumes from 1867 to 1894. Together with Engels, Marx also wrote a short pamphlet, *The Communist Manifesto*, in 1848. In this work, Marx and Engels aligned themselves with the communists, who aimed for the abolition of private property and the creation of a totally egalitarian society. Famously, *The Communist Manifesto* asserts that all human history has been the history of struggle between social classes. The work can be viewed as representative of mid-nineteenth century European thought on the problems of the working class.

PRIMARY SOURCE

Does it require deep intuition to comprehend that man's ideas, views and conceptions, in one word, man's consciousness, changes with every change in the conditions of his material existence, in his social relations and in his social life?

What else does the history of ideas prove, than that intellectual production changes its character in proportion as material production is changed? The ruling ideas of each age have ever been the ideas of its ruling class.

When people speak of ideas that revolutionize society, they do but express the fact, that within the old society, the elements of a new one have been created, and that the dissolution of the old ideas keeps even pace with the dissolution of the old conditions of existence.

When the ancient world was in its last throes, the ancient religions were overcome by Christianity. When Christian ideas succumbed in the 18th century to rationalist ideas, feudal society fought its death battle with the then revolutionary bourgeoisie. The ideas of religious liberty and freedom of conscience merely gave expression to the sway of free competition within the domain of knowledge.

"Undoubtedly," it will be said, "religious, moral, philosophical and juridical ideas have been modified in the course of historical development. But religion, morality philosophy, political science, and law, constantly survived this change."

"There are, besides, eternal truths, such as Freedom, Justice, etc. that are common to all states of society. But Communism abolishes eternal truths, it abolishes all religion, and all morality, instead of constituting them on a new basis; it therefore acts in contradiction to all past historical experience."

What does this accusation reduce itself to? The history of all past society has consisted in the development of class antagonisms, antagonisms that assumed different forms at different epochs.

But whatever form they may have taken, one fact is common to all past ages, viz., the exploitation of one part of society by the other. No wonder, then, that the social consciousness of past ages, despite all the multiplicity and variety it displays, moves within certain common forms, or general ideas, which cannot completely vanish except with the total disappearance of class antagonisms.

The Communist revolution is the most radical rupture with traditional property relations; no wonder that its development involves the most radical rupture with traditional ideas.

But let us have done with the bourgeois objections to Communism.

We have seen above, that the first step in the revolution by the working class, is to raise the proletariat to the position of ruling as to win the battle of democracy.

The proletariat will use its political supremacy to wrest, by degrees, all capital from the bourgeoisie, to centralize all instruments of production in the hands of the State, i.e., of the proletariat organized as the ruling class; and to increase the total of productive forces as rapidly as possible.

Of course, in the beginning, this cannot be effected except by means of despotic inroads on the rights of property, and on the conditions of bourgeois production; by means of measures, therefore, which appear economically insufficient and untenable, but which, in the course of the movement, outstrip themselves, necessitate further inroads upon the old social order, and are unavoidable as a means of entirely revolutionizing the mode of production.

These measures will of course be different in different countries.

Nevertheless in the most advanced countries, the following will be pretty generally applicable.

1. Abolition of property in land and application of all rents of land to public purposes.
2. A heavy progressive or graduated income tax.
3. Abolition of all right of inheritance.
4. Confiscation of the property of all emigrants and rebels.
5. Centralization of credit in the hands of the State, by means of a national bank with State capital and an exclusive monopoly.
6. Centralization of the means of communication and transport in the hands of the State.
7. Extension of factories and instruments of production owned by the State; the bringing into cultivation of waste-lands, and the improvement of the soil generally in accordance with a common plan.
8. Equal liability of all to labor. Establishment of industrial armies, especially for agriculture.
9. Combination of agriculture with manufacturing industries; gradual abolition of the distinction between town and country, by a more equable distribution of the population over the country.
10. Free education for all children in public schools. Abolition of children's factory labor in its present form. Combination of education with industrial production, etc., etc.

The Communist Manifesto and other items captured by police when they arrested a striking electrical plant worker in 1954. © BETTMANN/ CORBIS.

When, in the course of development, class distinctions have disappeared, and all production has been concentrated in the hands of a vast association of the whole nation, the public power will lose its political character. Political power, properly so called, is merely the organized power of one class for oppressing another. If the proletariat during its contest with the bourgeoisie is compelled, by the force of circumstances, to organize itself as a class, if, by means of a revolution, it makes itself the ruling class, and, as such, sweeps away by force the old conditions of production, then it will, along with these conditions, have swept away the conditions for the existence of class antagonisms and of classes generally, and will thereby have abolished its own supremacy as a class.

In place of the old bourgeois society, with its classes and class antagonisms, we shall have an association, in which the free development of each is the condition for the free development of all.

SIGNIFICANCE

Throughout the second half of the nineteenth century, socialism and socialist parties spread rapidly throughout Europe and the United States. The doctrines of Marx and Engels came to dominate European and international socialist thought. Revolutionary socialists like Marx and Engels urged workers to seize control of the state, confiscate the means of production, and redistribute wealth equitably throughout society. Such a revolutionary takeover occurred in Russia, leading to the creation of the communist Soviet Union that controlled much of Eastern Europe until 1989. The collapse of the Soviet model has given support to evolutionary socialists who argue that socialists should work through representative governments to elect legislators who support socialist reforms.

Despite the apparent failure of revolutionary socialism, *The Communist Manifesto* remains one of the most widely read secular books in any language. The work has maintained a substantial worldwide readership as a classic of political philosophy and a crucial historical document, while remaining key to many popular struggles for liberation. With major international movements forming around fair trade, ecology and sustainability, and economic and political justice, interest in *The Communist Manifesto* is higher at the turn of the millennium than it has been since the 1970s.

FURTHER RESOURCES

Books

Cowling, Mark, ed. *The Communist Manifesto: New Interpretations.* Washington Square, N.Y.: New York University Press, 1998.

Hamori, Paul A. *The Communist Manifesto: A Framework for a Critical Analysis and a Cursory Interpretation.* Muncie, Ind.: Ball State University, 1974.

Hodges, Donald Clark. *The Literate Communist: 150 Years of the Communist Manifesto.* New York: P. Lang, 1999.

The People's Legal Right to Freedom

Magazine article

By: Zhinazi

Date: 1903

Source: Angle, Stephen, and Marina Svensson. *The Chinese Human Rights Reader.* Armonk, N.Y.: M.E. Sharpe, 2001.

About the Author: "Zhinazi" is a pseudonym for an unknown Chinese political thinker writing in 1903.

INTRODUCTION

Chinese thought on the subject of human rights has developed along partly independent lines from Western thought, although, over the last two centuries, there has been considerable Western influence. This article is a manifesto proclaiming what the author believed to be essential human rights, especially appealing to the standards of what the author repeatedly describes as "civilized" states, namely European states. This article was first published in 1903 in a magazine called *Zhejiang Chao*, which was produced for one year by a group of Chinese men studying in Japan.

PRIMARY SOURCE

The right to freedom (ziyou quan) is one of the rights (quanli) that people hold against the state (guojia). If we examine the history of Europe, we will see that this right could not have been obtained if [European] states had not gone through numerous revolutions and their people had not gone through endless bloodshed. Uncivilized, despotic states feared only one thing: the freedom of their people, which would be able to limit the states' despotic powers. So long as the people's knowledge was deficient, their intellectual and physical strengths did not suffice to defy their states, and therefore they could not but lower their heads and obey [their rulers]. As people became more civilized, and also as they were pushed by the trends of the times and pressed by social changes, they were no longer willing to be fooled and manipulated. They mounted opposition movements aimed at recovering the rights that they ought to enjoy (yingxiang zhi quanli). The people of modern civilized countries are all [able to] bustle about under the aegis of their constitutions. Their states not only do not dare to interfere arbitrarily, but actually pay particular attention to protecting them. Isn't all this the result of fantastically ardent efforts by their predecessors?

Alas, our people always speak of freedom, freedom. Yet what after all is the right to freedom? And what eventually distinguishes the limit of freedom? I am afraid that our people are still utterly ignorant of these things....

Here I list the kinds of rights to freedom below.

1. The freedom of residence and movement. The most essential among people's rights to freedom is the right of residence. The state is composed of people. Whoever resides in the territory of a state is its subject. Therefore the state allows its people to freely move without any restriction within its territory.

2. The freedom of physical security. In a civilized country people have noble personalities. Even a hair or a tress should not sustain any unreasonable restraint, so the state does not dare to improperly act to arrest, imprison, or punish anyone. Crimes in violation of the law, of course, are separate matters.

3. The freedom of safe residence. "Residence" is the place that people use for their daily living. Legally speaking, "[safe] residence" means not to damage a person's safety within his abode. So long as people are not suspected of a crime, the state ought not to intrude upon and search their residence without a reason, in order to protect their safety.

4. The freedom of secrecy in correspondence. "Correspondence" is when a particular person conveys his ideas to another particular person in written words. It is sealed carefully, unlike public mass advertisements that are intended to be known to all people. Thus the state's

administrative organs, except as required by law, should not purposely open correspondence or show it to others, no matter what the enclosed content.

5. The freedom of assembly and association. "Assembly" is the gathering of a large number of people for a common end. "Association" is a contractual relationship; in order to fulfill their common end, a large number of people gather and contract to permanently and continuously seek their objective. During the old despotic era, the state prohibited and forcefully guarded against this right, fearing that people would initiate acts of resistance. In modern constitutional states, on the other hand, so long as the peace and order of the state and society are not harmed, the state should never interfere with this right.

6. The freedom of thought and expression. Certainly the law has no way to interfere with a person's inner thoughts. Only after the thought is published externally does it become the object of law and the state is able to limit or protect it. That which is put forth orally is called speech; that which is put forth in written words or illustrations is called writing; that which is put forth using stone-block, wood-block, or lead-block [printing] is called printed matter. So long as they do not transgress the limits of law, the state ought not arbitrarily interfere.

7. The freedom of ownership. The right to ownership (suoyou quan) is a relation between individuals in public law. As stipulated in the constitution, the right to ownership has two meanings. The first restricts the operation of the state's power, making it unable to violate people's freedom of ownership. The second protects people's freedom; if the state's administration violates [someone's property], [he or she] is permitted to be compensated by way of an administrative lawsuit.

8. The freedom of worship. Prior to the eighteenth century, the power of the Roman Pope was unlimited. Even all the rulers of European countries were subject to his power. Therefore politics and religion were subject to his power. Therefore politics and religion were hardly separable, and his strength was able to force the people not to convert to their religions [sic]. In the modern age, after many revolutions and with the advancement of civilization, the state's politics and religion have become absolutely separate and independent. The state grants its people freedom of worship and does not interfere, though [religious activities] should not cross the boundary of peace and order.

In all, then, there are eight kinds of rights to freedom. They are set down in the law code, declared in the constitution, and all have sworn to comply and do not dare to disobey. But where are these rights [actually] respected?

Alas, when I think about this, I cannot help sighing deeply. Please consider: have the four hundred million people of our China completely enjoyed these rights? Should our citizens desire to put into practice their freedom of assembly and association, and so gather a large number of people to form an organization, the government would certainly label it as a rebellion, uprising, or riot, and would employ its despotic force to dispel them, arrest them, imprison them, and would not stop until all are stamped out. Should our citizens desire to put into practice their freedom of thought and expression to make manifest the common principles of mankind, the government would definitely hold [the principles] to be rumors, heterodoxies, insults to the court, or sacrilege, and would proscribe them, destroy them, and would not be content until the principles can no longer be heard.

I do not blame the arbitrariness of the government, though: I only blame the ignorance of our citizens. Which among the so-called civilized governments was not barbaric and despotic before their reforms? Why is rights consciousness (quanli sixiang) so weak in the minds our citizens? Why do they treat rights so casually that they do not fight to reform the law, to stipulate clearly the limits of law, and hence to recover the rights due to them (yingyou zhi quanli)?

I cannot but blame those today who call themselves advocates of freedom (ziyouzhe). They do not have a sense of the civic consciousness (gonggongxin) nor a capability for self-rule (zizhi). They make the destruction of the community their purpose and regard the transgression of rules as freedom. They indulge themselves in individual selfishness and harm the rights of the commonality. Even up to the day they lose both fortune and honor, they still speak boastfully to others about "freedom, freedom," whereas they have degraded the value of freedom to nothing. Could they possibly know that what is called freedom and what are called rights in civilized states are [in each case] acknowledged by the law that has been approved publicly by the citizens? People together make up a state. If the elements of a state are all [passive and lacking in rights consciousness,] as I described above, then there will never be a day when the citizens recover their freedom. If the elements [have no civic consciousness nor sense of self-rule,] as I just described, then there will never be a day when the citizens peacefully enjoy their freedom. Civilized countries have no people who merely fulfill duties, nor do they have governments that exclusively enjoy rights. Those under heaven most capable of fulfilling duties while not enjoying rights are slaves and animals. If our citizens are willing to be slaves or animals, and allow a shepherd to reprimand them and thrash them, then there is nothing more to say. Otherwise, they should rise up at once.

SIGNIFICANCE

At the time this article was written, China was governed by its next-to-last emperor, Emperor Zaitian of the Qing dynasty. China had been ruled by emperors of various dynasties for approximately 2,000 years. The last emperor (Puyi) conceded in 1908 that a constitution was needed, and, in 1910, even took steps toward convening a national parliament, but these half-hearted measures never took shape. Puyi abdicated in 1912, and, from 1912 to 1916, China was governed by its first republic. The constitution of this republic explicitly recognized some of the principles articulated in this rights manifesto by Zhinazi, including freedom of religion.

However, the recognition of rights in constitutional documents does not necessarily correspond to reality. The Constitution of the People's Republic of China, enacted in 1982, states that "citizens of the People's Republic of China enjoy freedom of speech, of the press, of assembly, of association, of procession, and of demonstration," but in practice, citizens of China are routinely jailed and tortured or executed for practicing forbidden religions or criticizing the government. Hundreds of peaceful demonstrators were massacred in Tiananmen Square in the capital city of Beijing in 1989. It is one thing to proclaim rights in a constitution and another for them to be available to citizens.

Chinese thought on the subject of human rights dates to the sixteenth century, when neo-Confucian philosophers debated the subject of "legitimate desires" and "legitimate interests." In this setting, a right is seen as a means to an end (the realization of a legitimate desire or protection of a legitimate interest) rather than as an end in itself. In the nineteenth century, partly under influence from Europe and Japan, the concepts of "rights" (quanli, the word used by the writer of this primary source) and "people's [political] rights" (minquan) were articulated. Early in the twentieth century, about the time this manifesto was written, the term *renquan* came into use, which is usually used in modern Chinese to signify rights. According to China scholars, the concept of rights that developed at this time was—in keeping with its Confucian heritage—oriented toward ends and interests, including economic ends and interests, rather than toward absoluteness and innateness, as in much Western thought. In the nationalistic May Fourth Movement in China from 1919 to the mid-1920s, intellectual freedoms were a central concern. The idea that religion should be forbidden as irrational and harmful superstition co-existed in the Movement with ideals of freedom of speech, association, and the like.

Despite China's long history of intellectual engagement with the concept of human rights, the government of China today systematically violates many human rights. Some writers have argued that China should not be held to Western standards in such matters. They contend that the concept of human rights is relative, not absolute, and has evolved over the last few centuries of Western intellectual history. It would, therefore, be a form of cultural imperialism to impose Western ideals about freedom on the Chinese people. By protecting law and order and seeing to the orderly economic development of China, the government of China is protecting human rights according to Chinese rights. The Chinese government itself makes this argument. Its delegation to a U.N. human rights meeting in 1993 said, "The concept of human rights is a product of historical development.... Different historical development stages have different human rights requirements." China also accuses the West of hypocrisy, pointing to recent U.S. claims that human rights can be violated in the name of "the war on terrorism."

As noted above, there has, indeed, been a distinct school of Chinese thought on the nature of human rights for centuries. However, as documents such as this primary source and the constitution of the People's Republic of China show, the ideals articulated by that Chinese school of thought do not differ radically from those that are generally held in the West.

Western Internet companies such as Yahoo! and Google, which have cooperated with the Chinese government in censoring the Internet inside China, offer a rights-through-development argument that echoes that of the Chinese government. These Western companies and others that do business with the Chinese security apparatus argue that the best way to help human rights advance inside China is to speed China's economic development—while, of course, making a profit. U.S. foreign policy has usually reflected a similar philosophy, with China retaining Normal Trade Relations status (formerly Most Favored Nation trading status) despite its numerous human rights violations in occupied Tibet and within its own borders.

FURTHER RESOURCES

Books

Svensson, Marina. *Debating Human Rights in China: A Conceptual and Political History.* Lanham, Md.: Rowman & Littlefield, 2002.

Periodicals

Cody, Edward. "China, Others Criticize U.S. Report on Rights: Double Standard at State Dept. Alleged." *Washington Post* (March 4, 2005).

Web sites

Calvin College. "Human Rights, Religious Freedom, and Chinese Christians." February 19, 2004. <http://www.calvin.edu/minds/vol01/issue02/chinese-christians.php> (accessed May 3, 2006).

Niagara's Declaration of Principles

Declaration

By: Anonymous

Date: July 1905

Source: "Niagara's Declaration of Principles." Niagara Movement, July 1905.

About the Author: When first published in 1905, the *Declaration of Principles* was attributed to the Niagara Movement, a new organization committed to obtaining civil, legal, and social rights for African-Americans. Although they were not personally credited, it was clear that the new general secretary, W.E.B. Du Bois, and the new chairman of the Press and Public Opinion Committee, William Monroe Trotter, co-authored the *Declaration.* Historical research into the letters and documents of the Niagara Movement's members confirm this assumption. William Edward Burghardt Du Bois (1868–1963) and Monroe Trotter (1872–1934), as Trotter was known, were both African-Americans from Massachusetts. Du Bois received his doctorate from Harvard University in 1895, the same year that Trotter earned his bachelor's degree there. Du Bois became a scholar specializing in the history, economics, and sociology of black Americans, and in 1901 Trotter founded the *Guardian,* an influential Black weekly newspaper published in Boston. Both Du Bois and Trotter were prolific writers as well as controversial activists. Trotter was seen as the more radical of the two, mainly due to the vitriolic editorials he wrote for the *Guardian,* which he edited until his death in 1934. Du Bois was one of the founders of the NAACP (National Association for the Advancement of Colored People) in 1909 and served as the editor of its magazine, *The Crisis,* from 1910 to 1934. Du Bois was also the author of many important books, including *The Souls of Black Folk* (1903), *Darkwater* (1920), *Black Reconstruction in America* (1935), and *Dusk of Dawn* (1940). In 1958, Du Bois emigrated to Ghana, where he died in 1963.

INTRODUCTION

The Niagara Movement was the first African-American organization to demand equality in all spheres of contemporaneous life. Its *Declaration of Principles* was drawn up at the organization's first conference, which took place in July 1905 at the Erie Beach Hotel in Fort Erie, Ontario, a Canadian resort area across the falls from Buffalo, New York. The *Declaration* was notable not only for being the first collective black claim to equal rights, but for its explicit, controversial, and detailed description of the different areas of concern to black Americans. Its demand for social equality openly defied current Jim Crow laws, and its language, which spoke of protest, oppression, and agitation, was bold, if not radical.

The *Declaration* was written in pointed contrast to the policies and demeanor advocated by Booker T. Washington and his followers at the Tuskegee Institute in Alabama. As the era's leading black spokesman, Washington's political and social influence was enormous. The Tuskegee Institute was well-funded by white philanthropists that approved of Washington's gradual, non-threatening programs for social change, as exemplified by the famous speech Washington gave in 1895, known as the Atlanta Compromise. The Niagara Movement deliberately opposed the Atlanta Compromise and the Tuskegee Machine (as Du Bois called Washington's organization) in addition to white racism.

■ PRIMARY SOURCE

Progress: The members of the conference, known as the Niagara Movement, assembled in annual meeting at Buffalo, July 11th, 12th and 13th, 1905, congratulate the Negro-Americans on certain undoubted evidences of progress in the last decade, particularly the increase of intelligence, the buying of property, the checking of crime, the uplift in home life, the advance in literature and art, and the demonstration of constructive and executive ability in the conduct of great religious, economic and educational institutions.

Suffrage: At the same time, we believe that this class of American citizens should protest emphatically and continually against the curtailment of their political rights. We believe in manhood suffrage; we believe that no man is so good, intelligent or wealthy as to be entrusted wholly with the welfare of his neighbor.

Civil Liberty: We believe also in protest against the curtailment of our civil rights. All American citizens have the right to equal treatment in places of public entertainment according to their behavior and deserts.

Co-chairmen of the Niagara Centennial Committee Todd Bolton (left) and George Rutherford (right) stand between a picture of the 1906 Niagara Movement founding members. The movement held its second annual meeting, the first in the United States, on the Storer College campus in Harper's Ferry, West Virginia. AP IMAGES.

Economic Opportunity: We especially complain against the denial of equal opportunities to us in economic life; in the rural districts of the South this amounts to peonage and virtual slavery; all over the South it tends to crush labor and small business enterprises; and everywhere American prejudice, helped often by iniquitous laws, is making it more difficult for Negro-Americans to earn a decent living.

Education: Common school education should be free to all American children and compulsory. High school training should be adequately provided for all, and college training should be the monopoly of no class or race in any section of our common country. We believe that, in defense of our own institutions, the United States should aid common school education, particularly in the South, and we especially recommend concerted agitation to this end. We urge an increase in public high school facilities in

the South, where the Negro-Americans are almost wholly without such provisions. We favor well-equipped trade and technical schools for the training of artisans, and the need of adequate and liberal endowment for a few institutions of higher education must be patent to sincere well-wishers of the race.

Courts: We demand upright judges in courts, juries selected without discrimination on account of color and the same measure of punishment and the same efforts at reformation for black as for white offenders. We need orphanages and farm schools for dependent children, juvenile reformatories for delinquents, and the abolition of the dehumanizing convict-lease system.

Public Opinion: We note with alarm the evident retrogression in this land of sound public opinion on the subject of manhood rights, republican government and human brotherhood, and we pray God that this nation will not degenerate into a mob of boasters and oppressors, but rather will return to the faith of the fathers, that all men were created free and equal, with certain unalienable rights.

Health: We plead for health—for an opportunity to live in decent houses and localities, for a chance to rear our children in physical and moral cleanliness.

Employers and Labor Unions: We hold up for public execration the conduct of two opposite classes of men: The practice among employers of importing ignorant Negro-American laborers in emergencies, and then affording them neither protection nor permanent employment; and the practice of labor unions in proscribing and boycotting and oppressing thousands of their fellow-toilers, simply because they are black. These methods have accentuated and will accentuate the war of labor and capital, and they are disgraceful to both sides.

Protest: We refuse to allow the impression to remain that the Negro-American assents to inferiority, is submissive under oppression and apologetic before insults. Through helplessness we may submit, but the voice of protest of ten million Americans must never cease to assail the ears of their fellows, so long as America is unjust.

Color-Line: Any discrimination based simply on race or color is barbarous, we care not how hallowed it be by custom, expediency or prejudice. Differences made on account of ignorance, immorality, or disease are legitimate methods of fighting evil, and against them we have no word of protest; but discriminations based simply and solely on physical peculiarities, place of birth, color of skin, are relics of that unreasoning human savagery of which the world is and ought to be thoroughly ashamed.

"Jim Crow" Cars: We protest against the "Jim Crow" car, since its effect is and must be to make us pay first-class fare for third-class accommodations, render us open to insults and discomfort and to crucify wantonly our manhood, womanhood and self-respect.

Soldiers: We regret that this nation has never seen fit adequately to reward the black soldiers who, in its five wars, have defended their country with their blood, and yet have been systematically denied the promotions which their abilities deserve. And we regard as unjust, the exclusion of black boys from the military and naval training schools.

War Amendments: We urge upon Congress the enactment of appropriate legislation for securing the proper enforcement of those articles of freedom, the thirteenth, fourteenth and fifteenth amendments of the Constitution of the United States.

Oppression: We repudiate the monstrous doctrine that the oppressor should be the sole authority as to the rights of the oppressed. The Negro race in America stolen, ravished and degraded, struggling up through difficulties and oppression, needs sympathy and receives criticism; needs help and is given hindrance, needs protection and is given mob-violence, needs justice and is given charity, needs leadership and is given cowardice and apology, needs bread and is given a stone. This nation will never stand justified before God until these things are changed.

The Church: Especially are we surprised and astonished at the recent attitude of the church of Christ—of an increase of a desire to bow to racial prejudice, to narrow the bounds of human brotherhood, and to segregate black men to some outer sanctuary. This is wrong, unchristian and disgraceful to the twentieth century civilization.

Agitation: Of the above grievances we do not hesitate to complain, and to complain loudly and insistently. To ignore, overlook, or apologize for these wrongs is to prove ourselves unworthy of freedom. Persistent manly agitation is the way to liberty, and toward this goal the Niagara Movement has started and asks the cooperation of all men of all races.

Help: At the same time we want to acknowledge with deep thankfulness the help of our fellowmen from the Abolitionist down to those who today still stand for equal opportunity and who have given and still give of their wealth and of their poverty for our advancement.

Duties: And while we are demanding, and ought to demand, and will continue to demand the rights enumerated above, God forbid that we should ever forget to urge corresponding duties upon our people:

> The duty to vote.
> The duty to respect the rights of others.
> The duty to work.
> The duty to obey the laws.
> The duty to be clean and orderly.
> The duty to send our children to school.
> The duty to respect ourselves, even as we respect others.

This statement, complaint and prayer we submit to the American people, and Almighty God.

SIGNIFICANCE

Historian David L. Lewis describes the Niagara Movement as part of the Talented Tenth's response to growing discontent with Booker T. Washington's policies, as well as a reaction to the increasing racism, violence, and oppressive laws that followed the end of Reconstruction in the American South. The Talented Tenth was the phrase that W.E.B. Du Bois coined to describe an emerging black professional class. As epitomized by the members of the Niagara Movement, most of the Talented Tenth had some education in

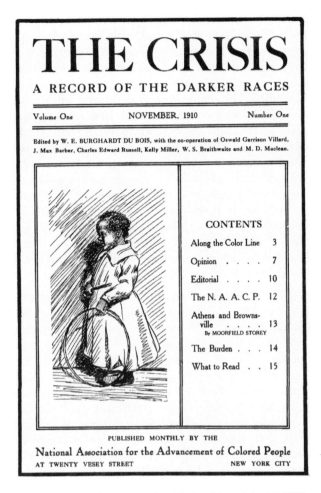

THE CRISIS

A RECORD OF THE DARKER RACES

Volume One   NOVEMBER, 1910   Number One

Edited by W. E. BURGHARDT DU BOIS, with the co-operation of Oswald Garrison Villard, J. Max Barber, Charles Edward Russell, Kelly Miller, W. S. Braithwaite and M. D. Maclean.

CONTENTS

Along the Color Line	3
Opinion	7
Editorial	10
The N. A. A. C. P.	12
Athens and Brownsville	13
By MOORFIELD STOREY	
The Burden	14
What to Read	15

PUBLISHED MONTHLY BY THE

National Association for the Advancement of Colored People
AT TWENTY VESEY STREET   NEW YORK CITY

The front cover of the November 1910 edition of the NAACP's monthly magazine *The Crisis.* This was the first edition of what would become one of the most important publications of the civil rights movement. PUBLIC DOMAIN.

the liberal arts. Many were college graduates who valued higher education for their race, as shown by the paragraph on education in the *Declaration.* This was in marked contrast to the Tuskegee Institute's focus on industrial education.

Booker T. Washington had already asked for Du Bois's help in organizing a conference of black leaders to be held in January of 1904, despite the fact that Du Bois had criticized Washington and his accommodationism in 1903 in *The Souls of Black Folk.* Du Bois's experience at this conference and his frustration with serving on the Committee of Twelve—the political action group organized by Washington—led Du Bois to consult with Monroe Trotter, Minnesota lawyer Frederick L. McGhee, and Chicago doctor Charles E. Bentley about forming a more radical black organization. As Fox describes in Trotter's biography, the

four planned a secret meeting for the summer of 1905. Du Bois invited fifty-nine men to come join "organized, determined, and aggressive action on the part of men who believe in Negro freedom and growth." Twenty-nine men attended the historic conference which resulted in the *Declaration of Principles.*

Although some accounts of the Niagara Movement's first meeting claim that it was scheduled to be held in Buffalo and that the men were denied hotel rooms because of their race, or because of a shortage of rooms caused by an Elks Club convention, there is no documented evidence for this. Buffalo residents and Du Bois supporters Mary Burnette Talbert and William H. Talbert may have suggested the Fort Erie resort location to Du Bois, who made the arrangements. Interestingly, there is some evidence that Booker T. Washington's followers kept all but a few newspapers from reporting on the Niagara Movement.

The Niagara Movement was officially incorporated in January 1906. By the time of its second conference in Harper's Ferry, West Virginia, in August 1906, the group had about 170 members in thirty branches and had distributed over ten thousand pieces of literature, including their *Declaration.* Despite the fact that the Niagara Movement only survived a few more years as an organization, Du Bois used both the organization's framework and its principles as the blueprint for a new, hugely successful group, the NAACP, in 1909.

FURTHER RESOURCES

Books

Fox, Stephen R. *The Guardian of Boston: William Monroe Trotter.* New York: Athenueum, 1970.

Harlan, Louis R. *The Booker T. Washington Papers,* Vol. 3. Urbana, Ill.: University of Illinois Press, 1974.

Lewis, David L. *W.E.B. Du Bois—Biography of a Race, 1868–1919.* New York: Henry Holt, 1993.

Periodicals

Bauerlein, Mark. "Washington, Du Bois, and the Black Future." *Wilson Quarterly* 28, 4 (2004): 74–86.

Four Freedoms

President Franklin Delano Roosevelt's State of the Union Address

Speech

By: Franklin Delano Roosevelt

Date: January 6, 1941

Source: Roosevelt, Franklin Delano. "The Four Freedoms: President Franklin Delano Roosevelt, State of the Union Address." *Congressional Record.* 44 (January 6, 1941).

About the Author: Franklin Delano Roosevelt (FDR) was born in 1882 in New Hyde Park, New York. During his youth, he played sports and remained active, but at age thirty-nine, he contracted poliomyelitis (polio). The disease caused him to loose the full use of his legs, and throughout the rest of his life, he used a wheelchair and crutches for mobility. Upon his 1932 election to the presidency, he became the first United States President with a physical disability, which he took great steps to conceal. FDR led the United States through the Great Dperession and World War II (1941–1945). He won the presidency for four consecutive terms—the only president to do so—and he died on April 12, 1945 of a cerebral hemorrhage. Franklin D. Roosevelt is also the fifth cousin of Theodore Roosevelt, U.S. president from 1901 to 1909.

INTRODUCTION

President Franklin Delano Roosevelt gave his Four Freedoms Speech as a State of the Union address to the U.S. Congress on January 6, 1941. In this speech, he outlined a plan for the United States to sustain economic recovery and to help Europe (particularly Great Britain) in war. The Great Depression of the 1930s, with the Stock Market Crash of October 1929 frequently noted as the catalyst for the nation's and world's economic crisis, sent the United States economy into a downward spiral. President Herbert Hoover initially asked the country to rely upon volunteerism to stabilize the economy, but Roosevelt took a drastically different approach after taking office in 1933. Roosevelt set up a series of New Deal programs that brought federal funding and aid to local communities. These moneys then established jobs and economic infrastructures that enabled individuals to earn a living, communities to maintain and establish economic growth, and with time, they allowed the national economy to rebuild itself. These types of programs, federal aid and help while letting individuals work and rebuild on their own, are synonymous with FDR's presidency. Thus, his Four Freedoms Speech established the Lend-Lease Bill with Great Britain and stated the Four Freedoms.

The Lend-Lease Bill provided that the United States would lend destroyers, and other weapons, to Great Britain on the condition that the United States could lease military bases from Great Britain. The Lend-Lease plan developed from the Neutrality Acts (beginning in 1935), which said the United States

would not intervene in European conflicts. But, as per the agreement, the United States would sell weaponry and raw material to belligerent countries on a cash and carry basis. With the start of World War II in September 1939, the United States took a stand of neutrality. The intent of the Lend-Lease Bill was to help Great Britain—the war greatly drained its resources—but the United States could not sign a bill directly aimed at Great Britain because the United States had taken a stand of neutrality. Hence, the bill said the United States and Great Britain were leasing and loaning property without the intent for war. The Lend-Lease Bill reflects Roosevelt's New Deal liberalism by helping without being hands on and giving aid too freely, and the core of this speech—the Four Freedoms—reflected the nation and the international community.

The four key points of the speech based themselves on key ideals of the American Constitution and on human desires. The first two points of the speech utilized the first and second amendments (freedom of speech and expression and freedom of religion), and the last two freedoms proposed alleviating the freedom from want and the freedom from fear. These elements of the speech reflected the American psyche and the turmoil of the Great Depression. Americans had not previously experienced such economic devastation, and they were not used to asking for help. In reaction to the Labor Struggles of the 1920s and the economic crisis of the 1930s, many Americans firmly believed in isolationism. This belief also grew from the aftermath of World War I when economic theories like The Merchant of Death Thesis said that big business had lured Americans into fighting so that they could make money. Hence, FDR knew that he had to rally the nation into supporting a European conflict, and with the Neutrality Acts and then the Lend-Lease Bill he was easing the American public's mind into the conflict. The insertion of the Four Freedoms then allowed FDR to bring the hopes and desires of Americans into an international arena, comparing them to U.S. Allies, and showing that Americans and non-Americans desire the same rights.

PRIMARY SOURCE

Let us say to the democracies, "We Americans are vitally concerned in your defense of freedom. We are putting forth our energies, our resources and our organizing powers to give you the strength to regain and maintain a free world. We shall send you in ever-increasing numbers, ships, planes, tanks, guns. That is our purpose and our pledge."

In fulfillment of this purpose we will not be intimidated by the threats of dictators that they will regard as a breach of international law or as an act of war our aid to the democracies which dare to resist their aggression. Such aid is not an act of war, even if a dictator should unilaterally proclaim it so to be.

When the dictators are ready to make war upon us, they will not wait for an act of war on our part. They did not wait for Norway or Belgium or the Netherlands to commit an act of war.

Their only interest is in a new one-way international law which lacks mutuality in its observance and, therefore becomes an instrument of oppression.

The happiness of future generations of Americans may well depend on how effective and how immediate we can make our aid felt. No one can tell the exact character of the emergency situations that we may be called upon to meet. The nation's hands must not be tied when the nation's life is in danger.

We must all prepare to make the sacrifices that the emergency—as serious as war itself—demands. Whatever stands in the way of speed and efficiency in defense preparations must give way to the national need.

A free nation has the right to expect full cooperation from all groups. A free nation has the right to look to the leaders of business, of labor and of agriculture to take the lead in stimulating effort, not among other groups but within their own groups.

The best way of dealing with the few slackers or trouble makers in our midst is, first, to shame them by patriotic example; and if that fails, to use the sovereignty of government to save government.

As men do not live by bread alone, they do not fight by armaments alone. Those who man our defenses and those behind them who build our defenses, must have the stamina and the courage which come from unshakable belief in the manner of life which they are defending. The mighty action that we are calling for cannot be based on a disregard of all the things worth fighting for.

The nation takes great satisfaction and much strength from the things which have been done to make its people conscious of their individual stake in the preservation of democratic life in America. Those things have toughened the fiber of our people, have renewed their faith and strengthened their devotion to the institutions we make ready to protect.

Certainly this is no time for any of us to stop thinking about the social and economic problems which are the root cause of the social revolution which is today a supreme factor in the world.

There is nothing mysterious about the foundations of a healthy and strong democracy.

The basic things expected by our people of their political and economic systems are simple. They are:

Equality of opportunity for youth and for others.

Jobs for those who can work.

Security for those who need it.

The ending of special privilege for the few.

The preservation of civil liberties for all.

The enjoyment of the fruits of scientific progress in a wider and constantly rising standard of living.

These are the simple, the basic things that must never be lost sight of in the turmoil and unbelievable complexity of our modern world. The inner and abiding strength of our economic and political systems is dependent upon the degree to which they fulfill these expectations.

Many subjects connected with our social economy call for immediate improvement.

As examples:

We should bring more citizens under the coverage of old-age pensions and unemployment insurance.

We should widen the opportunities for adequate medical care.

We should plan a better system by which persons deserving or needing gainful employment may obtain it.

I have called for personal sacrifice. I am assured of the willingness of almost all Americans to respond to that call.

A part of the sacrifice means the payment of more money in taxes. In my Budget Message I shall recommend that a greater portion of this great defense program be paid for from taxation than we are paying for today. No person should try, or be allowed to get rich out of this program; and the principle of tax payments in accordance with ability to pay should be constantly before our eyes to guide our legislation.

If the congress maintains these principles, the voters, putting patriotism ahead of pocketbooks, will give you their applause.

In the future days which we seek to make secure, we look forward to a world founded upon four essential human freedoms.

The first is freedom of speech and expression everywhere in the world.

The second is freedom of every person to worship God in his own way everywhere in the world.

The third is freedom from want, which, translated into world terms, means economic understandings which will secure to every nation a healthy peacetime life for its inhabitants everywhere in the world.

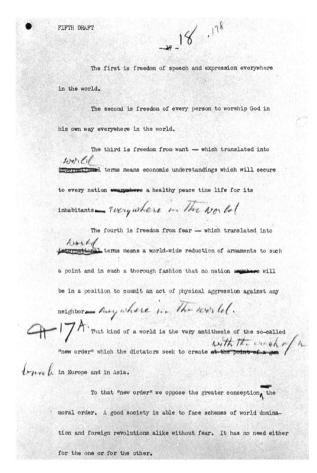

FIFTH DRAFT

The first is freedom of speech and expression everywhere in the world.

The second is freedom of every person to worship God in his own way everywhere in the world.

The third is freedom from want — which translated into world terms means economic understandings which will secure to every nation a healthy peace time life for its inhabitants— *everywhere in the world*

The fourth is freedom from fear — which translated into world terms means a world-wide reduction of armaments to such a point and in such a thorough fashion that no nation will be in a position to commit an act of physical aggression against any neighbor— *Anywhere in the world.*

That kind of a world is the very antithesis of the so-called "new order" which the dictators seek to create *with the crash of a bomb* in Europe and in Asia.

To that "new order" we oppose the greater conception, the moral order. A good society is able to face schemes of world domination and foreign revolutions alike without fear. It has no need either for the one or for the other.

A draft copy, with handwritten notes, of President Franklin D. Roosevelt's famous "Four Freedoms" speech. PHOTO BY HERBERT ORTH//TIME LIFE PICTURES/GETTY IMAGES.

The fourth is freedom from fear, which, translated into world terms, means a world-wide reduction of armaments to such a point and in such a thorough fashion that no nation will be in a position to commit an act of physical aggression against any neighbor—anywhere in the world.

That is no vision of a distant millennium. It is a definite basis for a kind of world attainable in our own time and generation. That kind of world is the very antithesis of the so-called "new order" of tyranny which the dictators seek to create with the crash of a bomb.

To that new order we oppose the greater conception—the moral order. A good society is able to face schemes of world domination and foreign revolutions alike without fear.

Since the beginning of our American history we have been engaged in change—in a perpetual, peaceful revolution—a revolution which goes on steadily, quietly, adjusting itself to changing conditions—without the concentration camp or the quick-lime in the ditch. The world order which we seek is the cooperation of free countries, working together in a friendly, civilized society.

This nation has placed its destiny in the hands and heads and hearts of its millions of free men and women; and its faith in freedom under the guidance of God. Freedom means the supremacy of human rights everywhere. Our support goes to those who struggle to gain those rights and keep them. Our strength is our unity of purpose.

To that high concept there can be no end save victory.

SIGNIFICANCE

The United States officially entered World War II in December 1941, after the Japanese attack on Pearl Harbor, and it became a central leader in forming the United Nations. The United Nations, an extension of President Woodrow Wilson's League of Nations following World War I, established a council for nations to settle their disputes. More importantly, the United Nations had the support of the world's major powers (the United States, Great Britain, the Soviet Union, and China), and it set up a system for embargos and penalties against countries that did not comply to international guidelines of warfare and human respect.

After the initial postwar period, the United Nations continued to develop and refine its role with world affairs. Since its creation, the United Nations has helped enforce such international laws as the Treatment of Prisoners of War (adopted August 1949 and entered into force in October 1950) and the Universal Declaration of Human Rights (adopted December 1948). First Lady Eleanor Roosevelt used the Four Freedoms Speech as her inspiration and catalyst for the drafting and signing of the United Nations Declaration of Human Rights, and the United Nations has parts of the Four Freedoms speech as a central element of its directive.

The Four Freedoms Speech also inspired four paintings by American artist Norman Rockwell. *The Saturday Evening Post* published this series of paintings in 1943 on February 20, February 27, March 6, and March 13. The Office of War Information also used the Rockwell paintings in their campaign to sell war bonds for World War II, and the four paintings are attributed with selling about $130,000,000 in war bonds.

The Franklin and Eleanor Roosevelt Institute pays yearly accolades to individuals who commit their lives to the ideals of the Four Freedoms. Some recipients of the Four Freedoms Award are Coretta Scott King (wife of civil rights leader Martin Luther King, Jr.) and Mikhail Gorbachev (former President of the

Soviet Union who worked with U.S. President Ronald Reagan to help end the Cold War).

FURTHER RESOURCES

Books

Dallek, Robert. *Franklin D. Roosevelt and American Foreign Policy, 1932–1945: With a New Afterword*. Oxford University Press, 1995.

Kimball, Warren B. *The Juggler: Franklin Roosevelt as a Wartime Statesman*. Princeton University Press, 1991.

Periodicals

Johnson, M. Glen. "The Contributions of Eleanor and Franklin Roosevelt to International Protection for Human Rights." *Human Rights Quarterly*. 9 (1987): 19–48.

Web sites

Franklin D. Roosevelt Presidential Library and Museum with Marist College and IBM. "Franklin D. Roosevelt Presidential Library and Museum." <http://www.fdrlibrary.marist.edu/> (accessed April 22, 2006).

Punishment and Prevention of War Crimes

Resolution

By: League of Nations

Date: October 10, 1943

Source: League of Nations. "Resolutions of the Executive Committee of the League of Nations Union." Executive Committee of the League of Nations Union, October 10, 1943.

About the Author: The League of Nations formed in 1919 as part of the postwar accords from World War I. U.S. President Woodrow Wilson first presented the idea of the League in his Fourteen Points Speech on January 8, 1918. Wilson initially called his plan The Covenant of the League of Nations, and through his work the League became Section I of the Treaty of Versailles. January 10, 1920 saw the ratification of the treaty, and the official formation of the League of Nations. It first met in Geneva on November 15, 1920, and twenty nations joined. The League was intended to prevent future hostilities through mediation and non-violent intervention, but many countries withdrew from the League and the United States never joined. Scholars note that the United States' failure to join the League caused many countries to withdraw their support for it. During World War II, the allied powers still worked under the auspices of the League until the formation of the United Nations at the Yalta Conference in February 1945. The United Nations replaced the League of Nations after World War II.

INTRODUCTION

During World War II, technology increased the intensity of warfare, and racial and ethnic divisions heightened the level of wartime brutalities. Operation Barbarossa saw Soviet Union troops and German troops committing highly intense acts of wartime cruelties upon each other. Postwar testimonies from German and Soviet soldiers attest that both sides used dead bodies as target practice, large massacres of civilians and troops took place, and other atrocities occurred. In the battle between the United States and Japan, scholars have deemed it a "war without mercy." Popular magazines captured cover images of women proudly holding up the skulls of Japanese soldiers. These skulls, and other bones, had been shipped to them from their Marine fiancés and husbands. President Franklin Roosevelt refused to accept a letter opener carved from the bones of a Japanese soldier, and keeping bones and body parts as souvenirs was so customary that customs officials had to ask individuals to declare their bones upon entry into the country.

In addition to the hostilities of the battlefield, and the efforts of soldiers to elevate their morale and feel justified in their actions, the general public became more aware of the German atrocities of war. Scholars do not know when the Germans decided to massacre Jews, nor do they know how the decision was made. Historians debate if Hitler initiated the extermination programs of the Third Reich or if his subordinates encouraged the idea, but they generally agree that at some point Hitler approved of the program. In the summer of 1941, indiscriminate killing of Jews officially began in conquered areas of the Soviet Union, and at the Wannsee Conference (a suburb of Berlin) the details of the Final Solution were laid out. The plan called for the continued deportation of Jews to Concentration Camps, immediate death for the very young, old, or those unable to work, segregation by gender, and death through forced labor and lack of food. Finally, any remaining Jews would be killed at the end of the war.

As the Nazis pushed forward on their plans for Jewish extermination, Allied leaders began to receive more concrete evidence concerning the German Concentration Camps and extermination facilities. More so, in 1943 the Germans began losing ground in the war; they were no longer gaining territory, their economy was suffering from overexertion, and

Survivors of the Nazi concentration camp at Buchenwald, after their liberation by the Allies on April 16, 1945. Elie Wiesel, the future Nobel Prize winning author, is on the second bunk from the bottom, sixth from the left. NATIONAL ARCHIVES AND RECORDS ADMINISTRATION.

Germany began to lose some of its war gains. The turn in the German warfront caused Hitler and his leaders to intensify their plans for exterminating the Jews. News from liberated zones and camps quickly spread to world media outlets, and the international public outcry against the treatment of European Jews superseded many local racisms and hostilities. For instance, in the United States, long-standing fears and hatred of Jews and other ethnic groups prohibited certain individuals from obtaining jobs and housing. Yet, the news of the Holocaust (that is, Germany's Concentration Camps and extermination programs) forced President Roosevelt to reverse national policy. Previously, the United States had refused entry to European refugees, and in February 1942 Roosevelt ordered the internment of Japanese-Americans living on the west coast.

In 1943, the federal government began allowing internees to leave Internment Camps. Initially, they were not allowed to return to the west coast, but in early 1944 this policy changed. Some individuals were allowed to return to their previous homes. In June 1944, Roosevelt brought one thousand refugees from Europe to the United States as his personal guests in Washington DC. These policy changes reflected the international community, the lack of tolerance for the unlawful imprisonment of individuals, and an international desire to end the hostilities of World War II—locally and internationally. The world community had grown tired of warfare, and the escalating brutalities of the battlefield shocked individuals. Additionally, policy changes reflected international agreements that aimed to prevent future retribution by victims of war crimes.

PRIMARY SOURCE

RESOLUTIONS OF THE EXECUTIVE COMMITTEE OF THE LEAGUE OF NATIONS UNION

Punishment of War Criminals The Executive Committee of the League of National Union recognizes that war cannot be made humane. But acts of violence permissible to a belligerent are strictly defined and limited by rules of International Law.

The charge against the Germans and their Allies is that, in defiance of these rules, they have carried out a system of terrorism by slaughter, outrage and torture, not to speak of robbery and destruction, unjustified by any military necessity and aimed at men, women and children of all ages and in certain cases dictated by racial or religious prejudice as in the wholesale massacre of Jews.

In order to re-establish the principles of Law, to satisfy the legitimate indignation cause by these horrors, and to prevent retaliatory massacres, the Executive Committee believes that it is essential that those individuals, whoever they may be, who are accused of having ordered or carried out such crimes should be brought before courts of justice which shall, after open and rigorously fair trial, pass sentence on any persons convicted of the offenses charged against them.

Where possible, the Committee hopes that the Courts will be international in character.

The Committee welcomes the assurance by the Government that they are taking preparatory steps in the direction indicated and it trusts that, as and when enemy-occupied territory comes under United Nations control, they will secure all known suspected persons there. It also hopes that it may be possible to prevent such persons escaping from justice into neutral territory and that, if they do so escape, the United Nations will require their surrender.

Prevention, where possible, of further War Crimes The Committee considers that it is of the utmost importance that all possible steps should be taken by the United Nations to remove persons criminally threatened with violence in the countries occupied by Nazi forces. In particular, as territories are in process of liberation, the strongest pressure should be put on those still in control of them to abstain for any violence against the inhabitants, to remove all discriminative measures, especially those against the Jews, and to rescue as many as possible who might still be in danger of attack.

At the same meeting it was resolved that,

The Committee is of opinion that no person figuring on the list of wanted war criminals of any of the United Nations should, on grounds of military expediency or for any other reason, be entrusted with any post of confidence.

SIGNIFICANCE

The Nuremburg Trials were held in Nuremburg, Germany from October 1945 to October 1946. The trials maintained the League's affirmations that those responsible for the Holocaust and various other war crimes of World War II would be held liable. War crimes brought before international courts tended to be of the worst kind. The most notable of these crimes were the German Concentration Camps. The first of these war crime trials occurred in Krasnodar, Soviet Union, in July 1943. Thirteen Soviet citizens were tried for more than seven thousand acts of murder. Three of the individuals received twenty-year prison sentences, and eight were hanged.

After the Nuremburg Trials, numerous other trials occurred. These cases were tried in a variety of places where the crimes occurred, such as France, Italy, and the Soviet Union. After 1946, most of those tried were not high-ranking officials, and many participants and facilitators of war crimes never faced charges.

After World War II, the United Nations continued to develop treaties and organizations and implemented measures to prevent future wartime atrocities. The Geneva Convention, being the most notable of the post-World-War-II actions, drafted concise definitions for the treatment of wartime prisoners, the execution of international and wartime criminals, and other aspects of war actions. The Geneva Convention drafted its articles in August 1949, and on October 21, 1950, the United Nations entered them into force. These measures have strengthened the international community and helped to define acts of torture and inhumane treatment that still occur—in 1999, hundreds of ethnic Albanians were executed in conflicts with Serbian police forces and the Kosovo Liberation Army. As recently as March 2006, U.S. Marines received indictments for the deaths of Iraqi civilians and soldiers. The outcomes of these trials have not yet been determined.

FURTHER RESOURCES
Books

Browning, Christopher R. *The Path to Genocide: Essays On Launching the Final Solution*. Cambridge, U.K. and New York: Cambridge University Press, 1992.

Gruber, Ruth. *Haven: The Dramatic Story of 1,000 World War II Refugees and How They Came to America*. New York: Three Rivers Press, 2000.

Periodicals

Combs, Nancy Amoury. "Copping a Plea to Genocide: The Plea Bargaining of International War Crimes." *University of Pennsylvania Law Review*. 151, 1 (November 2002): 1–157.

Web sites

Office of the High Commissioner for Human Rights. "International Human Rights Instruments." <http://www.unhchr.ch/html/intlinst.htm> (accessed May 3, 2006).

U.S. Department of State. "War Crime Issues." <http://www.state.gov/s/wci> (accessed May 3, 2006).

Creation of UN Commission on Human Rights

Resolution

By: United Nations

Date: June 21, 1946

Source: United Nations Economic and Social Council. "Creation of UN Commission on Human Rights." (June 21, 1946).

About the Author: The phrase "United Nations" was used during World War II (1939–1945) to describe the dozens of nations allied together to fight Germany and Japan, most notably including China, France, Great Britain, the Soviet Union, and the United States of America. These allies decided to develop a new organization to facilitate international cooperation and help prevent future wars. It would replace the League of Nations, which had failed to prevent World War II. They called it the United Nations (UN). The UN Charter was ratified on October 24, 1945. In the years since the UN has served as a forum for international negotiation and cooperation on many issues, including international security, human rights, trade and economics, and the environment.

INTRODUCTION

The mass genocide of the Jewish people, Roma people, homosexuals, communists, and other targeted groups during World War II (1938–1945) under the orders of Adolph Hitler, led to a call for greater international oversight and monitoring of human rights issues. By the end of World War II, leaders from countries worldwide called for an international body with greater powers than the League of Nations, which had formed in 1919 but had failed in its primary mission to control aggression, as evidenced by the Axis Powers' invasions leading to World War II. In 1945, more than fifty countries joined the newly created United Nations, which inherited many of the functions and agencies from the League of Nations, but which also included the membership of the United States and a broader coalition of countries.

The United Nations Commission on Human Rights (UNCHR) was created less than one year after the formation of the United Nations. The UNCHR is an independent commission under the umbrella of the UN Economic and Social Council and was established as part of the UN charter at its founding in 1945. The topic of human rights was paramount as calls for war crime trials increased in the late 1940s; German and Japanese military officers faced charges ranging from genocide to torture to institutionalized rape of Japanese "comfort women," to the murder of children and unarmed non-combatants.

The primary function of the UNCHR is to monitor human rights abuses, policies, procedures, and law in member countries. The Commission originally included eighteen member states; as the number of UN members increased, the UNCHR membership increased proportionally as well. In 2005, there were fifty-three member states comprising the commission, elected for three-year terms.

At its creation, the UNCHR's first function was to compile all existing laws, treaties, and policies concerning human rights in member countries. Over time, that mission has expanded to include the consistent monitoring of human rights topics including freedom of expression, access to healthcare, proper nutrition, education, and freedom from violence in member countries, and to create annual reports describing and detailing current human rights circumstances in each country.

PRIMARY SOURCE

2. Composition (a) The Commission on Human Rights shall consist of one representative from each of eighteen members of the United Nations selected by the Council.

(b) With a view to securing a balanced representation in the various fields covered by the Commission, the Secretary-General shall consult with the governments so selected before the representatives are finally nominated by these governments and confirmed by the Council.

(c) Except for the initial period, the term of office shall be for three years. For the initial period, one-third of the members shall serve for two years, one-third for three years, and one-third for four years, the term of each member to be determined by lot.

(d) Retiring members shall be eligible for re-election.

(e) In the event that a member of the Commission is unable to serve for the full three-year term, the vacancy thus arising shall be filled by a representative designated by the Member Government, subject to the provisions of paragraph (b) above.

3. Working Groups of Experts The Commission is authorized to call in *ad hoc* working groups of non-governmental experts in specialized fields or individual experts, without further reference to the Council, but with the approval of the President of the Council and the Secretary-General.

4. Documentation The Secretary-General is requested to make arrangements for:

the compilation and publication of a year-book on law and usage relating to human rights, the first edition of which should include all declarations and bills on human rights now in force in the various countries;

the collection and publication of information on the activities concerning human rights of all organs of the United Nations;

the collection and publication of information concerning human rights arising from trials of war criminals, quislings, and traitors, and in particular from the Nuremberg and Tokyo trials;

the preparation and publication of a survey of the development of human rights;

the collection and publication of plans and declarations on human rights by specialized agencies and non-governmental national and international organizations.

5. Information Groups Members of the United Nations are invited to consider the desirability of establishing information groups or local human rights committees within their respective countries to collaborate with them in furthering the work of the Commission on Human Rights.

6. Human Rights in International Treaties Pending the adoption of an international bill of rights, the general principle shall be accepted that International treaties involving basic human rights, including to the fullest extent practicable treaties of peace, shall conform to the fundamental standards relative to such rights set forth in the Charter.

7. Provisions For Implementation Considering that the purpose of the United Nations with regard to the promotion and observance of human rights as defined in the Charter of the United Nations, can only be fulfilled if provisions are made for the implementation of human rights and of an international bill of rights, the Council requests the commission on Human Rights to submit at an early date suggestions regarding the ways and means for the effective implementation of human rights and fundamental freedoms, with a view to assisting the Economic and Social Council in working out arrangements for such implementation with other appropriate organs of the United Nations.

8. Sub-Commission on Freedom of Information and of the Press
(a) The Commission on Human Rights is empowered to establish a Sub-Commission on Freedom of Information and of the Press.

(b) The function of the Sub-Commission shall be, in the first instance, to examine what rights, obligations, and practices should be included in the concept of freedom of information, and to report to the Commission on Human Rights on any issues that may arise from such examination.

9. Sub-Commission on Protection of Minorities a) The Commission on Human Rights is empowered to establish a Sub-Commission on the Protection of Minorities.

(b) Unless the Commission otherwise decides, the function of the Sub-Commission shall be, in the first instance, to examine what provisions should be adopted in the definition of the principles which are to be applied in the field of protection of minorities and to deal with the urgent problems in this field by making recommendations to the Commission.

10. Sub-Commission on the Prevention of Discrimination (a) The Commission on Human Rights is empowered to establish a Sub-Commission on the prevention of discrimination on the grounds of race, sex, language, or religion.

(b) Unless the Commission otherwise decides, the function of the Sub-Commission shall be, in the first instance, to examine what provision should be adopted in the definition of the principles which are to be applied in the field of the prevention of discrimination, and to deal with the urgent problems in this field by making recommendations to the Commission.

SIGNIFICANCE

The UNCHR met every March and April, convening for six weeks, with a rotating chair system; different countries from varying continents served as the Commission's chair each year. As of 1993, the UNCHR began to report to the newly created position of UN High Commissioner for Human Rights. As an Under Secretary within the UN system, the High Commissioner's mandate includes the promotion of human rights in international treaties, the protection of human rights, education on human rights issues, and the management of all human rights issues related to the UN.

An inmate in Trinidad's Carrera Island prison. In 2000, a report to the UN Commission on Human Rights alledged that the mentally ill were being mixed with the general prison population here and not given any treatment for their condition. © SMAILES ALEX/CORBIS SYGMA.

Since 1993, UN High Commissioners for Human Rights have come from Latin America, Western Europe, Africa, and North America; as of 2004, the position was held by Louise Arbour of Canada. In 2001, the UNCHR, for the first time since 1947, did not include the United States as a commission member. Many member states in Europe were not pleased with the United States' objections to the creation of an International Criminal Court. By 2003, the United States had been reinstated to the UNCHR. In 2004, Sudan was voted onto the commission, prompting outcries from international human rights groups, as Sudan is accused of sanctioning the ongoing extermination of non-Muslims in its Darfur region. The UNCHR has come under sharp criticism as well for including such member nations as China, Russia, Pakistan, Saudi Arabia, Cuba, and Zimbabwe on the commission; the human rights abuse records in these countries have led critics to charge that the UNCHR lacks credibility and has become a political pawn in international politics.

On March 15, 2006, the United Nations General Assembly voted to create a new body, the UN Human Rights Council, to replace UNCHR. International human rights organizations such as Amnesty International and Human Rights Watch strongly endorsed the new Human Rights Council and expressed opposition to the United States' refusal to vote for the new council. One hundred seventy member nations voted for the change, while Israel and the United States voted against it. The United States claimed the change did not go far enough in tightening human rights oversight. The new UNHRC includes forty-seven member nations, uses secret ballot procedures in the General Assembly to elect members, and creates a system for suspending members for human rights abuses. The final Commission on Human Rights meeting—its sixty-second—ended on March 27, 2006. The first meeting of the Human Rights Council was held in April 2006.

FURTHER RESOURCES
Books

Donnelly, Jack. *Universal Human Rights in Theory and Practice*. Ithaca, New York: Cornell University Press, 2002.

Ishay, Micheline. *The History of Human Rights: From Ancient Times to the Globalization Era.* University of California Press, 2004.

Steiner, Henry and Philip Alston. *International Human Rights in Context: Law, Politics, Morals.* Oxford University Press, U.S.A., 2000.

Web sites

United Nations. "Human Rights." <http://www.un.org/rights/> (accessed May 7, 2006).

UN Universal Declaration of Human Rights

Declaration

By: United Nations General Assembly

Date: December 10, 1948

Source: United Nations General Assembly. "UN Declaration of Human Rights. General Assembly Resolution 217 A (III). December 10, 1948.

About the Author: The phrase "United Nations" was used during World War II (1939–1945) to describe the dozens of nations allied together to fight Germany and Japan, most notably including China, France, Great Britain, the Soviet Union, and the United States of America. These allies decided to develop a new organization to facilitate international cooperation and help prevent future wars. It would replace the League of Nations, which had failed to prevent World War II. They called it the United Nations (UN). The UN Charter was ratified on October 24, 1945. In the years since the UN has served as a forum for international negotiation and cooperation on many issues, including international security, human rights, trade and economics, and the environment.

INTRODUCTION

By the end of World War II (1938–1945), the issue of human rights was central to the creation of an international organization that would include member states from around the globe. The League of Nations, the brainchild of United States President Woodrow Wilson, was founded in 1919 as an international organization that would help to prevent aggression, provide a mediator between nations, and help to maintain peace. When World War II began and Axis Powers invaded parts of Europe, Asia, and Africa, the League of nation's efficacy lost credibility, and a new international organization emerged: the United Nations.

One of the primary topics built into the United Nations charter in 1945 was human rights; by 1946 the UN created the UN Commission on Human Rights, an independent commission under the auspices of the UN Economic and Social Council. The genocide of World War II, Hitler's eugenics programs, and issues with refugees, sexual slavery in Asia, and other human rights concerns sparked international conversations about the definition of human rights, cultural attitudes toward such definitions, and simple questions of humanity. The United Nations charter had outlined the principles of human rights in its charter, but member nations and UN officials felt a need to clarify those principles by providing specific definitions of what universal human rights constituted.

The primary writer of the Declaration of Human Rights was Canadian John Humphrey, a professor of law at McGill University. His efforts were joined by Rene Cassin of France, Eleanor Roosevelt of the United States, Charles Malik of Lebanon, and P.C. Chang of China, providing involvement from member nations in North America, Asia, the Middle East, and Western Europe.

On December 10, 1948, the United Nations General Assembly unveiled the Declaration of Human Rights as a common goal for all member states.

▮ PRIMARY SOURCE

PREAMBLE Whereas, recognition of the inherent dignity and of the equal and inalienable rights of all members of the human family is the foundation of freedom, justice and peace in the world,

Whereas, disregard and contempt for human rights have resulted in barbarous acts which have outraged the conscience of mankind, and the advent of a world in which human beings shall enjoy freedom of speech and belief and freedom from fear and want has been proclaimed as the highest aspiration of the common people,

Whereas, it is essential, if man is not to be compelled to have recourse, as a last resort, to rebellion against tyranny and oppression, that human rights should be protected by the rule of law,

Whereas, it is essential to promote the development of friendly relations between nations,

Whereas, the peoples of the United Nations have in the Charter reaffirmed their faith in fundamental human rights, in the dignity and worth of the human person and in the equal rights of men and women and have determined to promote social progress and better standards of life in larger freedom,

Whereas, Member States have pledged themselves to achieve, in co-operation with the United Nations, the promotion of universal respect for and observance of human rights and fundamental freedoms, Whereas a common understanding of these rights and freedoms is of the greatest importance for the full realization of this pledge,

Now, Therefore THE GENERAL ASSEMBLY proclaims THIS UNIVERSAL DECLARATION OF HUMAN RIGHTS as a common standard of achievement for all peoples and all nations, to the end that every individual and every organ of society, keeping this Declaration constantly in mind, shall strive by teaching and education to promote respect for these rights and freedoms and by progressive measures, national and international, to secure their universal and effective recognition and observance, both among the peoples of Member States themselves and among the peoples of territories under their jurisdiction.

Article 1. All human beings are born free and equal in dignity and rights. They are endowed with reason and conscience and should act towards one another in a spirit of brotherhood.

Article 2. Everyone is entitled to all the rights and freedoms set forth in this Declaration, without distinction of any kind, such as race, colour, sex, language, religion, political or other opinion, national or social origin, property, birth or other status. Furthermore, no distinction shall be made on the basis of the political, jurisdictional or international status of the country or territory to which a person belongs, whether it be independent, trust, non-self-governing or under any other limitation of sovereignty.

Article 3. Everyone has the right to life, liberty and security of person.

Article 4. No one shall be held in slavery or servitude; slavery and the slave trade shall be prohibited in all their forms.

Article 5. No one shall be subjected to torture or to cruel, inhuman or degrading treatment or punishment.

Article 6. Everyone has the right to recognition everywhere as a person before the law.

Article 7. All are equal before the law and are entitled without any discrimination to equal protection of the law. All are entitled to equal protection against any discrimination in violation of this Declaration and against any incitement to such discrimination.

Article 8. Everyone has the right to an effective remedy by the competent national tribunals for acts violating the fundamental rights granted him by the constitution or by law.

Article 9. No one shall be subjected to arbitrary arrest, detention or exile.

Article 10. Everyone is entitled in full equality to a fair and public hearing by an independent and impartial tribunal, in the determination of his rights and obligations and of any criminal charge against him.

Article 11. (1) Everyone charged with a penal offence has the right to be presumed innocent until proved guilty according to law in a public trial at which he has had all the guarantees necessary for his defence.

(2) No one shall be held guilty of any penal offence on account of any act or omission which did not constitute a penal offence, under national or international law, at the time when it was committed. Nor shall a heavier penalty be imposed than the one that was applicable at the time the penal offence was committed.

Article 12. No one shall be subjected to arbitrary interference with his privacy, family, home or correspondence, nor to attacks upon his honour and reputation. Everyone has the right to the protection of the law against such interference or attacks.

Article 13. (1) Everyone has the right to freedom of movement and residence within the borders of each state.

(2) Everyone has the right to leave any country, including his own, and to return to his country.

Article 14. (1) Everyone has the right to seek and to enjoy in other countries asylum from persecution.

(2) This right may not be invoked in the case of prosecutions genuinely arising from non-political crimes or from acts contrary to the purposes and principles of the United Nations.

Article 15. (1) Everyone has the right to a nationality.

(2) No one shall be arbitrarily deprived of his nationality nor denied the right to change his nationality.

Article 16. (1) Men and women of full age, without any limitation due to race, nationality or religion, have the right to marry and to found a family. They are entitled to equal rights as to marriage, during marriage and at its dissolution.

(2) Marriage shall be entered into only with the free and full consent of the intending spouses.

(3) The family is the natural and fundamental group unit of society and is entitled to protection by society and the State.

Article 17. (1) Everyone has the right to own property alone as well as in association with others.

(2) No one shall be arbitrarily deprived of his property.

Article 18. Everyone has the right to freedom of thought, conscience and religion; this right includes freedom to change his religion or belief, and freedom, either alone or in community with others and in public or private, to manifest his religion or belief in teaching, practice, worship and observance.

Article 19. Everyone has the right to freedom of opinion and expression; this right includes freedom to hold opinions without interference and to seek, receive and impart information and ideas through any media and regardless of frontiers.

Article 20. (1) Everyone has the right to freedom of peaceful assembly and association.

(2) No one may be compelled to belong to an association.

Article 21. (1) Everyone has the right to take part in the government of his country, directly or through freely chosen representatives.

(2) Everyone has the right of equal access to public service in his country.

(3) The will of the people shall be the basis of the authority of government; this will shall be expressed in periodic and genuine elections which shall be by universal and equal suffrage and shall be held by secret vote or by equivalent free voting procedures.

Article 22. Everyone, as a member of society, has the right to social security and is entitled to realization, through national effort and international co-operation and in accordance with the organization and resources of each State, of the economic, social and cultural rights indispensable for his dignity and the free development of his personality.

Article 23. (1) Everyone has the right to work, to free choice of employment, to just and favourable conditions of work and to protection against unemployment.

(2) Everyone, without any discrimination, has the right to equal pay for equal work.

(3) Everyone who works has the right to just and favourable remuneration ensuring for himself and his family an existence worthy of human dignity, and supplemented, if necessary, by other means of social protection.

(4) Everyone has the right to form and to join trade unions for the protection of his interests.

Article 24. Everyone has the right to rest and leisure, including reasonable limitation of working hours and periodic holidays with pay.

Article 25. (1) Everyone has the right to a standard of living adequate for the health and well-being of himself and of his family, including food, clothing, housing and medical care and necessary social services, and the right to security in the event of unemployment, sickness, disability, widowhood, old age or other lack of livelihood in circumstances beyond his control.

(2) Motherhood and childhood are entitled to special care and assistance. All children, whether born in or out of wedlock, shall enjoy the same social protection.

Article 26. (1) Everyone has the right to education. Education shall be free, at least in the elementary and fundamental stages. Elementary education shall be compulsory. Technical and professional education shall be made generally available and higher education shall be equally accessible to all on the basis of merit.

(2) Education shall be directed to the full development of the human personality and to the strengthening of respect for human rights and fundamental freedoms. It shall promote understanding, tolerance and friendship among all nations, racial or religious groups, and shall further the activities of the United Nations for the maintenance of peace.

(3) Parents have a prior right to choose the kind of education that shall be given to their children.

Article 27. (1) Everyone has the right freely to participate in the cultural life of the community, to enjoy the arts and to share in scientific advancement and its benefits.

(2) Everyone has the right to the protection of the moral and material interests resulting from any scientific, literary or artistic production of which he is the author.

Article 28. Everyone is entitled to a social and international order in which the rights and freedoms set forth in this Declaration can be fully realized.

Article 29. (1) Everyone has duties to the community in which alone the free and full development of his personality is possible.

(2) In the exercise of his rights and freedoms, everyone shall be subject only to such limitations as are determined by law solely for the purpose of securing due recognition and respect for the rights and freedoms of others and of meeting the just requirements of morality, public order and the general welfare in a democratic society.

(3) These rights and freedoms may in no case be exercised contrary to the purposes and principles of the United Nations.

Article 30. Nothing in this Declaration may be interpreted as implying for any State, group or person any right to engage in any activity or to perform any act aimed at the destruction of any of the rights and freedoms set forth herein.

SIGNIFICANCE

The Universal Declaration of Human Rights passed a vote in the General Assembly with forty-eight votes for, and eight abstentions. Articles 3 and 25 of the Declaration of Human Rights address the most basic rights; article three states that "Everyone has the right to

A gypsy child stands amid garbage near a gypsy camp outside of Salonica, Greece, on December 10, 1998. Human rights groups are protesting poor conditions at the camp. The date is the fiftieth anniversary of the Universal Declaration of Human Rights. AP IMAGES.

life, liberty and security of person," an echo of the United States Declaration of Independence and France's Declaration of the Rights of Man and of the Citizen. Article twenty-five addresses basic living conditions and medical care as universal human rights: "(1) Everyone has the right to a standard of living adequate for the health and well-being of himself and of his family, including food, clothing, housing and medical care and necessary social services, and the right to security in the event of unemployment, sickness, disability, widowhood, old age or other lack of livelihood in circumstances beyond his control.

(2) Motherhood and childhood are entitled to special care and assistance. All children, whether born in or out of wedlock, shall enjoy the same social protection." By enumerating and describing what should be basic rights for all human beings, the Universal Declaration of Human Rights created an ideal to which governments were supposed to aspire.

The document's simple language is meant to be accessible for all readers, and the Universal Declaration of Human rights has been translated into more than three hundred languages and dialects. The Declaration is not a legally binding contract for UN member nations, but governments are expected to treat it as a strong guideline in crafting internal human rights policy and law.

The Declaration is one of three documents that together constitute the International Bill of Rights. The other two documents, the Optional Protocol and the International Covenants on Human Rights, were adopted in 1976. The Optional Protocol and the Covenants expand on the Universal Declaration of Human Rights and provide member nations with further clarity in creating treaties and laws that respect the universal rights of human beings.

In 1968, at the UN International Conference on Human Rights, the members agreed that following the Universal Declaration of Human Rights was an obligation for all member nations, to ensure fair treatment of all peoples worldwide, within their own borders and in other countries as well.

Many UN documents addressing the issue of rights, such as the 1952 Convention on the Political Rights of

Women and the 1981 Declaration on the Elimination of All Forms of Intolerance and of Discrimination Based on Religion or Belief are based on the principles in the Universal Declaration of Human Rights; the 1948 Declaration acts as a compass for international law and relations regarding human rights.

FURTHER RESOURCES

Books

Donnelly, Jack. *Universal Human Rights in Theory and Practice*. Ithaca, New York: Cornell University Press, 2002.

Ishay, Micheline. *The History of Human Rights: From Ancient Times to the Globalization Era*. University of California Press, 2004.

Steiner, Henry and Philip Alston. *International Human Rights in Context: Law, Politics, Morals*. Oxford University Press, U.S.A., 2000.

Web sites

United Nations. "Human Rights." <http://www.un.org/rights/> (accessed May 7, 2006).

Adoption of the Declaration of Human Rights

Speech

By: Eleanor Roosevelt

Date: December 9, 1948

Source: Roosevelt, Eleanor. "Adoption of the Declaration of Human Rights." Speech to United Nations General Assembly, December 9, 1948.

About the Author: Eleanor Roosevelt (1884–1962) is best known for being an activist First Lady during the presidential administration of her husband, Franklin D. Roosevelt. A diplomat and humanitarian, she devoted the years of her widowhood helping to shape the human rights agenda of United Nations.

INTRODUCTION

As U.S. delegate to the United Nations (UN), former First Lady Eleanor Roosevelt was credited with being the leading spirit behind the adoption of the Universal Declaration of Human Rights. It is a document that serves as the basis for efforts to internationalize the concept of human rights.

In January 1947, Roosevelt was elected chair of the Human Rights Commission that had been established

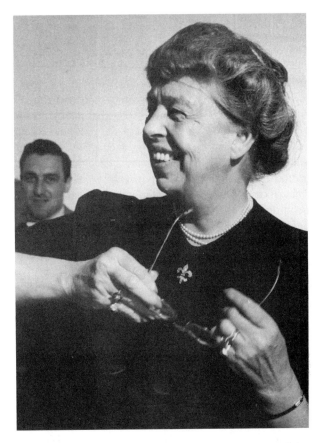

The former First Lady Eleanor Roosevelt, Chairwoman of the Committee of Human Rights, attends a meeting at the United Nations in January 1950. PHOTO BY JEAN MANZON/PIX INC./TIME LIFE PICTURES/GETTY IMAGES.

to work on the declaration. As chair, she split the commission into three committees. The committee that she led drafted the declaration, the statement of general principles that was ratified by the General Assembly of the UN. Roosevelt later wrote that she considered this work to be the most important task completed in her life.

Roosevelt encouraged the drafting committee to reach a realistic compromise without sacrificing principle. The declaration would assert for all humankind the fullest listing of human rights that the entire world community could be persuaded to adopt in principle but that no country at the time would fully meet. To increase acceptance of a fuller range of rights, the principles were phrased in general terms rather than in binding language. The other two Human Rights Commission committees developed binding human rights covenants on civil, political, cultural, and economic rights. On December 10, 1948, the General Assembly passed the Universal Declaration of Human Rights.

PRIMARY SOURCE

The long and meticulous study and debate of which this Universal Declaration of Human Rights is the product means that it reflects the composite views of the many men and governments who have contributed to its formulation. Not every man nor every government can have what he wants in a document of this kind. There are of course particular provisions in the declaration before us with which we are not fully satisfied. I have no doubt this is true of other delegations, but taken as a whole the Delegation of the United States believes that this is a good document—even a great document—and we propose to give it our full support. The position of the United States on the various parts of the declaration is a matter of record in the Third Committee. I shall not burden the Assembly, and particularly my colleagues of the Third Committee, with a restatement of that position here.

Certain provisions of the declaration are stated in such broad terms as to be acceptable only because of the limitations in article 29 providing for limitation on the exercise of the rights for the purpose of meeting the requirements of morality, public order, and the general welfare. An example of this is the provision that everyone has the right of equal access to the public service in his country. The basic principle of equality and of nondiscrimination as to public employment is sound, but it cannot be accepted without limitations. My government, for example, would consider that this is unquestionably subject to limitation in the interest of public order and the general welfare. It would not consider that the exclusion from public employment of persons holding subversive political beliefs and not loyal to the basic principles and practices of the constitution and laws of the country would in any way infringe upon this right.

Likewise, my Government has made it clear in the course of the development of the declaration that it does not consider that the economic and social and cultural rights stated in the declaration imply an obligation on governmental action. This was made quite clear in the Human Rights Commission text of article 23 which served as a so-called "umbrella" article to the articles on economic and social rights. We consider that the principle has not been affected by the fact that this article no longer contains a reference to the articles which follow it. This in no way affects our whole-hearted support for the basic principles of economic, social, and cultural rights set forth in these articles.

In giving our approval to the declaration today it is of primary importance that we keep clearly in mind the basic character of the document. It is not a treaty; it is not an international agreement. It is not and does not purport to be a statement of basic principles of law or legal obligation. It is a declaration of basic principles of human rights and freedoms, to be stamped with the approval of the General Assembly by formal vote of its members, and to serve as a common standard of achievement for all peoples of all nations.

We stand today at the threshold of a great event both in the life of the United Nations and in the life of mankind, that is the approval by the General Assembly of the Universal Declaration of Human Rights recommended by the Third Committee. This declaration may well become the international Magna Carta of all men everywhere. We hope its proclamation by the General Assembly will be an event comparable to the proclamation of the Declaration of the Rights of the Man by the French people in 1789, the adoption of the Bill of Rights by the people of the United States, and the adoption of comparable declarations at different times in other countries.

At a time when there are so many issues on which we find it difficult to reach a common basis of agreement, it is a significant fact that 58 states have found such a large measure of agreement in the complex field of human rights. This must be taken as testimony of our common aspiration first voiced in the Charter of the United Nations to lift men everywhere to a higher standard of life and to a greater enjoyment of freedom. Man's desire for peace lies behind this declaration. The realization that the fragrant violation of human rights by Nazi and Fascist countries sowed the seeds of the last world war has supplied the impetus for the work which brings us to the moment of achievement here today.

In a recent speech in Canada, Gladstone Murray said:

"The central fact is that man is fundamentally a moral being, that the light we have is imperfect does not matter so long as we are always trying to improve it . . . we are equal in sharing the moral freedom that distinguishes us as men. Man's status makes each individual an end in himself. No man is by nature simply the servant of the state or of another man . . . the ideal and fact of freedom—and not technology—are the true distinguishing marks of our civilization."

This declaration is based upon the spiritual fact that man must have freedom in which to develop his full stature and through common effort to raise the level of human dignity. We have much to do to fully achieve and to assure the rights set forth in this declaration. But having them put before us with the moral backing of 58 nations will be a great step forward.

As we here bring to fruition our labors on this Declaration of Human Rights, we must at the same time rededicate ourselves to the unfinished task which lies before us. We can now move on with new courage and inspiration to the completion of an international covenant on human rights and of measures for the implementation of human rights.

In conclusion I feel that I cannot do better than to repeat the call to action by Secretary Marshall in his opening statement to this Assembly:

> "Let this third regular session of the General Assembly approve by an overwhelming majority the Declaration of Human Rights as a statement of conduct for all; and let us, as Members of the United Nations, conscious of our own short-comings and imperfections, join our effort in all faith to live up to this high standard."

SIGNIFICANCE

The Universal Declaration of Human Rights emphasizes that human rights are basic to the human condition. It has focused attention on freedom of speech and expression, freedom of worship, and freedom from fear. Since its passage in 1948, governments, international organizations, and ordinary people have asserted Universal Declaration provisions in situations where no binding human rights laws exist. In this manner, the declaration has become recognized as the preeminent human rights document in the world.

The declaration has led to other binding human rights agreements, notably the International Convention on Elimination of Racial Discrimination in 1965, the Covenant on Civil and Political Rights in 1966, the International Convention on Elimination of Discrimination against Women in 1979, the International Convention Against Torture in 1984, and the International Convention on Rights of the Child in 1989. At the same time, numerous citizens' organizations have sprung up to support human rights, including Amnesty International and Human Rights Watch. These groups build on the concepts pioneered in the Declaration by internationalizing human rights. The international condemnation of abusive governments that has become a feature of the world since 1948 is one of the most important legacies of the declaration. To a large extent, Roosevelt's dream of a worldwide creation of cultures of human rights has been achieved.

FURTHER RESOURCES
Books

Alfredson, Gudmundur and Asbjorn Eide. *The Universal Declaration of Human Rights: A Common Standard of Achievement.* The Hague: Martinus Nijhoff, 1999.

Ramcharan, B. G. *Human Rights: Thirty Years After the Universal Declaration.* The Hague: Martinus Nijhoff, 1979.

Robinson, Nehemiah. *The Universal Declaration of Human Rights: Its Origin, Significance, Application, and Interpretation.* New York: Institute of Jewish Affairs, 1958.

Fifty Years After the Declaration: The United Nations' Record on Human Rights, edited by Teresa Wagner and Leslie Carbone. Lanham, Md.: University Press of America, 2001.

Geneva Convention Relative to the Treatment of Prisoners of War

Convention

By: United Nations

Date: October 21, 1950

Source: United Nations. "The Geneva Convention Relative to the Treatment of Prisoners of War." Diplomatic Conference for the Establishment of International Conventions for the Protection of Victims of War, October 21, 1950.

About the Author: The phrase "United Nations" was used during World War II (1939–1945) to describe the dozens of nations allied together to fight Germany and Japan, most notably including China, France, Great Britain, the Soviet Union, and the United States of America. These allies decided to develop a new organization to facilitate international cooperation and help prevent future wars. It would replace the League of Nations, which had failed to prevent World War II. They called it the United Nations (UN). The UN Charter was ratified on October 24, 1945. In the years since the UN has served as a forum for international negotiation and cooperation on many issues, including international security, human rights, trade and economics, and the environment.

INTRODUCTION

The Geneva Conventions of 1949 were created by the members of the United Nations under the guidance of the International Committee of the Red Cross (ICRC) and took effect on October 21, 1950. The provision to protect prisoners of war recognizes that while nations are quite capable of committing gross abuses of human rights in peacetime, wartime creates an especially fertile ground for horrendous attacks on individuals. The hatred, tension, and upheaval inherent in armed conflicts, particularly civil wars, has led to the murder or ill-treatment of prisoners of war throughout history.

Prisoners of war are defined as combatants who have fallen into the hands of the enemy. They are among the most vulnerable group for potential abuse by authorities.

International disgust at the brutal treatment accorded to prisoners of war by the Germans and Japanese during World War II led to a push to codify the proper behavior of states toward prisoners. The idea of protecting prisoners of war was not a new one. The Geneva Conventions of 1949 built upon the 1929 Geneva Convention on the Treatment of Prisoners of War and the Hague Conventions of 1899 to 1907 that covered the conduct of war.

The 1949 prisoner of war convention reflects innovations by applying to all international armed conflicts, regardless of any formal state of war; elaborating basic principles for non-international armed conflict; and providing a list of grave breaches for which countries are obligated to enact penal legislation and prosecute or extradite individual offenders. The grave breaches include willful killing, torture or inhumane treatment, willfully causing great suffering or serious injury to body or health, compelling a prisoner of war to serve in the forces of the hostile power, willfully depriving a prisoner of war of the rights of a fair and regular trial, and unlawful deportation of a protected person. Civilian internees, such as the Japanese Americans during World War II, enjoy similar protections to those granted to prisoners of war.

■ PRIMARY SOURCE

GENEVA CONVENTION RELATIVE TO THE TREATMENT OF PRISONERS OF WAR

GENERAL PROTECTION OF PRISONERS OF WAR

ARTICLE 12 Prisoners of war are in the hands of the enemy Power, but not of the individuals or military units who have captured them. Irrespective of the individual responsibilities that may exist, the Detaining Power is responsible for the treatment given them.

Prisoners of war may only be transferred by the Detaining Power to a Power which is a party to the Convention and after the Detaining Power has satisfied itself of the willingness and ability of such transferee Power to apply the Convention. When prisoners of war are transferred under such circumstances, responsibility for the application of the Convention rests on the Power accepting them while they are in its custody.

Nevertheless if that Power fails to carry out the provisions of the Convention in any important respect, the Power by whom the prisoners of war were transferred

shall, upon being notified by the Protecting Power, take effective measures to correct the situation or shall request the return of the prisoners of war. Such requests must be complied with.

ARTICLE 13 Prisoners of war must at all times be humanely treated. Any unlawful act or omission by the Detaining Power causing death or seriously endangering the health of a prisoner of war in its custody is prohibited, and will be regarded as a serious breach of the present Convention. In particular, no prisoner of war may be subjected to physical mutilation or to medical or scientific experiments of any kind which are not justified by the medical, dental or hospital treatment of the prisoner concerned and carried out in his interest.

Likewise, prisoners of war must at all times be protected, particularly against acts of violence or intimidation and against insults and public curiosity.

Measures of reprisal against prisoners of war are prohibited.

ARTICLE 14 Prisoners of war are entitled in all circumstances to respect for their persons and their honour. Women shall be treated with all the regard due to their sex and shall in all cases benefit by treatment as favourable as that granted to men. Prisoners of war shall retain the full civil capacity which they enjoyed at the time of their capture. The Detaining Power may not restrict the exercise, either within or without its own territory, of the rights such capacity confers except in so far as the captivity requires.

ARTICLE 15 The Power detaining prisoners of war shall be bound to provide free of charge for their maintenance and for the medical attention required by their state of health.

ARTICLE 16 Taking into consideration the provisions of the present Convention relating to rank and sex, and subject to any privileged treatment which may be accorded to them by reason of their state of health, age or professional qualifications, all prisoners of war shall be treated alike by the Detaining Power, without any adverse distinction based on race, nationality, religious belief or political opinions, or any other distinction founded on similar criteria.

PART III

CAPTIVITY
SECTION I
BEGINNING OF CAPTIVITY
ARTICLE 17

Every prisoner of war, when questioned on the subject, is bound to give only his surname, first names and rank, date of birth, and army, regimental, personal or serial

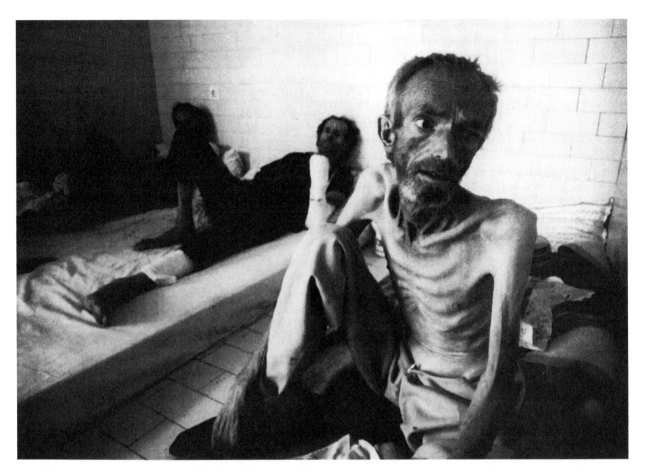

One of the Bosnian Muslims held prisoner by Serbian forces at their Trnopolje detention camp, near Banjaluka, Bosnia-Herzegovinia, August 12, 1992. AP/WIDE WORLD PHOTOS. REPRODUCED BY PERMISSION.

number, or failing this, equivalent information. If he willfully infringes this rule, he may render himself liable to a restriction of the privileges accorded to his rank or status.

Each Party to a conflict is required to furnish the persons under its jurisdiction who are liable to become prisoners of war, with an identity card showing the owner's surname, first names, rank, army, regimental, personal or serial number or equivalent information, and date of birth. The identity card may, furthermore, bear the signature or the fingerprints, or both, of the owner, and may bear, as well, any other information the Party to the conflict may wish to add concerning persons belonging to its armed forces. As far as possible the card shall measure 6.5 x 10 cm. and shall be issued in duplicate. The identity card shall be shown by the prisoner of war upon demand, but may in no case be taken away from him.

No physical or mental torture, nor any other form of coercion, may be inflicted on prisoners of war to secure from them information of any kind whatever. Prisoners of war who refuse to answer may not be threatened,

insulted, or exposed to any unpleasant or disadvantageous treatment of any kind.

Prisoners of war who, owing to their physical or mental condition, are unable to state their identity, shall be handed over to the medical service. The identity of such prisoners shall be established by all possible means, subject to the provisions of the preceding paragraph.

The questioning of prisoners of war shall be carried out in a language which they understand.

SIGNIFICANCE

The convention has received near-universal acceptance, giving it a strong claim to represent customary law. However, rogue nations and countries experiencing a collapse of internal structures do not always obey the rules of war with respect to prisoners. In African countries experiencing civil war, such as Sierra Leone and Liberia in the 1990s, prisoners of war were tortured, mutilated, killed, or forced to serve as soldiers for the side of their captors. With international reluctance to send troops to mediate such conflicts, the abuses have continued. In situations where troops are attempting to halt civil unrest, such as Iraq at the millennium, terrorists have abused prisoners of war to make political points.

In the 1990s, the UN Security Council began establishing criminal tribunals with international judges to prosecute those who had committed human rights abuses in the context of war. In 2002, the countries of the world met in Rome to establish the International Criminal Court (ICC). In contrast to the UN tribunals, the ICC is the first global permanent court with jurisdiction to prosecute individuals for crimes of greatest concern to the international community: genocide; crimes against humanity; and war crimes. The United States has yet to sign the ICC treaty.

American officials fear that an independent prosecutor, motivated by anti-Americanism, might single out U.S. military personal and senior government officials for persecution. They argue that Americans should not be placed at risk of criminal prosecution for national security decisions involving such matters as responding to acts of terrorism, preventing the proliferation of weapons of mass destruction, and deterring aggression. Any American prosecuted by the ICC would be denied procedural protections guaranteed to all U.S. citizens under the Bill of Rights, such as the right to trial by jury. In 2002, in response to these concerns, the United States Congress passed the American Service Members' Protection Act, declaring that the United States will not recognize the jurisdiction of the ICC over American nationals.

FURTHER RESOURCES
Books

Berkowitz, Peter. *Terrorism, the Laws of War, and the Constitution: Debating the Enemy Combatant Cases.* Stanford, Calif.: Hoover Institution Press, 2005.

Byers, Michael. *War Law: Understanding International Law and Armed Conflict.* New York: Grove Press, 2006.

Jinks, Derek. *The Rules of War: The Geneva Convention in the Age of Terror.* New York: Oxford University Press, 2005.

Equal Rights Amendment

Legislation

By: Martha Griffiths, Birch Bayh and Marlow Cook

Date: 1972

Source: 92nd U.S. Congress. Equal Rights Amendment. *United States Statutes at Large.* volume 86, pages 1523–1524, 1972.

About the Author: Democratic United States Representative Martha Griffiths of Michigan, Democratic Senator Birch Bayh of Indiana, and Republican Senator Marlow Cook of Kentucky took the language of the Equal Rights Amendment, originally written in 1921 and substantially revised in 1950, and made changes to help foster its successful passage in both the House and Senate in 1972.

INTRODUCTION

Alice Paul, a highly educated Quaker woman who earned five degrees, including a master of laws and a Ph.D. in economics, joined the National American Women's Suffrage Association in 1910; she left six years later to found the National Women's Party. In 1921, one year after the Nineteenth Amendment guaranteed women the right to vote, Paul penned the "Equal Rights Amendment," which read: "Men and women shall have equal rights throughout the United States and every place subject to its jurisdiction. Congress shall have power to enforce this article by appropriate legislation." Paul read the proposed amendment at a 1923 convention in Seneca Falls, New York, during the seventy-fifth anniversary of the first women's rights convention in the same town in 1848.

Designed to give American women equal protection under the law in such areas as employment, family law, education, and civil society, the Equal Rights Amendment was introduced to Congress in 1923 by Senate Republican Whip Charles Curtis and Representative Daniel R. Anthony, Susan B. Anthony's nephew. For the next forty-nine years proponents of the amendment submitted it to Congress for passage; finally in 1972 the joint efforts of Democratic Representative Martha Griffiths, Democratic Senator Birch Bayh, and Republican Senator Marlow Cook led to a draft of language that helped facilitate its passage. Griffiths had been widely credited with inserting language on gender protection into the Civil Rights Act of 1964, and the ERA helped reinforce her reputation as a women's rights legislator.

Senator Sam Ervin and Representative Emmanuel Cellar added a seven-year clause to the amendment: Thirty-eight states had to ratify the ERA within seven years for the amendment to be added to the Constitution. This tactic had been used on the Nineteenth Amendment as well, though many women's groups viewed it as unfair. March 22, 1979 became the ERA deadline.

Supporters of the Equal Rights Amendment rally in front of the Statue of Liberty on August 10, 1970. © BETTMANN/CORBIS. REPRODUCED BY PERMISSION.

PRIMARY SOURCE

SECTION 1. Equality of rights under the law shall not be denied or abridged by the United States or by any State on account of sex.

SECTION 2. The Congress shall have the power to enforce, by appropriate legislation, the provisions of this article.

SECTION 3. This amendment shall take effect two years after the date of ratification.

SIGNIFICANCE

In 1972, Phyllis Schlafly, best-selling conservative author and activist, created the National Committee to Stop the ERA and established the Eagle Forum, a conservative response to the Equal Rights Amendment.

Schlafly's primary argument against the ERA was that the 1963 Equal Pay Act and the 1964 Civil Rights Act provided enough gender protection for women; the ERA would not only duplicate those laws, but would also, by using the word "sex" in the amendment, open the door for federal acceptance of gay rights.

By 1977, thirty-five states had ratified the Equal Rights Amendment; with three more the amendment's adoption would be complete. The National Organization for Women, founded in 1966, poured money and time into grass roots campaigns in each state to push for ratification. Rallied by the amendment and the belief that the ERA would be the final push for legislative equality, in February 1977 NOW encouraged a boycott of all states that had not ratified the amendment.

At the same time, Phyllis Schlafly and other conservative groups worked to prevent the ERA's ratification. By arguing that gender equality would force women into the military, including combat, and to lose preferential treatment in child custody cases, Schlafly and her organizations helped stall the ERA's momentum. Despite a three-year extension, the ERA never gained the thirty-eight states needed, remaining instead three states shy. As of June 30, 1982, the Equal Rights Amendment officially timed out.

On March 15, 2005, Democratic Senator Ted Kennedy of Massachusetts and Democratic Representative Carolyn Maloney of New York introduced the Equal Rights Amendment to Congress once again using the "three-state strategy," an argument written by law students in 1995. This maintains that the Twenty-Seventh Amendment—the 1992 amendment regarding Congressional pay raises—actually began its ratification process in 1789 and was not fully ratified until 203 years later. Using this precedent, the strategy further maintains that the original thirty-five state ratifications are still valid and that time should be extended indefinitely to allow three more to ratify the amendment. Despite legal challenges and questions, feminist groups and supporters continue to push for the ERA's adoption using this argument.

FURTHER RESOURCES
Books

Becker, Susan D. *The Origins of the Equal Rights Amendment: American Feminism Between the Wars*. Westport, CT: Greenwood Press, 1981.

Cobble, Dorothy Sue. *The Other Women's Movement: Workplace Justice and Social Rights in Modern America*. Princeton, NJ: Princeton University Press, 2004.

Felder, Deborah G. *A Century of Women: The Most Influential Events in Twentieth-Century Women's History.* Kensington Publishing Corp., 1999.

Friedan, Betty. *The Feminine Mystique.* New York: W.W. Norton, 2001.

Millet, Kate. *Sexual Politics.* Champlaign, IL: University of Illinois Press, 2000.

Web sites

Ms. Magazine. "Her Story: 1971—Present" <http://www.msmagazine.com/about.asp> (accessed April 17, 2006).

National Women's Political Caucus. <http://www.nwpc.org> (accessed April 17, 2006).

Beauty Will Save the World

Speech excerpt

By: Aleksandr Solzhenitsyn

Date: 1974

Source: Solzhenitsyn, Aleksandr, translated by Thomas P. Whitney. "Beauty Will Save the World." In *The World Treasury of Modern Thought*, edited by Jaroslav Pelikan. New York: Harper and Row, 1974.

About the Author: Born in 1918, Alexander Solzhenitsyn was a Russian author who spent eight years in Russian leader Joseph Stalin's (1878–1953) prison camps. He was awarded the Nobel Prize for literature in 1970. Following the publication of *The Gulag Archipelago* in 1974, he was charged with treason and exiled from the Soviet Union.

INTRODUCTION

Aleksandr Solzhenitsyn (1918–) spent much of his adult life under arrest, in exile, or in fear. His *The Gulag Archipelago*, a three-volume series published between 1973 and 1978, exposed the history of the police state in the Soviet Union. Its most remarkable point showed that labor and political prisoner camps came from the theologies of Vladimir Lenin—the Communist founder of the Soviet Union—and not Joseph Stalin. Yet, it was not the publication of *The Gulag Archipelago* that made Solzhenitsyn a political target in the Soviet Union. Rather, his political chastisement, imprisonments, and eventual exile began in 1945.

In February 1945, the KGB (the Russian-language abbreviation for Secret Security Committee) arrested Solzhenitsyn for criticisms he had made about Stalin. Solzhenitsyn had written these remarks in letters to a school friend between 1944 and 1945, and his arrest came on the frontlines. He had been commanding an artillery-position-finding company in East Prussia for the Soviet Army during World War II. He achieved the rank of captain during the war, and his service earned him two wartime decorations. This arrest sent him to detention camps for eight years. Then, one month after his prison sentence ended, the administration decided that he would be exiled for life to Kok-Terek (in present-day Kazahkstan). This exile lasted until March 1953. In 1953, Solzhenitsyn was diagnosed with cancer, and he fought this battle until 1954 when the cancer went into remission.

During his exile, Solzhenitsyn turned toward his writing as a way to console and express himself. He wrote in secret and feared showing his works to even his closet friends because of continual government observation of his activities. It wasn't until much later that Solzhenitsyn broke his silence with *One Day in the Life of Ivan Denisovich* published in 1962. This work portrayed one day of life in a Soviet prison camp. The story erupted as a sensational piece, with numerous translations to follow. By 1964, Solzhenitsyn's writings and plays were censored, and in 1965 his book *The First Circle* and his papers were seized.

Solzhenitsyn's writings marked the beginning of Soviet prison camp literature, and his political criticism of the Soviet regime sparked the interest of the Western world. His writings spoke of the everyman, captured the reader through their direct language and narration, and the characters explored questions on life, death, and politics. These topics, particularly his political criticism, caused the KGB to censor his writings, seize his manuscripts, and halt his publications. From 1963 to 1966, he only published four short stories, and in 1969 the Writer's Union expelled him. Even though he faced a continual surge of governmental harassment, Solzhenitsyn continued to write. In 1971, he began smuggling his manuscripts into the West, and the story of how he smuggled his Nobel Lecture from Moscow showcased his drive to overcome his oppression.

Solzhenitsyn received the Nobel Prize in Literature in 1970, and his enemies in the Soviet Union used it as more fuel to condemn him. They saw the award as praising a traitor. Thus, Solzhenitsyn decided not to go to Stockholm, Sweden to accept the award for fear that he would not be allowed back into his country. Even though the Soviet Union's government harassed, quarantined, and censored him, he could not fathom severing

Russian novelist Alexander Solzhenitsyn in 1963. © BETTMANN/ CORBIS.

himself from his homeland. Once Solzhenitsyn decided to not accept the award in Sweden, officials talked of presenting him the prize at the Swedish Embassy in Moscow in April 1972. This plan fell through when the Swedish Ambassador insisted that the award be merely handed to Solzhenitsyn, and that he would not give his Nobel Lecture. Solzhenitsyn took offense to this demand, and he refused to accept the award there. In 1972, Solzhenitsyn met Swedish news correspondent Stig Fredrikson, and during the course of the next year the two would meet in secret locations and pass messages and packages to one another. Solzhenitsyn used Fredrikson to smuggle his writings from Moscow, and he used him to obtain correspondence from his lawyer and publishers in the West. Most importantly, Solzhenitsyn gave Fredrikson a series of negatives that contained his Nobel Lecture. From these negatives, his speech was given to the Swedish Academy and reproduced and published in later works. Its message spoke of political dissent, censorship, and of the human spirit. These are the same themes that Solzhenitsyn used in writings that won him the award in 1970.

■ PRIMARY SOURCE

I have climbed my way up to this lectern from which the Nobel Lecture is read, a lectern not granted to every writer and once only in a lifetime, not just up three or four specially erected steps but hundreds and even thousands of them—unyielding, steep, frozen, out of the dark and the cold where I was fated to survive and where others, who possessed perhaps greater talent and were stronger than I, perished. I met only a few among them in the Gulag Archipelago scattered over a wide-spread multitude of islands. And beneath the millstone of police surveillance and mistrust I did not speak face to face with all those who were there either. Of some I only heard at second hand and about others I only guessed. Those who fell into that abyss who already had made a name in literature are at least known to us—but how many were unknown, had never been published! And so very few, almost no one, managed to survive and return. A whole national literature remained behind, buried not only without coffins and graves, but even without underwear, naked except for an identification tag on the toe. Russian literature never ceased for one moment! Yet from outside it seemed a desert. Where a thick forest might have grown there remained, after all the timbering, only two or three trees which had missed being cut down.

And today how am I, accompanied as I am by the spirits of those who perished, my head bowed as I let pass before me up to this lectern others who were earlier worthy of it, how am I here today supposed to divine and express that which *they* would have wished to say?

This duty has long weighed upon me, and I have understood it. In the words of Vladimir Soloviev:

In chains, too, we must close the circle

Which the gods have drawn for us.

■

SIGNIFICANCE

After the 1973 publication of *The Gulag Archipelago*, Solzhenitsyn faced increased harassment and criticism from the Soviet Union's government. The book provided a detailed account of the Soviet prison and labor camps and did not show the Soviets in a kind light. He was arrested and charged with treason, which resulted in his expulsion from the Soviet Union in 1974. Soviet officials stripped him of his citizenship and deported him to West Germany. Once banished from his homeland, Solzhenitsyn first moved to Switzerland. In 1976, he came to the United States. While in the United States, in Vermont, he continued to write history and political pieces. He finished the *The Gulag Archipelago* series and also completed *The Red Wheel*. *The Red Wheel* detailed the Russian Army's defeat in East Prussia, and once again the history that Solzhenitsyn told did not glorify Soviet leadership.

When the Soviet Union collapsed in 1991, the political tide for Solzhenitsyn began to soften. In 1990, new leader Mikhail S. Gorbachev offered to restore his citizenship, and the following year Solzhenitsyn toured Siberia to promote his writings. In 1994, he resettled in Moscow where he continued his political writings condemning Western materialism. His later writings show a reflection of late-twentieth-century Russian culture and a desire for the return of pre-communist Russian culture. These later writings have not gained the same popularity and praise in Western societies as his earlier works, but he continues to gain respect and acclaim in the former Soviet Union. As of 2006, Solzhenitsyn lives with his family in Moscow.

FURTHER RESOURCES

Books

Mahoney, Daniel J. *Aleksandr Solzhenitsyn: The Ascent from Ideology*. New York: Rowman & Littlefield Publishers, Inc., 2001.

Pontuso, James F. *Assault on Ideology: Aleksandr Solzhenitsyn's Political Thought*. Los Angeles: Lexington Books, 2004.

Periodicals

Rowley, David G. "Aleksandr Solzhenitsyn and Russian Nationalism." *Journal of Contemporary History* 32, 3 (July 1997): 321–337.

Web sites

The *New York Times*. "Featured Author: Aleksandr Solzhenitsyn." 1997. <http://www.nytimes.com/books/98/03/01/home/solz.html> (accessed May 6, 2006).

The Final Act of the Conference on Security and Cooperation in Europe

Helsinki Declaration

Declaration

By: Conference on Security and Co-operation in Europe

Date: August 1, 1975

Source: The Final Act of the Conference on Security and Cooperation in Europe, 14 I.L.M. 1292. August 1, 1975.

About the Author: The Conference on Security and Co-operation in Europe was established in 1973 by a group of thirty-five nations and states for the purpose of examining issues of European security. After the collapse of the Soviet Union in 1991, the group became known as the Organization for Security and Co-operation in Europe. It is currently headquartered in Vienna and has fifty-five member states.

INTRODUCTION

In 1970, on a visit to Poland, the West German Chancellor Willy Brandt kneeled in front of a monument for victims of the Warsaw ghetto. This action was an example of Ostpolitik, or an effort by West Germany to advance relations with Eastern bloc, or Warsaw Pact countries. The Cold War (1947–1991) had created a climate of conflict throughout the international community and the measure of a state's security and strength was found in its alliances. However, a movement toward détente facilitated the environment for cooperation between rival nations. In 1972, preparations began for a conference among states. During that same year, the two nations leading the Cold War, United States and the Union of Soviet Socialist Republics, signed the SALT I (Strategic Arms Limitation Talks) to freeze the number of strategic ballistic missile launchers. By 1973, oil-producing Arab states launched an embargo against the United States, Europe, and Japan for those nations support for Israel. This global energy crisis sparked continued movement toward cooperation in the international community. As a result, on July 1, 1973, the Conference on Security and Co-operation in Europe (CSCE) opened in Helsinki. The conference met in Geneva from September 18, 1973 through July 21, 1975 and concluded on August 1, 1975 in a meeting in Helsinki. Representatives participated from Austria, Belgium, Bulgaria, Canada, Cyprus, Czechoslovakia, Denmark, Finland, France, the German Democratic Republic, the Federal Republic of Germany, Greece, the Holy See, Hungary, Iceland, Ireland, Italy, Liechtenstein, Luxemburg, Malta, Monaco, the Netherlands, Norway, Poland, Portugal, Romania, San Marino, Spain, Sweden, Switzerland, Turkey, USSR, United Kingdom, United States, and Yugoslavia. In addition, non-participating Mediterranean states that contributed to the conference were Algeria, Egypt, Israel, Morocco, Syria and Tunisia.

President Gerald Ford signs the Final Act of the Conference on Security and Cooperation in Europe, in Finland, on August 1, 1975.
© CORBIS.

At the close of the conference, the participating members signed the Helsinki Declaration, also called the Helsinki Final Act or Helsinki Accord. The agreement that emerged from the conference was intended to facilitate improved relations between Eastern and Western nations. The declaration identified that participating states possessed shared interests in creating security through confidence building measures rather than through the environment of force that prevailed during the Cold War. The agreement asserts detailed principles for relations between states. Intended to broaden peace and stability through cooperation in Europe, the agreement promoted détente by identifying a common purpose among participating states to create closer relations among nations, and asserted the recognition of a common history, tradition, and values within European states. The principles set out by the declaration include a respect for respective nation's sovereignty, the renunciation of force as a means to resolve disputes, the policy of non-intervention in internal affairs, acknowledgement of territorial integrity of states and inviolability of frontiers, and respect for human rights. In addition, the agreement affirmed the role of the United Nations in creating peace, justice, and security.

PRIMARY SOURCE

VII. Respect for human rights and fundamental freedoms, including the freedom of thought, conscience, religion or belief The participating States will respect human rights and fundamental freedoms, including the freedom of thought, conscience, religion or belief, for all without distinction as to race, sex, language or religion.

They will promote and encourage the effective exercise of civil, political, economic, social, cultural and other rights and freedoms all of which derive from the inherent dignity of the human person and are essential for his free and full development.

Within this framework the participating States will recognize and respect the freedom of the individual to profess and practice, alone or in community with others, religion or belief acting in accordance with the dictates of his own conscience.

The participating States on whose territory national minorities exist will respect the right of persons belonging to such minorities to equality before the law, will afford them the full opportunity for the actual enjoyment of human rights and fundamental freedoms and will, in this manner, protect their legitimate interests in this sphere.

The participating States recognize the universal significance of human rights and fundamental freedoms, respect for which is an essential factor for the peace, justice and well-being necessary to ensure the development of friendly relations and co-operation among themselves as among all States.

They will constantly respect these rights and freedoms in their mutual relations and will endeavour jointly and separately, including in co-operation with the United Nations, to promote universal and effective respect for them.

They confirm the right of the individual to know and act upon his rights and duties in this field.

In the field of human rights and fundamental freedoms, the participating States will act in conformity with the purposes and principles of the Charter of the United Nations and with the Universal Declaration of Human Rights. They will also fulfil their obligations as set forth in the international declarations and agreements in this field, including inter alia the International Covenants on Human Rights, by which they may be bound.

VIII. Equal rights and self-determination of peoples The participating States will respect the equal rights of peoples and their right to self-determination, acting at all times in conformity with the purposes and principles of the Charter of the United Nations and with the relevant norms of international law, including those relating to territorial integrity of States.

By virtue of the principle of equal rights and self-determination of peoples, all peoples always have the right, in full freedom, to determine, when and as they wish, their internal and external political status, without external interference, and to pursue as they wish their political, economic, social and cultural development.

The participating States reaffirm the universal significance of respect for and effective exercise of equal rights and self-determination of peoples for the development of friendly relations among themselves as among all States; they also recall the importance of the elimination of any form of violation of this principle.

SIGNIFICANCE

The initial thirty-five members of the Conference on Security and Co-operation in Europe met throughout Europe in its movement toward the Helsinki Final Act. These meetings resulted in a series of non-binding agreements between states on international issues such as human rights. The meetings and agreements that came from the meetings, especially the Helsinki Final Act, displayed a consensus throughout participating countries that had never been seen before. This consensus was based on the ideological link between security and cooperation between states. In a press briefing recognizing the 30th anniversary of the signing of the Act, the White House stated that the declaration was a factor in "undermining despotism with ideals of freedom and human rights . . . premised on the belief that security should be defined by the ways that countries treat their own citizens and cooperate with their neighbors." As a result, the CSCE evolved from a diplomatic entity to an international organization. The group began by bringing 1975 Cold War rivals into a similar organization thereby creating channels of communication between opposing states. In addition, the CSCE brought human rights to the forefront of international relations. With the collapse of communism, the CSCE convened in Paris in 1990 to restructure its organization. As a result, by January 1995, the CSCE became the Organization for Security and Co-operation in Europe. In July 2005, parliamentarians from Europe and North America convened in Washington, DC to promote continued involvement in the OSCE. As a result, the group reaffirmed the principles of international law set out in the Helsinki Final Act. In addition, the members once again identified human rights as a global foreign policy concern and adopted a resolution promoting women's involvement in the OSCE.

The Organization for Security and Co-operation in Europe emerged from the CSCE into the Western world's largest intergovernmental organization. In its support of the principles set out in the Helsinki Final Act, the OSCE has observed elections in eight regional countries and has monitored human rights in the region and continues to promote human rights and fundamental freedoms.

FURTHER RESOURCES
Web sites
Department of State. "OSCE Parliamentarians Reaffirm Helsinki Final Act Principles." July 2005. <http://usinfo.state.gov/eur/Archive/2005/Jul/06-473450.html> (accessed April 30, 2006).

Economic Reconstruction and Development in South East Europe. "The Helsinki Final Act." <http://www.seerecon.org/region/sp/helsinki.htm> (accessed April 30, 2006).

Eurasianet.org. "The 25th Anniversary of the Helsinki Final Act: Evaluating Human Rights." July 31, 2000. <http://www.eurasianet.org/departments/rights/articles/eav073100.shtml> (accessed April 30, 2006).

The Organization for Security and Co-operation in Europe. "CSCE/OSCE Timeline." <http://www.osce.org/item/15801.html> (accessed April 30, 2006).

The White House. "Statement on the 30th Anniversary of the Helsinki Final Act." August 1, 2005. <http://www.whitehouse.gov/news/releases/2005/08/20050801-3.html> (accessed April 30, 2006).

Convention against Torture and Other Cruel, Inhuman, or Degrading Treatment or Punishment

Declaration

By: United Nations

Date: December 10, 1984

Source: United Nations General Assembly. "Convention against Torture and Other Cruel, Inhuman, or Degrading Treatment or Punishment" General Assembly Resolution 39/46. December 10, 1984.

About the Author: The phrase "United Nations" was used during World War II (1939–1945) to describe the dozens of nations allied together to fight Germany and Japan, most notably including China, France, Great Britain, the Soviet Union, and the United States of America. These allies decided to develop a new organization to facilitate international cooperation and help prevent future wars. It would replace the League of Nations, which had failed to prevent World War II. They called it the United Nations (UN). The UN Charter was ratified on October 24, 1945. In the years since the UN has served as a forum for international negotiation and cooperation on many issues, including international security, human rights, trade and economics, and the environment.

INTRODUCTION

The United Nations Convention against Torture and Other Cruel, Inhuman, or Degrading Treatment or Punishment is a treaty that had been signed and ratified, as of April 2006, by 141 member nations, signed but not ratified by another ten, and unsigned by forty-one.

The convention was adopted by the UN General Assembly (the voting body consisting of all UN member states' representatives) on December 10, 1984, and entered into force on June 26, 1987. The first UN instrument to ban torture, adopted in 1948, was the Universal Declaration on Human Rights, which stated that "[n]o one shall be subjected to torture or to cruel, inhuman or degrading treatment or punishment." However, the word "torture" was not defined. The UN's 1966 International Covenant on Civil and Political Rights repeated the 1948 language and added that "no one shall be subjected without his free consent to medical or scientific experimentation" but still did not define the word "torture."

Not until the UN's 1975 Declaration on the Protection of All Persons from Being Subjected to Torture and Other Cruel, Inhuman, or Degrading Treatment or Punishment, which resembles the convention in many of its provisions, was "torture" defined. This definition was adopted as Part I, Article 1 of the Convention against Torture, with the addition of language specifying that for the purposes of the convention—that is, to be considered a state crime, as opposed to a crime against humanity (a broader category)—torture must be inflicted by a government official. Further, the convention added language specifying that pain "inherent in or incidental to lawful sanctions" is not torture. For example, the suffering of an enemy soldier shot in combat is not considered torture. The convention requires every signatory nation to ban and actively prevent torture and to not send any prisoner to a country "where there are substantial grounds for believing that he would be in danger of being subjected to torture." It also forbids the invocation of "exceptional circumstances" such as national emergencies to justify torture.

In the words of a UN fact sheet, "the United Nations did not merely put in writing in a series of articles a body of principles and pious hopes, the implementation and observance of which would not be guaranteed by anything or anyone." To encourage compliance, Article 17 of the convention established the UN Committee against Torture.

Committee members—ten experts in human rights who are citizens of nations signatory to the convention ("State Parties")—are elected every four years by a secret vote of all State Parties. The committee, which began to function on January 1, 1988, meets twice a year but can convene special sessions. It submits an annual report to all State Parties and the General Assembly. Each State Party is supposed to submit a report once every four years, starting within one year after signing the convention, describing actions taken to fulfill its obligations. Complaints by individuals or states can be filed formally with the committee, and the committee can institute investigations of its own accord.

PRIMARY SOURCE

Office of the High Commissioner for Human Rights

Convention against Torture and Other Cruel, Inhuman, or Degrading Treatment or Punishment

Adopted and opened for signature, ratification, and accession by General Assembly resolution 39/46 of 10 December 1984

entry into force 26 June 1987, in accordance with article 27 (1)

The States Parties to this Convention,

Considering that, in accordance with the principles proclaimed in the Charter of the United Nations, recognition of the equal and inalienable rights of all members of the human family is the foundation of freedom, justice and peace in the world,

Recognizing that those rights derive from the inherent dignity of the human person.

Considering the obligation of States under the Charter, in particular Article 55, to promote universal respect for, and observance of, human rights and fundamental freedoms,

Having regard to article 5 of the Universal Declaration of Human Rights and article 7 of the International Covenant on Civil and Political Rights, both of which provide that no one shall be subjected to torture or to cruel, inhuman or degrading treatment or punishment,

Having regard also to the Declaration on the Protection of All Persons from Being Subjected to Torture and Other Cruel, Inhuman or Degrading Treatment or Punishment, adopted by the General Assembly on 9 December 1975,

Desiring to make more effective the struggle against torture and other cruel, inhuman or degrading treatment or punishment throughout the world, Have agreed as follows:

PART I

Article 1

1. For the purposes of this Convention, the term "torture" means any act by which severe pain or suffering, whether physical or mental, is intentionally inflicted on a person for such purposes as obtaining from him or a third person information or a confession, punishing him for an act he or a third person has committed or is suspected of having committed, or intimidating or coercing him or a third person, or for any reason based on discrimination of any kind, when such pain or suffering is inflicted by or at the instigation of or with the consent or acquiescence of a public official or other person acting in an official capacity. It does not include pain or suffering arising only from, inherent in or incidental to lawful sanctions.

2. This article is without prejudice to any international instrument or national legislation which does or may contain provisions of wider application.

Article 2

1. Each State Party shall take effective legislative, administrative, judicial or other measures to prevent acts of torture in any territory under its jurisdiction.

2. No exceptional circumstances whatsoever, whether a state of war or a threat of war, internal political in stability or any other public emergency, may be invoked as a justification of torture.

3. An order from a superior officer or a public authority may not be invoked as a justification of torture.

Article 3

1. No State Party shall expel, return ("refouler") or extradite a person to another State where there are substantial grounds for believing that he would be in danger of being subjected to torture.

2. For the purpose of determining whether there are such grounds, the competent authorities shall take into account all relevant considerations including, where applicable, the existence in the State concerned of a consistent pattern of gross, flagrant or mass violations of human rights.

Article 4

1. Each State Party shall ensure that all acts of torture are offences under its criminal law. The same shall apply to an attempt to commit torture and to an act by any person which constitutes complicity or participation in torture.

2. Each State Party shall make these offences punishable by appropriate penalties which take into account their grave nature.

Article 5

1. Each State Party shall take such measures as may be necessary to establish its jurisdiction over the offences referred to in article 4 in the following cases:

(a) When the offences are committed in any territory under its jurisdiction or on board a ship or aircraft registered in that State;

(b) When the alleged offender is a national of that State;

(c) When the victim is a national of that State if that State considers it appropriate.

2. Each State Party shall likewise take such measures as may be necessary to establish its jurisdiction over such offences in cases where the alleged offender is present in any territory under its jurisdiction and it does not extradite him pursuant to article 8 to any of the States mentioned in paragraph I of this article.

3. This Convention does not exclude any criminal jurisdiction exercised in accordance with internal law.

Article 6

1. Upon being satisfied, after an examination of information available to it, that the circumstances so warrant, any State Party in whose territory a person alleged to have committed any offence referred to in article 4 is present shall take him into custody or take other legal measures to ensure his presence. The custody and other legal measures shall be as provided in the law of that State but may be continued only for such time as is necessary to enable any criminal or extradition proceedings to be instituted.

2. Such State shall immediately make a preliminary inquiry into the facts.

3. Any person in custody pursuant to paragraph I of this article shall be assisted in communicating immediately with the nearest appropriate representative of the State of which he is a national, or, if he is a stateless person, with the representative of the State where he usually resides.

4. When a State, pursuant to this article, has taken a person into custody, it shall immediately notify the States referred to in article 5, paragraph 1, of the fact that such person is in custody and of the circumstances which warrant his detention. The State which makes the preliminary inquiry contemplated in paragraph 2 of this article shall promptly report its findings to the said States and shall indicate whether it intends to exercise jurisdiction.

Article 7

1. The State Party in the territory under whose jurisdiction a person alleged to have committed any offence referred to in article 4 is found shall in the cases contemplated in article 5, if it does not extradite him, submit the case to its competent authorities for the purpose of prosecution.

2. These authorities shall take their decision in the same manner as in the case of any ordinary offence of a serious nature under the law of that State. In the cases referred to in article 5, paragraph 2, the standards of evidence required for prosecution and conviction shall in no way be less stringent than those which apply in the cases referred to in article 5, paragraph 1.

3. Any person regarding whom proceedings are brought in connection with any of the offences referred to in article 4 shall be guaranteed fair treatment at all stages of the proceedings.

Article 8

1. The offences referred to in article 4 shall be deemed to be included as extraditable offences in any extradition treaty existing between States Parties. States Parties undertake to include such offences as extraditable offences in every extradition treaty to be concluded between them.

2. If a State Party which makes extradition conditional on the existence of a treaty receives a request for extradition from another State Party with which it has no extradition treaty, it may consider this Convention as the legal basis for extradition in respect of such offences. Extradition shall be subject to the other conditions provided by the law of the requested State.

3. States Parties which do not make extradition conditional on the existence of a treaty shall recognize such offences as extraditable offences between themselves subject to the conditions provided by the law of the requested State.

4. Such offences shall be treated, for the purpose of extradition between States Parties, as if they had been committed not only in the place in which they occurred but also in the territories of the States required to establish their jurisdiction in accordance with article 5, paragraph 1.

Article 9

1. States Parties shall afford one another the greatest measure of assistance in connection with criminal proceedings brought in respect of any of the offences referred to in article 4, including the supply of all evidence at their disposal necessary for the proceedings.

2. States Parties shall carry out their obligations under paragraph I of this article in conformity with any treaties on mutual judicial assistance that may exist between them.

Article 10

1. Each State Party shall ensure that education and information regarding the prohibition against torture are fully included in the training of law enforcement personnel, civil or military, medical personnel, public officials and other persons who may be involved in the custody, interrogation or treatment of any individual subjected to any form of arrest, detention or imprisonment.
2. Each State Party shall include this prohibition in the rules or instructions issued in regard to the duties and functions of any such person.

Article 11

Each State Party shall keep under systematic review interrogation rules, instructions, methods and practices as well as arrangements for the custody and treatment of persons subjected to any form of arrest, detention or imprisonment in any territory under its jurisdiction, with a view to preventing any cases of torture.

Article 12

Each State Party shall ensure that its competent authorities proceed to a prompt and impartial investigation, wherever there is reasonable ground to believe that an act of torture has been committed in any territory under its jurisdiction.

Article 13

Each State Party shall ensure that any individual who alleges he has been subjected to torture in any territory under its jurisdiction has the right to complain to, and to have his case promptly and impartially examined by, its competent authorities. Steps shall be taken to ensure that the complainant and witnesses are protected against all ill-treatment or intimidation as a consequence of his complaint or any evidence given.

Article 14

1. Each State Party shall ensure in its legal system that the victim of an act of torture obtains redress and has an enforceable right to fair and adequate compensation, including the means for as full rehabilitation as possible. In the event of the death of the victim as a result of an act of torture, his dependants shall be entitled to compensation.
2. Nothing in this article shall affect any right of the victim or other persons to compensation which may exist under national law.

SIGNIFICANCE

Most countries are signatories of the Convention against Torture. Although many countries still practice torture, it has become, for the most part, politically unacceptable to openly defend the practice of torture. This is a historic novelty; torture was not always considered abhorrent. On the contrary, it has been openly and officially practiced by most states throughout history. Torture has been employed to enforce conformity to religious orthodoxies, for ritual purposes, and to punish various crimes. However, following the European Enlightenment in the 1700s, torture has gradually come to be seen as unacceptable by the majority of the world's population. In some democratic states, including the United States, public debate over the permissibility of torture under special circumstances—the usual hypothetical scenario being prevention of a massive terrorist attack—revived during the early 2000s.

Whether the Convention against Torture and the Committee Against Torture have been effective in decreasing the amount of torture practiced in the world is difficult to know. The Committee has no direct enforcement powers, but by making credible, independent information about torture practices widely available and by publicly calling on states to change their practices, the Committee may be able reinforce political processes that can cause some states to reduce or eliminate torture.

Scores of countries have been criticized for torture by the Committee Against Torture, but criticism of the United States by the Committee has received special attention because of the U.S.'s uniquely prominent role in international affairs. In 2005, the United States admitted in its second periodic report to the Committee (the first had been delivered in 1999, almost five years overdue) that prisoners had been tortured at U.S. military facilities in Guantanamo (Cuba), Afghanistan, and Iraq. It denied, however, that any of the torture had been officially permitted. In April 2006, the Committee demanded more information on the treatment of prisoners in these facilities and in alleged secret detention facilities worldwide run by the United States. The United States was due to send a delegation of officials to argue its case before the Committee in May 2006. The Committee also criticized U.S. practices of jailing juveniles with adults and allowing some states to put prisoners in chain gangs. Envoys from the International Committee of the Red Cross had already concluded in 2004 that officially permitted interrogation techniques at Guantanamo were "tantamount to torture," as had a delegation from the UN Commission on Human Rights in February 2006. The United States maintains

Ablavi Haden, a native of Togo, at the Dallas County Jail on December 2, 1998. She is seeking asylum in the United States under the Convention Against Torture, and fighting against the Immigration and Naturalization Service attempt to deport her back to Togo. AP IMAGES.

that its policies are in agreement with all treaty obligations and domestic laws.

FURTHER RESOURCES

Books

Karen, Greenberg J., ed. *The Torture Debate in America*. New York: Cambridge University Press, 2006.

Periodicals

Farley, Maggie. "Report: U.S. Is Abusing Captives." *The Los Angeles Times*. February 13, 2006.

Web sites

Office of the High Commissioner for Human Rights, United Nations. "Fact Sheet No.17, The Committee against Torture." <http://www.unhchr.ch/html/menu6/2/fs17.htm> (accessed April 20, 2006).

Office of the High Commissioner for Human Rights, United Nations. "Convention against Torture and Other Cruel, Inhuman or Degrading Treatment or Punishment." 1984. <http://www.unhchr.ch/html/menu3/b/h_cat39.htm> (accessed April 20, 2006).

Reuters. "UN Torture Panel Presses US on Detainees." April 18, 2006. <http://go.reuters.com/> (accessed April 20, 2006).

Israel's Knesset Debates the Adoption of a Human Rights Charter

Book excerpt

By: Netanel Lorch

Date: January 15, 1964

Source: Lorch, Netanel., ed. *Major Knesset Debates: 1948–1981*. Lanham, MD., University Press of America, 1993.

About the Author: Netanel Lorch is a former Secretary-General of the Knesset and author of several books about Israel's military history. The Knesset [trans. 'Assembly'] is the Israeli Parliament. First convened in February 1949, it consists of 120 elected members. In the source below, members are discussing the proposals of the Knesset member, Professor Yitzhak Klinghoffer (1905–1990), for a Human Rights Charter. Born in Austria, Klinghoffer fled to France then Brazil to avoid the Nazi annexations of 1938 and 1940 before settling in Israel in the 1950s. Klinghoffer was an expert on constitutional law and a founder of Israel's Liberal Party in 1961.

INTRODUCTION

When the state of Israel was proclaimed in 1948, one of the key differences that emerged between its founding fathers rested on the issue of a constitution. Though it had been promised in Israel's Proclamation of Independence, those who sought to bring in a formal written constitution were opposed by orthodox Jews, who opposed the notion of a secular document having higher authority than religious texts, such as the Torah and Talmud. In 1949, the first Knesset arrived upon the Harari Decision, by which Israel would forgo a formal constitution but instead formulate "Basic Laws" which would form the key component of Israel's unwritten constitution. Between 1958 and 1992, eleven Basic Laws would be passed, covering everything from the designation of Jerusalem as Israel's rightful capital to the role of the army. Although non-codified, combined they provided one of the most comprehensive constitutional documents in the World.

The debate about incorporating a human rights element into the Basic Laws was one of the most perennial in Israel's first fifty years. Although most democracies, including Israel, adhered to the principles of human rights law as expressed in the United Nations Universal Declaration of Human Rights, few had it enshrined in their constitutions or had adopted their own charter. Constitutional law is normally marked by its brevity: adding clauses which are open to interpretation is seen as a way of inviting a multitude of challenges to legislative law.

Liberal minded Israelis, such as Professor Yitzhak Klinghoffer, a constitutional law expert and member of the Knesset, however, believed a human rights element should be essential to Israel's constitution. Klinghoffer drafted a comprehensive Human Rights Charter which he put before the Knesset. He viewed its adoption as being the first step towards the Basic Laws assuming a Human Rights aspect.

PRIMARY SOURCE

Human Right's Charter

Introduction

It will be recalled that the work of the Constituent Assembly convened in 1949 ended with a compromise, namely, that the formal constitution be written over time, one chapter at a time. This was done, and in fact is still being done at the time of writing. The lack of a Bill of Rights has been a sore point for years. Professor Kinghoffer, himself a teacher of Constitutional Law, proposed such a bill. His proposal was rejected by the Minister of Justice, a distinguished jurist in his own right.

Sitting 320 of the Fifth Knesset
15 January 1964 (1 Shevat 5724)

The Speaker, B. Idelson: We now proceed to MK Klinghoffer's bill on the Basic Law: Charter of Basic Human Rights, 5724–1963.

I. Klinghoffer (Liberals): Madam Speaker, distinguished Knesset, not only is the proposal which I have the honor of bringing before the Knesset long and complex . . . but each of its component topics is important and raises problems which should be discussed extensively. . . .

Obviously, the time allotted for presenting a private bill . . . is insufficient for conducting an exhaustive discussion of all these problems, but submitting it gives me an opportunity to attempt to convince the House that it should be transferred to one of the Knesset committees so that it may be prepared for a first reading.

I will try to do so by limiting myself to two aspects of the overall subject . . . namely, giving a brief review of the history of the idea of determining basic human rights in law or a special Basic Law, and stressing what I regard as the need for according the charter of basic rights a rigid character and supremacy within Israel's legal system.

The idea of a charter of basic human rights is based on the constitutional tradition which has taken root throughout the world in the last two hundred years. It was preceded by quasi-constitutional documents in English constitutional history, although the first in the series of modern human rights charters guaranteeing the individual areas of freedom in which the authorities may not interfere was the State of Virginia's Bill of Rights of 1776, which served as the pattern for many others all over the world. . . .

The first country to introduce a legal basis for safeguarding basic social rights was Mexico, which included them in its constitution in 1917. . . . The countries of Europe began including basic social rights in democratic constitutions at a later date. . . . Since the end of the Second World War . . . there has been . . . international concern to ensure basic human and social rights. . . . This was reflected in certain passages of the United Nations charter and the World Proclamation of Human rights of 10 December 1948. This is not a convention, it is not a binding document, but it has moral and educational value and several new countries have incorporated recognition of its principles into their constitutions. Since 1954, the U.N. has been preparing two international agreements, one regarding civil and political rights and the other regarding social, economic and cultural rights. The contribution of Israel's representatives to this committee should be noted.

Against this background . . . it is somewhat surprising that Israel has no constitutional law assuring these rights. Is it not paradoxical that the Jewish people, which has always fought in the diaspora for human rights, has not yet attained a charter of basic rights in its fifteen years of independent existence in its own land? My proposal represents an attempt to put an end to this regrettable situation. The fact that the Government has refrained from taking any initiative in this may be due to its allergy to the principle of introducing a rigid constitution which would supercede other laws, as well as to its recognition . . . of the fact that a regular law ensuring basic human rights will have no legal value. . . . We must emerge from this deadlock. If groups within the government are still considering adopting a charter of basic rights in the form of a law which can be amended or annulled, like any other law, by a simple majority in the Knesset . . . they would do well to pay heed to well-known jurists who have completely rejected that approach. . . .

In my view, it is time that Israel adopted a charter of basic human rights . . . which should supersede regular legislation. I assume that these two questions are the central ones which could arise in any argument on matters of principle in Israel concerning the constitutional guaranteeing of basic human rights. . . . The actual details of my proposal to assure basic human social, economic and educational rights . . . will, I hope, be discussed in the parliamentary stages which will follow this preliminary debate. I will add only that the U.N. Secretary-General, U Thant, designated 1964 as Human Rights Year throughout the world. We should respect that pronouncement by passing a Basic Law of a charter of basic human rights which will be worthy of its name and will bring us honor. I asked the Knesset to decide to transfer my proposal to the Constitution, Law and Justice Committee so that a first reading may be prepared.

The Minister of Justice, D. Joseph: Professor Klinghoffer's proposal . . . is not original and has been preceded by several others, though these have not been debated by the Knesset. . . . I and the staff at my Ministry have examined MK Klinghoffer's proposal, and have noted various positive and negative aspects of it, but I will concentrate here on the matters of principle. . . .

The Knesset has already passed several constitutional laws, such as the Basic Law on the Knesset, the transition Law, with its various amendments . . . the Judges Law . . . the Law of Return, etc. . . . My Ministry has also prepared a chapter on human rights for the Basic Law but not in a form which they will destroy existing legislation by proclaiming its supremacy, as MK Kinghoffer advocates. His suggestion will enable any judge to decide that the law which has been in force since the establishment of the state . . . is invalid, thereby leading to general confusion. . . . Behind the fine and supposedly self-evident phrases of MK Klinghoffer's proposal hides a revolution in the country's constitutional basis and a blow to the Knesset's authority. Thus, the Knesset which is responsible for legislation, and the government, which is responsible for proposing the laws and the country needs to the Knesset, are working to prepare all the constitutional laws which, in accordance with the decision of the Knesset, will one day form Israel's constitution.

My question is whether in these circumstances it is necessary for a Member of the Knesset to interfere in this process and take the initiative for proposing laws of this kind, unless the intention is to act demonstratively and goad the Government. Even if the Knesset were to accept the proposal, the Constitution, Law and Justice committee would not deal with it until it had completed its work on the Basic Law: the president of the state . . . not to mention the Basic Law: the Government, which will soon be submitted. I do not think that his is an efficient or desirable way of managing our legislative affairs, and for that reason alone I will propose that the Knesset remove it from the agenda.

I . . . do not want the mistaken impression to be created that a member of the Knesset has proposed something good, a charter of human rights, a large part of the fine constitution which the country needs, and for some unaccountable reason the Government is not prepared to accept it. . . . In my view there is a fundamental mistake in professor Klinghoffer's approach to our constitutional problem . . . namely, that he wants to introduce into Israel, which is a unique and Unitarian state, something which is appropriate for a federal state. In a federal state it is necessary to ensure that the constitution is not subject to the legislatures of either the federal body or any one its component provinces or states. Then it is also necessary to determine who will decide whether a given law clashes with the constitution or departs from the rights of the state, the federal government or any individual province or their governments. In a Unitarian state, like Israel, there is no need or justification for that. On the contrary, no institution should be placed above the legislature, which should be enabled to adapt the constitution to the country's changing needs from time to time, even if the constitution is contained within one document.

This fundamental distinction between a federal and a Unitarian state seems to have escaped professor Klinghoffer, who wants our legislature to be subject to the decision of any court, because he does not propose who will decide whether a given law contradicts the proposals contained in his bill . . .and any judge—not even nine Supreme Court judges, as in the case in the U.S.—may overturn a law which has been passed by the Knesset.

P. Rosen (Liberals): Would you agree to that?

The Minister of Justice, D. Joseph: I will answer you if you come to my Ministry, because that is not MK Klinghoffer's proposal. I do not propose setting nine judges above the 120 elected representatives, when the nation can replace the latter but not the former . . . though what we are talking about is five judges out of nine.

J. Sapir (Liberals): There is a certain lack of politeness in that. . . .

The Minister of Justice, D. Joseph: Isn't my Ministry an appropriate place for discussing a subject of that kind?

J. Sapir (Liberals): The Knesset is here and you are replying to it.

The Minister of Justice, D. Joseph: . . .In his explanation, Professor Klinghoffer said that Israel's Declaration of Independence is not a substitute for a document of that kind because the Supreme Court, has decided that that document "expresses the nation's vision and credo, but does not in practice determine anything about the existence or annulment of laws." Exactly the same may be said of MK Klinghoffer's proposal, which does not determine what should be in the law but merely contains a long list of fine statements about rights which should be enacted in other laws, and which have in effect already been set out in detail in many existing laws. . . .To act as if we had before us a *tabula rasa*, as if nothing existed in the state and we had to begin with that law, with all due respect—I do not wish to speak sharply.

I completely reject NK Klinghoffer's claim that "the objective can be attained solely by legislating a Basic Law which will supercede the general legislation." I maintain that that can be achieved, as has in effect been done, by observing the prevailing law and amending it from time to time by regular legislative procedures.

How can one ignore the special reality of our life in Israel when, because of our unfortunate security situation, since we are surrounded by enemies who seek to destroy us, at any moment a situation might arise in which special legislation is required, and the majority in the Knesset will wish to do what is necessary to defend the state, but the Knesset will be free to act only with two-thirds majority?

And we know the secret, we know how often there are 81 members in the Knesset when the vote is taken.

I also disagree with the legislative system underlying MK Klinghoffer's proposal. The first few paragraphs reflect their German origin, in my view.

A. Ben-Eliezer (Herut): Do you regard that as positive?

The Minister of Justice, D. Joseph: No. the first three and the sixth paragraphs read as if they were translated from the West German Basic Law of 1949 . . . and a phrase like "the freedom to develop one's personality" is not recognized by us as a legal concept. . . .

I doubt whether the statements MK Kinghoffer desires us to make in his bill will bring us honor, since many people will regard them as mere empty phrases, without any practical value or content. For example, what does "Human dignity should not be harmed" mean? That one should not insult someone? Whom does it help, and how, if no accompanying sanctions are prescribed by law? . . . Who needs a declaration that "Every man has the right to develop his personality"? . . .

What is the value of the pronouncement that "Human life is sacred" if it means that one must not kill . . . that is evident from our criminal law regarding murder. . . . What is the point of saying that one must not strike a person? Will that stop a father from striking his son? . . . . If the intention of the bill is serious, would it not be better to determine a penalty? Our criminal law has already dealt with this. . . .

As a leading British jurist has said, without a clear and precise criminal law the citizens of a country will not benefit from declarations of this kind, apart from a general feeling of well-being. But that does not guarantee the public welfare. What point is there in declaring that science is free? Is it not free anyway? Do we make it free by declaring it to be so? And what does "teaching is free" mean? Does it mean that every teacher is free to teach what he wishes in school? . . .I believe that teaching is not free. Teaching is limited to what we determine by law. . . .Teachers are limited by the curriculum of the schools. . . .

What is the value of saying that "The freedom to strike is guaranteed," if this is qualified by the phrase "and may be used in accordance with the law". This means that the law, not the fine constitution, will determine to what extent the right to strike exists. That being so, what is the value of the fine phrase in the constitution? . . .What is important is not fine phrases but good laws, which are clear and precise and as detailed as possible. . . .

Thus, Professor Kinghoffer presents a series of rights which he supposedly wishes to guarantee, while they have always existed and are clearly guaranteed by law. . . . His bill also contains detailed provisions which suffer from the same defects, and will have an adverse effect on existing law if they are accepted....I am not concerned only that certain provisions will be annulled by the bill—Knesset can be warned of those dangers and appropriate solutions found—but that from time to time a clever lawyer will discover that a given law or clause contradicts the Charter of Basic Human Rights...and the courts will be obliged to annul laws which neither MK Klinghoffer nor the Knesset intended to harm....And even if the discrepancy is resolved, the state of confusion which will prevail until matters are settled will undermine the stability of Israeli law....It is not by chance that the great charters were written after revolutions, when nations were prepared to divest themselves of outdated legal systems. The State of Israel has no need of a legislative revolution. It needs continuity of law, carefully considered changes and organic development....

Professor Klinghoffer's bill proposes that the courts be authorized to examine whether a regular law accords with the Charter of Human Rights. In other words, every judge...will be entitled to declare a given law invalid, or reverse the decision of another judge....Is that the attitude to legislation which should be granted by the Knesset after several readings in the plenum and a careful examination in committee?...The issue of the examination of laws by the courts is one of the most serious of our day. In England the courts do not have the right to examine parliament's legislation, but would anyone say that human rights are not guaranteed in England. In the U.S. the Supreme Court has taken it upon itself to supervise the legislature...in accordance with the constitution. It has happened there in the last two decades that many laws which we intended to achieve social progress were obstructed by the court, until its composition changed. The court blocked laws prohibiting the employment of children and restricting hours of work....On the other hand, despite the fact that their Constitution states that no man's right to vote may be restricted by race or color, and despite the right of the Supreme Court to act against violations of the Constitution, we know that in certain states Negroes are unable to use their right to vote. What, then, is the value of the fine phrase which has been in their Constitution for almost a hundred years?...

I do not want what I am saying to be interpreted as meaning that the courts always obstruct social progress or protect the enemies of democracy...the U.S. Supreme Court is the rock of freedom of its citizens, even though some of its decisions raise doubts in our minds. Our Supreme Court has made an important contribution to preserving human rights, although this does not make it the supervisor of the legislature...for "who will supervise the supervisors?" The supreme authorities of the state must be independent of one another, each one being subject solely to itself and

its conscience. One cannot place human rights in the hands of one of them alone and rely on it to restrain the others; only if they all respect those rights is their existence assured. In that the courts are no better or superior to the legislature. I have every confidence that if the Knesset promulgates a charter of human rights it will not deliberately infringe it....If in the future the Knesset sees fit to limit one of the rights which at present we think should be protected, it alone can judge the situation which will prevail then....We must educate our sons to freedom and respect for the rights of others, but we must not tie their hands. That is why what is needed is a less rigid charter of rights, like the one my Ministry is preparing, and whose completion will not take long, I hope....I propose that the bill under review be removed from the agenda....

I. Klinghoffer (Liberals): Time does not permit me to answer all the Minister of Justice's criticisms of the content of my bill...though I will focus on a few of them. He said that it is not true that neither England nor Israel has a constitution. I know that there are differences of opinion on this point centering on the distinction between a material and a formal constitution. We have constitutional law in the material sense, but when one debates a constitution one is referring to a formal one, which neither Israel nor England has. The lack of a constitution in Israel negates the assurance given in the Declaration of Independence....It is true that a Constituent assembly was elected, but it did not promulgate a constitution....

The Minister regards my bill as an attempt to revolutionize our constitutional basis, since it could annul laws or provisions of laws and there is no knowing what this will lead to....I would like to say that had it not been for this effect of the Charter I propose it would have been possible to ask what it was worth....Its entire object is to be binding on the regular legislature and to bring about the consequent reexamination of the laws. That is why, at this point, I accept the Minister's criticism, which in my view emphasizes this positive aspect of my bill....

The Minister of Justice fears that the charter I propose will restrict the legislature and hereby undermine our constitutional foundations. I would like to say that I propose nothing of the sort. I am proposing only that in every instance the legislature be identified with the regular majority of the House, with any quorum. Two-thirds of all the members of the Knesset also constitute the Knesset, they are the legislature. In what way does this discriminate against the Knesset? You identify the Knesset with its regular majority when it makes decisions with any quorum....

I regret the fact that the Minister of Justice saw fit to single out two or three paragraphs (out of more than seventy) of my bill which he regards as having been copied from the basic law of West Germany. The fact that I included those paragraphs does not indicate that I am influenced by the

Palestinian People's Party activists burn an effigy representing closure, settlements, collaborators and occupation, during a rally held in the West Bank town of Nablus on February 10, 2001. AP IMAGES.

Germans....Those provisions, or ones very similar to them, are to be found in other documents which are international, not German, and include the term "dignity of man...."

In conclusion, as regards the Minister of Justice's remark...about the court's supervision of the constitutionality of the laws, he asks "who will supervise the supervisors?" The answer is that when the courts examine whether a given law accords with what is in the constitution or not they are merely fulfilling a purely legal role....Comparing laws is, in effect, what judges do every day....That is the right of every court of law in Israel. It is not concentrated solely in the hands of the Supreme Court, although by appeals and taking matters to the highest court the uniformity of decisions is ensured. The function which the court fulfills when it examines the validity of laws does not differ essentially from its function when it examines whether a certain law accords with the provisions of the constitution. That is basically the same function, as regards both thinking and law.

As regards the emphasis the Minister has placed on the need to educate the generations to come, I do not see,

within the framework of the Knesset's activities, a more appropriate opportunity of attaining that objective than by passing the Basic Law determining a charter of basic human rights, which without a doubt will be of the greatest educational value in enhancing the nation's political culture.

The Speaker, B. Idelson: We will now vote on MK Klinghoffer's proposal to transfer his bill to the Constitution, Law and Justice committee.

The Vote
Those in favor of the proposal: 21
Those against: 35
(The proposal is not adopted.)

SIGNIFICANCE

In 1992, Israel finally adopted a Basic Law covering "Human Dignity and Liberty." It proclaimed that: "Fundamental human rights in Israel are founded upon recognition of the value of the human being, the sanctity of human life, and the principle that all persons are free; these rights shall be upheld in the spirit of the principles set forth in the Declaration of the Establishment of the State of Israel." By then, however, Israel had become embroiled in one of the most controversial, widely reported and longest running human rights crises in modern history.

Three years after the Knesset rejected the adoption of a human rights charter discussed above, in June 1967, Israel fought what became known as the Six Day War, a three fronted pre-emptive strike against Egypt, Jordan and Syria. Israel astonished the world with the speed and effectiveness of the attack and in a swoop, through annexations, it increased its territorial size three times after seizing the Sinai Desert, Gaza, the West Bank, and the Golan Heights. Although it gave up most of the Sinai after the 1973 Yom Kippur War and Gaza in 2005, it has held onto most of the other occupied territories, thus giving rise to a series of human rights crises and global condemnation.

Arrest without charge, torture, targeted killings, the illegal settlement of occupied territories, onerous restrictions on freedom of movement, the ghettoising of entire towns are just some of the human rights violations of which Israel has been accused in the four decades it has held the occupied territories. The situation deteriorated markedly in the second Intifada (2000–2004) during which Israeli security forces would routinely carry out missions in the occupied territories, and prevent the passage of Palestinians into Israel itself, where many held jobs.

The U.S. State Department, which is usually one of Israel's more ardent defenders, has admitted that Israel's human rights record in the occupied territories is poor. Its criticism of occupying forces has in recent years been tempered by the apportionment of blame for human rights failures on the Palestinian Authority, which is supposed to govern Gaza and the West Bank. Nevertheless, in its 2005 *Country Report on Human Rights Practices*, the State Department noted that Israeli occupying forces stood accused of the following human rights abuses: "damage to civilians in the conduct of military operations; numerous, serious abuses of civilians and detainees; failure to take disciplinary action in cases of abuse; improper application of security internment procedures; use of temporary detention facilities that were austere and overcrowded; and limited cooperation with nongovernmental organizations (NGOs)."

To what extent the adoption of a Human Rights Charter in 1964 or an earlier Basic Law on "human dignity and liberty" would have improved the lot of those living in the occupied territories remains to be seen. Through its Basic Laws Israel came to protect and ensure the human rights of its citizens more comprehensively than almost any other country in the world. This is nevertheless a moot point. The problem facing those who live and who have lived in the occupied territories is that they are effectively stateless: though in Israeli held territory they are not seen as citizens of Israel; and although they had previously lived in Egyptian or Jordanian territory, most of their populations had been regarded as refugees after Israel's independence and the end of the Palestinian Mandate in 1948. The presence of Israeli settlers, who maintain their rights as citizens in the occupied territories, in contravention of international law exacerbates tensions.

More than a million Arabs living in Israel (though not the occupied territories) do so as Israeli citizens and are afforded the same rights under the country's Basic Laws as Israel's Jewish majority. The one exception in law is that Israeli Arabs are not obliged to undertake compulsory military service, although they are entitled to opt in. In practice, however, Israel's Arab citizens are subject to informal discrimination in education, employment, social policy provision and are under-represented in most professions and in government. Most notably, policies prohibiting the transfer of land to non-Jews in Israel make Arab land ownership problematic.

Discussion about human rights and Israel invariably invites questions about its treatment of its Arab population, both inside Israel itself and the occupied

territories. Yet the Arab context and the problems Israel faces because of its regional politics blur an otherwise generally sound human rights record. Indeed, taken in the context of the constitutional protection it gives its citizen's human rights, Israel stands up to comparison with most western democracies. Many of these countries are still to enact any form of statutory protection for its citizen's human rights comparable to Israel's Basic Laws.

FURTHER RESOURCES

Gilbert, Martin. *Israel: A History*. London: Doubleday, 1998.

Schulze, Kirsten E. *The Arab Israeli Conflict*. Harlow. Longman, 1999.

Shlaim, Avi. *The Iron Wall: Israel and the Arab World*. London: Penguin, 2001.

Web sites

The Knesset. "Israel's Basic Laws: an introduction." 2003. <http://www.knesset.gov.il/description/eng/eng_mimshal_yesod.htm> (accessed April 27, 2006).

Human Rights Watch. "Israel and the Palestinian Authority Reports." 2006. <http://www.hrw.org/campaigns/israel/> (accessed April 27, 2006).

Responding to Complex Humanitarian Crises and Massive Abuses of Human Rights

Reflections On the Legal, Political, and Humanitarian Framework

Speech

By: Joelle Tanguy

Date: September 16, 1998

Source: Tanguy, Joelle. "Responding to Complex Humanitarian Crises and Massive Abuses of Human Rights: Reflections On the Legal, Political and Humanitarian Framework." Doctors Without Borders, September 16, 1998.

About the Author: Joelle Tanguy is the U.S. Executive Director for Doctors Without Borders (also known as Médecins Sans Frontièrs, or MSF). She received her MBA from France's Institut Supérieur des Affaires, attended Stanford Business School, and has a background in computer science. After accepting her first assignment in Armenia, Tanguy continued with the organization. She has served in several locations where MSF has delivered aid.

INTRODUCTION

Doctors Without Borders (*Médecins Sans Frontières*) has worked as an independent, nonpolitical organization since its founding in France in 1971. MSF volunteers, composed of medical and non-medical professionals and laymen, work alongside local volunteers in areas of Africa, Australia, Asia, Europe, and the Americas. The organization's work primarily rests with bringing medical aid to conflict-ridden areas and locations where adequate supplies and medical facilities are not fully functioning.

As Doctors Without Borders works to alleviate suffering in impoverished, war-laden, and underdeveloped countries, it also strives to stay outside of local and international political debates. The organization does this in order to provide the most aid without having to play favorites to party lines, but this sense of political autonomy does leave the organization reliant upon private donor donations. These donations support MFS's work, but are also dependent upon the relative success of field operations and of public knowledge of crisis situations throughout the world. For instance, mainstream media reports may neglect coverage of hostilities and social crises in areas that the United States or other Western nations do not have direct control or major economic interests in.

In 1998 and 1999, U.S. troops under the support of the United Nations entered Kosovo on a peacekeeping mission. Prior to UN intervention and U.S. troop deployment, U.S. media accounts did not pay particular attention to the escalating conflict between the Kosovo Liberation Army and the standing regime in Yugoslavia. Even after UN and U.S. intervention, media accounts still paid little attention to the area. This lack of coverage for world events, particularly those concerning tribal and clan rivalries, leaves organizations like Doctors Without Borders vulnerable. Since the organization relies upon donations, it needs the public to be informed and concerned about international events. When individuals do not know about crises in places like Kosovo, the organization must attempt to educate them on the need and purpose for medical supplies and food relief efforts.

Other instances that put organizations like MSF in jeopardy can be seen with Saddam Hussein in the 1980s. Saddam Hussein, then-leader of Iraq, used chemical weapons against the Kurds in 1987. The persecution of Kurds in Iraq had been ongoing, and the targets of most of the attacks were male Kurds. Hussein's government-sanctioned genocide went

ignored by the United Nations. The United Nations refusing or neglecting to impose economic sanctions against Iraq for its use of chemical weapons, in this case poison gas, proves fateful for the support of the international community. Hussein's government continued to execute, imprison, and torture individuals who opposed his regime. Kurds and non-Kurds were routinely tortured and killed. Finally, after Iraq invaded Kuwait in 1991, the United States deployed troops to cease the hostilities. The Gulf War, a battle of about sixty days, ensued, and in its aftermath Hussein stayed in power and the United Nations placed economic sanctions against Iraq. These sanctions, while aiming to halt a destructive government, did more harm to the average citizen of Iraq than to the Iraqi government. The children and poorer citizens of Iraq were the ones who went without food, water, and medical supplies. The enforcement of humanitarian laws and the non-enforcement of these legislations created a protracted battle in places like Iraq. Reasons why the United Nations took so long in enforcing sanctions against Iraq for its treatment of Iraqis and Kurds is unknown, but effects of the sanctions solidify what non-governmental agencies continually claim. They report that sanctions do not always stop an oppressive government. Instead, they allow a government to maintain control through politically and economically oppressed people.

◼ PRIMARY SOURCE

RESPONDING TO COMPLEX HUMANITARIAN CRISES AND MASSIVE ABUSES OF HUMAN RIGHTS: REFLECTIONS ON THE LEGAL, POLITICAL, AND HUMANITARIAN FRAMEWORK

Two years ago, the United Nations classified 26 conflicts in the world as "complex emergencies" and quantified their impact: some 59 million people affected—the majority in Africa. Civilians accounted for 90% of the victims—half of those who died were children. To their side, relief teams such as those of Doctors Without Borders/Médecins Sans Frontières (MSF), attempt to alleviate the suffering.

CNN may portray our volunteers as physicians, stethoscope in hand, treating patients in a remote or besieged health-post, but the day to day challenge of humanitarian workers is not just in providing medical care. It also means to negotiate access to populations at risk and to fuel or confront media reporting on the crises we witness. It means to advocate for the respect of basic human rights and humanitarian law, and, hopefully, through our presence, to help in the protection of civilians.

The key message that our teams have learned, if not the intellectual framework that Médecins Sans Frontières

Doctors Without Boarders (MSF) medic Isabelle Yersin helps a potential cholera-victim, Domingo Mucatobusi, after he was airlifted to higher ground from a flooded area on March 4, 2000 in Chibuto, Mozambique. © REUTERS/CORBIS.

started with, is that effective humanitarian action demands an acute awareness of human rights and a vigilant sensitivity to the interaction of the humanitarian agenda with political, military, legal and economic arenas.

Building on the experience of our teams worldwide, I've identified three key issues that we need to address if we want the international community to successfully tackle the wave of "uncivil" civil wars and their appalling human rights records: the lack of an effective conceptual framework; the relativity of humanitarian law; and the ambiguous dynamics of the mediating actors.

LACK OF AN EFFECTIVE CONCEPTUAL FRAMEWORK First I would like to remark on the lack of an effective conceptual framework. As Rony Brauman points out in *Humanitaire: Le Dilemne* (Textuel, 1996), three concepts of peace have

been developed and adapted at different times over the last three centuries.

The first one, that of Montesquieu, of the British Liberals, is that of "peace by commerce": that business interests will ultimately arbitrate the destructive passions of man. It is the classical liberal paradox that the sum of private selfishness provides for the public well being.

The second concept, which appeared in the 19th century, is "peace by reason." That is, that the progress of knowledge would fight ignorance, the real cause of suffering and violence.

The third concept, mostly illustrated in today's debate about the International Criminal Court on this the 50th anniversary of the Universal Declaration of Human Rights, was that of "peace by law," as guaranteed by institutions.

All three concepts still have strong footing these days, sometimes merge, but often conflict. When seeking to improve international crisis response, the lack of an all-encompassing policy framework is appalling and the divide between the various actors is great.

What is the point of a humanitarian actor using the concept of "peace by law" to argue for the protection of Rwandan refugees in the Democratic Republic of Congo? The massacres orchestrated with the complicity of the country's political leadership who should be made accountable, but the formula adopted by the member states supporting this leadership is that of "peace by commerce!"

How do the World Bank, the IMF, on one hand, and the UNHCR on the other hand, coordinate their response to complex emergencies when their conceptual frameworks are so different, and their approaches to the crises entirely specialized? They don't!

THE RELATIVITY OF HUMANITARIAN LAW My second comment is on the (unfortunate) relativity of humanitarian law.

The Geneva Conventions, the Convention against Torture, the Convention for the Prevention and Repression of Genocide, the UN Charter and a number of other documents seem to protect civilians. Yet during the Cold War, we watched as state and international institutions used the precarious balance of power to flaunt these conventions and never once enacted them against Brezhnev, Pol Pot, Argentinian or Pakistani generals. Even in the 1980's after the Cold War was over, when it came to Saddam Hussein—then a Western ally—using chemical weapons against the Kurds, the conventions were still ignored. And the same thing happened in Chechnya and Rwanda. The noble declarations of intentions, enshrined in the texts of humanitarian law, flourish in UN conferences and international fora, but the practice and logic of member states remain unchanged.

THE AMBIGUOUS DYNAMICS OF MEDIATING ACTORS And finally I must mention the third factor, the ambiguous dynamics of the mediating actors.

The mediating actors are partly represented around this room: the United Nations, the Member States, and the NGOs. Let's not also forget key local actors such as the military and political leadership, as well as intellectual and community leaders, regional leadership, and others. And, of course, catalysts at every stage are the local and international media outfits.

Let us take a closer look at the humanitarian actors: What is our true ability to work in total independence and strictly according to humanitarian principles? How much influence can donor countries buy with their funding of our humanitarian operations? You will never find it

acknowledged, but the "N" of non-governmental does not always stand strong!

Institutions established by the UN charter and associated agencies, have also become suspect of capitulating to the pressures of donor states rather than advocating for the causes enshrined in their mandates. A case in point was the move by UNHCR in 1992 to propose temporary protection as a response to asylum seekers from Bosnia, while these were mostly fully eligible to standard and full asylum procedures according to the convention. Repeatedly, in recent years, and especially in the Rwanda-Zaire-Congo crisis which is still a hot preoccupation for us, we have felt that the Executive Committee and key funding member states exercised undue pressure on the UNHCR that resulted in an agency policy in the field that offered little support to the refugee populations caught in violence.

Probably among the most fiercely independent NGOs, Médecins San Frontières has had to build a large base of independent, individual donors over the years, hoping that this general public support will not impose politically on our operational deployment. But, we often ask, can't we lose what we have gained in political independence, by our total dependency on whether the media brings a given crisis to public attention? When the US media editorial policy ignores Rwanda, the Sudan or Kosovo because of O.J. Simpson or Monica Lewinsky, what recourse is left to invite private philanthropy, stir indignation and stimulate action?

CONCLUSION To conclude, I should like to stress that these same three factors who hinder effective response to the crises—the lack of an effective conceptual framework, the relativity of humanitarian law and the ambiguous dynamics of the mediating actors—actually also make prevention quite a challenging task if not an impossible one. Let me quote some examples:

Even though our first appeal for the Balkans dates back to the fall of Vukovar, even though the fall of Srebrenica and the collapse of the so-called "safe heavens" had a rehearsal a year earlier with the bombing of Gorazde, even though the Bosnian disaster was "en marche" since the recognition of Croatia, how long did it take for a significant military and political involvement in Bosnia? And who is listening to the calls from Pristina today? The Kosovo is the issue of the day, but, like Bosnia, the international community will wait till it's too late.

Working in Kigali at the height of the genocide, we were first hand witnesses to the fact that the Genocide Convention might not be worth the paper it is printed on. Warnings that impunity would further fuel violence in the region, were ignored too, and the Western Rwanda—Eastern DRC region all the way to Kinshasa—is still in the grasps of civil war.

Working in Mogadishu, we were, again, first hand witnesses to the failure of a peace-enforcement mission. The US and UN military and political leadership had ignored the warning given by humanitarian actors who saw the writing on the wall with regards to the escalation of violence that finally ended the mission and sent the chills through the spines of the most eager interventionists.

But across the years, and despite these failures, we have retained our commitment. This commitment is often fueled and inspired by the special courage of those men and women whom we meet, who in the midst of war, when their societies are torn apart and they are facing great personal risks, still stand up for the values they uphold, and advocate for the respect of human rights and humanitarian law.

Our commitment is also forged by our volunteers in the field, who remain pragmatic idealists despite the complex realities they face in dealing with humanitarian crises around the world.

I will end on the words of one of these volunteers, Dr. Zachariah:

"...what we saw in Rwanda proved to us that our bandages, our sutures, can never heal the deep wounds of Rwanda. What they need is justice. [...] All those people, all those patients that I had treated have been killed. The lives we had saved were killed before our eyes.

"I lost my friends, my colleagues, everything. And this is why, when I was on the bridge that separated Rwanda and Burundi, standing on this bridge counting the bodies, watching the corpses of mutilated children and women, thinking of the thousands and thousands of bodies I had seen, I swore to myself that if there is a judicial system in this world, those people will pay for their crime."

SIGNIFICANCE

Complexities concerning the application of humanitarian laws, political actors and agendas, and instituting peace accords and justice continue to perplex the role of humanitarian aid workers throughout the world. In March 2000, several relief organizations withdrew from the southern Sudan because they refused to allow rebel groups in the region to have control of relief agency operations. Eleven groups rejected the mandate of the Sudanese People's Liberation Army, and one of these groups was MFR. Adding complexity to the situation, U.S. considerations of sending aid directly to the rebels pointed to the dilemma of contradictory agendas in conflict zones. The promise of state-funded aid allowed rebel factions to gain a strengthened sense of superiority and power. While the U.S. relief plans stemmed from good intentions, the possible fallout of these measures was potentially catastrophic. With rebel forces controlling the relief programs, those in greatest need and those opposing the dominant rebel parties could be left without. Hence, organizations like MSF decided to withdraw from the area because its continual mission is to not entangle its relief efforts with politics.

Events like those in Sudan continually threaten the neutrality of humanitarian workers, and in the Middle East governmental investigative committees are forming to explore the patronage and personnel of non-governmental organizations (NGOs). Countries like Egypt and Israel have established offices to examine all humanitarian aid groups that want entry to the country. These offices examine the organizations funding and the background of its workers. These investigations of NGOs come from the rise in humanitarian aid organizations posing as neutral parties, when in fact they are politically oriented and government-funded. The Tunisian government committed such an act with its creation of *Jeunes Médecins Sans Frontières* (Young Doctors Without Borders). This group was composed of Tunisian spies and government actors who would frequent conferences hosted by humanitarian organizations. The group sought to gather information about neighboring countries so that it could use this knowledge to divide governments and instigate hostilities. The true identity of the Tunisian organization came to light when MSF began sending letters of protest to humanitarian conference organizers saying that the MSF was not affiliated with this newer organization.

Despite these conflicting agendas, humanitarian organizations still push forward. The United Nations and numerous governments throughout the world work closely with these groups to enable them access to war-torn areas. With the 2003 U.S. invasion of Iraq, the U.S. government approached the MFR and other humanitarian groups before the hostilities commenced. The United States asked if these organizations wanted to come into Iraq for humanitarian purposes—by asking these groups beforehand, policy leaders sought to mend the gap between aid workers and government initiatives. In 1999, Doctors Without Borders earned the Nobel Peace Prize for its continual efforts to bring non-political aid to individuals in need.

FURTHER RESOURCES
Books

Bortolotti, Dan. *Hope in Hell: Inside the World of Doctors Without Borders*. Buffalo, N.Y. and Richmond Hill, Ontario: Firefly Books Ltd., 2004.

Terry, Fiona. *Condemned to Repeat?: The Paradox of Humanitarian Action.* Ithaca, N.Y.: Cornell University Press, 2002.

Periodicals

Redfield, Peter. "Doctors, Borders, and Life in Crisis." *Cultural Anthropology* 20, 3 (August 2005): 328–361.

Weiss, Thomas G. "Principles, Politics, and Humanitarian Action." *Ethics and International Affairs* 13 (1999): 1–22.

Web sites

United Nations Office for the Coordination of Humanitarian Affairs. "IRIN Web Special on Civilian Protection in Armed Conflict." 2003. <http://www.irinnews.org/webspecials/civilprotect/sec1cp1.asp> (accessed May 6, 2006).

Fiftieth Anniversary of the Universal Declaration of Human Rights

Magazine article

By: David Manasian

Date: December 3, 1998

Source: Manasian, David. "50th Anniversary of the Universal Declaration of Human Rights." *The Economist.* (December 3, 1998).

About the Author: David Manasian is the Senior Editor for the London-based news magazine *The Economist.*

INTRODUCTION

The 1948 Universal Declaration of Human Rights, adopted by the United Nations General Assembly on December 10, 1948, ushered in a new era in human rights expectations and humanitarian law worldwide. The United Nations' 1945 charter itself including provisions creating bodies designed to monitor human rights abuses. The traditional notion among many countries that a nations's sovereignty superceded the human rights of its citizens and guests was rejected firmly with the creation of the Universal Declaration of Human Rights.

Written on the heels of World War II (1938–1945) with its dramatic human rights abuses involving concentration camps, mass genocide, forced sexual slavery, and other war crimes, the Universal Declaration of Human Rights was a joint effort that included drafters from North America, Western Europe, Latin America, Asia, and the Middle East.

Announced in 1948, the Universal Declaration of Human Rights was part of the International Bill of Rights, a United Nations project that also included the Optional Protocol and the International Covenants on Human Rights, which include the International Covenant on Civil and Political Rights and the International Covenant on Economic, Social and Cultural Rights. The Optional Protocol and the Covenants were adopted in 1976, after nearly a decade of consideration by member states. The UN hears cases of human rights abuses via a Human Rights Committee; this committee manages affairs related to the International Covenant on Civil and Political Rights, the Committee on the Elimination of Racial Discrimination, and the Committee on Torture.

Until the passage of the 1948 Universal Declaration, no such international document defining universal human rights existed. As the following article notes, the 50th anniversary of the Universal Declaration of Human Rights triggered praise for the document and its impact, while examining ongoing human rights abuses in member states.

■ PRIMARY SOURCE

Can international law establish universal human rights? After fifty years of treaty-making, writes David Manasian, it is at last beginning to get somewhere.

This has been a year of speeches, declarations, resolutions, conferences, concerts, meetings and campaigns marking an event of which the general public remains largely oblivious. Celebrations of the 50th anniversary of the Universal Declaration of Human Rights—a sweeping list of fundamental civil, political, social and economic rights—will reach a climax with a special session of the United Nations General Assembly on December 10th, the day the declaration was adopted by the same assembly in 1948. Bill Clinton, along with scores of other world leaders, will make yet more speeches. And nearly ten million people have already signed Amnesty International's pledge to do what they can to implement the declaration.

But the posters and petitions may have been preaching mainly to the converted. Most people remain unaware of the declaration, and many of those who know about it are unimpressed by righteous resolutions by politicians and do-gooders. Besides, what is there to celebrate? Human-rights abuses around the world are reported by newspapers and television every day of the week. Massacres in Kosovo. Slaughter in Algeria. Torture in Turkey. Chronic violence in Colombia. The jailing of dissidents in China, Myanmar and a dozen other countries. There seems no end to the terrible things people do to other people.

And yet, paradoxically, this constant stream of reports about human-rights abuses is itself a tribute to the Universal Declaration, and to the international human-rights movement it helped to spawn. Repeated misbehaviour by any government is now almost always picked up by some international group. Professions of concern about human rights, whether sincere or not, accompany almost any debate about world politics. For any western politician visiting China, raising the question of human rights with Chinese leaders has become a necessary ritual, rather like the obligatory state banquet or visit to the Beijing opera. Such concerns have also prodded reluctant governments into risky armed interventions in Somalia, Rwanda, Bosnia and Kosovo, mostly with mixed results.

A stealthy revolution Over the past few decades, a small army of non-governmental organisations (NGOs) advocating, monitoring and lobbying for human rights, led by bodies such as Amnesty International and Human Rights Watch, have become serious participants in international affairs. Linked with these larger international groups, and often sponsored or encouraged by them, are thousands of indigenous NGOs in poorer countries, gathering information on particular issues and pressing their governments to live up to international standards. Human rights has become a mainstream subject at law schools, and the number of lawyers specialising in it has soared. Harried by NGOs and consumer groups in rich countries, many multinational companies too have felt compelled to formulate human-rights policies, and to answer publicly for the effects of their commercial activities. But the NGOs' main targets remain governments, the key guarantors—and usually the key abusers—of human rights.

With talk about human rights so pervasive, it is easy to forget that the adoption of the Universal Declaration launched a revolution in international law. It may not be as famous as America's constitution, the French revolution's Declaration of the Rights of Man, or Britain's Magna Carta; but together with the United Nations Charter (the UN's founding document), the Genocide Convention and the four Geneva Conventions updating the laws of war, all roughly contemporaneous, it marked a decisive change with the past.

Until the end of the second world war, international relations were based on the idea of a society of sovereign states, as they had been ever since the rise of the European nation-state centuries earlier. There was little to challenge state sovereignty, either in international law or in the way that most governments behaved. True, philosophical appeals for what today might be described as universal human rights have been heard since the time of the ancient Greek Stoics; but such ideas played almost no part in international politics.

The United States and the European powers had sometimes intervened in the civil strife of other countries to protect their own nationals, as they did in the Chinese and Ottoman empires; but there was general agreement that whatever states did to their own nationals was their business. So long as they were able to maintain physical control over their territory, they remained sovereign. They answered to no higher political or moral authority. Nineteenth-century attempts to abolish the slave trade through international agreements achieved little. Instead, slavery waned because it became uneconomic. Efforts to codify the laws of war paid careful heed to state sovereignty, restricting only what a state could do to enemy soldiers or foreign nationals, not to its own. For the most part, individuals had no standing in international law: their fate lay in the hands of their governments.

The devastation of the second world war, the Jewish Holocaust and the violence inflicted on occupied populations by the Germans and the Japanese prompted a profound reconsideration of the relationship between human rights and international peace. The United Nations, like the League of Nations which had failed so abysmally before it, was meant to be a collective security arrangement, with the five permanent members of the Security Council, the world's major powers at the time, pledged to act together to punish breaches of the peace. But there was also a new element. For the first time, a state's treatment of its own citizens officially became a subject of international concern. Regimes which treated their citizens abominably would, it was recognised, eventually pose a threat to other countries too.

The UN Charter, signed in June 1945, is unequivocal about this. Its preamble pledges the organisation "to reaffirm faith in fundamental human rights," and article 1 cites "promoting and encouraging respect for human rights and for fundamental freedoms for all without distinction as to race, sex, language or religion" as one of the UN's principal purposes, along with peacekeeping. But the Universal Declaration goes further, explicitly linking respect for human rights as necessary to the maintenance of international peace.

The limits of sovereignty In retrospect, it seems amazing that Stalin's Soviet Union, which egregiously abused human rights, should have agreed to any reference to them in the UN Charter. But even in the long and bitter debates that accompanied the drafting of the Universal Declaration, the Soviets never repudiated the concept of universal rights as such. They argued only about the relative importance of different rights, and about the weight that should be given to individual rights and the conflicting doctrine of national sovereignty. The UN Charter embodies this contradiction, proclaiming that the UN is based on the

On July 21, 1999, Kosovar Albanians bury 75 victims of a massacre perpetrated five months earlier by Serbian troops. © PATRICK ROBERT/ SYGMA/CORBIS.

"sovereign equality of all its members," even while championing universal rights.

When the declaration was drafted, the cold war had already begun to blight post-war hopes that international co-operation would prevail over great-power rivalry. The declaration was passed unopposed, but the entire Soviet block abstained, along with Saudi Arabia. And yet, remarkably, even in the depths of the cold war a stream of human-rights treaties was still being signed. Some of the main ones are listed in table 1.

This large body of international human-rights and humanitarian law (the modern term for the laws of war) is historically unprecedented. It has developed alongside a similar body of international law governing trade, finance, and the exploitation of natural resources such as the sea. But in these other areas, international law is more akin to contractual agreements, in which benefits are reciprocal and national sovereignty remains largely unaffected. Human-rights law is different. It touches governments at their most sensitive point: how they exercise power over their own citizens. Never before have states agreed to accept so many restrictions on their domestic behaviour, or to submit to international scrutiny.

But has it done any good? Abuses of human rights have remained widespread in the past fifty years. Governments have evaded or ignored their obligations under these treaties with depressing regularity. Even as humanitarian law has been refined, many armed conflicts have been waged as indiscriminately as ever. The overwhelming majority of casualties are now civilians, not soldiers. International human-rights law did nothing for the post-war victims of the Soviet gulag, China's Cultural Revolution, Argentina's "dirty war" and Cambodia's killing fields. The end of the cold war in 1989 raised hopes that human rights would be more widely respected, and the 1990s became the decade of democracy—yet it also brought horrors such as the Rwandan genocide and the ethnic cleansing of the Balkans.

Sceptics (and there are many) could be forgiven for concluding that the frenzy of treaty-making which followed the Universal Declaration has mocked such continued and widespread suffering. Indeed, they might ask, does it make sense to call these treaties "law" at all, if there is no direct way of enforcing them? For all the human-rights legislation now in place, they would claim, the only genuine guides to international behaviour are still national interest and military power.

Such arguments should be treated with respect. Human rights have undeniably been widely abused, and are still being flouted in many parts of the world. Nevertheless, this survey will argue that human-rights law, for all its failures, has marked a genuine turning point in world affairs. It has had an influence on countries' behaviour in the past and could play a bigger role in the future. To make that admittedly difficult case, the best place to start is to see how human-rights law works in practice.

SIGNIFICANCE

As Manasian points out, one of the greatest criticisms of the Universal Declaration of Human Rights is that there is no mechanism for enforcing it. In the half-century following the Universal Declaration of Human Rights, a series of UN member states faced human rights crises, including military dictatorships in Chile and Argentina with accompanying torture of civilians, Pol Pot's regime in Cambodia, the Tutsi-Hutu genocidal conflict in Rwanda, war and ethnic cleansing in the Balkans, and famine in Eastern Africa. Within the context of diplomatic history, prior to the 1948 Universal Declaration, many governments would have limited their discussions with other countries to matters of diplomacy, trade, and war. As the creation of the United Nations and the documents that make up the International Bill of Rights, UN monitoring bodies and special rapporteurs—experts appointed by the Commission on Human Rights—investigate and report on human rights issues in member states, uncovering information and details about internal human rights situations. The systematic documentation of such internal issues is one of the primary functions of the UN agencies and councils that support human rights compliance and those issues outlined in the International Bill of Rights.

In 2005, the UN General Assembly voted to change the human rights oversight structure within the UN. The United Nations Commission on Human Rights, part of the UN since 1946, had become highly politicized in the eyes of many member nations. Membership included countries with strong human rights abuse records, and in 2004, United States UN Ambassador and Representative to the Economic and Social Council Sichan Siv walked out of the UNCHR meeting when Sudan's membership was approved. Ambassador Siv stated that the UN should "*not* elect a country to the only global body charged specifically with protecting human rights, at the precise time when thousands of its citizens are being murdered or risk starvation." The newly created Human Rights Council convened its first meeting in April 2006; the membership process involves a secret ballot in the General Assembly, requiring a simple majority for membership, and establishes a protocol for removing HRC members when severe human rights violations are documented.

As the Universal Declaration of Human Rights continues into the twenty-first century, its role in international affairs remains a crucial link in keeping human rights at the forefront of political, social, and civil society. While member nations may argue over cultural differences, legal definitions, and committee procedures, the issue of human rights has now become firmly established as part of international and humanitarian policy. The Declaration provides member nations, leaders, and individuals with a cohesive set of principles to guide treaties, policy, and human behavior.

FURTHER RESOURCES

Books

Donnelly, Jack. *Universal Human Rights in Theory and Practice*. Ithaca, New York: Cornell University Press, 2002.

Ishay, Micheline. *The History of Human Rights: From Ancient Times to the Globalization Era*. University of California Press, 2004.

Steiner, Henry and Philip Alston. *International Human Rights in Context: Law, Politics, Morals*. Oxford University Press, U.S.A., 2000.

Web sites

United Nations. "Human Rights." <http://www.un.org/rights/> (accessed May 7, 2006).

The Menace That Wasn't

Magazine article

By: Anonymous

Date: November 11, 2004

Source: "The Menace That Wasn't" *The Economist*. November 11, 2004.

About the Author: This article is an unsigned editorial by an editor of *The Economist*, a London-based weekly magazine devoted to economic and political subjects.

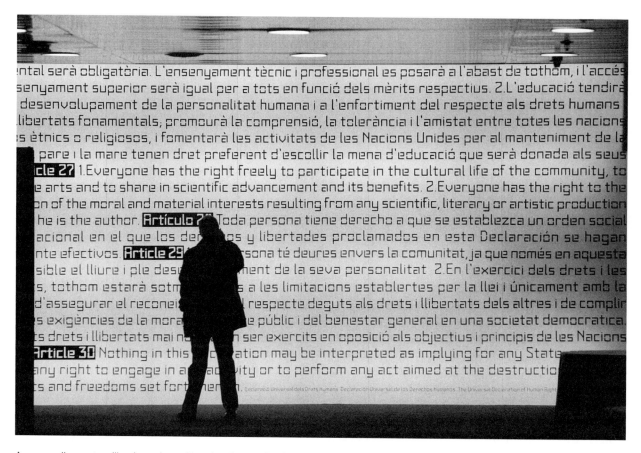

A man walks past an illuminated panel bearing the words of the Universal Declaration of Human Rights at the international convention centre in Barcelona, Spain, during the Euromed summit on November 27, 2005. ADRIAN DENNIS/AFP/GETTY IMAGES.

INTRODUCTION

The 1998 Human Rights Act, passed in 1998 and entered into force in October 2000, incorporated the provisions of the European Convention on Human Rights directly into British law. The convention is a legal instrument adopted by the Council of Europe in 1950. The Council of Europe is not to be confused with the European Union; the Council of Europe was formed in 1949, whereas the European Union was formed in 1992. Confusingly, at least to non-Europeans, both are headquartered in Strasbourg, France; moreover, the Council operates the European Court of Human Rights (established by the European Convention on Human Rights), while the European Union operates the European Court of Justice. The two organizations are completely distinct, apart from some overlap in membership.

The convention, which was the basis of the 1998 act, contains a number of articles: right to life, prohibition of torture, prohibition of slavery, right to liberty and security, right to a fair trial, no punishment without law, right to respect for private life, right to

freedom of thought, right to freedom of conscience and religion, right to freedom of expression, right to freedom of assembly and association, right to marry, right to an effective remedy, and prohibition of discrimination. All of these prohibitions are now part of British law. The significance of this, however, is debated.

■ PRIMARY SOURCE

The Menace That Wasn't: The Human Rights Act Has Not Lived up to Expectations. Good.

TAKE a common law system steeped in precedent and tradition and add a dash of fundamental rights. What do you get? Four years ago, Jack Straw, then the home secretary, made a confident prediction. By incorporating the European Convention on Human Rights (ECHR) into English law, he claimed, the nation would acquire something like America's Bill of Rights. Public authorities and the government would henceforth be bound by a "fairness guarantee" and would no longer be able to treat ordinary citizens according to whim. More than that, a Human Rights Act would create universal values for all and "act as a compass as society moves through the uncharted waters created by global change."

A less benign, but equally confident, view is that the human rights compass has led Britain astray. Tabloid newspapers report that the Human Rights Act has brought nothing but chaos. Undesirable minorities such as asylum-seekers, gypsies, and prisoners are said to have harnessed innocent-seeming "rights" to liberty and family life in such a way as to trample everyone else's liberties. Ever on the lookout for an issue with popular traction, the Conservative Party has pledged to review the Human Rights Act with the strong hint that some of its provisions will be undone.

This is splendid politics, but the problem is that the incorporation of the ECHR into domestic law has not come close to meeting reformers' hopes—nor has it confirmed conservative fears. "It has been a bit like the millennium bug," says Luke Clements, who follows human rights law at Cardiff University. Even Dominic Grieve, the Conservative shadow attorney-general, concedes: "the view was that it was going to lead to a legal free-for-all, and I don't think that has happened."

A count of cases heard in the high courts of England and Wales between 2000 and 2002 found that human rights claims were considered in 431 cases and upheld in just 94. Keir Starmer, a barrister who contributed to the study, says things have moved on since then: he has four appeals pending, all of which involve human rights in some way. But just because judges now have a new standard by which to assess the claims of plaintiffs doesn't mean they will reach a different decision. "Hand on heart," Mr Starmer says, the Human Rights Act has changed the outcome of only a very few cases.

That is partly because the common law turned out to be more accommodating than many reformers or tradition-alists suspected. Four years ago, some feared that, because Britain lacks a written constitution or bill of rights, the stark language of the ECHR would sweep aside centuries of legal precedent. Faced with a potential clash between two traditions, though, judges have simply declared them to be complementary, or even claimed that the ECHR "reveals" ambient human-rights principles in the common law.

For the most part, such philosophical niceties are unnecessary. Away from the high courts and the few London legal chambers that specialise in human rights cases, ECHR principles are rarely invoked. When they are, says Tony Kershaw, the principal solicitor at West Sussex county council, they are invariably "bolted on" to mundane claims in order to make them seem more solid. "No lawyer can hope to win a case based solely on human rights," he believes.

That holds true even for lawyers representing gypsies and travellers, who often assert the right to private and family life when facing eviction from illegally occupied land. Chris Johnson, a solicitor who represents gypsies, says that many people (including his clients) believe cases are transformed by "a sprinkling of magic human-rights dust." They are usually disappointed. The Human Rights Act has neither enabled more cases to be brought, nor made them much easier to win, since judges are still obliged to weigh individual rights against the common good. Even when decisions go the gypsies' way, they turn out to have limited application. Mr Johnson believes that a new planning bill will have a greater effect than all the court cases put together.

On the rare occasions when human rights have upset the apple cart there was usually a pressing need for change. A good example is privacy law: cases brought by Naomi Campbell, a model, and Princess Caroline of Monaco have recently jeopardised the trade in paparazzi photographs. Legislation could swiftly resolve the issue one way or the other, but the government is loth to cross the newspapers. So human rights law must clean up the mess.

Even in Westminster the Human Rights Act has been domesticated. Every item of legislation is now scrutinised by the Joint Committee on Human Rights to see if it complies with the ECHR. Some of the Home Office's wilder initiatives—such as a proposal to deny housing to asylum-seekers unless they do community work—have failed that test. But what looks like a clash between parliamentary sovereignty and fundamental rights is in fact just a new front in an old political battle. As Lord Lester, a committee member and a long-time campaigner for human rights, puts it, the committee supplies weapons—in the form of critical reports—which other parliamentarians use to attack legislation.

The mythical status of the Human Rights Act is such that almost every unpopular decision is now blamed on it. But Mr Clements, at Cardiff, believes there may be a more mundane explanation for the liberal drift in judicial thinking: staff turnover. "These days," he says, "there are simply more right-wing judges than very right-wing judges."

SIGNIFICANCE

The Human Rights Act was passed by the Labour Party after it took control of Parliament in 1997; passage of the act had been a campaign promise of the party. A white paper issued by the new government explained that although the UK was bound by international law to observe the European Convention on Human Rights, there was no means of applying the convention directly in British courts. With the bill's passage, it would be "unlawful for [British] public authorities to act in a way incompatible with the convention rights." Where previously it would have taken a great deal of time and money for a British citizen to take a case based on the convention to the European Court of Human Rights in Strasbourg, it would now be possible for that citizen to take the same case to a UK court.

Since its passage, the act has been invoked in relatively few British cases. Perhaps most significant have been challenges to alleged antiterrorism provisions of British law enacted since September 11, 2001. Thirteen foreign terror suspects were, as of 2004, being held without charge in a London jail on the strength of emergency detention measures passed as part of the Terrorism Act in 2001. The House of Lords ruled in December 2004 that their detention without charge violated the Human Rights Act of 1998. The Labour government's response was to pass (with difficulty) the Prevention of Terrorism Act of 2005, which among other provisions states that the British home secretary, who is roughly the equivalent of the U.S. attorney general, the primary government official responsible for law enforcement, can putatively issue antiterror "control orders" that bypass human rights laws. Passage of the controversial bill pitted the House of Lords against the House of Commons, creating a legislative crisis. The Prevention of Terrorism Act has been widely criticized by groups such as Human Rights Watch.

Many members of the Conservative party vigorously oppose the Human Rights Act. In 2005, party leader Michael Howard stated that "[t]here are too many people in Britain today who hide behind so-called human rights to justify doing the wrong thing. 'I've got my rights' has become the verbal equivalent of two fingers [an obscene gesture] to authority." In particular, Conservatives have claimed that gypsies are empowered by the Human Rights Act to trespass on public land. Several lower courts upheld an appeal by a gypsy family against an eviction order by the city of Leeds in 2005, but the appeal was ultimately overturned by a court of seven members of the House of Lords (March 2006). This would seem to uphold *The Economist*'s thesis that the Human Rights Act has not greatly changed British law.

FURTHER RESOURCES

Books

Feldman, David. *Civil Liberties and Human Rights in England and Wales.* New York: Oxford University Press, 1993.

Web sites

Council of Europe. "Convention for the Protection of Human Rights and Fundamental Freedoms as Amended by Protocol No. 11." <http://conventions.coe.int/treaty/en/Treaties/Html/005.htm> (accessed May 2, 2006).

Secretary of State for the Home Department (U.K.). "Rights Brought Home: The Human Rights Bill." October 1997. <http://www.archive.official-documents.co.uk/document/hoffice/rights/rights.htm> (accessed May 2, 2006).

Slavery and Genocide

Slavery and Genocide

Personal freedom is an essential cornerstone of human rights. The most basic aspect of personal freedom is self-ownership, meaning no human being may own another as property or in bondage for his or her labor. The United Nations Universal Declaration states that "[n]o one shall be held in slavery or servitude; slavery and the slave trade shall be prohibited in all their forms."

This chapter primarily addresses African slavery in England and the Americas from 1800 to 1865. Before the mid-twentieth century, human rights issues were often debated within the context of religion or morality. The article "Slaveholding Not Sinful" presents a nineteenth-century argument that slaveholding is consistent with Christian theology. Conversely, most abolitionist literature of the day was bolstered by religious teachings against slavery.

Slavery is not an historical relic. While slavery was outlawed in the United States in 1864 by the Emancipation Proclamation (included in this chapter), many forms of slavery still exist in the twenty-first century. Chattel slavery—the actual ownership of another human being is rare—but bondage slavery, owning a person's labor contract is alarmingly common. No nations recognize slavery as a legal institution, but some human rights groups assert that as of 2006, nearly 30 million people across the globe may be living in some form of slavery. Labor and sex slavery is a growing international problem. The article on comfort women discusses forced sex slavery. Issues involving labor slavery are discussed in the chapter "Working Conditions and Labor."

Slavery dehumanizes the enslaved. It fosters the notion of inferior classes of human beings, likens people to chattel, and undermines a crucial moral barrier that prevents most people from abusing or murdering others. Slavery turns people into a commodity, one that can be bought and sold for economic gain. Further dehumanization of a group of people—members of a certain race, ethnicity, or religion for example—can yield catastrophic consequences. The ability to strip target victims of their humanness is a necessary prelude to genocide, the mass killing of a target group with common characteristics.

Genocide is specifically defined by international treaty. The Convention on the Prevention and Punishment of the Crime of Genocide defines genocide as:

> Any of the following acts committed with intent to destroy, in whole or in part, a national, ethnical, racial or religious group, as such:
>
> (a) Killing members of the group;
> (b) Causing serious bodily or mental harm to members of the group;
> (c) Deliberately inflicting on the group conditions of life calculated to bring about its physical destruction in whole or in part;
> (d) Imposing measures intended to prevent births within the group;
> (e) Forcibly transferring children of the group to another group.

Included in this chapter are entries highlighting the horrors of the Holocaust, the "Killing Fields" of Cambodia, Kosovo, and Sudan.

The editors have chosen to adopt a broad definition of genocide to highlight, not only international wrangling over terminology, but also the prevalence of mass killings. Terminology carries consequences for policy and intervention, but it does not alter the horror of such crimes against humanity.

Handbill Offering a Reward for a Runaway Slave

Photograph

By: Louie Psihoyos

Date: October 21, 1835

Source: © Louie Psihoyos/Corbis.

About the Photographer: Louie Psihoyos was a staff photographer for *National Geographic* magazine and the recipient of numerous awards. His work includes a wide array of nature photography, as well as Hollywood campaigns and stock photography, including pictures of historical documents.

INTRODUCTION

America's first federal fugitive slave law was enacted in 1793, stating that no person "shall entertain, or give countenance to, the enemies of the other, or protect, in their respective states, criminal fugitives, servants, or slaves, but the same to apprehend and secure, and deliver to the state or states, to such enemies, criminals, servants or slaves." Although the issues of slavery and escaped slaves had been addressed in the Constitution, conflict still remained; the 1793 law was sparked by a clash between residents of Pennsylvania and Virginia.

Most successful escapes were made from slave states that bordered free states; the further south a slave lived, the less likely his or her chances of reaching freedom. In addition, slaves were usually required to produce documentation from their master permitting them to travel off the plantation; any slave caught without these papers was apprehended, returned to his master, and usually subjected to harsh punishment. Because so few slaves could read or write, forging such documents was nearly impossible. In his 1845 autobiography, Frederick Douglass, a former slave who could both read and write, detailed an event in which he forged papers for himself and fellow slaves as they prepared to escape from Maryland. When their plot was discovered, the slaves burned or ate the papers in an effort to hide the evidence; literacy was illegal for slaves, and the combination of an escape attempt and known literacy could have cost them their lives.

The Underground Railroad, a series of safe houses and havens for escaped slaves, was a loose system of abolitionists and others who helped escapees find their way to freedom in the northern United States

or Canada. From 1810 to 1850 the Underground Railroad helped more than 6,000 slaves escape, aided by former slaves such as Harriet Tubman, religious groups such as the Quakers, and abolitionist sympathizers. Fugitive slaves numbered more than 30,000 in Canada by the end of the Civil War.

In the 1830s, abolitionist sentiment grew, and tension between the North and South increased. Lecture circuits were filled with antislavery speakers, publications spoke of the institution's evils. This handbill, dated 1835, was printed and posted more than twenty-five years before the start of the Civil War. Similar items were printed by slave owners seeking their escaped slaves and offering rewards to those who helped return them.

■ PRIMARY SOURCE

Handbill Offering a Reward for a Runaway Slave
See primary source image.

SIGNIFICANCE

The description of Frank Mullen's clothing suggests that he was a household slave rather than a field hand; household slaves escaped less frequently than other slaves, in part because their treatment was generally better, and in part because they were under greater direct supervision. Slaves who drove carriages, cleaned the main house, worked as cooks, or cared for children were on more intimate terms with their owners and often received better clothing and rations than other slaves.

The bounty for Frank Mullen was set at $100–200; such rewards spawned an entire industry of slave hunters. In some instances, bounty hunters captured any black person without documentation they could find and turned the assumed slave over to authorities for a reward. Though rare, this practice led to the re-enslavement of some free blacks.

The Fugitive Slave Law of 1793 compelled citizens to hand over fugitive slaves, but many northerners refused to do so, and those in the Underground Railroad and other slave assistance organizations actively flouted the law. An 1842 Supreme Court decision, *Prigg v. Pennsylvania*, declared that states did not have to aid in the capture and delivery of an escaped slave, in effect nullifying portions of the 1793 law.

In 1850, Congress passed an updated Fugitive Slave Law; this new version required law enforcement officials to turn over any fugitive slave, with harsh

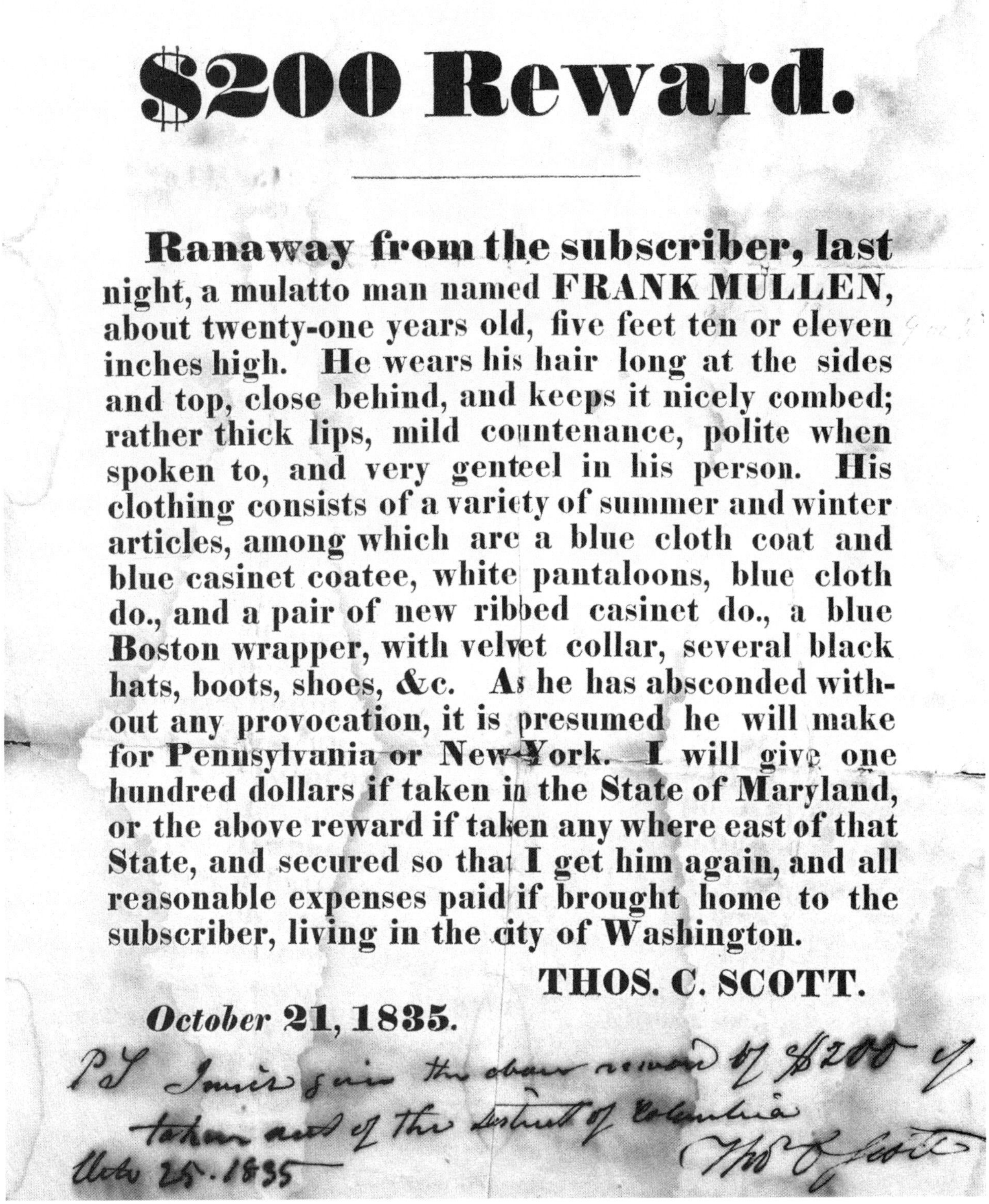

$200 Reward.

Ranaway from the subscriber, last night, a mulatto man named **FRANK MULLEN**, about twenty-one years old, five feet ten or eleven inches high. He wears his hair long at the sides and top, close behind, and keeps it nicely combed; rather thick lips, mild countenance, polite when spoken to, and very genteel in his person. His clothing consists of a variety of summer and winter articles, among which are a blue cloth coat and blue casinet coatee, white pantaloons, blue cloth do., and a pair of new ribbed casinet do., a blue Boston wrapper, with velvet collar, several black hats, boots, shoes, &c. As he has absconded without any provocation, it is presumed he will make for Pennsylvania or New-York. I will give one hundred dollars if taken in the State of Maryland, or the above reward if taken any where east of that State, and secured so that I get him again, and all reasonable expenses paid if brought home to the subscriber, living in the city of Washington.

THOS. C. SCOTT.

October 21, 1835.

P.S. I will give the above reward of $200 if taken out of the District of Columbia
Octo 25. 1835 Thos C Scott

PRIMARY SOURCE

Handbill Offering a Reward for a Runaway Slave: An 1835 handbill offering a reward for the return of Frank Mullen, a runaway slave. Such handbills were commonly posted in public areas and along suspected travel routes of escaped slaves. © LOUIE PSIHOYOS/CORBIS.

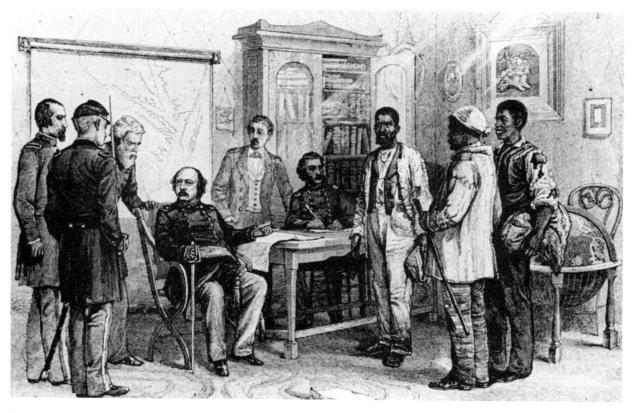

An illustration depicting former runaway slaves, now free men, meeting with Union officers during the Civil War. Under a policy developed during the Civil War, slaves who escaped from Confederate territory were treated as "contraband of war," with the effect that they were set free from slavery. © BETTMANN/CORBIS.

penalties for those who did not. In addition, the law provided a direct "finder's fee" for those who captured slaves, taking the informal system on handbills and making it part of the law.

By 1850, abolitionist sentiment in the North was reaching fever pitch. William Lloyd Garrison's abolitionist newspaper *The Liberator* published stories of fugitive slaves, their living conditions in the South, and powerful editorials fulminating against the slave system. Over the next decade, the 1850 Fugitive Slave Law became a source of escalating tension and aggression as the United States headed toward the Civil War.

FURTHER RESOURCES

Books

Davis, David Brion. *Inhuman Bondage: The Rise and Fall of Slavery in the New World*. New York: Oxford University Press, 2006.

Douglass, Frederick. *A Narrative of the Life of Frederick Douglass, An American Slave*. Dover, 1995.

Horton, James Oliver, and Lois E. Horton. *Slavery and the Making of America*. Oxford, New York: Oxford University Press, 2004.

Kolchin, Peter. *American Slavery: 1619–1877*. New York: Hill & Wang, 2003.

Websites

University of Oklahoma. College of Law. "The Fugitive Slave Law of 1793." <http://www.law.ou.edu/ushistory// fugslave.shtml> (accessed May 3, 2006).

Proceedings of the Anti-slavery Convention of American Women

Pamphlet

By: Anonymous

Date: May 1838

Source: *Proceedings of the Anti-Slavery Convention of American Women, Held in Philadelphia, May 15th, 16th, 17th, and 18th, 1838*. Philadelphia, PA: Merrihew & Gunn, 1838.

About the Author: The Anti-slavery Convention of American Women was organized by Lucretia Mott and other women after they were denied full membership to the American Anti-slavery Society.

INTRODUCTION

While abolitionism—the end of the institution of slavery or the enslavement of any human being—gained power in the United States in the late 1820s and early 1830s, pro-abolition groups and laws existed in the colonies long before noted abolitionists such as William Lloyd Garrison, Lucretia Mott, John Brown, or Frederick Douglass gained national attention.

Famous ministers such as Jonathan Edwards, Jr., published anti-slavery articles in newspapers such as *The Connecticut Journal* and the *New-Haven Post-Boy* in 1773 and 1774. Georgia's charter prohibited slavery. In 1774, Rhode Island abolished slavery, and in 1775 the first American abolition organization, the Society for the Relief of Free Negroes Unlawfully Held in Bondage, formed in Philadelphia. Many colonists believed slavery to be immoral and unethical; over time, northern colonies and states abolished or severely limited slavery, while in the south slaves provided an increasing amount of manual labor that sustained skyrocketing exports of cotton, tobacco, and sugar crops.

Congress declared the slave trade illegal by 1808, and in 1820 engaging in the slave trade was deemed piracy, punishable by death. Many abolitionists worked to abolish the slave trade itself, with the horrific "Middle Passage" in which newly captured slaves were crammed into ship hulls to be shipped to the Americas, fed erratic meals, and in which disease ran rampant, killing as much as twenty percent of the captives. With the banning of the slave trade and the north beginning to use a wage labor system vs. the slave labor system used by the agricultural south, the northern cry for abolitionism increased.

By the 1830s, a new opportunity for women's expression in civil society emerged. As the "cult of domesticity," which held the domestic and family sphere sacred for the middle and upper class woman, gained power in society, many women found an outlet for organization through the use of Christian motherhood ideals. As abolitionist ministers used the bully pulpit to preach against slavery, women rose to the call, organizing in unprecedented numbers to fight against slavery. The following is an excerpt from the Anti-slavery Convention of Women, held from May 15–18, 1838.

■ PRIMARY SOURCE

Resolved, That whatever may be the sacrifice, and whatever other rights may be yielded or denied, we will maintain practically the right of petition, until the slave shall go free, or our energies, like Loveyjoy's, are paralyzed in death.

Resolved, That for every petition by the National Legislature, during their late session, we will endeavor to send five the present year; and that we will not cease our efforts until the prayers of every woman within the sphere of our influence shall be heard in the halls of Congress on this subject.

On motion, the business of the Convention was suspended for a short time to give instructions to the committee appointed to make arrangements for the future meetings.

On motion of Mary Spencer,

Resolved, That we regard the right of petition as clear and inalienable, and so far from glamouring a dictatorial spirit, it is the refuge of the most humble and powerless, and greatness would never turn away from such appeals.

Mary Grew offered the following resolution,

Whereas, The principles of Christ are commanded to have no fellowship with the "unfruitful works of darkness;" and, whereas, union in His church is the strongest expression of fellowship between men; therefore, Resolved, That it is our duty to keep ourselves separate from those churches which receive to their pulpits and their communion tables, those who buy, or sell, or hold as property, the image of the living God.

This resolution was supported by the mover, Lucretia Mott, Abby Kelly, Maria W. Chapman, Anne W. Weston, Sarah T. Smith, and Sarah Lewis; and opposed by Margaret Dye, Margaret Prior, Henrietta Willcox, Martha W. Storrs, and Juliana A. Tappan, and was adopted.*

[Note: *Those who voted in the negative on the above resolution, fully concur with their sisters, in the belief that slaveholders and their apologists are guilty before God, and that, with the former, Northern Christian should hold no fellowship; but as it is their full belief that there is still moral power sufficient in the church, if rightly applied, to purify it, they cannot feel it their duty to withdraw until the utter inefficiency of the means used, shall constrain them to believe the church totally corrupt. Martha W. Storrs, Margaret Prior, Elizabeth M. Southard, Margaret Dye, Charlotte Woolsey.] Adjourned to meet in Pennsylvania Hall, on Thursday morning, May 17th.

Thursday Morning, May 17.

LADIES' DEPARTMENT.

'Am I not a Woman and a Sister?'

White Lady, happy, proud and free,
Lend awhile thine ear to me ;
Let the Negro Mother's wail
Turn thy pale cheek still more pale.
Can the Negro Mother joy
Over this her captive boy,
Which in bondage and in tears,
For a life of wo she rears ?
Though she bears a Mother's name,
A Mother's rights she may not claim ;
For the white man's will can part,
Her darling from her bursting heart.

From the Genius of Universal Emancipation.

LETTERS ON SLAVERY.—No. III.

A poem, "Am I not a Woman and a Sister?" published in the "Ladies' Department" of the anti-slavery newspaper *The Liberator*, 1849. © BETTMANN/CORBIS.

The Convention was called to order, in the Pennsylvania Hall, at 10 o'clock, A.M.

A portion of Scripture was read, and prayer offered by the President.

Lucretia Mott made some impressive remarks respecting the riot of the preceding evening, and exhorted the members of the Convention to be steadfast and solemn in the prosecution of the business for which they were assembled.

On motion of Margaret Dye,

Resolved, That the Anti-Slavery enterprise presents one of the most appropriate fields for the exertion of the influence of woman, and that we pledge ourselves, with divine assistance, never to desert the work, while an American slave groans in bondage.

On motion of Abigail B. Ordway,

Resolved, That every mother is bound by imperative obligations, to instruct her children in the principles abolition, by teaching them the nature and sanctity of human rights, and the claims of the great law of office, as binding alike on every member of the human family.

On motion of Mary Grew,

Resolved, That in view of unparalleled sufferings of the slave, and also in relation to the oppression of the nominally free people of color in the United States, it becomes us, as women and as Christians, to invoke the special aid of Almighty God for the speedy deliverance of this people from their oppressions, in that way which will most glorify Himself.

On motion of Henrietta Willcox,

Resolved, That in view of the exigencies of the times, and the loud call for money to aid in the dissemination of truth, this Convention recommend to Female Anti-Slavery Societies to take immediate measures for the formation of cent-a-week societies, on the plan proposed by the Executive Committee of the American Anti-Slavery Society. [Note: *Persons wishing to obtain cards and tracts, and any information respecting the system, and referred to Nathaniel Southard, 143 Nassau Street, New York.]

On motion of Margaret Dye,

Resolved, That the system of American slavery is contrary to the laws of God, and the spirit of religion, and that the church is deeply implicated in this sin, and that it therefore becomes the imperative duty of all her members to petition their ecclesiastical bodies to enter their decided protests against it, and exclude slaveholders from their pulpits and communion tables.

Adjourned to meet in the same place at 4 o'clock, P.M.

Thursday Afternoon, May 17.

The Convention was called to order at 4 o'clock, P.M. The President read the 6th chapter of 2d Cor., and Sarah M. Grimké offered prayer.

Sarah T. Smith, on behalf of the Business Committee, presented an address to Anti-Slavery Societies, which was read and adopted.

On motion of Thankful Southwick,

Resolved, That it is the duty of all those who call themselves abolitionists to make the most vigorous efforts to procure for the use of their families the products of free labor, so that their hands may be clean, in this particular, when inquisition is made for blood.

Esther Moore made some remarks upon the importance of carrying into effect the resolutions that had been passed.

Adjourned to meet in Temperance Hall on Friday morning at 9 o'clock.

Friday Morning, May 18.

The Convention met pursuant to adjournment at Temperance hall, but found the doors closed by order of the managers. *A member of the Convention offered the use of a school-room, where the meeting was called to order at 10 o'clock, A. M.

[Note: *The Pennsylvania Hall having been burned by a mob, on Thursday evening, and much excitement still prevailing, the managers of Temperance Hall, fearing for the safety of their building, refused to open the doors.] The President read the 4th chapter of 2d Cor., and prayer was offered by Juliana A. Tappan, and Mary E. Smith.

On motion of Lucretia Mott, Angelina E. G. Weld was appointed Vice-President.

On motion of Sarah R. Ingraham,

Resolved, That in view of the manifestation of public sentiment, as recently exhibited in the outbreakings of a lawless mob, resulting in insult and abuse towards all abolitionists, and personal injury to some of our colored friends, the case of the latter be earnestly commended to God, and prayer be offered that He will redress their wrongs, and protect them from the dangers to which they may be in future exposed.

Sarah T. Smith, in behalf of the Business Committee, presented an address to the free colored people of the United States, and an address to the Senators and Representatives of the free States in Congress, which were read and adopted.

Abby Kelly offered the following resolution, which was adopted:

Whereas, A vast portion of the wealth of the North has accrued, and is still accruing, from the slave system, either directly in the holding of slaves, by Northern citizens, or indirectly by our social and commercial intercourse with slaveholding communities; therefore, Resolved, That we are very deeply implicated in the sin of using our brother's service without wages, and of holding in our hands the gains of oppression; consequently it is our duty to bring forth fruits meet for repentance, by laboring devotedly in the service of the spoiled, and by contributing with unsparing liberality to the treasury of the slave.

On motion of Sarah M. Grimké,

Resolved, That prejudice against color is the very spirit of slavery, sinful in those who indulge it, and is the fire, which is consuming the happiness and energies of the free people of color.

That it is, therefore, the duty of abolitionists to identify themselves with these oppressed Americans, by sitting with them in places of worship, by appearing with them in our streets, by giving them our countenance in steamboats and stages, by visiting them at their homes and encouraging them to visit us, receiving them as we do our white fellow citizens.*

[Note : *Not unanimous—a number voted in the negative, believing that a resolution couched in such phraseology, might, by being misapprehended, injure the abolition cause.]

On motion of Sarah M. Grimké,

Resolved, That those of our Southern brethren and sisters who feel and mourn over the guilt of slavery, while circumstances impose on them the necessity of remaining witnesses of its evils and its horrors, are entitled to our sympathy and prayers, and that we encourage them to walk with weeping and supplication before God, that His judgments may be averted from our beloved country.

On motion, the following resolution was adopted:

Resolve, That in this Convention, met together to consider the solemn subject of American slavery, it is cause of grateful acknowledgement that sectarian feeling has been so far laid aside as to enable us to meet together as Christians, and we recommend to all similar bodies to keep in mind, that sects are no part of the glorious gospel of Christ, but that love to our fellow men is the test of religion. "Whoso dwelleth in love, dwelleth in God, and God in him."

The following resolution was offered by Sarah M.Grimké and adopted:

Resolved, That we hail with joy the triumphant success of immediate emancipation in the islands of Antigua and Bermuda, which has been most forcibly set forth in the journal of Kimball and Thome. We recommend this work to the perusal of Americans, as calculated to remove every objection to the fundamental principles of abolitionism, and to strengthen every one who is laboring for the slave's redemption.

On motion of Angelina E.G. Weld,

Resolved, That did we need other stimulus than the example of Him who came to preach deliverance to the captive, we possess it in the disinterested and untiring efforts of our sisters across the Atlantic, in this sacred cause, and in the success that has crowned them.

Resolved, That the voice of joy and freedom as it rings up from the British West Indies, resounds through our land, is a triumphant proof of the safety of immediate emancipation; and, while it inspires us with confidence, should so attune our spirits to gentleness and love, that the most obdurate may be moved by our entreaties, and the most captious find nothing to blame.

Catherine M. Sullivan offered the following resolution, which was adopted:

Believing the principles of the Anti-Slavery cause to be identical with those on which the whole gospel rests, and that the constant and vigorous propagation of them will equally advance the kingdom of Christ, in the hearts and outward lives of men; therefore,

Resolved, That we increase our efforts for the spiritual and temporal salvation of the slave, knowing that such labors will involve the salvation of the master, the good of our own souls, the general promotion of peace, moral reform, temperance; the circulation of the Scriptures, the education of youth, and the exaltation of our country to so high a standard of morals and religion, that its example shall go forth unto all the earth and recommend the gospel to every creature.

SIGNIFICANCE

Just five years before this convention, William Lloyd Garrison, Arthur Tappan, Lewis Tappan, and others formed the American Anti-slavery Society; abolition became a strong force in American society, pushing the issue to the forefront of American politics. Many men questioned having women play a public role in the abolition movement, claiming that politics was too worldly and crude for delicate and pure women to work within. Sarah and Angela Grimke, the first female speakers on the American lecture circuit, traveled throughout the United States in 1837, visiting Congregationalist churches to denounce slavery and race prejudice. By 1838, the same year as the Anti-slavery Convention of American Women, thousands of lecture attendees listened to the Grimke sisters, both devout Quakers shunned for the public displays of their beliefs.

The tone of female abolitionism was distinct; many women used emotional appeals to highlight the dark side of slavery. Female abolitionists invoked images of female slaves forced to give up children, be separated from husbands, or to face rape at the hands of immoral white owners. By appealing to women to look at female slaves as fellow *women* and not just black slaves, northern middle class organizers used their role as holders of moral and religious purity to invoke anti-slavery sentiment.

Women's work in abolitionism gave participants valuable organizational and political skills; over time, many female abolitionists and followers began to analyze the concept of civil rights and to examine the role of women in civil and political society. Future women's rights activists such as Lucretia Mott and Elizabeth Cady Stanton began their political involvement while working on abolitionist causes.

Female abolitionists often worked with former slaves such as Sojourner Truth and Frederick Douglass, providing white, middle class, northern women the opportunity to meet, converse, and lecture with African Americans not as slave owners but as people. Within ten years of the Anti-slavery Convention of American Women, the first women's rights convention convened in Seneca Falls, New York. Efforts to gain the vote for former slaves in the late 1860s brought abolitionist women into conflict with many black rights activists; Horace Greeley and Frederick Douglass, for instance, supported the black male vote, but not female suffrage at that time. Upset with their loss, many female abolitionists shifted their energies toward female suffrage, a right they would achieve fifty years later.

FURTHER RESOURCES
Books

Horton, James, and Lois E. Horton. *Slavery and the Making of America.* New York: Oxford University Press, 2004.

Jeffrey, Julie Roy. *The Great Silent Army of Abolitionism: Ordinary Women in the Antislavery Movement.* Chapel Hill, NC: University of North Carolina Press, 1998.

Lerner, Gerda. *The Grimke Sisters from South Carolina: Pioneers for Women's Rights and Abolition.* Chapel Hill, NC: University of North Carolina Press, 2004.

Mayer, Henry. *All on Fire: William Lloyd Garrison and the Abolition of Slavery.* New York: St. Martin's Griffin, 2000.

Copper Slave Tags

Photograph

By: Louie Psihoyos

Date: 1840

Source: "Copper Slave Tags." © Louie Psihoyos/ Corbis. 2006.

An illustration of the U.S. slave trade used by the abolitionist movement to raise anti-slavery awareness. © CORBIS.

About the Photographer: Louie Psihoyos was a staff photographer for *National Geographic* magazine and the recipient of numerous awards. His work includes a wide array of nature photography, as well as Hollywood campaigns and stock photography, including pictures of historical documents.

INTRODUCTION

These copper slave tags, dating from 1831–1840, were worn by slaves in Charleston, South Carolina. These slaves were hired out by their masters for work at the trades shown on the tags, occasionally receiving some portion of the wages themselves. They were required to wear the tags, purchased annually from the city treasurer's office, or risk jail with fines levied on the masters. The "hire badges" or "slave tax badges," as they were also called, served to differentiate slaves that were legally "jobbing out" from Black freedmen, runaway slaves, slaves attempting to earn money on their own, and those whose masters did not pay the required tax.

As one of the few enduring artifacts possessed by individual slaves, these tags have become increasingly valuable to both collectors and scholars. Although hiring out slaves for wage labor was common throughout the southern United States before the Civil War, contracts or paper tickets usually documented it. Metal tags, stamped with "Charleston," the year, a

trade, and a sequential number for each trade, were issued only in Charleston from 1783–1790 and from 1800–1865.

PRIMARY SOURCE

COPPER SLAVE TAGS
See primary source image.

SIGNIFICANCE

Charleston's slave tags are unique amongst slavery's artifacts. They evoke some of the horror and fascination of the other material remains, like shackles, but also prompt speculation on those who wore and perhaps lost or discarded their badges. These individuals included house servants, porters (who moved cargo on the docks), fishermen, fruit sellers ("hucksters" or "fruiterers"), carpenters, masons, tailors, and a host of other skilled tradesmen.

Urban slaves constituted only about five percent of the U.S. slave population, and these men and some women were more likely to have the skilled jobs that free citizens required on a part-time basis than those enslaved in the rural South. According to Theresa Singleton, urban slaves also had more access to other

PRIMARY SOURCE

Copper Slave Tags: When slave owners wished to hire out their slaves to work for others in Charleston, South Carolina, the slaves were required to wear these copper slave tags for identification purposes. Slaves without tags or identification papers were put in jail.
© LOUIE PSIHOYOS/CORBIS.

people, including free Blacks, as well as "education, opportunities for self-hire and self-purchase, and the privilege of 'live-out' in separate sections of town." As such, the badges were not perceived as shameful by their bearers, but were highly sought after, as described by Greene, Hutchins, and Hutchins in their book on the tags and their legal underpinnings.

Greater freedom, coupled with the hired slaves' economic competition with white artisans, resulted in increasingly complex laws regarding slave hiring from 1800 through 1866, culminating in Charleston's badges. Originally, freedmen were also required to display badges, and a few "Freedman" badges dating from 1783–1790 have been found. After 1800, only "jobbing slaves" needed badges. All slaves except house servants were required to display the tags, either strung around the neck or sewn onto clothing, and fees and penalties associated with breaking the slave hire laws increased.

A limited number of these tags were made. For example, Greene, Hutchins, and Hutchins estimate less than five thousand were issued in 1850, with about 2,400 for servants. Since tags were probably melted and re-used each year, the fraction of tags that have been discovered is quite small. Fewer than four hundred have been found, mostly in Charleston.

As symbols of slavery, these tags have been sought after since the early 1900s, although their use was not widely understood. Counterfeit badges were marketed as early as 1903. In 2002, a huckster's badge from 1803 brought more than $26,000 at an auction, and there has been a corresponding increase in forgery, as well as more interest and understanding of the role they played in one aspect of "the peculiar institution" of slavery.

FURTHER RESOURCES

Books

Greene, Harlan, Harry S. Hutchins, Jr., and Brian E. Hutchins. *Slave Badges and the Slave-Hire System in Charleston, South Carolina, 1783–1865*. Jefferson, N.C.: McFarland, 2004.

Periodicals

Singleton, Theresa A. "The Slave Tag: An Artifact of Urban Slavery." *South Carolina Antiquities* 16 (1984): 41–65.

Web sites

Dawson, Victoria. *Smithsonian Magazine*. "Cast in Bondage." <http://www.smithsonianmag.com/issues/2003/february/object.php> (accessed April 30, 2006).

Appellants, vs. Cinque, and Others, Africans, Captured in the Schooner *Amistad*

Argument Before the Supreme Court

Speech

By: John Quincy Adams

Date: March 1, 1841

Source: Adams, John Quincy. *Argument of John Quincy Adams, before the Supreme Court of the United States, in the Case of the United States, Appellants, vs. Cinque, and others, Africans, Captured in the Schooner Amistad...* New York: S. W. Benedict, 1841.

About the Author: John Quincy Adams (1767–1848) the sixth president of the United States and the son of the second president, spent most of his post-presidential career opposing the institution of slavery. As an attorney, he argued for the rights of Africans in the 1841 *Amistad* case before the U.S. Supreme Court.

INTRODUCTION

On June 18, 1839, the Spanish ship *Amistad* sailed from Havana, Cuba, with a cargo of fifty-three illegally imported Africans belonging to José Ruiz and Pedro Montes. The Africans were to be sold as slaves in Puerto Príncipe in east-central Cuba. Four nights later, the Africans freed themselves from their chains, mutinied, killed the ship's captain and cook, sent two crewmen overboard, and instructed two surviving crewman to sail for Africa. The mutineers were led by Joseph Cinque (1811?–1852?), also known as Sing-gbe, a native of present-day Sierra Leone and member of the Mende tribe.

The *Amistad* landed at Long Island, New York on August 26, after being seized in the Atlantic by a U.S. Coast Guard brig under the command of Lieutenant Thomas Gedney. The U.S. State Department recommended that the Spanish minister take custody of the *Amistad* and its jailed cargo. When the Africans were indicted for piracy, Lewis Tappan and other abolitionists established the Amistad Committee to raise money for their defense. Meanwhile, the Spanish government claimed the Africans as its property and demanded their return. The case moved from district court to circuit court and arrived before the Supreme Court in late 1840.

Antislavery activists took an interest in the case and convinced Adams to defend the Africans. Adams had not practiced law in years. He hesitated to take such an emotional case in part because he feared that his anti-slavery zealotry would diminish his ability to provide a cool, rational defense. Nevertheless, Adams stood before the Supreme Court for over four hours on February 24, 1841, and again on March 1 to present arguments that ranged from the minute wording of shipping laws to the ideals of the Declaration of Independence. On March 9, 1841, Chief Justice Roger B. Taney, a Maryland slave-owner who later decided the 1857 Dred Scott case, found the Africans innocent of murder and piracy. He ruled that they were free and should be allowed to return to Africa. The thirty-five surviving Africans, aided by the defense committee and Yale University's Divinity School, sailed for Sierra Leone in November 1841 to serve as Christian missionaries and positive examples of returned-to-Africa blacks for the American Colonization Society.

▇ PRIMARY SOURCE

...I appear here on the behalf of thirty-six individuals, the life and liberty of every one of whom depend on the decision of this Court....Three or four of them are female children, incapable, in the judgment of our laws, of the crime of murder or piracy, or, perhaps, of any other crime. Yet, from the day when the vessel was taken possession of by one of our naval officers, they have all been held as close prisoners, now for the period of eighteen long months....

The Constitution of the United States recognizes the slaves, held within some of the States of the Union, only in their capacity of persons—persons held to labor or service in a State under the laws thereof—persons constituting elements of representation in the popular branch of the National Legislature persons, the migration or importation of whom should not be prohibited by Congress prior to the year 1808. The Constitution no where recognizes them as property. The words slave and slavery are studiously excluded from the Constitution. Circumlocutions are the fig-leaves under which the parts of the body politic are decently concealed. Slaves, therefore, in the Constitution of the United States are persons, enjoying rights and held to the performance of duties.

...The persons aforesaid, described as slaves, are Negroes and persons of color, who have been transported from Africa in violation of the laws of the United States... The Court should enable the United States to send the Negroes home to Africa...in pursuance of the law of Congress passed March 3, 1829, entitled "An act in addition to the acts prohibiting the slave-trade."

...The President...signed [an] order for the delivery of MEN to the control of an officer of the navy to be carried beyond seas...The District Judge, contrary to all [the] anticipations of the Executive, decided that the thirty-six Negroes...brought before the Court...were FREEMEN; that they had been kidnapped in Africa; that they did not own...Spanish names;...that they were not correctly described in the passport, but were new Negroes bought by Ruiz in the depot of Havana, and fully entitled to their liberty.

...Well was it for the country—well was it for the President of the United States himself that he paused before stepping over this Rubicon!...The indignation of the freemen of Connecticut, might not tamely endure the sight, of thirty-six free persons, though Africans, fettered and manacled in their land of freedom, to be transported beyond the seas, to perpetual hereditary servitude or to death, by the servile submission of an American President to the insolent dictation of a foreign minister.....

[President Van Buren informed his subordinates that] if the decree of the Judge should be in our favor, and you can steal a march upon the Negroes by foreclosing their right of appeal, ship them off without mercy and without delay: and if the decree should be in their favor, fail not to enter an instantaneous appeal to the Supreme Court where the chances may be more hostile to self-emancipated slaves.

Was ever such a scene of Lilliputian trickery enacted by the rulers of a great, magnanimous, and Christian nation? Contrast it with that act of self-emancipation, by which the savage, heathen barbarians Cinque and Grabeau liberated themselves and their fellow suffering countrymen from Spanish slave traders, and which the Secretary of State...denominates lawless violence. Cinque and Graveau are uncouth and barbarous names. Call them Harmodius and Aristogiton, and go back for moral principle three thousand years to the fierce and glorious democracy of Athens. They too resorted to lawless violence, and slew the tyrant to redeem the freedom of their country....

I said, when I began this plea, that my final reliance for success in this case was on this Court as a court of JUSTICE; and in the confidence this fact inspired, that, in the administration of justice, in a case of no less importance than the liberty and the life of a large number of persons, this Court would not decide but on a due consideration of all the rights, both natural and social, of everyone of these individuals....I have avoided, purposely avoided, ... a recurrence to those first principles of liberty which might well have been invoked in the argument of this cause. I have shown that Ruiz and Montes, ... were acting at the time in a way that is forbidden by the laws of

John Quincy Adams, diplomat, congressman, and sixth president of the United States. © BETTMANN/CORBIS.

Great Britain, of Spain and of the United States, and that the mere signature of the Governor General of Cuba ought not to prevail over the ample evidence in the case that these Negroes were free and had a right to assert their liberty. . . .

. . . On the 7th of February, 1804, now more than thirty-seven years past, my name was entered, and yet stands recorded, on both the rolls, as one of the Attorneys and Counsellors of this Court. . . . I stand before the same Court, but not before the same judges—nor aided by the same associates—nor resisted by the same opponents. As I cast my eyes along those seats of honor and public trust, now occupied by you, they seek in vain for one of those honored and honorable persons whose indulgence listened then to my voice. Marshall—Cushing—Chase—Washington—Johnson—Livingston—Todd—Where are they? . . . Gone! Gone! All gone! . . . In taking, then, my final leave of this Bar, and of this Honorable Court, I can only ejaculate a fervent petition to Heaven, that every member of it may go to his final account with as little of earthly frailty to answer for as those illustrious dead . . . .

SIGNIFICANCE

The *Amistad* case remained a contentious point in antebellum U.S.-Spanish relations. From 1844 until 1860, when Spain abandoned its claims in the *Amistad* case, every American president suggested that the United States should compensate Spain for the Africans and mentioned the event in his state-of-the-union address.

The subsequent lives of Cinque and the other *Amistad* survivors are not well-documented. Cinque is the best known of the Africans. Some accounts claim that he died barely a decade after his return to Africa, while other records indicate that he lived until 1879 and was buried on the grounds of the American Missionary Association compound in Sierra Leone.

Regardless of the ultimate fate of Cinque and his African companions, they remained important symbols for slaves in the United States because they seized their freedom. After the end of slavery, the *Amistad* mutineers continued to serve as examples of the will to persevere for justice against great odds.

FURTHER RESOURCES
Books

Cable, Mary. *Black Odyssey: The Case of the Slave Ship* Amistad. New York: Viking Press, 1971.

Hoyt, Edwin. *The* Amistad *Affair*. New York: Abelard-Schuman, 1970.

Jones, Howard. *Mutiny on the* Amistad: *The Saga of a Slave Revolt and Its Impact on American Abolition, Law, and Diplomacy*. New York: Oxford University Press, 1987.

Am I Not a Man and a Brother?

Illustration

By: Anonymous

Date: 1837

Source: The Library of Congress.

About the Artist: The Society for Effecting the Abolition of the Slave Trade was formed in Britain in 1787 for the purpose of distributing anti-slavery literature and rousing public opinion against the slave trade. The primary source image was inspired by their official seal.

INTRODUCTION

Long before the U.S. Civil War (1861–1865), the Quakers—also known as the Society of Friends—were staunch Abolitionists (opponents of slavery) both in the United Kingdom and in the United States. In 1787, a group of Quakers in London formed an organization called the "Society for Effecting the Abolition of the Slave Trade." As part of the creation of the Society, several members designed a distinctive seal for its use, intended to be emblematic of its mission and belief system. The image they created was that of a kneeling African male, shackled at the wrists and ankles, bound by chains, bearing the caption "Am I not a man and a brother?" It was then made into a metal engraving that was used by the Society, and eventually adopted as emblematic of the cause of Abolitionists in the United Kingdom, the United States, and elsewhere. The phrasing of the emblem ("Am I not a man and a brother?") took on progressively more philosophical and political meaning over time.

It is noteworthy that the original intent of the Society for Effecting the Abolition of the Slave Trade was purported to be much more specific than abolition of slavery—it was intended merely to focus attention on the malfeasance of process of the African slave trade—but not to abolish the whole of slavery, although that is what the logo that they commissioned came to symbolize. There is, however, considerable disagreement in that regard recorded in historic documents attributed to individual members of the Society, many of whom were completely opposed to slavery.

PRIMARY SOURCE

AM I NOT A MAN AND A BROTHER?
See primary source image.

SIGNIFICANCE

As was the case in the United States, the history of the abolition of slavery in the United Kingdom progressed through several phases. In 1807, the importation of slaves to the British colonies was formally halted, although slaves remained in servitude throughout the British Empire. In 1833, all aspects of slavery were outlawed, both importation and ownership. However, slave owners were paid large sums of money (typically reported to be on the order of twenty million pounds) as part of the abolition, and they were permitted to retain their former slaves in a form of indentured servitude (an unpaid apprenticeship) for a period of one dozen years.

At a convention at Exeter Hall, London, in 1837, there was much outcry against the perceived unfairness of the apprenticeship programs, with many reports that they amounted to slavery under a different name. At that conference, the Central Emancipation Committee (CEC) was formed, with the goal of complete emancipation of all slaves throughout the British Empire. Again, the plantation owners and others who owned slaves were offered financial incentives for cooperation.

The British and Foreign Anti-Slavery Society (BFASS) got its start at Exeter Hall in 1839, The goals of the BFASS were similar to those of the CEC but with a more global perspective—although much of their work continued to be focused on the British colonies for the next decade. Essentially, it was this group's mission to prevent former slave owners from imposing indentured servitude on the freemen (and women), and to raise money so as to offer financial assistance to former slaves who wished to establish independent living and working situations. The organization helped large numbers of former slaves relocate to Jamaica and the West Indies, to form small farming communities there.

The design portrayed in "Am I not a man and a brother?" became symbolic of a larger ideal, and made its way into the upper echelons of society. In effect, it transitioned from the simple insignia of a particular organization to an artistic and political statement adopted by people around the world who were opposed to slavery. The seal became a design imprinted on a Wedgewood cameo, and a considerable number of the cameos were shipped from the United Kingdom to the United States. From there, the design was made into medallions that were copied onto all manner of accessories, from bracelets to hair clips. The designs were worn by the populace who desired to make personal anti-slavery statements. That trend has continued, symbolically, to the present day, wherein people express their philosophical and political sentiments by displaying or wearing colored ribbons or bands associated with various causes ranging from cancer awareness to support for the Armed Forces.

FURTHER RESOURCES
Books

Bennett, C.L. *Africa in America: Slave Acculturation and Resistance in the American South and the British Caribbean.* Chicago, Illinois: University of Illinois Press, 1995.

Brougham, Henry Peter. *Opinions of Lord Brougham on Politics, Theology, Law, Science, Education, Literature, Etc., Etc.* Boston, Massachusetts: Adamant Media, Elibron Classics Division, 2005.

■ **PRIMARY SOURCE**

Am I Not a Man and a Brother? This woodcut version of the iconic anti-slavery symbol of a slave in chains asking to be treated as a human being appeared as an illustration to an 1837 broadside of John Greenleaf Whittier's anti-slavery poem: "Our Countrymen in Chains." THE LIBRARY OF CONGRESS.

Civil rights protestors march in support of a sanitation worker's strike in Memphis, Tennessee, 1968. National Guardsmen and tanks flank the protestors. © BETTMANN/CORBIS. REPRODUCED BY PERMISSION.

Fladeland, Betty. *Men and Brothers: Anglo-American Anti-Slavery Cooperation.* Urbana, IL: University of Illinois Press, 1972.

Ripley, C. Peter, Ed. *The Black Abolitionist Papers, Volume One: The British Isles, 1830–1865.* Chapel Hill, North Carolina: The University of North Carolina Press, 1985.

Periodicals

Howard, Percy. "The Passing of Exeter Hall." *The Civil Service Observer.* 13(5) (1907): Inclusive.

Web sites

Privy Council Office. "Office Objectives and Structure.". <http://www.privy-council.org.uk/output/page2.asp> (accessed April 25, 2006).

The Library of Economics and Liberty. "Contributor's Forum: The Secret History of the Dismal Science: Economics, Religion and Race in the 19th Century." January 22, 2001. <http://www.econlib.org/LIBRARY/Columns/LevyPeartdismal.html> (accessed April 25, 2006).

Country, Conscience, and the Anti-Slavery Cause

An Address Delivered in New York, New York, May 11, 1847

Magazine article

By: Frederick Douglass

Date: May 13, 1847

Source: Douglass, Frederick. "Country, Conscience, and the Anti-Slavery Cause: An Address Delivered in New York, New York, May 11, 1847." *New York Daily Tribune* (May 13, 1847).

About the Author: Frederick Douglass was born in February 1818, on Maryland's Eastern Shore, with the name Frederick Augustus Washington Bailey. His mother, a slave, said his father was a white man whose identity remains unknown. In September 1838, he fled to New York City; once free, he changed his name to Frederick Douglass. He traveled to New England, pursued an education, and joined the fight to end slavery. In 1845, he published his autobiography and two years later began publishing his antislavery newspaper the *North Star*. Douglass was a key leader in the abolitionist movement and the first black American to gain significant government appointments.

INTRODUCTION

The early years of Frederick Douglass's life were not that different from other slave children. He lived with his grandparents and an aunt, in slave quarters on a large plantation, and he saw his mother only a few times before her death. At eight years old, he was removed from his family and was sent to Baltimore to work for the ship carpenter Hugh Auld. Douglass learned to read and write while working for Auld and later noted that his Baltimore years gave him the desire and ability to escape his servitude and fight against slavery. After Auld's death, the sixteen-year-old Douglass was returned to the plantation to work as a field hand, forcing him to endure the brutal privations of slavery. He became determined to obtain his freedom.

Douglass first attempted to escape in 1833, but his owner learned of the plans and jailed him on the property, eventually releasing him only to rejoin the other field hands. In 1838, Douglass successfully fled to New York and settled in New Bedford, Massachusetts, with his bride Anna Murray a few weeks later. Once in Massachusetts, Douglass continued his education, joined a black church, and became an active member of the community.

He read abolitionist writings, heard key leaders like William Lloyd Garrison speak, and soon began speaking and writing against slavery himself. In 1845, he published his autobiography *Narrative of the Life of Frederick Douglass, an American Slave*, even though he knew its publication would endanger his freedom. Slaveholders paid bounty hunters to return escaped slaves, and no law protected him from being recaptured. To make matters worse, in 1850 Congress signed the Fugitive Slave Act, which mandated the return of escaped slaves to their owners and rewarded anyone who captured runaways. Thus, Douglass and other escaped slaves lived in perpetual fear of being captured; not surprisingly, many worked for the abolitionist movement.

Douglass's public stature made him an especially tempting prize for slave catchers. To avoid being

A portrait of American abolitionist and writer Frederick Douglass (1817–1895). © BETTMANN/CORBIS.

returned to his owner, who he'd named in his book, Douglass embarked on a speaking tour of England and Ireland. There, he found the treatment of blacks and attitudes against slavery to be far more enlightened. In 1847, upon returning to the United States, Douglass moved his family to Rochester, New York, where he began publishing his weekly abolitionist newspaper the *North Star*. The paper successfully expanded the abolitionist cause, and Douglass continued an active career of speaking against slavery. In 1858, the militant abolitionist John Brown tried to recruit Douglass for his ill-fated raid on Harper's Ferry. Although Douglass declined the offer, he continued his public fight against slavery, expressing his longing for a country that treated its people as equals.

▪ PRIMARY SOURCE

4. You are aware, doubtless, that my object in going from this country was to get beyond the reach of

the clutch of the man who claimed to own me as his property. I had written a book giving a history of that portion of my life spent in the gall and bitterness and degradation of Slavery, and in which I also identified my oppressors as the perpetrators of some of the most atrocious crimes. This had deeply incensed them against me and stirred up within them the purpose of revenge, and, my whereabouts being known, I believed it necessary for me, if I would preserve my liberty, to leave the shores of America and take up my abode in some other land, at least until the excitement occasioned by the publication of my *Narrative* had subsided. I went to England, Monarchical England, to get rid of Democratic Slavery, and I must confess that, at the very threshold, I was satisfied that I had gone to the right place. Say what you will of England—of the degradation—of the poverty—and there is much of it there—say what you will of the oppression and suffering going on in England at this time, there is Liberty there, there is Freedom there, not only for the white man but for the black man also. The instant that I stepped upon the shore and looked into the faces of the crowd around me, I saw in every man a recognition of my manhood, and an absence, a perfect absence, of everything like that disgusting hate with which we are pursued in this country. (Cheers.) I looked around in vain to see in any man's face a token of the slightest aversion to me on account of my complexion. Even the cabmen demeaned themselves to me as they did to other men, and the very dogs and pigs of old England treated me as a man! I cannot, however, my friends, dwell upon this anti-Prejudice, or rather, the many illustrations of the absence of Prejudice against Color in England, but will proceed, at once, to defend the Right and Duty of invoking English aid and English sympathy for the overthrow of American Slavery, for the education of Colored Americans, and to forward, in every way, the interests of humanity; inasmuch as the right of appealing to England for aid in overthrowing Slavery in this country has been called in question, in public meetings and by the press, in this City.

5. I cannot agree with my friend Mr. Garrison in relation to my love and attachment to this land. I have no love for America, as such; I have no patriotism. I have no country. What country have I? The Institutions of this Country do not know me—do not recognize me as a man. I am not thought of, spoken of, in any direction, out of the Anti-Slavery ranks, as a man. I am not thought of or spoken of, except as a piece of property belonging to some *Christian* Slaveholder, and all the Religious and Political Institutions of this Country alike pronounce me a Slave and a chattel. Now, in such a country as this I cannot have patriotism. The only thing that links me to this land is my family, and the painful consciousness that here there are 3,000,000 of my fellow creatures groaning beneath the iron rod of the worst despotism that could be devised even in Pandemonium,— that here are men and brethren who are identified with me by their complexion, identified with me by their hatred of Slavery, identified with me by their love and aspirations for Liberty, identified with me by the stripes upon their backs, their inhuman wrongs and cruel sufferings. This, and this only, attaches me to this land, and brings me here to plead with you, and with this country at large, for the disenthrallment of my oppressed countrymen, and to overthrow this system of Slavery which is crushing them to the earth. How can I love a country that dooms 3,000,000 of my brethren, some of them my own kindred, my own brothers, my own sisters, who are now clanking the chains of Slavery upon the plains of the South, whose warm blood is now making fat the soil of Maryland and of Alabama, and over whose crushed spirits rolls the dark shadow of Oppression, shutting out and extinguishing forever the cheering rays of that bright Sun of Liberty, lighted in the souls of all God's children by the omnipotent hand of Deity itself? How can I, I say, love a country thus cursed, thus bedewed with the blood of my brethren? A Country, the Church of which, and the Government of which, and the Constitution of which are in favor of supporting and perpetuating this monstrous system of injustice and blood? I have not, I cannot have, any love for this country, as such, or for its Constitution. I desire to see it overthrown as speedily as possible and its Constitution shivered in a thousand fragments, rather than that this foul curse should continue to remain as now. (Hisses and cheers.)

6. In all this, my friends, let me make myself understood. I do not hate America as against England, or against any other country or land. I love Humanity all over the globe. I am anxious to see Righteousness prevail in all directions. I am anxious to see Slavery overthrown here; but, I never appealed to Englishmen in a manner calculated to awaken feelings of hatred or disgust, or to inflame their prejudices toward America as a nation, or in a manner provocative of national jealousy or ill-will; but I always appealed to their conscience—to the higher and nobler feelings of the people of that country, to

enlist them in this cause. I always appealed to their manhood, that which preceded their being Englishmen, (to quote an expression of my friend Phillips), I appealed to them as men, and I had a right to do so. They are men, and the Slave is a man, and we have a right to call upon all men to assist in breaking his bonds, let them be born when and live where they may.

7. But it is asked, "What good will this do?" or "What good has it done?" "Have you not irritated, have you not annoyed your American friends and the American people rather than done them good?" I admit that we have irritated them. They deserve to be irritated. I am anxious to irritate the American people on this question. As it is in physics, so in morals, there are cases which demand irritation and counter-irritation. The conscience of the American public needs this irritation, and I would *blister it all over from center to circumference,* until it gives signs of a purer and a better life than it is now manifesting to the world.

8. But why expose the sins of one nation in the eyes of another? Why attempt to bring one people under the odium of another people? There is much force in this question. I admit that there are sins in almost every country which can be best removed by means confined exclusively to their immediate locality. But such evils and such sins pre-suppose the existence of a moral power in their immediate locality sufficient to accomplish the work of renovation. But, where, pray, can we go to find moral power in this nation sufficient to overthrow Slavery? To what institution, to what party shall we apply for aid? I say we admit that there are evils which can be best removed by influences confined to their immediate locality. But in regard to American Slavery it is not so. It is such a giant crime, so darkening to the soul, so blinding in its moral influence, so well calculated to blast and corrupt all the humane principles of our nature, so well adapted to infuse its own accursed spirit into all around it, that the people among whom it exists have not the moral power to abolish it. Shall we go to the Church for this influence? We have heard its character described. Shall we go to Politicians or Political Parties? Have they the moral power necessary to accomplish this mighty task? They have not. What are they doing at this moment? Voting supplies for Slavery— voting supplies for the extension, the stability, the perpetuation of Slavery in this land. What is the press doing? The same. The pulpit? Almost the same. I do not flatter myself that there is moral power in the land sufficient to overthrow Slavery, and I welcome the aid of England. And that aid will come. The growing intercourse between England and this country, by means of steam navigation, the relaxation of the protective system in various countries in Europe, gives us an opportunity to bring in the aid, the moral and Christian aid, of those living on the other side of the Atlantic. We welcome it in the language of the resolution. We entreat our British friends to continue to send their remonstrances across the deep against Slavery in this land. And these remonstrances will have a powerful effect here. Sir, the Americans may tell of their ability, and I have no doubt they have it, to keep back the invader's hosts, to repulse the strongest force that its enemies may send against this country. It may boast, and *rightly* boast of its capacity to build its ramparts so high that no foe can hope to scale them—to render them so impregnable as to defy the assaults of the world. But, Sir, there is one thing it cannot resist, come from what quarter it may. It cannot resist TRUTH. You cannot build your forts so strong, nor your ramparts so high, nor arm yourselves so powerfully, as to be able to withstand the overwhelming MORAL SENTIMENT against Slavery now flowing into this land. For example: Prejudice against Color is continually becoming weaker in this land; and why? Because the whole European Continent denounces this sentiment as unworthy a lodgment in the breast of an enlightened community. And the American abroad dares not now, even in a public conveyance, to lift his voice in defence of this disgusting prejudice.

SIGNIFICANCE

In addition to his writings and speeches, Douglass worked with others in the antislavery movement. One such individual was William Lloyd Garrison, whom Douglass considered his mentor despite their divergent views of the Constitution and the best way to end slavery. Garrison, a radical abolitionist who believed the Constitution was irredeemably proslavery, felt that the Union should separate into pro- and antislavery sections. In contrast, Douglass believed that the Constitution could be amended to ban slavery and publicly supported an intact Union.

Douglass, who served as an advisor to President Abraham Lincoln, continued to fight for civil rights even after the war ended. In 1870, he and his sons began publishing the *New National Era* in Washington DC. This newspaper, along with his career in public life, led him to a series of public offices. The first of these came in 1877 when President Rutherford B. Hayes appointed him U.S. Marshal for the District of Columbia. Until about two years before his death, other offices ranged from the Recorder of Deeds in Washington, DC, to the minister-resident and consul-general to the Republic of Haiti.

FURTHER RESOURCES

Books

Douglass, Frederick. *Narrative and Life of Frederick Douglass, An American Slave: Written by Himself.* New Haven: Yale University Press, 2001.

Bender, Thomas. *The Antislavery Debate: Capitalism and Abolitionism as a Problem in Historical Interpretation.* Berkeley: University of California Press, 1992.

Periodicals

Sweeney, Fionnghuala. "The Republic of Letters: Frederick Douglass, Ireland, and the Irish Narratives." *Eire-Ireland: A Journal of Irish Studies* (Spring-Summer 2001): 47–65.

Web sites

National Park Service. "The Life of Frederick Douglass." <http://www.nps.gov/frdo/fdlife.htm> (accessed April 18, 2006).

A British View on America's Slave Trade

Book excerpt

By: The British and Foreign Anti-Slavery Society

Date: May 10, 1853

Source: British and Foreign Anti-Slavery Society. *Fourteenth Annual Report of the British and Foreign Anti-Slavery Society.* London: British and Foreign Anti-Slavery Society, 1853.

About the Author: The British and Foreign Anti-Slavery Society formed on April 17, 1839, with the aim of abolishing slavery throughout the world. It grew out of the Society for Mitigating and Gradually Abolishing Slavery throughout the British Dominions, created in 1823. The society initially focused on slavery in British India and Ceylon. After 1850, it focused on abolishing slavery in the United States.

INTRODUCTION

Early British abolitionists inveighed against the slave trade, not slavery itself. While they viewed the institution as evil because of the human horrors and the moral degradation associated with it, they argued that if the supply of slaves were halted, then the value of the slave would be increased and the planters in the British colonies would be obliged to treat slaves more humanely.

Supporters of slavery countered with an economic argument: Planters needed a ready supply of slave labor in the colonies to ensure that they could provide England with much-needed raw materials. In addition, British national interests would be seriously damaged unless all nations—including France, Spain, and other slave-owning rivals—emancipated their slaves at the same time. To that end, the British government tried to negotiate with other European nations to suppress the slave trade, but it was unsuccessful.

In addition to such setbacks, abolitionists realized that simply ending the slave trade would do little to better the life of the average British slave. This led to the creation of the Society for Mitigating and Gradually Abolishing Slavery Throughout the British Dominion.

Great Britain ended its slave trade in 1807 and abolished slavery in the British Empire with the Emancipation Act of August 29, 1833. British abolitionists then turned their energies to slavery in Europe and the United States. Americans finally abolished slavery in 1865 with the Thirteenth Amendment to the Constitution.

■ PRIMARY SOURCE

In the history of great questions there are seasons when those who are engaged in the advocacy of a catholic principle, are especially required to take a retrospect of the cause they are advocating.

The present is one of the most momentous periods in the annals of the Abolition movement. The public mind has never been so thoroughly alive to the magnitude of the evils of Slavery, nor has a more favourable opportunity ever presented itself of directing public opinion, in the full force of its mighty power, against this gigantic inquiry.

With especial reference, however, to the present healthy tone of general sentiment on the subject of Slavery, your Committee would recur with satisfaction to the past labours of those eminent individuals in this country and in America, and of the earlier associations which they originated, through whose instrumentality public attention was first powerfully directed to this subject. Your Committee would remind you of a time when the Slave-trade was not illegal, and when Slavery was a domestic institution in many of our colonies—when the principal maritime powers of Europe, with Great Britain at their head—the United States of America and the other countries of that immense continent and the colonies adjacent, were extensively engaged in the abominable traffic in human beings; when scarcely any portion of its

Engraving of an anti-slavery public meeting held in 1842 in Exeter Hall, London, by the African Civilization Society. © CORBIS.

mainland, or of the beautiful islands that fringe its coasts, and in which Europeans were settled, were unpolluted with Slavery; when nearly the whole of our imports of sugar, rice, tobacco, coffee and indigo, were the produce of Slave-labour; and when the public sentiment of this country was as opposed to the abolition of the Slave-trade and of Slavery, as it is now unanimous in condemnation of both. Your committee would next revert to the efforts which at that early period were made by a few earnest-minded men, to create a sound public opinion on these subjects, and stimulate it to stem the torrent of iniquity, that had already disfigured so fair a portion of the earth, and threatened rapidly to overspread contiguous territories. At first these efforts met with but indifferent success. Arrayed against them, in formidable combination, and goaded into the most resolute opposition by the powerful party whose interests were supposed to be identified with the continuance of Slavery, were the parliament, the clergy, the Press, and even the People. All of these had to be enlightened, and converted to the cause of the slave: a process which was found extremely slow, and

was oftentimes discouraging. It required, indeed, half a century of patient and indefatigable labour. But the national conscience was at length aroused, and the work was done—England renounced the Slave-Trade and Slavery.

Your committee, however, whilst dwelling on this grand moral triumph, would emphatically remind you, that notwithstanding the unwearied efforts of the Abolitionists, and their co-adjutors, to awaken the public opinion of this country to a sense of the enormous iniquities of Slave-holding, little real progress was made in this direction, until the principle was asserted of immediate and unconditional emancipation, on the ground that "Slavery is a sin and a crime before God." This doctrine it was that first startled the conscience of the nation. It smote its ear as an unbearable reproach on a professing Christian people, and aroused the religious feelings of the community. It led to investigation; conviction speedily followed. In vain Slavery asserted the rights of property in defiance of the laws of God. Such rights were indignantly denied to exist, when that property meant man: and thus, the principle that man cannot hold property in man, became the corner-stone of the Abolition movement.

The greatly improved state of public opinion, which resulted from the maintenance of this principle, finally led to the extinction of Slavery in the British colonies. Many of the northern States of the American Union had, indeed, already set a worthy example in this respect, and the odious institution would probably have been rapidly abolished throughout the entire federation, had not the value of slave-labour become greatly enhanced, by the extraordinary demand that unexpectedly arose for the chief products of that labour, and had not the monetary interest concerned in the support of Slavery been enabled, in consequence, to trample upon the greater interests of humanity. It is, nevertheless, encouraging to reflect, that the northern limit of Slavery in the American Union was finally fixed by an Act of Congress, so that in one direction at last, its area is circumscribed. Mexico, and the smaller republics of South America, also, from the first recognized the right of the slave to emancipation. In these States it no longer exists, or is in rapid process of extinction. It was, subsequently, abolished in the small island of St. Bartholomew, belonging to the King of Denmark, whilst in 1847 an act was passed for the emancipation of the slaves in the Danish West India Islands; though it is to be lamented that the labouring population has since been subjected to a code of regulations of a semi-slavery character. The following year the then Provisional Government of France gave immediate freedom to 300,0000 slaves in her colonial dependencies, and there is some reason to hope that Portugal will speedily banish Slavery from her Indian and African possessions. In the Dutch colonies it still exists; but the question of emancipation is occupying the attention of the home and colonial authorities, and will, it is expected, soon be officially discussed, with a view to its final adjustment. Thus, the principal territories in which this unrighteous system is now firmly maintained, on any very extended scale, are the Southern States of the American Union, Brazil, and a few minor States of South America, the Spanish colonies of Cuba and Porto [sic] Rico, and to a limited extent, in the colonies belonging to Holland. In all of these, the entire number of human beings held in bondage does not fall short of eight millions, thus distributed:—in the American Slave States, three million, three hundred thousand; in Brazil, about the same number; in the Spanish colonies probably above half a million; in the Dutch colonies, and the Portuguese settlements, about two hundred and fifty thousand; the remainder being spread over the South American Republics, and other territories. . . .

Your Committee would next refer to the Address they have recently issued, calling the attention of Christians of all denominations in the United Kingdom, and especially of Christian ministers, to the position of the American churches, and of the principal religious associations of the United States, with reference to the monstrous evil which they are cherishing in their midst. Upwards of five thousand copies of this Address, with a Statistical Appendix, have been distributed amongst the various religious denominations in the United Kingdom and the ministers connected with them. This measure has been attended with the most encouraging results. Resolutions have been founded upon them, and passed unanimously in public meetings and congregational gatherings, and earnest appeals to corresponding denominations in America have been adopted, and forwarded to your Committee, to be transmitted to the United States. The subject has also been adverted to at the annual meetings of some of our religious and benevolent associations, and public attention has thus been forcibly directed to the monstrous anomaly existing in America, of professedly Christian ministers openly defending the abomination of slavery, as a Divine institution, or observing upon the subject a scarcely less culpable silence. Towards such individuals as are identified with so deplorable a state of things, the religious sentiment of this country has suggested thee observance of a line of conduct which, it is hoped, may prove alike a solemn rebuke and a significant warning.

And here your committee would advert to the strenuous efforts which the slave-power in the United States is making to consolidate the iniquitous institution, against which public opinion is now so thoroughly aroused. Not only have several of the States passed new and most oppressive laws, involving the liberties and the rights of the free coloured population . . .Jamaica, however, pursues her career of disaster and decay, without making any visible efforts at self-improvement. Possessing within herself, every clement of wealth, nothing seems wanting to secure her commercial prosperity, but that whilst claiming aid from the mother country, she should assume the initiative in those measures which are essential to her welfare, and which includes the emendation of her vicious constitution, and a more economical expenditure. Unfortunately, Jamaica has been made to represent the British West Indies, and her actual condition is pointed at by slave-holders, as proof of the failure of Negro Emancipation. Her own mismanagement however, consequent on the non-residence of her proprietors, has reduced her to a position of comparatively small importance; her export of sugar being now far below that of the small island of Barbadoes.

Your Committee regret to have their attention still directed to attempts on the part of some of the colonial Legislatures to pass laws oppressive in their operation on the labouring classes, and measures to effect immigration, and to control the immigrants, which are of a most objectionable character. Your committee, however, will continue to watch this subject, and strenuously oppose the introduction of any measures likely to interfere with the just rights of the emancipated classes, or to retard their religious and social advancement....

Your committee would here refer, with much satisfaction, to those noble Addresses from the Women of England to the Women of America, on the subject of American Slavery, which have recently been presented to an eminent lady, now sojourning in this country, and who has kindly undertaken to lay them before her country-women.—To those distinguished personages who originated this expression of womanly sentiment, especially to Her Grace the Duchess of Sutherland, and to the Earl of Shaftesbury; and to those ladies who so gracefully seconded their efforts, and were instrumental in procuring the large number of nearly six hundred thousand signatures, a special tribute is due. When those whom a kind Providence has so highly favoured, are thus forward in promoting good works, oppressed humanity has reason to hope that the day of its deliverance is at hand.

But although your Committee have reason to be grateful for the large measure of success with which their labours have been crowned hitherto, the desperate efforts which the Slave power in America is making to extend and perpetuate the hateful institution of Slavery, demands increased watchfulness, and unabated exertion on the part of your Society. If it be objected that Slavery has been removed from British soil, and therefore it is not our province to interfere, in order to effect its eradication in foreign lands, the emphatic reply is; that no civilized nation can remain unaffected by a system, which, though operating afar off, brings disgrace on civilization; and that no professedly Christian community can view the perpetration of an enormous iniquity by another people professing the same religion, without feeling that their common faith is outraged and scandalized. Your Committee, therefore assert, that for the credit of civilization, for the welfare of humanity, and for the honour and the interests of Religion, we are bound to employ all moral and pacific means to extirpate that unrighteous system, which so long as it exists inflicts the foulest outrage upon them all. But your society can only hope to achieve this great object, through the same pubic opinion, which, in modern times, has been found so potent to accomplish the mightiest changes, and which, sustained by correct religious sentiment, has proved irresistible. Looking, therefore, to the influence of public opinion, as the chief means by which Slavery is to be abolished, yet fully alive to the extreme difficulty of impressing society at large, with the sense of the importance and efficacy of a simultaneous demonstration of sentiment on this question, your committee have hailed with heartfelt satisfaction, the appearance of those noble

works which are identified with the name of Harriet Beecher Stowe, works which by their intrinsic excellence and truthfulness have deservedly achieved a success unprecedented in the annals of literature, and aroused a universal spirit of opposition to Slavery, that they trust will not again slumber, until this monster iniquity shall be utterly suppressed. For having accomplished this so effectually and in so eminently a Christian spirit, the cause of the slave owes Harriet Beecher Stowe a deep debt of gratitude, which the emancipated generations of a degraded and despised people now held in ignominious bondage will repay with unnumbered blessings, whilst cherishing, as household words, her works and her name in their hearts....

SIGNIFICANCE

The British and Foreign Anti-Slavery Society remains in existence because slavery remains in existence even at the millennium. By the 1890s, the members of the society had focused their energies on the ill treatment of indigenous peoples. In 1909, the society merged with the Aborigines's Protection Society to form the Anti-Slavery and Aborigines' Protection Society. In 1990, the organization became Anti-Slavery International (ASI).

ASI addresses slavery, forced and bonded labor, child labor, and the trafficking of human beings, abuses that can be found around the world. Chattel slavery, or the sale and ownership of one person by another, exists in the Sudan and Mauritania. In India, Pakistan, and Nepal, children are forcibly employed in the handmade woolen carpet industry. In Iraq, women and girls have been abducted and forced to work as sex slaves. In the United States, female immigrants from Latin America and Asia have been forced into prostitution. In African countries torn by civil war, children are routinely forced to serve as soldiers.

Despite widespread evidence of bondage around the world, slavery fails to ignite major protests such as those sparked by globalization. The United Nations has formed a Working Group on Contemporary Forms of Slavery, but most people in developed nations continue to regard slavery as an issue that was resolved in the nineteenth century.

FURTHER RESOURCES
Books
Miers, Suzanne. *Britain and the Ending of the Slave Trade*. London: Longman, 1975.

Temperley, Howard. *British Antislavery, 1833–1870*. London: Longman, 1972.

Web sites

Anti-Slavery International. "The History of Anti-Slavery International." April 20, 2006. <http://www.antislavery.org/homepage/antislavery/history.htm> (accessed May 1, 2006).

Slaveholding Not Sinful

Slavery, the Punishment of Man's Sin, its Remedy, the Gospel of Christ

Book excerpt

By: Samuel Blanchard How

Date: 1856

Source: How, Samuel Blanchard. *Slaveholding Not Sinful: Slavery, the Punishment of Man's Sin, its Remedy, the Gospel of Christ.* New Brunswick, N.J.: J. Terhune's Press, 1856.

About the Author: Samuel Blanchard How served as the head of the Grammar School at Dickinson College in Carlisle, Pennsylvania and later became it's president in 1830, serving through 1832. A minister as well as an educator, How served in churches in Savannah, Georgia from 1823–1829 and in the First Dutch Reformed Church in New Brunswick, New Jersey, from 1832–1861.

INTRODUCTION

Pro-slavery arguments in the Ante-bellum South of the United States centered largely on economic, racial, and religious issues. Economic arguments examined the need for labor for cash crops such as cotton and tobacco; such labor-intensive crops needed a ready supply of cheap labor, and pro-slavery arguments focused on the potential collapse of the southern economy should slavery be abolished. In addition, as Chancelor Harper notes in his 1860 essay "Slavery in the Light of Social Ethics," "Our slavery has not only given existence to millions of slaves within our own territories, it has given the means of subsistence, and therefore, existence, to millions of freemen in our confederate States; enabling them to send forth their swarms to overspread the plains and forests of the West, and appear as the harbingers of civilization." Slavery, according to Harper, granted other men freedom, enabling white men to fulfill the principle of Manifest Destiny.

Racial prejudice and paternalism emerged as an argument, shored up by pseudoscientific arguments, such as those based on physiognomy, in which the character and/or intelligence of a person or race allegedly could be determined by physical characteristics. Richard H. Colfax, in his 1833 book *Evidence Against the Views of the Abolitionists, Consisting of Physical and Moral Proofs, of the Natural Inferiority of the Negroes,* applies physiognomy to the discussion of African facial characteristics—and the moral conclusions that result—in the following passage: "His lips are thick, his zygomatic muscles, large and full* (*"These muscles are always in action during laughter and the extreme enlargement of them indicates a low mind." Lavater)—his jaws large and projecting,—his chin retreating,—his forehead low, flat and slanting, and (as a consequence of this latter character,) his eyeballs are very prominent,—apparently larger than those of white men;—all of these peculiarities at the same time contributing to reduce his facial angle almost to a level with that of the brute—Can any such man become great or elevated?"

Colfax's viewpoint was shared by many who accepted physiognomy to be an accurate method for understanding a person's or a race's moral character and intellectual capabilities. The forerunner to eugenics, physiognomy-based arguments were used to legitimize slavery; if slaves were "brutes," then providing hard labor in exchange for food and housing, went the owners' arguments, was the slave's rightful role in society.

The biblical argument for slavery was the third primary message that pro-slavery activists used in arguing for the institution of slavery. Ministers in churches in the southern United States used biblical passages that refer directly to slavery as a defense against abolitionists; if the *Bible* gives specific rules for treatment of slaves and punishments, they asked, how can slavery be wrong?

In the excerpt below, Samuel Blanchard How, a minister in the First Dutch Reformed Church in New Brunswick, New Jersey, writes about the biblical argument that justifies slavery.

■ PRIMARY SOURCE

Mr. President: Two principal objections have been made against receiving into our Church the Classis of North Carolina. The first objection is, that if we do so, we shall destroy the peace of our Church, and introduce among ourselves distraction and division by the agitation of the slavery question. The second objection is, that slaveholding is a sin, and that therefore, we ought not to admit slaveholders into our Church. I shall attempt, first of all, to show that slaveholding is not a sin, and that therefore, there is no reason to exclude slaveholders, simply because they are slaveholders,

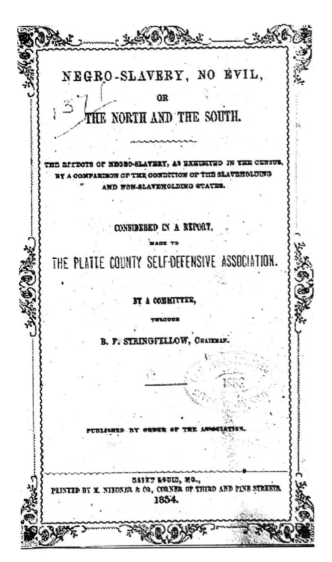

The title page of "Negro Slavery, No Evil; or the North and the South," a pro-slavery pamphlet published in 1854. © CORBIS.

from union and communion with us. If this is established, then both objections necessarily fail: for it would be alike absurd and wicked to disturb the peace of the Church for that which the Scriptures teach us is not a sin, and which was no bar to church-fellowship with the Apostles of Christ.

1. The Holding of a slave not a sin.

It has been said that "American Slavery is at war with the Declaration of Independence, the Constitution of the United States, natural justice, and Christianity—that slavery is a sin against God and a crime against man, etc." To these bold statements we reply, that the mass of the American people have never considered the holding of slaves as at war with the Declaration of Independence; that the Supreme Court of the Nation has declared that it is

not against the Constitution of the United States; and that it is not against natural justice and Christianity, we shall now endeavor to prove. We admit that it is an evil much to be lamented, but we deny that it is a sin against God and a crime against man.

As I am addressing the Supreme Ecclesiastical Court of the Reformed Protestant Dutch Church, my final appeal shall be to the Holy Scriptures as the inspired world of God, the only infallible and perfect rule of right and wrong, truth and error, in matters of religious faith and duty. We all profess to believe that "the law and the testimony of God" are the standard of duty and the rule of faith, and that if any "speak not according to this word, it is because there is no light in them."

That the holding of slaves is not a sin we prove from the following passages of Scripture:

> 1. 1 Tim. 6: 1–5: "Let as many servants as are under the yoke count their own masters worthy of all honor, that the name of God and his doctrine be not blasphemed. And they that have believing masters, let them not despise them, because they are brethren; but rather do them service, because they are faithful and beloved, partakers of the benefit. These things teach and exhort. If any man teach otherwise, and consent not to wholesome words, even the words of our Lord Jesus Christ, and to the doctrine which is according to godliness; he is proud, knowing nothing, but doting about questions and strifes of words, whereof cometh envy, strife, railings, evil surmising, perverse disputings of men of corrupt minds, and destitute of the truth, supposing that gain is godliness: from such withdraw thyself."

We begin with the New Testament to obviate an objection that might be urged if we should begin with the Old Testament, that the Christian dispensation has greater light and freedom and privileges than were enjoyed under the Jewish dispensation, and that therefore, though slavery might have lawfully existed under the latter, that can not be pleaded in favor of its existing under the former. Our endeavor will be to show that they both entirely agree on the point before us.

The term "servants" in this passage of sacred Scripture is in the original Greek *"douloi"* the primary meaning of which, Robinson in his Greek and English Lexicon of the New Testament, gives as "a bondsman, slave, servant, pr. By birth; diff. from *andrapodon*, one enslaved in war."—He says: "In a family the *doulos* was one *bound to serve, a slave,* and was the property of his master, 'a living possession,' as Aristotle calls him."—Schleusner gives as the meaning of the term—1. proprie: servus, minister, *homo non liber, nec sui juris et opponitur aleutheros,* that is, "its first and proper signification is that of a slave, a serving man, a man who is not free and at his own disposal."

But to put his meaning beyond doubt, the Apostle adds the words, "under *the yoke,*" which is an emblem of servitude or of the rule to which any one is subject. He here unquestionably speaks of slaves who are under bondage to their maters. Bloomfield says: "The commentators are not sufficiently aware of the strength of this expression, in which there is a blending of two expressions to put the case in its strongest point of view (supposing even the harshest bondage) in order to make the injunction to obedience the more forcible." These slaves the Apostle commands to "count their own masters, whether heathen or Christians or Jews, worthy of all honor," and the reason that he gives for this is, "that the name of God and his doctrine be not blasphemed." It was lawful by the law of Moses, to make of the heathen bondmen for life, and to hold their children in bondage. But not so with one who was born a Jew. He was permitted to serve only for six years, and it is quite possible that there were some false teachers who asserted that, as no Jew was to remain a slave for life, so ought no Christian.

This sentiment, if it had prevailed among those slaves who were Christians, would have caused them to despise and hate their masters, and to withhold from them the respect and obedience which they owed to them. They would thus bring a reproach on the Gospel as if it were a doctrine that taught men contempt for their superiors, and disobedience to their lawful commands. From speaking of the duty which slaves owe to their masters in general, the Apostle passes on to speak to those who have believing masters who are their brethren in Christ. Here the questions whether the holding of slaves is a sin, and whether we should hold Christian communion with slaveholders, are fairly met. Does the Apostle then teach the slaves that they ought to be free? that their Christian masters sin in holding them in bondage? and does he, with apostolic authority and in the name of Jesus Christ, command the masters to give them their freedom? He does nothing of the kind. He not only does not require these Christian masters to set their slaves at liberty, but he speaks of them as "faithful and beloved" brethren, "partakers of the benefit," and for this very reason he exhorts Christian slaves not to despise them, but rather to do them service. It seems impossible for the question before us to be more fully and directly settled. But the Apostle proceeds further. He says that "if any man teach, otherwise," that is, if there is any Abolitionist among you, and Immediate Emancipationist, who says that no Christian can, without sin, hold a slave; that if he holds any, he is bound in duty immediately to liberate them, and if he does not, then true Christians are bound to refuse church-fellowship and communion with him lest they should partake of his sin—if any man teach these things, then he does "not consent to wholesome words, even the words of our Lord Jesus

Christ, and to the doctrine which is according to godliness." This we should suppose would have been a sufficient rebuke. But to show the criminality of the doctrine of these early Abolitionists in the Christian church, the Apostle proceeds to say, that he who teaches their doctrine "is proud, knowing nothing, but doting about questions and strifes of words, whereof cometh envy, strife, railings, evil surmisings, perverse disputings of men of corrupt minds, and destitute of the truth, supposing that gain is godliness." He, then, is a most marked manner, shows the falseness and danger of their sentiments by commanding Timothy, "from such withdraw thyself," that is, hold no intercourse with them. We shall not inquire how far this precept extends, nor whether it is a prohibition against holding church communion with Abolitionists; nor whether the Apostle does not mean to teach us that their sentiments are so revolutionary, so subversive of the established order of society, so calculated to produce discontent and resentment in the minds of the slaves as to endanger not only public but domestic peace and safety, and to produce by stirring up the slaves to insurrection, massacres and horrors, like those of the Massacres of St. Domingo, in the year 1790. Certain it is, that he commands us to withdraw from them.

SIGNIFICANCE

How's work, published in 1856 and delivered before an audience at the General Synod of the German Reformed Church in 1855, was controversial. While his comments were not original arguments, it was his choice to deliver such a message in the North, where abolitionist thought dominated that was surprising. How's pro-slavery views may have been shaped by his six years as a minister in Georgia in the 1820s, though he was born and raised in the North, and spent most of his life there. Regardless, How pushed conventional standards with the delivery of a pro-slavery speech in the North and later the publication of such a message just a few years before the start of the Civil War (1861–1865).

Certain passages from the Old and New Testaments of the *Bible* were popular and quoted frequently in pro-slavery arguments. Writers used 1 Tim. 6: 1–5, which How uses above, as well as Luke 12:45–48, which not only specifically describes slavery as an institution, but also discusses a slave's whipping: "The lord [owner] of that servant will come in a day when he looketh not for him, and at an hour when he is not aware, and will cut him in sunder, and will appoint him his portion with the unbelievers. And that servant, which knew his lord's will, and prepared not himself, neither did according to his will, shall be beaten with many stripes. But he that knew not, and did commit things worthy of stripes, shall be beaten with few stripes. For unto whomsoever much is given, of him shall be much required: and to whom men have committed much, of him they will ask the more." In passages such as these pro-slavery lecturers, ministers, and writers found justification for slavery itself, slave conditions, terms of use, and punishments.

Abolitionists roundly criticized the use of the *Bible* to build the case for slavery, pointing instead to such passages as Exodus 21:16: "And he that stealeth a man, and selleth him, or if he be found in his hand, he shall surely be put to death." The "man stealers" were defined by abolitionists as being involved in human slavery, and the death sentence a sign of the Bible's rejection of human bondage.

Abolitionists and pro-slavery activists alike used different sections of the *Bible* to suit each side's rhetorical needs. How's remarks were directed at his church's decision whether to include a North Carolinian congregation. How's audience confronted the question: if slavery were a sin, could the General Synod reasonably welcome sinners into their fold? Although the very close vote favored inclusion of the North Carolina Classis of the German Reformed Church, the North Carolinians withdrew their request as a result of the discord and conflict between churches with slaveholders and those with abolitionists, just six years before north/south divisions would erupt into civil war.

FURTHER RESOURCES
Books

Bolokitten, Oliver, Esq. (pseudonym). *A Sojourn in the City of Amalgamation.* New York: self-published, 1835.

Colfax, Richard H. *Evidence Against the Views of the Abolitionists, Consisting of Physical and Moral Proofs, of the Natural Inferiority of the Negroes.* New York: James T. M. Bleakley Publishers, 1833.

Horton, James Oliver and Lois E. Horton. *Slavery and the Making of America.* New York: Oxford University Press, 2004.

Hosmer, William. *Slavery and the Church.* New York: W. J. Moses, 1853.

Link, William A. *Roots of Secession: Slavery and Politics in Antebellum Virginia (Civil War America).* Chapel Hill, NC: University of North Carolina Press, 2005.

The Emancipation Proclamation

Declaration

By: Abraham Lincoln

Date: 1863

Source: Lincoln, Abraham. "The Emancipation Proclamation." U.S. National Archives and Records Administration, 1863.

About the Author: Abraham Lincoln (1809–1865) rose to prominence as an attorney and orator whose hallmark was his opposition to slavery. Lincoln helped to found the Republican Party, and in 1860 he was that party's presidential candidate. At the time, the United States was deeply divided over the issues of state's rights and slavery. When Lincoln won the presidential election, many slave-holding Southern states that believed strongly in state' rights responded by seceding from the United States to form a new country. The result was the U.S. Civil War (1861–1865). Lincoln is renowned for successfully guiding the United States to victory in that conflict, as well as the wisdom and humanity he displayed while in office. Shortly after the end of the war, Lincoln was shot by a symphatizer with the Southern cause. He died on April 15, 1865.

INTRODUCTION

During the Hartford Convention in December 1814 and January 1815, the word "secession" was mentioned some forty-six years before the Civil War in the United States. Concerns over the high cost of the War of 1812 weighed heavily on the minds of New Englanders, and New England proposed secession from the Union. By convention's end the New England delegates rejected secession, but thirteen years later, in 1828, South Carolina's Senator John C. Calhoun would utter the word again in his famous arguments against the financial hardships imposed on the south with the Tariff of 1828.

South Carolina became the first state to secede from the Union thirty-three years later, the catalyst in starting the Civil War. Seven states—South Carolina, Mississippi, Florida, Alabama, Georgia, Louisiana, and Texas—broke off initially, later joined by Arkansas, Tennessee, and North Carolina. The eleven states formed the Confederate States of America, led by President Jefferson Davis.

The primary cause of the war was states' rights: did each state have an inherent right to set the laws and

A.A. Lamb's painting "The Emancipation Proclamation" depicts President Lincoln holding the proclamation while a female figure symbolizing emancipation rides past, to the cheers of soldiers and freed slaves. © FRANCIS G. MAYER/CORBIS. REPRODUCED BY PERMISSION.

policies that would govern the behavior of its citizens? Did federal law trump state law? Meanwhile, the continuation of the slave society of the south, where labor demands were met by ownership and use of slaves of African ancestry, generated civil rights questions for abolitionists. What rights did human beings have? Was skin color a determining factor in retaining—or removing—natural rights as human beings? Were slaves of African ancestry worth less than white owners? If the Constitution counted slaves as three-fifths of a person for House of Representatives districting, but the slaves could not vote, what roles and rights did slaves have in American government and civil society, if any? These rights issues set the stage for secession and war.

On April 12, 1861, just six weeks after President Abraham Lincoln's inauguration, the first battle of the Civil War took place at Fort Sumter; the Confederacy won. As war began, four "slave states" did not secede: Delaware, Kentucky, Maryland, and Missouri remained a part of the Union, in part because President Lincoln used a variety of legal maneuvers, including the suspension of *habeus corpus*, to force these border states to remain within the Union. While Lincoln had promised

not to abolish slavery in slave states during his campaign for the presidency, in spite of his personal belief in freedom for slaves, his commitment to the Union was stronger than his belief in states' rights.

In 1861, Congress passed an act stating that all slaves employed against the union were to be freed, and in 1862 a similar act, freeing slaves of men who supported the Confederacy, passed Congress as well. By 1863, with strong support in the north for abolition, Lincoln wrote and published The Emancipation Proclamation.

■ PRIMARY SOURCE

By the President of the United States of America: A Proclamation
Whereas, on the twenty-second day of September, in the year of our Lord one thousand eight hundred and sixty-two, a proclamation was issued by the President of the United States, containing, among other things, the following, to wit:

"That on the first day of January, in the year of our Lord one thousand eight hundred and sixty-three, all persons held as slaves within any State or designated part of a

State, the people whereof shall then be in rebellion against the United States, shall be then, thenceforward, and forever free; and the Executive Government of the United States, including the military and naval authority thereof, will recognize and maintain the freedom of such persons, and will do no act or acts to repress such persons, or any of them, in any efforts they may make for their actual freedom.

"That the Executive will, on the first day of January aforesaid, by proclamation, designate the States and parts of States, if any, in which the people thereof, respectively, shall then be in rebellion against the United States; and the fact that any State, or the people thereof, shall on that day be, in good faith, represented in the Congress of the United States by members chosen thereto at elections wherein a majority of the qualified voters of such State shall have participated, shall, in the absence of strong countervailing testimony, be deemed conclusive evidence that such State, and the people thereof, are not then in rebellion against the United States."

Now, therefore I, Abraham Lincoln, President of the United States, by virtue of the power in me vested as Commander-in-Chief, of the Army and Navy of the United States in time of actual armed rebellion against the authority and government of the United States, and as a fit and necessary war measure for suppressing said rebellion, do, on this first day of January, in the year of our Lord one thousand eight hundred and sixty-three, and in accordance with my purpose so to do publicly proclaimed for the full period of one hundred days, from the day first above mentioned, order and designate as the States and parts of States wherein the people thereof respectively, are this day in rebellion against the United States, the following, to wit:

Arkansas, Texas, Louisiana, (except the Parishes of St. Bernard, Plaquemines, Jefferson, St. John, St. Charles, St. James Ascension, Assumption, Terrebonne, Lafourche, St. Mary, St. Martin, and Orleans, including the City of New Orleans) Mississippi, Alabama, Florida, Georgia, South Carolina, North Carolina, and Virginia, (except the forty-eight counties designated as West Virginia, and also the counties of Berkley, Accomac, Northampton, Elizabeth City, York, Princess Ann, and Norfolk, including the cities of Norfolk and Portsmouth[)], and which excepted parts, are for the present, left precisely as if this proclamation were not issued.

And by virtue of the power, and for the purpose aforesaid, I do order and declare that all persons held as slaves within said designated States, and parts of States, are, and henceforward shall be free; and that the Executive government of the United States, including the military and naval

authorities thereof, will recognize and maintain the freedom of said persons.

And I hereby enjoin upon the people so declared to be free to abstain from all violence, unless in necessary self-defence; and I recommend to them that, in all cases when allowed, they labor faithfully for reasonable wages.

And I further declare and make known, that such persons of suitable condition, will be received into the armed service of the United States to garrison forts, positions, stations, and other places, and to man vessels of all sorts in said service.

And upon this act, sincerely believed to be an act of justice, warranted by the Constitution, upon military necessity, I invoke the considerate judgment of mankind, and the gracious favor of Almighty God.

In witness whereof, I have hereunto set my hand and caused the seal of the United States to be affixed.

Done at the City of Washington, this first day of January, in the year of our Lord one thousand eight hundred and sixty three, and of the Independence of the United States of America the eighty-seventh.

By the President: ABRAHAM LINCOLN

WILLIAM H. SEWARD, Secretary of State.

SIGNIFICANCE

Misinterpretation of The Emancipation Proclamation is common; the document did not free all slaves. Only those slaves held in areas under rebellion as of January 1, 1863, were freed by Lincoln; ironically, some slaves in southern rebel areas under Union control were not free. Lincoln exempted the four border slave states, Tennessee, forty-eight counties in Virginia that later became West Virginia, and portions of New Orleans as well.

Initially, slave owners ignored the terms of The Emancipation Proclamation, and word of the declaration spread slowly among slaves. As the union army gained control over more lands, waves of slaves were freed gradually. Many detractors stated that the proclamation was too timid and applied only to those areas not under Union control in places where Lincoln had no power. As the news spread among slaves, however, abolitionists hoped that slaves would have a stake in ending the war and helping the Union to victory. By offering "that such persons of suitable condition, will be received into the armed service of the United States to garrison forts, positions, stations, and other places, and to man vessels of all sorts in said service" Lincoln issued a direct call to

A group of African American men, former slaves freed by the Civil War and its aftermath, gather to look for work at a harbor. U.S. SIGNAL CORPS, NATIONAL ARCHIVES AND RECORDS ADMINISTRATION

action to slaves—and more than 200,000 took him up on his offer.

By war's end, four million slaves were freed, with a combined financial value of over $3 billion. Property seized by the Union when secession occurred led to massive property transfers—goods, land, farm equipment, and houses. British support for the South vanished; although the British textile industry suffered without Southern cotton, British support for abolition was stronger.

Lincoln campaigned in 1864 on the promise to push through a constitutional amendment giving slaves their freedom. Fearful of a Supreme Court reversal of the proclamation, Lincoln made plans in April 1865, as the war ended, to give former slaves the right to vote. In his last official speech before his death, President Lincoln announced on April 11, 1865, his intention to enfranchise former slaves. John Wilkes Booth, an actor, was in the audience that day; three days later he assassinated Lincoln in Ford's Theater.

The Thirteenth Amendment to the Constitution, which outlawed slavery, was ratified by twenty-seven of the thirty-six states on December 6, 1865, nearly eight months after Lincoln's death. The amendment

was not formally ratified by the state of Mississippi, the last of the thirty-six states in existence in 1865, until 1995.

FURTHER RESOURCES

Books

Foote, Shelby. *The Civil War: A Narrative*. New York: Vintage Books USA, 1986.

Goodwin, Doris Kearns. *Team of Rivals: The Political Genius of Abraham Lincoln*. New York: Simon & Shuster, 2005.

Guelzo, Allen C. *Lincoln's Emancipation Proclamation: The End of Slavery*. New York: Simon & Shuster, 2004.

Thirteenth Amendment

Legislation

By: U.S. Congress

Date: January 31, 1865

Source: U.S. Congress. Thirteenth Amendment to the Constitution of the United States, 1865. Available online at <http://www.ourdocuments.gov/> (accessed May 1, 2006).

About the Author: The thirty-eighth Congress passed the Thirteenth Amendment in January 1865. President Abraham Lincoln submitted the proposed amendment to the states for ratification on February 1, 1865. By December 6, 1865, the necessary number of states had ratified the amendment.

INTRODUCTION

The North American colonies of the seventeenth and eighteenth centuries, as well as the new American nation during its first century, relied on a complex system of labor that included slaves. Manual labor, supplied by hired hands, owners, children, indentured servants, and slaves, fueled economic development and allowed not only for cash crops to be exported to European colonial powers (and later, equal trading partners), but for societies to form and flourish in both the northern and southern sections of the United States.

By the mid-1700s, the southern colonies of Georgia, North Carolina, and South Carolina, as well as areas such as Mississippi, Alabama, and Florida, relied on slave labor for cash crops such as cotton, indigo, and tobacco. In the South, the transition from a "society with slaves" to a "slave society," in which slave labor provided more than fifty percent of all labor, stood in stark contrast to the North, which, by the third decade of the nineteenth century, had embraced industrialization and relied on a wage labor system and industrial export for economic growth.

Government policies and legislative maneuvers, including an 1828 tariff that helped the northern manufacturing economy (while hurting southern planters), the 1846 Wilmot Proviso, which attempted to ban slavery in Texas before its inclusion in the United States, and the ongoing battle over new states admitted to the Union and their "slave" vs. "free" status, opened the wedge between the North and the South.

This division set the stage for Civil War from 1861–1865. Abolitionists had been fighting against slavery for decades; the four million slaves of African ancestry in the South represented more than one-third the total population, and southern owners feared massive uprisings if slaves were granted any rights, however nominal. President Abraham Lincoln had campaigned in 1860 on a platform that sought to bridge the two positions; no new slave states, but slavery could remain in existing slave states. Six weeks into his new administration the first battle of the Civil War broke out at Fort Sumter. By the end of the war, over

580,000 men had died, and the Union emerged victorious, though the United States of America remained fractured.

President Lincoln had freed slaves in rebel-controlled areas with his 1863 Emancipation Proclamation; before his assassination on April 13, 1865 he had expressed the need for a constitutional amendment to free all slaves. The Thirteenth Amendment was ratified on December 6, 1865.

■ PRIMARY SOURCE

AMENDMENT XIII

Section 1. Neither slavery nor involuntary servitude, except as a punishment for crime whereof the party shall have been duly convicted, shall exist within the United States, or any place subject to their jurisdiction.

Section 2. Congress shall have power to enforce this article by appropriate legislation.

■

SIGNIFICANCE

The Thirteenth Amendment nullified a wide range of state laws as well as Supreme Court decisions, including the 1857 Supreme Court decision *Dred Scott v. Sanford*, in which Chief Justice Roger B. Taney wrote in the court's majority opinion: "In the opinion of the court, the legislation and histories of the times, and the language used in the declaration of independence, show, that neither the class of persons who had been imported as slaves, nor their descendants, whether they had become free or not, were then acknowledged as a part of the people, nor intended to be included in the general words used in that memorable instrument... It is too clear for dispute, that the enslaved African race were not intended to be included, and formed no part of the people who framed and adopted this declaration." Dred Scott was a slave who had lived in a free state, then moved to a slave state; Taney's opinion declared that Scott did not even have the standing to bring suit, as technically the U.S. Constitution did not recognize Scott as a citizen. The Thirteenth Amendment ended slavery, and the Fourteenth Amendment, ratified in 1868, granted direct citizenship to all former slaves. It also required all states to provide equal protection to all people—not just citizens—within their boundaries.

With slavery now illegal and the Civil War ended, the painful process of Reconstruction began for the South. The four million slaves in the former "slave" states made a variety of choices for survival. Some

An engraving showing the celebration of the African American community of Washington, D.C., during the fourth anniversary of the April 19, 1862, law that abolished slavery in the District of Columbia. PHOTO BY MPI/GETTY IMAGES.

stayed on the plantations where they had worked and were hired on as low-paid wage earners, others moved north to find work in factories or at ports, and still others migrated to land that the U.S. government offered to former slaves. Government agencies, such as the Bureau of Refugees, Freedmen and Abandoned Lands, commonly called the Freedmen's Bureau, provided former slaves with food, clothing, and assistance in finding places to settle. The Freedmen's Bureau did not last long; when President Andrew Johnson, a southerner, became president after Lincoln's assassination, much of the Reconstruction that had been planned was dismantled.

Within a decade "black codes" appeared in states, limiting labor options, housing choices, schooling options, and other rights for former slaves. The black codes, over time, evolved into Jim Crow laws, which segregated restaurants, movie houses, hotels, restroom facilities, and neighborhoods in the former slave states.

While the Thirteenth Amendment codified the end of slavery in the United States, society, especially in the South, followed the letter—though not the spirit—of the law.

FURTHER RESOURCES
Books

Jeffrey, Julie Roy. *The Great Silent Army of Abolitionism: Ordinary Women in the Antislavery Movement.* Chapel Hill, N.C.: University of North Carolina Press 1998.

Lerner, Gerda. *The Grimke Sisters from South Carolina: Pioneers for Women's Rights and Abolition.* Chapel Hill, N.C.: University of North Carolina Press 2004.

Mayer, Henry. *All on Fire: William Lloyd Garrison and the Abolition of Slavery.* New York: St. Martin's Griffin, 2000.

Tsesis, Alexander. *The Thirteenth Amendment and American Freedom: A Legal History.* New York: New York University Press, 2004.

League of Nations Convention to Suppress the Slave Trade and Slavery

Declaration

By: League of Nations

Date: September 25, 1926

Source: League of Nations. Convention to Suppress the Slave Trade and Slavery. September 25, 1926. Available online at *Yale Law School*. "The Avalon Project." May 28, 2006. <http://www.yale.edu/lawweb/avalon/league/lea001.htm> (accessed May 29, 2006).

About the Author: The League of Nations formed in 1919 as part of the postwar accords from World War I. U.S. President Woodrow Wilson first presented the idea of the League in his Fourteen Points Speech on January 8, 1918. Wilson initially called his plan The Covenant of the League of Nations, and through his work the League became Section I of the Treaty of Versailles. January 10, 1920 saw the ratification of the treaty, and the official formation of the League of Nations. It first met in Geneva on November 15, 1920, and twenty nations joined. The League was intended to prevent future hostilities through mediation and non-violent intervention, but many countries withdrew from the League and the United States never joined. Scholars note that the United States' failure to join the League caused many countries to withdraw their support for it. After the outbreak of World War II (1939–1945) most saw the League as a failure. It was replaced by the United Nations after the war.

INTRODUCTION

The League of Nations was an outcome of the four years of destruction and the tens of millions of lives lost in Europe during World War One (1914–1918). The Treaty of Versailles was the peace settlement negotiated between the Allied forces and Germany and its allies in 1919 that formally ended the First World War. The treaty contained a specific covenant that provided the basis for the creation of the League of Nations, a group of nations whose primary aim was the prevention of future war through cooperation.

The League of Nations was founded upon four essential principles as set out in the Versailles covenant. The first principle was the notion that independent nation states, as opposed to large colonial empires, would be the desired political entities of the world in this post-war era. Flowing from the nation state concept was the desire among the signatories to the Versailles treaty that open discussions of regional and international issues was far preferable to the secret diplomacy practiced particularly by the Great Powers (England, France, Germany, Russia) prior to 1914.

The Versailles covenant next provided for the elimination of the large military alliances where war might be declared as a reflex action to an ally becoming involved in an armed dispute. It was this complex and rigidly formulated alliance structure that drew so many European countries inexorably into war in 1914. The signatory nations to the Versailles treaty agreed to develop an alternative to the alliance system, through the creation of a more flexible network of international agreements designed to preserve the collective security of its members.

The last of the four cornerstones upon which the League of Nations was constructed was the desire to facilitate international disarmament and to create an international climate where an arms buildup would be discouraged in any League member.

The League of Nations was formally constituted in 1920, when the representatives of forty-one member nations met in Geneva. The President of the United States, Woodrow Wilson (1856–1924), had advocated American participation in the League, and he personally supported the Treaty of Versailles. However, sentiment in the United States at the end of WWI in 1918 was strongly isolationist. In deference to public opinion, the United States Senate would not ratify the Versailles Treaty, thereby excluding the United States from League of Nations membership.

Consumed by its 1917 revolution and the aftermath of that conflict, Russia was never a signatory to the treaty.

The members of the League of Nations also sought to advance a number of broad international social initiatives after 1920. The most far reaching and the most forceful of these efforts was the League's denunciation of the slave trade and slavery. The 1926 Convention to suppress the slave trade and slavery was signed by forty countries; the Convention built upon the historical precedent of 1889-90 Brussels Conference where slavery was repudiated, as well as the investigative report commissioned by the League in 1924.

■ PRIMARY SOURCE

ALBANIA, GERMANY, AUSTRIA, BELGIUM, the BRITISH EMPIRE, CANADA, the COMMONWEALTH OF AUSTRALIA, the UNION OF SOUTH AFRICA, the DOMINION OF NEW ZEALAND, and INDIA, BULGARIA, CHINA,

COLOMBIA, CUBA, DENMARK, SPAIN, ESTONIA, ABYSSINIA, FINLAND, FRANCE, GREECE, ITALY, LATVIA, LIBERIA, LITHUANIA, NORWAY, PANAMA, THE NETHERLANDS, PERSIA, POLAND, PORTUGAL, ROUMANIA, the KINGDOM OF THE SERBS, CROATS AND SLOVENES, SWEDEN, CZECHOSLOVAKIA and URUGUAY,

Whereas the signatories of the General Act of the Brussels Conference of 1889-90 declared that they were equally animated by the firm intention of putting an end to the traffic in African slaves;

Whereas the signatories of the Convention of Saint-Germain-en-Laye of 1919, to revise the General Act of Berlin of 1885, and the General Act and Declaration of Brussels of 1890, affirmed their intention of securing the complete suppression of slavery in all its forms and of the slave trade by land and sea;

Taking into consideration the report of the Temporary Slavery Commission appointed by the Council of the League of Nations on June 12th, 1924;

Desiring to complete and extend the work accomplished under the Brussels Act and to find a means of giving practical effect throughout the world to such intentions as were expressed in regard to slave trade and slavery by the signatories of the Convention of Saint-Germain-en-Laye, and recognising that it is necessary to conclude to that end more detailed arrangements than are contained in that Convention;

Considering, moreover, that it is necessary to prevent forced labour from developing into conditions analogous to slavery,

Have decided to conclude a Convention and have accordingly appointed as their Plenipotentiaries: [here follow the names of 40 envoys, omitted] Who, having communicated their full powers, have agreed as follows:

Article 1.

For the purpose of the present Convention, the following definitions are agreed upon:

1. Slavery is the status or condition of a person over whom any or all of the powers attaching to the right of ownership are exercised.
2. The slave trade includes all acts involved in the capture, acquisition or disposal of a person with intent to reduce him to slavery; all acts involved in the acquisition of a slave with a view to selling or exchanging him; all acts of disposal by sale or exchange of a slave acquired with a view to being sold or exchanged, and, in general, every act of trade or transport in slaves.

Article 2.

The High Contracting Parties undertake, each in respect of the territories placed under its sovereignty, jurisdiction, protection, suzerainty or tutelage, so far as they have not already taken the necessary steps:

(a) To prevent and suppress the slave trade;
(b) To bring about, progressively and as soon as possible, the complete abolition of slavery in all its forms.

Article 3.

The High Contracting Parties undertake to adopt all appropriate measures with a view to preventing and suppressing the embarkation, disembarkation and transport of slaves in their territorial waters and upon all vessels flying their respective flags.

The High Contracting Parties undertake to negotiate as soon as possible a general Convention with regard to the slave trade which will give them rights and impose upon them duties of the same nature as those provided for in the Convention of June 17th, 1925, relative to the International Trade in Arms (Articles 12, 20, 21, 22, 23, 24, and paragraphs 3, 4 and 5 of Section II of Annex II), with the necessary adaptations, it being understood that this general Convention will not place the ships (even of small tonnage) of any High Contracting Parties in a position different from that of the other High Contracting Parties.

It is also understood that, before or after the coming into force of this general Convention the High Contracting Parties are entirely free to conclude between themselves, without, however, derogating from the principles laid down in the preceding paragraph, such special agreements as, by reason of their peculiar situation, might appear to be suitable in order to bring about as soon as possible the complete disappearance of the slave trade.

Article 4.

The High Contracting Parties shall give to one another every assistance with the object of securing the abolition of slavery and the slave trade.

Article 5.

The High Contracting Parties recognise that recourse to compulsory or forced labour may have grave consequences and undertake, each in respect of the territories placed under its sovereignty, jurisdiction, protection, suzerainty or tutelage, to take all necessary measures to prevent compulsory or forced labour from developing into conditions analogous to slavery.

It is agreed that:

1. Subject to the transitional provisions laid down in paragraph (2) below, compulsory or forced labour may only be exacted for public purposes.
2. In territories in which compulsory or forced labour for other than public purposes still survives, the High Contracting Parties shall endeavour progressively and as soon as possible to put an end to the practice.

So long as such forced or compulsory labour exists, this labour shall invariably be of an exceptional character, shall always receive adequate remuneration, and shall not involve the removal of the labourers from their usual place of residence.

3. In all cases, the responsibility for any recourse to compulsory or forced labour shall rest with the competent central authorities of the territory concerned.

Article 6.

Those of the High Contracting Parties whose laws do not at present make adequate provision for the punishment of infractions of laws and regulations enacted with a view to giving effect to the purposes of the present Convention undertake to adopt the necessary measures in order that severe penalties may be imposed in respect of such infractions.

Article 7.

The High Contracting Parties undertake to communicate to each other and to the Secretary-General of the League of Nations any laws and regulations which they may enact with a view to the application of the provisions of the present Convention.

Article 8.

The High Contracting Parties agree that disputes arising between them relating to the interpretation or application of this Convention shall, if they cannot be settled by direct negotiation, be referred for decision to the Permanent Court of International Justice. In case either or both of the States Parties to such a dispute should not be parties to the Protocol of December 16th, 1920 relating to the Permanent Court of International Justice, the dispute shall be referred, at the choice of the Parties and in accordance with the constitutional procedure of each State either to the Permanent Court of International Justice or to a court of arbitration constituted in accordance with the Convention of October 18th, 1907, for the Pacific Settlement of International Disputes, or to some other court of arbitration.

Article 9.

At the time of signature or of ratification or of accession, any High Contracting Party may declare that its acceptance of the present Convention docs not bind some or all of the territories placed under its sovereignty, jurisdiction, protection, suzerainty or tutelage in respect of all or any provisions of the Convention; it may subsequently accede separately on behalf of any one of them or in respect of any provision to which any one of them is not a party.

Article 10.

In the event of a High Contracting Party wishing to denounce the present Convention, the denunciation shall be notified in writing to the Secretary-General of the League of Nations, who will at once communicate a certified true copy of the notification to all the other High Contracting Parties, informing them of the date on which it was received.

The denunciation shall only have effect in regard to the notifying State, and one year after the notification has reached the Secretary-General of the League of Nations.

Denunciation may also be made separately in respect of any territory placed under its sovereignty, jurisdiction, protection, suzerainty or tutelage.

Article 11.

The present Convention, which will bear this day's date and of which the French and English texts are both authentic, will remain open for signature by the States Members of the League of Nations until April 1st, 1927. The Secretary-General of the League of Nations will subsequently bring the present Convention to the notice of States which have not signed it, including States which are not Members of the League of Nations, and invite them to accede thereto.

A State desiring to accede to the Convention shall notify its intention in writing to the Secretary-General of the League of Nations and transmit to him the instrument of accession, which shall be deposited in the archives of the League.

The Secretary-General shall immediately transmit to all the other High Contracting Parties a certified true copy of the notification and of the instrument of accession, informing them of the date on which he received them.

Article 12.

The present Convention will be ratified and the instruments of ratification shall be deposited in the office of the Secretary-General of the League of Nations. The Secretary-General will inform all the High Contracting Parties of such deposit.

The Convention will come into operation for each State on the date of the deposit of its ratification or of its accession.

In faith whereof the Plenipotentiaries have signed the present Convention.

DONE at Geneva the twenty-fifth day of September, One thousand nine hundred and twenty-six, in one copy, which will be deposited in the archives of the League of Nations. A certified copy shall be forwarded to each signatory State.

SIGNIFICANCE

The League of Nations is regarded in many scholarly reviews as a body that was founded upon laudable ideals, but an organization that ultimately lacked the cohesion and the political clout to effectively maintain world peace. Critics point to the absence of the United States in the League membership as a key reason for the pronounced gap between principles and progress in the League efforts to settle international conflicts, particularly in the 1930s. It is notable in this context that the League of Nations was not defeated in battle so much as it simply faded away when it became plain the League had no real military means with which it could even threaten a response to aggression. The Japanese incursion into Manchuria in 1931 and the German occupation of Czechoslovakia in 1938 are the most prominent examples of such aggression.

The League was successful in its Convention to suppress slavery, although not in the fashion necessarily intended by the League member nations. The primary significance of the 1926 Convention was the subsequent importance that came to be attached to this international statement of opposition to slavery. The United Nations (UN) embraced the principles of the Convention when the UN crafted its Universal Declaration of Human Rights in 1948.

The language used by the drafters of the Convention is also illustrative of their broader and enlightened purpose. The Convention extended the commonly accepted definition of slavery from beyond simple ownership of a person, to the concept of forced labor. The Convention is clear that compulsory labor in anything except public purposes required careful examination as to whether such practices were in fact slavery. In 1926, the best-known public purposes where labor was forced were the armed forces or the prisons of a nation. The Convention also endeavored to eliminate any possible gaps in the definition of slave trade; the section cast a seemingly broad net over any activity, deliberate or innocent, that worked to advance slavery practices.

The concern of forced labor as de facto slavery is an issue that resonates today. Concerns have been raised periodically with China that its prisoners are required to perform labor and receive no remuneration for their work. Further, as evidenced by the enactment of legislation such as the United States Trafficking Victims Protection Act, 2000, the broad definition of slavery first advanced by the Convention of 1926 is accepted as the global standard today. In the American legislation (other countries such as Canada, Germany, and Great Britain have passed similar rules), there are provisions to combat the trade in both workers who are involuntarily held or where the worker is forced to work in the sex trade. Child labor and the participation of children in armed forces are extensions of the original definition consistent with modern developments. United States government statistics suggest that between 700,000 and four million persons per year are victims of human trafficking for a variety of forced labor and sex trade purposes.

The 1926 Convention also contemplated that issues arising from any practice related to slavery would be determined by a Permanent Council of International Justice. This body was also a forerunner to the modern World Court and its structure, based in the Hague.

FURTHER RESOURCES

Books

Gide, Andre. *Travels in the Congo.* Berkley; University of California Press, 1962.

Miers, Susan. *Slavery in the Twentieth Century: The Evolution of a Global Problem.* Walnut Creek, California; Altamira Press, 2003.

Pollock, Frederick. *The League of Nations.* Clark, New Jersey; Lawbook Exchange, 2003.

Periodicals

Irwin, Mary Ann. " 'White Slavery'as a Metaphor/Anatomy of Moral Panic." *Ex Post Facto The History Journal, San Francisco State University.* Vol. V (1996).

Web sites

British Broadcasting Corporation. "The League of Nations and the United Nations." May 29, 2006. <http://www.bbc.co.uk/history/state/nations/league_nations_01.shtml> (accessed May 29, 2006).

United Nations High Commissioner for Human Rights. "Contemporary Forms of Slavery." January 1, 2006. <http://193.194.138.190/html/menu6/2/fs14.htm> (accessed May 29, 2006).

Fate Did Not Let Me Go

A Letter from Valli Ollendorff to Her Son

Letter

By: Valli Ollendorff

Date: August 24, 1942

Source: Ollendorff, Valli. "Fate Did Not Let Me Go." Tenafly, N.J.: Ollendorff Center for Religious and Human Understanding, 1942.

About the Author: Valli Ollendorff (1874–1942) was born in Breslau, Germany as Valli Alexander, a woman of Jewish descent. She married Doctor Arthur Ollendorff in 1936 with whom she had three sons, Gerhard, Ulrich and Wolfgang. Arrested by the Nazis in August of 1942, Valli Ollendorf was sent to Theresienstadt concentration camp and was killed on October 16, 1942. Her second son, Ulrich, was the only member of the family to survive the holocaust.

INTRODUCTION

The letter below was written by Valli Ollendorff to her middle son, Ulrich, on August 24, 1942, during the Second World War. Ulrich had previously fled Nazi Germany to the United States, while his mother remained behind with other family members. Just days after composing these words, she was sent to the Theresienstadt concentration camp, where she died on October 16, 1942. The letter was lost in transit and eventually was found, forty-three years later in South America, and delivered to Ulrich Ollendorff when he was seventy-nine years old. Upon Ulrich's death in 1998, the Ollendorff family asked that the letter be read publicly at his funeral. The touching words of love from mother to son, in the midst of war and hatred, were an inspiration to those who heard them. Recognizing the extraordinary power of the letter and its story, Valli Ollendorff's descendents established the Ollendorff Center for Religious and Human Understanding and published the letter in a book for public access. Proceeds raised by the sale of the book go to non-profit agencies working for the promotion of human rights and religious tolerance around the world.

■ PRIMARY SOURCE

Tormensdorf—24th day of August, 1942.

My beloved, my good boy, within two days we are going away from here, and the future lies so dark in front of us that the thought comes up that the new place will be the last one which we reach on our migration. And if you my boy will hold this letter in your hands, then we are not chased from place to place, then all the suffering will have an end. Also, the restlessness and peace will be around us and in us.

Be happy that I have this rest and this peace, my good boy, and don't be too sad. Believe me, this is the best that could happen. I was, anyway, at the end of my life and the mother which you knew, my beloved son, was not any more the same.

Too much suffering, too much psychological pain and stress came over me, and I cannot get over Wolfgang's death which will be one year on the 27th of August. The suffering gets bigger day by day. The letters that I received from his friends speak of him with so much honor, friendship, respect and affection.

The letters show me only what he became and still could have become and achieved, and how much joy, spiritual wealth and wisdom he had and passed onto others. His letters to his father and me contained touching gratitude for his childhood and youth.

Also, you, my beloved boy, can carry the knowledge through your life that you through all your life were a source of purest joy for your parents, and that you, even in the times in which you like other boys of the same age were difficult, never gave your character cause for annoyance or hurt feelings. I wish your life will go from success to success, my beloved boy, and that you stay so good, so modest, and so grateful for all the good and beautiful things like you did already as a child. We wish for you to have with your child as much joy as we had with you. May the blessings, which I pray for you, come.

And I wish to your Anne, your loyal life partner, with whom you brought us a beloved daughter in our home, and your child a happy and joyful life together. The fact that I could not be a witness to your life in America was much more sad for me than you believed it my boy. All your letters born by a deep child's love called me to you and the joy of seeing you again, and the echo of the longing, and the possibility of living with you caused that I did all that was necessary to come to you.

If I did not write so often from all of my longing for you, it was done from love to you, because I believed it was better for you. Also, today I repeat to you and I know that you will understand me, I was and I am daily happy even longing very much for you and your life.

However, fate did not let me go. I was a necessity for Aunt Ella and I think that will console you. I wish it so very much. And now my beloved boy, I will take leave from you. I will thank you a thousand times for all the love, for all the gratitude, for all the joy and sunshine which you brought into your father's and my life, starting from the day of your birth. May the memory of your parent's house and your childhood shine like a bright lucky star over you, my beloved, good, precious boy.

Mother.

SIGNIFICANCE

In the period from 1939 to 1945, six million Jews were murdered by the Nazis as a part of Adolph Hitler's "final solution" to exterminate Europe's Jewish population. Hitler's victims faced the terrible conditions of concentration camps, starvation, cruel experiments, beatings, executions and the separation of families. The Holocaust, or Shoah, is generally regarded as the single largest genocide in modern history and it has left its mark on thousands of survivors, their families and descendents.

Adolph Hitler came to power in Germany in 1933. Almost immediately, the persecution of Jews and revocation of their civil rights began. Jews were prohibited from owning land (1933), denied national health

A courtyard in the Nazi concentration camp at Theresienstadt, Czechoslovakia, in 1946, after its liberation. A sign at the end of the yard states "Arbeit Macht Frei" ("Work Makes You Free"). © CORBIS.

insurance (1934), prohibited from serving in the military (1935), banned from employment in a range of professional occupations such as medicine, dentistry, accounting, teaching and law (1937–1938). The Nazis also implemented a range of policies to ensure that Jews could be easily identified, including the requirement for Jewish women to add the name 'Sarah' and Jewish men to add the name 'Israel' to their given name on legal identification and passports (1938), stamping a large red 'J' on the passports of Jews (1938) and requiring all Jews over the age of ten to wear a yellow star on their clothing (Polish Jews in 1939 and German Jews in 1941).

Germany invaded and occupied Poland in September of 1939, subjecting Polish Jews to the same restrictions of freedoms and revocations of citizenship rights. In early 1940, Hitler began the deportation of German Jews into occupied Poland, stripping them of their possessions, forcing them to live in ghettos and participate in hard labor. By 1941, France, Holland, Belgium, Croatia, Slovakia, Romania and Hungary were under the Nazi regime. Concentration camps had been established across Germany and Poland. In 1941, the Nazi government established the first death camp at Chelmno, Poland. Jews in concentration camps were forced into hard labor, many died of disease, starvation, or maltreatment. The death camps, however, were established for rapid and immediate execution. Most who arrived at the death camps were dead a day after their arrival. The largest of the extermination camps was Auschwitz-Birkenau in Poland. Mass executions of Jews and other minority groups at the Auschwitz facility began in earnest in January of 1942 by means of asphyxiation using Zyklon-B gas. By the time Auschwitz was liberated in January of 1945, an estimated two million people had been executed at the camp.

The voices and stories of many Jewish victims have been silenced forever, lost to history—many survivors and descendents have no idea how their family members died, what they were thinking and feeling and what they endured. The voices of women, with the notable exception of Anne Frank and her famous diary, are particularly absent in historical accounts of the Holocaust. For example, it is known that some Jewish women were forced into brothels at concentration camps, but what exactly happened to them and how they were treated, is largely unrecorded. Valli Ollendorff's letter to her son is particularly poignant in its candid description of her emotional experience as she faced impending death at the hands of the Nazis. The letter offers a snapshot of one victim's journey as a testament to the suffering of many and stands as a memorial for Holocaust victims and as a rebuttal to those who deny its reality.

To honor the memory of Valli Ollendorff, her grandson Stephen A. Ollendorff established the Ollendorff Center for Religious and Human Understanding. The organization is dedicated to promoting religious tolerance and human rights and the elimination of anti-Semitism. One notable undertaking of the Center is the Menorah Project, which endeavours to rebuild relations between Jews and Christians and to unite people of all faiths in remembering the events of the Holocaust. Monuments, crafted by Israeli sculptor Aharon Bezalel, in the shape of the Menorah (a ceremonial candelabra) have been erected at Catholic Centers across North America, recognizing the efforts of Pope John Paul II (1920–2005) to fight anti-Semitism through rebuilding diplomatic relations with Israel and issuing a statement emphasizing the non-culpability of the Jewish people in the crucifixion of Jesus Christ. The Ollendorff Center also provides resources to educate children about the Holocaust and about the dangers of prejudice.

In the aftermath of the tragic events of the Second World War, the international community has made efforts toward preventing further abuses of human rights. The United Nations' Universal Declaration of Human Rights was created in 1948 as a direct response to the Holocaust and the Nazi dehumanization of Jews. The Nuremburg Trials were also held to prosecute Nazi officers who were instrumental in perpetrating the genocide of European Jews.

FURTHER RESOURCES
Books

Dwork, Deborah, ed. *Voices & Views: A History of the Holocaust.* The Jewish Foundation for the Righteous, 2002.

Headland, Ronald. *So Others Will Remember: Holocaust History and Survivor Testimony.* Véhicule Press, 1999.

Ofer, Dalia and Lenore J. Weitzman, eds. *Women in the Holocaust.* Yale University Press, 1998.

Tec, Nechama. *Resilience and Courage: Women, Men, and the Holocaust.* Yale University Press, 2003.

Periodicals

Levy, Daniel and Natan Sznaider. "The institutionalization of cosmopolitan morality: the Holocaust and human rights." *Journal of Human Rights.* 3(2) (2004): 143–157.

Popkin, Jeremy D. "Holocaust Memories, Historians' Memoirs: First-Person Narrative and the Memory of the Holocaust." *History & Memory.* 15(1) (2003): 49-84.

Web sites

United Nations. "Universal Declaration of Human Rights." December 10, 1948. <http://www.un.org/Overview/rights.html> (accessed May 5, 2006).

Cambodia's Killing Fields

Photograph

By: Denis D. Gray

Date: April 17, 1981

Source: Gray, Denis D. "Cambodia's Killing Fields." Associated Press, 1981.

About the Photographer: Denis D. Gray is a reporter best known for covering events in Southeast Asia for the Associated Press (AP), a worldwide news agency based in New York.

INTRODUCTION

From 1975 to 1979, a Communist political party known as the Khmer Rouge ruled the nation of Cambodia, a country directly to the west of southern Vietnam. The Khmer Rouge (Khmer is the ethnicity of ninety-five percent of Cambodians and "rouge" is French for "red," the color usually associated with Communism) preached a radical philosophy of class warfare and social purification. City dwellers, college-educated people, scholars, Buddhist monks, persons connected in any with the previous government or foreigners, and many others were considered enemies of the new society, which, the Khmer Rouge announced, would count its calendar starting with "Year Zero" in the year of their victory. In pursuit of this utopian vision, the Khmer Rouge declared money, private property, religion, and books illegal and committed massive atrocities. The capital city of Cambodia, Phnom Penh (pronounced *pih-nom pen*), fell to Khmer Rouge forces on April 17, 1975. They ordered the city's two million inhabitants to evacuate to the countryside; many thousands died of exposure

PRIMARY SOURCE

Cambodia's Killing Fields: The skulls of victims of the Khmer Rouge, in Phnom Penh, Cambodia, April 17, 1981. AP IMAGES.

and starvation as a result of this forced exodus. Persons were also urged to confess their crimes against the state and were promised forgiveness from the new government, but in reality, those who identified themselves as members of a suspect group were taken away to remote rural locations, "killing fields," and executed, often after being tortured.

The rule of the Khmer Rouge ended in 1979 when the forces of Communist Vietnam—united as a single country since the defeat of the Americans at the end of the Vietnam War in 1975—invaded. The Vietnamese established a conventional Communist government in Cambodia and the genocide ceased. The Khmer Rouge became a guerrilla force once again and continued to pay a major role in Cambodian politics until the late 1990s. In 1996, about half the remaining Khmer Rouge forces surrendered in exchange for amnesty. Their founder and leader, Pol Pot, died in 1998.

In their few years in power, the Khmer Rouge killed over a million people, some by hand in the "killing fields" and many more through famine: estimates vary widely, from 1.2 million (U.S. State Department), 1.4 million (Amnesty International), or 1.7 million (Yale Cambodian Genocide Project) to 2.3 million (the scholar Francois Ponchaud). The bones shown in this photograph were uncovered and arranged a few years after the ousting of the Khmer Rouge by the Vietnamese in order to document their atrocities.

PRIMARY SOURCE

CAMBODIA'S KILLING FIELDS
See primary source image.

SIGNIFICANCE

The crimes committed by the Khmer Rouge show how geopolitical power struggles can prepare the conditions for genocide, and reconcile even nations that value human rights to genocidal regimes.

Most historians agree that U.S. actions during the Vietnam War helped the Khmer Rouge rise to power, though other factors contributed as well. The Khmer Rouge began fighting in the country-side as a small guerrilla force in 1963, but made little progress. In 1969, the U.S. Air Force began bombing raids on Cambodia that were allegedly targeted at Viet Cong military camps. The United States had been bombing the neighboring country of Laos since 1964. By 1973, over two million tons of bombs had been dropped on Laos and over half a million tons on Cambodia, more tonnage than had been dropped in all of World War II by all sides combined. In Cambodia, between 150,000 and 500,000 Cambodian civilians were killed by the bombing. The Khmer Rouge, which was receiving aid from China and North Vietnam, exploited the resulting chaos, social breakdown, and anger to its advantage, becoming a more formidable fighting force. The exiled Cambodian King, Sihanouk, declared his support for the Khmer Rouge, further boosting their popularity. In 1975, the Khmer Rouge took power and began to take people to the killing fields.

At that time, the United States saw Cambodia as a regional counterbalance to North Vietnam, which was supported by Soviet Russia; in 1975, U.S. President Gerald Ford and Secretary of State Henry Kissinger explained to the dictator of Indonesia, Suharto, that the United States was unwilling to oppose the Khmer Rouge government for this reason. President Ford told Suharto that "there is ... resistance in Cambodia to the influence of Hanoi 'North Vietnam.' We are willing to move slowly in our relations with Cambodia, hoping perhaps to slow down the North Vietnamese." When these words were spoken on December 6, 1975, the Khmer Rouge genocide had been underway for about eight months.

After the Vietnamese conquered Cambodia in 1979, China and the United States gave aid to an anti-Vietnamese resistance coalition formed by King Sihanouk and the Khmer Rouge. The Khmer Rouge, which U.S. President Jimmy Carter had called "the worst violater of human rights in the world" in 1978, thus became the indirect recipient of tens of millions of dollars of U.S. aid starting in 1979. The United States under Presidents Carter and Reagan also supported the retention of Cambodia's seat at the United Nations by Khmer Rouge representatives.

Vietnam left Cambodia in 1989. In 1992, United Nations peacekeeper forces oversaw a transition to a constitutional monarchy, and the following year Sihanouk was re-installed as king. In 2003, the United Nations, with U.S. support, signed an agreement with Cambodia to hold a tribunal to try former officials of the Khmer Rouge for genocide and crimes against humanity. As of early 2006, no trials had yet been held.

FURTHER RESOURCES

Books

Chomsky, Noam, and Edward Herman. *After the Cataclysm*. South End Press, 1979.

Periodicals

Scheffer, David J. "Justice for Cambodia." The *New York Times*. (December 21, 2002).

Web sites

CBS. "Remembering the Killing Fields." <http://www.cbsnews.com/stories/2000/04/15/world/main184477.shtml> (accessed April 24, 2006).

The Jurist. "High Time for Justice: The US and the Khmer Rouge Tribunal." <http://jurist.law.pitt.edu/forumy/2006/01/high-time-for-justice-us-and-khmer.php> (accessed April 24, 2006).

Letter to the Former Comfort Women

Letter

By: Junichiro Koizumi

Date: 2001

Source: Koizumi, Junichiro. *Letter from Prime Minister Junichiro Koizumi to the Former Comfort Women*. Ministry of Foreign Affairs, Japan, 2001.

About the Author: Junichiro Koizumi became Prime Minister of Japan in 2001. During his tenure in office the issue of "comfort women" became a diplomatic concern in Japan's relationship with South Korea.

INTRODUCTION

From approximately 1931 to 1946, the Japanese army and navy set up a network of official "comfort stations," designed to provide sexual services to soldiers. In the early years, the military advertised for prostitutes and willing sex workers to work in the brothels; workers found by middlemen and volunteers filled the brothels initially. The Japanese military assumed that by providing these sex services directly to soldiers, they would boost morale and control sexually transmitted diseases.

Over time, unscrupulous middlemen kidnapped young girls for use as "comfort women," or poor parents sold their daughters to middlemen with the understanding that their daughters would be given jobs. Women from China, Japan, Korea, Taiwan, Vietnam, Indonesia, Philippines, and Malaysia were used as comfort women, though the majority came from Korea and Japan. As World War II (1938–1945) progressed, Japanese soldiers would capture women from villages during invasions. Military recruiters were given specific instruction for detention and set-up of comfort stations.

The daily experience for these captured women varied, but each day multiple soldiers—sometimes forty to fifty per day—raped the women. The women were forced to travel with troops, living in poor conditions and in danger on battlefields. Within a few weeks, the women—occasionally girls as young as twelve-years-old—normally acquired a sexually transmitted disease. Many died or became infertile as a result of syphilis or gonorrhea. Fresh recruits and captives were popular with soldiers, who believed them to be less likely to have a sexually transmitted disease. Virgins were prized. Scholars estimate that the number of comfort women used ranged from 100,000–200,000 during World War II.

When the war ended, the comfort women, who had received military provisions as they were forced to travel with the Japanese military, were summarily abandoned on site. Thousands of miles from home, diseased, abused, and without money or goods, tens of thousands of comfort women struggled to return home. For those in the Philippines, a return home could lead to accusations of being a Japanese sympathizer or a spy, resulting in banishment or death. Once home, former comfort women faced shame in their villages for their experiences.

After World War II, more than fifty military tribunals took place in Asia; only one addressed the issue of comfort women. Dutch authorities tried and later executed one Japanese officer for his role in forcing thirty-five Dutch women in Jakarta into sexual slavery as comfort women. Western authorities, including the United States, knew about the extensive network of hundreds of thousands of comfort women used by the Japanese military; after Japan's defeat, Allied Forces landing in Japan were offered comfort women as part of official Japanese diplomatic policy. However, this Dutch comfort women case is the only prosecution of its kind.

In 1990, former comfort women in Korea created the Korean council for Women Drafted for Military Sexual Slavery and filed suit against the Japanese government. Japan denied the official use of comfort women, instead blaming independent contractors and brothel owners for supplying such women to soldiers. Historians revealed defense documents proving official government responsibility for the management of brothels; in 1992, Prime Minister Miyazawa formally expressed regret to the Korean people for Japan's treatment of comfort women.

In this 2001 letter from Prime Minister Koizumi, the Prime Minister makes reference to the Asian Women's Fund. In 1995, the Japanese government created the Asian Women's Fund as a non-profit entity to channel money to comfort women survivors.

PRIMARY SOURCE

The Year of 2001

Dear Madam,

On the occasion that the Asian Women's Fund, in cooperation with the Government and the people of Japan, offers atonement from the Japanese people to the former wartime comfort women, I wish to express my feelings as well.

The issue of comfort women, with an involvement of the Japanese military authorities at that time, was a grave affront to the honor and dignity of large numbers of women.

As Prime Minister of Japan, I thus extend anew my most sincere apologies and remorse to all the women who underwent immeasurable and painful experiences and suffered incurable physical and psychological wounds as comfort women.

We must not evade the weight of the past, nor should we evade our responsibilities for the future.

I believe that our country, painfully aware of its moral responsibilities, with feelings of apology and remorse, should face up squarely to its past history and accurately convey it to future generations.

Furthermore, Japan also should take an active part in dealing with violence and other forms of injustice to the honor and dignity of women.

Standing beside a portrait of the late "comfort woman" Kim Hak-Sun of South Korea, activists take part in a demonstration at the national parliament in Tokyo on August 10, 2005. They are demanding the Japanese government apologize for forcing women to work as sex slaves for Japanese soldiers during World War II, and offer them compensation. TORU YAMANAKA/AFP/GETTY IMAGES.

Finally, I pray from the bottom of my heart that each of you will find peace for the rest of your lives.

Respectfully yours,
Junichiro Koizumi
Prime Minister of Japan

SIGNIFICANCE

The Asian Women's Fund drew sharp criticism from both comfort women activists as well as conservatives who argued that Japan had committed no war crime and bore no responsibility to the comfort women. The Japanese government claimed that all legal questions and reparations between Korea and Japan had been settled in the 1965 Treaty on Basic Relations and Agreement of Economic Cooperation and Property Claims Between Japan and the Republic of Korea. By issuing regrets and creating the Asian Women's Fund, Japan acknowledged moral responsibility but refused to accept legal responsibility.

Accepting legal responsibility after the treaty could open Japan up to claims from other countries for various wartime activities, a diplomatic and financial dilemma Japan wished to avoid.

The International Commission of Jurists' 1994 report "Comfort Women: An Unfinished Ordeal" notes that neither the 1965 treaty nor a 1956 treaty with the Philippines addresses human rights violations. Reparations for forced sexual slavery, according to the report, should be provided by the Japanese government, with "adequate shelter, medical aid and a decent standard of living. Having regard to the years of neglect already suffered by the women, an immediate interim payment of U.S. $40,000 per victim is warranted."

By the 1990s, the youngest comfort women were already in their sixties; by 2001, when Koizumi wrote his letter regarding the Asian Women's Fund, most survivors were in their seventies. Comfort women activists accuse the Japanese government of playing a time game; the longer they wait, the fewer survivors they must pay. Japan, on the other hand, claims that the

Asian Women's Fund is sufficient. In a 1997 survey in Japan, 50.7 percent of respondents believed the Japan should formally apologize to the comfort women and take full legal and financial responsibility. Conservatives—many war veterans—claim that the comfort women system was voluntary for the women and that its purpose was to prevent the rape of women in conquered territories.

In 2000, in Tokyo, a non-governmental organization created the Women's International War Crimes Tribunals on Japan's Military Sexual Slavery, an unofficial tribunal which found the Japanese government responsible for the rapes and sexual slavery of comfort women. The 1992 expression of regret by then Prime Minister Miyazawa had long been considered insufficient by comfort women activists. The word he used, "owabi," can be translated similarly to the words "excuse me" or "pardon me" in English. Prime Minister Koizumi's expressed apology in this 2001 letter gave the remaining 136 documented comfort women the first official apology from the Japanese government for its creation and management of the comfort stations.

FURTHER RESOURCES

Books

Dolgopol, Ustinia. *Comfort Women: An Unfinished Ordeal.* International Commission of Jurists, 1994.

Hicks, George L. *The Comfort Women: Japan's Brutal Regime of Enforced Prostitution in the Second World War.* London: W. W. Norton, 1997.

Schellstede, Sangmie Choi. *Comfort Women Speak: Testimony by Sex Slaves of the Japanese Military: Includes New United Nations Human Rights Report.* New York: Holmes & Meier, 2000.

Yoshimi, Yoshiaki, and Suzanne O'Brien. *Comfort Women.* New York: Columbia University Press, 2002.

Web sites

Japan Policy Research Institute. "Japan's Responsibility Toward Comfort Women Survivors." May, 2001. <http://www.jpri.org/publications/workingpapers/wp77.html> (accessed April 26, 2006).

Pacifique Mukeshimana

Genocide in Rwanda, 1994

Interview

By: Public Broadcasting Service (PBS)

Date: December, 2003

Source: Public Broadcasting System (PBS). *Frontline.* "Portraits/Pacifique Mukeshimana." December, 2003.

About the Author: The Public Broadcasting Service (PBS) is a non-profit media network owned and operated by the approximately 350 public television stations based in the United States. Since 1983, PBS has produced *Frontline*, a television newsmagazine and public affairs program.

INTRODUCTION

Rwanda is a nation located in east central Africa. A Belgian protectorate at the end of World War I (1918), Rwanda was granted its independence by Belgium in 1962. The population of the country, numbering approximately seven million persons, is almost entirely comprised of two ethnic groups, the majority Hutu, and the minority Tutsi peoples.

Rwanda had been the subject of serious internal divisions in the early 1990s, including military action taken by an opposition group known as the Rwandan Popular Front, a Tutsi-centered political party that operated in exile. In 1993, an accord was negotiated between the Rwandan government and its various opponents. The United Nations (UN) authorized the deployment of a peace keeping force to Rwanda to assist in the implementation of the peace accord.

In early 1994, the Rwandan government increased its efforts to perpetuate an ethnic division between Hutus and Tutsis, as a means of circumventing its obligations to include Tutsi political parties in the Rwandan government. On April 6, 1994, an aircraft carrying Rwandan President Habyarinana was shot down, an event that precipitated the coordinated actions of the Hutu-dominated government against the Tutsi minority.

The commanders of the United Nations forces in Rwanda had expressed concerns to the UN leadership that hostilities in Rwanda appeared ready to escalate in April 1994. Requests were made by the Rwandan UN commander that the UN force be strengthened, as fears were expressed to the UN leadership that the Tutsi population was in peril. The UN forces were ordered to remain in their barracks in April 1994, when the first genocidal actions were taken by the Rwandan government. The UN forces were later permitted only to assist in the evacuation of foreigners from Rwanda.

Commencing in mid-April 1994, the Rwandan government directed its armed services, local militia, and police to drive Tutsi people from their homes, for the purpose of looting their property and killing them. Civilians were encouraged to participate in the killings, in exchange for a share of the murdered person's

In 1994, fleeing from Rwanda's civil war, refugees pass corpses lying by the side of a road. © DAVID TURNLEY/CORBIS.

belongings. It is estimated that between 500,000 and 800,000 persons were murdered in Rwanda between April 1994 and the end of July 1994, ninety percent of whom were Tutsi.

Pacifique Mukeshimana, the subject of the documentary prepared by PBS for the program *Frontline* in December 2003, was a twenty-year-old Hutu civilian at the time of the Rwandan genocide. Mukeshimana was one of the thousands of Hutus co-opted into the genocide process commenced by the Rwandan government against the Tutsi minority.

■ PRIMARY SOURCE

Pacifique Mukeshimana, 20 years old during the 1994 genocide, admits that he killed two people during the bloodletting. After spending seven years in prison, he returned home to his village in May 2003 as part of a program that granted early release to prisoners who have confessed their crimes.

THE PERPETRATOR:

I participated in the genocide. I killed a man's wife—named Karuganda—with one other person. I hit her with a club and the other one finished her with a knife.

I also killed a man named Muzigura. I joined a crowd of people at around 2 P.M. These people were shouting loudly, and when I got there I realized they were holding Muzigura. I got a machete from one of the men who were there and then I hit Muzigura, cutting him on the thigh. Another man finally hit Muzigura on the head with a pickaxe and he died.

I knew the people I killed. They weren't hidden. One was caught by a crowd of people and the other was sitting outside her house.

I got involved, first of all, because of ignorance. Second, people got involved because of the temptation to loot the victims' belongings. Then finally, there were bad authorities who were teaching people that they had to kill their [Tutsi] enemies. People got involved because they believed in it. Most people participated massively. I believe it was because the government kept on encouraging people to kill. Most of my friends were involved.

At the end of the genocide, I fled to Congo. I came back with the help of the U.N. High Commission for Refugees. They brought me back to Kigali and I was arrested there. There were people who knew me and they denounced me.

I was in prison for seven years. I want to thank the organizations, such as the National Unity and Reconciliation Commission, which taught us the importance of confessing. I was convinced that it was important to confess because I became a Christian. Reconciliation is not possible if there is no truth. Rwandans were the source of this genocide. I killed my fellow Rwandans and so the solution has to come from Rwandans. On April 15, 2000, I decided to confess and apologize for what I did.

I was released and sent to the solidarity camp in January this year. What they taught us in the camp was wonderful. We were taught how one should behave with those he hurt. One has to go and apologize for the things he did. One has to know how to behave in the presence of survivors. Some don't want to forgive, others forgive easily, and others are still angry. One has to know how to behave in front of these different kinds of people and show in his behavior that he's completely changed.

I came home in May, two months ago. I appeared before the gacaca court, confessed and asked pardon from the victims' relatives. They forgave me. I encouraged other people to (confess) because reconciliation will not be possible without recognizing one's crimes. Some people claimed reparations for their things, and my parents sold part of our farm in order to pay back what I destroyed.

I have no vision for the future. To prepare for the future, you need a foundation or a base. We can ask for aid from the National Unity and Reconciliation Commission to restart our lives. I really hope for nothing.

SIGNIFICANCE

The Rwandan genocide directed at its Tutsi population by the Hutu-dominated government is among the most extreme mass killings since the Holocaust was perpetrated during World War II (1938–1945). Unlike the other notable mass killings on the basis of race or religious belief that have occurred in human history, the slaughter of Tutsis by Hutu forces involved persons of very similar backgrounds. The Hutu and the Tutsi people had occupied the same region of Africa for centuries, they spoke the same language, and both groups possessed similar cultural traditions.

The involvement of Pacifique Mukeshimana is also in contrast to the patterns of mass killing previously recorded in history. Mukeshimana had no apparent ideological connection to the actions initiated by the Rwandan government against the Tutsis. He was persuaded to become involved in a horrific killing scene on the promise of looted spoils. There is no

suggestion of any personal enmity between the murder victims and Mukeshimana or his co-perpetrators. Given that the murder victims were known to him and his neighbors, it is reasonable to conclude that this man would not have been a likely perpetrator of such acts absent the government decision to move against the Tutsi people.

There is a significant contrast between how Mukeshimana's actions would have been judged in a Western court and the ultimate sentence imposed upon him in Rwanda. The perpetration of an unprovoked double homicide in the United States, Canada, England, or France would attract sanctions ranging from a life sentence, with minimum parole eligibility of twenty-five years, to the death penalty in some American states. Mukeshimana spent seven years in jail, before being returned to his community to be sentenced by the local court.

The function of the local court, the *gacaca* is intended to achieve the dual purposes of community based justice and the reality of dealing with tens of thousands of persons, such as Mukeshimana, who were complicit in the genocide at a purely local level. Approximately 130,000 such persons were detained in Rwanda, a significant number in proportion to a population of approximately seven million persons. It was estimated that if all of the alleged perpetrators of genocidal acts were the subject of a trial in the normal course, given Rwanda's limited judicial resources, the proceedings could take two hundred years to complete. Further, the country had the dual specter of this significant number of imprisoned persons permanently removed from the workforce and the concurrent cost of feeding and securing them in jail.

Approximately 11,000 gacaca were established throughout Rwanda to deal with the consequences of the genocide. The decisions of the gacaca balance a victim-centered restorative justice approach with that of reconciliation between the perpetrator, his victim, and the community at large. Mukeshimana returned to the village where his crimes occurred, and he is reintegrating himself into the community with the blessing of the elected judges of the gacaca.

The international political significance of the Rwandan genocide continues to reverberate. The International Criminal Tribunal has focused upon the prosecution of the leadership of the genocide, a number that will not exceed 200 cases. Like the Nuremberg war crimes trials (1945–1949) held at the conclusion of the Second World War, the International Criminal

Tribunal is seeking to create an incontrovertible historical record of the Rwandan genocide.

The most enduring significance of the Rwandan genocide may be what the United Nations and its various member nations chose not to do as the crisis unfolded with increasing speed in April 1994. There is considerable evidence that the genocide could have been at the least limited had the UN increased its existing military presence as its commander requested. The various governments with an interest in the Rwanda situation did not publicly refer to the mass killings as genocide until the immediate crisis was over in August 1994. Former U.S. President Bill Clinton described the Rwanda genocide as the greatest error in American foreign policy during his presidency.

FURTHER RESOURCES

Books

Barnett, Michael. *Eyewitness to a Genocide: The United Nations and Rwanda.* Ithaca, New York; Cornell University Press, 2002.

Kuperman, Allan J. *The Limits of Humanitarian Intervention: Genocide in Rwanda.* Washington; Brookings Institute Press, 2001.

Web sites

Human Rights Watch. "Leave None to Tell the Story: Genocide in Rwanda." April 1, 2004. <http://hrw.org/reports/1999/rwanda> (accessed May 29, 2006).

United Nations. "International Criminal Tribunal for Rwanda." May, 2006. <http://69.94.11.53/default.htm> (accessed May 29, 2006).

U.S. Congress Terms Situation in Darfur "Genocide"

Senate, House Pass Concurrent Resolutions on Darfur

News article

By: Charles W. Corey

Date: July 23, 2004

Source: *USINFO: International Information Programs.* "U.S. Congress Terms Situation in Darfur 'Genocide': Senate, House Pass Concurrent Resolutions on Darfur." July 23, 2004. <http://usinfo.state.gov/is/Archive/2004/Jul/26-233176.html> (accessed April 24, 2006).

About the Author: Charles W. Corey is a journalist who works as a Washington file staff writer for the U.S. Department of State's Bureau of International Information Programs.

INTRODUCTION

In December 1948, the United Nations General Assembly created a definition for genocide, describing it as an intentional obliteration of a "national, ethnical, racial or religious group" by literal extermination, psychological or emotional devastation, complete geographical displacement, forced sterilization or otherwise causing zero population growth, marginalizing to the point of elimination, or complete removal and repatriation of offspring to a desired group. The 1948 Convention came about as a result of the actions of the Nazis against members of the Jewish faith (and other so-called undesirables) during World War II. In the present day, the annihilation of civilians and the forced encampment or relocation of survivors in Darfur has been termed genocide by the U.S. federal government, among others.

Historically, genocide is a crime that has received extensive social and media attention, but relatively little effective criminal prosecution. Often, this is due to the chaotic situation in the regions affected by the crime and an inability to muster sufficient resources to effectively adjudicate the genocide cases. In part to address this issue, an International Criminal Court was established in The Hague, Netherlands. This court only hears four types of extremely serious and globally important cases—war crimes, crimes against humanity, crimes of aggression, and genocide.

There is a long history of civil unrest between Arab and non-Arab factions in the Sudan, fueled by poverty and a scarcity of natural resources. The current situation in Darfur began in 2003 as a conflict between the government of the Republic of the Sudan (also referred to as the GOS)—made up of persons of Arabic heritage and of professional guerilla-style militias—and non-Arab rebels and civilians. The conflict has been occurring principally in the Darfur region of the Sudan, which has a predominantly non-Arab population. The nature of the crimes reported, particularly single and mass murders, razing of villages, rapes and sexual assaults, the use of racist language by invading militias, loss of livelihood and forced removal or destruction of property (including business and livestock theft), and looting and vandalism of personal property, are consistent with the international crime of genocide. Several hundred villages in Darfur have been destroyed or significantly damaged, more than a million non-Arab people have been

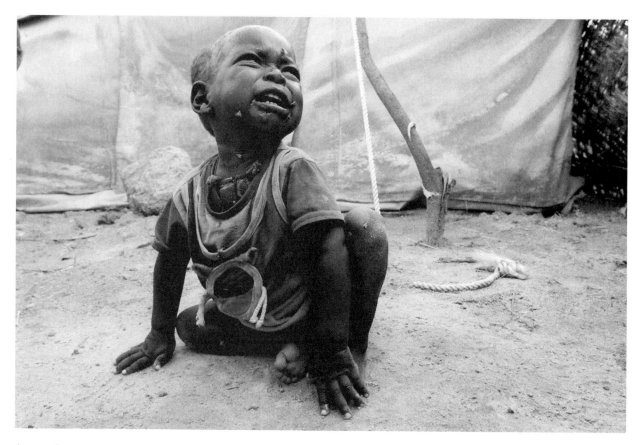

A young Sudanese refugee cries for his mother at a refugee camp across the border from Sudan's Darfur region in Frachana, Chad. He is one of millions of black Sudanese inhabitants who have been attacked and driven from their homes in what the U.S. Congress deems an act of genocide. © STEPHEN MORRISON/EPA/CORBIS.

displaced from their homes to other parts of the country, and hundreds of thousands have fled the Sudan to refugee camps in Chad and elsewhere. There is widespread famine, lack of adequate water, and sharply increased infant mortality, as well as increased rates of infection, illness, and mortality among the affected population.

The Arab militia group considered primarily responsible for the violence is called the Jingaweit or Janjaweed, and it works in tandem with GOS military forces in Darfur. Despite international efforts to bring an end to the hostilities, there are reports of continuing crimes against humanity, as well as genocide in Darfur. Also of international concern is the acute health crisis engendered by lack of food and water and conditions of overcrowding in refugee camps that the conflict has spawned.

◾ PRIMARY SOURCE

Washington—Both chambers of the U.S. Congress adopted concurrent resolutions July 22 condemning the continuing atrocities in the Darfur region of western Sudan as "genocide" and asking the international community to join with the United States to help bring an end to the humanitarian catastrophe that is under way there.

The U.S. House of Representatives passed its version (House Concurrent Resolution 467) in a vote of 422-0, with the U. S. Senate approving its version (Senate Concurrent Resolution 133) by voice vote. A concurrent resolution is a legislative proposal that requires the approval of both houses but does not require the signature of the president and does not have the force of law. These resolutions are often used to express the sentiments of both the House of Representatives and the Senate.

In debate in the House of Representatives preceding the vote, the chairman of the Subcommittee on Africa, Ed Royce (Republican-California), said that with the vote, "the House of Representatives will go on record declaring the atrocities being committed in the Darfur region of Sudan to be 'genocide.' H. Con. Res. 467 is a statement for the world, and a stark warning to the Sudanese government."

"We've heard about the atrocities government-backed militias are perpetrating in Darfur," he told his fellow lawmakers. "This resolution cites an estimated 30,000 innocent civilians brutally murdered, more than 130,000 people fleeing to neighboring Chad, and more than one million people internally displaced."

Royce reminded the lawmakers that the Subcommittee on Africa has held several hearings on Sudan.

"We've heard about the human suffering. We have also heard about how this killing is targeted and systematic. Villages are razed, crops are burned, and wells are poisoned. I fully support this resolution's determination that genocide is occurring in Sudan, as it played out in Rwanda 10 years ago!"

"Those doing the killing need to understand that the world is changing," Royce said. He reminded everyone: "We have international courts to hold human rights criminals accountable. Information is being collected. The days of impunity are ending. That is a message that this resolution sends."

"H. Con. Res. 467 deplores the failure of the United Nations Human Rights Commission to take appropriate action on Darfur," he declared.

Royce said the commission failed earlier this year to support a United States-led effort to strongly condemn gross human-rights violations in Darfur.

He credited the Bush administration with taking the lead in "seeking an end to the slaughter in Darfur" and addressing the humanitarian crisis there.

"Indeed, the administration deserves much credit for achieving a North-South Peace Accord in Sudan. It has played a very good hand with the cards it was dealt. Congress has been supportive of these negotiations, including with the Sudan Peace Act."

"It's cliché," he said, "but in Darfur, Khartoum is showing its true colors. Today, that government is hearing loud and clear that there will be no U.S. aid or improved relations, no support for the peace process, as long as the killing continues in Darfur."

Also on July 22, Secretary of State Colin Powell traveled to U.N. headquarters in New York to discuss the situation in Darfur with U.N. Secretary-General Kofi Annan and to press for Security Council action to pressure the Sudanese government to disarm the Jingaweit militia.

Talking with journalists after their private meeting, Powell and Annan said they had come together not just to put pressure on the government but also to help the hundreds of thousands in need.

Both Powell and Annan stressed that they will continue to insist that Khartoum honor the commitment it made to the two leaders when they visited Sudan in early July.

"We both agree that the international community must insist that the Sudanese government honor the commitments it gave when we both visited Sudan," Annan said. "It is important that the internally displaced people and the villages be protected. It is the sacred responsibility of the government of Sudan to do that and eventually disarm the Jingaweit and the other militias in the region."

Powell said that Khartoum should not look on the U.N. efforts as meddling, but "an effort to save people who are in desperate trouble."

There is no reason why Khartoum can't disarm the Jingaweit militias that have perpetrated large-scale atrocities against Sudanese civilians, Powell told his audience.

The United States has presented a second draft of a resolution on Darfur to the Security Council, both Powell and Annan told reporters.

Powell did not go into specifics on the new draft but said that it "puts down timelines and sets sanctions" if the timelines are not met.

The secretary of state said that since his visit there has been "some modest improvement" in access for aid workers, the delivery of humanitarian supplies, and the number of African Union monitors in the area.

"We are still, it is safe to say, not satisfied with the security situation," Powell said.

Asked about whether the situation in Darfur can be called genocide, Powell responded that the United States is examining the issue very carefully.

State Department officials have been in the Darfur region, interviewing victims in the camps and villages and sending reports back to Washington that will be used to make the legal judgment on whether to classify the situation as genocide.

Nevertheless, Powell said, "whatever you call it, it's a catastrophe."

SIGNIFICANCE

Although there is semantic debate regarding whether the conflict in Darfur meets technical definitional criteria for genocide or for crimes against humanity, the human toll has continued to rise. Between February of 2003 and the end of the first quarter of 2006, more than 200,000 people in Darfur were reported to have died, more than three million (of an estimated 7 million in total) persons were displaced, either internally or outside of Darfur, and most were starving. There have been numerous cease-fire orders and at least six rounds of formal peace talks involving the government of Sudan, the Jingaweit, and the non-Arab rebel forces, none of which have been successful thus far.

Conflicts between the Arab and non-Arab (rebel) factions in the Sudan have occurred intermittently for the past few decades. Government supported anti-rebel violence has been reported for the same length of time in the region. In addition, the Sudanese government has been alleged to have supported and trained various militia groups, the Jingaweit among them.

One distinguishing feature of the conflict in Darfur, which sets it apart from political machinations or civil war, is the lack of organized resistance by the non-Arab peoples. The vast majority of those impacted by the fighting have been civilians, large numbers of whom are women and children. The U.S. government, in partnership with several NGOs (non-governmental organizations) conducted a large-scale (more than 1,000 participants) random sampling survey of displaced residents of Darfur at a variety of locations in Chad about eighteen months after the most recent episodes of violence began. More than ninety percent of those interviewed stated that their villages, when attacked by the GOS soldiers, the Jingaweit, or both forces, were able to offer no resistance or defense. Ninety percent stated that there were no rebel military or militia forces present in their villages before the invasion or episodes of violence. It was the firm and independent conviction of those interviewed that the violence was ethnically based and consisted of attacks against non-Arab citizens.

The widespread violence has made it difficult for NGOs and other humanitarian, crisis, and relief agencies to provide adequate nourishment and medical care, and the United Nations Security Council has repeatedly requested that humanitarian access be facilitated. The lack of access to aid, as well as the other crimes against humanity and acts of genocide, is now considered differently than in the past, in no small measure because of the atrocities that occurred in Rwanda in 1994. With the advent of the International Criminal Court, crimes against humanity and acts of genocide can potentially be adjudicated in an international setting and appropriate penalties imposed.

As of 2006, the violence in the Sudan continues, as do attempts to bring the parties in the conflict together for peace-talks. The non-Arab citizens of Darfur continue to be victimized, displaced, and killed. They still lack food, potable water, access to adequate medical care, and the relief that humanitarian agencies, international governments, and NGOs seek to provide.

FURTHER RESOURCES

Books

Rome Statute of the International Criminal Court. The Hague, Netherlands: Public Information and Documentation Section of the International Criminal Court, 2002.

Totten, Samuel, William S. Parsons, and Israel W. Charny, eds. *A Century of Genocide: Critical Essays and Eyewitness Accounts.* Second edition. New York: Routledge, 2004.

U.S. Department of State. *Documenting Atrocities in Darfur.* U.S. Department of State Publication Number 11182. Washington, D.C.: U.S. Government Printing Office, 2004.

Periodicals

Graditzky, Thomas. "Individual Criminal Responsibility for Violations of International Humanitarian Law Committed in Non-International Armed Conflicts." *International Review of the Red Cross* 322 (March 31, 1998): 29–56.

Schabas, William A. "National Courts Finally Begin to Prosecute Genocide, the 'Crime of Crimes'." *Journal of International Criminal Justice* 1 (April 2003): 39–63.

Web sites

ReliefWeb. "Darfur: Humanitarian Emergency Fact Sheet # 3 (FY 2004)." April 30, 2004. <http://www.reliefweb.int/rw/rwb.nsf/AllDocsByUNID/383daba36e89935185256e86006c1f21> (accessed May 12, 2006).

United Nations. "Convention on the Prevention and Punishment of the Crime of Genocide." August 16, 1994. Last edited on January 27, 1997. <http://www.hrweb.org/legal/genocide.html> (accessed April 28, 2006).

Colombia: Displaced and Discarded

The Plight of Internally Displaced Persons in Bogotá and Cartagena

Report

By: Anonymous

Date: October 14, 2005

Source: "Colombia: Displaced and Discarded: The Plight of Internally Displaced Persons in Bogotá and Cartagena." *Human Rights Watch* 17 (October 14, 2005).

About the Author: Human Rights Watch is an independent human rights organization based in the United States. Founded in 1978, the organization sends fact-finding teams to sites of potential human rights abuses and then publicizes the results in the national and international media to put pressure on governments to institute change.

INTRODUCTION

Colombia, the only country in South America that borders two oceans, is a country rich in natural resources, scenic beauty, and violent history. It is one of the world's bloodiest places, with murder ranking as the number one killer of young adults. The violence has forced the displacement of millions of Colombians and has given Colombia the second largest displacement crisis in the world behind Sudan.

The trouble in Colombia is a direct result of cocaine trafficking. In the 1980s, cocaine became a drug of choice and cocaine trafficking became one of the major Columbian industries. In areas where peasants grew coca as a cash crop, guerillas from the Revolutionary Armed Forces of Colombia (FARC) protected them. FARC, founded in 1966 to create an independent republic south of Bogotá, violently opposes the Colombian government. The FARC grew to an estimated twenty thousand fighters who continued to harass landowners and engage in the lucrative activity of kidnapping. In turn, these actions by FARC adversely affected the drug traffickers who had become large landowners. The traffickers funded death squads in the 1980s to attack FARC and its peasant supporters. These squads gelled into a fairly cohesive right-wing force, the United Self-Defense Forces of Colombia (AUC). Negotiations between the government, AUC, and FARC have not proved fruitful. At one point, Colombia ceded a large tract of land to FARC, then rescinded the cession and reoccupied the territory. In 2002, independent candidate Alvara Uribe was elected president on the promise to gain the upper hand in the conflict.

As of 2006, the violence in Colombia is continuing. Various human rights organizations, including U.S.-based Human Rights Watch, have reported that right-wing death squads are targeting peasants who are suspected of supporting FARC, while FARC death squads are killing peasants who are suspected of supporting the right-wingers. The result is a massive displacement of peasants.

■ **PRIMARY SOURCE**

COLOMBIA: DISPLACED AND DISCARDED

The Plight of Internally Displaced Persons in Bogotá and Cartagena Human Rights Watch October 2005 Vol. 17, No. 4(B)

I. Summary "The *autodefensas* arrived at 5 a.m.," M.D. told Human Rights Watch, explaining why she and her family fled their homes in Putumayo in 1999. (*Autodefensas* are members of paramilitary groups.) "They called all of us into a room. There was an elderly man, eighty years old—they killed him. They cut off his head and began to play football with it ... They killed five of us in all, including the one whose head they cut off. Another man, they cut his arm off at the shoulder." The paramilitaries took the oldest of her seven children, a thirteen-year-old boy. The rest of the family fled to Bogotá.

Her husband, L.D., interrupted her account to say, "We've been here one month. It's the second time that we've been displaced." He told our researcher that the Social Solidarity Network (Red de Solidaridad Social), the government agency to coordinate humanitarian relief for the enormous number of Colombians who have been driven from their homes during the conflict, helped them relocate to the department of Nariño, to the west of Putumayo along the border with Ecuador. At the end of 2003, the *autodefensas* forced them to flee again, he said. They received help from strangers after they fled, spending one night sleeping in coffins at a funeral home and another night at a hotel after somebody gave them money for a room. "We found our way here," L.D. said. They had just begun to register with the Social Solidarity Network, a process that by law can take up to fifteen business days to complete. Asked what the Social Solidarity Network had given them to meet their immediate needs during this time, L.D. replied, "Nothing. Nothing."

Human Rights Watch interviewed the couple in a makeshift shelter in a shantytown on the fringes of Bogotá. Established by a group of individuals who had themselves been forced to flee their homes because of the conflict, the three-story house had no running water and no mattresses or blankets for the new arrivals referred there by the Social Solidarity Network. The couple and their children slept on the floor.

After Sudan, Colombia has the world's largest internal displacement crisis. In the last three years alone, nearly 5 percent of Colombia's 43 million people has been forcibly displaced in much the way that this family was—uprooted from their homes and deprived of their livelihoods because of the country's armed conflict. It is likely that more than half of all displaced persons are children under the age of eighteen.

Officials in the government of President Álvaro Uribe Vélez frequently describe displaced persons as economic migrants. This attitude ignores the reality that many have fled after receiving specific threats or because family members or neighbors were killed by guerrillas or members of paramilitary groups.

Indeed, government officials have suggested that programs to address the needs of displaced persons discriminate against other poor Colombians by, they say, arbitrarily singling out one group of impoverished people for assistance. In fact, displaced families are worse off by any measure—quality of housing, access to sanitation, level of education, and access to employment—than other poor families that have not been displaced, the government Social Solidarity Network found. They face the enormous challenge of finding new homes and employment at the same time that they are struggling to cope with the events that caused them to flee their communities.

Reflecting the mistaken view that most displaced persons have chosen to relocate for economic reasons rather than because of the armed conflict, President Uribe's government has promoted return to home communities as the principal response to internal displacement. Displaced persons, nongovernmental observers, and officials with many international agencies have been sharply critical of this approach, noting that lack of security in many areas often prevents safe return.

In this report, Human Rights Watch examines the hurdles internally displaced persons face in two cities, Bogotá and Cartagena, in access to humanitarian assistance, education, and health care. Internal displacement is a complex phenomenon, one that this report does not attempt to address comprehensively. Instead, this report examines the immediate needs of displaced families once they arrive in their new communities.

Displaced families often confront urgent challenges in providing for their basic necessities once they arrive in their new communities. In a typical account, E.B., an adult man living in the Nelson Mandela barrio on the outskirts of Cartagena, identified immediate humanitarian assistance, shelter, health services, and education as the principal needs he and his displaced neighbors faced.

Colombia is one of a handful of countries that have enacted legislation to protect the internally displaced. Under its Law 387, displaced families are entitled to humanitarian assistance, for example. But the registration process for these benefits can be confusing and cumbersome, despite efforts by the Social Solidarity Network to streamline the process. The office of the U.N. High Commissioner for Refugees found in December 2004 that only half of the families registered over a two-year period actually received humanitarian assistance. For those that do, assistance is limited in most cases to three months.

Displaced children are entitled to attend schools in their new communities, but in practice they face significant hurdles in continuing their education. Some children are turned away because they are asked to produce school records or forms of identification they no longer possess. Others are denied enrollment because schools have no room for them. In many cases, the matriculation fees and related costs of schooling prevent them from attending.

Displaced families have particular health needs, and under Colombian law they should receive free basic health care. Even so, many displaced families are not covered by Colombia's subsidized public health system, not because they do not qualify for coverage but simply because the system is at full capacity. They should be able to receive emergency care, but they are often turned away when they seek medical attention because hospitals have no incentive to provide services for which they will never receive payment. Those who are enrolled in the subsidized health care system must still pay for medications, which may be beyond the reach of the incomes of displaced families.

Because internally displaced persons have not crossed an international border, they are not refugees as that term is used in international law, and the international protections offered to refugees do not apply to them. Their situation as internally displaced persons is addressed in a separate, nonbinding set of international standards, contained in the Guiding Principles on Internal Displacement.

The Guiding Principles call on states to safeguard the liberty and personal security of displaced persons, guarantee them treatment equal to that given to those who are not displaced, ensure free primary education for their children, and offer them necessary humanitarian assistance, among other safeguards. The state should promote the return of displaced persons to their home communities only when such returns are voluntary and can be accomplished in safety and with dignity.

On paper, Colombia's Law 387 guarantees many of these safeguards. "In Colombia, the laws are very advanced," said Marta Skretteberg, then the head of the Colombian office of the Norwegian Refugee Council. "It has one of the most modern laws with regard to internal displacement. In reality, it's not implemented." As one European official commented, one of the law's chief weaknesses is its failure to give clear responsibility to a single government agency, with the result that "nobody was responsible for the problem." In early 2004, the system of attention for the displaced population had reached such a state of crisis that the Colombian Constitutional Court declared that it was in a "state of unconstitutional affairs" and ordered the state to take corrective measures within one year.

As the office of the U.N. High Commissioner for Refugees notes, the government has undertaken some important initiatives to safeguard the well-being of persons who are forcibly displaced. The state has established an early warning system, for example, and has improved its capacity to provide emergency humanitarian assistance to those in immediate need. In response to the Constitutional Court's 2004 decision, the government announced in August 2004 that it would increase the number of places available to displaced students in the country's public schools and would also increase the national health system's coverage of displaced persons. In February 2005 the government adopted a new National Plan of Attention to the Displaced Population (Plan Nacional para la Atención Integral a la Población Desplazada). The government has substantially increased the budget for its programs for displaced persons.

Despite these measures, the failure of local officials to act on information gathered by the early warning system has undermined its effectiveness. As this report documents, many displaced youths have not benefited from the education and public health initiatives. Indeed, the Constitutional Court concluded in September 2005 that the measures taken by the government to comply with its 2004 decision were insufficient both in terms of resources and institutional will.

Implementing the provisions of Law 387 to provide all internally displaced families with humanitarian aid and access to education and health services would be costly. The various Colombian government agencies responsible for implementing the law spent over 436,500 million pesos, about U.S. $175 million, between 2000 and 2003, and the government has allocated 474,000 million pesos (some U.S. $191 million) for 2005. Even so, the General Comptroller of the Republic (Contraloría General de la República) found that actual expenditures for the years 2001 and 2002 were 32 percent less than the funds allocated for assistance to internally displaced persons. If the same is true for the years going forward, these agencies have additional resources that they can draw upon to comply with the Constitutional Court's 2004 decision and address the urgent needs of Colombia's displaced population.

The United States is the most influential foreign actor in Colombia. In 2004 it provided more than U.S. $700 million to the government, mostly in military aid. Although 25 percent of the security assistance included in this package is formally subject to human rights conditions, the conditions have not been enforced. In August 2005, for example, U.S. Secretary of State Condoleezza Rice "determined that there is sufficient progress to certify to Congress that the Colombian Government and Armed Forces are meeting statutory criteria related to human rights and severing ties to paramilitary groups." Such certifications have meant that the full amount of aid continues to flow to Colombia even though the government has failed to break ties between the military and abusive paramilitary groups.

Although most U.S. assistance is in the form of military aid, the Internally Displaced Persons Program of the U.S. Agency for International Development (USAID) will provide some U.S. $33 million in FY 2005 and is expected to continue to provide support at least through 2010. In October 2005, USAID entered into an agreement with the International Organization for Migration (IOM) and the Pan American Development Foundation (PADF) under which USAID will provide U.S. $100 million over the next five years to fund a joint IOM/PADF project to provide assistance to internally displaced persons and other vulnerable groups.

The European Union has pledged over €330 million (U.S. $410 million) in aid to Colombia in a package that ends in 2006. Unlike U.S. funding, which mainly goes to Colombia's armed forces, nearly all of the European aid goes to civil society and to the United Nations office in Colombia. In addition to their support through the European Union's programs, several E.U. member states, including the Netherlands, Spain, and the United Kingdom, provide significant bilateral assistance. Canada and Japan also provide bilateral assistance to Colombia.

Human Rights Watch conducted research for this report in and around Bogotá and Cartagena in July and August 2004, with a follow-up visit to Bogotá in September 2005. During our field investigation, we interviewed over seventy adults and children who had been forcibly displaced from their homes because of the conflict. (The names of all children and many of the adults who were forcibly displaced have been changed or withheld to protect their privacy.) We also conducted over fifty other interviews for this report, speaking to teachers, health care providers, activists, academics, lawyers, and government officials.

We assess the treatment of displaced persons according to the standards set forth in the U.N. Guiding Principles on Internal Displacement and that of children according to international law, as set forth in the Convention on the Rights of the Child and other human

The remains of people killed by street violence in Bogota, Colombia, lie in the back of a Instituto de Medicina Legal truck on January 7, 2000. PHOTO BY PIERO POMPONI.

rights instruments. In this report, the word "child" refers to anyone under the age of eighteen.

SIGNIFICANCE

The idea of forcing populations of people out of an original habitat and into a new one is as old as human history. As a concept, the term "displaced people" was first used at the end of World War II to define people liberated from the Nazi concentration camps and not yet relocated into a stable environment. Currently, "displaced populations" is used to designate categories of populations that are forcibly displaced from their environment for different causes. Given the vast numbers of people in such situations, population displacement constitutes a major international concern.

Displaced Colombian people have sought refuge in Venezuela, Ecuador, Panama, and Costa Rica. Many more have fled to the United States, with several thousand granted asylum. There have been repeated calls by human rights groups for the United States to grant Colombians Temporary Protected Status, a categorization available to persons who cannot return home safely because of conflict or other civil disturbances. As of mid-2006, the U.S. had yet to do so. While the U.S. can absorb large numbers of Colombians, the economies of the weaker Latin American countries cannot easily withstand such an influx. The Colombian displacement has increased border tensions with Colombia's neighbors.

The vast majority of forced migrants remain within Colombian borders, however. The Colombian government has attempted to enact a system that helps the displaced. Comprehensive legislation has specified the rights of the displaced and the responsibilities of government entities at all levels. The system is coordinated by the Network of Social Solidarity (RSS), created in 1994. RSS gives basic services to the displaced for free for three months and thereafter for a small charge. The sheer numbers of the displaced have overwhelmed the system and the situation shows no signs of improving in the near future.

FURTHER RESOURCES

Books

Richani, Nazih. *Systems of Violence: The Political Economy of War and Peace in Colombia*. Albany, N.Y.: The State University of New York Press, 2002.

Stafford, Frank and Marco Palacios. *Colombia: Fragmented Land, Divided Society*. New York: Oxford University Press, 2002.

Violence in Colombia, 1990–2000, edited by Charles Bergquist, Ricardo Peñaranda, and Gonzalo Sànchez. Wilmington, N.C.: SR Books, 2001.

Milosevic Case Information Sheet

Document

By: United Nations International Criminal Tribunal for the Former Yugoslavia

Date: April 5, 2005

Source: United Nations International Criminal Tribunal for the Former Yugoslavia. Milosevic Case Information Sheet (IT-02-54) "Bosnia and Herzegovina." The Hague, April 5, 2005.

About the Author: The phrase "United Nations" was used during World War II (1939–1945) to describe the dozens of nations allied together to fight Germany and Japan, most notably including China, France, Great Britain, the Soviet Union, and the United States of America. These allies decided to develop a new organization to facilitate international cooperation and help prevent future wars. It would replace the League of Nations, which had failed to prevent World War II. They called it the United Nations (UN). The UN Charter was ratified on October 24, 1945. In the years since the UN has served as a forum for international negotiation and cooperation on many issues, including international security, human rights, trade and economics, and the environment.

INTRODUCTION

On January 15, 1999, forty-five ethnic Albanian civilians died in an attack on Racak, a village in Kosovo. These slayings came from a long history of violence and brutality in the region. Kosovo traditionally marked the geographic boundary between Orthodox Christian and Ottoman Muslim populations in the Balkans. It is a predominantly ethnic Albanian state, and when the Serbs obtained Kosovo from the Ottoman Empire in 1912–1913 ethnic lines proved to be a central point of contention. These battles began the history of selective and gender coded killings. The prime targets, for Serbian violence, were Albanian men. In one instance, Serbian military commanders invited peaceful Albanian men to their homes. When the Albanians arrived, they were executed. This legacy of violence and intense ethnic hostilities laid the framework for the massacres of the late 1990s. The rise to power of Serbian leader Slobodan Milosevic in 1987–1989 brought the plight of ethnic Albanians to the center of the human rights debates.

Milosevic's control of power led to the 1989 removal of Kosovo's provincial status within the Yugoslav Federation of States and was followed with Milosevic's orchestration of a police state within the territory. Milosevic empowered Serbs to migrate to Kosovo and brutalize ethnic Albanians because the region provided an extension of Serbian influence. Also, many Serbs viewed Kosovo as essential to their national identity. Albanians outnumbered Serbs by nine to one in Kosovo, which led to ferocious acts by Serbs for control in the region. Serbs viewed Kosovo in the same manner that Adolf Hitler and Nazi Germany previously viewed Chezkoslovakia, Austria, and other countries surrounding Germany. Furthermore, many of the tactics that the Serbs used against Albanians mirrored those of World War II Germany's policy towards Jews. This police state forced ten of thousands of ethnic Albanians from their homes and jobs, saw a mass exodus of ethnic Albanians from Kosovo, and brought forth one of the largest diaspora communities. These diaspora communities referred to the displaced citizens of Kosovo who fled throughout Europe and North America. They fled because of political and economic repression, and they also left their homeland for fear of their safety. Milosevic's regime continued to commit atrocities against ethnic Albanians, and between 1987 and 1997, more than half of the adult male Albanian population was arrested, remanded, or interrogated.

In 1998, major uprisings occurred in Kosovo, with the first beginning in February. An excess of two thousand people died in the conflict, with seven hundred unaccounted for and another one thousand detained by Serbs. The 1998 uprisings stemmed from the formation of the Kosovo Liberation Army (KLA). The KLA first appeared in 1992, and it generally took a non-violent stance for resisting Serbian political control. In 1995, it officially changed tactics, and it began actively and openly committing acts of retribution and aggression against Serbs. The year 1995 proved a turning point for the KLA because the question of

Kosovo's status was ignored at the Dayton Peace talks. The Dayton Peace Accords (drafted at the Dayton Air Force Base in Dayton, Ohio) established boundaries and settlements to end the fighting between Bosnia and Herzegovina. Bosnia and Herzegovina are also in the Balkans, bordering Yugoslavia. The KLA felt that in order for the international community to take Kosovo's claims of sovereignty seriously, its citizens had to make a public fight. When the KLA began committing acts of violence to support their fight for Kosovo's political independence, the Serbian government labeled them as terrorists, and the killings in Kosovo increased.

In 1998, both the Serbian army and the KLA both committed atrocious acts upon one another. On several occasions, international investigators attempted to enter the area to examine the conflict, but Serbian authorities prevented representatives from the International Criminal Tribunal for the Former Yugoslavia (ICTY) from entering the region. In January 1999, the KLA killed three Serbian policemen, and the Racak attack occurred just a few days later. The Racak attack shows the intensity of the Serbian-Albanian fights, and it also demonstrates the mass exodus of ethnic Albanians from the area. In August 1999, almost two thousand people resided in the village; by the following January, about three hundred remained.

Former Yugoslav President Slobodan Milosevic waits for the start of his defense case at the Yugoslav war crimes tribunal in Hague, the Netherlands on July 5, 2004. © BAS CZERWINSKI/POOL/REUTERS/CORBIS.

PRIMARY SOURCE

THE INDICTMENT "KOSOVO"

Factual allegations: The Second Amended Indictment, confirmed on 29 October 2001, alleges that, between 1 January 1999 and 20 June 1999, forces of the FRY [Federal Republic of Yugoslavia] and Serbia acting at the direction, with the encouragement, or with the support of the Accused, executed a campaign of terror and violence directed at Kosovo Albanian civilians.

It is alleged that the operations targeting the Kosovo Albanians were undertaken with the objective of expelling a substantial portion of the Kosovo Albanian population from Kosovo in an effort to ensure continued Serbian control over the province. The Indictment goes on to describe a series of well-planned and coordinated operations undertaken by the forces of the FRY and Serbia.

Approximately 800,000 Kosovo Albanian civilians were expelled from the province by their forced removal and subsequent looting and destruction of their homes, or by the shelling of villages. Surviving residents were sent to the borders of neighbouring countries. En route, many were killed, abused and had their possessions and identification papers stolen. Furthermore, specific massacres allegedly committed by Serb forces in places such as Djakovica/Gjakovë, Suva Reka/Suharekë, Racak/Reçak, Bela Crkva/Bellacërkë, Mala Krusa/Krusëe Vogël, Velika Krusa/Krushë e Madhe, Padaliste/Padalishtë, Izbica/Izbicë, Vucitrn/Vushtrri, Dubrava/Dubravë Prison complex, Meja/Mejë and Kacanik/Kacanik are listed in the Indictment.

The Accused are charged by virtue of their positions, as follows: Slobodan Milosevic as President of the FRY, Supreme Commander of the VJ, President of the Supreme Defence Council and pursuant to his de facto authority; Milan Milutinovic as President of Serbia, member of the Supreme Defence Council and pursuant to his de facto authority; Dragoljub Ojdanic as Chief of General Staff of the VJ; Nikola Sainovic as Deputy Prime Minister of Serbia; Vlajko Stojiljkovic as Minister of Internal Affairs of Serbia.

Charges: The Indictment charges Slobodan Milosevic, Milan Milutinovic, Dragoljub Ojdanic, Nikola Sainovic and Vlajko Stojiljkovic on the basis of individual criminal responsibility (Article 7(1) of the Statute) and superior criminal responsibility (Article 7(3) thereof) with: one count of violations of the laws or customs of war (Article 3 - murder), and four counts of crimes against humanity (Article 5—deportation; murder; persecutions on political, racial or religious grounds; other inhumane acts).

THE INDICTMENT "CROATIA"

Factual allegations: The Second Amended Indictment was filed by the Prosecution on 26 July 2004 and ordered the operative Indictment by the Trial Chamber on 28 July 2004. According to the Indictment, Slobodan Milosevic participated in a "joint criminal enterprise" between at least 1 August 1991 and June 1992. The purpose of this enterprise was the forcible removal of the majority of the Croat and other non-Serb population from approximately one-third of the territory of the Republic of Croatia, an area he planned to become part of a new Serb-dominated state. This area included those regions that were referred to by Serb authorities as the "Serbian Autonomous District ("SAO") Krajina," the "SAO Western Slavonia," and the "SAO Slavonia, Baranja and Western Srem" (collectively referred to by Serb Authorities after 19 December 1991 as the "Republic of Serbian Krajina ("RSK")) and "Dubrovnik Republic."

It is alleged that, during the above period, Serb forces, comprised of the Yugoslav People's Army ("JNA") units, local Territorial Defence ("TO") units and TO units from Serbia and Montenegro, local and Serbian Ministry of Internal Affairs ("MUP") police units and paramilitary units, attacked and took control of towns, villages and settlements in the territories listed above. After the takeover, the Serb forces, in cooperation with the local Serb authorities, established a regime of persecutions designed to drive the Croat and other non-Serb civilian population from these territories.

This regime included the extermination or murder of hundreds of Croat and other non-Serb civilians, including women and elderly persons, the deportation or forcible transfer of at least 170,000 Croat and other non-Serb civilians and the confinement or imprisonment under inhumane conditions of thousands of Croat and other non-Serb civilians. As a result, virtually the whole of the Croat and other non-Serb civilian population were forcibly removed, deported or killed in the "Serbian Autonomous District ("SAO") Krajina," the "SAO Western Slavonia," and the "SAO Slavonia, Baranja and Western Srem" regions.

Further, public and private property in all the relevant areas was intentionally and wantonly destroyed and plundered, including homes, religious, historical and cultural buildings.

According to the Indictment, during the relevant period, Slobodan Milosevic was President of the Republic of Serbia and as such exercised effective control or substantial influence over the participants of the joint criminal enterprise and, either alone or acting in concert with others, effectively controlled or substantially influenced the actions of the Federal Presidency of the Socialist Republic of Yugoslavia ("SFRY") and later the Federal Republic of Yugoslavia ("FRY"), the Serbian MUP, the JNA, the Serb-run TO staff in the relevant territories, and the Serb volunteer groups.

Charges: The Indictment charges Slobodan Milosevic on the basis of individual criminal responsibility (Article 7(1) of the Statute) and superior criminal responsibility (Article 7(3) thereof) with: nine counts of grave breaches of the 1949 Geneva Conventions (Article 2 thereof—wilful killing; unlawful confinement; torture; wilfully causing great suffering; unlawful deportation or transfer; extensive destruction and appropriation of property, not justified by military necessity and carried out unlawfully and wantonly),

Thirteen counts of violations of the laws or customs of war (Article 3 thereof - murder; torture; cruel treatment; wanton destruction of villages, or devastation not justified by military necessity; destruction or wilful damage done to institutions dedicated to education or religion; plunder of public or private property; attacks on civilians; destruction or wilful damage done to historic monuments and institutions dedicated to education or religion; unlawful attacks on civilian objects), and

Ten counts of crimes against humanity (Article 5 thereof - persecutions on political, racial or religious grounds; extermination; murder; imprisonment; torture; inhumane acts; deportation; inhumane acts (forcible transfers)).

THE INDICTMENT "BOSNIA AND HERZEGOVINA"

Factual allegations: Individual Criminal Responsibility (Article 7(1) of the Statute) According to the Amended Indictment filed on 22 November 2002 and confirmed on 21 April 2004, from 1987 until late 2000, Slobodan Milosevic was the dominant political figure in Serbia and the SFRY/FRY. It is alleged that Slobodan Milosevic, acted alone and in the joint criminal enterprise in the following ways:

(a) He exerted effective control over the elements of the Yugoslav People's Army ("JNA") and the Yugoslav Army ("VJ") which participated in the planning, preparation, facilitation and execution of the forcible removal of the majority of non-Serbs, principally Bosnian Muslims and Bosnian Croats, from large areas of Bosnia and Herzegovina.

(b) He provided financial, logistical and political support to the Bosnian Serb Army ("VRS"). These forces subsequently participated in the execution of the joint criminal enterprise.

(c) He exercised substantial influence over and assisted the political leadership of the "Republika Srpska" in the planning, preparation, facilitation and execution of the take-over of municipalities in Bosnia and Herzegovina and the subsequent forcible removal of the majority of non-Serbs.

(d) He participated in the planning and preparation of the take-over of municipalities in Bosnia and Herzegovina and the subsequent forcible removal of the majority of non-Serbs. He provided the financial, material and logistical support for such a take-over.

(e) He participated in the formation, financing, supply, support and direction of special forces of the Republic of Serbia Ministry of Internal Affairs ("MUP"). These special forces participated in the execution of the joint criminal enterprise.

(f) He participated in providing financial, logistical and political support and direction to Serbian irregular forces or paramilitaries. These forces participated in the execution of the joint criminal enterprise.

(g) He controlled, manipulated or otherwise utilised Serbian state-run media to spread exaggerated and false messages of ethnically based attacks by Bosnian Muslims and Croats against Serbs intended to create an atmosphere of fear and hatred among Serbs living in Serbia, Croatia and Bosnia and Herzegovina which contributed to the forcible removal of the majority of non-Serbs.

Superior Criminal Responsibility (Article 7(3) of the Statute) The Indictment further alleges that Slobodan Milosevic, while holding positions of superior authority, is also responsible for the acts and/or omissions of his subordinates, pursuant to Article 7(3) of the Statute. A superior is responsible for the criminal acts of his subordinates if he knew or had reason to know that his subordinates were about to commit such acts or had done so, and the superior failed to take the necessary and reasonable measures to prevent such acts or punish the perpetrators.

According to the Indictment the Federal Presidency had effective control over the JNA as its "Commander-in-Chief" and other units under the supervision of the JNA. Generals Veljko Kadijevic and Blagoje Adzic, who directed and supervised the JNA in Bosnia and Herzegovina, were in constant communication and consultation with the Accused.

On 27 April 1992, the Supreme Defence Council was formed. As a member of the Supreme Defence Council and as President of the FRY, Milosevic had de jure and de facto control over the JNA and later the VJ.

The Indictment also alleges that Milosevic exercised control over key figures in the Serbian MUP as well as in the State Security (Drzavna bezbednost, DB). The MUP and the DB directed the actions of the special forces and Serb paramilitary groups operating in Bosnia and Herzegovina.

Charges: The Indictment charges Slobodan Milosevic on the basis of individual criminal responsibility (Article 7(1) of the Statute) and superior criminal responsibility (Article 7(3) thereof) with:

Two counts of genocide and complicity in genocide under Article 4 of the Statute;

Ten counts of crimes against humanity involving persecution, extermination, murder, imprisonment, torture, deportation and inhumane acts (forcible transfers) under Article 5 of the Statute;

Eight counts of grave breaches of the Geneva Conventions of 1949 involving wilful killing, unlawful confinement, torture, wilfully causing great suffering, unlawful deportation or transfer, and extensive destruction and appropriation of property under Article 2 of the Statute, and;

Nine counts of violations of the laws or customs of war involving inter alia attacks on civilians, unlawful destruction, plunder of property and cruel treatment under Article 3 of the Statute.

SIGNIFICANCE

In response to the 1998 conflicts in Kosovo, culminating with the Racak attack, United States troops entered the region under the flag of the United Nations. The U.S. troops had the mission of acting as peacekeepers. The Serbs continued their attacks against the KLA and ethnic Albanians, and they concentrated their efforts to the semi-circular part of western Kosovo that bordered Albania. In addition to international military presence, the North Atlantic Treaty Organization (NATO) initiated a series of air strikes on Yugoslavia for its role in the acts of genocide and suppression of ethnic Albanians. Citizens of Yugoslavia viewed these attacks as unfair and aggressive, since it was the actions of the Milosevic regime and not them that brought the violence to Kosovo. Additionally, the air strikes caused considerable damage to Yugoslavian communities and civilians.

As of 2006, the exact number of Serbs and ethnic Albanians killed in the protracted dispute is unknown, and speculation states that Serbs went to considerable efforts to cover up the bodies of Albanians. In May 1999, the ICTY charged Milosevic with war crimes in Kosovo. This action marked the first time a sitting head of state was charged with violations of humanitarian law. In 2000, Milosevic was usurped from office, and refugees slowly began to return to their homes. As ethnic Albanians returned to Kosovo, over 100,000 Serbs fled the province in fear of relation by the KLA.

Kosovo, as of May 2006, is an autonomous province within the Former Republic of Yugoslavia. The United Nations continues to monitor Kosovo. As of May 2006, international talks on the future of Kosovo have not concluded with any resolution. These UN-sanctioned talks began on February 20, 2006.

FURTHER RESOURCES

Books

Independent International Commission on Kosovo. *Kosovo Report: Conflict * International Response * Lessons Learned*. Oxford and New York: Oxford University Press, 2001.

Judah, Tim. *Kosovo: War and Revenge*. New Haven, CT: Yale University Press, 2002.

Periodicals

Anonymous. "Iraq and Kosovo: A Meditation on American Power." *New Perspectives Quarterly*. 22.4 (Fall 2005): 27-30.

Johnstone, Ian. "The Plea of Necessity in International Legal Discourse: Humanitarian Intervention and Counter-terrorism." *Columbia Journal of Transnational Law*. 43.2 (2005): 337-88.

Web sites

United Nations. "United Nations Interim Mission in Kosovo." May 5, 2006. <http://www.unmikonline.org/> (accessed May 5, 2006).

Mass Grave Near Samawa in the Muthanna Province in Iraq

Photograph

By: Anonymous

Date: April 21, 2005

Source: AP Images.

About the Photographer: This image was taken by a staff photographer for the Associated Press, a worldwide news agency based in New York.

INTRODUCTION

In April 2005, an international team of forensic experts began to examine the site of a mass grave in the town of Samawa, some 230 miles (370 kilometers) southeast of Baghdad, Iraq. Its purpose was to collect evidence for the legal prosecution of Saddam Hussein (ruler of Iraq, 1979–2003) and his top officers for these and other killings. Hussein's trial began in July 2004 and was ongoing as of early 2006.

The mass grave near Samawa is located near the Euphrates River. The dead were originally placed in eighteen trenches. Clothing and artifacts found with the bodies make it clear that most of the victims were Kurds, that is, members of the ethnic-national Kurdish people, whose area is partly occupied by Turkey and partly by Iraq. Because of Kurdish agitation for an independent homeland, they have been harshly persecuted both in Turkey and, under Saddam Hussein, in Iraq. Under Hussein, some Kurdish communities were forcibly removed from their villages in order to repopulate them with Arab settlers loyal to the Hussein regime. Displacement of Kurds and the use of poison gas to kill approximately five thousand Kurds in the town of Halabja in 1988 were among the charges brought against Hussein during his trial.

Exhumation of remains began at Samawa in early April 2005. By the end of the month, investigators had recovered the remains of about 113 victims. All but five were women and children. It is likely that the victims were made to dig the graves, then forced to stand at the edge and shot so that they would fall directly in. This technique was also used extensively by Nazi forces massacring Jews in Eastern Europe during World War II.

Only after the removal of the Hussein regime in 2003 was it possible to access the mass grave at Samawa and the approximately three hundred others that have been tentatively identified in Iraq. Because of continued instability in the country, investigation of mass graves has been slow; as of April 30, 2005, over two years after the invasion, investigators had only begun work on two such sites. Relatives of the missing, anguished by uncertainty over their loved ones' fate, had begun amateur exhumations of some mass graves. Experts point out that this disturbs evidence, making it more difficult to identify many bodies and potentially invalidating the gravesite as evidence against Hussein and his officers.

■ PRIMARY SOURCE

MASS GRAVE NEAR SAMAWA IN THE MUTHANNA PROVINCE IN IRAQ

See primary source image.

■

SIGNIFICANCE

The human rights group Amnesty International states that tens or hundreds of thousands of Iraqis, including many Kurds, were killed by Iraqi security forces during the reign of Saddam Hussein. The use of

■ **PRIMARY SOURCE**

Mass Grave Near Samawa in the Muthanna Province in Iraq: During an April 21, 2005 excavation, a pathologist and archaeologist examine human remains found in a mass grave near Samawa, in the Muthanna Province of Iraq. They are collecting evidence to use in prosecuting Saddam Hussein and his top lieutenants for the mass killings of ethnic Kurds and Shiites during his more than 30 year reign as dictator. AP IMAGES.

torture and rape was also widespread and systematic under Hussein. Disappearances and mass executions were, according to Amnesty International, at their heaviest during the years of the Iran-Iraq war, 1980–1988.

Hussein's atrocities are significant in ongoing political debates about whether the invasion and occupation of Iraq were justified. The U.S.-led invasion of Iraq in March 2003 was justified at the time by U.S. officials on several grounds, including Iraq's alleged possession of "weapons of mass destruction"; alleged Iraqi ties to Al Qaeda and other terrorist organizations to which, it was said, Hussein might pass some of his weapons of mass destruction for use against the United States; and humanitarian relief for the Iraqi people. In the years following the invasion, no weapons of mass destruction or devices for the production of such weapons were found in Iraq, nor was any evidence of ties between Hussein and terrorist groups responsible for the September 11, 2001 attacks or other attacks on the United States found. These deficits have caused the humanitarian rationale—remove the tyrant, bring democracy—to become more important as a justification of U.S. actions. Exhumation of mass graves and revelations of torture chambers maintained by the Hussein regime have often been cited as evidence that "the world is better off without Saddam Hussein" (President George Bush during a debate with Sen. John Kerry, September 30, 2004) and that the U.S. invasion was justified regardless of whether Iraq was a military threat to the United States.

However, most of the killings by the Hussein regime took place during the 1980s, during which period he was actually a recipient of diplomatic and material support from the Reagan administration. In 1982, the U.S. State Department removed Iraq from its list of states supporting terrorism. During Hussein's reign, the U.S. government saw to it that Iraq received U.S. loans, provided Iraq with military intelligence, and in 1984 sent Donald Rumsfeld (later the second Bush administration's Secretary of Defense) to meet personally with Hussein and assure him that U.S. official condemnation of Iraqi use of chemical weapons against Iran should not cause Hussein to fear that the United States would cease positive relations. Critics of the Iraq invasion have pointed to these facts in support of the view that U.S. concern for Hussein's victims was not a motive for invading Iraq in 2003. Defenders of U.S. Iraq policy point to ongoing revelations of Hussein's brutality, including the bodies exhumed at Samawa, to justify the 2003 invasion, arguing that Iraq is better off

today, despite widespread civil violence, than before the invasion.

FURTHER RESOURCES

Books

Human Rights Watch. *Human Rights in Iraq.* New Haven, Conn.: Yale University Press, 1990.

Subcommittee on the Middle East and Central Asia of the Committee on International Relations, U.S. House of Representatives. *Human Rights Violations under Saddam Hussein: Victims Speak out.* Washington, D.C.: U.S. Government Printing Office, 2004.

Periodicals

Loeb, Vernon. "Rumsfeld Visited Baghdad in 1984 to Reassure Iraqis, Documents Show." The *Washington Post* (December 19, 2003).

Web sites

CNN.com. "Experts Combing Through Mass Grave in Iraq." April 30, 2005. <http://edition.cnn.com/2005/WORLD/meast/04/30/iraq.main> (accessed May 5, 2006).

National Security Archive, George Washington University. "Shaking Hands with Saddam Hussein: The U.S. Tilts Toward Iraq, 1980–1984." February 25, 2003. <http://www.gwu.edu/~nsarchiv/NSAEBB/NSAEBB82> (accessed May 5, 2006).

PEN Protests Charges Against Turkish Author Orhan Pamuk

Press release

By: PEN American Center

Date: September 2, 2005

Source: PEN American Center. "PEN Protests Charges Against Turkish Author Orhan Pamuk." Press Release, September 2, 2005.

About the Author: PEN American Center, the largest chapter of the human rights organization International PEN, began in 1922 to advance literature, defend free speech, and foster international literary fellowship. It has a membership of 2,900 writers, editors, and translators.

INTRODUCTION

Orhan Pamuk, the best-selling novelist in Turkish history and a major international literary figure, remarked to a Swiss interviewer in February 2005 that a million Armenians had been killed and he was the only Turk who dared to talk about it. By doing so, Pamuk highlighted Turkey's repression of free speech. He faced trial in 2006 for publicly denigrating Turkish identity.

For centuries, the Turks ruled over Armenia. When nationalistic Armenians began to press for greater rights in the 1870s, the leaders of the Ottoman Empire repressed them in various violent ways. During World War I, the Russian government recruited thousands of Armenians to join the army and fight against the Ottoman Empire. In 1915, leaders in Constantinople decided that the two million Armenians living within Turkey were a threat that needed to be eliminated. The Turkish rulers found a pretext for the massacre in the claim that the Armenians were openly supporting the Russians.

The Turkish government planned to proceed in stages. First, they would kill the chief Armenian leaders. The Turks would then disarm Armenian soldiers in the Ottoman army and place them in battalions on the railroads, where they might be killed off in small groups. The Turks would then move against outlying Armenian villages, killing every adult and teenaged male inhabitant in sight. The women and children who remained would be sent on forced marches to the eastern desert areas. Worn down by exhaustion and starvation, only a minority were expected to survive.

On the night of April 23, 1915, a coordinated Turkish government operation led to the arrest of hundreds of Armenian leaders. Many were executed or soon died in confinement. Next, the government ordered local authorities to forcibly relocate Armenians in Anatolia to Alleppo and then to remote mountainous or desert locations in the Mesopotamian desert. These relocations were actually extermination marches during which most of the Armenians were murdered, beaten, and raped by Kurds or vengeful Turks. Estimates of the number of Armenians who died from violence, starvation, or disease as a result of Turkish actions ranges from 600,000 to 1.5 million people. As of 2006, the Turkish government denies that any wartime massacre of Armenians ever occurred.

■ PRIMARY SOURCE

New York, New York, September 2, 2005—PEN American Center expressed shock today that world-famous Turkish writer Orhan Pamuk will be brought before an Istanbul court on December 16 and that he faces up to three years in prison for a comment published in a Swiss newspaper earlier this year.

Orhan Pamuk. PHOTOGRAPH BY SOPHIE BASSOULS. © CORBIS. REPRODUCED BY PERMISSION.

The charges stem from an interview given by Orhan Pamuk to the Swiss newspaper Tages Anzeiger on February 6, 2005, in which he is quoted as saying that "thirty thousand Kurds and a million Armenians were killed in these lands and nobody but me dares to talk about it."

Pamuk was referring to the killings by Ottoman Empire forces of thousands of Armenians in 1915–1917. Turkey does not contest the deaths, but denies that it could be called "genocide." The "30,000" Kurdish deaths refers to those killed since 1984 in the conflict between Turkish forces and Kurdish separatists. Debate on these issues has been stifled by stringent laws, which often result in lengthy lawsuits, fines, and prison terms.

Orhan Pamuk will be tried under Article 301/1 of the Turkish Penal Code, which states, "A person who explicitly insults being a Turk, the Republic or Turkish Grand National Assembly, shall be imposed to a penalty of imprisonment for a term of six months to three years." To compound matters, Article 301/3 states, "Where insulting being a Turk is committed by a Turkish citizen in a foreign country, the penalty to be imposed shall be increased by one third." Thus, if Pamuk is found guilty, he faces an additional penalty for having made the statement abroad.

PEN finds it extraordinary that a state that has ratified both the United Nations International Covenant on Civil and Political Rights, and the European Convention on Human Rights, both of which see freedom of expression as central, should have a Penal Code that includes a clause that is so clearly contrary to these very same principles. . . .

The trial against Orhan Pamuk is likely to follow the pattern of those against other writers, journalists and publishers similarly prosecuted in Turkey.

Karin Clark, Chair of PEN's Writers in Prison Committee, noted that "PEN has for years been campaigning for an end to Turkish courts trying and imprisoning writers, journalists and publishers under laws that clearly breach international standards to the Turkish government itself has pledged commitment."

Although the numbers of convictions and prison sentences under laws that penalize free speech in Turkey has declined in the past decade, PEN currently has on its records over fifty writers, journalists and publishers before the courts. This is despite a series of amendments to the Penal Code in recent years aimed at meeting demands for human rights improvements as a condition for opening talks into Turkey's application for membership of the European Union. . . .

Orhan Pamuk is one of Turkey's most well known authors, whose works have been published world wide in over twenty languages. In 2003 he won the International IMPAC award for *My Name is Red*. His 2004 novel *Snow* has met with similar acclaim. His most recent book, *Istanbul*, is a personal history of his native city.

In early 2005, news of the interview for which Pamuk will stand trial led to protests in Turkey that included reports that copies of his books were burned. He also suffered death threats from extremists. PEN members world-wide then called on the Turkish government to condemn these attacks.

SIGNIFICANCE

Pamuk's statement about the Armenian genocide is accepted by most historians as an accurate summary of Ottoman treatment of the Armenians. It is not accepted as truthful by the Turks. In Turkey, newspapers launched hate campaigns against Pamuk with some columnists even suggesting that he should be silenced. Pamuk also received specific death threats.

His books and his posters were burned at rallies. Fearful for his life, he went into hiding. In late 2005, the Turkish government made all insults to the state punishable by three years imprisonment. Pamuk then emerged into the open to join sixty other writers and journalists in awaiting trial for state defamation. He joked that friends had told him that he was, at last, a real Turkish writer.

Pamuk's trial in December 2005 was adjourned within minutes when the judge passed the matter to the justice minister. In January 2006, the justice minister passed the case back to the judge, who decided that there was no case to answer. The Turkish government, concerned about derailing its decade-long effort to join the European Union (EU), did not want to further inflame the international condemnation triggered by Pamuk's prosecution. The Pamuk charges appeared in international headlines just weeks before Turkey planned to seek approval to enter the EU. Turkey's pro-European Islamist government had been implementing reforms at a rapid rate in order to qualify for EU membership. It did not want to allow conservatives in Europe to portray Turkey as undeserving of EU membership or conservatives at home to invent a humiliation to serve ultra-rightwing, nationalistic causes. Within Turkey, conservative forces were already angry about perceived EU interference in Turkish affairs.

While Pamuk's case ended on a technicality, dozens of other writers went to jail for insulting Turkish identity or the country's state institutions. The Turkish government, despite the embarrassment caused by Pamuk's prosecution, remains unwilling to remove the law that bars freedom of expression. The EU has been watching these cases and the episodes have badly damaged Turkey's chances of joining the union.

FURTHER RESOURCES
Books

Tamer Akcam. *A Shameful Act: The Armenian Genocide and the Question of Turkish Responsibility*. New York: Metropolitan Books, 2006.

Donald Bloxham. *The Great Game of Genocide: Imperialism, Nationalism, and the Destruction of the Ottoman Armenians*. New York: Oxford University Press, 2005.

Orhan Pamuk. *Istanbul: Memories and the City*. New York: Knopf, 2005.

Web sites

PEN American Center. "News at PEN." <http://www.pen.org/> (accessed May 6, 2006).

Nashi ("Ours")

Photograph

By: Denis Sinyakov

Date: 2006

Source: AFP/Getty Images, 2006.

About the Photographer: Denis Sinyakov is a contributing photographer for Agence France-Presse (AFP), the world's oldest established news agency, founded in 1835. The photograph is part of the collection at Getty Images, a worldwide provider of visual content materials to such communications groups as advertisers, broadcasters, designers, magazines, new media organizations, newspapers, and producers.

INTRODUCTION

The young Russian man in the photograph is a member of the nationalist Russian youth group Nashi, which means "ours" or "our side" in Russian. He is handing out information leaflets on the Holocaust, the mass killing enterprise run by the Nazis during World War II that killed roughly ten million persons, including approximately six million Jews. The display and leaflets are evidently designed to counter Holocaust denial in Russia. Holocaust denial is the claim that the Holocaust did not really happen but is a product of Jewish propaganda. Holocaust denial is protected by the First Amendment in the United States, like other offensive speech, but is illegal in most of Europe. Since it is not illegal in Russia, many Holocaust deniers and other anti-Semites have recently taken refuge there, provoking counter-efforts such as that shown in the photograph.

Nashi has at least three thousand members. It was founded in the spring of 2005 and is funded by the Russian government.

PRIMARY SOURCE

NASHI ("OURS")

See primary source image.

SIGNIFICANCE

This photograph of a young Russian man passing out leaflets commemorating the Holocaust illustrates that in Russian politics, perhaps even more so than in the politics of other countries, things are not always what they seem. Nashi is not primarily a Holocaust memorial organization or human-rights organization;

it is pro-Putin and pro-Kremlin. (Vladimir Putin, born 1952, has been President of the Russian Federation since 1999.) In the rhetoric of Nashi, most persons who oppose the Putin government in whatever political mode are "fascists," including the left-liberal party Yabloko; the group has declared its opposition to "the anti-Fatherland union of oligarchs, anti-Semites, Nazis, and liberals."

Nashi's anti-Holocaust-denial activities must therefore be read in the context of Russian politics. The Holocaust was the work of bona fide fascists, the Nazis, who were also the mortal enemies of Russia during World War II (during which Russia suffered twenty-one million dead). Therefore, insisting on the gravity of Nazi crimes tends to validate Nashi's claim to be anti-fascist. Yet Nazis are not the political opponents that Nashi actually faces: its real opposition consists primarily of reformist youth groups, left-liberal parties calling for democratization, and old-age pensioners angered by Putin's 2005 announcement that pension benefits dating to the Soviet era are to be terminated.

Nashi's promotion of accurate information about the Holocaust is therefore not a sufficient guide to the organization's political character. In the Russian political context, defending the reality of the Holocaust can (and here, does) serve as secondary propaganda designed to bolster the credibility of a group that wishes to credential itself as "anti-fascist" and therefore pro-Russian.

The rise of youth as a major political force in Russia is recent. A number of Russian youth groups have been formed to press for government reforms, including greater democracy. These are modeled on the "orange revolution" that took place in the neighboring country of Ukraine in 2004–2005, when hundreds of thousands of Ukrainians peacefully protested government corruption and assured the electoral victory of opposition candidate Viktor Yushchenko. Nashi was created by the Russian government expressly to counter these "orange" groups in the run-up to the Russian presidential elections of 2008.

Critics of Nashi say that its real purpose is to recruit ex-skinheads for street attacks on pro-democratization groups. Nashi leaders have called for "intimidation" of opposition parties and one of the founders of Nashi, Vasily Yakemenko, said in 2005 in an interview with a Russian newspaper that "It is necessary to make short work of traitors."

FURTHER RESOURCES
Books
Russian Politics Under Putin, edited by Cameron Ross. New York: Manchester University Press, 2004.

PRIMARY SOURCE

Nashi ("Ours"): A member of a Kremlin-backed youth group called Nashi ("Ours") hands out leaflets outside the Moscow Choral Synagogue. He is standing in front of a replica of a Holocaust period Jewish room, a commemoration of the six million Jews who died in the Holocaust. DENIS SINYAKOV/AFP/GETTY IMAGES.

Periodicals

Finn, Peter. "Another Russian Revolution? Youth Movement Adopts Spirit of Uprisings Nearby." The *Washington Post* (April 9, 2005).

Lipman, Masha. "Preempting Politics in Russia." The *Washington Post*, (July 25, 2005).

Peterson, Scott. "New Political Force in Russia: Youths." *Christian Science Monitor* (March 16, 2005).

Web sites

BBC News. "Russian Youth on Political Barricades." <http://news.bbc.co.uk/2/hi/europe/4308655.stm> (accessed May 1, 2006).

3 Imprisonment

Imprisonment

Seldom is an individual more vulnerable to neglect or abuse than while imprisoned. The treatment of prisoners is one of the most debated and monitored areas of current human rights advocacy.

Even before the modern conception of "human rights" arose, there was concern over the condition of prisons and the treatment of prisoners. The sweeping prison reform movements of the nineteenth and early twentieth centuries in Britain and the United States advocated that prisoners—regardless of offense—were entitled to adequate food and clothing, medical care, exercise, sanitary living conditions, and freedom from physical abuse. The most controversial aspects of the early prison reform movement centered on the prevention of maltreatment and physical abuse. For some reformers, this meant only freedom from physical torture. Others crusaded for the abolishment of hard labor, strip searches, and solitary confinement cells.

The international interest in the conditions of imprisonment began after World War II. The horrors of the Nazi forced labor camps (featured in this chapter) prompted international action to guard the rights of prisoners of war. The seminal documents protecting the human rights of prisoners of war and providing for the punishment of war criminals are in the chapter *Development of Human Rights*, but the incidents that inspired their drafting and fuel current debate are included here.

This chapter also highlights human rights issues that arise from imprisonment outside of the context of war. Criminal imprisonment and the debate over the use of capital punishment in the United States are discussed in "We, On Death Row". Interrogation, imprisonment, and execution by police states are highlighted in the article on Pinochet's persecution of political dissidents in Chile. "Open Letter to Deng Xiaoping" furthers discussion of prisoners of conscience—individuals jailed for their political, social, or religious associations and speech.

Debate continues over the rights of prisoners (detainees) held in conjunction with the War on Terror. The decision of several nations, including the United States, to indefinitely detain some terror suspects garnered international criticism. Several articles underscore the debate over prisoners at the U.S. naval base at Guantanamo Bay, Cuba.

Hanging A Woman

Book excerpt

By: Karl Heinzen

Date: July 29, 1855

Source: Heinzen, Karl. *The Rights of Women and the Sexual Relations.* Chicago: Charles H. Kerr & Co., 1898.

About the Author: Karl Heinzen, (1809–1880), represented part of the radical German immigrant community in the United States in the latter nineteenth century. These German radicals fled Germany for political reasons in 1848, and even though they never represented a large part of the immigrant population, they took on the name Forty-Eighters. Their writings and works, like Heinzen's, adamantly called for the removal of slavery and the expansion of religious and civil rights in the United States.

INTRODUCTION

When Henrietta Robinson sat trail in 1853 for poisoning Timothy Langan and the attempted poisoning of another woman, she sat solemn with a heavy veil covering her face. Throughout the locally sensationalized trial, her identity remained hidden, and the press dubbed her the Veiled Murderess. The story of her crime was sensational for the 1850s because a woman on trial for murder seemed preposterous. Victorian Ideals of women held them to be pious and pure, and Robinson's crime of murder shook the foundations of that belief. Robinson murdered Langan by poisoning his beer, and at trail, her lawyers pled a case for insanity. On May 27, 1854, the jury found her guilty, and the following year, the judge sentenced her to death by hanging. On 27 July 1855, however, New York Governor Myron H. Clark commuted her sentence to life imprisonment, at Sing Sing Prison. Eventually, Robinson was transferred to a state mental hospital for mentally insane criminals. Yet, the foundations of her case from Troy, New York shocked her community, and her case represented events occurring on the larger political framework.

The 1850s marked an escalating point in pre-Civil War political debates. The Compromise of 1850 (also called the Pearce Act) admitted California as a free state, slave trade was abolished in Washington D.C., New Mexico, and Utah organized themselves under the guidelines of popular sovereignty, the Fugitive Slave Act went into force, and Texas was required to give up claims to western land. These highly debated legislative decisions came on the heels of a society that was bracing for and revisiting modernity. The Industrial Revolution, and new technologies like Eli Whitney's cotton gin, increased production. As products were made by cheaper and more rapid processes, consumers had more options of products to buy. Technology also boosted transportation, as steam engines and railroads allowed individuals to travel across states and regions in a few days rather than weeks. As politics collided with private life, particularly in the case of slavery, the rights of states to be slaveholding states or free states, and technological advances made mobility and accessibility easier the daily lives of individuals changed.

Women, who had always had networks of support through charity and church groups, began to advocate for more causes of social reform. Their words quickly turned into political activism, and in 1848, the Seneca Falls Convention laid the framework for the twentieth century's women's movement. Elizabeth Cady Stanton led the program, and its culminating moment was the signing and release of the Declaration of Women's Rights and Grievances. Here, women asked for the rights to property ownership, the right to vote, and other basic rights within civil society. These grievances did not become laws until the next century, but female activists did not stand alone in society. Instead, much like the political divisions in the U.S. Congress (and the brawls that occurred on the Congressional floor) mirrored the actions of mainstream society, the Seneca Falls Convention showed dissolving gendered barriers.

News accounts of husbands murdering their wives increased, and in New York the number of female homicides increased from seven to fifteen in the years of 1841 to 1860. These were killings where women committed the act of murder, and these New York statistics reflected a nationwide trend. Violent crime and acts of aggression increased, and men and women discussed their unhappy marriages with friends and persons outside their immediate family. More so, the fate of the unhappy marriage lay on the woman. Social mandates required her to keep the home happy and healthy, and when she could not do so she was often judged. Women who did not or could not provide the image of a happy and healthy family were deemed unfit, even sometimes sent to mental institutions. Women's magazines and news stories continually reminded women to separate their passions from their intellect so that they could keep an ordered and happy life. Women that deviated from the social norms of piety and purity were deemed to be passion-driven and without sound moral judgment. After all, women were thought to be delicate and weak. Hence, when women committed crimes, their actions were shocking to the public's mind. Critics against women rights used cases like Robinson to rebuke a woman's potentially productive role outside the home, and proponents for women's rights used female crimes as reasons why women should be treated equally. In the case of Robinson, German writer Karl Heinzen discussed how a cruel and unjust society could turn a woman into a murderer. His discussion of her commuted sentence reflected social expectations of women and of society's maltreatment of the female.

PRIMARY SOURCE

In Troy, N.Y., a Mrs. Robinson, who has poisoned her husband, has been sentenced to be hanged on the third of August. Now the governor is besieged from all sides with petitions for pardon, because the feelings revolt at the thought of having a woman hanged. What delicacy of feeling in a country where hanging partly takes the place of national holidays! Would not the hanging and dangling of a female prisoner, especially if she were pretty, afford a moist piquant excitement for the savage taste of the criminal mob?

What real motive dictates this petition to the governor? Is it American gallantry? Hardly, for this is usually practised where something is to be gained thereby, were it only the approval of fashion. Is it the disgrace fro the feminine sex which is to witness on of its highly honored members ending on the gallows? Possibly; although at other times we are not so zealous in warding off disgrace from the sex. But the chief motive is presumably a natural aversion towards hanging, which has come into consciousness and reached such a degree of intensity that it at last had to vent itself in petitions for pardon when the spectacle of a feminine delinquent presented itself. And since at the same time the consciousness arose that this aversion had not made itself felt on occasions of the hanging of men, its manifestation is now brought forward under the pretext that it is inhuman or unmanly to hang a woman. If a woman had not suffice to disgust our republican gentlemen with a hanging, a beautiful maiden, or perhaps a child, would have been required to at last universally awaken the consciousness that capital punishment, especially hanging, is a barbarity, nay, even a bestiality. That this recognition could be held in abeyance until a woman became the means of bringing it to light; that the gallows adorned with a male corpse could hitherto be considered as a show, or at least as an interesting spectacle, and was advanced to the dignity of a tragedy only at the thought of a hanged female, proves only how vulgar and unrepublican our popular consciousness still is; for capital punishment, especially hanging, is as great an anomaly in a republic as, for instance, torture for the "religion of love." Perhaps Mrs. Robinson will have

the honor of involuntarily having given the impulse towards the abolition of capital punishment in the chief State of the Union. To be sure, it is no flattering testimony for our worthy law-givers that it required the instruction of a poison-mixer to teach them to become humane!

But apart from this point, and assuming that capital punishment were generally justifiable and ought to be upheld, there is still another ground for protest against the hanging of Mrs. Robinson. This ground lies in the criminal irresponsibility of women as against men. I do not want to make the statement that everything is permissible for a woman to do against a man, but I do want to maintain what holds for women as well as for slaves, that the criminal can be held responsible only to such a degree as he is free. Therefore, whoever wants bondage must be contented to take crime into the bargain; whoever wants the right to punish crime must first concede liberty.

Strictly considered, no member of a political community is responsible before the criminal court, for the moral standard of every individual is only a product of the general standard, so that the responsibility really always falls back upon the community. This reason alone already suffices to stamp everything that we call punishment and the right to punish as nonsense and barbarity.

But if this doubt is thrown in general upon the responsibility of the individual, how much more must this be the case where the ruling portion takes away the responsibility from a class or a sex by disenfranchisement, by limitation, or by neglect! Whoever rules is responsible, for whoever rules is free. But women are ruled, and whoever is ruled is not only not free, but is always the suffering party, and is therefore always thrown back upon the revolution. Woman and the revolution are the most natural confederates. Probably that is the reason why the revolution is always represented as a woman. But ruling man would make woman as well as the slave responsible, although he will not grant them the conditions which make responsibility possible, and thus he punishes in them really himself, i.e., his own wrongdoing. In how far the actions of the suffering party are a necessary reaction against oppression, justifiable acts of defence against inflicted injustice, natural attempts at compensation for rights withheld, a forcibly sought outlet for a nature perverted by force, unavoidable outbreaks of inclinations falsely directed by binding circumstances,—this our present courts of justice shrink from investigating, because such an investigation would overthrow our entire barbaric justice, together with its barbaric foundation. But what the administration of justice neglects to do, the critic, the publicist must at least strive to make good.

Unbiased justice must always be predisposed to take the side of the weaker party, because in a conflict of rights the presumption must generally be that the weaker party has suffered a wrong or has been incited to do a wrong.

"The Execution of Mrs. Hibbins." © BETTMANN/CORBIS.

Women are almost always in that case. For all the wrong that is done by women the men as a rule ought to bear the blame, be it directly on account of their treatment or indirectly through their education of, and the position they impose upon, women. I am not acquainted with Mrs. Robinson's history, and do not remember the proceedings concerning the circumstances and motive of her deed. But so much I do know, that a woman is not by nature designed for a criminal, and that her heart must be wounded or hardened by very peculiar inducements or influences if she can resolve to commit a murder. . . .".

When the men have become so depraved that they must stop to think to which species of beast they belong, it is always the woman who still represents the human species and who still upholds human feelings. When the father has become a beast, the mother saves him again by the birth of a human being.

I do not want to use the moral expression that the woman is "better" than the man, but she certainly is more humanely organized, and in the retirement to which she is condemned she is less exposed to the hardening and demoralizing influences of the vulgar atmosphere in which the male sex at present still disports itself. A crime committed by a woman will, therefore, generally have more cogent and deeper motives than the same crime committed by a man. How often we hear in this country of men who have murdered their wives; and how rare is the opposite case! But who is there to maintain that men have to suffer more at the hands of the women than the women at the hands of the men? This juxtaposition alone proves the weaker disposition of the feminine nature towards criminal deeds; consequently the necessity of applying a different standard in the judging or condemning of a Mrs. Robinson than of a Mr. Whiskeyson or of any wife-murderer by whatsoever name he may be called. A husband may perhaps slay his wife for some pat rejoinder; the wife poisons her husband only after her feelings, her love, her pride, tortured perhaps through all grades of despair, has killed all womanliness within her, and has left nothing of it except the feeling of revenge. . . .".

SIGNIFICANCE

The sensationalism of women committing acts of murder, and other crimes, continued to shock the American public. By the 1890s, increasing numbers of middle-class women were being arrested for shoplifting, even though they could afford the items they stole. These women, labeled as kleptomaniacs, confused the public because middle and upper class women were supposed to have a stronger sense of morality and shame than the working class and poor. Psychiatrics argued that these women needed medical treatment, and they said that the abundance of consumer goods forced people into a sense of hysteria. Of course, the hysteria syndrome stuck to the female gender because it reflected unstable and weak emotions.

In August 1892, Lizzie Borden discovered her father and stepmother murdered in their home. She stood trial for the murders in June 1893, but an all male jury acquitted her after little more than an hour of deliberations. Her trial became a sensational news story covered in many national newspapers, a first for crime stories. Even though she was found not guilty, a large amount of doubt surrounded her. Many members of society found it difficult to believe a woman would kill two people with an axe. While Borden remained in prison, she held special privileges. Borden was allowed to bring her own furniture into her cell, and there are accounts of her wandering through the jail unaccompanied. In contrast to the Robinson defense of insanity, Borden's lawyers painted her as a devout daughter who had remained unmarried to care for her parents. This statement helped ease questions about her spinsterhood, and it helped eradicate skepticism that she could have been a weak and immoral woman. Nonetheless, the Borden trial put key questions into the American legal and social framework. Questions of a woman's legal standing, her ability to commit a crime, and punishment played heavily on the public's mind.

The rise in women's crimes and their fight for political equality saw excessive measures taken to quell their unusual behavior. Women were given hysterectomies to calm them and cure mental ailments like depression, and females who did not fit social orders received electrical shock, water treatments, and large doses of medications. As criminal behavior increased, with men and women, state and local courts slowly began treating a woman the same as a man. As of May 2006, forty-nine women remain on death row in the United States, and the last execution of a female prisoner occurred in October 2002 in Georgia.

FURTHER RESOURCES

Books

Abelson, Elaine S. *When Ladies Go A-Thieving: Middle-Class Shoplifters in the Victorian Department Store.* Oxford and New York: Oxford University Press, 1989.

Edwards, Susan S. M. *Women on Trial: A Study of the Female Suspect, Defendant and Offender in the Criminal Law and Criminal Justice System.* Dover, NH: Manchester University Press, 1984.

Periodicals

Ritter, Gretchen. "Jury Service and Women's Citizenship Before and After the Nineteenth Amendment." *Law and History Review.* 20.3 (Autumn 2002): 479–515.

Kessler-Harris, Alice. "In the Nation's Image: The Gendered Limits of Social Citizenship in the Depression." *The Journal of American History.* 86.3 (December 1999): 1251–1279.

Web sites

Sean T. Moore and SUNY at Plattsburgh. "Husband Murder, Seduction, and Female Violence in New York State, 1790–1860." 2004. <http://faculty.plattsburgh.edu/sean.moore/Chapter%204-Extract%20from%20dissertation.htm> (accessed May 7, 2006).

Executive Order 9066

Resulting in the Internment of Japanese Americans

Executive order

By: Franklin D. Roosevelt

Date: February 19, 1942

Source: Roosevelt, Franklin D. "Executive Order No. 9066." February 19, 1942.

About the Author: Franklin Delano Roosevelt (FDR) was born in 1882 in New Hyde Park, New York. During his youth, he played sports and remained active, but at age thirty-nine, he contracted poliomyelitis (polio). The disease caused him to loose the full use of his legs, and throughout the rest of his life, he used a wheelchair and crutches for mobility. Upon his 1932 election to the presidency, he became the first United States President with a physical disability, which he took great steps to conceal. FDR led the United States through the Great Depression and World War II (1941–1945). He won the presidency for four consecutive terms—the only president to do so—and he died on April 12, 1945 of a cerebral hemorrhage. Franklin D. Roosevelt is also the fifth cousin of Theodore Roosevelt, U.S. president from 1901 to 1909.

INTRODUCTION

On December 7, 1941, Japan launched a surprise attack on the U.S. Pacific Fleet at Pearl Harbor in Hawaii. The attack sank or disabled eighteen ships, killed more than 2,400 Americans, and almost crippled U.S. war-making capacity in the Pacific. Determined that the bombing of Pearl Harbor would not be followed by more sneak attacks, military and political leaders on the West Coast targeted persons of Japanese ancestry as potential saboteurs.

About 320,000 people of Japanese descent lived in the United States in 1941, with two-thirds of them residing in Hawaii. The Hawaiians largely escaped persecution because they were essential and valued members of society. On the mainland, Japanese Americans were a tiny minority. Although an official military survey concluded that Japanese Americans posed no danger, popular hostility fueled a campaign to round up all mainland Japanese Americans, a majority of whom were U.S. citizens. Many Americans simply did not accept that Asians could be loyal Americans.

On February 14, 1942, General John DeWitt, commander of the Western Defense Command, persuaded President Franklin Roosevelt to issue an executive order authorizing the removal of mainland Japanese Americans. Roosevelt issued the order on February 19. On March 21, 1942, Congress enacted the major provisions of 9066 into law and added stringent penalties for those who resisted relocation. As a result, 110,000 men, women, and children were forced to move to internment camps. Although relocated families could stay together, they had to leave their

In San Francisco, California on April 6, 1942, a Japanese boy awaits the return of his parents. They are at an assembly point for the forcible relocation effort that sent thousands of Japanese and Japanese-Americans to camps during World War II. AP IMAGES.

homes and jobs. Property owners suffered enormously because they had to dispose of their holdings in a matter of days and accept whatever price that they could get. Inside the camps, which were ringed with guard towers and fences topped with barbed-wire, the Japanese Americans had little to do. Most cooperated with government authorities.

A few Japanese Americans and their supporters resisted the internment order in the courts as a violation of fundamental constitutional rights. Fred Korematsu, an American citizen who was turned down because of ulcers when he volunteered for the army, refused to leave the war zone. In *Korematsu v. United States* (1944), the Supreme Court upheld the internment of the Japanese Americans on the grounds of "pressing public necessity" though it also declared that legal restrictions that limit the civil rights of a single group are immediately suspect as possible violations of the Equal Protection Clause of the Constitution. The Japanese American internment program officially ended on January 2, 1945 when the government released Japanese Americans from concentration camps and permitted them freedom of movement throughout the country.

PRIMARY SOURCE

Executive Order No. 9066

The President

Executive Order

Authorizing the Secretary of War to Prescribe Military Areas

Whereas the successful prosecution of the war requires every possible protection against espionage and against sabotage to national-defense material, national-defense premises, and national-defense utilities as defined in Section 4, Act of April 20, 1918, 40 Stat. 533, as amended by the Act of November 30, 1940, 54 Stat. 1220, and the Act of August 21, 1941, 55 Stat. 655 (U.S.C., Title 50, Sec. 104);

Now, therefore, by virtue of the authority vested in me as President of the United States, and Commander in Chief of the Army and Navy, I hereby authorize and direct the Secretary of War, and the Military Commanders whom he may from time to time designate, whenever he or any designated Commander deems such action necessary or desirable, to prescribe military areas in such places and of such extent as he or the appropriate Military Commander may determine, from which any or all persons may be excluded, and with respect to which, the right of any person to enter, remain in, or leave shall be subject to whatever restrictions the Secretary of War or the appropriate Military Commander may impose in his discretion. The Secretary of War is hereby authorized to provide for residents of any such area who are excluded therefrom, such transportation, food, shelter, and other accommodations as may be necessary, in the judgment of the Secretary of War or the said Military Commander, and until other arrangements are made, to accomplish the purpose of this order. The designation of military areas in any region or locality shall supersede designations of prohibited and restricted areas by the Attorney General under the Proclamations of December 7 and 8, 1941, and shall supersede the responsibility and authority of the Attorney General under the said Proclamations in respect of such prohibited and restricted areas.

I hereby further authorize and direct the Secretary of War and the said Military Commanders to take such other steps as he or the appropriate Military Commander may deem advisable to enforce compliance with the restrictions applicable to each Military area hereinabove authorized to be designated, including the use of Federal troops and other Federal Agencies, with authority to accept assistance of state and local agencies.

I hereby further authorize and direct all Executive Departments, independent establishments and other Federal Agencies, to assist the Secretary of War or the said Military Commanders in carrying out this Executive Order, including the furnishing of medical aid, hospitalization, food, clothing, transportation, use of land, shelter, and other supplies, equipment, utilities, facilities, and services.

This order shall not be construed as modifying or limiting in any way the authority heretofore granted under Executive Order No. 8972, dated December 12, 1941, nor shall it be construed as limiting or modifying the duty and responsibility of the Federal Bureau of Investigation, with respect to the investigation of alleged acts of sabotage or the duty and responsibility of the Attorney General and the Department of Justice under the Proclamations of December 7 and 8, 1941, prescribing regulations for the conduct and control of alien enemies, except as such duty and responsibility is superseded by the designation of military areas hereunder.

Franklin D. Roosevelt

The White House,

February 19, 1942.

SIGNIFICANCE

The Japanese American internment program and the Supreme Court's approval of it have been generally condemned in the years since World War II. It is commonly agreed that the there was no military necessity for interning people of Japanese ancestry. Historian Peter Irons and other scholars have examined government documents to show how great a role racial stereotyping played in the internment decision. However, Milton Eisenhower, who briefly headed the War Relocation Authority that supervised the internment, has argued that military, political, economic, emotional, and racial forces combined to plunge American society off course.

Following the civil rights movements of the 1950s and 1960s, prejudice against Japanese Americans began to decrease. Starting in the 1970s, a drive began to secure government recognition of the wrong done to Japanese Americans during WWII. On February 19, 1976, President Gerald R. Ford issued a formal apology on behalf of the U.S. government in regard to the internment policy. In 1980, the Commission on Wartime Relocation and Internment of Civilians was established to hear testimony, review wartime documents, and make a recommendation about reparations for the surviving evacuees. In 1983, the commission issued its report, *Personal Justice Denied*, in which it recommended that the United States acknowledge and apologize for the injustice of the internment, give presidential pardons to those who resisted internment, and establish a $1.5 billion fund to provide for redress. In 1988, Congress passed a bill that made these recommendations and President Ronald Reagan signed it into law.

FURTHER RESOURCES

Books

Daniels, Roger, Sandra C. Taylor and Harry H.L. Kitano. *Japanese Americans: From Relocation to Redress.* Seattle: University of Washington Press, 1991.

Daniels, Roger. *Prisoners Without Trial: Japanese Americans in World War II.* New York: Hill and Wang, 1993.

Irons, Peter. *Justice at War: The Story of the Japanese American Internment Cases.* New York: Oxford University Press, 1983.

Murray, Alice Yang. *What Did the Internment of Japanese Americans Mean?* Boston: Bedford/St. Martin's, 2000.

One Day in the Life of Ivan Denisovich

Book excerpt

By: Alexander Solzhenitsyn

Date: 1963 (English translation)

Source: Solzhenitsyn, Alexander (Ralph Parker, trans.). *One Day in the Life of Ivan Denisovich.* New York: E.P. Dutton, 1963.

About the Author: Born in 1918, Alexander Solzhenitsyn was a Russian author who spent eight years in Russian leader Joseph Stalin's (1878–1953) prison camps. He was awarded the Nobel Prize for literature in 1970. Following the publication of *The Gulag Archipelago* in 1974, he was charged with treason and exiled from the Soviet Union.

INTRODUCTION

Aleksandr Isayevich Solzhenitsyn was born in 1918. After earning a college degree in mathematics, he fought with the Russian army in World War II (1938–1945). In 1945, Solzhenitsyn penned a private letter to a friend criticizing Russian leader Joseph Stalin's persecution of the war; the letter was read by authorities who ordered his arrest. Solzhenitsyn spent the following eight years in labor camps and three years in exile.

The pre-revolutionary Russian government established numerous labor camps in Siberia. These camps housed those considered a threat to the state, and more than one million individuals served time there, including future revolutionaries such as Lenin and Stalin.

After the revolution, the labor camps were closed. But Stalin soon reopened the camps, now known as gulags, and filled them with those he labeled enemies of the state. Temperatures in the camps could reach ninety degrees below zero, and death rates in some reached 30% per year. Stalin's purges extended beyond political leaders, and the arts were subjected to severe restrictions, including a prohibition of all experimental art. Solzhenenitsyn was only one of numerous writers sent to the gulags, where many eventually died.

Solzhenitsyn survived his imprisonment and exile, and upon his release in 1956 became a mathematics teacher. In the following years, Solzhenitsyn wrote extensively about his experiences, and in 1962, he submitted a novel to a popular Soviet literary magazine. Based on Solzhenitsyn's own experiences in the gulags, the novel provided an intimate glimpse into the daily routine of a political prisoner named Ivan Denisovich. The story was an immediate hit, both with readers, who found it both entertaining and powerfully written, and with the government, which was busily distancing itself from the abuses of the Stalin regime. Almost overnight, Solzhenitsyn was transformed from a simple math teacher into an international literary sensation.

The release and popularity of *Ivan Denisovich* launched a flood of books describing the inhumane conditions in Stalin's labor camps. While an exact total remains difficult to reach, estimates of the death toll in the camps range from 1.5 to three million people.

■ PRIMARY SOURCE

At five o'clock that morning reveille was sounded, as usual, by the blows of a hammer on the length of rail hanging up near the staff quarters. The intermittent sounds barely penetrated the windowpanes on which the frost lay two fingers thick, and they ended almost as soon as they'd begun. It was cold outside, and the camp guard was reluctant to go on beating out the reveille for long.

The clanging ceased, but everything outside still looked like the middle of the night when Ivan Denisovich Shukhov got up to go to the bucket. It was pitch dark except for the yellow light east on the window by three lamps—two in the outer zone, one inside the camp itself.

And no one came to unbolt the barracks door; there was no sound of the barrack orderlies pushing a pole into place to lift the barrel of excrement and carry it out.

Shukhov never overslept reveille. He always got up at once, for the next ninety minutes, until they assembled for work, belonged to him, not to the authorities, and any old-timer could always earn a bit—by sewing a pair of mittens for some one out of old sleeve lining; or bringing some rich

A Soviet prison labor site, off the main square of Birobidjan, the capital of the Jewish Autonomous Oblast in Eastern Siberia, Soviet Union. AP IMAGES.

loafer in the squad his dry valenki—right up to his bunk, so that he wouldn't have to stumble barefoot round the heap of boots looking for his own pair; or going the rounds of the warehouses, offering to be of service, sweeping up this or fetching that; or going to the mess hall to collect bowls from the tables and bring them stacked to the dishwasher—you're sure to be given something to eat there, though there were plenty of others at that game, more than plenty—and, what's worse, if you found a bowl with something left in it you could hardly resist licking it out. But Shukhov had never forgotten the words of his first squad leader, Kuziomin—a hard-bitten prisoner who had already been in for twelve years by 1943—who told the newcomers, just in from the front, as they sat beside a fire in a desolate cutting in the forest:

"Here, men, we live by the law of the taiga. But even here people manage to live. The ones that don't make it are those who lick other mens' leftovers, those who count on the doctors to pull them through, and those who squeal on their buddies."

As for squealers, he was wrong there. Those people were sure to get through camp all right. Only, they were saving their own skin at the expense of other people's blood.

Shukhov always arose at reveille. But this day he didn't. He had felt strange the evening before, feverish, with pains all over his body. He hadn't been able to get warm all through the night. Even in his sleep he had felt at one moment that he was getting seriously ill, at another that he was getting better. He had wished morning would never come.

But the morning came as usual.

Anyway, where would you get warm in a place like this, with the windows iced over and the white cobwebs of frost all along the huge barracks where the walls joined the ceiling!

He didn't get up. He lay there in his bunk on the top tier, his head buried in a blanket and a coat, both feet stuffed into one tucked-under sleeve of his wadded jacket.

He couldn't see, but his ears told him everything going on in the barrack room and especially in the corner his squad occupied. He heard the heavy tread of the orderlies carrying one of the big barrels of excrement along the passage outside. A light job, that was considered, a job for the infirm, but just you try and carry out the muck without spilling any. He heard some of the 75th slamming bunches of boots onto the floor from the drying shed. Now their own men were doing it (it was their own squad's turn, too, to dry valenki). Tiurin, the squad leader, and his deputy Pavlo put on their valenki without a word but he heard their bunks creaking. Now Pavlo would be going off to the bread-storage and Tiurin to the staff quarters to see the P.P.D.

Ah, but not simply to report as usual to the authorities for the daily assignment. Shukhov remembered that this morning his fate hung in the balance: they wanted to shift the 104th from the building shops to a new site, the "Socialist Way of Life" settlement. It lay in open country covered with snowdrifts, and before anything else could be done there they would have to dig holes and put up posts and attach barbed wire to them. Wire themselves in, so that they wouldn't runaway. Only then would they start building.

There wouldn't be a warm corner for a whole month. Not even a doghouse. And fires were out of the question. There was nothing to build them with. Let your work warm you up; that was your only salvation.

No wonder the squad leader looked so worried, that was his job—to elbow some other squad, some bunch of suckers, into the assignment instead of the 104th. Of course with empty hands you got nowhere. He'd have to take a pound of salt pork to the senior official there, if not a couple of pounds.

There's never nay harm in trying, so why not have a go at the dispensary and get a few days off if you can? After all, he did feel as though every limb was out of joint.

Then Shukhov wondered which of the campguards was on duty that morning. It was "One-and-a-half" Ivan's turn, he recalled. Ivan was a thin, weedy, dark-eyes sergeant. At first sight he looked like a real bastard, but when you got to know him he turned out to be the most good-natured of the guards on duty: he didn't put you in the guardhouse, he didn't haul you off before the authorities. So Shukhov decided he could lie in his bunk a little longer, at least while Barracks 9 was at the mess hall.

The whole four-bunk frame began to shake and sway. Two of its occupants were getting up at the same time: Shukhov's top-tier neighbor, Alyosha the Baptist, and Bunovsky, the ex-naval captain down below.

The orderlies, after removing both barrels of excrement, began to quarrel about which of them should go for hot water. They quarrel naggingly, like old women.

"Hey you, cackling like a couple of hens!" bellowed the electric welder in the 20th squad. "Get going." He flung a boot at them.

The boot thudded against a post. The squabbling stopped.

In the next squad the deputy squad leader growled quietly: "Vasily Fyodorovich, they've cheated us again at the supply depot, the dirty rats. They should have given us four twenty-five-ounce loaves and I've only got three. Who's gong to go short?"

He kept his voice down, but of course everyone in the squad heard him and waited fearfully to learn who would be losing a slice of bread that evening.

Shukhov went on lying on his sawdust mattress, as hard as a board from long wear. If only it could be one thing or the other—let him fall into a real fever or let his aching joints east up.

Meanwhile Alyosha was murmuring his prayers and Buinovsky had returned from the latrines, announcing to no one in particular but with a sort of malicious glee: "Well, sailors, grit your teeth. It's twenty below, for sure."

Shukhov decided to report sick.

At that very moment his blanket and jacket were imperiously jerked off him. He flung his coat away from his face and sat up. Looking up at him, his head level with the top bunk, was lean figure of The Tartar.

So the fellow was on duty out of turn and had stolen up.

"S 854," The Tartar read from the white strip that had been stitched to the back of his black jacket. "Three days' penalty with work."

The moment they heard that peculiar choking voice of his, everyone who wasn't up yet in the whole dimly lit barracks, where two hundred men slept in bug-ridden bunks, stirred to life and began dressing in a hurry.

"What for, citizen chief?" asked Shukhov with more chagrin than he felt in his voice.

With work—that wasn't half so bad. They gave you hot food and you had no time to start thinking. Real jail was when you were kept back from work. . . .

"Well," he said conclusively, "however much you pray it doesn't shorten your stretch. You'll sit it out from beginning to end anyhow."

"Oh, you mustn't pray for that either," said Alyosha, horrified. "Why do you want freedom? In freedom your last grain of faith will be choked with weeds. You should rejoice that you're in prison. Here you have time to think about your soul. As the Apostle Paul wrote: 'Why all these tears? Why are you trying to weaken my resolution? For my part I am ready not merely to be bound but even to die for the name of the Lord Jesus."

Shukhov gazed at the ceiling in silence. Now he didn't know either whether he wanted freedom or not. At first he'd longed for it. Every night he'd counted the days of this stretch—how many had passed, how many were coming. And then he'd grown bored with counting. And then it became clear that men like him wouldn't ever be allowed to return home, that they'd be exiled. And whether his life would be any better there than here—who could tell?

Freedom meant one thing to him—home.

But they wouldn't let him go home.

Alyosha was speaking the truth. His voice and his eyes left no doubt that he was happy in prison.

"You see, Alyosha," Shukhov explained to him, "somehow it works out all right for you: Jesus Christ wanted you to sit in prison and so you are—sitting there for His sake. But for whose sake am I here? Because we weren't ready for war in forty-one? For that? But was that *my* fault?"

"Seems like there's not going to be a recount," Kilgas murmured from his bunk.

"Yeah," said Shukhov. "We ought to write it up in coal inside the chimney. No second count." He yawned. "might as well get to sleep."

And at that very moment the door bolt rattled to break the calm that now reigned in the barracks. From the corridor ran two of the prisoners who'd taken boots to the drying shed.

"Second count," they shouted.

On their heels came a guard.

"All out to the other half."

Some were already asleep. They began to grumble and move about, they put their boots on (no one ever took his wadded trousers off at night—you'd grow numb with cold unless you wore them under your blanket).

"Damn them," said Shukhov. Mildly, because he hadn't gone to sleep yet.

Tsezar raised a hand and gave him two biscuits, two lumps of sugar, and a slice of sausage.

"Thank you, Tsezar Markovich," said Shukhov, leaning over the edge of his bunk. " Come on now, hand up that sack of yours. I'll put it under my mattress."(It's not so easy to swipe things from the top bunks as you go by. Anyway, who'd look for anything in Shukhov's bunk?)

Tsezar handed up his sack and Shukhov hid it under the mattress. Then he waited a little till more men had been sent out—he wouldn't have to stand barefoot so long in the corridor. But the guard scowled at him and shouted: "Come on, you there in the corner."

Shukhov sprang lightly to the floor (his boots and footrags were so well placed on the stove it would be a pity to move them). Though he'd made so many slippers for others he hadn't a pair of his own. But he was used to this—and the count didn't take long.

They confiscate slippers too if they find them in daytime.

As for the squads who'd sent their boots to be dried, it wasn't so bad for them, now the recount was held indoors. Some wore slippers, some just their footrags, some went barefoot.

"Come one, come one," growled the guard.

"Do you want to be carried out, you s——?" the barracks commander shouted.

They shoved them all into the other half of the barracks, and loiterers into the corridor. Shukhov stood against the wall near the bucket. The floor was moist underfoot. An icy draft crept in from the porch.

They had them all out now and once again the guard and the orderly did their round, looking for any who might be dozing in dark corners. There'd be trouble if they counted short. It would mean still another recount. Round they went, round they went, and came back to the door.

"One, two, three, four...." Now they released you faster, for they were counting one by one. Shukhov managed to squeeze in eighteenth. He ran back to his bunk, put his foot on the support—heave, and he was up.

All right. Feet back into the sleeve of his jacket. Blanket on top. Then the coat. And to sleep. Now they'd be letting everybody from the other half of the barracks into our half. But that's not our worry.

Tsezar returned, Shukhov lowered his sack to him.

Alyosha returned. Impractical, that's his trouble. Makes himself nice to everyone but doesn't know how to do favors that get paid back.

"Here you are, Alyosha," said Shuhov, and handed him a biscuit.

Alyosha smiled, "Thank you. But you've got nothing yourself."

"Eat it."

(We've nothing but we always find a way to make something extra.)

Now for that slice of sausage. Into the mouth. Getting your teeth into it. Your teeth. The meaty taste. And the meaty juice, the real stuff. Down it goes, into your belly.

Gone.

The rest, Shukhov decided, for the morning. Before the roll call.

And he buried his head in the thin, unwashed blanket, deaf now to the crowd of zeks from the other half as they jostled between the bunk frames, waiting to be counted.

Shukhov went to sleep fully content. He'd had many strokes of luck that day; they hadn't put him in the cells; they hadn't sent his squad to the settlement; he'd swiped a bowl of kasha at dinner; the squad leader had fixed the rates well; he'd built a wall and enjoyed doing it; he smuggled that bit of hacksaw blade through; he'd earned a favor from Tsezar that evening; he'd bought that tobacco. And he hadn't fallen ill. He'd got over it.

A day without a dark cloud. Almost a happy day.

SIGNIFICANCE

Despite Solzhenitsyn's newfound fame, he was not immune to changes in government policy. Loosened restrictions on writing and expression were soon tightened again. After publishing a collection of short stories in 1963, Solzhenitsyn found himself increasingly harassed by government officials who viewed him as an outspoken critic of the regime. Solzhenitsyn was soon barred from publishing.

Despite the official ban, Solzhenitsyn continued writing, and his novels published outside the Soviet Union garnered him the 1970 Nobel Prize for Literature. In 1973, portions of a book entitled *The Gulag Archipelago* were published in France. The book, Solzhenitsyn's most ambitious effort to date, was a historical account of the extensive network of prison and labor camps established after the Russian Revolution and subsequently expanded under Joseph Stalin. The work provided graphic descriptions of arrests, interrogations, imprisonment, and torture, including many first-person accounts collected by Solzhenitsyn while imprisoned. Weeks after the book's publication, Solzhenitsyn was arrested and charged with treason. Twenty-four hours later, he was exiled from the Soviet Union.

In the years following his expulsion, Solzhenitsyn published the second and third installments of *The Gulag Archipelago* as well as a variety of other fiction and non-fiction works. With the collapse of the Soviet Union in 1991, Solzhenitsyn's works once again became widely available to readers in his home country. In 1990, his Russian citizenship was renewed, and four years later he returned to his homeland. In 1997, the Solzhenitsyn Prize for Russian writing was established in his honor.

In his 1968 volume *The First Circle*, Solzhenitsyn eloquently described the role he would play for most of his life: "A great writer is, so to speak, a second government in his country. And for that reason no regime has ever loved great writers, only minor ones." As he approaches his ninetieth birthday, Solzhenitsyn remains an outspoken critic of both Eastern and Western governments.

FURTHER RESOURCES

Books

Applebaum, Anne. *Gulag: A History*. New York: Doubleday, 2004.

Pearce, Joseph. *Solzhenitsyn: A Soul in Exile*. New York: Baker Books, 2001.

Solzhenitsyn, Alexander. *Russia in Collapse*. Wilmington, Delaware: Intercollegiate Studies Institute, 2006.

Periodicals

Brander, Michael. "Alexander Solzhenitsyn and the West." *Quadrant*. 49(2005):52–57.

Mahoney, Daniel J. "Empire-Slayer." *National Review*. 57(2005):113–114.

Web sites

Columbia University. "Text of address by Alexander Solzhenistsyn at Harvard Class Day Afternoon Exercises, Thursday, June 8, 1978." <http://www.columbia.edu/cu/augustine/arch/solzhenitsyn/harvard1978.html> (accessed May 30, 2006).

Oxford Blueprint. "Stalin's Gulags still used as prisons." January 31, 2002. <http://www.ox.ac.uk/blueprint/2001-02/3101/05.shtml> (accessed May 31, 2006).

Weekly Standard. "Solzhenitsyn, Again: The great Russian thinker foresaw the situation which now faces George W. Bush." March 12, 2003. <http://www.weeklystandard.com/Content/Public/Articles/000/000/002/347nmolx.asp> (accessed May 30, 2006).

Human Rights Abuses in Shahist Iran

Report

By: Amnesty International

Date: November 1976

Source: "Human Rights Abuses in Shahist Iran," *Amnesty International Briefing: Iran*. Amnesty International, November 1976.

About the Author: Amnesty International, founded in 1961, is an organization that campaigns globally for the abolition of torture, political imprisonment, and the death penalty.

INTRODUCTION

In 1979, radical Islamists overthrew the Iranian government ruled by the hereditary king or "shah" of Iran, Mohammed Reza Shah Pahlavi (1919–1980). One of the grievances that the rebels cited against his regime was its use of torture, especially by the secret police force SAVAK (*Sazeman-i Ettelaat va Amniyat-i Keshvar*, or Organization for Intelligence and National Security). In a 1976 document, Amnesty International detailed some of SAVAK's torture practices and stated that the shah's regime was one of the worst human rights violators in the world.

The shah's relationship with the United States and the United Kingdom was close, from his ascension to the throne in 1949 until his exile in 1979. During World War II, Iran was occupied by the United Kingdom and Soviet Union to preempt a Nazi invasion. During the occupation, the Allies forced the shah's father to abdicate, and the younger man was installed as constitutional monarch, sharing limited power with a national parliament and prime minister. In the early 1950s, the democratically elected Parliament and Prime Minister, Mohammad Mossadegh (1882–1967), nationalized the oil industry and made other nationalistic moves that displeased the United Kingdom and the United States. In 1953, a coup engineered by the Central Intelligence Agency (CIA) and British intelligence deposed Mossadegh and elevated the shah to supreme power. He ruled until his deposition in 1979.

SAVAK was established in 1967 with help from both the CIA and the Israeli intelligence agency, Mossad. Its first director, General Teymur Bakhtiar, was dismissed in 1961 and died in 1970, probably assassinated on orders from the shah. From 1963 to 1979, thousands of political prisoners were tortured and executed, dissent was suppressed, and traditional Muslims were alienated by the shah's support of votes for women. (Arguably, however, the votes had little power, becasue the shah forbade all political parties except one.) To this day, little public information is available about SAVAK. It monitored all journalists, professors, labor unions—indeed, organizations of every type.

SAVAK also spied extensively on the 30,000 or so Iranian students in the United States, with thirteen full-time case officers devoted to this task. Students were an important part of the revolution against the shah, and it was primarily they who took over and occupied the U.S. embassy in Iran in November 1979. The students cited the admission of the exiled shah (who was dying of cancer) into the United States as justification for the embassy takeover. They took fifty-two Americans hostages and held them for 444 days, releasing them on January 20, 1981.

■ PRIMARY SOURCE

Human Rights Abuses in Shahist Iran
5. Location of Prisons

Before trial, political prisoners are detained in one of two prisons in Teheran.... After trial prisoners are transferred to other prisons, either in Teheran or in the provinces. These include Quasar prison, in Teheran; Hazel Gale prison, Teheran' Barajas prison, Bandar-Abbes prison, Adel-Abed prison and Shiraz prison in Shiraz, Booster prison, Saharan prison, Mashed prison, Sunman prison, Haves prison, Rash prison, Ark prison, Tapirs prison, Malabar prison, and Resaca prison. In addition to these there are in every provincial capital and large city Joint Committee of SAVAK and Police prisons which are used for interrogations. As well, in large and medium-size cities there are police prisons where political prisoners are detained at time of large scale arrests.

6. Prison Conditions

As I have never been given an opportunity by the Iranian authorities to visit prisons in Iran, the following information has been provided by former prisoners and the families of prisoners.

Prisoners held in pre-trial detention in the Committee and Evin prisons have no contact with other prisoners, or with the outside world, and are subjected to torture. They are locked up in small, damp cells with only a straw mattress on which to sleep. In these prisons, as in others, the extremes of temperature in Iran are an important factor. Lack of heating in the winter or cooling in the summer create extra hardship frequently remarked upon by prisoners. Washing facilities are inadequate and opportunities for washing are infrequent. Food rations are small and inadequate and no opportunities are provided for exercise. Papers, pencils and books are not allowed and prisoners are not given an opportunity to join communal prayer.

After trial, prisoners may be transferred to any of the prisons mentioned above, regardless of where their families live. This means that in many cases prisoners are not able to see their families for very long periods of time, and even when members of families have travelled long distances to visit prisoners they are still restricted to 15 minutes' visiting time, or less. Food is usually inadequate and of poor quality and this often leads to malnutrition, food poisoning or chronic illness. Medical treatment is practically non-existent and prisoners are hardly ever seen by a doctor, sent to hospital or allowed to receive medicines. Discipline is severe and in cases of indiscipline prisoners may be put into solitary confinement for anything

A mob of Iranian demonstrators riot outside of a Beverley Hills, California, home on January 2, 1978. They are angered by the presence of the queen mother of Iran (the Shah's mother), who has taken sanctuary in the home to escape the violence of the Iranian revolution. © BETTMANN/CORBIS.

up to three or four months. Maltreatment and torture do not always cease after trial and in some cases prisoners who are regarded as being difficult are sent back to the Committee or Evin prisons for further torture. Former prisoners have stated that they are convinced that the harsh conditions and maltreatment are intended to break the prisoner, with the aim of making him or her recant. This view is supported by the appearance on television, from time to time, of political prisoners who repudiate their previously-held opinions and express their support for the Shah's policies.

Although article 131 of the Iranian Penal code expressly prohibits torture, the practice of holding prisoners incommunicado for long periods before trial, together with the importance for the prosecution of obtaining a confession, creates a situation in which prisoners are very likely to be ill-treated, and all the information received by AI over the past decade confirms that torture does invariably occur during the period between arrest and trial. All observers to trials since 1965 have reported allegations of torture which have

been made by defendants and have expressed their own conviction that prisoners are tortured for the purpose of obtaining confessions. Alleged methods of torture include whipping and beating, electric shocks, the extraction of nails and teeth, boiling water pumped into the rectum, heavy weights hung on the testicles, tying the prisoner to a metal table heated to white heat, inserting a broken bottle into the anus, and rape.

Maitre Nora Albia in his report on his mission to Iran in January/February 1972 on behalf of the international association of Democratic Lawyers, describes an exchange between a defendant, Masoud Ahmadzadeh, and the prosecutor in which Ahmadzadeh stated that his confession had been obtained by torture. During the course of the trial Ahmadzadeh, thinking that Maitre Albala was a foreign journalist, suddenly pulled off his sweater and showed the lawyer appalling burns on his stomach and back which appeared to be several months old. During a subsequent conversation with another defendant, Nasser Sadegh, Maitre Albala was told that Massoud Ahmadzadeh and other defendants had been burned by being placed on a table which was then heated to white heat, and that one of those so treated, Badizadeghan, had since then been paralysed in the lower limbs and could move only by crawling forward using his upper arms. Nasser Sadegh also said that he saw one prisoner, Behruz Tehrani, die near him in the torture room.

A recent, detailed account of his own torture and that of other prisoners has been given by Reza Baraheni, a released prisoner now resident in the United States of America.

> Most of the horrible instruments were located on the second floor. I was not taken there, but the office of my interrogator, Dr Rezvan, was next to this chamber, and one day when he was called to another office for some sort of consultation, I walked into the room, glanced round it and then went back. It resembles an ancient Egyptian tomb and is reserved for those suspected of being terrorists or accused of having made attempts on the life of the Shah or a member of the royal Family. Not every prisoner goes through the same process, but generally, this is what happens to a prisoner of the first importance. First he is beaten by several torturers at once, with sticks and clubs. If he doesn't confess, he is hanged upside down and beaten; if this doesn't work, he is raped; and if he still shows signs of resistance, he is given electric shock which turns him into a howling dog; and if he is still obstinate, his nails and sometimes all his teeth are pulled out, and in certain exceptional cases, a hot iron rod is put into one side of the face to force its way to the other side, burning the entire mouth and the tongue. A young man was killed in this way. . . .

Allegations of deaths under torture are not uncommon. One instance is cited above; another is the death of Ayatollah Haj Hosssen Ghafari Azar Shari, a religious leader in the city of Qom, who was arrested in August 1974 and died on 28 December 1974, following torture. Nine deaths which were announced in April 1975 of political prisoners who had been in prison since 1968 and were allegedly "shot while trying to escape" may have been due to torture. The official account of the deaths contained discrepancies and the families were never allowed to have the bodies for burial.

The renewed use of torture, after trial and conviction, is alleged to take place in Iran. In the case referred to above, the nine prisoners who died were part of a much larger group of prisoners who had been brought to Teheran from other prisons and were allegedly being tortured to persuade them to give support to the Shah's newly announced one-party state.

When questioned about the use of torture in his country, the Shah has never denied that it occurs. In a recent interview reported in *Le Monde* on 1 October 1976, the Shah replied to a question about the use of torture by

saying: "Why should we not employ the same methods as you Europeans? We have learned sophisticated methods of torture from you. You use psychological methods to extract the truth: we do the same."

8. Released Prisoners

Prisoners who have recanted may eventually be judged to have expiated their crimes and be allowed to live a normal life, but most released prisoners are kept under surveillance and suffer constant harassment from SAVAK, which extends to the treatment of their families. They are unable to obtain employment without the permission of SAVAK and this permission is rarely granted. Prisoners tried by military tribunals automatically suffer the loss of their civil rights for 10 years, regardless of the length of their sentence. . . .

In addition to the violations already referred to there is little respect demonstrated for human rights in many other areas of Iranian life. Freedom of speech and association are non-existent. The press is strictly censored and has been dramatically curtailed in recent years since the shah decreed that every newspaper with a circulation of less than 3,000 and periodicals with a circulation of less than 5,000 should be shut down. Trade unions are illegal and workers' protests are dealt with severely, sometimes resulting in imprisonment and deaths. Political activity is restricted to participation in the *Rastakhiz* Party. Some Iranians have difficulty in obtaining, or are refused, passports. This restriction on freedom of movement applies especially to released political prisoners and members of their families. Academic freedom is also restricted and students and university teachers are kept under surveillance by SAVAK. A recent account concerns a professor of literature who was harassed, beaten, arrested and tortured because his courses had been deemed as not conforming to the "ideology" of the "White Revolution" of the shah, in that he had failed to refer to it.

SIGNIFICANCE

Iran's revolution, which overthrew the shah, was the first Islamist revolution in modern times. It was the result of many factors, but hatred for SAVAK's cruelty was certainly a contributing factor. Iran's government has been passionately anti-American since 1979. Much of this history might have been different had the United States not contributed to the founding of SAVAK in the 1950s and publicly supported the shah throughout his increasingly cruel regime.

In 1978, President Jimmy Carter, who had said that human rights were the "soul of our foreign policy," praised the Shah as a wise ruler and, toasting the Shah during a state visit to Iran, told him that "Iran, because of the great leadership of the Shah, is an island of stability in one of the troubled areas of the world. This is a great tribute to you and to your majesty and to your leadership and to the respect, admiration, and love which your people give to you." In 1979, the former chief Iran analyst for the CIA, Jesse J. Leaf, told *New York Times* reporter Seymour Hersh that prior to 1973 the CIA had worked closely with SAVAK and the Shah had known of the torture of dissenters. Leaf also stated that a senior CIA officer had been "involved in instructing officials in the Savak on torture techniques … based on German torture techniques from World War II." Shredded documents from the captured U.S. embassy were painstakingly reassembled by hand after the revolution, producing documents that showed CIA collaboration with SAVAK.

Several writers have argued that the rise of anti-American terror organizations such as Al Qaeda in recent years is partly due to U.S. support for oppressive regimes in Islamic countries such as Iran. According to Stephen Kinzer, a former *New York Times* correspondent, "I think it's not an exaggeration to say that you can draw a line from the American sponsorship of the 1953 coup in Iran, through the Shah's repressive regime, to the Islamic revolution of 1979 and the spread of militant religious fundamentalism that produced waves of anti-Western terrorism." This thesis is controversial.

The Islamist Iranian revolutionary regime replaced SAVAK with a similar organization, VEVAK (*Vezarat-e Ettela'at va Amniat-e Keshvar*, Ministry of Intelligence and Security). According to a 2005 report by Amnesty International, the human rights situation in Iran continues to be grim; torture remains widespread, punishments such as beheading and amputation of the tongue have been introduced, and the death penalty "continues to be handed down for charges such as 'enmity against God' or 'morality crimes' that do not reflect internationally recognized criminal charges"

FURTHER RESOURCES
Books

Kinzer, Stephen. *All the Shah's Men: An American Coup and the Roots of Middle East Terror*. Hoboken, NJ: John Wiley & Sons, 2003.

Periodicals

Hersh, Seymour M. "Ex-Analyst Says CIA Rejected Warning on Shah." *New York Times*. (January 7, 1989): A3.

Web sites

Amnesty International. "Report 2005: Iran" <http://web.amnesty.org/report2005/irn-summary-eng> (accessed April 25, 2006).

U.S. Library of Congress. "Library of Congress Country Studies: Iran—Savak." December 1987 <http://lcweb2.loc.gov/cgi-bin/query/r?frd/cstdy:@field(DOCID+ir0187)> (accessed April 25, 2006).

The Visit

Magazine Article

By: Timothy Garton Ash

Date: 1993

Source: Ash, Timothy Garton. "The Visit." *Granta 43: Gazza Agnosties*. London.: Granta, Fall 1993.

About the Author: Timothy Garton Ash is the author of eight books of political writing or what he terms "history of the present," which have charted the transformation of Europe over the last twenty-five years. He is Professor of European Studies in the University of Oxford, Director of the European Studies Centre at St. Antony's College, Oxford, and a Senior Fellow at the Hoover Institution, Stanford University. He writes regularly for the *New York Review of Books* and he has a weekly column in the *Guardian* which is syndicated in Europe, Asia and the Americas.

INTRODUCTION

The German Democratic Republic (commonly known as East Germany or GDR) was a socialist state that existed between 1949 and 1990 in the former Soviet controlled zone of Germany. The state was declared in 1949, some five months after West Germany, and it was proclaimed fully sovereign in 1954, although Soviet troops remained there throughout its history, ostensibly as a counterbalance to NATO's (North Atlantic Treaty Organization) presence in West Germany.

With its capital, Berlin, cut in two by a great wall and a West Berlin marooned in the country's heart, East Germany was a strange part of Soviet-occupied Europe. On the one hand, its geography and history should have made it more open and receptive to outside influences, yet its leaders vigorously upheld their socialist principles and were arguably closer and more loyal to Moscow than other Soviet satellite nations. Indeed, of all the members of the Warsaw Pact—the name given to the Soviet military alliance designed as a counterbalance to NATO—East Germany was arguably the most repressive and authoritarian.

Amongst East Germany's dominant political influences, Erich Honecker stands tall. He was a classic communist party apparatchik, whose dedication to Moscow and the Soviet cause stifled progress and debate in East Germany and ultimately led to the country's fall. Born into a politically militant coal mining family in August 1912, Honecker was politically active from his early teens, joining the German Communist Party's (KPD) youth leagues and the party itself at the age of seventeen. As with many young socialists of the era, he was invited to Moscow to study communist doctrine and spent his late teens there. He returned to Germany in 1931 and was active in the KPD's unsuccessful political battles with Adolf Hitler's Nazi Party. Two years after Hitler took power, in 1935, Honecker was arrested and remained in prison until the end of the Second World War.

Liberated by Soviet troops in 1945, Honecker was thrust into mainstream politics in the political chaos that ensued in Germany's liberated sectors. When East Germany was proclaimed a nation in 1949, he became a member of the Communist Party's Central Committee [essentially East Germany's ruling council] and during the 1950s rose through its ranks. In 1961, he was charged with responsibility of building the Berlin Wall, the most famous symbol not just of East Germany, but the entire Soviet era. In 1971, Honecker became General Secretary of the Central Committee. Honecker became East Germany's President in 1976.

East Germany under Honecker initially experienced some improvements in its living standards and economic condition as he embraced a program of "consumer socialism"—which saw limited market reforms and some trade with the west (bringing in some much desired consumer goods). There was also recognition for the first time of West Germany, although its people could still not usually pass between the two. Increasingly, East Germany became a police state, with its secret police force, the Stasi, gaining in power and influence throughout the nation. When limited debate on political reforms and civil rights was permitted in Poland, Czechoslovakia and elsewhere in the 1980s, such talk was prohibited in East Germany. Even when the USSR under President Mikhail Gorbachev began to initiate political and economic reform under his program of *perestroika*, or "change." Honecker famously refused to follow, claiming East Germany had already done "its perestroika" in the 1970s.

Of all of Gorbachev's reforms, however, it was the abandonment of the "Brezhnev Doctrine" that had the widest implications. Under the terms of this doctrine, the USSR would intervene in Warsaw Pact countries—as it had done in Czechoslovakia in 1968—to uphold communist rule where necessary. By discarding it, client states were able to discuss and initiate reforms without threat of Soviet military intervention. Poland and Hungary led the way during 1989. In August 1989, Hungary removed its border restrictions, briefly allowing several thousand East Germans to flee over the Hungarian border and then onto Austria and West Germany.

Taking inspiration from this and of news of peaceful demonstrations elsewhere in eastern Europe, East Germans took to the streets over the fall of 1989 in a number of peaceful demonstrations. With power quickly slipping away, East Germany's politburo chiefs initiated a political coup on October 18, which forced Honecker's resignation and his replacement by his deputy Egon Krenz. This, however, was regarded as a mere sop, and three weeks later, on November 9, during demonstrations in East Berlin, border guards abandoned their posts and thousands began spilling over into the West. Most symbolically, demonstrators began hacking away at the Berlin Wall with pick axes and hammers. East Germany had collapsed; within a year Germany was reunified.

Honecker had spent much of this time in a Soviet military hospital outside Berlin. Then, when calls for his arrest came, he fled to Moscow. However, he was extradited to Germany in 1992 to face trial for an array of Cold War crimes, specifically for the deaths of 192 people who had been killed trying to cross the Berlin Wall into the West. The writer and academic Timothy Garton Ash visited Honecker whilst he awaited trial in Berlin's Moabit Prison in 1992.

■ PRIMARY SOURCE

"Are you bringing any laundry?" asks the porter at the fortified entrance to Moabit prison.

When I laugh, he says defensively, "I was only asking," and grimly stamps my permit to visit remand prisoner Honecker, Rich.

Into a waiting-room full of chain-smoking wives and spivs in black leather jackets. Wait for your number to be called from a loudspeaker. Through an automatic barrier. Empty your pockets and put everything in a locker. Body search. Another automatic barrier. Unsmiling guards,

Former East German communist leader Erich Honecker raises a clenched fist before the start of the fifth day of his manslaughter trial in Berlin on November 30, 1992. AP IMAGES.

barked orders. *Moment! Kommen Sie mit!* Then you've come to the wrong place. Collect all your belongings again. Pack up. Walk around the red-brick fortress to another gate. Unpack. Sign this, take that. Another huge metal door. The clash of bolts. A courtyard, then the corridor to the prison hospital, bare but clean.

Somehow all this seems increasingly familiar. I have been here before. But where and when? Then I remember. It's like crossing through the Friedrichstrasse underground frontier station into East Berlin, in the bad old days. West Germany has given Honecker back his Berlin Wall.

Inside it is warm and safe. There is food to eat; plain fare, to be sure, but regular and ample. There is basic, free medical care for all. Good books are to be had from the library, and there is guaranteed employment for men and women alike. And life is, of course, very secure. Just like East Germany.

The first time I saw, at close quarters, the Chairman of the Council of State of the German Democratic Republic and General Secretary of the Socialist Unity Party of Germany, Erich Honecker, was at the Leipzig trade fair in 1980. A horde of plains-clothes Stasi men heralded the arrival of the leader. Eastern functionaries, West German businessmen, British diplomats—all flapped and fluttered, bowed and scraped, as if at the Sublime Porte of Suleimana the Great. His every move, every tiny gesture, was studied and minutely interpreted, with all the arcane science of Sovietology. Significantly, graciously, the Chairman and General Secretary stopped at the Afghan stand, which displayed rungs and nuts. "And those are peanuts and those are salted peanuts . . .' came the breathless commentary of the rattled Afghan salesman. Graciously, significantly, the Chairman and General Secretary clapped him on the shoulder and said: "We regard your revolution as a decisive contribution to détente. All the best for your struggle!" Ah, happy days, the old style.

Now the door opens and there he stands in a tiny corner room, sandwiched between the doctor's washbasin and a table. He is very small, his face pallid and sweaty, but he still stands bold upright. "Bodily contacts are not permitted," says my permit. But he extends his hand—graciously, significantly—and I shake it. He is clad in khaki prison pyjamas, which remind me of a Mao suit. But on his feet he still wears, incongruously, those fine, black leather slip-on shoes in which he used to tread all the red carpets, not just in Moscow and Prague but in Madrid, in Paris and in Bonn. "Fraternal greetings, Comrade Leonid Hyitch,' and a smacking kiss on each cheek. "how do you do, Mr. President.' *'Guten Tag, Herr Bundeskanzler.* We sit down, our knees almost touching in the cramped room, and the accompanying warder wedges himself into a corner. All my notes and papers have been impounded at the gate, but fortunately the doctor has left some spare sheets of lined paper and a pencil. Fixing me with his tiny, intense eyes—always his most striking feature—Honecker concentrates on answering my questions. He talks at length about his relations with Moscow, his friendship with Brezhnev, his arguments with Chernenko and then Gorbachev. Even under Gorbachev, he says, the Soviet Union never ceased to intervene in East Germany. The Soviet embassy's consular officials behaved, he says, like provincial governors. So much for the sovereignty of the GDR that he himself had so long trumpeted! At one point he shows staggering (and I think genuine) economic naivete, arguing that East Germany's hard currency debt, in Deutschmarks, has to be set against its surplus in transferable rubles.

His language is a little stiff, polit-bureaucratic, but very far from being just ideological gobbledygook. Through it come glimpses of a real political intelligence, a man who knows about power. Was it his conscious decision to allow many more ordinary East Germans to travel to the West in the second half of the 1980s? Yes, definitely, a conscious decision. He thought it would make people more satisfied. But did it? *Nee*, he says, *offenischtlich nicht*. Nope, obviously not.

With the tiny pupils of his eyes boring into mine, he speaks with what seems like real, almost fanatical conviction—or at least with a real will to convince. This is somehow more, not less, impressive because of the humiliating prison surroundings, and because of the obvious physical effort it costs him. (He has cancer of the liver. The doctors give him only months to live.) Once he has to excuse himself to go to the lavatory, accompanied by the warder. "you noticed I was getting a little restless," he says apologetically on his return.

Then he resumed his defiant refrain. East Germany, he insists, was "to the end the only socialist country in which you could always go into a shop and buy bread, butter, sausage etc." Yet people wanted more? Yes, but now they regret it. Look at the unemployment in the former GDR! Look how few apartments are being built! He gets hundreds of letters from people in the east. They say they lived more *quietly* in the old days: *sie haben ruhiger gelebt*.

And look what's happening in the streets now, the racist attacks, the fascists. It reminds him of 1933. Really? 1933? Well, he concedes, perhaps 1923. Hitler's first attempt was also a flop. But look what happened then. He's warning us. We've been here before. At least: he's been here before. Which, indeed, he has: held as a remand prisoner in this very prison in the years 1935–37, after being caught working for the Communist resistance.

And now he is here again. West Germany's leaders denounce him as a criminal. Yet only yesterday those same politicians were competing for the privilege of being received in audience by him. Oh, the tales he could tell! His talks with West German Social Democrats were, he says, "comradely". Some other West German politicians were more reserved. He had great respect of Franz Joseph Strauss. Helmut Schmidt was the most reliable and punctilious partner. But he also got on well with Helmut Kohl. He had often talked on the telephone to Chancellor Schmidt, and to Chancellor Kohl. Why, he had even dialed the number himself.

Then the former Chairman of the council of State of the former German Democratic Republic and former General Secretary of the former Socialist Unity Party of Germany pulls out of the pocket of his prison pyjamas a slightly dog-eared card on which his former secretary had typed the direct telephone number to the Chancellor in Bonn. He places it before me, urges me to copy the number down. 0649 (West Germany) 228 9Bonn 562001.

A quarter-century of divided Germany's tragic, complex history is, it seems to me, concentrated in this one pathetic moment: the defiant, mortally sick old man in his prison pyjamas, the dog-eared card with the direct number to Chancellor Kohl.

What would happen, I wonder, if he rang that number now? Would it, perhaps, give the standard German recorded message for a defunct number: no *Anschluss* on this number? (The word *Anschluss* means simply connection, as well as territorial incorporation.) But no, I try it later, and it still takes you straight through to the Chancellor's office in Bonn.

The warder clears his throat and looks at his watch. Our time is up. Honecker rises, again standing almost to attention. A formal farewell. Then the bare corridors, the clashing gates, the unsmiling guards, the belongings from the locker, the fortified entrance. But now I *am* carrying laundry. Scribbled in pencil on a doctor's notepad: the dirty linen of history.

SIGNIFICANCE

Honecker's incarceration was unusually divisive for one who had ruled with such an iron fist. On the one hand, there was a feeling that he should pay for holding East Germany back; for the crimes of the Stasi; and for suffocating his people's liberty. On the other, there was a sense that the charges he faced—mostly concerning the deaths of those who had tried to violate the East-West Berlin border as a result of his shoot-to-kill policy—were wrong and punitive. It was pointed out that he had relinquished power to prevent East Germany from descending into violent revolution, as Romania did just weeks later. From a moral perspective, the righteousness of incarcerating an eighty year-old man who was by then ravaged by liver cancer was also called into question.

In the event, a Berlin court ruled in January 1993 that making Honecker stand trial would be in "violation of his human rights." He was freed and allowed to join his wife Margot Feist (who had been an East German education minister for twenty-six years) in exile in Chile. He died in Santiago of liver cancer in May 1994.

Honecker's successor Egon Krenz was sentenced to six-and-a-half years imprisonment in 1997 for electoral fraud and for the deaths of those who had tried to illegally cross the border into West Berlin. He served three years of his sentence from 2000 after losing an appeal, but was not alone in dismissing his punishment as a 'victors justice' in a 'Cold War court.'.

The most open wound following the collapse of East Germany remains that of the role of the Stasi. It directly employed up to 150,000 people (nearly one percent of East Germany's population) and during its history is believed to have held files on up to one third of the population. A substantial proportion of the East German population have also been implicated as direct or indirect informants. The Stasi was central to the suppression of democratic and opposition movements and implicated in tens of thousands of human rights violations, including imprisonment without trial, secret killings, spying on civilians and torture. Attempts to bring former Stasi members to justice have been slow and replete with controversy.

FURTHER RESOURCES

Books

Funder, Anna. *Stasiland*. London: Granta, 2004.

Crampton, R J. *Return to Diversity: A Political History of East Central Europe Since World War II*. London: Routledge, 1997.

Rothschild, Joseph. and Nancy M. Wingfield. *Return to Diversity: A Political History of East Central Europe Since World War II*. Oxford University Press, 2000.

Nigeria: On the Anniversary of Ken Saro-Wiwa's Execution, Human Rights Organizations Call for Reform

Press release

By: Amnesty International

Date: November 6, 1996

Source: *Amnesty International*. "Nigeria: On the Anniversary of Ken Saro-Wiwa's Execution, Human Rights Organizations Call for Reform." November 6, 1996. <http://web.amnesty.org/library/Index/ENG AFR440261996> (accessed May 1, 2006).

About the Author: Amnesty International, started in 1961 by British attorney Peter Benenson is an independent, worldwide movement of people who campaign for human rights. The organization has more than 1.8 million members in 150 countries and territories. It won the Nobel Peace Prize in 1977.

INTRODUCTION

A writer of satirical novels and plays, Ken Saro-Wiwa had achieved worldwide fame when he and eight fellow members of the Movement for the Survival of Ogoni People were hanged by the government of Nigeria on November 10, 1995 for environmental activism. Saro-Wiwa had spoken out against the exploitation of the Ogoni by the Royal Dutch Shell oil company in collaboration with the Nigerian government. His killing for reportedly murdering four of his Ogoni kinsmen sparked international outrage.

Born in Bane in Khana Local council of Rivers State in Nigeria's Niger Delta region, Saro-Wiwa had spent years campaigning against the ravages of uncontrolled oil development. He accused successive military governments and the giant Shell oil of contaminating the land of 500,000 Ogoni tribespeople. He charged them with committing "environmental genocide" against the Ogoni for depriving them of their means of livelihood—farming and fishing. Saro-Wiwa spearheaded a worldwide campaign to give the impoverished delta communities more access to the wealth produced on their land.

In 1994, the government of General Sani Abacha arrested Saro-Wiwa and fellow activists Dr. Barinem Kiobel, Saturday Dorbee, Paul Levura, Nordu Eawo, Felix Nuate, Daniel Gboko, John Kpuine, and Baribor Bera. The men were held without charges for more than a year. They were allegedly tortured, denied medical and legal aid, and deprived of contact with their families. In the meantime, Saro-Wiwa was nominated for the Nobel Peace Prize and won the prestigious Goldman Environmental Prize. As international calls for the release of the Ogoni Nine mounted, the group was accused of conspiring to murder four Ogoni activists. The resulting trial before a military tribunal was widely condemned as flawed and unfair. After their convictions, the men were denied all rights of appeal and hanged. The executions were so politically sensitive that Nigerian government officials refused to disclose the burial location or turn the bodies over to relatives. They feared that the graves would become a rallying point for anti-government activists. In November 2004, the remains of the Ogoni Nine were exhumed and returned to their families. Despite

Nigerian minority rights activist Ken Saro Wiwa. REUTERS/ARCHIVE PHOTOS INC. REPRODUCED BY PERMISSION.

widespread rumors that bodies were bathed in acid and burned, the bodies showed no indication of mutilation.

PRIMARY SOURCE

Lagos—[alternatively Johannesburg]—On the eve of the first anniversary of the execution of Ken Saro-Wiwa, Amnesty International, together with Nigerian human rights organizations, today called on the Nigerian government to end human rights violations.

An Amnesty International delegation is in the country to mark the 10th November anniversary, and to launch a campaign against human rights violations in Nigeria. Nigerian human rights organizations such as the Civil Liberties Organisation and the Constitutional Rights Project are supporting the campaign.

Ken Saro-Wiwa and his eight colleagues cannot be brought back to life, said Pierre Sané, Secretary General of Amnesty International, at a press conference. The best way to respond to the injustice of their trials and executions is for Nigerians to pledge that it will never happen again and then to take the necessary steps to ensure that it does not.

The Nigerian authorities clear disregard for the most basic and fundamental rights of their people can only result in scepticism about its proposed transition to civilian government by October 1998. One year after the trials, governments worldwide should be keeping up the pressure for improvement in the human rights situation and accept nothing less than substantial reforms from General Abachas government.

In new reports issued today, Amnesty International and the Nigerian human rights organizations are putting forward a ten point program for human rights reform. This program includes the release of all prisoners of conscience, the revocation of all military decrees which allow the indefinite or incommunicado imprisonment of political prisoners, the guarantee of fair trials for political prisoners, safeguards against torture and ill-treatment and abolition of the death penalty.

Despite the international outcry and condemnation of the executions, the situation in Nigeria remains grave, Mr. Sané said. Nigerians who have the courage to stand up for the human rights of their fellow citizens continue to pay a heavy price. Human rights defenders and journalists have been singled out for beatings, detention and harassment.

Former head of state General Olusegun Obasanjo and human rights defender Dr. Beko Ransome-Kuti remain imprisoned after secret and unfair trials by special military tribunals. Others have been detained for long periods without charge or trial. Many have been held in harsh conditions, denied the support of families and lawyers, their lives at risk from malnutrition and medical neglect.

Supporters of the Movement for the Survival of the Ogoni People (MOSOP) continue to face heavy repression by the authorities. At least nineteen Ogoni still face the prospect of unfair trial and execution on the same murder charges which were brought against Ken Saro-Wiwa, President of MOSOP, and his co-defendants. The government has made little progress towards bringing the Ogoni ninenteen to trial and has held them in such terrible prison conditions that one of them died in August 1995 and others are said to be in serious ill-health.

Amnesty International is particularly critical of the Civil Disturbances Special Tribunal which tried Ken Saro-Wiwa and the other Ogoni. Measures announced following a critical UN report in May 1996 have done little to reform the Tribunal. The removal of the one military member from the Tribunal does not affect the governments direct control over it while the right of appeal granted in July 1996 to prisoners convicted by future Civil Disturbance Special Tribunals allows an appeal only to another hand-picked special tribunal, a Special Appeal Tribunal, not to an independent higher court in the normal judicial system. Its convictions and sentences must still be confirmed by the military government.

Given that the Nigerian government appears unprepared to genuinely reform the Ogoni Civil Disturbances Special Tribunal, it should be abolished before the nineteen Ogoni prisoners suffer the same fate as Ken Saro-Wiwa and his colleagues, Mr. Sané said. Although there have been releases of a few detainees, measures announced by the government as reforms are a sham.

The government has revoked one military decree which specifically abolished the right of *habeas corpus* but has continued to flout court orders to release detainees or bring them before the court by invoking other military decrees which remove the courts jurisdiction. The promised reviews of political detentions have not been undertaken by an independent, judicial body but in secret by the security officials who ordered the detentions in the first place. The latest review panel announced in October 1996 is headed by senior security officers and its recommendations have to be approved by the head of state. Chief Gani Fawehinmi's detention was reportedly extended after such a secret review, which confers no rights on the detainee and does not prevent arbitrary and indefinite detention.

SIGNIFICANCE

The death of Saro-Wiwa has not changed much in Nigeria. The man who ordered his death, General Sani Abacha died suddenly of heart failure on June 8, 1998. Elections in May 1999 elevated a civilian to the presidency and ended sixteen years of consecutive military rule. However, corruption is so endemic that Nigeria's government is commonly referred to as a "kleptocracy." The civilian rulers have been unable to cure Nigeria of widespread poverty. Although the country is oil-rich, the wealth is still not filtering down to the people. In 2005, sixty-six percent of Nigeria's 110 million people lived below the poverty line. The Ogoni continue to complain that their land is devastated by Shell. The flaring of gas, sometimes in the middle of villages, has destroyed wildlife and plant life, poisoned the atmosphere, and made the residents half-deaf and prone to respiratory diseases. The problems that consumed Saro-Wiwa have not been resolved.

As of the early twenty-first century, in the absence of government programs, the major multinational oil companies launched their own community development programs. A new entity, the Niger Delta Development Committee, was created to help catalyze economic and social development in the region. At the same time, youths demanding jobs and more stake in Nigeria's wealth sporadically seized oil workers and oil installations. Anti-Western terrorists attacked oil pipelines running through Nigeria. The country's future is in doubt.

FURTHER RESOURCES

Books

Eshiet, Imo, Onookome Okome and Felix Akpan, eds. *Ken Saro-Wiwa and the Discourse of Ethnic Minorities in Nigeria*. Calabar, Nigeria: University of Calabar Press, 1999.

McLuckie, Craig W. and Audrey McPhail, eds. *Ken Saro-Wiwa: Writer and Political Activist*. Boulder: Lynne Rienner, 2000.

NaAllah, Abdul-Rasheed, ed. *Ogoni's Agonies: Ken Saro-Wiwa and the Crisis in Nigeria*. Trenton, NJ: Africa World Press, 1998.

Wiwa, Ken. *In the Shadow of a Saint: A Son's Journey to Understand His Father's Legacy*. South Royalton, VT: Steerforth Press, 2001.

U.N. Report on Torture and Other Cruel, Inhuman or Degrading Treatment or Punishment

Report

By: Nigel S. Rodley

Date: January 9, 1996

Source: Rodley, Nigel S. "U.N. Report on Torture and Other Cruel, Inhuman or Degrading Treatment or Punishment." United Nations Economic and Social Council, January 9, 1996.

About the Author: Sir Nigel S. Rodley, a citizen of the United Kingdom, served as Special Rapporteur on Torture for the United Nations Commission on Human Rights from 1993 to 2001. The job of the Special Rapporteur is to gather information about torture practices in various countries.

INTRODUCTION

The United Nations has several ways of monitoring the occurrence of torture worldwide. One is the Special Rapporteur on Torture, an agent of the U.N. Commission on Human Rights (CHR). The Special Rapporteur issues yearly reports on torture and other cruel, inhuman or degrading treatment or punishment around the world. Nations criticized in the reports are requested to respond officially. The Rapporteur may then issue a second report or addendum commenting on the responses received and making further recommendations or requesting more information. The 1996 report excerpted here, "Question of the Human Rights of All Persons Subjected to Any Form of Detention or Imprisonment, In Particular: Torture and Other Cruel, Inhuman or Degrading Treatment or Punishment," reviewed torture and other illegal practices in sixty-nine countries, including the United States.

In 1996, the Rapporteur's concerns with U.S. practice were primarily to do with the treatment of prisoners by police forces and prison systems. Specifically, the Rapporteur expressed concern that prisoners were held in positions that put them at risk of suffocating and that maximum-security conditions were excessively harsh or inhuman.

PRIMARY SOURCE

U.N. REPORT ON TORTURE AND OTHER CRUEL, INHUMAN OR DEGRADING TREATMENT OR PUNISHMENT

United States of America 182. The Special Rapporteur advised the Government that he had received information indicating that a police practice of placing suspects face down in restraints, usually while hogtied, had resulted in a substantial number of injuries and deaths in police custody in the country. Such practices, exercised in a number of jurisdictions, were said to restrict respiratory movement and occasionally to lead to death from "positional asphyxia." The risk of death was said to be exacerbated when the restrained person was in an agitated state or under the influence of drugs.

183. Conditions at certain maximum security facilities were said to result in the inhuman and degrading treatment of the inmates in those facilities. At the H-Unit in the Oklahoma State Penitentiary at McAlester, death row inmates were reportedly confined for 23 or 24 hours per day in windowless, sealed, concrete cells, with virtually no natural light or fresh air. The only time spent outside these cells was 1 hour per day on weekdays, when 4 prisoners at a time were able to exercise in a bare concrete yard with 18 foot solid walls giving no view of the outside. There was very little direct contact between prisoners and guards and no work, recreational or vocational programmes. Similarly, at the Special Housing Unit (SHU) of Pelican Bay prison in California, prisoners were reportedly confined, either alone or with one other prisoner, for 22 1/2 hours per day in sealed, windowless cells with bare white concrete walls. The cell doors were made of heavy gauge perforated metal

which, according to a federal district court, "blocks vision and light." A substantial number of prisoners in SHU were said to be suffering from mental illness, which had been caused or exacerbated by their confinement in the unit. In recent litigation, the federal district court concluded that conditions there "may press the outer bounds of what most humans can psychologically tolerate." A large number of prisoners were said to be assigned to the unit indefinitely.

184. On 21 November 1995 the Government sent a reply regarding the general concerns raised by the Special Rapporteur. The Constitution and laws of the United States and those of its constituent states prohibited torture and any form of cruel and unusual punishment; the Constitution protected every individual's right to bodily integrity and security of person, including the right to be free from excessively forceful arrest; and the law of the United States and of its constituent states provided numerous judicial, administrative and other remedies and avenues of recourse for individuals who claimed that, in the course of their arrest or detention, law enforcement officials had inflicted torture or cruel and inhuman treatment or punishment. In its reply, the Government went on to discuss and analyse particular legal standards and practices applicable to issues concerning segregation and solitary confinement, use of excessive force by prison guards, use of excessive force by police officers, as well as criminal and civil remedies available to alleged victims.

SIGNIFICANCE

From the viewpoint of later years, the remarkable thing about the 1996 report of the Special Rapporteur on Torture is that its concerns with U.S. treatment of prisoners were so few and minor. In his follow-up addendum ("Summary of communications transmitted to Governments and replies received," January 16, 1996), the Rapporteur described a handful of individual cases of suffocation and torture in police custody, all of which the United States agreed were illegal and in many of which the responsible officers had already been prosecuted. The United States responded with detailed legal arguments to criticisms of the conditions in maximum-security jails, arguing that these conditions did not constitute treatment forbidden by the U.S. Constitution or treaty law. The Rapporteur did not comment on the merit of these arguments. The Rapporteur's 1998 Report on Torture raised similar issues (the United States was not reviewed in the 1997 report) and added that it was concerned about the use of tasers or electric stun-guns against suspects (tasers had killed over 150 persons in the United States from 2001 to 2005).

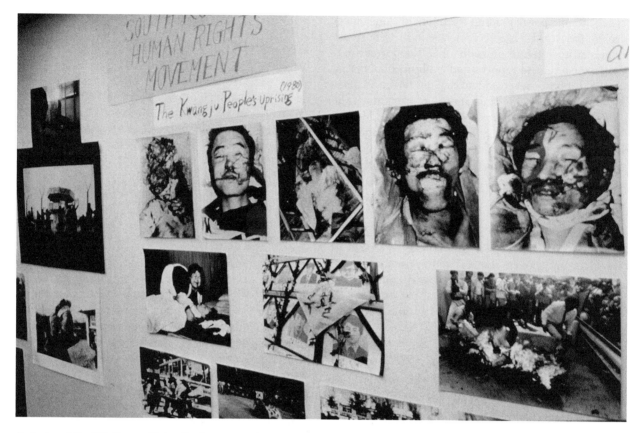

A display at the UN Human Rights Conference on June 14, 1993 titled "The Kwangju People's Uprising", which shows photos of violence, battered and presumably dead Chinese protestors. © VIENNAREPORT AGENCY/CORBIS SYGMA.

A decade later, the situation had changed dramatically. The permissibility of torture was being openly debated in U.S. media and government circles, and in its second four-year report to the U.N. Committee Against Torture (due, 1999; delivered, 2005), required by the U.N. Convention on Torture, the United States found it necessary to defend itself against the charge that it tortured prisoners or sent them to countries where they were likely to be tortured (a practice known as "special rendition"). The United States stated in this 2005 document that "The United States is unequivocally opposed to the use and practice of torture. No circumstance whatsoever, including war, the threat of war, internal political instability, public emergency, or an order from a superior officer or public authority, may be invoked as a justification for or defense to committing torture" (U.N. document CAT/C/48/Add.3, p. 4).

At the same time, however, high officials of the U.S. government were apparently advocating the view that torture is legal under certain circumstances. In 2002, a memo was drafted by the Justice Department

holding that the President can authorize agents of the U.S. government to violate anti-torture laws and treaties in the name of national security. In January 2005, Attorney General Alberto Gonzales said that the Administration held that anti-torture law did not restrain U.S. interrogators overseas (e.g., at Guantanamo) because the U.S. Constitution does not apply outside the borders of the United States. In 2005, when the U.S. Senate was considering an amendment by Sen. John McCain (R-AZ) to the Defense Department Authorization Bill that would ban torture and inhuman treatment by all U.S. agents, even overseas, Vice President Dick Cheney lobbied members of the Senate to exempt agents of the Central Intelligence Agency from the amendment. (The exemption was not granted.) The amendment passed 90–9, but when President George W. Bush signed the bill he issued a "signing statement" indicating that he believed he could ignore the bill whenever he deemed that national security was at stake. The U.N. Commission Against Torture has demanded explanations from the United States (due to be delivered at a meeting in Geneva, Switzerland in May 2006) of its practices and of its various statements that appear to defend the use of torture.

Moreover, starting in 2002, allegations were made by groups such as Amnesty International, Human Rights Watch, and the International Committee of the Red Cross that the United States was practicing torture and inhuman treatment at facilities in Guantanamo, Iraq, Afghanistan, and elsewhere. The U.N. Commission on Human Rights appointed a task force to study the situation of detainees in Guantanamo starting in June 2004. The task force included the Special Rapporteur on Torture.

In February, 2006, the team's report was released. It accused the United States of systematically inflicting both torture and "cruel, inhuman and degrading treatment" (also forbidden by law) on prisoners held at the U.S. naval base in Guantanamo, Cuba. The report found that excessive solitary confinement, exposure to extreme heat and cold, exposure to painfully loud noise and painfully bright light, forced shaving and other techniques designed to humiliate, and force-feeding of hunger strikers through violently inserted and removed nasal tubes amounted to inhuman and degrading treatment and, in some cases, torture.

The U.S. government stated that prisoner testimony received by the envoys was false or exaggerated. White House spokesman Scott McClellan said that "Al Qaeda is trained in trying to make wild accusations" and reiterated that "we do not condone torture, and we do not engage in torture."

The Rapporteur's regular annual reports after 2001 have borne little resemblance, at least regarding the United States, to those of the mid–1990s. Domestic U.S. prison conditions were not even mentioned in the 2005 report. Instead, the Rapporteur criticized the United States for its special rendition of Maher Arar, a Canadian sent by the United States to Syria where he was tortured. The Rapporteur also cited "Secret [CIA] detention centers under United States' authority in various parts of the world, in which an unknown number of persons are detained," noting that the Red Cross has no access to them and that "there is no oversight of the conditions of detention and the treatment of the detainees." He said this was of particular concern given Vice President Cheney's efforts to obtain an exemption for the CIA from the McCain anti-torture bill of 2005.

FURTHER RESOURCES

Books

Tolley Jr., Howard. *The U.N. Commission on Human Rights.* Boulder, Colo.: Westview Press, 1987.

Periodicals

Farley, Maggie. "Report: U.S. Is Abusing Captives." The *Los Angeles Times* (February 13, 2006).

Savage, Charlie. "Bush Could Bypass New Torture Ban." The *Boston Globe* (January 4, 2006).

Smith, R. Jeffrey, and Josh White. "Cheney Plan Exempts CIA From Bill Barring Abuse of Detainees." The *Washington Post* (October 25, 2005).

Web sites

United States Department of State. "Second Periodic Report of the United States of America to the Committee Against Torture." <http://www.state.gov/g/drl/rls/45738.htm> (accessed April 20, 2006).

Conditions in Primam Prison, Jeddah

Report

By: United Nations Economic and Social Council

Date: January 16, 1996

Source: United Nations Economic and Social Council: Commission on Human Rights (52nd Session). "Conditions in Primam Prison, Jeddah." January 16, 1996.

About the Author: The United Nations (UN) formed during World War II in an effort to prevent future hostilities between individual nations and conglomerates of nations. In addition to acting as a world peace-keeping force, the UN has also taken upon the task of patrolling and maintaining human rights.

INTRODUCTION

Saudi Arabia, an active participant in the international community, has continual allegations of human rights violations. These violations primarily reside in the nature, execution, and condition of the Saudi Arabian legal system. International human rights organizations like Amnesty International and Human Rights Watch have released several reports attesting to the conditions of Saudi Arabian prisons and to the maltreatment of detainees and prisoners.

Instances of prisoner neglect, abuse, and torture encompass a large net of human rights violations. Reports attest that individuals charged with petty theft have received seventy or more lashes, several years imprisonment, and, in some cases, death. Cases are heard in closed proceedings, lawyers and legal council are frequently denied to defendants, and a clear understanding of the legal process is not made. Along with charges of extreme punishment, former prisoners and detainees have remarked that many prisoners do not know the status of their case. Not knowing the status of their case relates to prisoners being held for days, weeks, and years before seeing a judge, and then when they do go to court they are not always informed on the outcome of the proceedings. For instance, if a prisoner disagrees with his or her sentence he can reject the punishment and verdict. Once a rejection has been placed, the case will go to appeal. But, the appeals process can take even longer than the sentence stipulated, and it can take longer than it took to get before the first judge. Hence, prisoners frequently opt to take a sentence for a crime they did not commit (they reject the guilty verdict but accept the sentence) so that they can get out of jail sooner. Donato Lana, a Filipino national who worked in Saudi Arabia, faced such an ordeal after his October 11, 1995 arrest. Two policemen came to his home and arrested him on charges of preaching Christianity. After being charged at the police station in Riyadh, the police transferred him to Malz Prison. Lama, who admitted to being a Christian but not a preacher, later signed a statement in Arabic claiming that he was a preacher. When he signed the statement, he believed it related to his release, and his signature came after several months of living in shackles and being beaten daily. When he took his sentence, but denied the guilty verdict, he had about four months left to serve. It was for one and a half years imprisonment and seventy lashes. His captors administered the lashes in one day, and he was not examined by a doctor after they were given.

Lana's case at the Malz Prison is just one example of the injustices in the Saudi Arabian legal system. Other instances of abuse are seen when prisoners see a judge and the accusers or witnesses are not in court. Without advice from a lawyer, or outside party, the prisoner often leaves court with the impression that their case is still in trial. Unfortunately, reports have shown that these prisoners learned that their case received a guilty verdict long after the fact.

The Priman Prison in Jeddah has proved to be the most noted case for prisoner maltreatment in Saudi Arabia. The use of beatings, shackles, and electrical torture has forced the international community to examine the conditions of Saudi Arabian prisons. The question still remains on how to enforce human rights statutes and mandates on the Saudi Arabian government.

■ PRIMARY SOURCE

Saudi Arabia
Information transmitted to the Government and replies received

578. By letter dated 18 September 1995 the Special Rapporteur advised the Government that he had received information indicating that the torture and ill-treatment of prisoners in Priman prison in Jeddah were widespread. It was reported that the prison had insufficient space for detainees to sleep, that temperatures sometimes reached as high as fifty-four degrees Celsius and that it lacked medical facilities to treat prisoners, many of whom were ill.

579. The Special Rapporteur also transmitted the individual cases described in the following paragraphs.

580. Four Christian prisoners, with the surnames Garcase (aged 89), Bile, Johanis and Caperey (correct spellings uncertain), were allegedly taken outside the prison on 13 July 1994 and severely beaten for failing to participate in a Muslim prayer session.

581. Muhammad Dahir Dualle, a national of Somalia, was reportedly arrested and beaten in Mecca on 14 August 1994 because he was not in possession of a passport. He was taken to Jeddah, and after failing to locate the house in which he had left the passport, was allegedly beaten severely, causing him to suffer a broken nose and profuse bleeding from his ears and nose. He was treated at hospital and taken to Priman prison. At the prison, he slipped and fell while carrying some books. In response, a soldier allegedly kicked him in the kidney and, as a result, he had to be transferred back to hospital. A doctor diagnosed a serious injury to his kidney and ordered that he refrain from normal work.

582. Gulam Mustafa, a national of Pakistan, was allegedly tortured on 23 May 1994 in a detention centre for drug offenders in Jeddah. Police personnel allegedly inserted an object into his penis and applied electric shocks, causing him to bleed. He was transferred to Priman prison with his penis bleeding heavily.

583. Osman Gheddi Guled, a national of Djibouti, was transferring planes for Cairo when he was arrested, reportedly after failing to pay a bribe to the authorities when khat, a herbal stimulant, was found in his luggage. His passport and luggage with a large sum of money were seized and he was placed in detention. Several days later, he was taken for interrogation and asked for his passport. When he replied that it had already been confiscated, he was allegedly beaten unconscious. He spent several months in Priman prison, where he was allegedly subjected to further beatings. He was released more than two months after being found innocent by a tribunal.

584. By the same letter the Special Rapporteur reminded the Government of information transmitted on 3 June 1994 concerning the alleged ill-treatment of Iraqi refugees, regarding which no reply had been received. On 27 October 1995 the Government replied that the authorities at the national and local levels had treated the refugees in the same way as Saudi citizens and in some cases had accorded them special privileges to help them to maintain their traditions and preserve their identity. The refugees were treated in accordance with customary international law and the Geneva Conventions concerning the law of war, when they had been considered prisoners of war. After they were recognized as refugees, the Government had treated them according to international instruments concerning refugees or Saudi national law, consisting in the Islamic Shari'a. Initially, there were a few incidents involving infringements by some soldiers with little or no experience of refugee problems, but persons responsible for those infringements were invariably punished in accordance with Islamic Shari'a, as a result of which the situation at the camps had been brought under control.

Refugees suspected of committing offences were investigated under the normal procedures in force in the country, in accordance with the Islamic Shari'a.

Contrary to allegations, no refugees had died as a result of the investigation methods applied. Corporal punishment might have been required under the terms of legal judgements handed down against law-breakers. However, the authorities had endeavoured to restrict and even avoid its application to the refugees in light of their particular status and the penalty had been commuted and was not used against any of the refugees.

585. In its reply, the Government also mentioned several individual cases transmitted by the Special Rapporteur—those of Hadi Nasi Hussein, Abbad Ali Mahawi, Muhammad Hassan, Ali Sabah Ward, Basim Youssuf Ibrahim al-Shaimari and Asaad Ali Hussein al-Bashama. With the exception of Ali Sabah, they had not complained of ill-treatment to the authorities concerned or to the Office of the United Nations High Commissioner for Refugees (UNHCR).

URGENT APPEALS

586. The Special Rapporteur sent three urgent appeals on behalf of the persons mentioned in the following paragraphs, all of whom had reportedly been sentenced to flogging. The dates on which the appeals were sent are mentioned in brackets at the end of each summary.

587. Mohammed 'Ali al-Sayyid, an Egyptian national, was reportedly sentenced to a prison term of seven years and four thousand lashes after being convicted of theft. He was allegedly removed with his legs shackled once every two weeks from al-Buraida prison in al-Qaseem province and taken to the marketplace, where he would receive from a police official fifty lashes with a bamboo cane of about one metre in length and one half centimetre in diameter. As a result of this treatment, he usually suffered bruised or bleeding buttocks, leaving him unable to sleep or sit for three or four days afterwards. He was said to have thus far received 3,400 lashes (2 August 1995).

588. Ibrahim 'Abd al-Rahman al-Hudayf was reportedly sentenced to three hundred lashes and eighteen years' imprisonment after being convicted in a secret trial of participation in the planning of an attack on a security officer and of membership in the Committee for the Defence of Legitimate Rights (17 August 1995).

SIGNIFICANCE

In January 1996, Saudi Arabia signed the UN Conventions on the Rights of the Child, and in August 1997 it joined the consortium of nations to ratify the UN Convention against Torture and Other Cruel, Inhuman, or Degrading Treatment or Punishment. These steps toward joining the international community to eradicate torture and inhumane punishment show steps in the Saudi Arabian government to eradicate its legacy of human rights violations. Unfortunately, the Saudi Arabian government has maintained a policy of trying criminals in closed courts, arresting individuals without warrants, and detaining people without disclosing the nature and purpose of the investigation.

The abuses of the Saudi Arabian legal system do not just pertain to men. Women and other disadvantaged groups are often targets of police brutality and court neglect. Saudi Arabian law prohibits women from driving cars, they must wear headscarves, and their clothing must cover their entire body. Women who are out alone, deemed to be wearing inappropriate clothing, or accused of immoral behavior face severe consequences in the legal system. Numerous cases show Saudi Arabian and foreign women have been arrested for charges like those mentioned here. Furthermore, the treatment of women prisoners and detainees is no better than for males. Cases show women being locked in cars for hours in extreme heat, being beaten, and being tried for murder without knowing their charges. As with the male cases, these victims often do not know the evidence or full charges against them, and when sentencing occurs they are often without knowledge of its severity or length.

As the international community continues to seek mandates and plans to eradicate human injustices, countries that continue to violate human rights come under more scrutiny. The United Nations has declared Saudi Arabia to be in serious violations of human rights, but no concrete action has been taken against its government. Countries like England and the United States have also publicly voiced concerns about Saudi Arabia's treatment of its citizens and non-nationals, but these governments have failed to politically reprimand Saudi Arabia for its actions. Reasons for the lack of international action against human rights violations vary from country to country. With Saudi Arabia, political analysts and skeptics have remarked that England and the United States fear offending Saudi Arabia because it supplies cheap crude oil. This fear might be the reason why UN embargos have not been enforced against Saudi Arabia, but other issues pertain to the matter.

In 1993, the United States Supreme Court declared that Scott Nelson could not sue the country of Saudi Arabia for torture, injury, and harm he encountered while jailed there. In *Saudi Arabia v Nelson*, Nelson sought financial retribution for the harm he and his wife encountered when he was jailed and arrested in Saudi Arabia. He worked for a state owned hospital there, as a safety engineer, and he claimed that after reporting safety violations he was arrested and tortured. The Court declared that the harm against Nelson did not fall within the bounds of commercial activity, which would have allowed Nelson to sue for damages. The court's 1993 decision to rule in the favor of Saudi Arabia mirrors the actions of the United Nations in failing to hold Saudi Arabia responsible to the world court.

FURTHER RESOURCES
Books

Brysk, Allison. *Globalization and Human Rights*. Los Angles: University of California Press, 2002.

Steiner, Henry and Philip Alston. *International Human Rights in Context: Law, Politics, Morals*. Oxford and New York: Oxford University Press, 2000.

Web sites

Amnesty International. "Behind Closed Doors: Unfair Trials in Saudi Arabia." November 25, 1997. <http://www.cdhrap.net/text/english/Reports%20%20Statements/Amnesty%20International/Behind%20Closed%20Doors.htm> (accessed May 8, 2006).

We, On Death Row

Journal article

By: Paul D'Amato

Date: February 2000

Source: D'Amato, Paul. "Benetton Produces "We, On Death Row." *The New Abolitionist*. (February 2000): 14.

About the Author: Paul D'Amato is a journalist who frequently writes about sociopolitical issues. He writes a biweekly column for the online journal *The Socialist Worker ONLINE*. He has also written for the political newsletter *counterpunch*.

INTRODUCTION

Capital punishment is a controversial subject with passionate debate on both sides. In many areas of the world, there is considerable opposition to the death penalty, with many groups pressing hard to put a global end to the practice. At the opposite end of the spectrum are countries where executions are still carried out in public places according to religious law.

The World Coalition Against the Death Penalty is a large abolition group, comprised of nearly fifty non-governmental organizations (NGOs), numerous bar associations (professional associations for attorneys), local and national government agencies, and unions. It was started in 2002, in Rome, Italy, subsequent to a 2001 World Congress held in order to express opposition to the death penalty and to form a united system to work for abolition of capital punishment. The World Coalition is supported and endorsed by the European Union as well as by the Council of Europe. It is the belief of the World Coalition that capital punishment is not a deterrent for future criminal activity (except for the person put to death). It purports that the act of human execution constitutes an act of revenge rather than one of punishment or of justice. It is considered by this group to be cruel, immoral, and inhumane, and an act tantamount to torture. A seminal point of the World Coalition's belief system is that "a society that imposes the death penalty symbolically encourages violence. Every single society that respects the dignity of its people has to strive to abolish capital punishment."

The United States is among the countries that still utilize the death penalty. It may be imposed at either the state or federal level, for a variety of different criminal acts. For the most part, it is first-degree murder, also called premeditated or aggravated murder

Photographer Oliviero Toscani stands in front of one of his pieces about death row inmates, at his exhibition "We, On Death Row," in London, December 13, 2004. PHOTO BY GARETH CATTERMOLE/GETTY IMAGES.

that merits a sentence of death—particularly death of a law enforcement professional or a political figure. Although thirty-eight of the fifty United States retain laws that permit capital punishment, few of them actually perform executions. Five states currently perform the preponderance of executions: Texas, Florida, Missouri, Oklahoma, and Virginia, with Texas having the greatest number in an average year. Although federal courts in America can invoke a sentence of death, it is relatively unusual for that to occur. According to statistics published by Amnesty International, there are just over thirty inmates housed on federal or military death rows. Of those prisoners, only one has been executed during the past four decades. There are, on average, nearly four thousand inmates living on death row in thirty-seven different states. Amnesty International states that some ninety percent of those individuals were either impoverished or otherwise unable to afford independent legal counsel at the time of their criminal trails and worked with court appointed attorneys. Nearly all death row inmates are male, and a disproportionate number of them are non-white (primarily African-American

and Hispanic, few Asians or Native Americans, in comparison).

PRIMARY SOURCE

A lot of good material has been published in the last several years exposing the injustices of the death penalty.

But a double take is in order when Benetton, one of Italy's leading clothes-makers, turns its advertising machine against capital punishment. In January, Benetton produced a one hundred page glossy magazine insert containing pictures and interviews with twenty-five death row inmates from around the U.S.

Entitled "We, On Death Row," the insert includes an interview with Illinois death row inmate Leroy Orange, one of the Death Row Ten convicted on the basis of a confession he gave after being tortured in Chicago's Area 2 police station under the direction of Commander Jon Burge. Leroy confessed to a murder after police placed a plastic bag over his head and applied electric shocks to his testicles.

Burge was thrown off the force in 1993 for directing the torture of scores of people in custody. But that hasn't yet helped Leroy and others convicted on false confessions.

Benetton is known for provocative, socially conscious advertising. Its chief creative director, Oliviero Toscani, said that he intends the supplement to encourage discussion about the human costs of executing criminals. "We will look back to this kind of justice one day, and we will consider ourselves very primitive," he said.

The Benetton ad reflects in part just how unpopular the death penalty is in Italy and Europe. And given the recent California poll showing a shift from three to one in favor of capital punishment to a fifty-fifty split, perhaps Benetton's campaign can be seen as a sign that at least one advertiser believes the tide of public opinion has shifted enough to speak out against the death penalty and still sell clothes.

SIGNIFICANCE

There was a moratorium on the use of capital punishment in the United States between 1972 and 1975. Capital punishment was reinstated in 1976. Since 1976, about one thousand people have been executed in America. In the United States, by far the most common means of execution is the lethal injection, followed by electrocution, lethal gas, hanging, and the firing squad. In lethal injection, the prisoner is strapped to a gurney (stretcher) and given a series of drugs that produce deep sedation prior to stopping the heart beat and respiration. Until relatively recently, the lethal injection was considered the most humane form of execution. However, recent legal challenges suggest that the initial sedatives may not be as effective as had been previously thought, causing the prisoner to die painfully and stressfully.

Around the world, there are seven main forms of death by execution. Hanging is considered to be humane if properly done. If the free fall distance is appropriate, death is swift and purportedly painless. If not, the person can either asphyxiate (if the fall is too short), or be forcibly beheaded (if the fall is too great). Many countries still use death by electrocution (also called the electric chair), which is strongly opposed by the American Civil Liberties Union. There is some evidence that it may take several episodes of application of electric shock before the inmate is actually killed, lasting anywhere from five to ten or more minutes. Because the individual typically wears a mask and hood, it is virtually impossible to know what is experienced prior to death. The firing squad is still employed in some places, with the bound and blindfolded prisoner being shot through the heart (there is a target pinned to his clothing) by a group of marksmen. The gas chamber, or use of lethal gas, is still used in a few places. In that scenario, some form of cyanide is dropped into an acid-filled container, producing hydrogen cyanide. This is considered to be a very slow and painful form of execution, and it is strongly opposed by many of the world's communities. The lethal injection is used most commonly by those countries that execute the death penalty. The guillotine is rarely utilized and is not used at all in North America. It functions by severing the head. It is reported to be a swift and apparently painless form of execution. Some Muslim and Middle Eastern countries still practice death by stoning. In that case, the individual is buried up to the neck and showered with rocks and stones. The premise is that the rocks are large enough to cause pain and significant bodily injury, but not immediate death.

Among the socially and philosophically controversial aspects of death by execution, in addition to the basic human rights issues, concern the matters of executing innocent people, or those who were denied adequate legal representation or truly fair trials; execution of those who were later found to be innocent by means of DNA exclusion or other incontrovertible evidence; carrying out a sentence of death for those who are mentally ill, mentally retarded, have suffered significant brain insult or injury, or those who are otherwise cognitively or psychologically disabled; and execution of those who committed capital crimes as children or youth. Although abolitionists, as well as a growing segment of the general population, favor ending the death penalty under all circumstances, the foregoing are considered the most egregious human rights concerns meriting a moratorium on the death penalty for all persons falling into those categories. Of concern as well is the number of countries that have utilized the practice of deportation of convicted capital criminals, a situation in which nations that have abolished the death penalty have sometimes sent such persons to countries that permit death by execution, under any circumstances.

According to the most recent statistics published by Amnesty International, well over half of the countries in the world have abolished the death penalty, either in fact of law or in practice (that is, having legislation that permits the imposition of the death penalty while choosing not to enforce it for at least the past decade.) According to their data, nearly ninety countries have abolished the death penalty for all crimes, more than ten have ceased it for all but very specific crimes (generally associated with wartime behavior), and close to thirty have capital punishment laws on their books but have carried out no executions for at least ten years. To date, nearly one hundred twenty-five countries have virtually eliminated the death penalty, either in fact or in practice.

Of those countries that still permit capital punishment, some ninety-seven percent of all executions occur in just four countries: China (reported figures range from five thousand to more than ten thousand per year), Viet Nam (estimated sixty to eighty annually), Iran (estimated one hundred and fifty to two hundred annually), and the United States of America (estimated fifty to sixty-five annually).

Although the originally stated premise in favor of capital punishment is that of deterrence, published statistics on the occurrence of violent crimes consistently fails to support this in any considerable degree. The United Nations has expressed the opinion that death by execution is no more a deterrent than life imprisonment. Research data published by Amnesty International suggests that the threat of life without parole has a greater deterrent effect than does the death penalty.

FURTHER RESOURCES

Books

Ancker, Carsten. *Determinants of the Death Penalty: A Comparative Study of the World*. New York, New York: Routledge, 2004.

Bedau, Hugo Adam, and Paul G. Cassell, eds. *Debating the Death Penalty: Should America Have Capital Punishment? The Experts on Both Sides Make Their Best Case*. New York, New York: Oxford University Press, 2004.

Hood, Roger. *The Death Penalty: A World-Wide Perspective*. Oxford, United Kingdom: Clarendon Press, 2002.

Johnson, Robert. *Death Work: A Study of the Modern Execution Process*. Pacific Grove, California: Brooks Cole Publishing Company, 1990.

O'Shea, Kathleen. *Women on the Row*. Ann Arbor, Michigan: Firebrand Books, 2000.

Prejean, Helen. *Dead Man Walking*. New York, New York: Vintage Books, 1994.

Web sites

Amnesty International. "The Death Penalty." <http://web.amnesty.org/pages/deathpenalty-index-eng> (accessed May 07, 2006).

World Coalition Against the Death Penalty. "First World Congress Against the Death Penalty." <http://www.worldcoalition.org/bcoal03decla.html> (accessed May 07, 2006).

Open Letter to Deng Xiaoping

Letter

By: Fang Lizhi

Date: January 6, 1989

Source: Angle, Stephen C. and Marina Svensson, ed. *Chinese Human Rights Reader*. Armonk, New York; M.E. Sharpe, 2001.

About the Author: Fang Lizhi is a Chinese physicist and political dissident whose writings, including his 1989 open letter to Deng Xiaoping, the leader of the Chinese government, contributed to the popular protest that culminated in the Tiananmen Square demonstrations in the spring of 1989. Fang obtained asylum in the United States in 1990, where he continued to participate in the Chinese democracy movement.

INTRODUCTION

In 1949, the Chinese Communist Party under the leadership of Mao Zedong (1893–1976) took control of China after a lengthy civil war. From that point, the Chinese government has been wary of dissent against governmental authority from any part of Chinese society, particularly with regard to opposition expressed by China's intellectual classes.

Prior to the demonstrations staged at Tiananmen Square in Beijing in 1989, organized opposition to government policy within China was invariably suppressed by the government. During the Cultural Revolution, a period of often violent purges of the ranks of the ruling Communist Party that began in 1966, intellectuals who had voiced even mild dissatisfaction with official government policies found themselves stripped of their status with the Party. Many of these persons were sent into the Chinese country side to work as manual laborers; Fang Lizhi, who had worked as a professor of physics prior to running afoul of the Communist Party, was one of those persons "rehabilitated" in this fashion.

Fang was deemed sufficiently rehabilitated that in the late 1970s he was restored to both Communist Party membership and his academic post. Deng Xiaoping (1904–1997), a politician regarded as a moderate, assumed leadership of the Communist Party in 1977, and there was a widespread assumption in the country that with Deng now in power, a greater tolerance would be shown by the Chinese government to the forces favoring greater democracy and freedom of expression in China.

The modern Chinese dissident movement received much of its impetus from a letter sent to Deng by Wie Jingsheng, a Chinese activist, in 1978. Deng had published his views regarding the advancement of China in a policy document entitled The Four Modernizations. Wie's letter, the Fifth Modernization, asserted that there could be no economic progress without democracy. Wie was branded a counter revolutionary and a traitor and was imprisoned for his views in 1979. Wie would remain in custody until 1997.

Fang supported the views of Wie and was outspoken regarding Wie's release. On January 6, 1989, Fang wrote to Deng Xiaoping in an open letter, urging the release of both Wie and all other political prisoners held in China. Fang's letter coincided with a growing unrest in China, particularly within the hundreds of thousands of students resident in and around Beijing. Increasingly bold displays of dissatisfaction with government policy culminated in the protests staged at Tiananmen Square, Beijing, in April 1989.

 PRIMARY SOURCE

January 6, 1989

Central Military Commission

Dear Chairman Deng:

This year marks the fortieth anniversary of the founding of the People's Republic, and the seventieth anniversary of the May Fourth movement. There must be many events commemorating these important dates, but the people are perhaps more worried right now about the future than about the past.

In order to better evoke the spirit of these days, I earnestly suggest that on the fortieth anniversary of this nation's founding, you grant a full amnesty, especially for political prisoners such as Wei Jingsheng. Whatever one's assessment of Wei Jingsheng might be, a full pardon for people like him who have already served ten years in prison would certainly be consistent with a spirit of humanity.

This year also marks the two hundredth anniversary of the French Revolution. Thanks to the inspiration it provides, liberty, equality, fraternity and human rights have received increasing respect over the passing years. I reiterate my sincere hope that you will consider my suggestion so that respect for these values may grow even more in the future.

My best regards,

Fang Lizhi

SIGNIFICANCE

The most obvious consequence of the letter from Fang to Deng Xiaoping was its contribution to anti-government feeling among China's intellectual and student groups in early 1989. The Chinese government were sufficiently persuaded as to Fang's influence with the student protestors at Tiananmen Square that Fang and his wife, Li Shuxian, were the persons that headed a "Most Wanted" list of suspected counter-revolutionaries published by the Chinese government after the protests were suppressed by the Chinese army on June 4, 1989. Fang and his wife were provided a safe haven within the United States embassy in Beijing until they were transported out of China by the United States in June 1990.

The open letter from Fang to Deng Xiaoping represented the first time any member of China's intellectual elite had publicly questioned the imprisonment of anyone. Fang's letter prompted others in the Chinese intellectual and academic classes to send their own letters to Deng Xiaoping.

The pro-democracy demonstrations at Tiananmen Square remain among the most profound and visible protest ever initiated within China against its political leadership. It was also the first demonstration within China that was the subject of relatively contemporaneous media coverage, albeit without the cooperation of Chinese authorities. Tiananmen Square focused international attention on China and its suppression of human rights in the name of Communist Party control. China was roundly condemned by other nations for the manner in which the demonstrations were terminated, including the firing of weapons into thousands of massed and unarmed demonstrators. Hundreds of protestors were killed by the military gunfire and upwards of 500 persons were imprisoned by the Chinese government for their part in the demonstrations.

Despite significant pressure from foreign governments and the international organizations that support the development of democracy in China, the Chinese government never conducted an investigation or an public inquiry into the events of June 4, 1989 at Tiananmen Square.

However, the protest climate that Fang's letter formed a part did not lead to any immediate changes in the dictatorial rule of the Chinese Communist Party into the 1990s. Wie, who remained in prison until 1997, wrote a further open letter to Deng Xiaoping in 1992 regarding the Chinese control of Tibet, a country first occupied by the Chinese in 1950; numerous international groups, including the Dalai Lama, had attacked China for its repression of Tibetan nationals. Fang was actively working from his home in exile in the United States to advance the cause for liberalization and democracy in China, without apparent concrete success.

Deng Xiaoping retired in 1989, and the economic reforms that were initiated in China continued with greater speed. China is now an overtly capitalistic and market driven economy. China has executed a series of bilateral trade agreements with the United States and numerous other Western countries since 1990 that have served as the backbone to a significant flow of trade between China and its economic partners. In a direct contrast to the anti-capitalism rhetoric directed against the Western world by China in the time of the Cultural Revolution, American commercial icons such as Kentucky Fried Chicken and McDonalds now have hundreds of outlets in China.

The flourishing trade has not been impaired by the concerns voiced from time to time by American and other nations regarding the absence of any significant democratic movements in China. Economic issues are of major importance in the current dealings between Western democracies and the Chinese government. Fang has attained iconic status in the academic literature that pertains to the events leading up to the Tiananmen Square protests in 1989. He published *Bringing Down the Great Wall: Writings on Science, Culture, and Democracy in China* in 1991.

FURTHER RESOURCES
Books

Lizhi, Fang. *Bringing Down the Great Wall: Writings on Science, Culture, and Democracy in China*. New York; Norton, 1992.

Miller, H. Lynn. *The Limits of Authority: Science and Dissent in Post-Mao China*. Seattle; University of Washington Press, 1996.

Perry, Elizabeth J., and Mark Selden. *Chinese Society: Change, Conflict, and Resistance (Asia's Transformations)*. New York; Routledge, 2000.

Web sites

Human Rights in China. "Background to the 1989 Democracy Movement." May 1, 2006. <http://www.hrichina.org/fr/downloadables/pdf/downloadable-resources/June-Fourth.pdf?revision-id=14517> (accessed May 29, 2006).

Expressing the Sense of the House of Representatives Regarding Several Individuals Who are Being Held as Prisoners of Conscience by the Chinese Government for Their Involvement in Efforts to End the Chinese Occupation of Tibet

Resolution

By: Tom Udall

Date: July 9, 2002

Source: Udall, Tom. "Expressing the Sense of the House of Representatives Regarding Several Individuals Who are Being Held as Prisoners of Conscience by the Chinese Government for Their Involvement in Efforts to End the Chinese Occupation of Tibet." Washington, D.C.: 107th Congress, July 9, 2002.

About the Author: Democratic Representative Tom Udall of New Mexico has represented New Mexico's third district since 1999 with a focus on civil liberties, the environment, and veteran's affairs.

INTRODUCTION

In 1949, the new Communist government of China chose to invade neighboring Tibet. Tibet had been a free, sovereign nation since 1911; the new Chinese government claimed that Tibet was merely a province of China, and that the Tibetan government was a "feudal regime." The fourteenth Dalai Lama—the spiritual and political leader of the Tibetans—was only fourteen years old, with Tibet under the control of a Regent until the Dalai Lama reached the age of 18. Shortly after the Chinese invasion, the Dalai Lama was made the full head of state with complete political powers.

In 1959, after nearly ten years of increasingly invasive Chinese control over Tibet, tensions escalated, a Tibetan guerilla movement used violence against Chinese soldiers, and the Chinese government ordered bombings and attacks that killed more than eighty-six thousand Tibetans. In March 1959, the Dalai Lama escaped from Tibet wearing a disguise; his fifteen-day trip from Tibet's capital city Lhasa to northern India was dangerous and covert; Tibetans did not know for two weeks whether he was dead or alive.

By 1960, the twenty-five-year-old Dalai Lama had set up a government in exile in India, leaving six million Tibetans in his homeland. Over time a steady trickle of Tibetan refugees settled in India, Nepal, and western Europe and the United States. Many of the refugees were monks and religious teachers, and they spread the teaching of Buddhism and and knowledge of Tibetan history and culture to regions that had previously known little about them. In part because of this, international sentiment turned against the Chinese government and in favor of a free Tibet.

The Chinese government reportedly imprisoned tens of thousands of Tibetans in the 1950s. Sentenced for opposition to the Chinese government or for "local nationalism," a second wave of imprisonments from Tibetan revolts in 1987–1989 included many nuns and monks who chose to peacefully demonstrate against the Chinese government. As of 2001, there were three hundred documented prisoners of conscience in Tibet; the numbers had dwindled as a result of completed sentences, early release, or death.

In 1989, Phuntsog Nyidron, then twenty-four years old, was one of fourteen Buddhist nuns imprisoned for peacefully protesting against the Chinese occupation of Tibet. Sentenced to nine years in the Drapchi prison, Nyidron was tortured while incarcerated. In 1993, audio tapes of the nuns singing songs and chants in praise of the Dalai Lama were smuggled from the prison. When the tapes were released to the public and the Chinese government was pressured to release the nuns, the government responded by charging the nuns with "spreading counter-revolutionary propaganda" and extended their sentences.

▮ PRIMARY SOURCE

IN THE HOUSE OF REPRESENTATIVES
JULY 9, 2002

Mr. UDALL of New Mexico submitted the following resolution; which was referred to the Committee on International Relations

RESOLUTION

Expressing the sense of the House of Representatives regarding several individuals who are being held as prisoners of conscience by the Chinese Government for their involvement in efforts to end the Chinese occupation of Tibet.

Whereas for more than 1,000 years Tibet has maintained a sovereign national identity that is distinct from the national identity of China;

Whereas armed forces of the People's Republic of China invaded Tibet in 1949 and 1950 and have occupied it since then;

Whereas according to the United States Department of State and international human rights organizations, the Government of the People's Republic of China continues to commit widespread and well-documented human rights abuses in China and Tibet;

Whereas the People's Republic of China has yet to demonstrate its willingness to abide by internationally accepted norms of freedom of belief, expression, and association by repealing or amending laws and decrees that restrict those freedoms;

Whereas the Chinese Government has detained several nuns, monks, and individuals as prisoners of conscience for their efforts in speaking out against the Chinese occupation of Tibet;

Whereas on October 14, 1989, Phuntsog Nyidron, a Tibetan Buddhist nun, and 5 other nuns from the Michungri Nunnery were arrested in Lhasa after chanting some slogans and marching in a procession as part of a peaceful demonstration that they organized to protest the Chinese occupation of Tibet;

Whereas Nyidron and the other nuns were kicked, beaten, and given electric shocks on their hands, shoulders, breasts, tongue, and face at the time of the arrest;

Whereas 4 years later, Nyidron and 13 other nuns sang and recorded songs about Tibetan independence in front of prison guards;

Whereas the Chinese Government determined that the public distribution of these songs constituted 'spreading counter-revolutionary propaganda' and on October 8, 1993, extended Nyidron's sentence by 8 years;

Whereas Nyidron is now serving a 17-year sentence, one of the longest reported sentences of any female prisoner of conscience in Tibet;

Whereas Phuntsog Nyidron was awarded the Reebok Human Rights Award in 1995;

Whereas Phuntsog Nyidron is just one of many individuals whom the Chinese Government has held as a prisoner of conscience;

Whereas the Chinese Government continues to imprison individuals as prisoners of conscience for involvement in efforts to end the Chinese occupation of Tibet; and

Whereas the Chinese Government continues to exert control over religious and cultural institutions in Tibet, abusing human rights through torture, arbitrary arrest, and detention without public trial of Tibetans who peacefully expressed their political or religious views: Now, therefore, be it

A member of Amnesty International displays a photo of, Gao Yu, a Chinese prisoner of conscience. ROBYN BECK/AFP/GETTY IMAGES.

Resolved, That it is the sense of the House of Representatives that the Government of the People's Republic of China should, as a gesture of good will and in order to promote human rights, release prisoners of conscience such as Phuntsog Nyidron.

SIGNIFICANCE

Representative Tom Udall, a Democrat from New Mexico, wrote this resolution for the United States House of Representatives in addition to cosponsoring a bill on Tibetan policy. On February 2, 2004, the resolution passed as House Resolution 157 with sixty-six cosponsors. It passed unanimously in the House of Representatives.

Twenty-four days later, Chinese authorities released Phuntsog Nyidron from Drapchi, one day after a United States Department of State report characterized China's treatment of Tibetan political prisoners as a gross human rights violation. The report

detailed summary executions, torture, lack of legal representation, arbitrary arrest, and extensions of sentences without due process.

Phuntsog Nyidron's release after fifteen years in prison was hailed as a diplomatic success; Udall's resolution, combined with the State Department report, was believed to have put enough pressure on China to compel her release. In addition, the United Nations Commission on Human Rights was set to convene the following month, in March 2004; China's choice to release Phuntsog Nyidron helped to quell complaints about the treatment of political prisoners in Tibet.

Phuntsog Nyidron was released to a home in Lhasa where she was kept under strict surveillance, denied a passport, and denied appropriate medical care for a kidney condition. On March 15, 2006, Phuntsog Nyidron was released to the International Campaign for Tibet staff and delivered to the United States, where she had an audience with the Dalai Lama and received medical care. Her release came one month before Chinese President Hu Jintao's summit with United States President George W. Bush.

At the time of Phuntsog Nyidron's release, human rights researchers estimated than 150 Tibetan political prisoners remained imprisoned by Chinese authorities, and approximately seventy-five percent of those prisoners were Buddhist monks and nuns convicted for peaceful demonstrations against the Chinese government.

FURTHER RESOURCES

Books

Avedon, John. *In Exile from the Land of Snows*. New York: Harper Perennial, 1997.

Lama, Dalai. *My Land and My People: The Original Autobiography of His Holiness the Dalai Lama of Tibet*. New York: Warner Books, 1997.

Shakya, Tsering. *The Dragon in the Land of Snows: A History of Modern Tibet Since 1947*. New York: Penguin, 2000.

Web sites

Human Rights Watch. "China and Tibet." <http://hrw.org/> (accessed May 5, 2006).

The Office of Tibet. "Invasion and Illegal Annexation of Tibet: 1949–1951." February 2, 1996. <http://www.tibet.com/WhitePaper/white2.html> (accessed May 5, 2006).

Coming Out of Solitary Confinement, Schlusselburg Fortress Prison, Russia, 1886

Book excerpt

By: Vera Figner

Date: ca. 1921

Source: Scheffler, Judith A. (ed). *Wall Tappings*. New York.: Feminist Press, 2002.

About the Author: Vera Figner (1852–1942) was a Russian revolutionary and prominent Soviet era writer. A member of Narodnaya Volya (People's Will), she was implicated in several plots to kill Tsar Alexander II (1818–1881). After he was killed in St Petersburg in 1881, a round up of People's Will members took place and many, including Vera Figner, were sentenced to death. Figner's sentence was later reduced to life imprisonment, but she was released in 1904 and went into exile for eleven years. After the 1917 Revolution, she found worldwide fame as a writer with the publication of her *Memoirs of a Revolutionist*.

INTRODUCTION

On March 1, 1881, while traveling through the streets of central St. Petersburg, the carriage of Tsar Alexander II was attacked and destroyed in a grenade attack carried out by Ignacy Hryniewiecki, a Polish member of the revolutionary organization, Narodnaya Volya (People's Will). It was the third time the People's Will had tried to kill Alexander II and the fifth attempt on his life. He was taken away from the scene seriously injured and died a few hours later.

In the months that followed his murder, police rounded up members of the People's Will and sent them to trial. Many were executed for either their involvement in Alexander's assassination or even simply for membership of the People's Will or other renegade organizations. Amongst those arrested was Vera Figner, a former medical student and long standing revolutionary. Figner was a member of the People's Will's executive committee and spent nearly two years on the run after Alexander's murder. She was arrested in Kharkov in February 1883 and placed in solitary confinement for twenty months.

At her trial, Figner was sentenced to death, but this was later reduced to life imprisonment, and she was sent to the Shlüsselburg Prison thirty miles east of St. Petersburg where she remained until her release in 1904.

■ PRIMARY SOURCE

I Acquire a Friend

Early in January, 1/28/86, knowing that Ludmila Alexandrovna Volkenstein, one of my co-defendants in the Trail of 14, was also in the Fortress, I asked the inspector whey they did not permit me to take my walks in company with one of the other prisoners. The inspector was silent for a moment, and then said, "WE can grant you this privilege, only you mustn't..." He bent his forefinger and tapped on the door jamb, imitating our fashion of carrying on conversations by tapping on the wall. I replied that I did very little tapping.

The interview went no further, and I was left in solitude as before. But on January 14, when they took me out for my walk, and the door into the little enclosure which we called "the first cage," opened, I beheld an unexpected figure in a short cloth coat, with linen handkerchief on her head, who swiftly embraced me, and I recognized with difficulty my comrade Volkenstein. Probably she also was as shocked by the change in my appearance...

We were like people shipwrecked on an uninhabited island. We had nothing and no one in all the world save each other. Not only people, but nature, colors, sounds, were gone, all of them. And instead there was left a gloomy vault with a row of mysterious, walled-in cells, in which invisible captives were pining; an ominous silence, and the atmosphere of violence, madness and death. One can see plainly that in such surroundings two friendly spirits must needs find joy in each other's company, and ever afterwards treasure a most touching remembrance of the association.

Any one who has been in prison knows the influence that the sympathetic tenderness of a comrade has on one's life while in confinement. In Polivanov's memoirs of his imprisonment in the Alexey Ravelin, there is a touching picture of Kolodkevich, hobbling up to the wall on crutches to console him with a few tender words. A brief conversation through the soulless stone that separated the two captives, who were dying from scurvy and loneliness, was their only joy and support. The author of the memoirs confessed that more than once Kolodkevich's kind words saved him from acute attacks of melancholy, which were tempting them to commit suicide. And indeed, loving sympathy works veritable wonders in prison; and were it not for those light tappings on the wall, which destroy the stone barrier separating man from man, the prisoner could not preserve his life or his soul. Good reason was there for the struggle to maintain the system of tappings, the very first struggle that a captive wages with the prison officials; it is an out-and-out struggle for existence, and every one who is walled up in a cell clutches at this device as at a straw. But when those sentenced to solitary confinement are permitted to meet their co-prisoners face to face, and to replace the symbolic tapping with living speech, then the warm-heartedness and kindness expressed in the tones of the voice, in an affectionate glance, and a friendly handshake, bring joy unknown to one who has never lost his freedom.

I do not know what I gave to Ludmila Alexandrovna, but she was my comfort, my joy and happiness. My nerves and general constitution had been completely unstrung. I was physically weak, and spiritually exhausted. My general state of mind was entirely abnormal; and lo! I found a friend whom prison conditions had not affected so profoundly and painfully as they had me; and this friend was the personification of tenderness, kindness, and humaneness. All the treasures of her loving spirit she gave to me with a generous hand. No matter how gloomy my mood when we met, she always knew how to dispel it in one way or another, and how to console ... Straightway I would begin to dream of our next meeting. We saw each other every other day; prison discipline evidently found it necessary to dilute the joy of our meetings, by making us pass a day in complete solitude. But perhaps this fact only made our longing to see

each other more keen, and accentuated our "holiday mood," which was so pleasant to recall afterwards.

SIGNIFICANCE

Although Vera Figner's political ideas were articulated in a particularly extreme manner, incarceration for political or anti-monarchy views in Tsarist Russia was by no means unique. Many of Figner's fellow prisoners at Shlüsselburg, notably Alexander Ulyanov (the brother of Lenin who was later hanged for his part in an attempt to assassinate Alexander III), were there for their political opinions, whether they had been expressed in a benign or violent way. Many thousands more were sent into exile in Siberia.

Russia in the late nineteenth century was a country caught between two worlds. Although monarchies existed in most of its European neighbors, nowhere was the monarch more absolute than in Tsarist Russia and in no other country did the aristocracy exert as much power over its people. Not until 1861 did feudalism end. Yet, at the same time, a wealthy, educated and highly cosmopolitan elite were imbued with the ideas and ideals of the rest of the world in which they traveled widely. Nationalistic and idealistic, they envisaged varying models of a modern liberal democracy existing in Russia. Political debate, however, was all but banned and the Tsar's extensive secret police force worked assiduously to infiltrate both formal and informal political organizations. As such, political expression was often pushed to extremes and groups like the People's Will sought to inspire political revolution by creating social upheaval. In effect, their actions merely served to polarize the situation, to increase the clampdown on political debate and further the numbers and pervasiveness of the Tsar's secret police. The prison population and numbers sent into exile in Tsarist Russia increased significantly in the last twenty years of the nineteenth century.

Alexander II had been one of the most liberal Tsars in history and was slowly setting Russia on the course of becoming a constitutional monarchy. He had been responsible for the emancipation of the serfs, the most significant reform in centuries, and had set about reforming Russia's judiciary based on the French model. One of the ironies of his assassination was that it inadvertently set reform in Russia back by years. He was replaced by Tsars Alexander III and Nicholas II whose reigns were far more despotic and repressive than his had ever been.

The political unrest of Nicholas II's reign, compounded by the appalling military losses and food

A jail cell in the old prison of the Pierre-and-Paul fortress in Saint Petersburg, Russia, 1991. PHOTO BY LIPNITZKI/ROGER VIOLLET/GETTY IMAGES.

shortages of the First World War, eventually gave way to revolution in February 1917. In the political chaos that followed, the Bolsheviks, a small socialist revolutionary party led by Vladimir Ulyanov (Lenin), seized political momentum and eventually power in October 1917 after staging a *coup d'etat*.

The Bolsheviks were the acknowledged successors of the People's Will, sharing many of the same influences and ideas. Despite the fact that many of its members had themselves suffered for their political beliefs, they were not in the business of enacting wholesale changes to the Russian judicial system nor of allowing their opponents—or even those within their own membership—any form of freedom of political expression. Lenin spoke of the necessity of discipline within his party ranks and the country as a whole and made no allowance for dissent, no matter how nuanced. One of his first acts as Russian leader was to establish the Council of People's Commissars (the Cheka, and later the NKVD), a secret police force whose pervasiveness and brutality very quickly outstripped that of the Tsarist police force.

To accommodate the large-scale arrest of Bolshevik opponents, something that increased exponentially after the succession of Lenin by Joseph Stalin in 1924 and continued until the 1980s, large-scale prison camps were set up across Siberia and beyond. Known as Gulags, the writer Alexander Solzhenitsyn accurately observed that these camps came to form an 'archipelago' across Russia. Forced labor, prison officer brutality, hunger and the harshness of Siberian climate made these amongst the most notorious prison conditions in history. The scale of these gulags was also immense. By the outbreak of World War II in 1939, 1.3 million people were incarcerated in them, and up to 20 million passed through them during Russia's Soviet era.

For her part, Vera Figner, whose earlier revolutionary activities had helped pave the way for the Bolsheviks and their repressive system, was a favorite of the new regime. Her memoirs made her famous in the USSR and across the world, although she herself maintained a distance from the Bolshevik government. In her later years, she was active in organizing famine relief for her fellow Russians and campaigned as far as she could to ease Russia's prison conditions.

FURTHER RESOURCES
Books

Applebaum, Anne. *Gulag: A History*. London: Penguin, 2004.

Figes, Orlando. *A People's Tragedy: The Russian Revolution 1891–1924*. London: Jonathan Cape, 1996.

Pipes, Richard. *Russia under the Old Regime*. London: Penguin, 1995.

A Passion for Solitude

Nawal El Saadawi's Memories of an Egyptian Prison

Book except

By: Nawal El Saadawi

Date: 2002

Source: El Saadawi, Nawal. "A Passion for Solitude" in Scheffler, Judith A., ed. *Wall Tappings: Women's Prison Writings*. New York: Feminist Press, 2002.

About the Author: The writer and feminist Nawal El Saadawi (b. 1931) had a distinguished career in public health in Egypt until 1973 when she was dismissed from her post as Director of Health Education in the Ministry of Health in Cairo. Eight years later, she was imprisoned for crimes against the state for advocating for women's liberation.

INTRODUCTION

Nawal El Saadawi, a physician and writer, went to prison in Egypt in 1981 for challenging the subordinate role of women in Middle Eastern society and within Islam. Born in 1931 in Kafr Tahla, a small village outside of Cairo to a large family, El Saadawi suffered female genital mutilation at the age of six. Her family was traditional in many ways, yet her father also accepted the importance of educating girls. El Saadawi attended the University of Cairo and graduated in 1955 with a degree in psychiatry. After completing her education, she practiced psychiatry and eventually rose to become Egypt's Director of Public Health. In the 1960s, she instituted a divorce against her first husband, a near impossibility in the Arab world. She subsequently married Sherif Hatata, a leftist physician who also suffered imprisonment for his political views.

The major theme of El Saadawi's work is Arab women's sexuality, which she views as part of the wider problem of women's subordinate social and legal status within the Arab world. Women's sexuality is a taboo subject in many Islamic countries, including Egypt in the 1970s. El Saadawi's writings were controversial and considered by many in authority to be dangerous. Her writings were banned in her native country. As a result, El Saadawi was forced to publish her works in Beirut, Lebanon. In 1972, she published her first work of non-fiction, *Women and Sex*. The book angered highly placed political and theological authorities to the extent that the Ministry of Health fired El Saadawi. Under similar pressures, she lost her post as Chief Editor of a health journal and as Assistant General Secretary in the Medical Association in Egypt.

El Saadawi had been warned by her husband about the "visitors of the dawn," the Egyptian secret police, yet she refused to be cowed. As a member of the Ain Shams University's Faculty of Medicine, she conducted research on women and neurosis. The results inspired her novel *Woman at Point Zero*, which was based on a female death row inmate convicted of murdering her husband that she met while conducting interviews. In 1977, El Saadawi published her most famous work, *The Hidden Face of Eve*. This book covered a host of topics relative to Arab women, such as aggression against female children and female genital mutilation, prostitution, sexual relationships, marriage and divorce, and Islamic fundamentalism. On September 6, 1981, El Saadawi sat at home alone reading a novel. The doorbell rang. The "visitors of the dawn" collected El Saadwi's books and papers and then took her to jail. She was released in 1982, after the assassination of President Anwar Sadat. In 1983, she published *Memoirs from the Women's Prison*, in which she continued her attacks on the repressive Egyptian government.

PRIMARY SOURCE

I had imagined prison to be solitude and total silence, the isolated cell in which one lives alone, talking to oneself, rapping at the wall to hear the responding knock of one's neighbour. Here, though, I enjoyed neither solitude nor silence, except in the space after midnight and before the dawn call to prayer. I could not pull a door shut between me and the others, even when I was in the toilet.

If Boduur ceased quarrelling with her colleagues, she would begin reciting the *Qur'an* out loud. And if Boduur went to sleep, Fawqiyya would wake up and begin to discuss and orate. If Fawqiyya went to sleep, Boduur would wake up to announce prayertime and the onset of night.

Outspoken Egyptian feminist Nawal Saadawi (left) with her husband Sherif Hetata on February 27, 1998. © REUTERS/CORBIS.

One night, the quarrel between Boduur and one of her comrades continued until dawn, ending only when Boduur fainted after she'd been hit by violent nervous convulsions. She tore at her hair and face with her fingernails, screaming until she lost consciousness.

As soon as the *shawisha* had opened the cell door in the morning, I called out to her. "I want to be transferred to a solitary cell. I don't want to stay in this cell any longer."

But the prison administration rejected my request. I came to understand that in prison, torture occurs not through solitude and silence but in a far more forceful way through uproar and noise. The solitary cell continued to float before me like a dream unlikely to be realized.

Since childhood, I've had a passion for solitude. I've not had a room in which I could shut myself off, for the number of individuals in every stage of my life has been greater than the number of rooms in the house. But I have always wrested for myself a place in which I could be alone

to write. My ability to write has been linked to the possibility of complete seclusion, of being alone with myself, for I am incapable of writing when I am unable to give myself completely to solitude.

After midnight, when the atmosphere grows calm and I hear only the sound of sleep's regular breathing, I rise from my bed and tiptoe to the corner of the toilet, turn the empty jerry can upside down and sit on its bottom. I rest the aluminum plate on my knees, place against it the long, tape-like toilet paper, and begin to write.

SIGNIFICANCE

El Saadawi's influence on Arab feminism has been profound. She is currently one of the most widely read of contemporary Egyptian authors. Her twenty-seven books have been translated into no fewer than twelve languages. In 1983, she founded the Arab Women's

Solidarity Association (AWSA), an international organization dedicated to "lifting the veil from the mind" of Arab women. In 1985, AWSA was granted consultant status with the Economic and Social Council of the United Nations as an Arab non-governmental association. Under pressure from Islamic fundamentalists, the Egyptian government closed AWSA down in 1991 and diverted its funds to a religious women's association. El Saadawi took the Egyptian government to court, but she did not win the case.

When Hosni Mubarak succeeded Anwar Sadat as President of Egypt on October 6, 1981, Mubarak promised to address Egypt's social problems. He released many of the political and religious leaders imprisoned by Sadat, including El Saadawi. Political parties created under Sadat were permitted to grow, publish newspapers, and promote candidates for legislative elections. Since 1992, however, the Mubarak government has limited the proliferation of parties, restricted freedom of the press, and curbed movements that it regards as subversive. For her writing and activism on behalf of women, El Saadawi discovered in June 1992 that she had been placed on a death list. On January 8, 1993, she fled Egypt for the United States. She subsequently returned home and unsuccessfully ran for president in 2004. In 2006, she continued to promote feminist issues from her home in Cairo.

The Mubarak government initially supported the resurgence of Islamist movements in Egypt, notably al-Jihad and the Muslim Brotherhood. In recent years, in the wake of an attempt on Mubarak's life, the government has attempted to crack down on Islamic fundamentalism. However, the movement has proven too deeply entrenched, especially in the professional associations. It is unlikely that an improvement in the situation of women, a goal long held by El Saadawi, will occur as long as Islamic fundamentalism remains strong in Egypt.

FURTHER RESOURCES
Books
El-Saadawi, Nawal. *The Hidden Face of Eve: Women in the Arab World*. London: Zed Books, 1980.

—— *The Nawal El Saadawi Reader*. London: Zed Books, 1997.

—— *Walking Through Fire: A Life of Nawal El Saadawi*. London: Zed Books, 2002.

Howland, Courtney W. *Religious Fundamentalism and the Rights of Women*. New York: St. Martin's Press, 1999.

By Right of Memory

Poem excerpt

By: Alexander Tvardovsky

Date: Date unknown; between 1968 and 1991

Source: Applebaum, Anne, ed. *By Right of Memory*. New York: Penguin, 2003.

About the Author: Alexander Tvardovsky was a Russian poet who received several official prizes from the Soviet regime, but late in his career assisted dissenters such as Alexander Solzhenitsyn.

INTRODUCTION

This scrap of poetry, which is an English translation of a Russian original, was found in the remains of the Soviet prison system known as the Gulag. The original text was an autobiographical poem by Alexander Tvardovsky (1910–1971), a Russian Soviet poet who received the Stalin Prize and Lenin Prize for works that praised the Soviet government but who supported dissent in the 1970s.

The word "Gulag" was originally an acronym for *Glavnoe Upravlenie Lagerei*, Russian for "Main Camp Administration." The Gulag was a system of geographically isolated prisons, camps, colonies, and villages in which a total of about twenty million persons were imprisoned throughout much of the Soviet era (early 1920s through 1991). Many thousands of persons were tortured and killed in the Gulag system; over a million died. Prisoners were expected to do hard work but were inadequately fed, leading to a high rate of death by disease. Families and children of persons accused of counterrevolutionary activity were also imprisoned, often in separate camps or colonies. Intellectuals were often assigned to forced psychiatric treatment designed not to cure mental disorders but to break down resistance. During World War II, many Gulag prisoners were drafted into penal battalions that were placed at the most dangerous parts of the front. (Russia suffered about ten million military dead and eleven million civilian dead in World War II, by far the greatest losses of any group or country in that period.).

Mass releases from the Gulag system occurred in the 1950s under Nikita Khruschev (1894–1971). The Gulag system was officially terminated in 1960, but many people remained imprisoned in parts of the system for years afterward.

The remains of a Gulag prison camp in Russian Siberia, 2000. © STAFFAN WIDSTRAND/CORBIS.

PRIMARY SOURCE

And fate made everybody equal
Outside the limits of the law
Son of a kulak or Red commander
Son of a priest or commissar . . .

Here classes were all equalized,
All men were brothers, camp mates all,
Branded as traitors every one. . . .

SIGNIFICANCE

The preservation by an inmate of a Soviet prison camp of a protest poem written by an official Soviet poet is a peculiar event. It reflects the complex personal story of the poem's original author, Alexander Tvardovsky, and hints at the slow-growing discontent that eventually brought about the collapse of the Soviet system in 1991.

The Soviet government was formally established in 1922. Although founded on a Communist ideology that originally appealed to the idea of universal fairness, it was a harshly repressive regime. Its vast secret-police apparatus sent millions of peasants, intellectuals, religious believers, and dissidents to the Gulag. The first major wave of Soviet forced-labor camps was engineered in the early 1930s to "liquidate" (the official Soviet term) the class of relatively well-to-do peasant farmers known in Russia as *kulaks*. Kulaks were considered "class enemies"—that is, government officials assumed that they would be less loyal to the new Soviet regime than poorer classes of farmers. It was decided by the Soviet government that the kulaks would be "liquidated as a class," that is, not necessarily massacred but forced to take up a lower social status. Those who resisted were shot. Forced movement of kulaks to collective farms resulted in many thousands of deaths and greatly expanded the incipient Gulag system.

The young poet Alexander Tvardovsky had been a fervent member of the Communist Youth League from age fifteen. When he was twenty-one and living away from home, his parents and brother were designated as kulaks and deported to forced labor in the Urals. Tvardovsky learned of their deportation in 1931 when they contacted him to plead for help. He responded in a letter that they should "be strong, be patient, and work" and later denounced his family as "enemies of the people." During World War II, his brother Ivan was drafted into the Soviet army; after the war, Ivan was sent to the Gulag (which he survived).

Tvardovsky, having renounced his family in favor of Soviet ideology, went on to become one of the most famous Soviet poets during World War II. Yet in the ideological thaw that began when Khrushchev denounced Stalin's crimes in a famous 1956 speech to Twentieth Congress of the Communist Party, Tvardovsky—by then editor of the literary journal *Novyi Mir* ("New World")—renounced Stalinism and helped to expose the Gulag. In his journal, he published what is still one of the most famous pieces of literature about the Gulag, *One Day in the Life of Ivan Denisovich* by Alexander Solzhenitsyn (1918–).

In 1968, Tvardovsky wrote a long autobiographical poem, "By Right of Memory," in which he confesses his guilt for renouncing family. This is the poem quoted in translation in this primary source. Tvardovsky was not allowed to publish the poem in *Novyi Mir* and was forced out of the editorship by the government. By the time he died in 1971, Tvardovsky had fallen definitively from official grace. He remained estranged from his brother, however, until his death.

The story of Tvardovsky reflects the larger arc of twentieth-century Russian history: early enthusiasm of large segments of the population for the Soviet project, followed by disillusionment and embitterment over decades of government oppression, corruption, and inefficiency. Increased political openness or *glasnost* under Mikhail Gorbachev (1931–) allowed discontent a louder voice. Solzhenitsyn's classic *The Gulag Archipelago* was finally published in Russia in 1989, sixteen years after it first appeared in translation in the West. The Soviet Union collapsed in 1991.

FURTHER RESOURCES

Books

Applebaum, Anne. *Gulag, A History*. New York: Doubleday, 2003.

Solzhenitsyn, Alexander. *The Gulag Archipelago*. New York: Harper & Row, 1978.

Periodicals

McFaul, Michael. "Camps of Terror, Often Overlooked." *The New York Times*. June 11, 2003.

Chile: Torture Testimonies To Be Concealed for Fifty Years

News article

By: Anonymous

Date: December 16, 2004

Source: "Chile: Torture Testimonies To Be Concealed for Fifty Years." *Human Rights News* (December 16, 2004).

About the Author: This article was published without a byline in *Human Rights News*, a publication of Human Rights Watch, the largest human rights organization in the United States. The author is not known.

INTRODUCTION

Chilean voters chose Popular Unity party candidate Salvador Allende to be their president on September 4, 1970. The Popular Unity party, composed of Socialist, Communist, Radical, and Social-Democratic Parties of Chile, represented a dramatic leftist set of political beliefs and policies. Allende's ascent to the presidency angered conservatives in Chile; upper class elites, landowners, and the Catholic Church formed an odd alliance with foreign investors and governments such as the United States in their joint disapproval of Allende's election. Shortly after Allende's win, President Richard Nixon, with his Secretary of State Henry Kissinger, ordered CIA Director Richard Helms to create an operation to bring down the presidency of Salvador Allende. The initial operation, Project FUBELT, failed, though Nixon authorized Helms to spend between $10 million and $21 million to destabilize Allende's administration.

Allende's socialist policies during his three years in power included land reform that gave peasants ownership over seized private land; greater rights for women in civil society and the political process; increased labor rights; and nationalization of such industries as banking, mining, and steel. Within one year of Allende's presidency, the government controlled more than ninety percent of all industry. A wide range of foreign investors and private international companies had removed operations from Chile with Allende's socialist victory, but those who did not faced the loss of capital through the Popular Unity's policies. The Popular Unity coalition claimed that their goal was to use democratic and constitutional means to accomplish socialist goals; nationalization of industry, according to their plans, gave workers greater economic security and stabilized the economy.

Inflation soared, foreign loans were difficult to obtain and credit constricted, and Washington DC worked to alienate Chile from international financial and diplomatic relationships. The country had been in economic crisis when Allende took over, and by mid-1973 it was still in economic crisis, though one that had redistributed wealth and alienated elites.

On September 11, 1973 in the Chilean capital of Santiago, fifty-seven-year-old General Augusto Pinochet, Commander in Chief of the Army, ordered the seizure of the port city of Valparaiso, shut down radio stations, and bombed, then captured La Moneda, the presidential palace. By day's end, Allende was dead; while some accounts report that he committed suicide, others insist that military forces killed him and staged his death to look like suicide.

Pinochet immediately took control and later installed himself as president. International credit lines opened up, and Pinochet embarked on an economic experiment, "The Chilean Miracle," which claimed to follow neoliberalism. Using the neoliberal economic theories of Milton Friedman, a University of Chicago economist, Pinochet reversed Allende's land reform and returned land to elite owners, removed many social programs that Allende had created, and let a "free market" approach reign. The effect on the poor and working-class elements in society was grim, with no financial safety net in place.

While the economic policies were harsh, Pinochet's human rights policies were even harsher. In an effort to destroy all leftist, socialist, or communist elements in society, Pinochet ordered the execution of many Marxist leaders and used public facilities such as the National Stadium to round up alleged leftists for detainment, torture, and at times execution. Wives were tortured and sexually assaulted in front of husbands; daughters in front of fathers; dogs used to sexually assault women; and electroshock devices were used by soldiers for torture.

Between 1973 and 1976, an alleged 40,000 Chilean citizens were tortured, and to date more than 4,000 remain "disappeared," their whereabouts unknown. Many leftists and accused leftists fled Chile during the coup and shortly after being released from detention centers. In 1978, Pinochet pushed through the Chilean legislature an act that granted all soldiers immunity for their actions.

In 1989, Pinochet permitted elections for the Presidency for the first time in sixteen years; he lost the election, and in 1990 handed over control of the highest office in Chile to Patricio Aylwin. Pinochet installed himself as a senator for life, and remained Commander in Chief of the Armed Forces until 1998.

PRIMARY SOURCE

A law approved last night by the Chilean Congress that denies courts access to the testimonies of thousands of torture victims gravely undermines efforts to prosecute abuses committed under the military government (1973–1990), Human Rights Watch said today. Last month a presidential commission released a report on the use of torture during the military dictatorship that was based on testimony gathered from thousands of victims. The law bars those testimonies from being divulged for 50 years and explicitly prohibits them from being revealed even to the courts.

The law was approved by both chambers of Congress in less than 48 hours and its secrecy provisions were scarcely debated.

"After refusing for years to investigate torture allegations, Chile has finally collected evidence that could help identify and prosecute those responsible for thousands of abuses," said José Miguel Vivanco, Americas director of Human Rights Watch. "It's incomprehensible that the government and congress have now deliberately prevented this from happening."

In recent years, Chilean judges have shown courage and tenacity in investigating the systematic human rights abuses of the military era, but these efforts will be seriously impeded by the secrecy rule.

The law provides reparations for more than 27,000 torture victims identified by the National Commission on Political Imprisonment and Torture, whose report President Ricardo Lagos made public on November 28. Victims will receive annual pensions of between 1,350,000 pesos and 1,550,000 pesos (approximately US$2,300 and US$2,600). Children born in prison or detained with their parents will receive a lump-sum payment of 4 million pesos (approximately US$6,800).

The law's preamble justifies the secrecy rule on the grounds that those who testified before the commission were told that their testimonies would remain confidential. It maintains that these reassurances of confidentiality gave victims confidence to testify and that the government is bound to honor its pledge. It also states that using the testimonies as evidence in judicial proceedings would distort the original purpose of the commission, which was solely to name victims and provide them with reparations.

In Santiago, Chile, on December 14, 1983, police use tear gas and a water cannon to disperse a demonstration by 1,650 priests, nuns and pacifists. They are protesting against the use of torture by Chile's Secret Police force. © BETTMANN/CORBIS.

"If victims want to keep their testimony private, their wish should be fully respected," said Vivanco. "But it is totally unacceptable to impose this secrecy rule on others who would prefer that their testimonies contribute to the prosecution of those who tortured them."

The Chilean government has clarified that individual victims are free to make their testimonies public or submit them to the courts if they wish to do so. Yet, without access to the testimonies, judges investigating torture cases will be prevented from identifying many victims who could contribute evidence as witnesses. And the victims themselves will not know of the relevance of their evidence to cases under investigation.

The government must ask those who testified whether they want their testimonies to be made available to the courts. The government, which formed the commission, has a responsibility to turn over this information to the courts, rather than put the onus on the victims.

After Chile's Truth and Reconciliation Commission in 1991 reported on human rights violations committed under the military government, it turned over its findings on individual cases to the courts.

Less than a week after the release of the torture commission's report in November, a group of lawyers presented a petition on behalf of 21 torture victims. The petition presents charges of torture and illicit association against former military ruler General Augusto Pinochet and Senator Sergio Fernández, who was an interior minister in the military government. The victims' lawyers have requested that Judge Joaquín Billard, who has been appointed by the Santiago Appeals Court to investigate the complaint, obtain relevant testimonies from the commission.

"The torture commission has helped uncover one of the most painful secrets of the military regime," said Vivanco. "If the evidence collected by the commission is kept secret for half a century, many of those responsible for the abuses will never be held accountable in their lifetime."

SIGNIFICANCE

On October 17, 1998, while recovering from back surgery in London, Pinochet was arrested in connection with the deaths of Spanish citizens during his years in power in Chile. Spain had contacted the United Kingdom to formally request extradition for the arrest.

The arrest sparked worldwide shock—and elation—in human rights groups. Pinochet, however, had engineered a change in the Chilean constitution giving him senator-for-life privileges, as well as immunity from any charges for actions during his time in power. The question in late 1998 was: did this immunity extend to foreign soil? Could Spain and the United Kingdom work together to charge and try him?

In his first public statement, on November 8, 1998, Pinochet announced, "I am at peace with myself and with the Chilean people." Margaret Thatcher, the former British Prime Minister, called for his release. In the ensuing months, Pinochet's lawyers used a variety of legal maneuvers, while Chile cancelled diplomatic meetings with the United Kingdom and threatened to suspend Chilean flights to the Falkland Islands in South America.

Pinochet publicly announced his ill health and advanced age of eighty three and pointedly used his health concerns as a justification for not being tried. In March of 2000, Pinochet was freed by the United Kingdom and declared "medically unfit" for trial. In the meantime, officials and judges in Chile worked to strip Pinochet of his immunity; bowing to pressures from torture victims and families of the "disappeared," by early 2001 Pinochet was in Chile and placed under house arrest for a growing number of charges, including kidnapping, from the years 1973 to 1990.

The Chilean court reversed its decision in 2002, declaring Pinochet "mentally unfit" to stand trial; by 2005, after the release of the Chilean National Commission on Political Imprisonment and Torture report, Pinochet once again was indicted. As of 2006, his case was still pending in Chilean courts.

By barring access to Chilean torture victims' testimony for fifty years, should Pinochet ever stand trial, those materials could not be used by prosecutors building a case against the former dictator. While the extension of torture survivor benefits acts as a recognition of the abuse suffered by citizens at the hands of the brutal military regime, the classification of a piece of Chile's recent-and painful-history closes off inquiry into an ongoing and relevant societal issue.

FURTHER RESOURCES

Books

Kornbluh, Peter. *The Pinochet File: A Declassified Dossier on Atrocity and Accountability*. New York: New Press, 2004.

Timerman, Jacobo. *Chile: Death in the South*. New York: Knopf, 1987.

Periodicals

Carrera, Carolina. "Secrets Revealed: Women Victims of Sexual Violence as Torture During Chile's Era of Political Repression, 1973–1990." *Women's Health Journal* 2005, 1 (January 1, 2005).

Web sites

Amnesty International. "An International Crime: Even One Torture Victim Is One Too Many." <http://web.amnesty.org/library/index/engamr220101999> (accessed April 30, 2006).

Last Secrets of Nazi Terror— an Underground Labor Camp

Article excerpt

By: Luke Harding

Date: October 25, 2005

Source: Harding, Luke. "Last Secrets of Nazi Terror— an Underground Labor Camp." *The Guardian*. October 25, 2005.

About the Author: This article was originally written by Luke Harding, a reporter for the BBC, the British Broadcasting Corporation, in 2005.

INTRODUCTION

In 2005, a retired mine-pit foreman who had worked in the potassium mines in Wansleben, Germany—apparently misidentified in this primary source as "salt" mines was looking for documents on the history of the mining industry in his area. For reasons that are not clear, he examined records of the Stasi, the secret police of the East German Communist regime (1945–1990). ("Stasi" was short for Staatssicherheit, from the official name of the organization, Ministerium für Staatssicherheit, "Ministry for State Security.") After East and West Germany were reunited as a single state in 1990, Stasi's vast records eventually became available to Western researchers.

The Stasi records discovered in 2005 revealed details of an operation at Wansleben am See

(Wansleben for short) overseen by the Nazi SS (Schutzstaffel or "defense squadron", a separate branch of the Nazi military). Starting in March 1944, the SS employed slave laborers, including at least some French prisoners of war, to dig additional chambers and tunnels in the mine. These spaces were then used for the manufacture of airplane engines for Junkers military aircraft and for the safe storage of valuable library books and art. The slave laborers used to enlarge and run the facility were housed aboveground. The facility at Wansleben was a small satellite camp of Buchenwald, a concentration camp designed primarily to provide slave labor for industrial facilities rather than as an extermination camp. About 1,500 laborers were typically kept at the Wansleben facility.

Late in the war, as Allied and Soviet troops converged on the area, mine laborers were forcibly evacuated to points further East. Most or all probably died there in the confusion of the final days of the war. The Soviets looted the mines of their books, machinery, and art, then allowed them to fill with water. Later, in the 1960s, the Soviet-controlled East German government re-investigated the mines, but it found nothing of value. The entrances to the Wansleben mines were thoroughly sealed using explosives in 1989; today, only rubble is visible on the surface at the site.

▮ PRIMARY SOURCE

Luke Harding in Wansleben am See
Tuesday October 25, 2005

As a small boy growing up during the second world war, Dieter Michaelis knew to keep away from the old salt mine. The only hint of what was going on inside came when prisoners wearing blue-striped uniforms arrived under SS guard to collect bread from the bakery.

"We were told they were bad people. They were enemies of Germany. They had to be locked up," Mr Michaelis, sixty-eight, said. "We didn't talk about it at school."

It was here in Wansleben am See that one of the last secrets of the Nazis was hidden. Now, sixty years after the war, documents found in the archive of East Germany's secret police, the Stasi, reveal how the Nazis used a vast subterranean complex as a concentration camp.

A retired pit foreman Horst Bringezu stumbled on evidence while researching a local history of the mining industry. Documents revealed that some 1,500 prisoners worked among its vaults; many died. They also revealed that the SS had used the secret tunnels linking two mine shafts to store rare books, priceless paintings and letters by Goethe—all now vanished.

In 1944, the SS picked three hundred workers from other camps, including Buchenwald seventy-five miles away, to hack out vast underground chambers. Out of reach of allied bombers, production equipment was lowered into the mine. Deep underground, the Polish, French and Russian workers—some Jewish—assembled parts for Germany's war industry.

"We worked in three shifts, 6PM and 10.

"One of my French friends tried to escape. He was captured three days later. He was brought back to the camp and hanged with two Russians. We all had to watch. The camp was not as terrible as others, like Auschwitz. But by March and April 1945 there was less and less to eat. The Germans had nothing to give us. The soup was clear."

Letters from inmates found in the Stasi archive paint the same grim picture. According to Karol Zeglicki, a Pole, prisoners worked in the gloom "with open wounds." Those too ill to work disappeared, their bodies apparently cremated in nearby Halle, in the state of Saxony-Anhalt. Some raw materials used to make weapons came from churches looted by the Nazis, Mr Zeglicki said. "There were crucifixes, candelabras, chalices, and candlesticks...."

Mr Michaelis, who still lives in the village, recalled: "After the Americans came, the prisoners came knocking on our door asking for clothes. My mother gave them some underpants. They were extremely thin." Days earlier, the SS commandant had stolen his father's car in an attempt to escape, he added.

The camp's existence was swiftly forgotten as US investigators concentrated on another camp in nearby Nordhausen, where sensational diagrams of Hitler's secret V2 rocket were found....

In the 1960s East Germany's communist regime launched a secret investigation into the mine. A Stasi investigator, Sgt Meyer, went down the pit and was confronted with "an evil smell" that probably came from the "corpses of former prisoners," he reported. He found a postcard from "a fourteen- to fifteen-year-old child—probably of Jewish origin"—and several sacks full of SS documents.... Communist officials sealed the mine, and its secrets, shortly afterwards.

...Today there is little to identify the old mine as a former Nazi camp. Above ground there are few clues: a cobbled street where the prisoners marched, a few outbuildings, and a railway cutting overgrown with bushes, brambles and apple trees. There is no monument.

"It's in very bad shape," said Ines Valhaus, a member of Wansleben's local history society, as she toured the bleak landscape. The lake was pumped dry in the nineteenth century. Since the fall of the Berlin Wall most jobs have

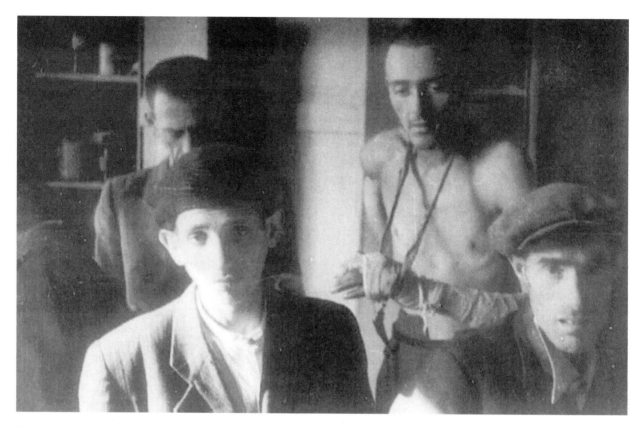

Ben Berkenwald, lower left, is pictured in the infirmary at the Ahlem labor camp near Hanover, Germany on April 10, 1945, after the camp's liberation by Allied forces. One of four children, Berkenwald was the only member of his family who survived the camp. AP IMAGES.

disappeared. "We would like to put up some kind of memorial here. But we don't have any money," she said.

"There is a monument in the village square erected under the communist regime to the "victims of fascism."

The world may have forgotten Wansleben but the prisoners who survived did not. "One of the overseers at the camp was a Herr Spiess," Mr. Michaelis said. "He fled to southern Germany after the war. He later came back heavily disguised and with a beard. One of the Poles who had been in the camp and stayed on in the village recognised Spiess. He killed him."

SIGNIFICANCE

The existence of underground facilities at Wansleben was a response to the threat posed by Allied bombers. It was a largely ineffective response against a largely ineffective bombing campaign.

During the first few years of World War II (1939–1945), British bombing policy was to destroy industrial facilities crucial to the German war effort. However, studies by the British Bomber Command found that only about twenty percent of British bombers were delivering their bombs within five miles of their targets, which was ineffective against objects as small as individual factories, mines, refineries, and the like. Therefore, after February 1942, the British bombing campaign officially switched from war production facilities to cities, which were large enough to strike reliably. The new goal was to break what British documents called the "morale of the enemy civil population" by killing large numbers of civilians. Although Allied bombers killed approximately 600,000 German civilians from 1942 to 1945 and precision bombing techniques for attacking specific facilities were developed in the last few years of the war, bombing did not succeed in either breaking German morale or reducing German production of war materiel.

The German response to Allied bombing was manifold. Fighter planes and antiaircraft guns directly attacked Allied bomber fleets. Camouflage, smoke screens, fake factories, dispersal of functions, and underground factories such as that at Wansleben were all used to evade Allied bombing. For example, another underground aircraft factory was built using slave labor at Rabstejn, today in the Czech Republic.

Unlike Wansleben, the Rabstejn underground system was never flooded or sealed, and in 2004 it was partly reopened to the public. One of the biggest underground slave factories was at Peenemunde, where the V-1 and V-2 "vengeance weapons" were built to harass the Allies in the closing days of the war. A prison camp named Dora, which was, like Wansleben, a satellite of Buchenwald, was built to support construction of an underground rocket factory at Nordhausen (the site mentioned in the primary source). Some 20,000 prisoners died in Dora. German rocket officers who were knowingly complicit in the use of slave labor for Nordhausen, especially SS officer Wernher von Braun (1912–1977), were captured by Allied forces at the end of the war and became honored leaders of the U.S. space effort through the 1960s.

The effectiveness of Germany's underground factories was questioned by the U.S. Air Force in the Summary Report of its Strategic Bombing Survey (Sep. 30, 1945): "Germany never succeeded in placing any substantial portion of her war production underground—the effort was largely limited to certain types of aircraft, their components, and the V weapons. The practicability of going underground as the escape from full and free exploitation of the air is highly questionable; it was so considered by the Germans themselves." The Report noted that although underground facilities were safe from direct damage, their operations were impacted by the bombing of surface transport systems.

The Nazi German government made extensive use of slave labor, and not only in underground facilities. At Auschwitz, the largest of the Nazi extermination camps, a separate camp called "I.G. Auschwitz" was built by the I.G. Farben corporation to house slave laborers for the manufacture of synthetic oil and rubber from coal. I.G. Farben also manufactured the Zyklon B poison gas that killed over a million people in the gas chambers of Auschwitz. Slave laborers were systematically starved and so were useful for only about three months; when they became too weak to work, they were sent to their death.

FURTHER RESOURCES

Web sites

Ceske Svykarska. "Rabstejn—a complex of underground aircraft factories from World War II." 2004. <http://www.cztour.cz/rabstejn/eng/index.html> (accessed April 7, 2006).

Detlef, Siebert. BBC. "British Bombing Strategy in World War II." August 1, 2001. <http://www.bbc.co.uk/history/war/wwtwo/area_bombing_03.shtml> (accessed April 13, 2006).

Question of Detainees in the U.S. Naval Base in Guantanamo

Resolution

By: Government of Cuba

Date: April 14, 2005

Source: "Question of Detainees in the U.S. Naval Base in Guantanamo." United Nations Economic and Social Council, April 14, 2005.

About the Author: Cuba is a Caribbean nation of approximately eleven million persons. Cuba is a close neighbor to the United States, and the two countries have a long and complicated history. The United States helped Cuba win independence from Spain in the nineteenth century, but kept part of the island known as Guantanamo Bay for itself. The United States often interfered in Cuban politics and society in the years thereafter. Relations between Cuba and the United States have been mutually antagonistic since Fidel Castro came to power and established Communist rule in Cuba during the late 1950s and early 1960s.

INTRODUCTION

This is a draft resolution tabled by Cuba on April 14, 2005 at the sixty-first session of the United Nations Commission on Human Rights (CHR) meeting in Geneva, Switzerland. It refers to several positions officially taken by the United Nations and the European Parliament expressing disapproval or concern about the United States Government's policy of holding prisoners at the U.S. Navy base at Guantanamo Bay, Cuba, and requests the United Nations High Commissioner for Human Rights make a report on the situation of the detainees at Guantanamo that is based on visits to the facility. The Office of the U.N. High Commissioner for Human Rights is a division of the U.N. Secretariat (the executive arm of the U.N.) and was established by General Assembly resolution in 1993; it is, in the words of its mission statement, "mandated to promote and protect the enjoyment and full realization, by all people, of all rights established in the Charter of the United Nations and in international human rights laws and treaties."

Guantanamo Bay Naval Base is an inholding of approximately 45 square miles (116 square kilometers) controlled by the United States and located on the southeastern coast of Cuba. It has been held by the United States since the Spanish-American War of

1898; since 1959, the Cuban Government has not acknowledged the legality of the lease by which the United States holds Guantanamo. Since 2002, camps at Guantanamo have been used as detention facilities for between five hundred and seven hundred prisoners captured by the United States abroad, primarily in Afghanistan and Iraq.

Relations between the United States and Cuba have been strained since 1959. The United States has maintained a trade embargo on Cuba since 1960 and forbids its citizens to travel there without a license from the Treasury Department. The United States also sponsored a failed military invasion of Cuba in 1961. The introduction of a resolution by Cuba demanding closer inspection of Guantanamo, with possibly embarrassing results for the United States, reflects this history of hostilities.

Cuba submitted a similar draft resolution to the CHR in 2004 but did not insist on having it put to a vote. The 2005 resolution was voted down on April 21, 2005 (8–22 with 23 abstentions). Cuba denounced the vote as "scandalous." All members of the European Union on the Committee voted against the measure, perhaps in order to avoid further antagonizing the United States, which lobbied strongly for its defeat; the European Parliament had already voted, in 2004, to allow a full and independent investigation of allegations of torture and other abuses at Guantanamo.

The U.N. Commission on Human Rights was established by the United Nations in 1946. It was superseded by the Human Rights Council in 2006 after concluding its sixty-second annual session.

A detainee's hand can be seen holding on to a chain-link fence, at Camp 4 of the maximum security prison Camp Delta at Guantanamo Naval Base in Cuba, August 26, 2004. MARK WILSON/ AFP/GETTY IMAGES.

■ PRIMARY SOURCE

QUESTION OF DETAINEES IN THE AREA OF THE UNITED STATES NAVAL BASE IN GUANTANAMO

Cuba: draft resolution *The Commission on Human Rights, Considering* the obligation of States under the Charter of the United Nations to promote universal respect for, and observance of, human rights and fundamental freedoms through international cooperation,

Aware that all persons are entitled to respect for *their* human rights as set forth in the Universal Declaration of Human Rights, and bearing in mind that several of these rights are non-derogable, and that their enjoyment cannot be restricted under any circumstances,

Recalling the duty of all States to respect and comply with their obligations under international instruments, including those relating to human rights, to which they are party,

Recalling also general comment No. 31 (2004) of the Human Rights Committee, adopted at its 2187th meeting on 29 March 2004,

Recalling further the request made to the Government of the United States on 25 June 2004 by four thematic procedures mandate holders of the Commission, with the objective of visiting the persons detained on grounds of terrorism, including in Guantanamo Bay,

Taking into account the statement made on 4 February 2005 by six special procedures mandate holders of the Commission, reaffirming their serious concern over the situation of detainees at the naval base in Guantanamo, despite some positive developments that had taken place on the issue in the last few months.

Taking into account also that a significant number of Governments and parliaments from all over the world have expressed their concern in this regard, among them the European Parliament which, in its resolution on Guantanamo adopted on 28 October 2004, called on the United States administration to allow an impartial and independent investigation into allegations of torture and mistreatment for all persons deprived of their liberty in United States custody.

Requests the Government of the United States of America to authorize for that purpose the Chairperson-Rapporteur of the Working Group on Arbitrary Detention, the Special Rapporteur on the question of torture, the Special Rapporteur on the right of everyone to the enjoyment of the highest attainable standard of physical and mental health and the Special Rapporteur on the independence of judges and lawyers to visit the detention centres that have been established on that base;

Requests the United Nations High Commissioner for Human Rights to prepare and submit to the Commission at its sixty-second session, a report on the situation of the detainees at the United States naval base in Guantanamo, based on the results of the findings of the visits to be conducted thereto by the mandate holders of the above-mentioned special procedures;

Decides to continue the consideration of this issue at its sixty-second session.

SIGNIFICANCE

The detention of prisoners at Guantanamo by the United States has been highly controversial, both internationally and within the United States. Only ten of the prisoners held at Guantanamo had, as of early 2006, been charged with a crime. The United States maintains that persons it holds at Guantanamo are not "prisoners of war" but "illegal combatants" or "enemy combatants" and are therefore not covered by the terms of the Third Geneva Convention on the treatment of prisoners of war (1929, revised 1949); it has also maintained that since the prisoners are not U.S. citizens and not held on U.S. soil, they have no standing in U.S. courts.

The treatment of prisoners at Guantanamo has been repeatedly criticized since 2002. Human rights groups, former Guantanamo prisoners, and several U.S. military officers who have served at Guantanamo have all claimed that the treatment of prisoners at the facility is torture. An agent of the U.S. Federal Bureau of Investigation (FBI) told his superiors in 2004 that military interrogators impersonating FBI agents had shackled detainees in fetal position for more than twenty-four hours at a time and allowed them to urinate and defecate on themselves; subjected them to extreme heat, cold and painfully loud levels of noise; deprived them of food and water; and threatened them with growling dogs during interrogations. Allegations of sexual humiliation, beatings, and deliberately violent force-feeding have also been made.

The U.S. government maintains that no prisoners have been treated illegally (not only torture but "inhuman and degrading treatment" are banned by treaties signed by the United States) and that its treatment of the detainees, although occasionally using "stress techniques," is justified by the exigencies of what it terms "the war on terror."

The significance of this Cuban draft resolution lay partly in its demand for on-site inspection of Guantanamo. Earlier, the CHR had already commissioned a five-member panel of envoys to examine the human rights situation in Guantanamo, but this panel did not make an on-site inspection of the base. The United States invited the envoys to visit Guantanamo but stated that they would not be allowed to meet with detainees. The envoys declined to visit on the grounds that without access to confidential testimony from prisoners their presence would constitute a "show tour" and thus violate CHR guidelines for prison visits. The envoys based their final report on interviews with former prisoners, detainees' lawyers, and U.S. officials and on other evidence. The report, which was released on February 15, 2006, declared that U.S. treatment of detainees at Guantanamo "must be assessed as amounting to torture" and called for Guantanamo to be closed. In reaction to the report, the European Parliament passed a resolution in February 2006 calling on the United States to close Guantanamo and to treat all prisoners "in accordance with international humanitarian law." The United States stated that the report's conclusions were invalid.

In 2006, the U.S. Supreme Court was to decide whether Guantanamo detainees have standing in U.S. courts.

FURTHER RESOURCES

Books

Saar, Erik and Viveca Novak. *Inside the Wire: A Military Intelligence Soldier's Eyewitness Account of Life at Guantanamo.* New York: Penguin Press, 2005.

Periodicals

Eggen, Dan and Jeffrey R. Smith. "FBI Agents Allege Abuse of Detainees at Guantanamo Bay." The *Washington Post* (December 21, 2004): A1.

Farley, Maggie. "Report: U.S. is Abusing Captives." The *New York Times* (February 13, 2006): A1.

Web sites

United Nations Economic and Social Council. "Situation of Detainees at Guanténamo Bay." <http://www.nytimes.com/packages/pdf/international/20060216gitmo_report.pdf> (accessed April 30, 2006).

Camp Delta Four in the Guantánamo Bay Naval Station, Cuba

Photograph

By: Andres Leighton

Date: July 6, 2005

Source: AP Images.

About the Author: Andres Leighton is a frequent contributor of photographs to The Associated Press, a worldwide news agency based in New York.

INTRODUCTION

This photograph shows a prisoner spending time outside of his cell at a detention camp at the Guantánamo Bay Naval Station, Cuba. The U.S. Navy base at Guantánamo is a coastal inholding that dates to the early twentieth century. Starting in 2002, the U.S. Government began imprisoning alleged terrorists at Guantánamo. Originally, prisoners were stored at a temporary facility called Camp X-Ray, but this facility was closed in 2002 and replaced by Camp Delta, which is shown in the photograph. Camp Delta is actually a complex of seven detention camps. Six of the camps are numbered; Camp Four, shown in the photo, is for compliant prisoners. Prisoners at Camp Four are allowed to wear white clothing and enjoy amenities such as books and showers. It should be noted that journalists cannot photograph the Guantánamo facilities at will; this photograph was reviewed and approved by the U.S. military before being released by the Associated Press.

From 2002 to late 2005, over 750 prisoners had been detained at Guantánamo for some period of time; as of late 2005, over 500 were still held. About five percent of detainees were captured by U.S. forces, while eighty-six percent had been captured by Pakistani or Northern Alliance (Afghani) forces. Only a handful have been charged formally with a crime. The U.S. Government has argued that the Geneva Conventions regarding the treatment of prisoners of war do not apply to the prisoners at Guantánamo and that because they are neither U.S. citizens nor on U.S. territory, no U.S. law applies to their condition. U.S. treatment of prisoners at Guantánamo has been criticized by human rights groups, the United Nations, and the International Committee of the Red Cross. The U.S. Government maintains that its treatment of the detainees has been humane and legal.

PRIMARY SOURCE

CAMP DELTA FOUR IN THE GUANTÁNAMO BAY NAVAL STATION, CUBA

See primary source image.

SIGNIFICANCE

The legality of the U.S. detention of alleged terrorists at Guantánamo has been repeatedly challenged, with mixed results. In *Rasul v. Bush* (2004), the U.S. Supreme Court ruled that foreign nationals imprisoned at Guantánamo were entitled to challenge their detention in U.S. courts. In response, the U.S. government began reviewing the status of detainees before military tribunals at Guantánamo. In *Hamdi v. Rumsfeld* (2004), the Supreme Court ruled that Hamdi, a U.S. citizen, could not be detained indefinitely without trial. Following *Hamdi v. Rumsfeld*, the government convened a series of Combatant Status Review Tribunals at Guantánamo in order to provide the required review of status. However, the tribunals were widely criticized because in them the accused could not call or cross-examine witnesses, often lacked counsel, and were not allowed to challenge the evidence against them. In February, 2005, a Federal judge ruled in *Hamdan v. Rumsfeld* (not to be confused with *Hamdi v. Rumsfeld*) that the tribunals were illegal and that the Guantánamo detainees must be allowed to challenge their detention in U.S. civilian courts, rather than before military tribunals. The decision was appealed, and a ruling was expected from the Supreme Court in June, 2006.

A number of human rights groups have accused the United States of subjecting detainees at Guantánamo to inhumane and degrading treatment, which is forbidden by treaties to which the United States is signatory. In 2005, the International Committee of the Red Cross (ICRC) concluded that some United States practices at Guantánamo were "tantamount to torture." The report, which was delivered confidentially to the U.S. Government, as are all ICRC reports on prison conditions, was leaked to the press.

In April 2005, the United Nations Committee on Legal Affairs and Human Rights released a report entitled "Lawfulness of detentions by the United States in Guantánamo Bay." The Committee concluded that "the circumstances surrounding detentions by the U.S.A. at Guantánamo Bay show unlawfulness on grounds including the torture and cruel, inhuman, or degrading treatment of detainees and violations of rights relating to prisoner-of-war status, the right to judicial review of the lawfulness of detention and the right to a fair trial." The Committee also found that

PRIMARY SOURCE

Camp Delta Four in the Guantánamo Bay Naval Station, Cuba: On July 6, 2005 a detainee spends time outside his cell at Camp Delta Four, a medium security facility for compliant detainees at the Guantanamo Bay Naval Station in Cuba. AP IMAGES.

"the U.S.A. has engaged in the unlawful practices of secret detention and 'rendition' (i.e. the removal of persons to other countries, without judicial supervision, for purposes such as interrogation or detention)."

In June 2004, the U.N. Commission on Human Rights appointed a task force to study the situation of Guantánamo detainees. In February 2006, the team accused the U.S. of exposing detainees at Guantánamo to excessive solitary confinement, exposure to extreme heat and cold, exposure to painfully loud noise and painfully bright light, forced shaving, and force-feeding of hunger strikers through nasal tubes. The Commission demanded that the United States close Guantánamo.

Then White House spokesman Scott McClellan replied that prisoner testimony received by the United Nations envoys was false, noting "al-Qaeda training manuals talk about ways to disseminate false information and hope to get attention." U.N. envoys had not visited Guantánamo prior to this statement. They were invited to visit but declined, according to the Commission, because the guidelines laid down by the U.S. military did not allow for confidential interviews with prisoners, which violates Commission guidelines for prison visits. McClellan said that "the military treats detainees humanely, as directed by the President of the United States" and reiterated that "we do not condone torture, and we do not engage in torture."

In May 2006, President George W. Bush said in an interview on German television that he wanted to close Guantánamo, but he was waiting for the Supreme Court's decision in *Hamdan v. Rumsfeld*.

It was not clear where the prisoners would be transferred to if Guantánamo was closed.

FURTHER RESOURCES

Books

Berkowitz, Peter, ed. *Terrorism, the Laws of War, and the Constitution: Debating the Enemy Combatant Cases*. Palo Alto: Hoover Institution Press, Stanford University, 2005.

Saar, Erik. *Inside the Wire: A Military Intelligence Soldier's Eyewitness Account of Life at Guantánamo*. New York: Penguin Press, 2005.

Periodicals

Farley, Maggie. "Report: U.S. Is Abusing Captives." *The Los Angeles Times*. February 13, 2006.

Lane, Charles. "Court Case Challenges Power of President: Military Tribunals' Legitimacy at Issue." *The Washington Post*. March 26, 2006.

Leonnig, Carol. "Judge Rules Detainee Tribunals Illegal." *The Washington Post*. February 1, 2005.

Lewis, Neil A. "Red Cross Finds Detainee Abuse in Guantánamo." *The New York Times*. November 30, 2004.

Web sites

CBS News. "Bush Says He Wants to Close Guantánamo." May 9, 2006. <http://www.cbsnews.com/stories/2006/05/08/politics/main1596464.shtml> (accessed May 9, 2006).

Council of Europe. "Lawfulness of detentions by the United States in Guantánamo Bay." April 8, 2005. <http://assembly.coe.int/Documents/WorkingDocs/Doc05/EDOC10497.htm> (accessed May 9, 2006).

Reuters. "UN Torture Panel Presses U.S. on Detainees." April 18, 2006. <http://go.reuters.com/> (accessed April 20, 2006).

4 Health and Housing

Health and Housing

The United Nations Universal Declaration of Human Rights, Article 25, states "everyone has the right to a standard of living adequate for the health and well-being of himself and of his family, including food, clothing, housing and medical care and necessary social services." Adequate food, water, and shelter are the building blocks of life, but famine and destruction are common global occurrences. Two billion people across the globe lack access to fresh water. War, profiteering, corruption, and a lack of adequate transport infrastructure (highways, trains, and airports) hamper delivery of food, water, and medical supplies to areas most in need.

Medical care is necessary to ensure both individual and public health. Absolute denial of medial care to a distinct group of people is a human rights crime. Similarly, historical violations of human rights have involved medical experimentation on unknowing persons. International accords—as well as western medical ethics—advocate that enemy combatants and prisoners of war receive emergency medical treatment. The documents enumerating rights to medical care are found in the chapter *Development of human Rights*. Highlighted in this chapter are violations of those rights, including the Taliban's denial of hospital serv-ices to Afghani women, the Tuskegee Syphilis study, and the destruction of hospitals and neglect of enemy combatants in Kashmir.

Several articles in this chapter discus issues of reproductive rights. Family limitation, abortion, and sterilization are all controversial topics with possible human rights implications. The editors have included an article on the *Rove v. Wade* decision permitting voluntary abortion in the United States as contrast to articles on forced sterilization and forced family limi-tation. "China's 'One Child Family' Policy" discusses the controversy over both the policy of government limits on family and the methods employed to ensure one-child families. The policy and its practice are highly controversial, but the editors have chosen to focus the discussion on human rights based criticism.

Finally, the movement to improve living condi-tions in the United States is briefly addressed in two articles. "The Moral and Sanitary Condition of New York City" is an example of the tenement and slum reform movement of the nineteenth century, while an article on the Fair Housing Act discusses twentieth-century codification of housing programs.

The Sanitary and Moral Condition of New York City

Magazine article

By: Anonymous

Date: August 1869

Source: Anonymous. "The Sanitary and Moral Condition of New York City." *Catholic World: A Monthly Magazine.* 53.9 (August 1869): 553–566.

About the Author: *Catholic World: A Monthly Magazine* is a religious publication which The Catholic Publication House in New York began printing in 1865. Fr. Isaac Thomas Hecker of the Paulist Fathers founded the magazine, set in a liberal theological tone, as an outlet for Catholic writers to express themselves within the scope of their faith.

INTRODUCTION

In 1865, as the Civil War ended in the United States, reformers in New York City embarked on an aggressive campaign to clean the city's streets from sewage, filth, and disease. The Association of New York issued its report on the condition of the city in 1863, and its three hundred plus page report detailed problems with the city's sanitation system, the perceived moral condition of the city's inhabitants, and the condition of housing. The three hundred page report often read like a laundry list of ills within the city, but the point and purpose of the Association's work was made clear. It wanted the inhabitants of New York City, and the city's government, to address issues of hygiene and safety so that inhabitants and visitors to the city could prosper. Additionally, the Association's remarks about urban sanitation were frequently linked with moral reform. These moral reforms referenced a higher rate of prostitution and child labor in New York City (and other urban areas). As a side note, child labor occurred in rural areas, but rural communities did not consider a child working on the farm or family business as labor. Rather, it was familial duty. But, children in urban areas often entered factories at young ages, or they took to earning money as street vendors. These jobs were noted in media accounts, and a variety of reform movements sought to halt child labor. These reforms ranged from groups focusing on family life, labor laws, to sanitary reform.

As immigration increased and urban areas continued to swell from new inhabitants and the rise of factories and industries, more reform organizations emerged. These groups varied widely in the agendas,

St. Patrick's Cathedral at Fifth Avenue between 50th and 51st streets in New York City, circa 1880. © CORBIS.

but some of the most prevalent concerned improving sanitary conditions for Americans. New York City took the lead in the sanitary reform movement, mostly because it was the largest U.S. city and held the highest ratio of new immigrants. In the 1850s, civic reform groups (mostly led by middle and upper class white women) began actively campaigning for municipal reform, and their actions went against the grain of middle and upper class society while also acting with it. This dichotomy occurred because the middle and upper classes had selectively withdrawn from politics, particularly in large urban areas like New York City, because they felt that the rise of immigrants increased corruption in politics. Individuals believed this because the middle and upper classes tended to view immigrants as unclean, slovenly, ignorant, and without morals. Thus, there was little concern for the poor, but issues like sanitary reform obviously benefited the wealthy and the poor.

The first of these municipal reforms, in New York City, developed as the 1857 creation of the Metropolitan Board of Police, and the New York Sanitary Association formed in 1859. The Sanitary

Association also received the backing of four physicians who were leaders in health reform. These individuals were John H. Griscom, Elisha Harris, Joseph M. Smith, and Stephen Smith. Municipal reforms aimed to create separate agencies for city growth and maintenance, and these newly founded offices were held accountable to the state and not the city's government. Hence, the middle and upper classes were seeking ways to over-ride the immigrant vote. Even though the Sanitary Association sought to improve the lives and cleanliness of the upwardly elite, it worked closely with the New York Association for Improving Conditions of the Poor (AICP). These two groups continued to hold the backing of prominent physicians, but they were mostly run by laypersons. The AICP desired to improve the conditions of the city's slums, but its work toward elevating living conditions of the poor and working poor also benefited the upper classes. Neighborhood improvements helped decrease filth in the streets, and the removal or repair of ramshackle buildings helped decrease the risk of fires.

As these civic organizations grew so did their support in local newspapers. The 1863 creation of the New York Citizen's Association merely reflected the growing desires and approval of the public. The Citizen's Association sought to expand the works of the Sanitary Association and the AICP by merging the agendas of both groups into a central agency. This statement does not mean that the Citizen's Association superseded previous reform organizations. Instead, all of these groups still worked as separate units, but as new groups formed they built upon previous organizations to make their causes more concise.

In 1865, New York City formed the Metropolitan Board of Health (MBH) to evaluate and handle issues concerning city health. These dilemmas concerned fires, sewage systems, running water, and adequate housing for urban residents. These organizations continued to work for city sewage systems, cleaner streets, and safer living conditions, and they made annual reports detailing their inspections of local neighborhoods—rich and poor—and of factories and streets.

■ PRIMARY SOURCE

A glance at New York city, embracing the entire of Manhattan Island, will show that its geological position, its advantages for sewerage and drainage, in fact for everything that would make it salubrious and healthy, cannot be surpassed by any city in this or any other country. And still, with its bountiful supply of nature's choicest gifts, many of our readers will be surprised to hear that our death-rate is higher than that of any city on this continent, or any of the larger cities of Europe....

There is one other subject we wish to mention before concluding this paper: it is, the condition of the night-lodgers at the station-houses. From the report of the Board of Metropolitan Police, we find that 105,460 persons were accommodated with lodgings at the various precincts during the last twelve months. Mr. S. C. Hawley, the very accommodating chief clerk of this department, informs us that the number this year will be much greater. Over 100,000 sought refuge in the station-houses, glad to obtain the bare floor to rest their weary limbs; but how many pace our streets nightly, poverty-stricken and despairing, but too proud to seek a shelter in these abodes of crime! It is a stigma on the fair fame of this great city that, throughout its length and breadth, there is not one refuge, established by religious or philanthropic efforts, where the homeless can find shelter from the wintry night blasts.

> "Our beasts and our thieves and our chattels
> Have weight for good or for ill;
> But the poor are only his image,
> His presence, his word, his will;
> And so Lazarus lies at our doorstep,
> And Dives neglects him still."

In Montreal, Canada, refuges are connected with the church property, and are superintended by the female religious orders, we think more particularly by the Gray Nuns. In 1860, the Providence Row Night Refuge was established in London, under the care of the Sisters of Mercy. There is no distinction made as regards religious creed, and the only requisites necessary for admission are, to be homeless and of good character. Before retiring, a half-pound of bread and a basin of gruel are given to each lodger, and the same in the morning, before they are allowed to commence another day's efforts to obtain work. What charity could so directly appeal to our hearts as this? Think how many men and women arrive daily in this metropolis, in search of employment! For days they eagerly seek it without success, hoarding their scanty means to the uttermost. Finally the time comes when the last dime is spent for bread, and they wander along, their hearts filled with dread, as night covers the earth with her sable mantle, knowing not whither they shall turn their weary steps. Think of the poor woman wending her way through the pelting storm; garments soaked and clinging to the chilled form; heart filled with despair, and crying to Heaven for shelter; head aching, temples throbbing, brain nearly crazed with terror; finally, crouching down under some old steps to wait the first gleam of day to relieve her from her agony. If one in such condition should reach the river-side, what a fearful temptation it must be to take that final leap which ends for ever earth's cares and sufferings, or, still worse for the poor female, the temptation to seek in sin the refuge denied her in every other way!

"There the weary come, who through the daylight
Pace the town and crave for work in vain:
There they crouch in cold and rain and hunger,
Waiting for another day of pain.
In slow darkness creeps the dismal river;
From its depths looks up a sinful rest.
Many a weary, baffled, hopeless wanderer
Has it drawn into its treacherous breast!
There is near another river flowing.
Black with guilt and deep as hell and sin:,
On its brink even sinners stand and shudder—
Cold and hunger goad the homeless in."

What a mute appeal for such institutions is the case of the little Italian boy found dead on the steps of one of our Fifth avenue palaces last winter! Think of this little fellow as he slowly perished that bitter night, at the very feet of princely wealth. How his thoughts must have reverted to his dark-browed mother in her far-off sunny home! And think of that mother's anguish, her wailing

"For a birdling lost that she'll never find."

when she heard of her boy's death, from cold and starvation, in the principal avenue of all free America! We consider we are safe in saying that in no other work of charity could a small amount of money be made to benefit so many as in the founding of these refuges.

In the police report it is recommended that "several of these be established in different parts of the city, to be under the supervision of the police." This is a great mistake. These people always associate station-houses and the police with crime; consequently it is bad policy for them to come constantly in contact with either. This is the objection to the lodging-rooms used in the various precincts. Official charity, as a rule, hardens those who dole it out, and degrades its recipients.

There are thousands of noble-hearted women attached to our different churches, who, if they once thoroughly understood this subject, would not cease their efforts until societies were established and refuges opened. How could it be otherwise! How could they nestle their little ones down to sleep in warm comfortable beds, and think of God's little ones freezing under their windows? How could they go to sleep themselves, and feel that some poor woman was probably wandering past their doorways, dying from want and exposure? We hope, before the chilling winds of next November remind us of the immensity of suffering the winter entails upon the poor, some philanthropic persons will have perfected this design, and have the refuges in working order. If such should be the case, the founders will find an ample reward in the words of Holy Writ, "He that hath mercy on the poor, lendeth to the Lord: and he will repay him."

If we could thus, by the adoption of every possible sanitary precaution, deprive our death-tables of all avoidable mortality; and by a proper religious influence elevate the moral character of the people, we should in the first place, save thousands of lives, now necessary to develop our vast resources; and, secondly, our advance toward perfection in healthfulness and public virtues would go hand in had with the gigantic strides being made in the adornment of our beautiful island. Our people would no longer seek other places in quest of health, as none more salubrious than New York could be found; and strangers, instead of saying, as is said of that most beautiful of Italy's fair cities, "See Naples, and die!" would exclaim, "Go to New York, and live!".

SIGNIFICANCE

The Metropolitan Board of Health, with noted sanitary reformer Stephen Smith, worked long and hard to clean the sewage and general filth from New York streets. Some of this filth derived from animal waste and by-products from factories overflowing into the streets. The work of Smith and the MBH set the framework for other cities to establish sanitary reforms. The MBH led to the formation of the American Public Health Association in 1872.

Chicago, like New York, faced a plethora of public health issues. In the 1850s, it fell prey to a series of cholera and dysentery epidemics. These health crises were attributed to the city's poor waste disposal system, and in response to the problem the city hired Boston city engineer Ellis Sylvester Chesbrough, in 1855, to devise a sewage plan for the city. Immediately, he proposed a plan, and the new sewer system was laid in place. He became the city's first Commissioner of Public Works, and his sewage system reversed the flow of the Chicago River. In 1879, he resigned the position, but he continued to plan sanitary and sewage systems for other cities.

The sewage system of Chicago, and later with other U.S. cities, was only one aspect of reform that derived from the works of sanitary reformers. The most noted sanitary reformers came from New York City, but this middle and upper class movement aided in city planning and areas of reform for the poor throughout the nation. Sanitary reform helped bring issues of immigrant and working poor living conditions to the forefront of U.S. media and politics, and individuals like Jacob A. Riis captured their disparity. Riis began lecturing about the living conditions of the poor, and after the invention of flash photography he began adding images to his talks. The work of Riis shows a continuation to the public health debate and sanitary reform era. And not to be forgotten, the publication of Upton Sinclair's *The Jungle* in 1906 added another catalyst to health reformers. Sinclair's book used the meat packing district of Chicago to display the horrid living and working conditions of immigrant workers and factories. The 1906 Federal Foods and Drug Act reflected the public outcry about deplorable conditions in factories.

The early twentieth century saw a number of public health reform measures pass through Congress and local municipalities, and into the modern era these reforms are still taking place. In the modern era, these reforms have evolved from the removal of sewage to the removal of chemicals in water supplies, the recycling of goods, and of how to deal with growing landfills.

FURTHER RESOURCES

Books

Christine Stansell. *City of Women: Sex and Class in New York, 1789–1860*. Champaign, IL: University of Illinois Press, 1987.

Nancy Tomes. *The Gospel of Germs: Men, Women, and the Microbe in American Life*. Cambridge, MA and London: Harvard University Press, 1988 and 1999.

Periodicals

Gostin, Lawrence O. and Scott Burris. "The Law and the Public's Health: A Study of Infectious Disease Law in the United States." *Columbia Law Review*. 99.1 (January 1999): 59–128.

Link, William A. "Privies, Progressivism, and Public Schools: Health Reform and Education in the Rural South, 1919–1920." *The Journal of Southern History*. 54.4 (November 1988): 623-642.

Web sites

American Chemical Society. "Apostles of Cleanliness." 2002. <http://pubs.acs.org/subscribe/journals/mdd/v05/i05/html/05ttl.html> (accessed April 30, 2006).

John W. Hartman Center for Sales, Advertising and Marketing History Rare Book, Manuscript, and Special Collections Library at Duke University. "Medicine and Madison Avenue." 2002. <http://scriptorium.lib.duke.edu/mma/> (accessed April 30, 2006).

Fair Housing Act

Legislation

By: United States Congress

Date: 1968

Source: United States Congress. "Fair Housing Act." Civil Rights Act, Titlle VIII, 1968.

About the Author: The Congress of the United States was established by Article 1 of the United States Constitution of 1787. It is the legislative arm of the U.S. Federal Government.

INTRODUCTION

As part of the civil rights movement, the United States government enacted the Fair Housing Act in 1968. It prohibits discrimination in sales and rentals of housing by landlords, real estate companies, home-owners' insurance companies, lending institutions, and municipalities. Complaints are typically filed with the Department of Housing and Urban Development and then prosecuted by the Department of Justice.

The Fair Housing Act is a means of promoting social integration. Such integration, which involves legislation in the workplace as well as housing, is seen by many governments and humanitarian organizations as critical to the development of broad values such as social justice, social harmony and unity, and interdependence and mutual respect. Housing is particularly important to social integration because the residential environment provides a setting in which contact between different cultural groups can grow into relationships that may defuse tensions and increase the possibility of sharing diverse experiences.

Historically, most housing discrimination has been racial in nature. The first official nationwide study of housing discrimination against blacks began in 1977. The Department of Housing and Urban Development sent staff from the National Committee Against Discrimination in Housing to test the implementation of the Fair Housing Act. Approximately three hundred whites and three hundred blacks in matched pairs shopped for housing advertised in metropolitan newspapers. Blacks were systematically treated less favorably and less courteously than whites. In the rental market, twenty-seven percent of agents discriminated against blacks, while fifteen percent of sales agents in the real estate market did the same. In subsequent years, such blatant discrimination became far less common but remained present at the millennium.

PRIMARY SOURCE

FAIR HOUSING ACT

SEC. 804. [42 U.S.C. 3604] DISCRIMINATION IN SALE OR RENTAL OF HOUSING AND OTHER PROHIBITED PRACTICES

As made applicable by section 803 of this title and except as exempted by sections 803(b) and 807 of this title, it shall be unlawful—

(a) To refuse to sell or rent after the making of a bona fide offer, or to refuse to negotiate for the sale or rental of, or

Members of CORE (Committee on Racial Equality) picket the home of a landlord for his refusal to rent apartments to African Americans.
PHOTO BY HERB SCHARFMAN//TIME LIFE PICTURES/GETTY IMAGES.

otherwise make unavailable or deny, a dwelling to any person because of race, color, religion, sex, familial status, or national origin.

(b) To discriminate against any person in the terms, conditions, or privileges of sale or rental of a dwelling, or in the provision of services or facilities in connection therewith, because of race, color, religion, sex, familial status, or national origin.

(c) To make, print, or publish, or cause to be made, printed, or published any notice, statement, or advertisement, with respect to the sale or rental of a dwelling that indicates any preference, limitation, or discrimination based on race, color, religion, sex, handicap, familial status, or national origin, or an intention to make any such preference, limitation, or discrimination.

(d) To represent to any person because of race, color, religion, sex, handicap, familial status, or national origin that any dwelling is not available for inspection, sale, or rental when such dwelling is in fact so available.

(e) For profit, to induce or attempt to induce any person to sell or rent any dwelling by representations regarding the entry or prospective entry into the neighborhood of a person or persons of a particular race, color, religion, sex, handicap, familial status, or national origin.

(f)

(1) To discriminate in the sale or rental, or to otherwise make unavailable or deny, a dwelling to any buyer or renter because of a handicap of—

(A) that buyer or renter,

(B) a person residing in or intending to reside in that dwelling after it is so sold, rented, or made available; or

(C) any person associated with that buyer or renter.

(2) To discriminate against any person in the terms, conditions, or privileges of sale or rental of a dwelling, or in the provision of services or facilities in connection with such dwelling, because of a handicap of—

(A) that person; or

(B) a person residing in or intending to reside in that dwelling after it is so sold, rented, or made available; or

(C) any person associated with that person.

(3) For purposes of this subsection, discrimination includes—

(A) a refusal to permit, at the expense of the handicapped person, reasonable modifications of existing premises occupied or to be occupied by such person if such modifications may be necessary to afford such person full enjoyment of the premises, except that, in the case of a rental, the landlord may where it is reasonable to do so condition permission for a modification on the renter agreeing to restore the interior of the premises to the condition that existed before the modification, reasonable wear and tear excepted.

(B) a refusal to make reasonable accommodations in rules, policies, practices, or services, when such accommodations may be necessary to afford such person equal opportunity to use and enjoy a dwelling; or

(C) in connection with the design and construction of covered multifamily dwellings for first occupancy after the date that is 30 months after the date of enactment of the Fair Housing Amendments Act of 1988, a failure to design and construct those dwelling in such a manner that—

(i) the public use and common use portions of such dwellings are readily accessible to and usable by handicapped persons;

(ii) all the doors designed to allow passage into and within all premises within such dwellings are sufficiently wide to allow passage by handicapped persons in wheelchairs; and

(iii) all premises within such dwellings contain the following features of adaptive design:

(I) an accessible route into and through the dwelling;

(II) light switches, electrical outlets, thermostats, and other environmental controls in accessible locations;

(III) reinforcements in bathroom walls to allow later installation of grab bars; and

(IV) usable kitchens and bathrooms such that an individual in a wheelchair can maneuver about the space.

SIGNIFICANCE

Race discrimination in housing continues as a major problem in the early twenty-first century. The majority of violations of the Fair Housing Act that are prosecuted by the Justice Department involve claims of race discrimination. However, all forms of discrimination are prosecuted, with disability becoming a protected class in 1988.

Implementation of the Fair Housing Act has changed considerably since the 1960s. In 1968, sexual harassment in housing received very little attention. Women, particularly those who were poor and with limited housing options, often had little choice but to tolerate sexual harassment in order to keep a roof over their heads and those of their children. The Justice Department established an enforcement program to obtain relief for tenants who have been mistreated by landlords and to deter other potential abusers. Other changes in enforcement protect people with blindness, hearing impairment, alcoholism, drug addiction, and mental illness. The legislation offers no protection to people who constitute a direct threat to other persons or property, but determination about a threat has to be made on an individual basis. Complications surrounding enforcement of this provision have led the Justice Department to focus on zoning regulations that might block group homes and multi-family housing construction that must be accessible for people with mobility issues.

Dramatic changes in the cities since the 1960s have also influenced housing integration. The movement of manufacturing jobs away from cities and the departure of middle-class taxpayers led to growing numbers of poor residents in need of expensive services just as city revenues were declining. Many cities experienced fiscal crises, losing federal dollars to fund infrastructure, education, and mass transit. As a result, cities became more polarized between the affluent and the poor, highlighted by the rise and concentration of poverty, homelessness, and crime.

The war on terrorism in the early twenty-first century has led to a rise in the number of hate crimes directed against people who possess a Middle Eastern appearance or background as well as those who follow Islam. It is likely that continuing conflict with the Arab world will lead to a shift in housing discrimination cases as discrimination based on national origin and religion emerges as a major concern.

FURTHER RESOURCES
Books

The Communist Manifesto: New Interpretations, edited by Mark Cowling. New York: New York University Press, 1998.

Maly, Michael T. *Beyond Segregation: Multiracial and Multiethnic Neighborhoods in the United States.* Philadelphia: Temple University Press, 2005.

Wienk, Ronald E., Clifford E. Reid, and John C. Simonson. *Measuring Racial Discrimination in American Housing Markets: The Housing Market Practices Survey.* Washington, D.C.: U.S. Department of Housing and Urban Development, 1979.

Roe v. Wade

Legal decision

By: U.S. Supreme Court

Date: January 22, 1973

Source: *Roe v. Wade* 410 U.S. 113 (1973). Available at: <http://supreme.justia.com/us/410/113/case.html> (accessed April 12, 2006).

About the Author: At the time of the *Roe v. Wade* decision, the U.S. Supreme Court was composed of Justices Warren Burger (Chief), William Douglas, William Brennan, Potter Stewart, Byron White, Thurgood Marshall, Harry Blackmun, Lewis F. Powell, and William Rehnquist. Justice Harry Blackmun, a Republican, served on the court from 1970–1994. Appointed to the court by President Richard Nixon, Blackmun's most famous written opinion for the court is *Roe v. Wade*. Blackmun continued to support abortion rights until his death in 1999.

INTRODUCTION

Abortion was legal in the United States from the country's founding until the 1820s, when some states began to pass legislation limiting the procedure. English common law, which provided the basis for many laws in the United States, had treated abortion before "quickening" or the feeling of fetal movement, as a misdemeanor, but post-quickening abortion was considered a felony or a capital offense. An 1803 English law, The Miscarriage of Women Act, made pre-quickening abortion a felony and post-quickening abortion a capital crime. American states began to follow England in codifying abortion law by the 1820s.

In 1861, England passed the Offenses Against the Person Act, declaring all abortions felonies, and, in 1869, Pope Pius IX, leader of the Roman Catholic Church, declared all abortion, regardless of circumstance or timing, to be grounds for excommunication. In addition, the Pope stated that any person involved in the act—including medical personnel and husbands—had also separated themselves from the Catholic Church by virtue of their choice.

By the early 1900s, abortion was illegal throughout most of the United States. Illegal abortions were commonly performed by midwives, some doctors, or any person who chose to perform the procedure; the practice was unregulated. Because abortion was criminalized, there were few incentives to report corrupt, "back alley" abortion providers or to name them

should a complication arise. Many such abortion providers charged large sums of money, performed the procedure with unsterilized equipment, and provided no follow-up care to check for infection, retained tissue, or other complications.

In the 1920s and 1930s, economic crises in the United States, coupled with the difficulty of accessing affordable birth control, led many women to seek abortions. Although abortion was illegal, many states had a clause permitting a physician to perform the procedure if the mother's life was in jeopardy. The American Medical Association had lobbied for criminalization of abortion in the late 1800s and early 1900s with a dual purpose of driving non-medical abortion providers out of business and making the procedure safer by forcing it to be performed by physicians only.

In 1935, Iceland became the first western country to permit abortions under certain specific medical circumstances; other countries, such as Britain, Canada, and Australia, followed throughout the 1930s, 1940s, and 1950s. In the United States, California and Colorado both made abortion legal in 1967, and New York decriminalized abortion in 1970.

Anti-choice advocates argued that life begins at conception, and ending that life is equivalent to murder. The Roman Catholic Church held this position as well. By 1970, when the *Roe v. Wade* case was filed, thirty-one states permitted abortion when the mother's life was in danger, and women seeking abortions often traveled across state lines or into Canada to seek elective abortions.

Norma McCorvey, the "Jane Roe" in *Roe v. Wade*, filed a lawsuit in Texas on the grounds that Texas law criminalizing abortion violated her rights under the First, Fourth, Fifth, Ninth, and Fourteenth Amendments. Abortion rights proponents had been searching for a case to take through the courts that would stand through repeated court battles; attorneys Sarah Weddington and Linda Coffee believed Norma McCorvey's case was the right choice. McCorvey claimed that her pregnancy was the result of a rape, a condition that some states would have accepted as justification for the abortion. Weddington did not make that fact public during the court case.

The case made its way to the U.S. Supreme Court in December 1971, but after initial arguments the court decided to have it reargued, to give new justices William Rehnquist and Lewis Powell the opportunity to hear the case. In October 1972, the U.S. Supreme Court heard the case again, and in January handed down its ruling, declaring the Texas state law banning abortion unconstitutional.

PRIMARY SOURCE

VIII

. . . .

This right of privacy, whether it be founded in the Fourteenth Amendment's concept of personal liberty and restrictions upon state action, as we feel it is, or, as the District Court determined, in the Ninth Amendment's reservation of rights to the people, is broad enough to encompass a woman's decision whether or not to terminate her pregnancy. The detriment that the State would impose upon the pregnant woman by denying this choice altogether is apparent. Specific and direct harm medically diagnosable even in early pregnancy may be involved. Maternity, or additional offspring, may force upon the woman a distressful life and future. Psychological harm may be imminent. Mental and physical health may be taxed by child care. There is also the distress, for all concerned, associated with the unwanted child, and there is the problem of bringing a child into a family already unable, psychologically and otherwise, to care for it. In other cases, as in this one, the additional difficulties and continuing stigma of unwed motherhood may be involved. All these are factors the woman and her responsible physician necessarily will consider in consultation.

On the basis of elements such as these, appellant and some amici argue that the woman's right is absolute and that she is entitled to terminate her pregnancy at whatever time, in whatever way, and for whatever reason she alone chooses. With this we do not agree. Appellant's arguments that Texas either has no valid interest at all in regulating the abortion decision, or no interest strong enough to support any limitation upon the woman's sole determination, are unpersuasive. The [410 U.S. 113, 154] Court's decisions recognizing a right of privacy also acknowledge that some state regulation in areas protected by that right is appropriate. As noted above, a State may properly assert important interests in safeguarding health, in maintaining medical standards, and in protecting potential life. At some point in pregnancy, these respective interests become sufficiently compelling to sustain regulation of the factors that govern the abortion decision. The privacy right involved, therefore, cannot be said to be absolute. In fact, it is not clear to us that the claim asserted by some amici that one has an unlimited right to do with one's body as one pleases bears a close relationship to the right of privacy previously articulated in the Court's decisions. The Court has refused to recognize an unlimited right of this kind in the past. Jacobson v. Massachusetts, 197 U.S. 11 (1905) (vaccination); Buck v. Bell, 274 U.S. 200 (1927) (sterilization).

We, therefore, conclude that the right of personal privacy includes the abortion decision, but that this right is not unqualified and must be considered against important state interests in regulation.

. . . .

Although the results are divided, most of these courts have agreed that the right of privacy, however based, is broad enough to cover the abortion decision; that the right, nonetheless, is not absolute and is subject to some limitations; and that at some point the state interests as to protection of health, medical standards, and prenatal life, become dominant. We agree with this approach.

. . . .

In the recent abortion cases, cited above, courts have recognized these principles. Those striking down state laws have generally scrutinized the State's interests in protecting health and potential life, and have concluded that neither interest justified broad limitations on the reasons for which a physician and his pregnant patient might decide that she should have an abortion in the early stages of pregnancy. Courts sustaining state laws have held that the State's determinations to protect health or prenatal life are dominant and constitutionally justifiable.

IX

The District Court held that the appellee failed to meet his burden of demonstrating that the Texas statute's infringement upon Roe's rights was necessary to support a compelling state interest, and that, although the appellee presented "several compelling justifications for state presence in the area of abortions," the statutes outstripped these justifications and swept "far beyond any areas of compelling state interest." 314 F. Supp., at 1222–1223. Appellant and appellee both contest that holding. Appellant, as has been indicated, claims an absolute right that bars any state imposition of criminal penalties in the area. Appellee argues that the State's determination to recognize and protect prenatal life from and after conception constitutes a compelling state interest. As noted above, we do not agree fully with either formulation.

A. The appellee and certain amici argue that the fetus is a "person" within the language and meaning of the Fourteenth Amendment. In support of this, they outline at length and in detail the well-known facts of fetal development. If this suggestion of personhood is established, the appellant's case, of course, collapses, [410 U.S. 113, 157] for the fetus' right to life would then be guaranteed specifically by the Amendment. The appellant conceded as much on reargument. On the other hand, the appellee conceded on reargument that no case could be cited that holds that a fetus is a person within the meaning of the Fourteenth Amendment. . . .

B. The pregnant woman cannot be isolated in her privacy. She carries an embryo and, later, a fetus, if one accepts the medical definitions of the developing young in the human uterus. See Dorland's Illustrated Medical Dictionary 478-479, 547 (24th ed. 1965). The situation therefore is inherently different from marital intimacy, or bedroom possession of obscene material, or marriage, or procreation, or education, with which Eisenstadt and Griswold, Stanley, Loving, Skinner, and Pierce and Meyer were respectively concerned. As we have intimated above, it is reasonable and appropriate for a State to decide that at some point in time another interest, that of health of the mother or that of potential human life, becomes significantly involved. The woman's privacy is no longer sole and any right of privacy she possesses must be measured accordingly.

Texas urges that, apart from the Fourteenth Amendment, life begins at conception and is present throughout pregnancy, and that, therefore, the State has a compelling interest in protecting that life from and after conception. We need not resolve the difficult question of when life begins. When those trained in the respective disciplines of medicine, philosophy, and theology are unable to arrive at any consensus, the judiciary, at this point in the development of man's knowledge, is not in a position to speculate as to the answer. [410 U.S. 113, 160].

It should be sufficient to note briefly the wide divergence of thinking on this most sensitive and difficult question. There has always been strong support for the view that life does not begin until live birth. This was the belief of the Stoics. It appears to be the predominant, though not the unanimous, attitude of the Jewish faith. It may be taken to represent also the position of a large segment of the Protestant community, insofar as that can be ascertained; organized groups that have taken a formal position on the abortion issue have generally regarded abortion as a matter for the conscience of the individual and her family. As we have noted, the common law found greater significance in quickening. Physicians and their scientific colleagues have regarded that event with less interest and have tended to focus either upon conception, upon live birth, or upon the interim point at which the fetus becomes "viable," that is, potentially able to live outside the mother's womb, albeit with artificial aid. Viability is usually placed at about seven months (28 weeks) but may occur earlier, even at 24 weeks. The Aristotelian theory of "mediate animation," that held sway throughout the Middle Ages and the Renaissance in Europe, continued to be official Roman Catholic dogma until the 19th century, despite opposition to this "ensoulment" theory from those in the Church who would recognize the existence of life from [410 U.S. 113, 161] the moment of conception. The latter is now, of course, the official belief of the Catholic Church. As one brief amicus discloses, this is a view strongly held by many non-Catholics as well, and by many physicians. Substantial problems for precise

definition of this view are posed, however, by new embryological data that purport to indicate that conception is a "process" over time, rather than an event, and by new medical techniques such as menstrual extraction, the "morning-after" pill, implantation of embryos, artificial insemination, and even artificial wombs.

In areas other than criminal abortion, the law has been reluctant to endorse any theory that life, as we recognize it, begins before live birth or to accord legal rights to the unborn except in narrowly defined situations and except when the rights are contingent upon live birth. For example, the traditional rule of tort law denied recovery for prenatal injuries even though the child was born alive. That rule has been changed in almost every jurisdiction. In most States, recovery is said to be permitted only if the fetus was viable, or at least quick, when the injuries were sustained, though few [410 U.S. 113, 162] courts have squarely so held. In a recent development, generally opposed by the commentators, some States permit the parents of a stillborn child to maintain an action for wrongful death because of prenatal injuries. Such an action, however, would appear to be one to vindicate the parents' interest and is thus consistent with the view that the fetus, at most, represents only the potentiality of life. Similarly, unborn children have been recognized as acquiring rights or interests by way of inheritance or other devolution of property, and have been represented by guardians ad litem. Perfection of the interests involved, again, has generally been contingent upon live birth. In short, the unborn have never been recognized in the law as persons in the whole sense.

X

In view of all this, we do not agree that, by adopting one theory of life, Texas may override the rights of the pregnant woman that are at stake. We repeat, however, that the State does have an important and legitimate interest in preserving and protecting the health of the pregnant woman, whether she be a resident of the State or a nonresident who seeks medical consultation and treatment there, and that it has still another important and legitimate interest in protecting the potentiality of human life. These interests are separate and distinct. Each grows in substantiality as the woman approaches [410 U.S. 113, 163] term and, at a point during pregnancy, each becomes "compelling."

With respect to the State's important and legitimate interest in the health of the mother, the "compelling" point, in the light of present medical knowledge, is at approximately the end of the first trimester. This is so because of the now-established medical fact, referred to above at 149, that until the end of the first trimester mortality in abortion may be less than mortality in normal childbirth. It follows that, from and after this point, a State may regulate the abortion procedure to the extent that the regulation reasonably relates to the preservation and protection of maternal health. Examples of permissible state regulation in this area are requirements as to the qualifications of the person who is to perform the abortion; as to the licensure of that person; as to the facility in which the procedure is to be performed, that is, whether it must be a hospital or may be a clinic or some other place of less-than-hospital status; as to the licensing of the facility; and the like.

This means, on the other hand, that, for the period of pregnancy prior to this "compelling" point, the attending physician, in consultation with his patient, is free to determine, without regulation by the State, that, in his medical judgment, the patient's pregnancy should be terminated. If that decision is reached, the judgment may be effectuated by an abortion free of interference by the State.

With respect to the State's important and legitimate interest in potential life, the "compelling" point is at viability. This is so because the fetus then presumably has the capability of meaningful life outside the mother's womb. State regulation protective of fetal life after viability thus has both logical and biological justifications. If the State is interested in protecting fetal life after viability, it may go so far as to proscribe abortion [410 U.S. 113, 164] during that period, except when it is necessary to preserve the life or health of the mother.

Measured against these standards, Art. 1196 of the Texas Penal Code, in restricting legal abortions to those "procured or attempted by medical advice for the purpose of saving the life of the mother," sweeps too broadly. The statute makes no distinction between abortions performed early in pregnancy and those performed later, and it limits to a single reason, "saving" the mother's life, the legal justification for the procedure. The statute, therefore, cannot survive the constitutional attack made upon it here.

SIGNIFICANCE

The court interpreted the right to obtain an abortion as an issue of personal privacy, grounded in the Fourteenth Amendment. In addition, Blackmun's written decision rejected the Texas law's claim that life begins at conception; the court ruled that viability, or the fetus's ability to live outside the womb, was the better benchmark for state involvement in regulating abortion.

Roe v. Wade set clear guidelines on the state's ability to set limits on abortion based on the viability of the fetus. (In 1973, a fetus was considered to be viable at approximately twenty-eight weeks of gestation.) Until the age of viability had passed, women could legally obtain abortions on demand. Once the

fetus was viable, the state could place restrictions on abortion.

Within seven years, European countries such as France, Italy, West Germany, and the Netherlands legalized abortion. In the United States, individual states responded to the *Roe v. Wade* decision by passing laws that required parental notification, informed consent, "cooling off" periods of twenty-four or more hours between the first consultation with an abortion provider and the actual procedure, and specific counseling information requirements.

The 1992 case *Planned Parenthood v. Casey* revisited Roe and provided a new court that included appointees from conservative presidents Ronald Reagan and George H. W. Bush with the opportunity to overturn Roe. Many legal scholars had argued that the U.S. Supreme Court had created a privacy right in the Fourteenth Amendment, arguing strenuously with the court's use of that justification for Roe. In *Planned Parenthood v. Casey* the court struck down portions of Pennsylvania's abortion restrictions, such as spousal notification laws, but upheld parental consent and "cooling off" periods. Anti-choice and pro-choice advocates alike had expected the court to overturn Roe; the court, however, did not do so.

Technological advances, such as RU-486, an abortion pill protocol, and neonatal care for premature infants have blurred the lines set by Roe in 1973. Viability comes at earlier stages more than thirty years after the *Roe v. Wade* decision was published; ten to forty percent of all babies born at twenty-three weeks survive, and survival rates increase to fifty to eighty percent for babies born at twenty-five weeks.

In February 2006, South Dakota passed a state law banning all abortions, with the only exception being to save the life of the mother. In April 2006, legislators in Ohio crafted a law making abortion illegal and criminalizing those who cross state lines for the purpose of obtaining an abortion. While *Roe v. Wade* struck down such laws in 1973, more than thirty years later the debate continues.

FURTHER RESOURCES
Books

Hull, N. E. H., and Peter Charles Hoffer. *Roe V. Wade: The Abortion Rights Controversy in American History.* Lawrence: University Press of Kansas, 2001.

Solinger, Rickie. *Abortion Wars: A Half Century of Struggle, 1950–2000.* Berkeley: University of California Press, 1998.

Weddington, Sarah. *A Question of Choice.* New York: Penguin, 1993.

A crowd of approximately 5,000 people march in front of the Minnesota Capitol building in St. Paul, Minn., on January 22, 1973. They are protesting the Supreme Court's decision legalizing abortion in *Roe v. Wade.* AP/WIDE WORLD PHOTOS. REPRODUCED BY PERMISSION.

China's "One-Child Family" Policy

Photograph

By: Owen Franken

Date: April 1985

Source: © Owen Franken/Corbis. Reproduced by permission.

About the Photographer: Owen Franken, the brother of political commentator, comedian, and author Al Franken, is a Paris-based photographer. Franken's work has appeared in *Time*, *Newsweek*, and *National Geographic* magazines.

INTRODUCTION

In 1949, when Mao Zedong's Communist Party assumed power in China, annual population growth hovered at two percent. This trend continued for the next twenty-five years as Mao encouraged Chinese citizens to give birth to more children. In 1950, the average Chinese woman had six children; by 2005, the rate was 1.8 children, a dramatic drop in fifty-five years.

In 1979, the new leader of China, Deng Xiaoping (1904–1997), instituted the "birth planning" program, limiting married couples to one child. Each town had a Birth Planning Commission with a Commissioner who monitors birth rates. The one-child policy is complex, with a variety of exceptions to the rule. In rural areas, if the first child is a girl, couples may have a second child three to four years after the first one.

Chinese tradition holds that sons take care of their parents, while girls help with the care of their in-laws; as such, boys are favored over girls by many people in Chinese society, especially in rural areas where male labor is viewed as essential for farming.

In addition, if both members of a married couple are only children themselves, the couple may have two children. The Chinese policy permitting two children in these circumstances helps to resolve the "one-two-four" problem, with one son caring for and supporting two parents and four grandparents.

By the mid–1970s, before Deng Xiaoping implemented the one-child policy, birth rates had already declined from five per woman to approximately 2.5 children per woman. The one-child policy offered economic and educational incentives for families willing to sign a one-child pledge. The goal was zero population growth by the year 2000; in 1979, population growth was approximately 1.5%, down from a steady two percent rate from 1949 through 1974.

PRIMARY SOURCE

CHINA'S "ONE-CHILD FAMILY" POLICY

See primary source image.

SIGNIFICANCE

The one-child policy was voluntary; couples in non-rural areas who wanted more than one child paid fines or lost economic incentives offered through a one-child pledge. Critics of the program claim that the policy, though voluntary, was coercive; fines were set at such high rates as to encourage abortions for couples unable to afford the fine. The Chinese government determined which form of birth control each woman could use. In many instances, sterilizations— with or without informed consent—were performed on women after giving birth to their second child. Unmarried women reportedly have been forced to undergo abortions; the one-child policy applies only to married couples, and unmarried women are not permitted to have children. In addition, couples were forced to apply for "birth permits" when they were ready to conceive.

The Chinese cultural preference for sons led to the abandonment and infanticide of baby girls in the initial years of the one-child policy. As prenatal technology such as ultrasounds became available in the 1980s, some women chose to abort female fetuses and to try again so that their one child would be a

PRIMARY SOURCE

China's "One-Child Family" Policy: A happy mother and her baby illustrate a Chinese government poster that promotes its "one child family" policy to encourage small families and limit population growth. © OWEN FRANKEN/CORBIS. REPRODUCED BY PERMISSION.

boy. Such efforts brought China to a gender imbalance; for every 100 girls born in China there are approximately 118 boys born. The average worldwide is 105 boys for every 100 girls.

Human rights groups have criticized the Chinese government's approach to those who choose to have more than one child, citing forced abortions, forced sterilizations, and the creation of a climate in which infanticide and abandonment at orphanages are the result of oppressive policies. In 2002, China passed the Law on Population and Birth Planning, which updated the 1979 policy, encouraging family planning education for women and providing a legal framework to prevent abuses of the one-child policy.

China's population reduction program was heralded when the country held off projections of 1.3 billion people by three to four years. The one-child

A Chinese family watches television together in Shanghai, China, 1996. One child families like these meet the government's ideal family size. © LIU LIQUN/CORBIS.

policy has reduced or maintained spending levels on social services and education for children, freeing up capital for other investments. In addition, women in the workforce face fewer absences with only one child, and the children in one-child families receive the benefit of their parents' full resources and attention. The darker side of such exclusive attention has been named the "little emperor" problem; with so many only children in China, many of them boys, these children become the sole focus of their parents' and grandparents' attention.

The United States has sharply criticized China's birth planning policies. In 2002, the United States withheld $34 million in United Nations family planning money, stating that programs in China violated the U.S. Kemp-Kasten provision, which prohibits the use of U.S. money on programs that include forced abortions or forced sterilizations. The United States has withheld that funding annually since 2002.

FURTHER RESOURCES

Books

Fong, Vanessa. *Only Hope: Coming of Age Under China's One-Child Policy*. Palo Alto: Stanford University Press, 2004.

United States Congress. *China: Human Rights Violations and Coercion in One-Child Policy Enforcement: Hearing Before the Committee on International Relations*. Washington, D.C.: U.S. Government Printing Office, 2005.

Periodicals

Greenhalgh, Susan. "Science, modernity, and the making of China's one-child policy: An article from: Population and Development Review." *The Population Council, Inc.* 29 (2003): 163.

Web sites

BBC News. "China steps up 'one child' policy." September 25, 2000. <http://news.bbc.co.uk/2/hi/asia-pacific/941511.stm> (accessed May 3, 2006).

Woman Cries With Her Dying Child

Famine in Somalia

Photograph

By: Andrew Holbrooke

Date: August 1, 1992

Source: © Andrew Holbrooke/Corbis.

About the Photographer: Andrew Holbrooke is a professional photojournalist based in New York. A graduate in film and television from the Tisch School of Arts, New York University, he has worked in troubled areas of the world, focusing on the hardships people face there. His work centers on natural and man-made disasters, political and social developments, and related themes. Holbrooke's work has been published in many international publications such as *The New York Times, The Boston Globe, Life, Time Magazine, Newsweek,* and the *U.S. World Report.* He also has won many prestigious and distinguished photojournalism awards in his career.

INTRODUCTION

Somalia is coastal country located in East Africa, a region that is also called the Great Horn of Africa. Initially colonized by the Italians and later the British, Somalia obtained independence in 1960. However, ever since the late 1960s, Somalia has been in political turmoil.

Following the assassination of Abdirashid Ali Shermarke—elected president in 1967—in a presidential coup in 1969, the country was taken over by a dictator, Mohamed Siad Barre, who remained in power until 1990. According to a report published by the Human Rights Watch, the devastation in Somalia has its roots in the twenty one-year rule of Siad Barre. The report points out that Siad Barre destroyed all independent institutions, making it difficult for moderate leaders to emerge. Moreover, his grip on power was ensured by his encouragement of regional feuds and manipulations of clan loyalties.

In an armed battle that started in the Somali capital of Mogadishu in December 1990, rebels forced Siad Barre to flee. Ali Mahdi, leader of the United Somali Congress (USC)—a prominent group that led the rebellion, and a previous opponent of Siad Barre came to power. However, due to stern opposition from General Mohamed Farah Aideed—leader of another faction of the USC—the country slid into a volatile battle for power. Civil war eventually broke in late 1991.

Political analysts state that the following years are considered to be the worst in Somali history. Famines, wars, and other crimes erupted. The food and medical situation in Somalia was visibly affected because of the ongoing war in the country. There were reported cases of Somali civilians suffering from severe malnutrition. The country faced acute water crisis due to lack of central electric power or water supply.

Moreover, because of frequent droughts, Somalia has historically been subjected to famines. According to Historical Survey of the Incidence of Drought in Northern Somalia, at least ten significant droughts occurred between 1918 and 1975. Droughts have also occurred in the periods between 1979 and 1980, 1983 and 1986, and 1989 and 1990. Shortage of food, water, and day to day living supplies along with frequent drought situations in the region have added to the burden of the Somali civilians. Reportedly, thousands of people have died due to starvation since the early 1980s.

The primary source is a photograph by Andrew Holbrooke taken during the 1992 famine that took the lives of more than 300,000 people. The photograph depicts the plight of a helpless woman begging for food.

PRIMARY SOURCE

WOMAN CRIES WITH HER DYING CHILD
See primary source image.

SIGNIFICANCE

Various policies enforced by Mohammed Aideed and the ongoing civil war crippled the state of agriculture and consequently the economy of Somalia in the 1990s. The extensive internal refugee problem created by the destructive civil war also devastated the Somali economy. Between 1991 and 1992, at least 350,000 Somalis reportedly died from disease and starvation. These events are considered extremely significant in Somalia's history as they ravaged the country. In modern times, no other country has reported such high number of deaths.

Somalia started receiving international aid. Led by the United States and supported by United Nations Operations in Somalia...UNOSOM 1..., operation Provide Relief began in August 1992. However, media reports indicate that nearly eighty percent of the food was stolen by warring clans, and

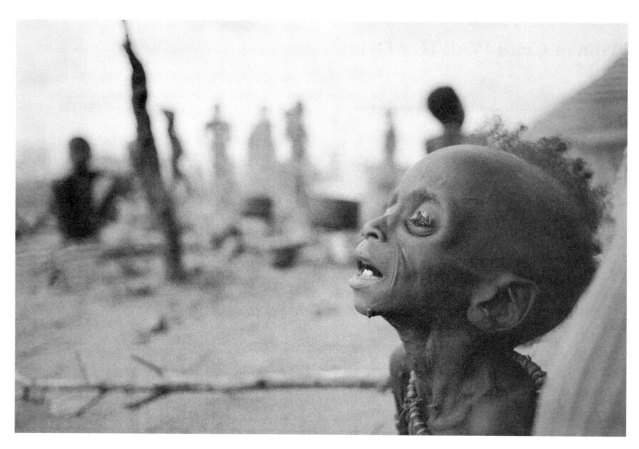

A starving boy cries inside a compound run by Doctors Without Borders (MSF), in Ajiep, within famine-torn Bahr el Ghazal province in south Sudan, July 26, 1998. AP IMAGES.

in many cases, was exchanged for weapons from neighboring regions. Consequently, the relief efforts proved to be inadequate.

In short time, another major coalition effort known as Operation Restore Hope was launched by the United States to restore humanitarian and relief activities in Somalia. However, in an event that took place in October 1993—later known as the Battle of Mogadishu—eighteen U.S. soldiers lost their lives and seventy five were wounded. Operation Restore Hope wound up in March 1994 as a result of continuing causalities and failure to accomplish designated objectives. The popular Hollywood movie "Black Hawk Down" is based on these incidents.

The events in Somalia have also given rise to an international refugee situation. Many Somalians have fled the country and have sought asylum in neighboring nations as well as other western countries. According to a 1996 consolidated UN report, up to 400,000 Somalis became refugees in the neighboring countries of Kenya, Ethiopia, and Djibouti during this period.

Since the early 2000s, a few Somali refugees have returned back to the country. The UN High Commissioner for Refugees (UNHCR) states that 11,633 Somali refugees were repatriated to Somaliland and Puntland areas during 2005. However, no significant changes have been observed by the UN independent expert on Human Rights in Somalia, in the situation of residents living in various settlements. As of 2006, these overcrowded settlements have poor sanitation and offer little or no access to employment and education. Moreover, malnutrition, drought, floods, ethnic fighting, the Indian Ocean tsunami, and the displacement of more than 400,000 people have intensified the country's already poor human rights situation. Besides, it is administered by a transitional government called the Somalia Transitional Federal Institutions (TFI), headed by transitional Federal President Abdullah Yusuf Ahmed.

In April 2006, Christian Balslev-Olesen, the United Nation's Acting Humanitarian Coordinator for Somalia, declared that to prevent a famine in

PRIMARY SOURCE

Woman Cries With Her Dying Child: A woman seeks help for her dying child at a Red Cross feeding center in Baidoa, Somalia, during a 1992 famine in which over 300,000 people died of starvation. © ANDREW HOLBROOKE/CORBIS.

2006, Somalia needs emergency funding of 326 million dollars. According to Balslev-Olesen, more than two million people out of an estimated population of nine million are on food aid, and more than ten thousand could die from starvation each month. Further, there are very few channels to deliver aid effectively. The continuing looting, extortion at roadblocks, and kidnappings has prevented relief and humanitarian efforts.

FURTHER RESOURCES

Books

Peter D. Little. *Somalia: Economy Without State (African Issues)*. Indiana University Press, November 2003.

Web sites

Country Studies US. "Somalia." <http://countrystudies.us/somalia> (accessed April 28, 2006).

Human Rights Watch Publications. "Somalia No Mercy in Mogadishu." March 26, 1992. <http://www.hrw.org/reports/1992/somalia> (accessed April 28, 2006).

Reuters. "Somalia needs $326 mln to ward off famine, UN says." April 4, 2006. <http://www.alertnet.org/thenews/newsdesk/N04222464.htm> (accessed April 28, 2006).

U.S. Committee for Refugees and Immigrants. "World Refugee Survey 2004 Country Report." <http://www.refugees.org/countryreports/> (accessed April 28, 2006).

U.S. Department of State. "Somalia." March 8, 2006. <http://www.state.gov/g/drl/rls/hrrpt/2005/61592.htm> (accessed April 28, 2006).

No Electricity, Running Water, and Almost No Medical Supplies

Photograph

By: David Turnley

Date: ca. August–September 1992

Source: © David Turnley/Corbis.

About the Photographer: This photograph is part of the Corbis collection of images, a worldwide source of visual content to advertisers, broadcasters, designers, magazines, new media organizations, newspapers, and producers. David Turnley is a Pulitzer Prize–winning independent photographer.

INTRODUCTION

Somalia is a country in Eastern Africa that borders the Gulf of Aden and the Indian Ocean on the east and Ethiopia on the west. When it gained its independence in 1960 after a legacy of English and Italian colonization, Mohamed Siad Barre assumed power as a dictator. His regime faced constant internal challenges, however. In the late 1960s, he jailed Mohamed Farah Aideed for plotting a coup, and in the Ogaden War (1977–1978) with Ethiopia, endured a devastating defeat.

Barre ruled by dividing citizens along clan lines—alliances and coalitions of families, friends, and neighbors. In this system of polygamy and segmentary

PRIMARY SOURCE

No Electricity, Running Water, and Almost No Medical Supplies: Xaawo Mohammed Hasan lies with her newborn in a hospital in Baidoa, Somalia, 1992. She was caught in a corssfire and injured during Somalia's civil war. The hospital is overwhelmed with famine and war victims and has no electricity, running water, and hardly any medicine. © DAVID TURNLEY/CORBIS.

lineage, a man's children born of different mothers will turn on one another, and continual infighting easily emerges. Barre used clan alliances to divide the populace, and the conflicts detracted attention from his dying regime.

In the 1980s, the Somali civil war began. Majeerteen clans in southern Somalia began fighting Barre's regime, known as the Somali Salvation Democratic Front (SSDF). Isaaq clans in the north, known as the Somali National Movement (SNM), also initiated an uprising. Barre fought back, using his militia to engage in torture, mutilation, and murder. Whole villages were exterminated. Women were raped, a double crime that produced "unpure" children. By May 1988, the fighting had destroyed Hargeysa, the country's second-largest city, and Burao, the provincial capital. A year later, the Hawiye clans began yet another rebellion as the United Somali

Congress (USC). Soon, six distinct political groups were fighting Barre and each other. When Barre's regime finally fell in 1991, Mohamaed Farak Aideed and the USC took charge.

Western media accounts showed images of malnourished Somali children forced into the conflict as both combatants and victims. In 1991, the United Nations opened an office in the Somali capital, ostensibly to supply food and other forms of aid; in 1992, it began sending peacekeeping troops as well. American troops arrived in December 1992 to protect food and humanitarian relief shipments. Many Somalis, however, saw the troops as a threat to their independence and feared becoming a UN trustee.

Even with international aid, the violence in Somalia continued to escalate. Militia groups continued to torture and kill civilians and hijacked

The corpses of famine and disease victims are loaded into a truck near Baidoa, Somalia, late Summer 1992. © DAVID TURNLEY/CORBIS.

desperately needed supplies intended for the general populace. The fighting, destruction of land, and food shortages created a severe famine.

PRIMARY SOURCE

No Electricity, Running Water, and Almost No Medical Supplies
See primary source image.

SIGNIFICANCE

In the summer of 1993, several Pakistani UN peacekeepers were killed, and an American helicopter mistakenly fired on a group of Somali civilians. In October 1993, U.S. forces seeking Aideed's senior officials were caught in a shootout that left eighteen American soldiers and hundreds of Somali civilians dead. The body of a dead American solider was dragged through the streets of Mogadishu. In March 1994, UN troops withdrew from Somalia, and much of the fighting temporarily ceased. Aideed died in August

1996 from a gunshot wound, and his son, a former U.S. Marine, was chosen to take his place.

In 1996, the Ethiopian government brought most of the clans together, but Aideed's son boycotted the conference. A year later, clan representatives met in Cairo to discuss Somalia's future but made little headway. In August 2000, they elected Addigasim Salad Hasan as Somalia's new president; he was sworn in on August 27, 2000. Hasan's election was a ray of hope for Somalia, but as of 2006, the country was still in a state of political chaos.

According to the Central Intelligence Agency, the government of Somalia remains unstable. The United Nations has deemed the country too hostile for humanitarian aid shipments, and as a result, the country lacks a sufficient food supply. In 2006, Somalia suffered one of the most devastating droughts in over a decade.

FURTHER RESOURCES
Books

Little, Peter D. *Somalia: Economy Without State*. Indianapolis: Indiana University Press, 2003.

Peterson, Scott. *Me Against My Brother: At War in Somalia, Sudan and Rwanda*. New York: Routledge, 2001.

Physicians for Human Rights. *No Mercy in Mogadishu: The Human Cost of the Conflict and the Struggle for Relief*. Boston: Physicians for Human Rights; New York: Africa Watch, c1992.

Periodicals

Besteman, Catherine. "Representing Violence and 'Othering' Somalia." *Cultural Anthropology*. 11, no.1 (February 1996): 120–133.

Klarevas, Louis J. "Trends: The United States Peace Operation in Somalia." *The Public Opinion Quarterly*. 64.4 (Winter 2000): 523–540.

Web sites

Laitin, David D., *Columbia International Affairs Online*. "Somalia: Civil War and International Intervention." February 1997. <http://www.ciaonet.org/conf/iwp01/iwp01ad.html> (accessed May 4, 2006).

Indian Government's Comments on Asia Watch-Physicians for Human Rights Report "The Crackdown in Kashmir"

Press release

By: Embassy of India, Washington, D.C.

Date: February 1993

Source: The Embassy of India. "Indian Government's Comments on Asia Watch-Physicians for Human Rights Report 'The Crackdown in Kashmir.'" Press release. February 1993. Reprinted in: Asia Watch and Physicians for Human Rights. *The Human Rights Crisis in Kashmir: A Pattern of Impunity*. New York: Human Rights Watch, 1993.

About the Author: The Indian Embassy in the United States is located in Washington D.C. As of 2006, Ronen Sen is Ambassador to the United States. The Ambassador and his staff act as representatives of the Indian government in the United States. They work to facilitate relations, travel, immigration, and trade between the two countries. Communicating and explaining the policies and actions of the Indian government is also among their responsibilities.

INTRODUCTION

Ever since independence from British rule in 1947, the region of Jammu and Kashmir has been at the heart of a territorial dispute between India and Pakistan. At the time of independence, British India was divided into two democratic countries—a Hindu-dominated India and a Muslim-dominated Pakistan. Both claimed the state of Kashmir to be a part of their country. Before independence, states in India had their own kings. Kashmir, though dominated by Muslims, had a Hindu king, Hari Singh. When the British granted independence to India, each king was given the right to choose whether his state would become part of Pakistan or India (or, with some restrictions, remain independent).

Kashmir was invaded by Pathan tribesmen intent upon coercing Hari Singh to accede to Pakistan. However, Singh signed the Instrument of Accession and acceded to India. Nevertheless, the invaders succeeded in capturing some of the northern territories in the state, thus creating an unofficial border between the two countries. The Indian Prime Minister at that time, Jawaharlal Nehru (1889–1964), referred the dispute to the United Nations. Three wars later, the Kashmir region is still in dispute. Owing to its beauty and strategic location, both India and Pakistan consider Kashmir to be a prized possession.

For more than fifteen years, the Kashmir valley region has witnessed an increase in violence and militant activities. The Indian government accuses its counterpart in Pakistan of sponsoring terrorism in the Indian-occupied portion of Kashmir—Jammu and Kashmir. The Pakistani government, however, maintains that these activities are carried out by independent rebels fighting for freedom. Thousands have been reportedly killed since the first incidents of terrorism in 1989. Moreover, the insurgency has significantly affected the tourism industry of Kashmir—an industry that fuels the state's economy.

The escalation of armed violence led the Indian government to deploy army troops in Jammu and Kashmir in 1990. However, the government's campaign to end militancy in Kashmir has been under scrutiny, especially from human rights groups. In the past, the Indian Army has been charged with unlawful detainment of innocent civilians, civilian massacre, anti-secularism, and other cases of human rights violations. Some human rights organizations allege that the army has been promoting counter-insurgency by training local forces of captured militants. The government of India, however, has denied all such allegations stating that the recruitment of former militants is merely for rehabilitation. In 1993, the government of

India also established the National Human Rights Commission with the aim of preserving human rights and civil liberties in the disputed region.

The primary source contains the official riposte of the Embassy of India in the United States to allegations of human rights abuses by the Indian Army in the state of Jammu and Kashmir. The Embassy states that the conclusions presented in the Boston-based Physicians for Human Rights (PHR) and Asia Watch report are flawed and unfairly interpreted.

■ PRIMARY SOURCE

The Indian Government had given detailed comments to Asia Watch-PHR on the findings in their Report on "The Crackdown in Kashmir—Torture of Detainees and Assaults on the Medical Community." Some of these comments have been incorporated, along with rebuttals by AW-PHR in the main body of the Report which is being released on February 28. A few of them have been distorted by AW-PHR to draw erroneous conclusions about Indian Government policy while some have been less than fairly interpreted.

In view of this it is felt necessary to respond to AW-PHR's observations on the Indian Government's initial response so as to put the facts in their correct perspective.

It is unfortunate that the Press Release starts with an attack against the Indian forces for having stepped up their "campaign of terror" against civilians. The use of the word "terror" to describe the difficult combat of the security forces against the large-scale violence in the Valley is all the more surprising because AW-PHR have carefully avoided using this word to describe the murderous activities of Pakistan-backed Muslim fundamentalist groups in Kashmir. To suggest that the only terrorism in Kashmir is the one at the hands of the security forces is to make a travesty of the real situation there. Apart from countless reports in the international media on terrorism in Kashmir by Muslim groups and recognition of this fact by several Governments, even the latest Report on Human Rights issued by the State Department has noted that the militants have maintained a reign of terror in the Kashmir Valley. The true picture is that the violence unleashed by the terrorists in Jammu and Kashmir has grown and in 1992, as compared to 1991, the total number of incidents of terrorist violence increased from 3,122 to 4,871 (Annexure-I). The question to ask is who is sustaining this growing terrorist activity? Where are the terrorists obtaining their arms and equipment, training and strategic direction from? What is the responsibility of the terrorists and their increasing activity in disrupting civilian life in the Valley, including health and medical services?

A claim has again been made that patients in hospitals have been disconnected from life sustaining treatments which had earlier been categorically denied. A similar claim has been made regarding shooting doctors on duty and torturing some others, which is also categorically denied. It is unfortunate that AW-PHR continue to make these groundless charges based on hearsay.

While dwelling at some length on the issue of medical neutrality and the Geneva Conventions, the Release accuses the Government of violations and denies that any legitimacy is being provided to terrorist groups, as indicated in our preliminary response. It goes on to say that as per the norms of medical neutrality medical personnel should be able to render medical care to all populations, on all sides of the conflict. While not entering into any argument on issues of principle, it may be mentioned that nowhere does the Report care to acknowledge the fact that treatment has been provided to the apprehended terrorists even in army hospitals, quite apart from the question that nothing in their Report or in our response suggests that the Government or the security forces as a matter of policy prevented treatment of injured terrorists in the hospitals.

A perturbing aspect of AW-PHR's Report is its tendency to reject evidence which may not fit in with the case it wants to project, or make categorical statements on matters that clearly they are not qualified to do as they cannot have full information with them. While the Release acknowledges killings of medical workers by the terrorists, it goes on to say that "there is no evidence that militants have done this" in the context of our observation that militants have used hospitals as sanctuaries and have even feigned injuries in this process. In fact, it claims that "hospitals are unlikely places for militants to seek refuge unless they are genuinely wounded." AW-PHR made this claim in the face of evidence of the recoveries made from the hospitals in the searches that were conducted in some of them. They assert that when security forces conduct such operations in hospitals in Kashmir, they don't do so on the basis of specific information. If such a format of reporting were to be acceptable, just about anything can be said and any claim could be made without there being any need for evidence for and to the contrary.

The Report says that while the authorities may prosecute health professionals for failing to provide information about persons in their care whom they believe may have committed crimes, they cannot physically abuse them for failing to do so. In fact, in our comments we had not referred to prosecution of health care professionals but to conditions in which most of them out of fear and some due to connivance, may not report medico legal cases as required under the law, which may lead to situations where it may become necessary to look for such criminals inside hospitals.

The Release says that the Report describes a number of incidents in which security forces opened fire inside hospitals, apparently to intimidate the medical staff to identify suspected militants. The Report mentions such incidents at two places and the number of times that a hospital may have been searched, but no specific incident has been narrated. The question of providing any explanation for such incidents, therefore, does not arise. However, in our comments, the incidents in which searches did take place in the hospitals were mentioned, including those cases where such searches may not have ended up in any recoveries. One specific incident taken out of our response and included in the Report, about firing from the premises of SKIMS, is only one of the numerous illustrative incidents that had been mentioned in our comments to show the type of activities that the terrorists have been indulging in from the premises of hospitals in Srinagar.

The Release also mentions two security laws currently in force in Kasmir, viz., The Armed Forces (Jammu & Kashmir) Special Powers Act and the Jammu & Kashmir Disturbed Areas Act, and has stated that these acts explicitly promote the use of lethal force against people who are not combatants and who do not pose a threat to the lives of the security forces. It has also been claimed that these laws permit immunity from prosecution to the security forces. Elsewhere it refers to our claim that we are trying to fight the terrorist menace by civilian law and order methods and concludes that the Government, by saying so, attempts to justify and excuse acts of gross violations as legitimate means of "law enforcement." Such a conclusion is astounding, to say the least. The fact of the matter is that the security forces in Kashmir or elsewhere are not a law unto themselves and none of these Acts provide any immunity to them. What they require is prior sanction for prosecution as is also provided under India's Criminal Procedure Code (Section 197). In actual fact, as mentioned in our previous comments, action has been taken against over 100 personnel of the Army and Para-Military forces which includes officers. This shows that neither does the Government excuse violations nor is there any immunity for errant officers or personnel who may be acting even within the powers conferred under these Acts. The suggestion that Government policy condones excesses is totally baseless.

The warning of the medical catastrophe, unless the Government grants immediate access to the ICRC, is deliberately alarmist. All the details in the AW-PHR's Report together do not point to any impending medical catastrophe. Despite all the difficulties created by terrorist activities, the authorities will continue to do their best to meet their responsibilities for providing health, medical and other facilities to the population of the affected area.

Brief comments have been given above only with respect to some of the specific points mentioned in the Release. There are many others which are general and speaking about wide-spread torture, maltreatment by the security forces etc., on which no specific comments are being made again. We would, however, like to strongly state that we do not make any excuses for violations of Human Rights just because the terrorists may be indulging in abuses. At the same time, the extremely difficult environment created by the indiscriminate and massive level of violence perpetrated by the terrorists has to be understood to appreciate that it may not be possible to deal with the situation, under the normal laws. Over 500 security force personnel have been killed by the terrorists, apart form a large number of politicians, press persons, Government officials and innocent citizens in the State (figures have been given earlier). Even so, the Special Laws referred to in the Release are not passed by any ad hoc draconian fiat, but after full deliberation in the Parliament, and are only temporary measures. In the prevailing environment, there can be possibilities where harassment may be caused to the civilian population on account of security operations and there may also be occasional cases of excesses. At the same time, we reiterate that we do not hesitate to take action against security force personnel where deliberate acts of excesses and cases of gross negligence and over-reaction etc., come to notice. The swift and firm response in the recent unfortunate incident at Sopore would bring this out clearly.

Finally, we note that in the chapter "Conclusions and Recommendations" of the Report, AW-PHR have made several critical comments against the Government of India of an all-embracing political nature on the problem in Kashmir, but have no advice to offer militant groups to put an end to terrorist activities in the context of Human Rights, other than merely urging them to desist from attacks against health services and health professionals. Can it be concluded that SW-PHR encourage or condone all other forms of violent activities by Muslim fundamentalist terrorist groups?

SIGNIFICANCE

According to the Indian government, militant organizations operating in Jammu and Kashmir have often targeted government officials, reporters, armed forces, peacekeepers, and civilians, including children and the disabled. The United States and other countries have also endorsed the Indian government's allegations. For instance, a 1997 report published by the U.S. Department of State concluded that militant groups in Jammu and Kashmir were responsible for innumerable acts of terrorism in the region.

However, as mentioned earlier, international human rights organizations, such as Amnesty International and Human Rights Watch, have also accused the Indian Army of violating human rights in order to suppress terrorism in the state. An Amnesty International Press Release stated that Indian Armed Forces were responsible for the killing of 250 civilians in 2003 alone. On its part, the Indian Government alleges that human rights activists have ignored the role of Pakistan in sponsoring terrorism in Indian occupied Kashmir.

The Indian government's stated position regarding the disputed Jammu and Kashmir region is that Kashmir is an integral part of India and that Parkistani occupation of a portion of that region is illegal. Further, the Indian government wants the government of Pakistan to stop supporting militant groups using terrorist tactics in an effort to unite Kashmir with Pakistan. For its part, the government of Pakistan supports holding a plebiscite that would allow the residents of Jammu and Kashmir to vote on which country they want to join. India is opposed to holding a plebiscite.

Clearly, the events in the Jammu and Kashmir region have been subject to a variety of interpretations by the many parties directly or indirectly affected by the conflict. Reaching a balanced and dispassionate assessment of these events and assigning responsibility for any civil or human rights abuses is an ongoing challenge. Unfortunately, as of 2006, the conflict in Jammu and Kashmir appeared to be no closer to a resolution than it was when the British withdrew from the Indian subcontinent nearly sixty years ago.

FURTHER RESOURCES
Books

Human Rights Watch. *Kashmir Under Siege: Human Rights in India*. New York: Human Rights Watch, 1991.

Ganguly, Sumit, and Lee H. Hamilton. *The Crisis in Kashmir: Portents of War, Hopes of Peace*. New York: Cambridge University Press, 1999.

Web sites

Amnesty International. "India: Jammu and Kashmir Government Must Uphold Promises to End Human Rights Abuses." December 3, 2003. <http://web.amnesty.org/library/index/> (accessed April 29, 2006).

Committee on Government Reform. "Decades of Terror: Exploring Human Rights Abuses in Kashmir and the Disputed Territories." May 12, 2004. <http://reform.house.gov/WHR/Hearings/

EventSingle.aspx?EventID=14204> (accessed April 29, 2006).

Crimes of War. "Kashmir and International Law: How War Crimes Fuel the Conflict." July 17, 2002. <http://www.crimesofwar.org/onnews/news-kashmir.html> (accessed April 29, 2006).

Embassy of India (Washington, D.C.). "Frequently Asked Questions on Jammu and Kashmir." <http://www.indianembassy.org/policy/Kashmir/FAQ-Kashmir.htm> (accessed April 29, 2006).

Human Rights Watch. "Violations By Indian Government Forces: State-Sponsored 'Renegade' Militas." <http://www.hrw.org/campaigns/kashmir/1996/India-07.htm> (accessed April 29, 2006).

International Committee of the Red Cross. "What Is International Humanitarian Law?" July 31, 2004. <http://www.icrc.org/web/eng/siteeng0.nsf/html/humanitarian-law-factsheet> (accessed April 29, 2006).

U.S. Department of State. "India: Country Report on Human Rights Practices for 1997." January 30, 1998. <http://www.state.gov/www/global/human_rights/1997_hrp_report/india.html> (accessed April 29, 2006).

U.S. Department of State. "India: Country Reports on Human Rights Practices, 2004." February 28, 2005. <http://www.state.gov/g/drl/rls/hrrpt/2004/41740.htm> (accessed April 29, 2006).

World Medical Association Resolution on the Prohibition of Access of Women to Health Care and the Prohibition of Practice of Female Doctors in Afghanistan

Resolution

By: World Medical Association

Date: November 1997

Source: *World Medical Association.* "World Medical Association Resolution on the Prohibition of Access of Women to Health Care and the Prohibition of Practice of Female Doctors in Afghanistan" (November 1997). <http://www.wma.net/e/policy/a12.htm> (accessed April 22, 2006).

About the Author: The World Medical Association, founded in 1947, is an international organization of physicians committed to promoting ethical standards, freedom of movement across borders for medical personnel, and helping physicians worldwide with professional health care issues.

INTRODUCTION

The 1979 invasion of Afghanistan by the Soviet Union and subsequent ten-year war led to chaos. The *mujahedin*—Muslims who fought against Soviet forces—received aid from the United States, China, Pakistan, and Saudi Arabia. When the Soviet Union left Afghanistan in 1989, the *mujahedin* split into two competing groups, the Afghan Northern Alliance and the Taliban. By 1996, the Taliban, whose name means "seeker" or "student of Islam," gained power in Afghanistan.

After it took the capital city of Kabul on September 26, 1996, the Taliban imposed *sharia*, or Islamic religious law, on all of Afghanistan. Women were harshly restricted and lost both civil and personal rights, such as the right to work, to vote, to be educated, or to be seen in public unescorted by a male relative. In addition, women were required to wear full body coverings called *burqa* and forbidden to wear white (the official color of the Taliban).

By 1997, the Taliban ordered hospitals to be segregated by gender and banned women from work in medicine and education. In Kabul, which had twenty-two hospitals, the city's more than 500,000 women were forced to use a single facility with limited supplies and no electricity. Many women whose husbands refused to let them be seen by male doctors were left without access to any health care at all.

Organized Afghan protests of this treatment were rare, although the Revolutionary Association of Women of Afghanistan, or RAWA, a women's rights organization founded in 1977, continued to work behind the scenes. The prodemocracy and antifundamentalist RAWA openly condemned the Taliban's oppressive rule; many women who spoke out faced the death penalty for their actions.

International human rights organizations such as Amnesty International and Human Rights Watch, as well as medical organizations such as Physicians for Human, also condemned the Taliban's treatment of women. The document below is a resolution passed by the World Medical Association.

◼ PRIMARY SOURCE

World Medical Association Resolution on the Prohibition of Access of Women to Health Care and the Prohibition of Practice by Female Doctors in Afghanistan Adopted by the 49th WMA General Assembly, Hamburg, Germany, November 1997

PREAMBLE

For years women and girls in Afghanistan have been suffering increasing violations of their human rights; In 1996 a general prohibition was introduced on practice by women, which affected more than 40,000 women. Human rights organisations call this a "human rights catastrophe" for the women in Afghanistan. Women are completely excluded from social life, girls' schools are closed, women students have been expelled from universities, and women and girls are stoned in the street. According to information from the United Nations on the human rights situation in Afghanistan (February, 1996) the prohibition on practice affects first of all women working in the educational and health sectors. In particular female doctors and nurses were prevented from exercising their profession. Although the health sector was on the brink of collapse under these restrictions, they have been eased only slightly. Without access to female doctors female patients and their children have no access to health care. Some female doctors have been allowed now to exercise their profession, but in general only under strict and unacceptable supervision (US Department of State, Afghanistan Report on Human Rights Practices for 1996, January 1997).

RECOMMENDATION

Therefore, the World Medical Association urges its national member associations to insist and call on their governments:

—to condemn roundly the serious violations of the basic human rights of women in Afghanistan; and,

—to take worldwide action aimed at restoring the fundamental human rights of women and removing the provision prohibiting women from practising their profession.

—to insist on the rights of women to adequate medical care across the whole range of medical and surgical services, including acute, subacute and ongoing treatment.

◼

SIGNIFICANCE

A 1999 survey of Afghan women revealed "extraordinarily" high levels of mental stress and depression, with eighty-one percent reporting a decline in their mental condition over the past two years. Forty-two percent met the diagnostic criteria for post-traumatic stress disorder (PTSD), ninety-seven percent exhibited major depression, and eighty-six percent demonstrated significant symptoms of anxiety. Twenty-one percent indicated that they had suicidal thoughts "extremely often" or "quite often."

The ban on female physicians, which prevented female physicians from practicing, cut 40,000 medical professionals from Afghanistan's health care system and removed the only medical practitioners some female Muslims were permitted to access. The resulting crisis led to a higher mortality rate for women and infants and for widows and other women without male relatives to chaperone them.

The 2001 invasion of Afghanistan by United States forces in the wake of the September 11, 2001 bombings in the United States by Al-Qaeda, removed the Taliban from power, the first step to improving women's status in Afghanistan. As of April 2006, Afghanistan's infant mortality rate was the second highest in the world. For children under the age of five, the death rate was 257 per 1,000. Malnutrition, poor education rates for young mothers, and severe shortages of trained doctors and supplies continued to hamper health care efforts in Afghanistan.

FURTHER RESOURCES

Books

Brodsky, Anne E. *With All Our Strength: The Revolutionary Association of Women in Afghanistan*. Routledge, 2003.

Skaine, Rosemarie. *The Women of Afghanistan under the Taliban*. Jefferson, NC: McFarland & Company, 2001.

Web sites

Associated Press. "Mortality Rates Climb in Afghanistan." April 19, 2006. <http://hosted.ap.org/dynamic/stories/> (accessed April 21, 2006).

Physicians for Human Rights. "1999 Report: The Taliban's War on Women—A Health and Human Rights Crisis in Afghanistan." 1999. <http://www.phrusa.org/research/health_effects/exec.html> (accessed April 20, 2006).

U.S. Department of State. "Report on the Taliban's War against Women." November 17, 2001. <http://www.state.gov/g/drl/rls/c4804.htm> (accessed April 20, 2006).

Apology for Study Done in Tuskegee

Speech

By: William Jefferson Clinton

Date: May 16, 1997

Source: Clinton, William J. *Apology for Study Done in Tuskegee*. White House Office of Press Secretary, 1997.

About the Author: President William Jefferson Clinton was the forty-second president of the United States, serving from 1993 to 2001. During his tenure in office, President Clinton was very popular with African-American voters as a result of his efforts to reach out to the black community on political and cultural issues.

INTRODUCTION

In 1932, the United states Public Health Service recruited African-American men in Macon County, Alabama, for a study titled the "Tuskegee Study of Untreated Syphilis in the Negro Male." Researchers enrolled 600 men in the study; 399 with syphilis, 201 who were not infected with the disease. Syphilis treatment at the time was limited to the use of mercury and bismuth; the combination caused severe side effects in some patients, and the cure rate was approximately thirty percent. In the 1920s and 1930s, public health officials estimated that as much as one third of the U.S. population of reproductive age had syphilis. The epidemic was viewed as one of the primary health crises of the era.

In exchange for their enrollment in the planned six month study, African-American men would receive free medical care and exams, free meals, and burial insurance. In many instances, the enrollees—largely poor sharecroppers and laborers—were unaware that they had syphilis. Told they had "bad blood," a euphemism used for ailments such as anemia, syphilis, and exhaustion, the study's purpose was to follow the physical changes in men with syphilis without providing treatment, to examine the effects of syphilis on the body.

The disease progression for syphilis begins with lesions that develop on the patient's genitals; these sores are contagious, and contact with the sores spreads the disease. Once the sores heal, many patients with syphilis recover; others experience secondary syphilis, in which a flu-like illness develops accompanied by new sores. Again, the patient is contagious, and the disease is in the blood and lymph nodes. Most patients recover, though as many as twenty-five percent of untreated syphilis patients can develop tertiary syphilis, in which the disease attacks the organs, the hair, and the blood vessels. The heart is weakened, sores appear on the skin, and the breakdown of the nervous system leads to erratic gait, paralysis, incontinence, and later blindness. As the bones break down, the face and palate deteriorate; the combination of bone problems, skin lesions, organ complications and central nervous system dysfunction in untreated syphilis cases can lead to painful death.

By 1945, penicillin had been isolated as a known treatment for syphilis; the antibiotic killed the bacteria that caused the disease. The men in the Tuskegee Experiment were never told of the treatment, and doctors and nurses administering the Public Health Service experiment actively recruited local doctors' assistance in not treating or informing men with syphilis in the study. Concerned that such treatment would end the study, researchers followed the syphilis patients without providing treatment for more than twenty-five years during which a quick and simple cure—penicillin—was available for the patients' disease. When 250 of the men involved in the study were drafted in World War II and ordered to report for treatment for syphilis, the Tuskegee Study's researchers successfully exempted the men from military medical treatment via government channels. As one Public Health Service researcher reported, "So far, we are keeping the known positive patients from getting treatment."

On July 25, 1972, nearly forty years into the experiment—a former researcher named Peter Buxtun provided information to Associated Press reporter Jean Heller. The story exposed the study for the first time to a national audience. The U.S. Public Health Service defended the project, but it was closed immediately. After forty years, twenty-eight of the 399 men with syphilis had died of the disease, another 100 men had died of complications related to the disease, forty had passed the disease on to their wives, and nineteen children of diseased men had been born with congenital syphilis.

■ PRIMARY SOURCE

The East Room.

2:26 P.M. EDT.

THE PRESIDENT: Ladies and gentlemen, on Sunday, Mr. Shaw will celebrate his 95th birthday. I would like to recognize the other survivors who are here today and their families: Mr. Charlie Pollard is here. Mr. Carter Howard. Mr. Fred Simmons. Mr. Simmons just took his first airplane ride, and he reckons he's about 110 years old, so I think it's time for him to take a chance or two. I'm glad he did. And Mr. Frederick Moss, thank you, sir.

I would also like to ask three family representatives who are here—Sam Doner is represented by his daughter, Gwendolyn Cox. Thank you, Gwendolyn. Ernest Hendon, who is watching in Tuskegee, is represented by his brother, North Hendon. Thank you, sir, for being here.

And George Key is represented by his grandson, Christopher Monroe. Thank you, Chris.

I also acknowledge the families, community leaders, teachers and students watching today by satellite from Tuskegee. The White House is the people's house; we are glad to have all of you here today. I thank Dr. David Satcher for his role in this. I thank Congresswoman Waters and Congressman Hilliard, Congressman Stokes, the entire Congressional Black Caucus. Dr. Satcher, members of the Cabinet who are here, Secretary Herman, Secretary Slater, members of the Cabinet who are here, Secretary Herman, Secretary Slater. A great friend of freedom, Fred Gray, thank you for fighting this long battle all these long years.

The eight men who are survivors of the syphilis study at Tuskegee are a living link to a time not so very long ago that many Americans would prefer not to remember, but we dare not forget. It was a time when our nation failed to live up to its ideals, when our nation broke the trust with our people that is the very foundation of our democracy. It is not only in remembering that shameful past that we can make amends and repair our nation, but it is in remembering that past that we can build a better present and a better future. And without remembering it, we cannot make amends and we cannot go forward.

So today America does remember the hundreds of men used in research without their knowledge and consent. We remember them and their family members. Men who were poor and African American, without resources and with few alternatives, they believed they had found hope when they were offered free medical care by the United States Public Health Service.

They were betrayed.

Medical people are supposed to help when we need care but even once a cure was discovered, they were denied help, and they were lied to by their government. Our government is supposed to protect the rights of its citizens; their rights were trampled upon. Forty years, hundreds of men betrayed, along with their wives and children, along with the community in Macon County, Alabama, the City of Tuskegee, the fine university there, and the larger African American community.

The United States government did something that was wrong—deeply, profoundly, morally wrong. It was an outrage to our commitment to integrity and equality for all our citizens.

To the survivors, to the wives and family members, the children and the grandchildren, I say what you know: No power on Earth can give you back the lives lost, the pain suffered, the years of internal torment and anguish. What was done cannot be undone. But we can end the silence. We can stop turning our heads away. We can look at you in the eye and finally say on behalf of the American people, what the United States government did was shameful, and I am sorry.

The American people are sorry—for the loss, for the years of hurt. You did nothing wrong, but you were grievously wronged. I apologize and I am sorry that this apology has been so long in coming.

To Macon County, to Tuskegee, to the doctors who have been wrongly associated with the events there, you have our apology, as well. To our African American citizens, I am sorry that your federal government orchestrated a study so clearly racist. That can never be allowed to happen again. It is against everything our country stands for and what we must stand against is what it was.

So let us resolve to hold forever in our hearts and minds the memory of a time not long ago in Macon County, Alabama, so that we can always see how adrift we can become when the rights of any citizens are neglected, ignored and betrayed. And let us resolve here and now to move forward together.

The legacy of the study at Tuskegee has reached far and deep, in ways that hurt our progress and divide our nation. We cannot be one America when a whole segment of our nation has no trust in America. An apology is the first step, and we take it with a commitment to rebuild that broken trust. We can begin by making sure there is never again another episode like this one. We need to do more to ensure that medical research practices are sound and ethical, and that researchers work more closely with communities.

Today I would like to announce several steps to help us achieve these goals. First, we will help to build that lasting memorial at Tuskegee. (Applause.) The school founded by Booker T. Washington, distinguished by the renowned scientist George Washington Carver and so many others who advanced the health and well-being of African Americans and all Americans, is a fitting site. The Department of Health and Human Services will award a planning grant so the school can pursue establishing a center for bioethics in research and health care. The center will serve as a museum of the study and support efforts to address its legacy and strengthen bioethics training.

Second, we commit to increase our community involvement so that we may begin restoring lost trust. The study at Tuskegee served to sow distrust of our medical institutions, especially where research is involved. Since the study was halted, abuses have been checked by making informed consent and local review mandatory in federally-funded and mandated research.

Still, 25 years later, many medical studies have little African American participation and African American organ donors are few. This impedes efforts to conduct promising

research and to provide the best health care to all our people, including African Americans. So today, I'm directing the Secretary of Health and Human Services, Donna Shalala, to issue a report in 180 days about how we can best involve communities, especially minority communities, in research and health care. You must—every American group must be involved in medical research in ways that are positive. We have put the curse behind us; now we must bring the benefits to all Americans.

Third, we commit to strengthen researchers' training in bioethics. We are constantly working on making breakthroughs in protecting the health of our people and in vanquishing diseases. But all our people must be assured that their rights and dignity will be respected as new drugs, treatments and therapies are tested and used. So I am directing Secretary Shalala to work in partnership with higher education to prepare training materials for medical researchers. They will be available in a year. They will help researchers build on core ethical principles of respect for individuals, justice and informed consent, and advise them on how to use these principles effectively in diverse populations.

Fourth, to increase and broaden our understanding of ethical issues and clinical research, we commit to providing postgraduate fellowships to train bioethicists especially among African Americans and other minority groups. HHS will offer these fellowships beginning in September of 1998 to promising students enrolled in bioethics graduate programs.

And, finally, by executive order I am also today extending the charter of the National Bioethics Advisory Commission to October of 1999. The need for this commission is clear. We must be able to call on the thoughtful, collective wisdom of experts and community representatives to find ways to further strengthen our protections for subjects in human research.

We face a challenge in our time. Science and technology are rapidly changing our lives with the promise of making us much healthier, much more productive and more prosperous. But with these changes we must work harder to see that as we advance we don't leave behind our conscience. No ground is gained and, indeed, much is lost if we lose our moral bearings in the name of progress.

The people who ran the study at Tuskegee diminished the stature of man by abandoning the most basic ethical precepts. They forgot their pledge to heal and repair. They had the power to heal the survivors and all the others and they did not. Today, all we can do is apologize. But you have the power, for only you—Mr. Shaw, the others who are here, the family members who are with us in Tuskegee—only you have the power to forgive. Your presence here shows us that you have chosen a better path than your government did so long ago. You have not

President Bill Clinton and Vice President Al Gore meet with Herman Shaw, one of the victims of the Tuskegee Syphilis Study, on May 16, 1997. Clinton issued an apology to all of the study's participants. AP/WIDE WORLD PHOTOS. REPRODUCED BY PERMISSION.

withheld the power to forgive. I hope today and tomorrow every American will remember your lesson and live by it.

Thank you, and God bless you.

SIGNIFICANCE

In the aftermath of the revelations, calls for government investigations, reparations, and apologies were met with Congressional hearings. The Henderson Act of 1943 had required that all forms of venereal disease be documented and treated; the U.S. Surgeon General had sent letters of commendation to men enrolled in the study on its twenty-fifth anniversary in 1957; and the study violated the 1964 World Health Organization's Declaration of Helsinki, in which informed consent is required. All of these events pointed to a level of government involvement and neglect that led the National Association for the Advancement of Colored People (NAACP) to file a 1973 class-action lawsuit; in the end, survivors and enrollees' families received over nine million U.S. dollars in a settlement.

Prominent African-American leaders initially stated that the Tuskegee Experiment was perpetrated against African-American men by only white medical staff. While most of the clinicians who administered the study were white, one of the primary nurses involved in the study, Eunice Rivers, was an African-American woman who worked on the study for nearly forty years. In addition, from 1947 until its end, over 127 African-American medical students were involved in the project; African-American medical professionals' involvement in the mistreatment of African-American syphilis patients complicated the racist overtones of the study.

President Bill Clinton's apology was part of an effort on the part of the Clinton administration to reach out to African-American voters and to correct the omission of an apology from the federal government. In 1997, when President Clinton issued his apology, only 8 of the 399 study participants who had syphilis were still alive.

The primary legacy of the Tuskegee Experiment is African-American distrust of the medical establishment in the United States. The Tuskegee Experiment, in conjunction with such policies as forced sterilization from the 1920s through the 1970s in some states, created an atmosphere of fear and distrust among many minorities toward medical professionals and medical treatments. Public health officials believe that this distrust inhibits many low-income and minority patients from seeking early or preventive treatment, leading to higher morbidity and mortality rates.

FURTHER RESOURCES
Books
Jones, James H. *Bad Blood: The Tuskegee Syphilis Experiment.* Free Press, 1993.

Reverby, Susan M. *Tuskegee's Truths: Rethinking the Tuskegee Syphilis Study.* University of North Carolina Press, 2000.

Wailoo, Keith. *Drawing Blood: Technology and Disease Identity in Twentieth-Century America.* The Johns Hopkins University Press, 1999.

Web sites
Center for Disease Control and Prevention. "Tuskegee Syphilis Study." <http://www.cdc.gov/nchstp/od/tuskegee/> (accessed April 26, 2006).

Medical News Today. "Beliefs May Hinder HIV Prevention Among Africn-Americans." January 26, 2005. <http://www.medicalnewstoday.com/medicalnews.php?newsid=19276> (accessed April 26, 2006).

University of Virginia Health System. "Final Report of The Tuskegee Syphilis Study Legacy." <http://www.healthsystem.virginia.edu/internet/library/historical/medical_history/bad_blood/report.cfm> (accessed April 26, 2006).

Aid for Africa Development

Photograph

By: Antony Njuguna

Date: June 28, 2002

Source: © Reuters/Corbis.

About the Photographer: Antony Njuguna is a photographer with Reuters, a worldwide news agency. This photograph is part of the collection of the Corbis Corporation, headquartered in Seattle, with a worldwide archive of over seventy million images.

INTRODUCTION

Poverty is more severe in Africa than on any other continent. As of 2001, for example, 617 million people in sub-Saharan Africa survive on an average of seventy-five US cents per day. Increasingly, the poor of Africa live in vast slums built around large cities. This picture shows a lane in what is probably Kibera, Africa's largest slum. The area is home to between 500,000 and 750,000 people, one of 199 slums that surround Nairobi, Kenya's capital city. Forty-six percent of Nairobi's 3.5 million inhabitants—1.6 million people—live in slums, and forty-four percent of those live in Kibera. With about 3,000 people per hectare, Kibera may have the highest population density of any urban area in the world, according to Alioune Badiane, director of the U.N. Human Settlements Program. Most homes consist of a single room with dried mud walls, a mud floor, no windows, no toilet, no running water, no electricity, and a leaking roof. Nairobi's population is expected to double over the next twenty years.

One of the grimmest features of life in Kibera and other Nairobi slums can be seen in this photograph: the lack of any sanitation or drainage system. Human waste accumulates in the middle of every narrow lane and turns to a stew of sewage, garbage, and mud in the rainy season. In the Nairobi slum called Laina Saba, there were ten pit latrines for 40,000 people in 2002; about 4,000 would be appropriate for this many people. The open sewers breed malarial mosquitoes, typhoid, worm infestations, skin diseases, and other illnesses. Children brain-damaged from sniffing industrial solvents terrorize drivers that traverse the few passable roads through the slum by holding up handfuls of human excrement and threatening to throw them in the car if the driver does not give them money.

Incredibly, most of the structures in the slums are owned by landlords, almost sixty percent of whom are

PRIMARY SOURCE

Aid for Africa Development: A Kenyan slum dweller walks on the side of a road, with sewage and trash running down the street in the impoverished Kibera slums, outside Nairobi, Kenya on June 28, 2002. © REUTERS/CORBIS.

politicians or government officials. A 2001 statement by the Kenyan President Daniel arap Moi suggesting that slum landlords cut their rents in half led to major violence. When residents began to withhold rent, the police moved in, attacking homes and shops, stealing goods and money, beating residents, and allegedly raping residents.

Extreme immiserization of this kind, fairly common in sub-Saharan Africa, prompted African leaders to initiate an aid-and-development program in the early 2000s called the New Partnership for Africa's Development (NEPAD). In June 2002, NEPAD was endorsed by the Group of Eight (G8): Canada, France, Germany, Italy, Japan, the United Kingdom, the United States, and the Russian Federation, who promised financial aid to Africa as part of their endorsement.

PRIMARY SOURCE

Aid for Africa Development

See primary source image.

SIGNIFICANCE

The slums of Nairobi are a legacy of historic discrimination. Kenya was ruled by the United Kingdom from the 1890s to the 1950s[LG1], during which time official policies allocated land separately to Africans, Asians, and Europeans, with Africans receiving the poorest parcels. Today's slums have developed directly from the old African enclaves, although they are vastly more populous. For decades, the Kenyan government's response to the slums has been to simply demolish blocks of dwellings occasionally and hope that their residents would somehow go away. Instead, having nowhere to go, the dwellers rebuilt. It was only in 1996 that the Kenyan government and the city council of Nairobi officially abandoned the demolition method in favor of working with foreign-based nongovernmental organizations to form the Nairobi Informal Settlements Coordinating Committee to provide basic services to the slums. However, in 2004 the government announced plans to demolish much of Kibera to construct a bypass highway, a move that would leave approximately 350,000 people homeless. Construction was still on hold as of early 2006.

NEPAD has been widely criticized as inadequate. For example, the 2002 G8 summit allocated only $1 billion for debt relief (cancellation of debts owed by African governments to foreign financial institutions and governments) for all of Africa—about the cost of a single space shuttle launch. The only initiative at the summit regarding water supplies—an increasingly critical problem—involved privatization, that is, transfer of control of water supplies to private, for-profit companies. Privatization makes access to water even harder for the poorest of the poor, who in Africa have little or no money. The G8 endorsement of NEPAD was widely praised by government officials of participating nations, but the president of Oxfam International, one of the world's largest anti-poverty charity groups, said that the G8 nations had in effect "turned their backs on Africa."

Other organizations are also trying to help Africa. For example, the U.N. Human Settlements Program, the U.N. Children's Fund, and several private groups are working to improve basic conditions in Kibera and the other slums of Nairobi. Goals include the construction of pit latrines and the provision of safe drinking water.

The construction of better housing is the only way to replace the slums themselves. However, there are obstacles. Nairobi slum landlords, about half of whom are government officials, sometimes own as many as 1,000 dwellings apiece and reap high profits; they therefore form a constituency which has a straightforward interest in the slums' continued existence. In Nairobi, across Africa, and indeed around the world, indifference to suffering combines with financial interest in the status quo to perpetuate inequity.

FURTHER RESOURCES
Web sites

BBC News. "Bypass Threat to Nairobi's Giant Slum." April 30, 2004. <http://news.bbc.co.uk/2/hi/africa/3671837.stm> (accessed April 12, 2006).

BBC News. "Nairobi Slum Life: Kibera's Children." Oct. 10, 2002. <http://news.bbc.co.uk/2/hi/africa/2297265.stm> (accessed April 12, 2006).

United Nations Economic Partnership for Africa. UN Regional Consultations on NEPAD. "Summary Report of the first NEPAD Multi-Stakeholder Dialogue: Sandton, South Africa, 22–23 October, 2004.". <http://www.uneca.org/unregionalconsultations/documents/report_multistakeholder.htm> (accessed April 7, 2006).

Water: Two Billion People Are Dying for It

Photograph

By: Amit Dave

Date: June 1, 2003

Source: © Reuters/Corbis.

About the Photographer: Amit Dave is a photographer for Reuters, a worldwide news agency. This photo is part of the Corbis Corporation collection, whose worldwide archive contains over seventy million images.

INTRODUCTION

Areas of Pakistan and India suffered a protracted drought in the early 2000s. This image shows inhabitants of the village of Natwargadh in the state of Gujarat, western India, gathered around a large communal well on June 1, 2003. Temperatures rose as high as 111° F as people were forced to walk long distances—sometimes miles—to get drinking water.

The drought broke in July 2003, about a month after this picture was taken, when massive monsoon season rains swept the region. Suddenly floods and polluted water supplies were the problem rather than insufficient water; about 300 people drowned in India and Bangladesh, 300,000 were made homeless, and, when sewage mixed with rain water, 50,000 were sickened and 300 died in India's Assam province.

■ PRIMARY SOURCE

WATER: TWO BILLION PEOPLE ARE DYING FOR IT
See primary source image.

SIGNIFICANCE

Fresh water is essential for survival and basic to human society: It is needed for crops, sanitation, drinking, cooking, washing, and industry. Water covers about 70 percent of the world's surface in the form of oceans, rivers, lakes, and ice caps, but only about 2.5 percent is fresh, and two-thirds of that amount is frozen in glaciers and ice caps. As much as twenty percent of the world's fresh liquid water is in the Amazon River basin. About seventy percent of human fresh water use goes to agriculture, both livestock and irrigation.

PRIMARY SOURCE

Water: Two Billion People Are Dying for It: Hundreds of people gather around a huge well in Natwarghad, a town in arid western India, in the hopes of retrieving some water during a serious drought. © REUTERS/CORBIS.

As population increases worldwide, fresh water supplies are increasingly stressed. The plight of the villagers in this photograph typifies that of many people where water is running short, particularly the Middle East, north Africa, and large parts of India and China. The United Nations has declared a crisis in global fresh water supplies and predicts that by 2025 two-thirds of the world's population could experience "stress conditions" of water scarcity, while 1.8 billion people could face severe water scarcity. Three billion had no access to sanitation (which requires water) in 2000, according to a UN study: One billion had no access to safe drinking water. About 5,000 children a day die worldwide from preventable waterborne diseases.

As water becomes scarce, food supplies are endangered. Farmers can reduce water waste with more precise sprinklers and drip irrigation systems, which deliver water directly to crop roots rather than saturating whole areas of land. However, irrigation can have intrinsic long-term problems as well. When water is delivered to a land area and then evaporated from it, whatever minerals were dissolved in it—including salt—stay in the soil. If insufficient rain fails to dissolve the salt and wash it away, it accumulates, eventually rendering the soil unfit for crops.

Global climate change is likely to worsen the situation. In 2006, scientists at the Africa Earth Observatory Network released a study noting that the parts of the world already shortest on water are most likely to see a reduction in rainfall. They also found that seemingly small rainfall reductions can have a disproportionate effect on surface water supplies: In regions of Africa receiving 500 millimeters of rain annually, a ten percent reduction in precipitation

In the midst of the worst drought in over a decade, an Indian woman tries to collect water from the local well near the village of Natwarghad in western India, June 2003. © REUTERS/CORBIS.

would cut surface water in half. Water refugees and even water wars—military struggles over water supplies—may occur as water becomes scarce. Indeed, the Israeli/Palestinian conflict may already be partly a water war: Aquifers in the West Bank are currently processed through Israel's water system and distributed throughout the region. Any reduction in (or charge for) water from the West Bank might present a major crisis.

In 2003 the General Assembly declared 2005–2015 the "Water for Life" decade. During this time, the UN hopes "to reduce by half the proportion of people without access to safe drinking water … and to stop unsustainable exploitation of water resources." The basic problem, according to the UN, is not one of absolute water shortage, but of mismanaging what is available. Through improved management, much suffering can be alleviated, even as the planet's population continues to grow.

FURTHER RESOURCES
Web sites

BBC News. "World's Drinking Water Running Out." Dec. 15, 1999. <http://news.bbc.co.uk/1/hi/world/americas/566809.stm> (accessed April 12, 2006).

BBC News. "Food at Risk as Water Drips Away." July 17, 1999. <http://news.bbc.co.uk/1/hi/sci/tech/396270.stm> (accessed April 12, 2006).

United Nations–Water. ".International Decade for Action: Water for Life, 2005–2015". < http://www.un.org/waterforlifedecade/index.html gt; (accessed April 12, 2006).

Reuters Alertnet. "Climate Change to Create African [Water Refugees]—Scientists." (March 22, 2006) <http://www.alertnet.org/thefacts/reliefresources/114303555233> (accessed April 12, 2006).

Act for the Relief of the Parents of Theresa Marie Schiavo

Legislation

By: United States Congress

Date: March 19, 2005

Source: 109th United States Congress. Act for the Relief of the Parents of Theresa Marie Schiavo. S. 653. March 17, 2005.

About the Author: The 109th Congress convened for two sessions during its tenure from January 2005 to January 2007. The Republican Party held a majority of seats in the 109th Congress.

INTRODUCTION

When Theresa Marie Schindler Schiavo died on March 31, 2005, at the age of forty-one, she was at the center of a legal battle that had spanned seven years and incited political, ethical, and religious debate around the world. It was the longest right to die case in American history. The legal wrangling centered around whether or not Terri Schiavo was in a persistent vegetative state (PVS), whether she had irreversible brain damage and to what degree, and whether or not she would have wished to have her life prolonged by artificial means. In the end, her husband, who had asserted throughout that she would not have wanted to remain alive in her current state, won the right to have her feeding tube removed, and artificial feeding and hydration withdrawn. Schiavo died thirteen days after her feeding tube was removed.

Although there is some level of controversy surrounding the circumstances that caused the initial event, there is no doubt that Terri Schiavo experienced cardiac and respiratory arrest in the early morning hours of February 25, 1990. She was twenty-six years old. Her husband, Michael, reported being awakened by the sound of his wife falling to the floor. He found her unconscious and immediately called for emergency assistance. Schiavo was eventually resuscitated and taken to the hospital. However, her brain had been deprived of oxygen for about three quarters of an hour, and she remained in a deep coma for about ten weeks. Doctors later concluded that Schiavo remained in what is known as a persistent vegetative state: she was not conscious, she did not have volitional or purposeful movement, and she did not interact in a conscious or meaningful way with her environment or other people. The diagnosis of PVS was independently made by five different physicians, over the course of the first few years after the cardiac and respiratory arrests. The PVS was caused by the brain damage resulting from the extremely long period of oxygen deprivation to her brain—anoxic-ischemic encephalopathy, according to the autopsy report.

Schiavo's husband professed to know her wishes around the continuation of her life under circumstances in which she was not able to lead an independent existence. He spent years embroiled in legal cases with her parents, in which he asserted her right not to be kept alive when there was no reasonable or likely chance of recovery to a functional state.

Before Terri Schiavo's life ended, there had been vast amounts of media coverage, official acts of legislation, and commentary by sources as remote as Florida's Governor, the Pope, the United States Senate, the U.S. House of Representatives, the United States Congress, and the American President. Never before in American history had the private struggles of a family been made quite so public, for quite so long.

PRIMARY SOURCE

AN ACT For the relief of the parents of Theresa Marie Schiavo.

Be it enacted by the Senate and House of Representatives of the United States of America in Congress assembled,.

The United States District Court for the Middle District of Florida shall have jurisdiction to hear, determine, and render judgment on a suit or claim by or on behalf of Theresa Marie Schiavo for the alleged violation of any right of Theresa Marie Schiavo under the Constitution or laws of the United States relating to the withholding or withdrawal of food, fluids, or medical treatment necessary to sustain her life.

SEC. 2. PROCEDURE.

Any parent of Theresa Marie Schiavo shall have standing to bring a suit under this Act. The suit may be brought against any other person who was a party to State court proceedings relating to the withholding or withdrawal of food, fluids, or medical treatment necessary to sustain the life of Theresa Marie Schiavo, or who may act pursuant to a State court order authorizing or directing the withholding or withdrawal of food, fluids, or medical treatment necessary to sustain her life. In such a suit, the District Court shall determine de novo any claim of a violation of any right of Theresa Marie Schiavo within the scope of this Act, notwithstanding any prior State court determination and regardless of whether such a claim has previously been raised, considered, or decided in State court proceedings. The District Court shall entertain and determine the suit without any delay or abstention in favor of State court proceedings, and regardless of whether remedies available in the State courts have been exhausted.

SEC. 3. RELIEF.

After a determination of the merits of a suit brought under this Act, the District Court shall issue such declaratory and injunctive relief as may be necessary to protect the rights of Theresa Marie Schiavo under the Constitution and laws of the United States relating to the withholding or withdrawal of food, fluids, or medical treatment necessary to sustain her life.

SEC. 4. TIME FOR FILING.

Notwithstanding any other time limitation, any suit or claim under this Act shall be timely if filed within 30 days after the date of enactment of this Act.

SEC. 5. NO CHANGE OF SUBSTANTIVE RIGHTS.

Nothing in this Act shall be construed to create substantive rights not otherwise secured by the Constitution and laws of the United States or of the several States.

SEC. 6. NO EFFECT ON ASSISTING SUICIDE.

Nothing in this Act shall be construed to confer additional jurisdiction on any court to consider any claim related—.

1. to assisting suicide, or
2. a State law regarding assisting suicide.

SEC. 7. NO PRECEDENT FOR FUTURE LEGISLATION.

Nothing in this Act shall constitute a precedent with respect to future legislation, including the provision of private relief bills.

Nothing in this Act shall affect the rights of any person under the Patient Self-Determination Act of 1990.

On March 23, 2005, Christi Gourley stands in silence among a crowd with a piece of tape over her mouth in demonstration against euthanasing Terri Schiavo. AP IMAGES.

SEC. 9. SENSE OF THE CONGRESS.

It is the Sense of Congress that the 109th Congress should consider policies regarding the status and legal rights of incapacitated individuals who are incapable of making decisions concerning the provision, withholding, or withdrawal of foods, fluid, or medical care.

SIGNIFICANCE

After stabilization and recovery from her cardiac and respiratory arrests and ensuing coma, Schiavo was found to be unable to take hydration and nourishment orally, as she was unable to swallow voluntarily. As a result, she was given a percutaneous endoscopic gastrostomy (also called a PEG tube) in order to put nutrition and hydration directly into her digestive system. It was the placement of the PEG tube and the later requests by her husband, Michael Schiavo, to remove the tube that were the focal points of the controversy. Before all legal efforts ceased, there had been numerous court cases, the first of which was a malpractice case brought against Ms. Schiavo's previous physicians for failure to notice and appropriately respond to indications of her alleged eating disorder. The court cases, motions and appeals spanned local district, circuit, state, federal, and Supreme Court decisions. Governor Jeb Bush filed federal court papers supporting Schiavo's parents' endeavors to prevent removal of the PEG tube; various advocacy groups filed court petitions and briefs supporting them as well. It is very rare that a state governor becomes personally involved in a family medical matter. However, this case quickly rose from being a private family medical matter to the

status of a major international political and philosophical event.

The Florida House of Representatives enacted legislation referred to as "Terri's Law," allowing the governor to issue a stay preventing removal of nutrition and hydration tubes on a one-time basis. Various independent legal guardians were appointed by the court systems in order to assure that Ms. Schiavo's safety and well-being were properly considered. Among the many (in this instance, unsuccessful) legal precedents that were attempted in this case was one in which legislation was introduced by two Florida senators who proposed that artificial hydration and nutrition be mandatory in cases in which there was no Living Will in place, despite the wishes and beliefs held by next of kin or expressed by the patient and witnessed by others. Ultimately, "Terri's Law" was found by the Florida Supreme Court to be unconstitutional and was removed. Governor Bush petitioned the United States Supreme Court to overturn the ruling and re-institute "Terri's Law;" the U.S. Supreme Court refused the request to review the case.

In March of 2004, Pope John Paul II convened meetings regarding treatment of those considered to be in a persistent vegetative state and publicly decried any attempts to hasten the end of life by removal of artificial means of hydration and nutrition. This further raised the degree of public attention brought to the case of Terri Schiavo.

On March 17, 2005, the Schindlers were granted a Relief Act by the United States Government. The Relief Act was actually a "private bill" that applied solely to the Schiavo case. The United States Senate website refers to a private bill as one that "provides benefits to specified individuals (including corporate bodies). Individuals sometimes request relief through private legislation when administrative or legal remedies are exhausted. Many private bills deal with immigration—granting citizenship or permanent residency. Private bills may also be introduced for individuals who have claims again the government, veterans benefits claims, claims for military decorations, or taxation problems. The title of a private bill usually begins with the phrase, 'For the relief of....' If a private bill is passed in identical form by both houses of Congress and is signed by the President, it becomes a private law. On March 18, 2005, the PEG tube is removed from Terri Schiavo for the final time. Numerous appeals and attempts at legislation mandating re-insertion of the tube were filed, and all were denied. The tube remained out, and Terri Schiavo died on March 31, 2005. After the PEG tube was removed, there was a great deal of media attention focused both on the case and on the location of the hospice in which Schiavo was a patient. Threats were made against Michael Schiavo and his family, and arrests were made in connection with a plot to pay for Michael Schiavo's assassination.

Although there is still some debate regarding the legal and ethical decisions made in the case, some of the claims made against the diagnosis of PVS were silenced by the Medical examiner's autopsy report, in which statements were made regarding the permanent nature of Ms. Schiavo's brain damage, as well as the markedly decreased physical size of her brain. The Schiavo case renewed public discourse over whether there is a right to die. Public opinion remains sharply divided over whether to incorporate a right to die into U.S. law.

FURTHER RESOURCES

Books

Caplan, Arthur C., James J. McCartney, and Dominic A. Sisti. *The Case of Terri Schiavo: Ethics at the End of Life.* Amherst, New York: Prometheus Books, 2006.

Pearse, Richard L., Jr. *In Re: The Guardianship of Theresa Schiavo, An Incapacitated Person. Report of Guardian Ad Litem. Case No. 90-2908GD-003.* The Circuit Court for Pinellas County, Florida: Probate Division, December 29, 1998.

Schiavo, Michael & Michael Hirsch. *Terri: The Truth.* New York, New York: Dutton Adult, 2006.

Schindler, Mary, Robert Schindler, Suzanne Schindler Vitadamo & Bobby Schindler. *A Life That Matters: The Legacy of Terri Schiavo, A Lesson For Us All.* Clayton, Australia: Warner Books, 2006.

Periodicals

Annas, G.J. "Culture of life" politics at the bedside—the case of Terri Schiavo." *New England Journal of Medicine.* 352 (2005): 1710–1715.

Campo-Flores, Arian. "The Legacy of Terri Schiavo." *Newsweek.* April 4, 2005.

Editorial Opinion. "The sacred and the secular: the life and death of Terri Schiavo." *Canadian Medical Association Journal.* 172(9) (2005): 1149.

Web sites

Medical Examiner, District Six, Pasco & Pinellas Counties. "Report of Autopsy: Schiavo, Theresa." Date of Autopsy: April 01, 2005. <http://www.abstractappeal.com/schiavo/autopsyreport.pdf> (accessed April 28, 2006).

United States Senate. "Legislation, Laws and Acts: Chapter 1: Bills." <http://www.senate.gov/pagelayout/legislative/d_three_sections_with_teasers/bills.htm> (accessed April 28, 2006).

An Act to Provide Compensation to the Persons Sterilized Through the State's Eugenic Sterilization

Legislation

By: Larry Womble and Earl Jones

Date: July 1, 2005

Source: General Assembly of North Carolina. "An Act to Provide Compensation to the Persons Sterilized Through the State's Eugenic Sterilization." Session 2005. H1607, July 1, 2005.

About the Author: Democratic Representative Larry Womble, representing the Forsyth district in the General Assembly of North Carolina, and Democratic Representative Earl Jones of Guildford cosponsored the Sterilization Compensation bill, the first legislative act on the part of any state in the United States to make reparations for forced sterilization programs dating from the 1920s to the 1970s.

INTRODUCTION

Compulsory sterilization laws were in effect in the United States in thirty-three states from the beginning of the twentieth century through the 1970s. With their roots in the eugenics movement, forced sterilizations and sterilizations performed without informed consent were part of a stated policy to remove the "feeble minded" from the gene pool.

The United States was the first country to use forced sterilization, though Germany and Sweden employed the practice as well. The eugenics movement reached its peak in the 1920s and 1930s. Selective breeding, according to eugenics theory, could produce healthier, more intelligent, and more capable human beings. American proponents of eugenics included Alexander Graham Bell, who studied deafness rates in Massachusetts and concluded that deafness was hereditary; as a result, deaf people ought to be discouraged from marrying and breeding.

In the mid 1800s, homes for the mentally retarded were established by states to house people with mental disabilities. Concerns arose that the sexually active women who lived in these homes would bear children out of wedlock. Within a few decades, eugenics proponents proposed that sterilization would prevent these women from becoming pregnant and bearing children.

In 1869, Francis Dalton's book *Hereditary Genius* was published. The book's central thesis—rather than being victim to the theory of natural selection, human beings could use artificial and intentional selection to give offspring the best genetic qualities—created the grounds for examining human traits with a goal of increasing those that were outstanding and discarding those that were undesirable. Selective breeding, according to eugenics theory, could elevate human beings and improve intelligence and talent in the population.

Forced sterilizations—tubal ligations and vasectomies performed on people against their will or without their informed consent—typically were done on men and women who were classified as mentally retarded, insane, deaf, blind, or epileptic. Minorities, such as African Americans and Native Americans, were targeted as well. A very small number of convicts were also forcibly sterilized, but that practice was outlawed in 1942.

In 1896, Connecticut enacted the first marriage law based on eugenics, prohibiting mentally retarded and epileptic persons from marrying. By the end of the eugenics movement in the United States, more than thirty states had enacted eugenics-based laws. In 1927, the U.S. Supreme Court ruled in the *Buck v. Bell* case that forced sterilization of the mentally retarded or "feeble minded" was legal for the protection of the state's interests. In 1942, the U.S. Supreme Court ruled in *Skinner v. Oklahoma* that compulsory sterilization could not be used as a punishment for crimes committed; Oklahoma sterilized people convicted of crimes that were "felonies involving moral turpitude" as part of a eugenics program to remove certain people from the gene pool.

Hitler's rise to power in Germany, his strident anti-Semitism, and his espousal of eugenics to build a "master race," resulted in the forced sterilization of more than 400,000 Germans. As a result of Hitler's diabolical uses of eugenics, the movement's popularity had declined rapidly by the end of the 1940s. However, forced sterilization laws remained in effect in some states, such as Virginia and North Carolina, into the mid-1970s.

◾ PRIMARY SOURCE

Whereas, during the early part of the 20th century, social reformers advocated eugenic sterilization as a solution to problems such as mental retardation and mental illness; and.

Whereas, in 1907, Indiana was the first state to pass a eugenic sterilization program, and eventually more than 30 states passed these laws, with North Carolina following in 1929; and.

Whereas, from 1933 to 1974, North Carolina's Eugenics Board reviewed petitions for sterilizations, and sterilizations were ordered in more than 90% of the cases before the Board; and.

Whereas, researchers estimate that more than 7,600 people were sterilized in North Carolina between 1929 and 1974, ranking North Carolina third among the states operating eugenic sterilization programs; and.

Whereas, while most states sharply curtailed their sterilization programs after World War II, nearly four-fifths of sterilizations in North Carolina were performed after 1945, and by the late 1960s, more than 60% of those persons sterilized in the State were black and 99% were female; and.

Whereas, the governors of Virginia, Oregon, South Carolina, and North Carolina have issued apologies for these forced sterilizations, and Governor Michael F. Easley established a committee to investigate the eugenics program and consider compensation or counseling services for these persons; and.

Whereas, the General Assembly finds that persons sterilized as a result of the State's eugenics sterilization program should be compensated; Now, therefore,.

The General Assembly of North Carolina enacts:.

SECTION 1.(a) Any person who, as a result of the eugenic sterilization program in this State, was sterilized between the years 1929 and 1975 shall receive compensation as provided for in this section if the person submits a claim before June 30, 2009.

SECTION 1.(b) A claim under this section may be submitted to the Department of Health and Human Services. The claim shall be supported by appropriate verification and information as determined by the Department.

SECTION 1.(c) The Department shall determine the eligibility of a claimant to receive the compensation authorized by this section. The Department shall notify the claimant by mail of its determination regarding the claimant's eligibility.

SECTION 1.(d) The Department shall adopt rules that will assist in the fair determination of eligibility and the processing of claims. The Department, however, shall not be obligated to notify any person of possible eligibility for compensation.

SECTION 1.(e) A claimant under this section who is determined eligible by the Department shall receive twenty thousand dollars ($20,000). All claims which the Department determines are eligible for compensation

Rose Brooks and Jesse Meadows participate in the unveiling of a roadside historical marker, Thursday, May 2, 2002, in Charlottesville, Virginia. The marker commemerates Carrie Buck's forcible sterilization by the state of Virginia because she was considered "genetically inferior," an example of eugenics judged by the Supreme Court to be legal in the famous case Buck v. Bell (1927). AP IMAGES.

shall be immediately forwarded to the State Treasurer, who shall issue warrants in the appropriate amounts upon demand and verification of identity. If a claimant dies after filing a claim but before receiving payment, payments shall be made to the claimant's estate upon demand and verification of identity.

SECTION 2. There is established the Eugenic Sterilization Compensation Fund. Funds appropriated to this Fund shall not revert until the claims verified by the Department of Health and Human Services under Section 1 of this act are paid. The Fund shall be kept on deposit with the State Treasurer, as in the case of other State funds, and may be invested by the State Treasurer in any lawful security for the investment of State money. The Fund is subject to the oversight of the State Auditor pursuant to Article 5A of Chapter 147 of the General Statutes.

SECTION 3.(a) The Department of Health and Human Services shall report its estimate of the cost of providing health care, counseling, and educational assistance required as a result of sterilization under the State's eugenic sterilization program, to those persons who are eligible for compensation under this act. The Department shall report the result of its findings to the House of Representatives Appropriations Subcommittee on Health and Human Services, the Senate Appropriations Committee on Health and Human Services, and the Fiscal Research Division on or before January 1, 2006.

SECTION 3.(b) It is the intent of the General Assembly after receiving cost estimates to provide appropriate health care coverage, counseling, and educational assistance to persons who receive compensation under Section 1 of this act.

SECTION 4. There is appropriated from the General Fund to the State Treasurer the sum of sixty-nine million one hundred thousand dollars ($69,100,000) for the 2005–2006 fiscal year to fund the Eugenic Sterilization Compensation Fund. There is appropriated from the General Fund to the Department of Health and Human Services the sum of one hundred sixty-five thousand dollars ($165,000) for the 2005–2006 fiscal year and the sum of one hundred sixty-five thousand dollars ($165,000) for the 2006–2007 fiscal year to administer Section 1 of this act. There is appropriated from the General Fund to the Department of Health and Human Services the sum of fifty thousand dollars ($50,000) for the 2005–2006 fiscal year to implement Section 3 of this act.

SECTION 5. This act becomes effective July 1, 2005.

SIGNIFICANCE

In 2002, the *Winston-Salem Journal* published a series of articles that examined the North Carolina compulsory sterilization program. As the bill states, "more than 60% of those persons sterilized in the State were black and 99% were female." Slightly fewer than half of the estimated 7,600 people sterilized in North Carolina were still alive as of 2003, and state representatives Larry Wobble and Earl Jones cosponsored legislation to provide compensation.

Canada and Sweden both created extensive compensation funds for victims of forced sterilizations. In Sweden, claimants must prove that they did not provide permission for the sterilization procedure. The North Carolina Sterilization Compensation bill does not require such proof; claimants simply must prove that they were sterilized by the state. In some instances African-American girls as young as ten years of age were sterilized in North Carolina. North Carolina's compensation plan is the first in the country. Only Virginia and California performed more sterilizations than North Carolina.

In 2002, two stories concerning ongoing forced sterilizations became public. In Peru, during the presi-

dency of Alberto Fujimori, a government campaign was instituted in which more than 230,000 peasants were pressured to undergo sterilization between 1996 and 2000, leading to a dramatic rise in Peru's sterilization rates. Fujimori's government offered incentives such as food rations, and those who refused were threatened with fines. In Czechoslovakia, the Roma, or gypsy population, was subjected to forced sterilization during the Communist era. In 2002, news articles revealed that Roma sterilizations persisted long after the 1989 revolution that ended Communist rule. As in Peru, the Roma women were given incorrect information, threatened or intimidated, and given no legal recourse. While revelations that North Carolina's program continued as late as 1974 shocked American readers, the evidence indicates that forced sterilization continues to be used by some governments into the twenty-first century.

FURTHER RESOURCES

Books

Black, Edwin. *War Against the Weak: Eugenics and America's Campaign to Create a Master Race*. New York: Four Walls Eight Windows, 2004.

Bruinius, Harry. *Better for All the World: The Secret History of Forced Sterilization and America's Quest for Racial Purity*. New York: Knopf, 2006.

Web sites

BBC News. "Mass Sterilization Scandal Shocks Peru." <http://news.bbc.co.uk/1/hi/world/americas/2148793.stm> (accessed April 29, 2006).

CNN. "Swedish Panel Urges Compensation for Forced Sterilization Victims." <http://www.cnn.com/HEALTH/9901/26/sweden.sterilization/> (accessed April 29, 2006).

Eugenics Archive. "The Image Archive on the American Eugenics Movement." <http://www.eugenicsarchive.org/eugenics/> (accessed April 29, 2006).

Guardian Unlimited. "Gypsies Fight for Justice Over Forced Sterilization." <http://observer.guardian.co.uk/international/story/0,6903,1489524,00.html> (accessed April 29, 2006).

Labor and Working Conditions

Labor and Working Conditions

The United Nations Universal Declaration of Human Rights, Article 23, asserts that all persons have a right to work. Persons have the right to choose a field of employment, to receive fair and just compensation for their services, and to work in safe conditions. All laborers within an organization have the right to equal pay for equal work. The Universal Declaration further proclaims that workers have a right to organize into representative trade unions.

Throughout the world, all principals of Article 23 have yet to be realized. Sweatshops are as common now as they were at the turn of twentieth century, though almost all are now located in developing nations. Inhumane working conditions and low pay are all too common. Many workers are denied the right to organize, curtailing their ability to protest unfair wage and working conditions. Child labor (also addressed in *Children and Education*) continues in many parts of the word, despite being outlawed a century ago in Britain and the United States.

The factory is not the only venue of work prone to human rights abuses. Agricultural workers across the globe work long hours at physically demanding jobs for low pay. Even in the most developed nations, agricultural workers—many of whom are migrant workers or recent immigrants—enjoy a fraction of the legal protections offered to factory laborers.

Labor is also used as a form of punishment. "How Ireland Hid its Own Dirty Laundry" tells the story of Ireland's infamous Magdalene Laundries. The sweatshop laundries, most often run by the local Catholic Church, were staffed by prostitutes and young women who had given birth out of wedlock. Girls were often abandoned by their families to the care of the "asylums" and forced into silent, grueling labor. Another article included here discusses prison labor in Russian gulags. Forced labor or prison labor as a means of punishment, especially in the nineteenth and early twentieth centuries, is further addressed in the chapter *Imprisonment*.

Also included in this chapter are two articles on working conditions in the military. One article discusses the refusal to participate in military operations on the basis of conscious objection; another looks at the U.S. military's "stop-loss" policy issued in 2005. These two sources illustrate the most common exceptions to voluntary military service in the United States—the first through the draft of potential soldiers and the second by extending service obligations of current soldiers.

Finally, the article "Solidarity's First Congress" presents a compelling look at the potential political and social influence of trade unions. Solidarity led Poland's nationalist, pro-democracy reform movement in the 1980s and 1990s. The trade-union-turned-political-party sped the collapse of the Iron Curtain (the Soviet Union's network of communist satellite nations in Eastern Europe) and led the first democratic, independent Polish government in the post-Soviet era.

Labor Strikes and Their Effects on Society:

A Common Sense Discussion of the Rights and Relations of Labor and Capital

Book excerpt

By: Charles Henry Bliss

Date: 1902

Source: Bliss, Charles Henry. *Labor Strikes and Their Effects on Society: A Common Sense Discussion of the Rights and Relations of Labor and Capital.* Pensacola, Fla.: C. H. Bliss, 1902.

About the Author: Charles Henry Bliss (1860–1907) wrote several social policy essays. Many of his writings are maintained with the Florida Heritage Project.

INTRODUCTION

The struggle for labor rights and organization in the United States has been long and arduous. The history of labor organizations extends back to the founding days of the nation. The organizers and rebels who orchestrated the Boston Tea Party in 1773 were members of craft organizations. These craftsmen were pre-factory laborers with specific skills. Following the Revolutionary War (1775–1783), more craftsmen organized themselves. The first U.S. strike occurred in 1794, when New York printers used the phrase "pursuit of happiness" to demand shorter working hours. Two years later, cabinetmakers went on strike, demanding better pay and shorter hours. By the 1820s, unions began to take shape, and, by demanding ten- to twelve-hour working days, took up the struggle that would shape working conditions in the twentieth century.

Battles for labor rights continued, and, as industrialization expanded the number of factories and altered the skills required by the workers, more conflicts arose. From the 1880s through World War I (1914–1918), workers organized and developed a trade union system and political groups to protect their interests and promote their political goals. Initially, these unions formed according to trade and skill because many workers felt skilled labor was held in higher respect in society. Unskilled workers also organized themselves, and they subscribed to much the same ideology that skilled workers did. Both skilled and unskilled workers viewed their labor as essential to social growth, economic expansion, and economic productivity. However, businesspeople and company owners frequently resisted the growth of labor organizations.

Business owners largely felt that they should be able to pay their workers whatever wage they deemed appropriate. Also, these business owners subscribed to the same belief that the striking New York printers of 1794 did. They argued that their rights for happiness could not, and should not, be infringed upon by the working classes. The U.S. Congress acknowledged the need for labor regulation in 1884 with the formation of the Bureau of Labor.

In 1894, a labor dispute erupted that would shape the immediate future of labor laws. The 1894 Pullman Strike by railroad workers was broken when President Grover Cleveland (1837–1908) sent in the military. President Cleveland's use of military force traced its roots to the violent rail strikes of 1877. During those strikes, several workers died or were injured, and President Rutherford B. Hayes (1822–1893) used troops to prevent further destruction of the railroad lines. The 1877 and 1894 strikes contributed to the passage of the Erdman Act of 1898, which stipulated that the Commissioner of Labor and Chairman of the Interstate Commerce Commission would mediate strikes. The Erdman Act had not been tested when the coal strikes of 1900 and 1902 occurred.

The Coal Strike of 1900 occurred on the eve of a presidential election, and it also traced its roots to earlier strikes in the late 1890s. During the 1890s, an economic depression reduced wages, and mine owners hired large numbers of immigrants in an attempt to keep their wage costs low, thus angering many American miners. In addition, the hazardous nature of mining led many miners to demand higher wages. Concerned about the potential impact of the strike on the impending presidential election, Republican Senator Marcus A. Hanna acted as a mediator between the mine owners and the workers. Under this political pressure, the 1900 strike was settled. Coal operators posted pay increases and established a grievance procedure, but refused to recognize the union. The six-week strike ended just a week before the election, and William McKinley (1843–1901) was re-elected by a large margin.

The 1902 Coal Strike occurred for many of the same reasons as the 1900 strike. The miners demanded better pay, better working conditions, and union recognition. The coal companies maintained that they could not meet the miners demands because prices were low and an increase in wages would destroy their profit margins. On May 12, 1902, the miners struck. Initially the maintenance crews stayed on the job in the hope that a partial crew continuing to work would encourage the

A Manhattan ferry boat is packed with commuters on May 11, 1953, the result of a transit worker strike that closed the Hudson Tubes. © BETTMANN/CORBIS.

mine company to settle with the strikers. However, by June 2, the maintenance crews also joined the strike. The strikers became violent, and they attacked scabs (those working during the strike), scabs' families, and private police forces and armed guards. Theodore Roosevelt stepped in to settle the strike because he believed that both labor and the business owners had rights and responsibilities to the larger community.

On October 23, 1902, the 163-day strike officially ended. There were gains and concessions on both sides. The miners received a ten percent pay increase (they had asked for twenty percent), and the work day was set at nine hours (at a time when the standard work day was ten hours). Most importantly, both sides agreed that labor disputes should be brought to arbitration to prevent future strikes.

Even though the 1902 Coal Strike was settled with both the workers and mine owners relatively happy about the outcome, the fight for unions and labor rights continued to escalate. The popular press did not always portray labor disputes in a balanced manner. Writers like Charles Henry Bliss denounced strikers for interrupting production flow, and he (and others) argued that business owners should be able to pay their workers as they saw fit.

PRIMARY SOURCE

When strikes decree that no one shall work for another unless he belongs to their particular union or organization, they practically declare themselves a trust. In this case it is a labor trust. It is not anything but a trust for it seeks to attain the same end as do other trusts and by the same means. If there is any difference, the labor trust is the worse, for it seeks to interfere with the constitutional freedom of the individual and violates the fundamental principle of civil liberty.

The Constitution of the United States guarantees to each one life, liberty, and pursuit of happiness. But the strike organization steps in and says that anyone may pursue happiness providing he is a member of their particular union. In other words, the union asserts its authority to be above that of the Constitution of the United States. But that is not the worst of it for he usually cannot become a member of the union without paying a stipulated price, and if anyone for any reason sees fit to "blackball" him he cannot become a member of the union at all. So if the labor trust be permitted to exist and enforce its demands the constitutional liberty of many individuals would depend upon whether any striker was inclined to blackball him or not. That is constitutional liberty with a vengeance, yet it is precisely what is proposed by the striking fraternity.

I wish to state this matter in such language that the most obtuse of labor agitators may know exactly what I mean and for that reason I shall restate the matter in other language. Under the Constitution of the United States I am free to work for anyone that I may choose and on such terms as we may agree upon. It is nobody's business but our own and no one has any right to interfere in the matter. But the labor union steps in and asserts that I shall not work for whom I choose unless I am a union man and then only on such terms as they may dictate. It further says I cannot become a member of the union without first paying a stipulated price, no matter whether I am able to pay or not, and even then I cannot become a member unless the other members are willing. In this matter the labor trust instead of being a benefit to the workman it endeavors to destroy the liberty that is vouchsafed to him by the highest law of the country.

STRIKES INTERFERE WITH PROPERTY RIGHTS.

Sixth. It is not the intention to enter into an elaborate discussion of property rights but to make a few observations so that the point made will be clear and indisputable. The first right that one has is the right to life. Perhaps the next right that one has is the right to the means by which to live.

The means by which to live is a property right, and who shall say that it is not as sacred as the right to life itself, for what is the value of the right to life if one be deprived of the means to live? In fact who is able to draw the line between the two rights? How can one be said to have the right to live if he be deprived of the means of subsistence? It may be taken for granted that the property rights of the individual are just as sacred as the right to life itself.

Property exists in a multitude of forms. A man's property may consist of a quantity of corn. It is his and he alone has the authority to say what shall become of it. He may eat it or store it up for the future, or may sell it, or may give it away, or may feed it to the cattle of the street, or may cast it into the river, or do anything else that he pleases with it, so long as he does not infringe on the rights of others. If a man have money he has the right to keep it, give it away, spend it, invest it or do anything else that he may choose so long as he does not infringe on the rights of others. The workingman who has a dollar has a right to spend that dollar where, when and how he pleases, or keep it or dispose of it as he pleases. It is his property and no one has any right to dictate to him what he shall do with it. Any man who has a dollar or a number of dollars has the same right.

This is a beautiful theory and a beautiful practice but the striker asserts himself to change the order of things. He assumes to dictate to a man as to how he shall run his business and spend his money. He tells the man of money who he may or may not hire and what wage he shall pay him. This is an infringement on the constitutional property rights of the individual and the reason is sufficient to demand the abolition of the strike. The striker in interfering with the property rights of the individual attacks the very foundations upon which society is built.

SIGNIFICANCE

The 1902 Coal Strike marked the first time that the federal government intervened in a labor dispute as a peacemaker instead of as a strikebreaker. During the twentieth century, more strikes occurred, but the federal government did not always act as a peacemaker in these disputes. In 1908, the U.S. Supreme Court ruled against the American Federation of Labor's Hatters Union in the Danbury Hatters Case. The employees of Danbury hat manufacturer Dietrich Loewe struck when Loewe refused to recognize their union. Loewe hired scab workers to replace the strikers, causing the strikers to organize a secondary boycott against Loewe's products. Loewe then filed a suit against the union in compliance with the Sherman Antitrust Law of 1890. The suit alleged that the union restricted trade with its secondary boycott. The verdict in the Danbury Hatters Case levied a fine of $250,000 on the strikers, and, in 1915, the AFL organized Hatter's Day, asking its members to donate one hour of pay to raise money for the fine payment. The 1947 Taft-Hartley Act officially made secondary boycotts illegal.

Other laws that helped and hindered labor continued to be enacted throughout the twentieth century. In 1916, the Adamson Act mandated the eight-hour work day for the railroads. This act proved to be an important milestone because, through a series of strikes, the eight-hour day became accepted. The Fair-Labor Standards Act of 1938 reduced the work week to forty-four hours for interstate commerce, with another reduction to forty hours after two years of employment. Most importantly for the labor movement, the National Recovery Administration recognized the right of unions to exist and to negotiate with employers. Even though the NRA did not have an enforcement mechanism, many workers saw this recognition as a significant gain.

The gains of the early and mid-twentieth century benefited labor, but the fight for fair pay has not ended. Strikes continue to occur, and legislation, like the New York State Taylor Laws, prohibits public sector employees from striking. Public sector employees are allowed to join unions and to negotiate with employers, but if they strike they are subject to a variety of penalties, including fines, prison terms, and the loss of their jobs. A recent example of a labor dispute is the December 2004 Metropolitan Transit Authority strike in New York City. This three-day strike shut down the city's subway system, and labor leader Roger Toussaint received a ten-day jail sentence and a $1,000 fine for ordering the strike. As of May 2006, the MTA and its workers are still trying to devise a contract that suits the needs of all parties.

FURTHER RESOURCES

Books

Sanders, Elizabeth. *Roots of Reform: Farmers, Workers, and the American States, 1877–1917*. Chicago: The University of Chicago Press, 1999.

Zinn, Howard, Dana Frank, and Robin D. G. Kelley. *Three Strikes: Miners, Musicians, Salesgirls, and the Fighting Spirit of Labor's Last Century*. Boston: Beacon Press, 2001.

Periodicals

Barrett, James R. "Americanization From the Bottom Up: Immigration and the Remaking of the Working Class in the United States, 1880–1930." *Journal of American History* 79 (December 1992): 996–1020.

Hanes, Christopher, and John A. James. "Wage Adjustment Under Low Inflation: Evidence from U.S. History." *American Economic Review* 93 (November 2003): 1414–1424.

Web sites

U.S. Department of Labor. "The Coal Strike of 1902: Turning Point in U.S. Policy." <http://www.dol.gov/asp/programs/history/coalstrike.htm> (accessed April 28, 2006).

Keating-Owen Child Labor Act of 1916

Legislation

By: Edward Keating and Robert Owen

Date: December 6, 1915

Source: Sixty-fourth Congress of the U.S. "Keating-Owen Child Labor Act.". Keating-Owen Bill, 39 Stat. 675 (1916). Available online at <http://www.ourdocuments.gov/> (accessed April 24, 2006).

About the Author: Representatives Edward Keating of Colorado and Robert Owen of Oklahoma, both Democrats, co-sponsored the Keating-Owen Child Labor Act of 1916 after investigating child labor in manufacturing and industrial settings. This act was the first piece of federal legislation to address child labor practices in the United States.

INTRODUCTION

The concept of "child labor" as a distinct entity from adult labor resulted from the development of the factory system and industrialization in western Europe and the United States in the mid-nineteenth and early twentieth centuries. Before industrialization, children were part of the workflow of the family, on farms, in small shops, or hired out as domestic workers for needed wages in poorer homes. In all but the wealthiest families, by the time a child reached the age of four or five he or she would be expected to perform a variety of tasks, including caring for farm animals, finding fresh water, tending to fields, working with parents in retail shops or in skilled trades, or managing domestic tasks.

As the twin forces of industrialization and urbanization changed the structure of the family in the mid-nineteenth century, the concept of child labor changed. In textile factories children as young as five were used for loom work, small children worked in shipyards and mines. These children were paid a small percentage of the hourly rates adults earned. Nevertheless, poor families often relied on children's wages to get by in urban areas; in large families the older children and parents worked while girls as young as eight stayed home to care for babies and toddlers in the family.

Nineteenth century literary works such as Charles Dickens' *Oliver Twist* and Emile Zola's *Germinal* describe the plight of poor children in urban settings and in mining towns, with children dying from

A fourteen-year-old girl working as a spool tender in a Massachusetts cotton mill in 1916. AP IMAGES.

exhaustion, overwork, poor working conditions, and machinery accidents. By the turn of the twentieth century social reformers in the United States, working with immigrants and their children in inner city centers, targeted the issue of child labor as a major social problem for the country's children.

In parallel to the development of a factory system that used children's labor, many states passed compulsory education laws for children. In 1853, Massachusetts passed the first such statewide law, followed by New York in 1854. By 1918—two years after the Keating-Owen Child Labor Act took effect—all states had some form of compulsory education law in place. Despite the new laws, immigrant children—who were not bound by state laws in many instances—were least likely to attend school and most likely to be pushed into factory work as their families needed income.

In 1912, President William H. Taft created the Department of Labor's Children's Bureau, to track issues related to child labor and welfare. Following the issue of a Children's Bureau report on child labor, Democratic Representatives Edward Keating of Colorado and Robert Owen of Oklahoma crafted the language of the Keating-Owen Child Labor Act.

■ PRIMARY SOURCE

Sixty-fourth Congress of the United States of America; At the First Session, Begun and held at the City of Washington on Monday, the sixth day of December, one thousand nine hundred and fifteen. AN ACT To prevent interstate commerce in the products of child labor, and for other purposes.

Be it enacted by the Senate and House of Representatives of the United States of America in Congress assembled, That no producer, manufacturer, or dealer shall ship or deliver for shipment in interstate or foreign commerce, any article or commodity the product of any mine or quarry situated in the United States, in which within thirty days prior to the time of the removal of such product there from children under the age of sixteen years have been employed or permitted to work, or any article or commodity the product of any mill, cannery, workshop, factory, or manufacturing establishment, situated in the United States, in which within thirty days prior to the removal of such product there from children under the age of fourteen years have been employed or permitted to work, or children between the ages of fourteen years and sixteen years have been employed or permitted to work more than eight hours in any day, or more than six days in any week, or after the hour of seven o'clock postmeridian, or before the hour of six o'clock antemeridian: *Provided,* That a prosecution and conviction of a defendant for the shipment or delivery for shipment of any article or commodity under the conditions herein prohibited shall be a bar to any further prosecution against the same defendant for shipments or deliveries for shipment of any such article or commodity before the beginning of said prosecution.

SEC. 2. That the Attorney General, the Secretary of Commerce and the Secretary of Labor shall constitute a board to make and publish from time to time uniform rules and regulations for carrying out the provisions of this Act.

SEC. 3. That for the purpose of securing proper enforcement of this Act the Secretary of Labor, or any person duly authorized by him, shall have authority to enter and inspect at any time mines quarries, mills, canneries, workshops, factories, manufacturing establishments, and other places in which goods are produced or held for interstate commerce; and the Secretary of Labor shall have authority to employ such assistance for the purposes of this Act as may from time to time be authorized by appropriation or other law.

SEC. 4. That it shall be the duty of each district attorney to whom the Secretary of Labor shall report any violation of this Act, or to whom any State factory or mining or quarry inspector, commissioner of labor, State medical inspector or school-attendance officer, or any other person shall present satisfactory evidence of any such violation to cause appropriate proceedings to be commenced and prosecuted in the proper courts of the United States without delay for the enforcement of the penalties in such cases herein provided: *Provided,* That nothing in this Act shall be construed to apply to bona fide boys' and girls' canning clubs recognized by the Agricultural Department of the several States and of the United States.

SEC. 5. That any person who violates any of the provisions of section one of this Act, or who refuses or obstructs entry or inspection authorized by section three of this Act, shall for each offense prior to the first conviction of such person under the provisions of this Act, be punished by a fine of not more than $200, and shall for each offense subsequent to such conviction be punished by a fine of not

more than $1,000, nor less than $100, or by imprisonment for not more than three months, or by both such fine and imprisonment, in the discretion of the court: *Provided,* That no dealer shall be prosecuted under the provisions of this Act for a shipment, delivery for shipment, or transportation who establishes a guaranty issued by the person by whom the goods shipped or delivered for shipment or transportation were manufactured or produced, resident in the United States, to the effect that such goods were produced or manufactured in a mine or quarry in which within thirty days prior to their removal there from no children under the age of sixteen years were employed or permitted to work, or in a mill, cannery, workshop, factory, or manufacturing establishment in which within thirty days prior to the removal of such goods there from no children under the ages of fourteen years were employed or permitted to work, nor children between the ages of fourteen years and sixteen years employed or permitted to work more than eight hours in any day or more than six days in any week or after the hour of seven o'clock postmeridian or before the hour of six o'clock antemeridian; and in such event, if the guaranty contains any false statement or a material fact the guarantor shall be amenable to prosecution and to the fine or imprisonment provided by this section for violation of the provisions of this Act. Said guaranty, to afford the protection above provided, shall contain the name and address of the person giving the same: And provided further, That no producer, manufacturer, or dealer shall be prosecuted under this Act for the shipment, delivery for shipment, or transportation of a product of any mine, quarry, mill, cannery, workshop, factory, or manufacturing establishment, if the only employment therein within thirty days prior to the removal of such product there from, of a child under the age of sixteen years has been that of a child as to whom the producer, or manufacturer has in; good faith procured, at the time of employing such child, and has since in good faith relied upon and kept on file a certificate, issued in such form, under such conditions, and by such persons as may be prescribed by the board, showing the child to be of such an age that the shipment, delivery for shipment, or transportation was not prohibited by this Act. Any person who knowingly makes a false statement or presents false evidence in or in relation to any such certificate or application there for shall be amenable to prosecution and to the fine or imprisonment provided by this section for violations of this Act. In any State designated by the board, an employment certificate or other similar paper as to the age of the child, issued under the laws of that State and not inconsistent with the provisions of this Act, shall have the same force and effect as a certificate herein provided for.

SEC. 6. That the word "person" as used in this Act shall be construed to include any individual or corporation or the members of any partnership or other unincorporated association. The term "ship or deliver for shipment in interstate or foreign commerce" as used in this Act means to transport or to ship or deliver for shipment from any State or Territory or the District of Columbia to or through any other State or Territory or the District of Columbia or to any foreign country; and in the case of a dealer means only to transport or to ship or deliver for shipment from the State, Territory or district of manufacture or production.

SEC. 7. That this Act shall take effect from and after one year from the date of its passage.

Approved, September 1, 1916.

SIGNIFICANCE

Many states had child labor laws in place before the rapid industrialization of the late 1800s, and early trade unions, such as The Knights of Labor, advocated the abolition of child labor completely in the early 1870s. While some safeguards were in place to protect child laborers and encourage school attendance, children were largely at the mercy of parents and non-compliant employers.

Settlement house workers such as Lillian Wald, of Henry Street Settlement House in New York City, helped to establish the Children's Bureau and to argue that tighter regulation of compulsory schooling would help immigrant children to assimilate and to increase literacy rates in the United States. Photographer Lewis W. Hine was hired in 1908 by the National Child Labor Committee to travel across the country photographing children at work. From 1908 to 1912, he chronicled the lives of children working in factories, snapping photographs of children as young as three years old working long hours under poor conditions. When Hine published his first photo essay in 1909, the pictures garnered public sympathy and helped push for greater government involvement in controlling or eliminating child labor.

The Keating-Owen Child Labor Act established a minimum working age of fourteen (with exceptions for farm and family work), limited hours children could work, and attempted to regulate interstate commerce. The National Child Labor Committee hailed its passage, but in 1918 the United States Supreme Court, in *Hammer v. Dagenhart*, declared the Keating-Owen Child Labor Act unconstitutional on the grounds that it was overreaching in its attempts to regulate interstate commerce and that it did not permit a child to contract his or her own work.

Child labor activists continued to press for regulatory legislation, passing another child labor law in 1919 that was declared unconstitutional in 1922. In 1924, Congress passed a constitutional amendment that would have regulated child labor, but it was not ratified by a sufficient number of states.

During the Great Depression in the late 1920s and early 1930s, child labor rates dropped dramatically as adults, desperate for work, were willing to take jobs at the same low rate of pay as children. In 1938, twenty-three years after the Keating-Owen act had passed, Congress passed the Fair Labor Standards Act, which placed legal limits on child labor, permitting children thirteen and under to work for their parents or as babysitters, and placed specific hour limits on fourteen and fifteen year olds. Upheld in the courts, the Fair Labor Standards Act remains in force into the twenty-first century, as do compulsory schooling laws.

FURTHER RESOURCES

Books

Dubofsky, Melvyn. *Hard Work: The Making of Labor History.* Champaign, IL: University of Illinois Press, 2000.

Fantasia, Rick and Kim Voss. *Hard Work: Remaking the American Labor Movement.* University of California Press, 2004.

Hindman, Hugh D. *Child Labor: An American History.* M.E. Sharpe, 2002.

Web sites

Human Rights Watch. "Child Labor." <http://www.hrw.org/children/labor.htm> (accessed April 29, 2006).

Legal Recognition of Industrial Women

Pamphlet

By: Eleanor L. Lattimore

Date: 1919

Source: Lattimore, Eleanor L. *Legal Recognition of Industrial Women.* New York: Industrial Committee, War Work Council of the National Board of Young Women's Christian Associations, 1919.

About the Author: Eleanor L. Lattimore earned her doctorate degree in psychology from the University of Pennsylvania in 1916.

INTRODUCTION

Progressive Era reformers were most active between 1870 and 1920; highly educated reformers looked at such social issues as health, education, personal hygiene, childcare, maternity care and family planning, and the relationship between factory work, labor, and the family. Noted Progressive Era reformers such as Jane Addams and Lillian Wald established "settlement houses" for immigrants and the poor, where they offered a range of support services including food, medical care, shelter, and basic education. Organizations such as labor unions, children's protection societies, birth control and family planning groups, the National Association for the Advancement of Colored People, the National Women's Party, and professional groups including the American Medical Association all formed during this time.

While many female leaders in the Progressive Era focused on social issues directly related to the condition of women and children, other female leaders examined the role of women in the workforce, especially in industrial settings. Upton Sinclair's 1906 novel *The Jungle* exposed the living conditions for poor immigrants who worked in the Chicago stockyards and meat-packing plants; while the novel is famous for sparking food and safety legislation, the suffering experienced by women and children captured the hearts of Americans, and helped feed interest in social reform. The 1911 Triangle Shirtwaist Factory Fire, in which more than 140 women and girls died during a fire in a garment factory, sparked the rise of the International Ladies' Garment Workers' Union and brought greater attention to the role of women in factory work and the labor force in general.

By 1919, when *Legal Recognition of Industrial Women* was written, Congress had passed and President Woodrow Wilson had signed the 1916 Keating-Owen Child Labor Act, which provided protections for child labor in industrial settings. The United States Supreme Court had found the law unconstitutional in the 1918 decision *Hammer v. Dagenhart*. Other reform legislation protecting women and girls, such as mother's pensions, eight hour work days for women, and a minimum wage were sparked by female reformers in the parallel feminist movement which pushed for female suffrage.

As this excerpt from *Legal Recognition of Industrial Women* notes, many writers blended social reform with labor rights to open a dialogue into the role of the state in protecting female workers and their families.

PRIMARY SOURCE

...**Social Insurance.** There are six general classes of labor legislation: social insurance, minimum wage, hour regulations, safety, sanitation and health regulations, and

A World War I era poster encouraging women to join the workforce and support the war effort. © K.J. HISTORICAL/CORBIS.

child welfare laws. The most far-reaching of these groups is social insurance, which simply means that injuries and misfortunes are to be cared for by the community, and which applies to men, women and children. Workmen's compensation, health insurance, maternity benefits, mother's compensation are included in social insurance and are mutually dependent. Each kind of social insurance is administered separately and the expense of each is distributed differently.

(1) Workmen's compensation. Workmen's compensation laws in the United States were first passed in 1911, by Washington, Kansas and Wisconsin, though there had been attempts at some form of compensation laws since 1902. Thirty-five other states, the Federal Government, Porto Rico, Alaska and Hawaii have adopted compensation laws. Workmen's compensation should be compulsory and should cover all occupations, hazardous or non-hazardous. It is just, however, that "casual" labor be exempted, if it is carefully defined and limited. The application of the law is usually limited to workers receiving less than a certain salary, but the phrasing of that salary limit should take into consideration the rising cost of living and the underlying principle that the object

of compensation is not only the meeting of emergency expenses for illness, etc., but the maintenance of a proper standard of living.

It is evident that much depends upon the administration of compensation law, and so an industrial accident board should established. The expense of administration is borne by state, but the compensation is paid by the employer.

The justice of the claim that a workman injured in course of duty, through no fault of his own, is entitled to compensation, has not been denied, but courts have seldom granted damages, because of three defenses of the employer known as "assumed risk," "fellow servant," and "contributory negligence." The first means that when you take a job you do it voluntarily knowing the dangers involved and willing to take the risk. By "fellow servant" it is understood that the employer is not responsible if he can prove that the injury was due to the carelessness of any other of his employees. "Contributory negligence" is the court's way of saying that if the worker is in any way responsible for the accident, no matter what the other circumstances in the care are, he is not entitled to compensation. These three common law defenses arose before the days of factories and machinery, because of which workmen's compensation laws necessary. Courts have decided that workmen's compensation laws are constitutional, agreeing with the New York decision. "Surely it is competent for the State in the promotion of general welfare to require both employer and employee to yield something toward the establishment of a principle and a plan of compensation for their mutual protection and advantage."

(2) Health Insurance. Health insurance is a broadening of the principle and methods of the fraternal and labor benefit societies, so that all the people instead of only a few may receive needed help. Sweden was the first country to give state aid to the voluntary health associations. Compulsory health insurance exists in Great Britain, Norway, Sweden, Russia, Holland, Germany, Austria, Hungary, Roumania, Serbia and Luxemburg. In the United States, eight states, California, Connecticut, Illinois, Massachusetts, New Jersey, Ohio, Pennsylvania and Wisconsin, have appointed commissions to investigate health insurance, and bills providing for compulsory health insurance are before many state legislatures in 1919. To be effective, health insurance which is an extension of the principle and method of workmen's compensation, should be compulsory, the fund to be contributed by the employer, worker and the state. As with workmen's compensation, the law should be restricted to wage workers earning less than a given annual sum, but there should be no exceptions, and the dependents of the workers should be included. Health insurance supplements workmen's compensation by providing for occupational

diseases, very few of which have yet been interpreted as coming under the compensation laws.

Health insurance also will provide maternity benefits, both for insured women and the non-insured wives of insured men. Under an effective bill, both medical and nursing care and cash benefits should be included. Adequate provision should also be made, either through the administration of health insurance or through the health or educational branches of the state government, or through the state labor department or industrial commission, for full and well-directed health education in personal hygiene from an industrial standpoint, in the prevention and treatment of industrial disease (including of course first-aid instruction of a most practical kind), and in such principles of general community sanitation and public health as especially apply to industrial communities. Such educational effort should avail itself of all possible help from federal and state and private agencies who specialize in health education, but special attention should be devoted to the development of sound principles of maintaining health among industrial workers and their families.

Twenty-six weeks has been named provisionally as the period during which benefits are to be provided. The administration of health insurance should be through boards, consisting of employers and employed workers, with government supervision. Incomplete figures show in New York State alone an annual loss of $40,000.000 a year in wages because of sickness.

Present methods of dealing with this sickness problem are inadequate; charity and fraternal benefit societies reach a small minority of those needing help. A community spirit and better living conditions will follow the adoption and application of health insurance.

(3) Mother's Compensation. The form of social insurance most widely adopted as yet in the United States is mother's compensation. Its growth has been rapid, thirty states having made mother's pension or compensation provisions since 1911, although the sums allotted have been insufficient to fulfill their object, which is to make it possible for the mother to devote herself to the care of her children, instead of struggling along on heavy work and poor wages.

The laws have all taken the form of direct grants of money by the state, never more than $15.00 or $20.00 a month for one child. This sum, of course, cannot support one person, but it is a help. The plan of having the fund administered through the courts seems to have been satisfactory, though there should be a local board of child welfare to advise with the judge. Mother's compensation laws should be flexible, should permit the administrators to consider the welfare of the child, as does the Colorado law, for example, which reads, "to pay such parent or parents, or, if it seems *for the best interest of the child*, to some other person designated by the court for that purpose,"—

and in its final section, "This act shall be liberally construed for the protection of the child, the home and the state, and in the interest of the public morals, and for the prevention of poverty and crime." Mother's compensation scarcely needs discussion, since no one doubts that the future of society is dependent upon the children of today. As Judge Ben B. Lindsey says, "It is a recognition for the first time by society that the state is responsible, in a measure, for the plight of the mother."

What sickness means to an employer. One of the most serious industrial hazards an employer has to face is that of sickness on the part of his employees.

The absence of a workman, even for a short time, means an interruption of work—if piecework it means either that the progression of material through the factory is blocked by the lack of the workman to put in his particular bit of the process, or that the total production is decreased and machinery and equipment lie idle. Too much of this means loss of morale among employes, which every employer deplores.

If the illness is long or death occurs and the vacant place must be filled time and money are lost through the need of instructing and training a new worker (this is valued at from $30 to $5,000), through decreased production, through injury to machinery, accidents and delays, and through poor quality of work.

What sickness means to an employee. On the side of the employee sickness means a loss of income with poverty looming ahead, the possible loss of a job, the necessity of returning to work before he is able, thus continuing the illness. It means a shortage of funds when expenses are greatest. Mr. Frederick I. Hoffman says, "It has been said, and I believe it is, that the majority of our wage workers have not a single week's wage ahead." Sometimes $10 to $15 represents the margin between independence and dependency. From 75 to 80 percent of the relief given by the Charity Organization Societies of our large cities is due to illness. In this connection we must not overlook the psychological effect upon the worker of the mental turmoil and distress incident to facing poverty and unemployment, and the dragging of a wife and family along the same path. Thus John H. was a hard working New York truck-driver, whose family consisted of a wife and three children, the youngest a baby, four months old. He contracted influenza and had to stop work. His wife nursed him for two weeks, at the end of which time their small savings had been used up. Then the three children came down with the disease, and two days later the wife became very ill. When a neighbor finally referred the case to charity they were penniless, without medical care, the baby had died and the two older children had developed double pneumonia. The family were loaned money enough to pay for the burial of the baby, nursing care and food—which meant that John mortgaged his future earnings and went back to work burdened with a load of debt. What would have happened if a health insurance bill had been in effect? John would have been insured in a mutual health insurance fund at a cost to himself of about twenty-four cents a week, his employer paying an equal amount. This would have entitled him to call a doctor as soon as he was taken ill, to receive medicine, and if necessary to secure the services of a nurse to help his wife—all paid by the insurance fund. Sound medical advice might have prevented the illness of the rest of the family and saved the baby's life. Besides medical care, John would have received, after the first three days of illness, $8.00 a week as long as he was unable to work. This would have supplied food and prevented the discouraging debt with which the family is now struggling.

To the other employees in a plant sickness among their number means not alone the possibility of contagion for themselves and families, but delay and often times loss of piece-work wages by reason of the absence of the worker who should produce the material they work upon. Under the present system of trade union benefits only a man's fellow workers share in the burden of tiding him and his family over the period of financial difficulty due to his illness; under the health insurance the whole community shares the burden as they should also share in educational and other preventive measures, in the interest of the whole community's welfare.

SIGNIFICANCE

Lattimore addresses broad social policy themes to be funded by the government, such as health insurance, worker's compensation, maternity leave, child allowances, and other concepts that some western nations—most notably Scandinavian countries, Canada, Great Britain, Italy, France, the Netherlands, and Spain—began to embrace in the mid-twentieth century. In the United States such reforms were touched on with the New Deal legislation of the mid 1930s and early 1940s, but paid maternity leave, child allowances, and universal state health insurance for female workers have never been federal policy in the United States.

In 1920 the United States government created the Women's Bureau to address specific workforce concerns for female workers. Women's work in World War I expanded during the wartime economy; the Women's Bureau tackled issues such as African-American women's participation in the workforce, child care, hazardous job protection during pregnancy, and helped to pass the Fair Labor Standards Act of 1938, which finally created a federal law protecting child laborers.

Future laws such as the Equal Pay Act of 1963 gave women equal work for equal pay, but many of the reforms suggested in *Legal Recognition of Industrial Women* have never been passed in the United States, despite rich debate among legislators and in civil society. The Pregnancy Discrimination Law of 1978 protects pregnant women from being fired for their pregnant status, while the 1992 Family and Medical Leave Act provides all workers in businesses with fifty workers or more with up to thirteen weeks of unpaid leave per year without job loss. At the same time, as of 2005 more than forty million people in the United States—approximately fourteen percent of the population—do not have health insurance, the United States provides no mandated paid maternity leave, and worker policies for sick leave or child illness leave are on an employer-by-employer basis in the U.S.

The year after Lattimore wrote *Legal Recognition of Industrial Women* women gained the vote in the United States with the passage of the Nineteenth Amendment, giving women agency in government. More than eighty-five years after Lattimore laid out these policy statements, many of her recommendations remain part of the political discourse, though not part of federal policy.

FURTHER RESOURCES

Books

Dubofsky, Melvin. *Hard Work: The Making of Labor History*. Champaign, Illinois: University of Illinois Press, 2000.

Fantasia, Rick and Kim Voss. *Hard Work: Remaking the American Labor Movement*. University of California Press, 2004.

Felder, Deborah G. *A Century of Women: The Most Influential Events in Twentieth-Century Women's History*. Kensington Publishing Corp., 1999.

Rosen, Ellen Doree. *A Wobblie Life: IWW Organizer E.F. Doree*. Wayne State University Press, 2004.

Web sites

United States Department of Labor. "Women's Bureau." <http://www.dol.gov/wb/> (accessed May 8, 2006).

Conscientious Objector

Pacifism in America in the 1930s

Poem

By: Edna St. Vincent Millay

Date: 1934

Source: Millay, Edna St. Vincent. *Collected Poems*. New York; Harper and Row, 1956.

About the Author: Edna St. Vincent Millay (1892–1950) was among the most celebrated American female poets of her generation. In 1923, Millay became the first female winner of the Pulitzer Prize for poetry. Her work was widely published during her lifetime and her poems, particularly her sonnets, have been the subject of significant academic study since her death.

INTRODUCTION

Edna St. Vincent Millay was a life-long poet and literary figure. Her first work was published when Millay was twenty years old, and the themes explored throughout her career were often contentious, including her explorations of female sexuality, feminism, pacifism, and the American justice system.

Millay moved to the Greenwich Village district of New York City in 1920. Greenwich Village had developed at that time into a significant community of artists, writers, and intellectuals, and it was a relative hotbed of political radicalism. Millay was politically active after she was established in Greenwich Village, not seeking elected office or a leadership role in any organization, but supporter of a number of radical causes.

A notable example of a Millay cause was her opposition to the 1927 execution of Nicola Sacco and Bartolomeo Vanzetti, Italian immigrants and avowed anarchists who had been convicted in Boston of a robbery and subsequent murder on evidence that appeared to be significantly flawed. Millay's poem, 'Justice Denied in Massachusetts' captured the spirit of the protests that had engaged the attention of the radical aspects of American society.

In the 1930s, as the Great Depression gripped the United States in a prolonged period of economic stagnation, the focus of American government was the resolution of its pressing domestic problems. Public opinion in America favored isolationism with respect to the country's involvement in foreign disputes. Millay remained a committed pacifist during this period; her work "Conscientious Objector" was followed by a series of works where Millay comments upon the Spanish Civil War (1936–1939) and the rise of fascism in Europe.

Millay was an influential thinker and writer throughout her entire career. Her poems sold remarkably well; the book of sonnets including "Conscientious Objector" sold over 35,000 copies within the first two weeks of its release in 1934. Millay was voted one of the ten most famous women in America in

Edna St. Vincent Millay in 1929. THE LIBRARY OF CONGRESS.

1938; the United States Postal Service later issued a stamp in her honor.

PRIMARY SOURCE

Conscientious Objector
I shall die, but
that is all that I shall do for Death.
I hear him leading his horse out of the stall;
I hear the clatter on the barn-floor.
He is in haste; he has business in Cuba,
business in the Balkans, many calls to make this morning.
But I will not hold the bridle
while he clinches the girth.
And he may mount by himself:
I will not give him a leg up.

Though he flick my shoulders with his whip,
I will not tell him which way the fox ran.
With his hoof on my breast, I will not tell him where
the black boy hides in the swamp.
I shall die, but that is all that I shall do for Death;
I am not on his pay-roll.

I will not tell him the whereabout of my friends
nor of my enemies either.

Though he promise me much,
I will not map him the route to any man's door.
Am I a spy in the land of the living,
that I should deliver men to Death?
Brother, the password and the plans of our city
are safe with me; never through me Shall you be
overcome.

SIGNIFICANCE

As a literary creation, Millay weaves together references in "Conscientious Objector" to world conflict and the duty of the conscientious objector not to involve themselves in any capacity with the military actions of any power. This portrayal by Millay of the role of the pacifist when faced with the threat of armed conflict can be taken as a metaphor for the position of the United States in relation to international armed conflicts in the early 1930s. It is clear that for Millay, a conscientious objector and a pacifist would remain disengaged and aloof from any struggle.

When Millay wrote this work in 1934, a conscientious objector under American law had to demonstrate an appropriate religious belief as the underlying basis for their objection to military service. Millay's depiction of the conscientious objector as one motivated by a personal moral belief as opposed to a strictly religious basis anticipated the United States Supreme Court's 1970 ruling, where the Court held that a conscientious objection could be sustained absent religious grounds.

A companion notion expressed by Millay is the sense of brotherhood among those who oppose fighting and the resultant cost of human life. This sentiment was a cornerstone of the pacifist movement to which Millay was aligned. The supporters of pacifism believed that theirs was a philosophy that was not limited to a nation; it was a concept that transcended all borders.

The rise of fascism in Europe in the 1930s caused Millay and other pacifists to re-examine their world view. Fascism is a philosophy of government that places the interests of the nation-state ahead of those of the individual. Italy had been placed under a Fascist dictatorship by Benito Mussolini (1883–1945) by degrees in the early 1930s. The rise of Adolph Hitler (1889–1945) and his Nazi party in 1933 was the second example of the growth of fascism in Europe. The Spanish Civil War and the victory of the Fascist forces lead by General Francisco Franco (1892–1975) was a graphic example to American pacifists and isolationists alike that fascism posed a significant threat to personal freedoms and the security of the world. It had become apparent to Millay and others in America by 1939 that pacifism would be an inadequate response to the obvious ambitions of leaders such as Hitler and Mussolini.

In this context, "Conscientious Objector" takes on an additional significance. Millay expressed her opposition to the Spanish fascism in a series of poems published in 1939. She also became an advocate of an early entry by the United States into the European war that commenced in September 1939. Millay wrote poems commissioned by the United States government in 1941 to address various aspects of the war. The most powerful of these works was "Murder at Lidice," written in 1942 to describe the reprisal killings carried out by the German occupational forces in Lidice, Czechoslovakia, where members of the Czech underground had assisted in the killing of German Gestapo (secret police) chief Reinhardt Heydrich.

It is of interest that after World War II (1938–1945), Millay distanced herself artistically from these war works. She expressed the view that as they were essentially commissioned for wartime, they should have remained within the context of the war.

FURTHER RESOURCES

Books

Bennett, Scott H. *Radical Pacifism: the War Resisters League and Gandian Nonviolence in America, 1915–1963.* Syracuse, New York; Syracuse University Press, 2003.

Milford, Nancy. *Savage Beauty: The Life of Edna St. Vincent Millay.* New York; Random House, 2001.

Periodicals

Cook, Blanche Weisen. "Women and Peace: The Legacy." *Ms. Magazine.* Winter 2006.

Web sites

California State University, Stanislaus. "Perspectives in American Literature / Early 20th Century." January 7, 2003. < http://www.csustan.edu/english/reuben/pal/chap7/millay.html> (accessed May 29, 2006).

National Labor Relations Act

Legislation

By: Robert R. Wagner

Date: July 5, 1935

Source: 29th Congress of the United States. National Labor Relations Act. *United States Code.* Title 29, Chapter 7, Subchapter II. Available online at <http://www.ourdocuments.gov/> (accessed April 24, 2006).

About the Author: Senator Robert R. Wagner of New York, a Democrat who served from 1927 to 1949, was the author of the National Labor Relations Act and helped to create the National Labor Relations Board. Wagner sponsored the Social Security Act as well as a wide range of other New Deal reforms.

INTRODUCTION

Organized labor unions in the United States began to gain power in the 1850s, as industrialization grew in the northern states. While guilds had been present during the colonial era and into the early 1800s, organized unions for all trade workers did not emerge until the 1820s; early attempts to control shift length or women's hours led to some successes.

In 1852, the Typographical Union formed the oldest continuing national union in the United States. In 1859, in Philadelphia iron molders created a union, and in 1866, the first national union, the National labor Union, was founded in Baltimore, Maryland. The NLU was a federation of local unions; its primary success was the passage of an eight hour workday for federal workers. By 1873, the NLU lost power during an economic depression, while the Knights of Labor, a new union, rose to prominence.

The Knights of Labor formed in 1869 as a trade union open to women, minorities (in 1883), and immigrants as well as native-born white men. Founder Uriah Stevens, a member of the Garment Cutter's Association, helped bring the union's messages of social revolution—not just economic protection—to the public. By the mid 1880s, the Knights of Labor platform of the eight hour work day, the end of child labor, equal pay regardless of gender, age, or race, and the elimination of the private banking system contrasted with the new national union, the American Federation of Labor, which worked with employers on a more pragmatic level with no element of social change in their platform.

Although the Knights of Labor experienced some successful strikes, the 1886 Haymarket Square Riot, a labor protest of 1500 workers that turned violent when a bomb exploded and killed eleven people, twisted public sentiment against the Knights of Labor. The American Federation of Labor, however, stepped in to fill the gap, but did not permit women and minorities to join.

As industrialization increased in the early 1900s and factories needed large numbers of skilled and unskilled workers, loosely regulated capitalism, with no government safety oversight or bureau of labor, created workplaces with high injury and death rates, high turnover, and increasing tension between workers

Gathering at a Ford plant in River Rouge, Michigan, workers vote whether or not to have union representation under the National Labor Relations Act of 1935. PHOTO BY MPI/GETTY IMAGES.

and owners. The 1911 Triangle Shirtwaist Factory fire in which 150 women and girls were killed ignited public outrage; the doors had been locked and chained from the inside by managers to prevent theft. The next year more than 50,000 textile workers in Lawrence, Massachusetts, led by the Industrial Workers of the World, nicknamed the "Wobblies," went on strike. The strikers faced arrest, violence at the hands of police and militia, and women and children were attacked by police as they attempted to leave town. Local, state, and federal government officials and law enforcement found themselves caught between laborers and industrialists as labor conditions and corporate demands faced off in conflict.

The Department of Labor, founded in 1913, and the 1914 Clayton Act which protected the right to strike and boycott, helped labor unions to expand and advocate for workers. The economic boon of the 1920s, followed by the Great Depression, weakened unions; many employers took this opportunity to create "open shops" or only hire non-union members. Workers who attempted to join unions had faced opposition and intimidation at times throughout the development of unions; as anti-immigrant and anti-socialist sentiment increased in the United States during the 1920s and 1930s, some nativists began to equate unions with socialism and communism, using violence, strike breaking, and company unions to destroy the AFL and other unions.

In 1935, as part of the New Deal series of laws, President Franklin D. Roosevelt signed the National Labor Relations Act.

■ PRIMARY SOURCE

AN ACT To diminish the causes of labor disputes burdening or obstructing interstate and foreign commerce, to create a National Labor Relations Board, and for other purposes.

FINDINGS AND POLICIES Section 1. The denial by some employers of the right of employees to organize and the refusal by some employers to accept the procedure of collective bargaining lead to strikes and other forms of industrial strife or unrest, which have the intent or the necessary effect of burdening or obstructing commerce by (a) impairing the efficiency, safety, or operation of the instrumentalities of commerce; (b) occurring in the current of commerce; (c) materially affecting, restraining, or controlling the flow of raw materials or manufactured or processed goods from or into the channels of commerce, or the prices of such materials or goods in commerce; or (d) causing diminution of employment and wages in such volume as substantially to impair or disrupt the market for goods flowing from or into the channels of commerce.

The inequality of bargaining power between employees who do not possess full freedom of association or actual liberty of contract and employers who are organized in the corporate or other forms of ownership association substantially burdens and affects the flow of commerce, and tends to aggravate recurrent business depressions, by depressing wage rates and the purchasing power of wage earners in industry and by preventing the stabilization of competitive wage rates and working conditions within and between industries.

Experience has proved that protection by law of the right of employees to organize and bargain collectively safeguards commerce from injury, impairment, or interruption, and promotes the flow of commerce by removing certain recognized sources of industrial strife and unrest, by encouraging practices fundamental to the friendly adjustment of industrial disputes arising out of differences as to wages, hours, or other working conditions, and by restoring equality of bargaining power between employers and employees.

Experience has further demonstrated that certain practices by some labor organizations, their officers, and members have the intent or the necessary effect of burdening or obstructing commerce by preventing the free flow of goods in such commerce through strikes and other forms of industrial unrest or through concerted activities which impair the interest of the public in the free flow of such commerce. The elimination of such practices is a necessary condition to the assurance of the rights herein guaranteed.

It is declared to be the policy of the United States to eliminate the causes of certain substantial obstructions to the free flow of commerce and to mitigate and eliminate these obstructions when they have occurred by encouraging the practice and procedure of collective bargaining and by protecting the exercise by workers of full freedom of association, self-organization, and designation of representatives of their own choosing, for the purpose of negotiating the terms and conditions of their employment or other mutual aid or protection.

SIGNIFICANCE

The National Labor Relations Act created the National Labor Relations Board, a government body that provides oversight for collective bargaining and the creation of unions. In addition, the NRLB investigates labor abuses, union concerns, and disputes. The NLRB conducts secret ballot elections in companies with employees who wish to develop unions. The National Labor Relations Act also protects workers' rights not to join or create unions; union organizers and coworkers cannot pressure others into union creation or membership under the law.

In 1947 Congress amended the act to prohibit unionization in four industries—airlines, railroads, agriculture, and government. The revision of the National Labor Relations Act, commonly called the Taft-Hartley Act, also curtailed union practices such as closed shops and certain forms of boycotting. In addition, the Taft-Hartley Act gave the federal government the power to use an injunction to stop a strike or a lockout if the strike or lockout caused harm to national interests. President Harry S. Truman vetoed the Taft-Hartley Act but Congress overrode his veto and the changes to the original National Labor Relations Act took effect on June 23, 1947.

The National Labor Relations Act and the Taft-Hartley Act have a long history of use. The federal government has used injunctions more than thirty times since its passage in 1947; President Richard Nixon used an injunction to break a dock strike in 1971. President Jimmy Carter invoked the Taft-Hartley Act during coal miner strikes in 1977 and 1978, President William J. Clinton in 1997 to avert an airline pilot strike, and in 2002 President George W. Bush used the provisions in the Taft-Hartley Act to stop a lockout started by shipping companies on west coast docks.

The National Labor Relations Board processes more than 30,000 cases of alleged unfair labor practices each year as part of its express mission, written into the original act, to promote industrial peace.

FURTHER RESOURCES
Books

Dubofsky, Melvin. *Hard Work: The Making of Labor History*. Champaign, Illinois: University of Illinois Press, 2000.

Fantasia, Rick and Kim Voss. *Hard Work: Remaking the American Labor Movement*. University of California Press, 2004.

Rosen, Ellen D. *A Wobblie Life: IWW Organizer E.F. Doree*. Wayne State University Press, 2004.

Web sites

FDR Library. "Franklin Roosevelt's Statement on the National Labor Relations Act (The Wagner Act)." <http://www.fdrlibrary.marist.edu/odnlrast.html> (accessed April 24, 2006).

Equal Pay Act of 1963

Legislation

By: Edith Green and Edith Rogers

Date: June 10, 1963

Source: *Equal Pay Act of 1963*. Public Law 88–38. 29 U.S. Code Sec. 206(d).

About the Author: Representative Edith Green, a Democrat from Oregon, first crafted the Equal Pay bill in 1955 with co-author Edith Rogers, a Republican congresswoman from Massachusetts. Green served ten terms in the House of Representatives for the state of Oregon, while Rogers served thirty-five years for Massachusetts, the longest tenure of any woman representative. Rogers died in 1960, before the equal Pay Act was signed into law.

INTRODUCTION

The issue of equal pay legislation in the United States dates back to 1868, when newspapers such as *The Revolution*, published by women's rights activist Susan B. Anthony, advocated equal pay for equal work, an eight-hour work day, and the inclusion of women in labor unions. The ratification of the Fourteenth Amendment that same year, with its "equal protection" clause, inspired activists in search of equitable treatment for minorities and women.

World War I and, especially, World War II changed society's view of women as industrial workers. With the war industry experiencing sharp increases in labor needs at the same time that men were needed in the military, the U.S. government itself pushed to change the perception of factory work for women. The National War Labor Board recommended that men and women be paid equal wages during the war, and collective female labor experiences during the war years engineered social change in the coming decades.

Opponents of equal pay for equal work argued that federal laws were unnecessary. By 1963, over twenty states had laws on the books protecting equal pay, and corporate opponents of a federal law maintained that such laws were a matter for states, and not the federal government, to decide. In many states, women already enjoyed labor protections through legally mandated break periods that were longer or more frequent than those for men and shorter work days. In addition, opponents of equal pay legislation pointed to the expansion of federal bureaucracy necessary for the enforcement of any labor laws applying to women. Employers also noted the expense of creating separate restroom and changing facilities for women. According to opponents, the economics of equal pay would impose a financial burden on employers.

The persistent belief that a man should be the "provider" for his family, while his wife managed the domestic sphere fed the argument for lower wages for women. Many opponents of equal pay laws believed that single women needed less money because most of these women still lived with their parents, while married women should be housewives and mothers rather than working outside the home. The concept of a masculine "family wage" drove the cultural argument surrounding the wage gap.

Finally, opponents cited higher rates of absenteeism for female workers caused in part by pregnancy, child care issues, and medical concerns. This absenteeism, combined with existing state laws giving women more accommodations, made female workers a more expensive form of labor. Equal pay critics argued that paying women less was only fair, on balance, in light of these issues.

In 1961, President John F. Kennedy created the President's Commission on the Status of Women, which investigated issues of women's employment, health, education, and legal status. Chaired by former First Lady Eleanor Roosevelt, the Commission issued a report in 1963 with recommendations to improve the status of women in the United States, including such measures as anti-discrimination legislation, paid maternity and family leave, and access to affordable childcare. Indeed, 1963 became a transformative year for women's rights in America—the Commission on the Status of Women, the Equal Pay Act, and Betty Friedan's feminist book *The Feminine Mystique* all appeared during that year.

■ PRIMARY SOURCE

AN ACT

To prohibit discrimination on account of sex in the payment of wages by employers engaged in commerce or in the production of goods for commerce. June 10, 1963 [S. 1409].

Be it enacted by the Senate and House of Representatives of the United States of America in Congress assembled, That this Act may be cited as the "Equal Pay Act of 1963."

DECLARATION OF PURPOSE

SEC. 2. (a) The Congress hereby finds that the existence in industries engaged in commerce or in the production of goods for commerce of wage differentials based on sex—.

(1) depresses wages and living standards for employees necessary for their health and efficiency;

(2) prevents the maximum utilization of the available labor resources;

(3) tends to cause labor disputes, thereby burdening, affecting, and obstructing commerce;

(4) burdens commerce and the free flow of goods in commerce; and

(5) constitutes an unfair method of competition.

(b) It is hereby declared to be the policy of this Act, through exercise by Congress of its power to regulate commerce among the several States and with foreign nations, to correct the conditions above referred to in such industries.

SEC. 3. Section 6 of the Fair Labor Standards Act of 1938, as amended (29 U.S.C. et seq.), is amended by adding thereto a new subsection (d) as follows: Discrimination prohibited. 52 Stat. 1062; 63 Stat. 912.

(d)(1) No employer having employees subject to any provisions of this section shall discriminate, within any establishment in which such employees are employed, between employees on the basis of sex by paying wages to employees in such establishment at a rate less than the rate at which he pays wages to employees of the opposite sex in such establishment for equal work on jobs the performance of which requires equal skill, effort, and responsibility, and which are performed under similar working conditions, except where such payment is made pursuant to (i) a seniority system; (ii) a merit system; (iii) a system which measures earnings by quantity or quality of production; or (iv) a differential based on any other factor other than sex: Provided, That an employer who is paying a wage rate differential in violation of this subsection shall not, in order to comply with the provisions of this subsection, reduce the wage rate of any employee. 29 USC 206.

(2) No labor organization, or its agents, representing employees of an employer having employees subject to any provisions of this section shall cause or attempt to cause such an employer to discriminate against an employee in violation of paragraph (1) of this subsection.

(3) For purposes of administration and enforcement, any amounts owing to any employee which have been withheld in violation of this subsection shall be deemed to be unpaid minimum wages or unpaid overtime compensation under this Act.

(4) As used in this subsection, the term 'labor organization' means any organization of any kind, or any agency or employee representation committee or plan, in which employees participate and which exists for the purpose, in whole or in part, of dealing with employers concerning grievances, labor disputes, wages, rates of pay, hours of employment, or conditions of work. "Labor organization."

SEC. 4. The amendments made by this Act shall take effect upon the expiration of one year from the date of its enactment: Provided, That in the case of employees covered by a bona fide collective bargaining agreement in effect at least thirty days prior to the date of enactment of this Act, entered into by a labor organization (as defined in section 6(d)(4) of the Fair Labor Standards Act of 1938, as amended), the amendments made by this Act shall take effect upon the termination of such collective bargaining agreement or upon the expiration of two years from the date of enactment of this Act, whichever shall first occur. Effective date.

Approved June 10, 1963, 12:00.

■

SIGNIFICANCE

Proponents of equal pay legislation made one basic argument: equal pay for equal work. If a woman could do the same work that a man could perform, as women had shown themselves capable of doing during the wars, then she should be paid the same wage, regardless of marital status or gender. In 1955, Edith Rogers and Edith Green co-authored the first version of the Equal Pay Act; it passed in 1963, three years after Rogers' death. In 1963, the average working woman earned 59 cents for every dollar that the average working man earned.

Within seven years of the passage of the Equal Pay Act, forty states passed state-level versions of the Act. In the year following the passage of the Equal Pay Act, the 1964 Civil Rights Act created the Equal Employment Opportunity Commission to protect workers from discrimination based on sex and race.

The Equal Pay Act of 1963 and the Civil Rights Act of 1964 taken together provided stronger legal protections to women than ever before, but, in the coming decade, a cluster of laws and government actions granted women greater access to rights previously available to men only. President Lyndon Johnson's 1965 Executive Order 11375 ordered federal agencies to provide women with equal access to employment and educational opportunities; the 1972 Title IX law banned sex discrimination in schools; and the 1974 Equal Credit Opportunity Act required equal access to credit and financial services regardless of sex, marital status, race, age, or national origin.

Women's rights activist groups such as the National Organization for Women, the National Women's Political Caucus, and publications, such as *Ms. Magazine*, championed the labor rights of women. Workplace equity became the central tenet of the women's movement in the late 1960s and early 1970s, feeding into the push for an Equal Rights Amendment as well.

As other protections, including prohibitions against firing pregnant women and laws against sexual harassment, became standard practice in the American labor force, the wage gap gradually diminished. As of 2004, the average working woman earned 80 cents for every dollar that the average working man earned.

FURTHER RESOURCES

Books

Becker, Susan D. *The Origins of the Equal Rights Amendment: American Feminism Between the Wars*. Westport, Conn.: Greenwood Press, 1981.

Cobble, Dorothy Sue. *The Other Women's Movement: Workplace Justice and Social Rights in Modern America*. Princeton, N.J.: Princeton University Press, 2004.

Felder, Deborah G. *A Century of Women: The Most Influential Events in Twentieth-Century Women's History*. New York: Kensington Publishing Corp., 1999.

Friedan, Betty. *The Feminine Mystique*. New York: W.W. Norton, 2001.

Stetson, Dorothy M. *Women's Rights in the U.S.A.: Policy Debates and Gender Roles*. New York: Routledge, 2004.

Web sites

Ms. Magazine. <http://www.msmagazine.com/about.asp> (accessed April 17, 2006).

National Women's Political Caucus. <http://www.nwpc.org> (accessed April 17, 2006).

American Federation of Labor on President Johnson and Human Rights

Book excerpt

By: AFL–CIO

Date: February 23, 1968

Source: Fink, Gary M., ed. *AFL–CIO Executive Council Statements and Reports, 1956–1975*. Westport, CT: Greenwood Press, 1977.

About the Author: The first step toward organized labor in the United States occurred on November 15, 1881, when delegates from local units of the Knights of Labor met in Pittsburgh, Pennsylvania, to form the Federation of Organized Trades and Labor Unions. An eclectic group of cigar makers, merchant seamen, printers, and others, they wrote a constitution and set the eight-hour work day as a central part of their platform. The group was already popular among workers, but it lacked public backing. On December 8, 1886, members of the federation aligned with representatives from various other unions to form the American Federation of Labor (AFL) and quickly began to strike for the eight-hour work day and other issues. In 1935, AFL in-fighting led to the exodus of several key unions, who created the Committee for Industrial Organization (CIO). With the addition of several other unions, the CIO became the Congress of Industrial Organizations in 1938. The CIO and AFL disagreed bitterly, but they continued to make substantial gains for workers, including minimum wages, workers' and unemployment compensation, as well as other benefits. During World War II, the two organizations began to put their disagreements aside and work more closely together. In December 1955, they officially joined forces as the AFL–CIO. In the postwar years, the organization has added human rights to its agenda.

INTRODUCTION

The first International Conference on Human Rights met in Teheran, Iran, from April 22 to May 13, 1968, to review progress that had been made in the twenty years since Eleanor Roosevelt had first presented the 1948 UN Universal Declaration of Human Rights. The year was a pivotal one, as the Vietnam conflict brought international human rights into the spotlight.

The harsh and bloody North Vietnamese Tet offensive led to the war's escalation, and in 1969 news of the My Lai massacre became public. In addition to the war, the United States had also endured over a decade of civil rights strife, beginning with the 1957 desegregation of Little Rock, Arkansas schools. Protests for civil rights, women's rights, and other avenues of social discontent were led by civic and political groups including the AFL–CIO, which joined these campaigns for the same reasons that it mandated desegregation of unions: Human rights are part of workers rights.

■ PRIMARY SOURCE

In his formal proclamation of 1968 as Human Rights year, President Johnson emphasized that U.S. ratification of human rights treaties was long overdue. This ratification is all the more urgent because, otherwise, our government will not be able to participate effectively in the United Nations Conference on Human Rights to be held in Teheran next April.

American labor has had an unceasing interest in promoting and preserving human rights. Devoted to this course, the AFL–CIO Executive council strives to do its utmost to help assure the success of this historic conference which marks the 20th anniversary of the proclamation of the Declaration of Human Rights by the U.N. General Assembly. In this regard, we note that the initial drive for the adoption of this inspiring Declaration was provided by organized labor in the U.S.

Furthermore, over twenty years ago, in November 1947, American labor took the initiative in placing the issue of forced labor before the entire world community. We then petitioned the U.N. Economic and Social Council to request the International Labor Organization (ILC) to make a comprehensive survey of the extent of forced labor in the member States of the U.N. We proposed, at the same time, that positive procedures be established for revising the 1930 convention and that measures be taken for its implementation so as to eliminate forced labor.

We of the AFL–CIO are very much interested in our country playing the decisive role in making the Teheran sessions fruitful. With this in mind and in the spirit of President Johnson's aforementioned Proclamation, the Executive Council calls upon Chairman Fulbright of the Senate Foreign Relations Committee to cease all further delays in holding hearings on the ratification of the remaining human rights treaties. This Committee has, so far, reported favorably only on the supplementary convention on Slavery. I cannot afford to lose any more time in taking similar action on the other convention before it—as strongly urged by the late President Kennedy and President Johnson.

The Foreign Relations Committee must realize that it is no credit to our country that the U.S. is not one of the 71 nations which have approved the convention on the Prevention and Punishment of the Crime of Genocide that was unanimously recommended, on December 9, 1948, by the U.N. General Assembly for ratification by member states; the U.S. is not one of the 79 nations which have approved the Convention concerning the Abolition of Forced Labor; the U.S. is not among the 76 nations which have approved the Convention on Freedom of Association; and the U.S. is not among the 55 nations which have already approved the Convention on the Political Rights of Women.

Further delay by the Senate, which has the constitutional responsibility for ratification of the above Conventions, will place our country in an entirely unnecessary and dangerously ambiguous position—playing into the hands of the slanderers of the U.S. at home and abroad. Since the American people as a whole now enjoy the rights, freedoms and standards provided by these conventions, no member of the Senate Foreign Relations committee can, at this very late date, raise the question of the so-called sanctity of states' rights as an objection to their ratification.

We of American labor continue our uncompromising opposition to the use of totalitarian and other authoritarian methods for resolving, by force, social problems relating to work. In this light, we condemn unreservedly all political policies and economic procedures which provide for the employers (state) using organizations with workers in their ranks to police the factories—for instance, as in communist countries, to serve as instruments for speeding up the workers or, under the guise of new "codes of Work," to penalize them for what the employer (state) considers inadequate use of machinery.

We are especially distressed over the failure of the U.S. Senate to act with dispatch in promoting human rights, because, more recently, mankind has witnessed the frightening recurrence of a massive growth of the utterly inhumane practice of forced labor—particularly in the Soviet Union, Communist China and other totalitarian and tyrannical lands.

The Teheran conference provides our government with a unique opportunity to take the lead in seeking concrete worldwide implementation of the International Covenant on Human Rights which was adopted by the U.N. General Assembly in December 1966. Towards full utilization of this opportunity, the AFL–CIO Executive Council urges our government to take the initiative in proposing that the Teheran Conference take the following positive steps for implementing:

(1) Article 13 (2) of the Universal Declaration of Human Rights which provides that "Everyone has the right to leave any country, including his own, and to return to his country."

(2) Article 14 (1) of this Declaration which provides that "Everyone has the right to seek and enjoy in other countries asylum from persecution."

(3) The creation of more effective safeguards against the violation of human rights by establishing a Permanent U.N. Commission on the Preservation and Promotion of Human Rights, with authority to appoint Human Rights Observation Committees endowed with the rights and powers of investigation, surveillance and reporting.

(4) The elimination by the U.N. Member States of all legal, political, administrative, and police barriers to the widest freedom of circulation among their peoples of all U.N. publications, surveys, reports, and other documents acted upon by the General Assembly or any of its subdivisions.

(5) Enforcement of effective sanctions against repressive colonialist regimes in the African territories under Portuguese and Spanish administration, in Rhodesia, and South Africa.

(6) Preparation of a program for a more effective solution of all refugee problems (Arab and Jewish alike) by ratifying the October 4, 1967, protocol on Refugees which enlarged the scope of the 1951 Refugee convention.

Finally, we urge our government to include a representative of the AFL–CIO in the U.S. delegation to the Teheran Conference.

This seal became the official insignia for the American Federation of Labor—Congress of Industrial Organizations (AFL-CIO) when the two organizations mergered on Decemeber 5, 1955. © BETTMANN/CORBIS.

SIGNIFICANCE

The late 1960s and 1970s saw a rise in protests for women's, ethnic, and civil rights. The brutality of the Vietnam conflict (as well as numerous other conflicts in Africa, southeastern Europe, and Central America) forced the United Nations to add clauses to the Geneva Conventions, which are guidelines for acts of war and the treatment of prisoners.

As American labor union membership declined after World War II, the United States withdrew its support from the UN's International Labor Organization (ILO) in 1977, primarily because the AFL–CIO had traditionally avoided international committees and politics. Other reasons cited were political divisions in the organization and its shift from original goals. Two years later, the United States rejoined the organization when it reformed itself to its original plan of strengthening employer–employee relations to ensure and elevate human rights. Labor unions continued to decline in the United States, but such setbacks did not prevent the world community from pushing forward.

The United Nations began holding World Conferences for Women's Rights in 1975, and the first World Conference against Racism, Racial Discrimination, Xenophobia, and Related Intolerance in Durban, South Africa, in 2001. Like the women's rights conference, which addressed issues concerning discrimination and unequal treatment of women, the 2001 meeting sought to develop international mandates against racism. The conference also raised the issue of migrants and political refugees; clear and concise agendas for the treatment of such individuals is still under discussion.

FURTHER RESOURCES

Books

Mertus, Julie. *United Nations and Human Rights A Guide for a New Era.* New York: Routledge, 2005.

Steiner, Henry, and Philip Alston. *International Human Rights in Context: Law, Politics, Morals.* Oxford, New York: Oxford University Press, 2000.

Wehrle, Edmund F. *Between a River and a Mountain: The AFL–CIO and the Vietnam War.* Ann Arbor: University of Michigan Press, 2005.

Web sites

United Nations. "Key Conference Outcomes on Human Rights" <http://www.un.org/esa/devagenda/humanrights.html> (accessed April 22, 2006).

Solidarity's First Congress

Report

By: J. B. Weydenthal

Date: October 19, 1981

Source: de Weydenthal, J. B. From *RAD Background Report/291 (Poland)*. Radio Free Europe/Radio Liberty, 1981.

About the Author: J. B. Weydenthal is a long-serving Radio Free Europe Correspondent based in Eastern Europe. Radio Free Europe is a United States government-funded radio station that broadcasts throughout the world. Its mission is to: "promote democratic values and institutions by disseminating factual information." Radio Free Europe served Eastern Europe during the Cold War (1946–1991) era, when it would broadcast news otherwise censored by Soviet-backed governments.

INTRODUCTION

In the context of the Cold War, the 1970s began a period of détente between East and West. The era is also marked by economic hubris that occurred across the Union of Soviet Socialist Republics (USSR) and Eastern Europe. This economic mismanagement, which involved the taking on and wasting of large-sized western loans and the building up of huge trade deficits with the west, would help lead to a collapse in living standards across the region, the discrediting of the Soviet regime, and eventually, its collapse.

In Poland, the limitations of its planned economy gave its leaders few tools with which to correct economic distortions. One of the few ways in which they could bring in funds was to increase food prices. This was deeply unpopular, however, and had contributed to the fall of Wladyslaw Gomulka as Communist Party leader in 1970. When his successor, Edward Gierek, abruptly tried to do the same on June 24, 1976, he brought thousands of protesters onto the streets of Poland's cities and was forced to backtrack within twenty-four hours. Many of the demonstrators were incarcerated and hundreds were imprisoned.

This legitimacy took a further blow in October 1978 when Cardinal Karol Wojtyla of Krakow was elected Pope John II. His elevation to Pope unleashed an unprecedented sense of national and religious self-confidence. When he made a victorious return home the following June, the ecstatic reception that he met highlighted the contrast between his vibrant and charismatic papacy and the moribund and ineffectual leadership of the Communist Party.

The economic crisis came to a head in the summer of 1980. The inability of the Polish government to stem its economic deficit had seen its hard currency debt treble to more than 20 billion U.S. dollars in just five years. On the brink of economic collapse, on July 1, 1980, the Communist Government resorted to the tactic that had already twice failed and increased meat prices.

A wave of strikes and factory occupations began immediately, but whereas participants in previous protests—factory workers, students, intellectuals—had been divided, in 1980 they united in a solid phalanx. The spearhead of the protests was the Baltic shipyards, where workers were led by Lech Walesa, a former electrician. Walesa formed an Inter-Enterprise Strike Committee, which articulated the demands of 600 factories from all over Poland. Its extensive list of demands included calls for new and independent trade unions, the right to strike, an extension of the Catholic Church's freedom of expression, the freeing of political prisoners, improvement of social services, and a freer media. Disorientated by the extent of the protests, the Polish Government agreed to many of the demands in a series of accords in late August and early September 1980 that became known as the Gdansk Agreements. Buoyed by the success of the Inter-Enterprise Strike Committee, Walesa formed a national trade union based upon its organizational structure. Inaugurated on September 17, 1980, it was called Solidarity.

Over the following twelve months, the Solidarity movement led a period of political debate unparalleled in Poland's communist era. Aimed at shaping the country's political destiny, the freedoms enjoyed by Solidarity caused panic amongst Poland's Warsaw Pact allies, although the Soviet President, Leonid Brezhnev, ignored the calls of the East German leader, Erich Honecker, to send in Soviet tanks and restore order. Walesa became a globally recognized figure and even met Pope John Paul II in Rome in January 1981. Later on that year, from September 5–10 and September 26–October 7, Solidarity staged its first national congress. Walesa was elected its president.

■ PRIMARY SOURCE

The congress was a lengthy affair, lasting far beyond initial expectations. While the first stage lasted six days (September 5–10) instead of the planned three, the second session went on for twelve days (September 26 until October 7), whereas only seven or eight had been scheduled.

There were several reasons for the extension of the discussions; one of them was the scope of issues covered. They ranged from the general principles of the movement's future activities and its existing political and economic system to specific problems of internal organization. Draft proposals on those questions were presented to the delegates by special working teams formed during the first stage of the congress. (2) In addition, the congress devoted considerable time to

PAX SOVIETICA

A Polish Solidarity movement poster ironically suggests that the Soviet Peace ("Pax Sovietica") comes in the form of tanks. © STAPLETON COLLECTION/CORBIS.

discussing specific queries and demands raised from the floor by regional delegations or individual delegates with regard to their separate interests and problems.

This proliferation of issues was expected. Solidarity, a worker's protest movement that has developed in the course of the last year into a nationwide social movement, has always been regarded by its members as an organization symbolizing hopes and expectations that exceeded the functions of a mere labor union. Indeed, in the eyes of many, Solidarity is both the representative of society in general and the recipient of popular demands for change. The demands have come from many quarters. Since the congress provided the first opportunity ever to present and articulate those demands in a formal manner, n social group could have been expected to forego the chance of having its preferences embodied in Solidarity's future program. This inevitably resulted in interminable discussions, seemingly empty squabbles, and even occasional quarrels, all of which greatly contributed to the impression that the debates were chaotic and fruitless.

Another factor that prolonged the congress was the scrupulous attention to procedure, particularly over the

leadership elections. While the important position of Solidarity's chairman was filled relatively quickly, Lech Walesa having won after a single ballot, the selection of the members of the National and Audit commissions proved much more difficult. The election of 21 members of the Audit commission was, for example, completed only on October 5, following 4 rounds of balloting. As for the National commission, an important body charged with setting the main policies of the movement in the months to come, 64 out of 69 elective seats were filled after 2 rounds of voting; 4 of the remaining 5 required 5 ballots; and the last seat was filled only after 6 rounds of voting.

....On October 2, the sixth day of the session, Lech Walesa was elected chairman of Solidarity. The former electrician, who had headed Solidarity's National Coordinating Commission since its establishment in September 1980, outpolled three other contenders, drawing 462 votes, or 55.2% of the 844 ballots cast. His closest competitor, Marian Jurczyk, received 201 votes (24%), while Andrzej Gwiazda and Jan Rulewski received 74 (8.8%) and 52 (6.2%), respectively; 7 votes were declared invalid, and 48 delegates reportedly failed to vote, perhaps because of abstention. Walesa's victory had, of course, been expected. The already legendary leader of the successful August 1980 strikes in Gdansk, a seemingly simple man but also a remarkably skillful political tactician, a populist capable of attracting both workers and the intellectuals, and a tough negotiator with a strong pragmatic touch, Walesa had emerged in the course of the year both as Solidarity's most popular leader and as a personality who, in the eyes of many, symbolized the movement as a whole. Largely because of that Walesa had long been regarded by both domestic and foreign observers as the heavy favorite for the movement's chairmanship.

And yet, despite Walesa's popularity and prestige, the margin of his victory, while considerable by any democratic standards, was smaller than had been anticipated. This could be significant because it did not result from the competitive strength of his rivals. It is that Andrzej Gwiazda, a cofounder of the first free trade union movement in Gdansk in mid-1978, a leading organizer of the 1980 Gdansk strikes, and a man widely recognized as solidarity's principal ideologist, has long enjoyed nationwide prestige and respect. It is also that Marian Jurczyk, the main leader of the 1980 Szczecin strikes and the chairman of one of the movement's most successful regional organizations had been directly involved in several crucial negotiations with the authorities on issues of national importance. It is, finally, that Jan Rulewski, a victim of police brutality in the Bydgoszcz incident in March and a prominent solidarity activist involved in key areas of the movement's organizational and political work, had long enjoyed the political limelight. None of them, however, had ever been able to match Walesa's popularity or equal his prestige both within the movement and in relations with other groups or institutions.

As to the political implications of the election, Walesa's victory would seem to affirm what has been regarded as a "moderate" orientation that favors negotiation, rather than confrontation, with the authorities on various problems in Poland's public life. Over the past year, Walesa has established a solid record of dealing with the authorities, a record with numerous successes in hammering out compromises and agreements . . . .

The basic fact remains, however, that political moderation reflects not only the views and preferences of particular leaders of the movement, but also the authorities' behavior toward Solidarity. It has become clear in recent months that the political conflicts between solidarity and the authorities resulted not so much from the aggressiveness of the former as from the latters's reluctance to accept changes in the country's social and economic life. It is that those changes have been stimulated by the operations, and the very existence, of Solidarity. They have, nonetheless, materialized through society's pressures for

change in the existing system rather than calculated designs of the movement's leaders or its activists. There is no reason to assume that the essence of Poland's politics will change following these elections. The Solidarity leadership's future policy is likely to depend not so much on its own preferences or political predilections as on the attitudes of the public, and the willingness of the Polish party and state leaders to act as partners in good faith.

Perhaps the most important and politically significant decision of the congress was the adoption of Solidarity's program setting out policy and objectives for the next two years. The document consists of eight chapters, dealing with the movement's internal matters and its relations with other institutions as well as its views on the evolution of political, social, and economic relations in the country.

Defining Solidarity as "the greatest mass movement in Poland's history . . . a movement born from a revolt of a society that has been subjected over more than 30 years to violations of civil and human rights," the programmatic document said that his movement "unified people of different views and beliefs through a common protest against injustice, abuses of power, and autocracy." The objectives of the movement included work for "justice, democracy, truth, legality, freedom of opinion, and the renewal of the state" as well as for an improvement in economic conditions. (11) Both the origins of the movement and its objectives were said to have determined the role of Solidarity. It is to be that of both "a labor union" and "a social movement." The program said that it was precisely 'the inherent unity of those two aspects of Solidarity that has determined the importance of our organization and defined it's role in the nation's life," adding that through Solidarity "Poland's society has recovered its hopes . . . for a national renewal."

Expanding on solidarity's national role the program proclaimed that in the face of the current national tragedy, solidarity can no longer confine itself to waiting and exerting pressure on the authorities to meet their obligations stemming from the agreements between the labor movement and the government. We are the only guarantor for society for change in social and economic areas and that is why the union deemed it its basic duty to take all possible short and long-term steps to salvage Poland from ruin and society from poverty, despondency, and self-destruction. There is no other way to attain this goal but to restructure the state and the economy o n the basis of democracy and all-round social initiative.

More specifically, the program declared that "no support for the government's program of stabilization of the economy would be possible" unless "social control" were extended over all activities related to the resolution of difficulties and "individuals commanding social and professional respect were placed in directing positions in the economy."

At the same time, the program said that the process of innovation would have to take evolutionary rather than revolutionary forms. "The nation will never forgive anyone if his steps, born even from the best intentions, lead to bloodshed . . . we should implement our ideas gradually, so that each successful task has the public's support."

Underscoring Solidarity's insistence on the need for moderation in its political actions, was the program's approach to questions of Poland's relations with other countries. "Responsibility for the well-being of the country makes it imperative for us to acknowledge the alignment of forces existing in Europe since World War II, "the program stated; "we want to carry out the great transformation in domestic relations that has already been started by us without violating Poland's international alliances." At the same time, however, the program included a reminder that "Poland can serve as a valuable partner for others only if it defines by itself, and in full consciousness, it's own obligations."

Indeed, self-management and organizational autonomy provided the crucial elements behind the program's call for the establishment of a 'self-governing republic," that is, the introduction of major institutional changes within the system. In particular, the program said that Solidarity, acting on the principle that "public life should reflect the existing pluralism in social, political, and cultural areas," was determined "to support and defend civil activities aiming to present to society various political, economic, and social programs as well as to protect efforts at self-organization that would make it possible to implement those program."

Among the specific measures that could facilitate such a development, the program pledged Solidarity's support for reform of the penal system and the judiciary, for a reform of the educational system, for the full implementation of labor laws, and for a comprehensive restructuring of the country's institutions so that each would be accountable to the public and all of them would be equal before the law.

Furthermore, the program envisaged a major change in the country's legislative system that would both ensure the representative character of the parliamentary bodies and provide deputies with considerable prerogatives for independent activity. The program indicated that solidarity might make an effort to ensure that future elections to the Sejm and the local people's councils "include candidates nominated by various social organizations and civil groups" and that "no list would enjoy preferential treatment." Although the program stopped short of demanding free elections, the meaning of those declarations was clear. Until now, all candidates had to be proposed by the Front of National Unity, and within that body the communist

party candidates had obvious advantages over the others. Solidarity's proposal would place them on an equal footing with any prospective rivals. The next elections will take place in December and will involve the selection of public representatives in the local people's councils; the next parliamentary elections are scheduled for 1984.

On other matters, the program demanded the punishment of officials judged responsible for past repression of members of the public (1956, 1968, 1970, 1976). No specific names were mentioned, but the program said that "the investigation aimed at finding those who were responsible should not be subject to any restrictions, extending to individuals occupying the highest positions in the party and the government." Such demands have been repeatedly made by solidarity activists in the past. Equally consistent was the program's demand for the movement's access to the broadcasting media. Here, the program maintained Solidarity's well-established position that the broadcasting media should "serve society as a whole and should be placed under its direct control."

The program concluded with an appeal to the authorities to accept "a new social contract" with the public, a contract that would center on a threefold agreement. First, "an agreement to cope with the crisis," ensuring means of overcoming the difficulties of the coming winter and providing "the first indication of cooperation between the authorities and society." Secondly, 'an agreement on economic reform" which would imply official acceptance of "major economic changes." And thirdly, "an agreement on the self-governing republic," which would "chart the directions toward democratization of public life."

The program was officially adopted by the delegates by 455 to 65 votes with 91 abstentions.

SIGNIFICANCE

Solidarity's first congress increased the alarm the nascent trade union organization was sending across the Soviet-bloc. In particular, their message of fraternity addressed to workers across eastern Europe and the USSR antagonized Poland's neighbors. With the domestic situation deteriorating under Solidarity's increasingly unrealistic demands and Moscow putting pressure upon the Polish government, Poland's new Prime Minister, General Jaruzelski, declared martial law on December 13 and initiated a huge crack down on Solidarity members. Hundreds of strikes broke out across the country but were broken up by riot police. On several occasions, government forces opened fire on protesters.

Martial law lasted until July 1983, during which time Solidarity was banned and its assets seized. Walesa was just one of its many supporters imprisoned for much of its duration, but even after his release and the end of martial law he was banned in 1984 from collecting the Nobel Peace Prize that October. News of the Polish government's repression frequently made it to the west, and the 1984 kidnapping and murder of Father Jerzy Popieluszko, an outspoken pro-Solidarity priest, prompted a global outcry.

Solidarity continued to operate covertly throughout the mid–1980s, supported by the Catholic Church and the CIA. The Polish Government's repression of it earned it global condemnation and it faced economic sanctions, which worsened the country's already bleak economic condition.

In April 1988, with Poland's economy in tatters and the standard of living quickly deteriorating, a new wave of strikes broke out. By August they were nationwide, but rather than declare martial law again, the government this time opened talks with Walesa. Over the following six months, Solidarity was legalized and a schedule was made for parliamentary elections. Solidarity was only able to contest thirty-five percent of seats for Parliament's main house, the Sejm, but all of the 100 seats in the newly resurrected Senate.

At the open elections staged in June 1989, Solidarity won ninety-two of the 100 Senate seats and all but one of the 162 Sejm seats the party was allowed to contest. The Polish communist party still had sixty-five percent of Sejm seats that it had not opened up in the elections. Although General Jaruzelski was designated President on July 19, his power was tentative as several Communist Sejm designates defected to Solidarity. By August 24, this shift had become inexorable. Jaruzelski, seeking some form of political consensus, chose Tadeusz Mazowiecki, a leading Solidarity member, as the country's first non-communist Prime Minister since 1945.

Solidarity's significance extended far beyond ushering Poland out of its communist era, however. News of developments in Poland spread far beyond its borders and initiated profound change across Soviet-dominated eastern Europe. By the end of 1989, communism had fallen in Hungary, East Germany, Czechoslovakia, and Romania.

Unlike many other opposition groups in Europe at the time, notably Czechoslovakia, Solidarity was not a human or civil rights-based organization. It was a trade union, albeit one which placed considerable emphasis on human rights as part of its program for change. However, assuming that democracy is the first precondition for allowing human rights to flourish, it was a profoundly important organization. By enabling democracy to exist in Poland, and inspiring its spread elsewhere, Solidarity arguably did more to help free eastern Europe from the cloying grasp of Soviet rule than any other organization.

FURTHER RESOURCES
Books

Ost, David. *Solidarity and the Politics of Anti-Politics: Opposition and Reform in Poland since 1968*. Philadelphia: Temple University Press, 1990.

Rothschild, Joseph. and Nancy M. Wingfield. *Return to Diversity: A Political History of East Central Europe Since World War II*. Oxford University Press, 2000.

Weschler, Lawrence. *The Passion of Poland: From Solidarity Through the State of War*. New York: Pantheon, 1982.

Americans With Disabilities Act

Legislation

By: George H. W. Bush

Date: July 26, 1990

Source: *Americans With Disabilities Act*, Public Law 101–336, 42 U.S. Code Sec. 12101 *et seq.*

About the Author: President George H.W. Bush signed the Americans With Disabilities Act (ADA) into law on July 26, 1990. The U.S. Department of Justice bears primary responsibility for federal enforcement of the ADA. It provides technical assistance to businesses, state and local governments, and individuals with responsibilities under the legislation, but also files lawsuits to enforce compliance.

INTRODUCTION

The Americans With Disabilities Act (ADA) of 1990 marked the first time in history that disabled Americans received civil rights protections. Since World War II, disability rights activists had been pushing for legislation that provided services and partial rights in incremental steps. With the passage of the Civil Rights Act of 1964, some disability activists decided to push for a single, sweeping federal disability rights act. On July 12, 1990, the U.S. House of Representatives approved the ADA by a vote of 377 to 28. It passed the U.S. Senate by a vote of 91 to 6. On July 26, 1990, President George H. W. Bush signed the ADA into law.

The ADA, as passed, borrowed heavily from the regulatory parts of Section 504 of the Rehabilitation

Act of 1973 as well as from the Civil Rights Act. Along with regulations that apply to businesses, the ADA prohibits discrimination in public services provided by state and local governments. It mandates that public mass transportation be accessible, even if alterations must be made to existing bus and rail stations. Discrimination against people with disabilities is banned in public accommodations, such as restaurants, hotels, theaters, pharmacies, retail stores, health clubs, museums, libraries, parks, private schools, and day care centers. Private clubs and religious organizations are exempt, partly because opponents of the legislation did not want to force groups that are hostile to homosexuality to extend protections to gays with HIV/AIDS. Transvestites, transsexuals, pedophiles, exhibitionists, voyeurs, people with gender identity disorders, compulsive gamblers, kleptomaniacs, pyromaniacs, and individuals with psychoactive disorders resulting from the illegal use of drugs are not covered by the ADA. Additionally, insurance providers are permitted to use disability as a factor when refusing insurance or setting premiums.

Critics of the ADA had predicted that a flood of litigation would be brought under the legislation. However, in the first five years after passage, only a little over 600 lawsuits were filed. A Harris Poll commissioned by the National Council on Disability in 1995 found that more than ninety percent of business executives supported the antidiscrimination provisions of the ADA. However, proponents of smaller government continue to regard the legislation as wasteful and unnecessary.

PRIMARY SOURCE

SEC. 2. FINDINGS AND PURPOSES.
b) Purpose.—It is the purpose of this Act—.

(1) to provide a clear and comprehensive national mandate for the elimination of discrimination against individuals with disabilities;.

(2) to provide clear, strong, consistent, enforceable standards addressing discrimination against individuals with disabilities;.

(3) to ensure that the Federal Government plays a central role in enforcing the standards established in this Act on behalf of individuals with disabilities; and.

(4) to invoke the sweep of congressional authority, including the power to enforce the fourteenth amendment and to regulate commerce, in order to address the major areas of discrimination faced day-to-day by people with disabilities.

SEC. 3. DEFINITIONS.
As used in this Act:

(1) Auxiliary aids and services.—The term "auxiliary aids and services" includes—.

(A) qualified interpreters or other effective methods of making aurally delivered materials available to individuals with hearing impairments;.

(B) qualified readers, taped texts, or other effective methods of making visually delivered materials available to individuals with visual impairments;.

(C) acquisition or modification of equipment or devices; and.

(D) other similar services and actions.

(2) Disability.—The term "disability" means, with respect to an individual—.

(A) a physical or mental impairment that substantially limits one or more of the major life activities of such individual;.

(B) a record of such an impairment; or.

(C) being regarded as having such an impairment.

(3) State.—The term "State" means each of the several States, the District of Columbia, the Commonwealth of Puerto Rico, Guam, American Samoa, the Virgin Islands, the Trust Territory of the Pacific Islands, and the Commonwealth of the Northern Mariana Islands.

SEC. 101. DEFINITIONS.
As used in this title:

(1) Commission.—The term "Commission" means the Equal Employment Opportunity Commission established by section 705 of the Civil Rights Act of 1964 (42 U.S.C. 2000e-4).

(2) Covered entity.—The term "covered entity" means an employer, employment agency, labor organization, or joint labor-management committee.

(3) Direct threat.—The term "direct threat" means a significant risk to the health or safety of others that cannot be eliminated by reasonable accommodation.

(4) Employee.—The term "employee" means an individual employed by an employer.

(5) Employer.—.

(A) In general.—The term "employer" means a person engaged in an industry affecting commerce who has 15 or more employees for each working day in each of 20 or more calendar weeks in the current or preceding calendar year, and any agent of such person, except that, for two years following the effective date of this title, an employer means a person engaged in an industry affecting commerce who has 25 or more employees for each working day in each of 20 or more calendar weeks in the current or preceding year, and any agent of such person.

(B) Exceptions.—The term "employer" does not include—.

(i) the United States, a corporation wholly owned by the government of the United States, or an Indian tribe; or.

(ii) a bona fide private membership club (other than a labor organization) that is exempt from taxation under section 501(c) of the Internal Revenue Code of 1986.

(6) Illegal use of drugs.—.

(A) In general.—The term "illegal use of drugs" means the use of drugs, the possession or distribution of which is unlawful under the Controlled Substances Act (21 U.S.C. 812). Such term does not include the use of a drug taken under supervision by a licensed health care professional, or other uses authorized by the Controlled Substances Act or other provisions of Federal law.

(B) Drugs.—The term "drug" means a controlled substance, as defined in schedules I through V of section 202 of the Controlled Substances Act.

(7) Person, etc.—The terms "person," "labor organization," "employment agency," "commerce," and "industry affecting commerce," shall have the same meaning given such terms in section 701 of the Civil Rights Act of 1964 (42 U.S.C. 2000e).

(8) Qualified individual with a disability.—The term "qualified individual with a disability" means an individual with a disability who, with or without reasonable accommodation, can perform the essential functions of the employment position that such individual holds or desires. For the purposes of this title, consideration shall be given to the employer's judgment as to what functions of a job are essential, and if an employer has prepared a written description before advertising or interviewing applicants for the job, this description shall be considered evidence of the essential functions of the job.

(9) Reasonable accommodation.—The term "reasonable accommodation" may include—.

(A) making existing facilities used by employees readily accessible to and usable by individuals with disabilities; and.

(B) job restructuring, part-time or modified work schedules, reassignment to a vacant position, acquisition or modification of equipment or devices, appropriate adjustment or modifications of examinations, training materials or policies, the

provision of qualified readers or interpreters, and other similar accommodations for individuals with disabilities.

(10) Undue hardship.—.

(A) In general.—The term "undue hardship" means an action requiring significant difficulty or expense, when considered in light of the factors set forth in subparagraph (B).

(B) Factors to be considered.—In determining whether an accommodation would impose an undue hardship on a covered entity, factors to be considered include—.

(i) the nature and cost of the accommodation needed under this Act;.

(ii) the overall financial resources of the facility or facilities involved in the provision of the reasonable accommodation; the number of persons employed at such facility; the effect on expenses and resources, or the impact otherwise of such accommodation upon the operation of the facility;.

(iii) the overall financial resources of the covered entity; the overall size of the business of a covered entity with respect to the number of its employees; the number, type, and location of its facilities; and.

(iv) the type of operation or operations of the covered entity, including the composition, structure, and functions of the workforce of such entity; the geographic separateness, administrative, or fiscal relationship of the facility or facilities in question to the covered entity.

SIGNIFICANCE

Passage of the ADA brought with it some disillusionment. People who expected to see an overnight change in the way society treated those with disabilities were disappointed. Some protested that the law contained too many loopholes for those wishing to avoid providing access. It is clear, however, that the ADA has had a significant impact. Voting machines, sidewalks, and restrooms are just a few of the aspects of everyday life that have been modified to comply with ADA provisions.

Nevertheless, there is room for improvement. In 2001, there were 54 million Americans with varying degrees of disability. Many of them remain hampered by barriers. Students with disabilities graduate from high school and pursue college at a far lower rate than other students, making it difficult for them to achieve independence. The ADA mandates access to public transportation, but almost forty percent of rural counties throughout the United States have no public transportation. Those counties with public transportation

Disabled activists lobby Congress on Captial Hill on May 17, 1990, in an effort to get Congress to approve the Americans with Disabilities Act. PHOTO BY TERRY ASHE//TIME LIFE PICTURES/GETTY IMAGES.

do not typically have bus and train routes that stretch to every area. Americans with disabilities, particularly those who are low-income and older, are the least likely people to be able to provide or afford their own transportation. As a result, lack of transportation continues to inhibit the ability of people with disabilities to take advantage of job training, employment, and recreational opportunities.

In 2001, President George W. Bush pledged to fulfill America's promise to Americans with disabilities. The subsequent terrorist attacks shifted national focus, but the ADA has made disability rights a continuing part of the national agenda. This legislation has substantially helped to raise people with disabilities to full citizenship under the law in the United States.

FURTHER RESOURCES
Books
Francis, Leslie, and Anita Silvers, eds. *Americans with Disabilities: Exploring Implications of the Law for Institutions and Individuals*. New York: Routledge, 2000.

Perry, Greg M. *Disabling America: The Unintended Consequences of Government Protection of the Handicapped.* Nashville, Tenn.: WND Books, 2003.

Wehman, Paul, ed. *The ADA Mandate for Social Change.* Baltimore, Md.: P.H. Brookes, 1993.

Web sites
U.S. Department of Justice. "ADA Home Page." <http://www.usdoj.gov/crt/ada/> (accessed April 27, 2006).

Indian Child Labor

Photograph

By: Sophie Elbaz

Date: December 1990

Source: © Sophie Elbaz/Sygma/Corbis.

About the Photographer: Sophie Elbaz is a French photographer living in Marseilles, France. Throughout her professional career, Elbaz has held numerous exhibitions of her photographs. Most of these photographs depict events and lives of people, especially women and children the world over. According to Elbaz, her photographs symbolize human determination and courage.

INTRODUCTION

Child labor is a pervasive problem in most of the developing countries. Among these countries, India has a high number of child workers. Various organizations in the past have emphasized the prevalence of child labor in India. The United Nations reported that in 1996, India had at least fifty million children involved in labor work. As of the early 2000s, reports published by Human Rights Watch—a non-profit human rights organization—estimated the number of child workers in the range of sixty to 115 million.

Out of these, at least fifteen million are bonded laborers. Bonded laborers are those who work for meager wages, usually with the purpose of paying off a debt. This debt is often incurred as a result of a loan taken by the child's parents or guardians. Moreover, there has been a significant increase in child labor in the last decade. A census report published by Global March Against Child Labor showed that the magnitude of child labor has increased from 11.59 million in 1991, to 12.66 million in 2001. Some human rights organizations claim that the figure is higher, as child workers in the domestic and agriculture sector have not been covered in this census.

These reports also show that bonded child laborers, as young as eleven, often work for sixteen hours a day. Moreover, some are expected to work every day of the year. There are many reasons for such bonded child labor. These include poverty, weak implementation of child labor prevention laws, lack of alternative small-scale loans for poor people in the rural and urban areas, absence of a concerted social welfare scheme to safeguard against hunger and illness, and an imbalanced educational system especially in the rural regions. Further, fewer employment opportunities, corruption and apathy of government officials, caste-based discrimination, and indifference of the society forces the children to start working at an early age.

Over the years, various human rights organizations, within and outside India, have criticized the role of the Indian government in not being able to stop child labor. As mentioned above, numerous reports highlighting the rise of child labor in India have been published. The primary source is a photograph taken by Sophie Elbaz in December 1990, depicting an eleven-year-old orphaned child working in a stone mine in Gurgaon, northern India, to meet his daily needs.

■ PRIMARY SOURCE

INDIA'S BONDED CHILD LABORERS
See primary source image.

SIGNIFICANCE

Child labor is a socio-economic problem that is predominantly rooted in poverty. In its report, the Global March against Child Labor found that seventy percent of respondents—mainly parents of child laborers—cited poverty as the main cause of child labor in India. Studies also showed that illiteracy and unemployment are two more factors that are responsible for this growing scourge.

In rural India, there is an increasing trend of child labor as most of the people there depend on agriculture as the only source of livelihood. With no proper government schemes, especially on finance, the farmers keep on seeking loans from landlords who provide it at high interest rates. Many farmers fail to repay these loans and eventually pass it on to their children. As a result, these children have no alternative but to take up labor at a very young age. It deprives them of even the sparse educational opportunities available in their villages. According to the 2001 Census that was released in August 2005, out of 226 million children aged between six and fourteen years, 65.3 million children—thirty percent approximately—did not attend the school at all. The proportion of out-of-school boys was twenty five percent compared to thirty three percent for girls.

A nation's progress depends on the education of its younger generation. However, lack of education has diminished the job prospects of these children, even as the number of child labor keeps on escalating every year.

In order to improve the situation, the Indian government has, in the last decade, created some awareness among the masses and also initiated several steps mostly under the first Act on child labor—Enactment of Children Pledging of Labor—framed in February 1933. Since then, there have been nine different legislations relating to child labor. The Child Labor Act, 1986, seeks to ban employment of children working in certain hazardous occupations and also regulates the work of children in certain other industries.

PRIMARY SOURCE

India's Bonded Child Laborers: Eleven-year-old Jan Mornod is a bonded laborer from Rajasthan, India, who works in the Gurgaon stone mines. © SOPHIE ELBAZ/SYGMA/CORBIS.

The government has set up committees under the Ministries of Rural Development, Urban Affairs and Employment, Human Resources Development—Department of Education—Social Justice and Empowerment and the Department of Women and Child Development for the betterment of child laborers. Several benefits have been listed for the parents and family members of the children working under the poverty eradication and employment generation programs. Another program, the Integrated Child Development Service (ICDS), perhaps, the single largest program in the world is focused on pregnant mothers and children in terms of immunization, nutrition and pre-primary early childhood education. Approximately 600,000 schools have been set up with a purpose of providing free and compulsory primary education irrespective of caste, creed, and sex. The National Literacy Mission has been launched since 1988 to remove parental illiteracy.

Besides, projects to rehabilitate children working in hazardous industries like fireworks, glass, bangle making, gem cutting, and so on were started following the announcement of National Child Labor Policy of 1987. In 1994, then Prime Minister PV Narasimha Rao developed initiatives for taking out two million children of 'hazardous employment'. Hazardous employment, as the name suggests, indicates employment conditions that are unsafe for children. This figure—though in millions—encompasses only up to 3.3 percent of the nation's child laborers.

The Indian legal system prohibits bonded child labor and is a punishable crime with severe penalties. In 1996, the Supreme Court of India gave directions for immediate identification of children in hazardous occupations and their subsequent rehabilitation, including providing appropriate education to the released children. At the international level, India is signatory to the treaties framed under the International Labor

A teenage Kurdish girl harvests cotton in southeastern Turkey in 1993. © REZA; WEBISTAN/CORBIS.

Organization that guarantee rights of children. These treaties were drafted at the International Covenant on Economic, Social and Cultural Rights (ICESCR) 1966, and the Convention on the Rights of the Child, 1989.

The figures of child labor in India vary from organization to organization due to the methods adopted and the period selected for such surveys. However, the scourge of child labor continues unabated.

FURTHER RESOURCES
Books
Lakshmidhar Mishra. *Child Labor in India*. New York: Oxford University Press, 2000.

World Bank. *India: Achievements and Challenges in Reducing Poverty*. Geneva: World Bank Publications, June 1997.

Web sites
BBC News. "India's child labour laws failing." August 20, 2002. <http://news.bbc.co.uk/1/hi/world/south_asia/2206026.stm> (accessed April 27, 2006).

BBC News. "India 'losing' child-labour battle." May 6, 2002. <http://news.bbc.co.uk/1/hi/world/south_asia/1970708.stm> (accessed April 27, 2006).

Congressional Record. "The Exploitation of Child Labor in India." July 25, 1995. <http://www.dalitstan.org/journal/rights/104/250595.html> (accessed April 27, 2006).

Embassy of India, Washington, D.C. "Child Labor and India." <http://www.indianembassy.org/policy/Child_Labor/childlabor.htm> (accessed April 27, 2006).

Human Rights Watch. "The Small Hands of Slavery." September 1996. <http://www.hrw.org/reports/1996/India3.htm> (accessed April 27, 2006).

North American Secretariat on Child Labor and Education. "Review of Child Labour, Education and Poverty Agenda." <http://www.iccle.org/images/india-report.pdf> (accessed April 27, 2006).

UNICEF. "Child Protection: The Picture in India." <http://www.unicef.org/india/child_protection_152.htm> (accessed April 27, 2006).

World Bank. "Child Labor: Issues, Causes and Interventions." <http://www.worldbank.org/html/extdr/hnp/hddflash/workp/wp_00056.html> (accessed April 27, 2006).

How Ireland Hid its Own Dirty Laundry

Newspaper article

By: Mary Gordon

Date: August 3, 2003

Source: Gordon, Mary. "How Ireland Hid its Own Dirty Laundry." *The New York Times.* (August 3, 2003).

About the Author: Mary Gordon, critic, essayist and novelist, resides in New York City. Among her contributions to contemporary Irish-American literature are *Pearl* and *Final Payments.*

INTRODUCTION

Scottish director Peter Mullan's film *The Magdalene Sisters* opens with rhythmic music sounded by the bodhran drum, dancing, celebratory drinking, and a traditional wedding party. Soon, the priest's drumming and singing of "The Well Below the Valley," a song about Jesus Christ's encounter with Mary Magdalene, drowns out the sounds of the rape of a girl, Margaret (played by Ann-Marie Duff) by her cousin. Later, the young man endures no punishment, while the girl is shunned by her family, cast off to live with "the sisters." The priest's unintentional silencing of the victim through the noise of his druid-like chanting and drumming mirrors the actual Catholic Church's deliberate silencing of 30,000 young women during the late nineteenth and twentieth centuries. Women who were raped, became pregnant out of wedlock, were sexually active, or were simply considered too attractive or promiscuous to remain in open society were sent to institutions run by nuns where they were forced into hard labor without pay and leave. Their only chance for pardon was from a male relative—a rare occurrence because of the fear of shame begotten to the family. These girls were called the Magdalene Sisters, or Maggies for short.

Mary Gordon's New York Times article "How Ireland Hid Its Own Dirty Laundry," examines Mullan's film, which questions a culture that keeps history and family matters tightly lip-locked in such cases as the knowledge of the laundries.

Mullan's has said that his viewing of the televised documentary "Sex in a Cold Climate," in which four "ex-Maggies" are interviewed, led to a desire to treat the topic in a motion picture in order to reach a larger audience.

PRIMARY SOURCE

ONE of the most ancient and thriving products of Irish industry isn't mentioned in the tourist brochures, or the guidebooks, or the economic histories. I don't mean linen, tweed or Jameson's. What I have in mind is shame.

The Magdalene Sisters by the Scottish director Peter Mullan, which opened Friday, is a fictional rendering of a historical situation that could only take place in a culture of shame. The film follows three young Irish girls who are sent to one of the Magdalene Asylums, institutions run by nuns, primarily in Ireland, to house girls who got pregnant outside of marriage, or who were considered too sexual, too flirtatious or even too attractive. They were incarcerated in these asylums, which doubled as laundries, where they worked, unpaid, seven days a week, 364 days a year, with only Christmas day off.

Often the girls were put there by their families, in arrangements facilitated by the parish priest; if they escaped, they were returned by the police—a perfect collusion of family, church and state. Some girls spent years there; some a whole life. The laundries were founded in the mid–19th century; the last was closed only in 1996. It is said that 30,000 women passed through their doors.

Mr. Mullan's film raises the inevitable questions: how can this have been allowed to go on? Didn't anybody know what was happening? Part of the explanation lies in the fact that the soil in which the Magdalene laundries flourished was the soil of shamed silence, the kind of silence that allows words to be spoken but makes full understanding of them impossible. And so the answer to the question—didn't people know what was going on?—is yes and no.

Yes, in that the laundries' existence was well known enough to become part of the vernacular, to have generated nicknames, proverbs, cautionary tales: the domestic architecture of demotic speech. Girls who were sent to the laundries were known as Maggies. There was a saying, "Bad girls do the best sheets." Children who misbehaved were told to mend their ways or they'd be sent "to the laundries with the sisters." And no, in that all the Irish people I have asked have said that they had no idea of the conditions of the laundries themselves. The girls were literally kept behind stone walls; invisible, isolate.

And one of the most distressing aspects of the film is the girls' isolation: they seem so utterly unbefriended, even by one another. Women who spent time in the laundries say that one of the film's unrealistic touches is the conversations among the girls; these would never have been allowed. Silence was part of the penitential discipline that was meant to cleanse them—while keeping them, of course, from forming any sort of community. But we ask ourselves: didn't any of the women who escaped or left legitimately (any adult male relative could rescue them) tell anyone—a family member, a friend, a sympathetic confessor—what they had endured? The answer seems to be no, and the explanation lies in the particular flavor of Irish shamed silence.

Is the Irish mania for keeping things in the family explicable only by colonization, by poverty, by the prevalence of alcoholism? I'm not a good enough historian to trace the causes. But I do know this: one of the mistakes that people make about the Irish is to confuse their volubility with a sharing of information; the Irish believe that language is at least as much ornament as telegrapher, and one can be astonished at how many words one has heard at an Irish gathering without having learned the slightest thing about the speakers' lives.

All the ex-Magdalenes interviewed by historians and documentarians insisted that they never told anyone what had happened to them because they feared the stigma of being known as an "ex-Maggie" so intensely that they denied themselves the consolation of sharing their experience. They never spoke of it to their families, and their families never spoke of it to them, because they had endangered their families' position in the world, the future success and happiness of their siblings. In the film, the father of one of the girls who has tried to escape (he is played by Mr. Mullan himself) brings her back and beats her in front of the smirking mother superior while shouting: "You have no parents. You've killed your mother and me."

The moral horror of the Magdalene laundries is that the abuses they perpetrated were not the outgrowths of simple sadism, or even of unmindfulness, but of a belief that they were intended for the victims' own good. It is difficult to understand now that even in my childhood, people who were neither insane nor stupid believed in literal hell fire, a torment that was physical and spiritual and went on for all eternity. If you really believed this, it could certainly be seen as an act of kindness to lock someone up, even for life, to subject her to humiliation and deprivation, if that would purge her sin and wash her as white as the sheets she scrubbed.

And it is important to remember that the Magdalene laundries came into being in the social, political, and religious context of Victorian Ireland, and the defenders of the laundries say that we must also put them in their historical context. They say that we must remember that for some girls they were a refuge from a life on the streets, a shelter from death by starvation or the fate worse than death:

prostitution. When the laundries were founded, Ireland was a colony of England, its population halved by famine. The country's economic and social reality, and its image of itself, were closely tied to Mother England. It was a perverse relationship, as colonial relationships tend to be, a common-law marriage whose shaky legitimacy could be easily threatened.

For important segments of the Irish middle class, respectability was a tantalizing fruit always ready to be devoured by the savage maw of Irish instinctual life. The most visible sign of this threat was the sexually active woman; a pregnancy outside of marriage was a reminder of fecundity that could not be controlled by the mores of the widowed queen—even with the collusion of the church.

But if the relationship with Mother England was fragile and vexed, if the signals were confusing and shifting, there was the rock of Peter upon which the church stood. That need never be doubted: whatever the winds blowing across the Irish Sea, the breath of the Holy Spirit could be felt every time a nun or a priest opened his or her mouth.

The burden of these girls' shame was made heavier by their conviction that no one would believe them if they said that the nuns were cruel torturers rather than angelic saviors. Their abuse was hidden from the world by a wall of long-skirted, veiled Brides of Christ, who were themselves incarcerated: if it was good enough for them, why wasn't it good enough for ordinary sinners?

One of the most arresting scenes in the film is the one in which Sister Bridget, the Mother Superior, watches, in tears, while Ingrid Bergman, as Sister Benedict in *The Bells of St. Mary's,* weeps while she prays. We can see Sister Bridget's image of herself: rapt in her romance with the Divine, able to endure any hardship on earth for her Lover in heaven. The image was easily accessible to one type of Catholic imagination, for which the nun, in her consecrate virginity, was the only vessel in which femaleness could safely be contained without the contamination of sexuality. What hope could a tainted vessel have in testifying against a pure one?

My own experience with nuns left me dissatisfied with the heavy-handed burlesque of Geraldine McEwan's performance as Sister Bridget. I would have been more chilled if she had seemed less psychotic, more calmly sure in her role as handmaiden of the Lord. An obvious crazy is easier to deal with and then dismiss than a hyper-rational ice princess: an obvious crazy allows you to believe in the possibility that she may be wrong. The cool rationalist leaves you nowhere to turn, except against yourself. Sister Bridget's giving Harriet, the straight-haired, simpleminded girl (brilliantly played by a newcomer, Eileen Walsh), the name Crispina, which is Irish for curly-headed, and the girl's forced laughter at her own humiliation, was more horrifying to me than the scene in which the nun cruelly stabs at the eyes of another girl as she shears her victim's hair with her punishing scissors. Sister Bridget's cool insults, delivered with a hyper-genteel precision, striking at the girls' notions that they are of any value under the sun, seemed more parching to the soul than beatings or starvation rations. And there is almost no one who went through Catholic school who has not had at least one experience of the nun's special brand of styptic words and looks.

There is a cruel irony in choosing Magdalene as the patroness of the laundries' punishing enterprise. Jesus' dealings with Mary Magdalene are saturated with forgiveness; there is no hint of punishment. Magdalene, the prostitute, pours perfume over Jesus' feet and dries them with her hair. He gives her a place of honor—it is Judas who objects, and it is after the incident with Magdalene that he decides to betray Jesus. In the Gospel of John, Magdalene is the first to see Jesus after the Resurrection.

But no such reward has been given to modern Magdalenes by the Catholic Church or the State of Ireland. Because of this, Peter Mullan's movie sheds an essential light, however occasionally overheated, on this shameful transaction.

SIGNIFICANCE

The original intent of the institutions sprang forth from earlier "rescue movements" of both Ireland and Britain to "save" those women whose work was prostitution. This Victorian age of sexual repression also encapsulated the great potato famine that swept Ireland from shore to shore in the mid-nineteenth century, leading to desperation among Ireland's people to survive, thus producing more prostitution in the country. These early asylum women were, therefore, saved from prostitution and from starvation, and resulted in less available avenues for venereal disease transmission to the public.

However, the original intent of the laundries became blurred as women were brought to the asylums for reasons beyond that of prostitution. Numbers of voluntary inhabitants diminished and laundry profits plummeted, therefore, the criteria for confinement to the laundries widened. Women who had sex outside the sanctity of marriage, whether by consent or by rape, were also then shepherded into the profitable, soul-saving laundries. Additionally, the asylums were used to hide away young women with mental and physical disabilities less accepted by society, as characterized by Crispina in Mullan's film. "Maggies" were instructed not to leave the laundries for the sake of their souls and instead to commit to lives of silent penance, working for the church, in order to avoid the repercussion of Hell.

Ultimately, the advent of the washing machine spelled the end of the Magdalene asylums, as profits once again fell when large laundries became impractical and washing machines were plentiful. The kind of activity that is portrayed in the institutions in Mullan's film primarily ended in the 1970s. The last of the convent laundries belonging to the Convent of the Sisters of Our Lady of Charity on Sean Mac Dermott Street in Dublin did not officially close until 1996. Those who were found there were free to leave the convent, yet many opted to stay because they either had no surviving family or other prospects for living and working arrangements. According to Gary Culliton's 1996 *Irish Times* article entitled "Last Days of a Laundry", the convent was not referred to as a Magdalene Laundry in thirty years before its closing. "Magdalene means a public sinner. I'd be very wary who I'd call a sinner," commented Sister Lucy, a nun at the convent. "The term makes my gorge rise. In their young lives, these women were thrown aside by their families and by society. They feel it is so unfair to keep throwing that back at them."

In 1993, old memories of the Magdalene asylums resurfaced when a mass grave of 133 unmarked bodies of the once-incarcerated at the High Park laundry was found after the land was sold. The bodies were disinterred, cremated and reburied in a nearby cemetery. The Magdalene Name Project has been erected in hope of further research and recognition of the incarceration of these women, allowing families to claim acknowledgment of relatives and loved ones who worked within the halls of the laundries. A memorial plaque presented by the former Irish President Mary Robinson in 1996 resides in central Dublin and is inscribed "To the women who worked in the Magdalene laundry institutions and to the children born to some members of those communities—reflect here upon their lives."

FURTHER RESOURCES
Web sites

CBSnews.com. "The Magdalene Laundry." (August 3, 2003). <http://www.cbsnews.com/stories/2003/08/08/sunday/main567365.shtml> (accessed May 10, 2006).

Decent Films Guide. Greydanus, Steven, D. "The Magdalene Sisters Controversy" (2003). <http://decentfilms.com/sections/articles/2551> (accessed May 10, 2006).

The Irish Times. Culliton, Gary. "Last Days of a Laundry." September 26, 1996. <http://users.erols.com/bcccsbs/bass/new_lastdays.html> (accessed May 5, 2006).

Magdalenelaundries.com. "The Magdalene Name Project." <http://www.magdalenelaundries.com/name.htm> (accessed May 10, 2006).

Women at work in a New York City sweatshop, 1913. © BETTMANN/CORBIS. REPRODUCED BY PERMISSION.

The Victorian Web. "Prostitution in Victorian England." <http://www.victorianweb.org/gender/ prostitution.html> (accessed May 10, 2006).

International Convention on the Protection of the Rights of All Migrant Workers and Members of Their Families

Resolution

By: United Nations General Assembly

Date: July 1, 2003

Source: United Nations General Assembly. "International Convention on the Protection of the Rights of All Migrant Workers and Members of Their Families." General Assembly Resolution 45/158, July 1, 2003.

About the Author: The phrase "United Nations" was used during World War II (1939–1945) to describe the dozens of nations allied together to fight Germany and Japan, most notably including China, France, Great Britain, the Soviet Union, and the United States of America. These allies decided to develop a new organization to facilitate international cooperation and help prevent future wars. It would replace the League of Nations, which had failed to prevent World War II. They called it the United Nations (UN). The UN Charter was ratified on October 24, 1945. In the years since the UN has served as a forum for

Faubert Jean cuts cane on a batey, or sugar plantation, in the Dominican Republic. Like most cane cutters on the bateys, Jean is a migrant worker for Haiti, and faces frequent discrimination. © GIDEON MENDEL/CORBIS.

international negotiation and cooperation on many issues, including international security, human rights, trade and economics, and the environment.

INTRODUCTION

In the wake of the terrorist attacks on September 11, 2001, illegal immigration and a growing population of non-nationals have become serious problems for many countries. While greater restrictions are necessary to increase security, the backlash and fallout from these measures can hinder economic growth and infringe upon human rights. Debates concerning illegal immigration and migrant workers often lump the two categories together because both groups enter countries without official documentation.

Unlike illegal immigrants, migrant workers generally come for seasonal work such as harvesting crops and often return home after the work is done. Immigrants desire to relocate to a new nation, and the decision to move from their original country stems from reasons of economic hardship, religious intolerance, political suppression, to wanting to experience a new lifestyle. The International Organization for Migration estimates that about 175 million people worldwide live outside their country of birth.

Even though advocacy groups also maintain that the United States was founded by immigrants, many sectors of society fear unrestricted immigration into the United States. Hence, recent increased border patrols have brought the number of undocumented immigrants in the United States, estimated at eleven million people, into a heightened media spotlight. The added security measures aimed at preventing another terrorist attack have caused many immigrants and non-nationals to be detained at borders or within the United States for extended periods. Often their immigration hearings have been held in secret, they have been deported, and some detainees have testified to unacceptable conditions in their holding cells. Many of these detainees have been of Arab or Asian decent.

The United States is not the only country to have taken such extensive measures to curb illegal immigration and the flux of migrant workers. The European

Union mandated that asylum seekers and political refugees will not be returned to places where their lives will be at risk, although after a large influx of refugees from Northern Africa in the 1990s, some European countries such as Italy and France are struggling to incorporate the new residents into their economies. A few wealthier countries like the Netherlands and Spain have not given all refugees security from harm. Thus, the European Union is challenged in maintaining its own directive.

These continual struggles with immigration rights and the question of the rights of the undocumented laborer caused the United Nations to examine the issue in 2003. On July 1, 2003, the International Convention on the Protection of the Rights of All Migrant Workers and Members of Their Families treaty went into force. Over twenty years in its making, this treaty requires states to prevent and stop illegal migration and to inform migrants and employers of their rights.

▮ PRIMARY SOURCE

PART III HUMAN RIGHTS OF ALL MIGRANT WORKERS AND MEMBERS OF THEIR FAMILIES

Article 8.

1. Migrant workers and members of their families shall be free to leave any State, including their State of origin. This right shall not be subject to any restrictions except those that are provided by law, are necessary to protect national security, public order, public health or morals or the rights and freedoms of others and are consistent with the other rights recognized in the present part of the Convention.

2. Migrant workers and members of their families shall have the right at any time to enter and remain in their State of origin.

Article 9.

The right to life of migrant workers and members of their families shall be protected by law.

Article 10.

No migrant worker or member of his or her family shall be subjected to torture or to cruel, inhuman or degrading treatment or punishment.

Article 11.

1. No migrant worker or member of his or her family shall be held in slavery or servitude.

2. No migrant worker or member of his or her family shall be required to perform forced or compulsory labour.

3. Paragraph 2 of the present article shall not be held to preclude, in States where imprisonment with hard labour may be imposed as a punishment for a crime, the performance of hard labour in pursuance of a sentence to such punishment by a competent court.

4. For the purpose of the present article the term" "forced or compulsory labour" shall not include:

(a) Any work or service not referred to in paragraph 3 of the present article normally required of a person who is under detention in consequence of a lawful order of a court or of a person during conditional release from such detention;

(b) Any service exacted in cases of emergency or calamity threatening the life or well-being of the community;

(c) Any work or service that forms part of normal civil obligations so far as it is imposed also on citizens of the State concerned.

Article 12

1. Migrant workers and members of their families shall have the right to freedom of thought, conscience, and religion. This right shall include freedom to have or to adopt a religion or belief of their choice and freedom either individually or in community with others and in public or private to manifest their religion or belief in worship, observance, practice and teaching.

2. Migrant workers and members of their families shall not be subject to coercion that would impair their freedom to have or to adopt a religion or belief of their choice.

3. Freedom to manifest one's religion or belief may be subject only to such limitations as are prescribed by law and are necessary to protect public safety, order, health or morals or the fundamental rights and freedoms of others.

4. States Parties to the present Convention undertake to have respect for the liberty of parents, at least one of whom is a migrant worker, and, when applicable, legal guardians to ensure the religious and moral education of their children in conformity with their own convictions.

Article 13

1. Migrant workers and members of their families shall have the right to hold opinions without interference.

2. Migrant workers and members of their families shall have the right to freedom of expression; this right shall include freedom to seek, receive and impart information and ideas of all kinds, regardless of frontiers, either orally, in writing or in print, in the form of art or through any other media of their choice.

3. The exercise of the right provided for in paragraph 2 of the present article carries with it special duties and responsibilities. It may therefore be subject to certain restrictions, but these shall only be such as are provided by law and are necessary:

(a) For respect of the rights or reputation of others;

(b) For the protection of the national security of the States concerned or of public order or of public health or morals;

(c) For the purpose of preventing any propaganda for war;

(d) For the purpose of preventing any advocacy of national, racial or religious hatred that constitutes incitement to discrimination, hostility or violence.

Article 14

No migrant worker or member of his or her family shall be subjected to arbitrary or unlawful interference with his or her privacy, family, home, correspondence or other communications, or to unlawful attacks on his or her honour and reputation. Each migrant worker and member of his or her family shall have the right to the protection of the law against such interference or attacks.

Article 15

No migrant worker or member of his or her family shall be arbitrarily deprived of property, whether owned individually or in association with others. Where, under the legislation in force in the State of employment, the assets of a migrant worker or a member of his or her family are expropriated in whole or in part, the person concerned shall have the right to fair and adequate compensation.

Article 16

1. Migrant workers and members of their families shall have the right to liberty and security of person.

2. Migrant workers and members of their families shall be entitled to effective protection by the State against violence, physical injury, threats and intimidation, whether by public officials or by private individuals, groups or institutions.

3. Any verification by law enforcement officials of the identity of migrant workers or members of their families shall be carried out in accordance with procedure established by law.

4. Migrant workers and members of their families shall not be subjected individually or collectively to arbitrary arrest or detention; they shall not be deprived of their liberty except on such grounds and in accordance with such procedures as are established by law.

5. Migrant workers and members of their families who are arrested shall be informed at the time of arrest as far as possible in a language they understand of the reasons for their arrest and they shall be promptly informed in a language they understand of any charges against them.

6. Migrant workers and members of their families who are arrested or detained on a criminal charge shall be brought promptly before a judge or other officer authorized by law to exercise judicial power and shall be entitled to trial within a reasonable time or to release. It shall not be the general rule that while awaiting trial they shall be detained in custody, but release may be subject to guarantees to appear for trial, at any other stage of the judicial proceedings and, should the occasion arise, for the execution of the judgment.

7. When a migrant worker or a member of his or her family is arrested or committed to prison or custody pending trial or is detained in any other manner:

(a) The consular or diplomatic authorities of his or her State of origin or of a State representing the interests of that State shall, if he or she so requests, be informed without delay of his or her arrest or detention and of the reasons therefore;

(b) The person concerned shall have the right to communicate with the said authorities. Any communication by the person concerned to the said authorities shall be forwarded without delay, and he or she shall also have the right to receive communications sent by the said authorities without delay;

(c) The person concerned shall be informed without delay of this right and of rights deriving from relevant treaties, if any, applicable between the States concerned, to correspond and to meet with representatives of the said authorities and to make arrangements with them for his or her legal representation.

8. Migrant workers and members of their families who are deprived of their liberty by arrest or detention shall be entitled to take proceedings before a court, in order that that court may decide without delay on the lawfulness of their detention and order their release if the detention is not lawful. When they attend such proceedings, they shall have the assistance, if necessary without cost to them, of an interpreter, if they cannot understand or speak the language used.

9. Migrant workers and members of their families who have been victims of unlawful arrest or detention shall have an enforceable right to compensation.

SIGNIFICANCE

The 2003 migrant worker treaty only began the process toward global cooperation and understanding for the rights of migrants and other immigrants. As of this publication, no major Western nation has ratified the treaty. Smaller countries, and several developing countries, have signed the treaty. Some of these countries are Egypt, Mexico, and the Philippines. The countries that have signed the treaty are also those that see the highest number of individuals leave their nation every year.

The treaty is a major step in acknowledging the rights of migrants, but recent world events have also shown that there is more work to be done. In April 2006, intense Congressional debates, public protests (for and against), and media scrutiny concerned a proposal to provide amnesty for nearly eleven million undocumented illegal aliens in the United States. Advocacy groups remarked that this program would ease hostilities with targeted groups. Arab immigrants and Arab Americans have frequently stated that they are targeted in immigration investigations because of racist assumptions that they are terrorists. Also, advocates of the amnesty program claim that it would force employers to offer fair wages—instead of the lower wages that are traditionally given to undocumented individuals—, thus encouraging future immigrants to come to the United States legally. Opponents to the plan contend that amnesty could give terrorists an opportunity to infiltrate the United States—and that the plan would cause welfare and public assistance roles to swell.

FURTHER RESOURCES

Books

Cholewinski, Ryszard. *Migrant Workers in the International Human Rights Law: Their Protection in Countries of Employment*. New York: Oxford University Press, 1997.

Mitchell, Don. *The Lie of the Land: Migrant Workers and the California Landscape*. Saint Paul: University of Minnesota Press, 1996.

Periodicals

Cleveland, Sarah H. "Legal Status and Rights of Undocumented Workers: Advisory Opinion." *The American Journal of International Law*. 99:2 (April 2005): 460-465.

Helton, Arthur C. "The new convention from the perspective of a country of employment: the U.S. case. (Special Issue - U.N. International Convention on the Protection of the Rights of All Migrant Workers and Members of Their Families)." *International Migration Review*. 25.n4 (Winter 1991): 848–858.

Web sites

International Labor Organization. "General Activities: Social Protection." May 5, 2005. <http://www.ilo.org/public/english/dialogue/actrav/genact/socprot/migrant/> (accessed April 28, 2006).

Honduran Sweatshops

Photograph

By: Ginnette Riquelme

Date: October 29, 2003

Source: AP Images.

About the Photographer: The Associated Press is a worldwide news agency based in New York.

INTRODUCTION

The rap musician and businessman Sean P. Diddy Combs (1969–) is the owner of two fashion clothing lines, Sean John and Sean by Sean Combs. The workers in this picture are sewing shirts for the Sean John clothing line at a factory owned by Southeast Textiles, S.A. in Choloma, Cortés, Honduras. In 2003, the factory employed 380–400 workers in two buildings—an older building housing laundry, cutting, packing, and warehousing facilities and a newer building housing fifteen production lines, each employing fifteen to eighteen sewers. One of these production lines is pictured here. Eighty percent of the factory's output was Combs's Sean John clothing line (long-sleeved t-shirts and SJb9 Ski Division sweatshirts) and the remaining twenty percent was long-sleeved t-shirts for Rocawear, a clothing line co-founded by another rap artist, Jay-Z. Other Sean John clothing line items are made in Vietnam and China.

Controversy erupted around Combs when the National Labor Committee in Support of Human and Worker Rights (NLC) released a detailed report in 2003 stating that working conditions at Southeast Textiles were exploitative. The NLC is a New York-based, nonprofit labor-rights group founded in 1981 that says it "investigates and exposes human and labor rights abuses committed by U.S. companies producing goods in the developing world." The 2003 report included interviews with factory workers at Southeast Textiles, allegations about specific abusive working conditions, and an interview with the Human Rights Ombudsman of Honduras, Dr. Ramon Custodio. (The Human Rights Ombudsman's office is a Honduran government office set up in the 1990s to monitor human rights abuses in that country; about 100 nations, worldwide, have set up Human Rights Ombudsman's offices.) The NLC report was bolstered by pay stubs, bathroom passes, bills of lading, and other evidence.

According to the NLC, employees in the factory worked mandatory 11–12 hour shifts without overtime, were paid the Honduran equivalent of $0.75–$0.98 per hour, were required to sew a Sean John sweatshirt or long-sleeved t-shirt every 14.4 minutes or a short-sleeved t-shirt every 3.75 minutes, and were forbidden to talk. Drinking water supplied to workers sometimes contained excrement, women were required to take pregnancy tests and were fired if found to be pregnant, and no workers were entered in the Honduran Social Security Health Care system. Regarding the latter point, the Honduran Human Rights Ombudsman stated, "This is illegal, a violation of the law because every worker should have the protection of Social Security."

After the NLC report was released, several large U.S. news organizations picked up the story and it was widely reported that Combs was profiting from a sweatshop. (Any factory where workers work long hours, receive very low pay, and must endure dangerous, abusive, or otherwise illegal conditions is known as a sweatshop.) Combs held a press conference on October 28, 2003, in which he stated that he knew from his childhood "what it's like to struggle day after day in a job to put food on the table" and was unaware that his fashion lines might be produced using sweatshop labor. He promised to investigate the NLC's charges.

Later in 2003, the NLC reported that the most abusive supervisors at the Southeast Textiles factory had been fired, overtime was being paid, workers could use the bathroom without getting a pass, filtered drinking water was being supplied, air conditioning had been installed, workers were about to be entered in the Social Security system, workers believed that mandatory pregnancy testing was about to be ended, and a union had been organized and recognized. In a 2005 interview, the Director of the NLC said, "Sean Combs didn't pull out of the factory, and he did the right thing. But it took a lot of public embarrassment for him to make any improvements."

PRIMARY SOURCE

Honduran sweatshops: Workers at a Southeast Textiles International, S.A., in Choloma, Honduras, on October 29, 2003. They are sewing t-shirts for the clothing line of American entrepreneur Sean "P. Diddy" Combs. AP IMAGES.

PRIMARY SOURCE

HONDURAN SWEATSHOPS

See primary source image.

SIGNIFICANCE

Low wages for workers can translate directly into higher profits for manufacturers because low wages reduce the cost of production. For example, according to the NLC, each Sean John t-shirt produced by Southeast Textiles, S.A. cost only $3.65 for a wholesale buyer in the U.S. in 2003. This cost included labor, materials, shipping to the United States, and profits earned by Southeast Textiles. Since a worker was paid only $0.15 for sewing a shirt, labor comprised only four percent of the shirt's cost to the wholesale importer. The same shirts were sold in U.S. stores for $30 each, so the labor cost was less than one half of one percent of the final retail price. Other hip-hop focused clothing companies such as Perry Ellis, Karl Kani, and Timberland have also been accused of contracting with foreign factories that employ sweatshop labor. According to China Labour Watch, in 2004 workers were paid only $0.55 to produce a pair of Timberland boots that retails for up to $85.

The controversy over the production of apparel in sweatshops is part of a larger controversy about economic globalization. Critics of the globalization of manufacturing and marketing argue that manufacturers locate their factories in countries where workers are so desperate for income that they will endure extremely low wages and abusive conditions. Defenders of globalization argue that foreign employers pay higher wages than local ones and actually raise living standards by establishing their factories in foreign countries.

Family members arrive at a New York City morgue to identify the bodies of victims of the Triangle Shirtwaist Company fire. The infamous fire killed 146 factory workers, mainly young immigrant women, in March 1911, and led to workplace safety reforms in the United States. © BETTMANN/CORBIS.

Efforts to produce clothing lines without using sweatshop labor have been made. For example, No Sweat, a clothing line of "urban apparel" based in Bangor, Maine, features only clothes made by unionized workers. Opponents of such efforts argue that withdrawing business from low-wage factories in poorer countries—whether these factories can technically be classed as sweatshops or not—actually harms poor workers rather than helping them. Some sweatshop opponents reply that their efforts are aimed at improving working conditions in these factories, rather than at closing them.

FURTHER RESOURCES
Books

Esbenshade, Jill Louise. *Monitoring Sweatshops: Workers, Consumers, and the Global Apparel Industry*. Philadelphia: Temple University Press, 2004.

Ross, Robert J. S. *Slaves to Fashion: Poverty and Abuse in the New Sweatshops*. Ann Arbor: University of Michigan Press, 2004.

Periodicals

Garcia, Michelle, and Michael Powell. "P. Diddy Feels the Heat Over Sweatshop Charge." *The Washington Post* (October 29, 2003): C3.

Web sites

National Labor Committee. "Sean John's Sweatshops." October 2003. <http://www.nlcnet.org/campaigns/setisa/> (accessed April 18, 2006).

Judge Rejects Lawsuit Challenging Army "Stop Loss" Policy

Newspaper article

By: The Associated Press

Date: February 8, 2005

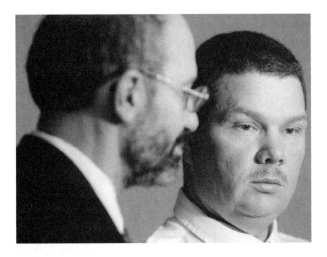

In Washington on December 6, 2004, a news conference announced a lawsuit challenging the military's "stop loss" policy of involuntarily extending service in Iraq. Present was one of the seven plaintiffs, U.S. Army National Guard Specialist David Qualls, pictured right, who is seeking a court order requiring immediate release from military service. AP IMAGES.

Source: The Associated Press

About the Author: This article was written by a contributor to the Associated Press, a worldwide news agency based in New York.

INTRODUCTION

Thousands of United States servicemen and women were forced to remain in the military beyond their scheduled retirement or discharge after the September 11, 2001 terrorist attacks. The "stop loss" orders issued by the U.S. government indefinitely suspended the date that military personnel could leave the armed forces because an insufficient number of Americans had volunteered to replace them in the ranks. To critics of the policy, the government turned its own soldiers into prisoners of war.

At the start of the war on terror in 2001, fewer than half of one percent of Americans served in the armed forces. During the Vietnam War, five percent of Americans served in the military while twelve percent of Americans put on a uniform during World War II. In September 2001, the Air Force became the first service branch to issue a stop loss order when it blocked eleven thousand people from leaving. In subsequent months, the Army, Navy, and Marines also imposed stop loss orders.

In 2004, the Pentagon relaxed the stop loss rules. In the wake of this decision, more special operations personnel left the military than at any time since the

September 11 terrorist attacks. These personnel were Army Special Forces, known as Green Berets, and Naval Special Warfare personnel, known as SEALS. Nearly thirteen percent of Army-enlisted commandos left the service in 2004, compared with about six percent in 2003. Nearly ten percent of 1,237 sergeants in Special Forces with fourteen to nineteen years of experience left the service in 2004 compared with only thirteen leaving in 2003. The former commandos were recruited by private security firms working in Iraq and Afghanistan that could pay far higher wages than those offered by the U.S. military. These losses meant that younger, less-experienced special operations personnel were being promoted to leadership roles more quickly than in the past. High attrition also meant that if a shortage of Navy SEALS or Green Berets existed, a mission was not completed or the wrong personnel was sent.

■ PRIMARY SOURCE

JUDGE REJECTS LAWSUIT CHALLENGING ARMY "STOP LOSS" POLICY

WASHINGTON (AP)—A federal judge on Monday dismissed a lawsuit challenging the Army's right to force soldiers to serve past the dates of their enlistments, the so-called "stop loss" policy that can keep men and women in uniform during war or national emergencies.

Spc. David Qualls had sought a preliminary injunction to prevent the Army from forcing him to remain on active duty, claiming his enlistment contract was misleading. He signed up for a one-year stint in the Arkansas National Guard in July 2003 but was later told he would remain on active duty in Iraq until 2005.

U.S. District Judge Royce C. Lamberth for the District of Columbia said the enlistment contract does notify those who sign up that the government could extend their terms of service. While acknowledging minimal harm to the Army if he ordered Qualls released, Lamberth said similar claims could lead to substantial disruption and diversion of military resources.

The enlistments of an estimated 7,000 active-duty soldiers have been extended under the policy, which the Army says is needed to provide experienced soldiers for battle. As many as 40,000 reserve soldiers could be ordered to stay longer.

Qualls and seven other soldiers serving in Iraq or en route to Iraq had asked the judge to order the Army to release them from service immediately. They contended the enlistment contracts make no explicit reference to the stop loss policy.

The government maintained that the enlistment contract provided that soldiers may be involuntarily ordered to active duty in case of war, national emergency or any other condition required by law, which the government contended would include extensions of existing contracts.

Qualls was ordered in December to return to Iraq while Lamberth reviewed his lawsuit. In January, Qualls volunteered for another six-year stint in the Guard.

SIGNIFICANCE

The U.S. government took several steps other than stop loss orders to remedy the troop shortages. The Pentagon began an involuntary recall of soldiers who left active service, raised the eligibility age for the Reserve forces, and eased standards for new recruits. It also considered implementing a shortened, fifteen-month enlistment policy that had been used to disastrous effect during the Vietnam War. To immediately address the problem of a troop shortage, Pentagon officials in 2005 offered re-enlistment bonuses of $8,000 for one year to $150,000 for six more years. It is doubtful if such bonuses substantially influenced enlistments. Private security firms offered $33,000 per month in 2005 with some former commandos earning $200,000 or more per year for essentially the same work they performed as soldiers.

The shortage of Americans willing to put life and limb at risk at the going pay rate and the urgency of having enough troops to fight in Iraq and other global hot spots has renewed calls for a draft. The military has long resisted a draft since an all-volunteer military provides better-quality soldiers. Draftees historically are less committed to the mission and less willing to obey orders. Politicians are also not especially eager to institute a program that will be politically unpopular. Yet the commitment to Iraq and the fight against terrorism are long efforts that will require a substantial number of military personnel. Without a draft, stop loss orders are the only means of obtaining sufficient numbers of soldiers for these battles.

FURTHER RESOURCES
Books

Buzzell, Colby. *My War: Killing Time in Iraq*. New York: Putnam, 2005.

Crawford, John. *The Last True Story I'll Ever Tell: An Accidental Soldier's Account of the War in Iraq*. New York: Riverhead, 2005.

Hartley, Jason Christopher. *Another Soldier: A Year on the Ground in Iraq*. New York: Harper Collins, 2005.

Undocumented Migrant Farm Workers

Photograph

By: Andrew Lichtenstein

Date: August 10, 2005

Source: © Andrew Lichtenstein/Corbis.

About the Photographer: This image was taken by Andrew Lichtenstein, a documentary photographer based in New York. The photograph is part of the collection of the Corbis Corporation, headquartered in Seattle, with a worldwide archive of over seventy million images.

INTRODUCTION

Over thirty-five million new immigrants entered the United States in the four decades after the Immigration Act of 1965 reformed the immigration process. The new law abolished the discriminatory quota based on national origins that had governed immigration policy since the 1920s. It treated all nationalities and races equally. In place of national quotas, Congress created hemispheric ceilings on visas issued with only 120,000 people from the Western Hemisphere permitted to enter the United States. The legislation also stipulated that no more than twenty thousand people could come from one country each year. However, more than 120,000 immigrants from Latin America wanted to enter the United States, and those denied legal entrance became undocumented workers.

In states like California and Texas, both documented and undocumented immigrants became targets of those who feared dramatic social changes. Conservative politicians mounted "English-only" campaigns, opposed bilingual education, lobbied to remove all welfare benefits from undocumented immigrants, and campaigned to sharply restrict benefits for legal immigrants. Leaders opposed to immigration charged that the waves of immigrant workers were undermining the United States as a European nation and the principal guardian of Western civilization. Latinos and Latinas came under particular target for taking jobs from American citizens. Conservatives called for greatly increased border patrols and suggested the possibility of building a fence across the long U.S.-Mexican border to thwart immigrants.

The conservative victory in the 1994 congressional elections led to the enactment of the Illegal

PRIMARY SOURCE

Undocumented Migrant Farm Workers: Undocumented migrant workers carry eggplants out of a field in Sampson County, North Carolina, August 10, 2005. © ANDREW LICHTENSTEIN/CORBIS.

Immigration Reform and Immigrant Responsibility Act of 1996. This legislation increased the border patrol, expanded Immigration and Naturalization Service (INS) powers to deport immigrants, and sharply increased penalties for illegal immigration. However, employers of illegal immigrants faced few penalties. Additionally, they could report undocumented workers to the INS when they sought improved wages and work conditions. As a result, immigration reform did little to slow the great numbers of illegal immigrants who could make more money in the United States than they ever could in Latin America, albeit at low-paying, exploitative jobs.

PRIMARY SOURCE

UNDOCUMENTED MIGRANT FARM WORKERS

See primary source image.

SIGNIFICANCE

By the start of 2006, over thirty-five million people living in the United States were born in other countries. This equals about twelve percent of the American population, the highest percentage of foreign-born since 1920. Of these people, an estimated eleven to twelve million are illegal immigrants, with Mexico as the largest source of these immigrants. Three in four illegal immigrants come from Latin America, with a little more than half hailing from Mexico. About a quarter of these immigrants enter the United States legally and then overstay their visas. Undocumented workers make up about five percent of the American workforce. Nearly two-thirds of illegal immigrants have offspring born in the United States, making the children American citizens and greatly complicating the problem of return to Mexico.

The rise in immigration has made the topic of undocumented workers a matter of increasing national concern. In 2006, a series of massive immigrant marches focused attention on the rights of immigrants at the same time that Congress debated legislation that would make illegal immigration into a federal felony, tighten border control, and crack down on employers who hire undocumented workers. The marches, sponsored by unions, religious organizations, and immigrant rights groups such as United Farm Workers and Hermandad Mexicana, were designed to show that Latin American immigrants had made substantial contributions to the United States. The marches were publicized through Spanish-language media. Participants were encouraged to carry American flags to show patriotism. However, many marchers carried flags of their countries of origin. Worsening the situation, a media group released a Spanish-language version of the American national anthem, "The Star-Spangled Banner." Many Americans viewed these developments as evidence that Mexican immigrants were refusing to assimilate into the United States and were intent on changing American culture into Mexican culture. In 2006, immigration remained a very hot political topic.

FURTHER RESOURCES
Books

Acuna, Rodolfo. *Occupied America: A History of Chicanos*. New York: Pearson Longman, 2004.

Daniels, Roger. *Coming to America: A History of Immigration and Ethnicity in American Life*. New York: Harper Perennial, 2002.

Mitchell, Don. *The Lie of the Land: Migrant Workers and the California Landscape*. Minneapolis. Minn.: University of Minnesota Press, 1996.

Ngai, Mae M. *Impossible Subjects: Illegal Aliens and the Making of Modern America*. Princeton, N.J.: Princeton University Press, 2005.

6 Civil and Political Rights

Civil and Political Rights

To speak of civil and political rights without speaking of human rights is impossible. Most of the rights enumerated in the United States Bill of Rights are also enumerated in the United Nations Universal Declaration of Human Rights. Civil rights are those rights codified and protected under the law. Most often, these are rights such as freedom of speech, religion, movement, employment, and education; privacy, access to courts, due process, property ownership, commerce, and non-discrimination.

Political rights involve one's ability to interact with their government. Political rights include the civil rights of free speech, voting, but specifically refer to one's ability to participate in government (vote and hold office), criticize government, and advocate change without risk of government repression. While civil rights—as human rights—are universal, political rights are often limited to citizens.

African slavery is covered in the chapter *Slavery and Genocide*. This chapter chronicles key events in the century-long African-American struggle for civil rights from the Dred Scott decision of 1856 to the height of the civil rights movement in the 1950s and 1960s. To provide a global context for the Black civil rights movement, "Nelson Mandela's Second Court Statement" and "Appeal for Action to Stop Repression and Trial in South Africa" look at the anti-Apartheid movement in South Africa.

The capstone of this chapter's discussion of political rights is the 1989 pro-democracy demonstrations in Tiananmen Square, Beijing, China. The event provided one of the iconic images of the political protest, a lone man halting a line of tanks. The Tiananmen protest was eventually met with a brutal response from the Chinese government, but not before items like the "Tiananmen Square Declaration of Human Rights" circulated widely among Beijing students and political dissidents.

The editors have chosen to include a limited number of articles on Women's rights. The rights to participate in government (vote), hold employment, own property, marry, and found families are all enumerated in the United Nations Universal Declaration of Human Rights. Attainment of these human rights is the core struggle of many movements for social equity.

Dred Scott v. Sanford

Legal decision

By: Roger B. Taney

Date: 1856

Source: *Dred Scott v. Sanford.* Supreme Court of the United States 60 U.S. 393, December 1856.

About the Author: Chief Justice Roger B. Taney served on the United States Supreme Court from 1836 until his death in 1864. Widely criticized for the *Dred Scott* decision, Taney's personal views and actions on slavery contradicted the decision; Taney emancipated his own slaves and provided pensions for those too ill or old to work.

INTRODUCTION

In 1834 Dred Scott, a slave owned by army physician Dr. John Emerson, traveled with Emerson to Illinois, a free state in which slavery was not permitted, and later to the Wisconsin Territory, a free territory. While in the Wisconsin Territory, in an area that is in modern-day Minnesota, Scott met and married fellow slave Harriet Robinson. (Marriage of slaves in slave states was prohibited, for it implied that slaves had legal rights or standing.) Dr. Emerson bought Robinson, and the couple soon had their first child. Emerson himself met and married Irene Sandford in 1838.

After Dr. Emerson's death in 1843, Dred Scott, Harriet Robinson, and their child moved to St. Louis, Missouri, where Dr. Emerson's widow lived. Scott and Robinson worked for Irene Emerson for three years before asking to buy their freedom. Scott offered $300 but Mrs. Emerson refused. Scott then decided to sue for his freedom.

Abolition sentiment in the north was running high in the mid-1840s; lecture circuit stars such as the Grimke sisters, Frederick Douglass, and Sojourner Truth brought the issues of slavery and abolition into the public spotlight, and editor William Lloyd Garrison's *The Liberator* published articles and editorials against slavery and the slave system of labor. Dred Scott argued that his time living in Illinois and the Wisconsin territory, where slavery was illegal, nullified his status as a slave.

Dred Scott's initial lawsuit, filed in Missouri, was dismissed for Scott's failure to prove that the Emersons owned him. In 1850 the St. Louis Circuit Court ruled that Scott and his family were free. In 1852

the Missouri Supreme Court reversed the lower court ruling, and Scott's case made its way to the federal courts. The children of Scott's first owner, Peter Blow, helped pay Scott's legal fees.

After an 1854 decision by the United States Circuit Court found for Mrs. Emerson, Scott appealed to the United States Supreme Court. The court heard the case in 1856 and made a public declaration in early 1857.

■ PRIMARY SOURCE

DRED SCOTT, PLAINTIFF IN ERROR, v. JOHN F. A. SANDFORD. SUPREME COURT OF THE UNITED STATES

60 U.S. 393; 15 L. Ed. 691

DECEMBER, 1856 Term

OPINION: Mr. Chief Justice TANEY delivered the opinion of the court....

The question is simply this: Can a negro, whose ancestors were imported into this country, and sold as slaves, become a member of the political community formed and brought into existence by the Constitution of the United States, and as such become entitled to all the rights, and privileges, and immunities, guaranteed by that instrument to the citizen? One of which rights is the privilege of suing in a court of the United States in the cases specified in the Constitution....

The words "people of the United States" and "citizens" are synonymous terms, and mean the same thing. They both describe the political body who, according to our republican institutions, form the sovereignty, and who hold the power and conduct the Government through their representatives. They are what we familiarly call the "sovereign people," and every citizen is one of this people, and a constituent member of this sovereignty. The question before us is, whether the class of persons described in the plea in abatement compose a portion of this people, and are constituent members of this sovereignty? We think they are not, and that they are not included, and were not intended to be included, under the word "citizens" in the Constitution, and can therefore claim none of the rights and privileges which that instrument provides for and secures to citizens of the United States. On the contrary, they were at that time considered as a subordinate and inferior class of beings, who had been subjugated by the dominant race, and, whether emancipated or not, yet remained subject to their authority, and had no rights or privileges but such as those who held the power and the government might choose to grant them.

It is not the province of the court to decide upon the justice or injustice, the policy or impolicy, of these laws.

Dred Scott. PUBLIC DOMAIN.

The decision of that question belonged to the political or law-making power; to those who formed the sovereignty and framed the Constitution. The duty of the court is, to interpret the instrument they have framed, with the best lights we can obtain on the subject, and to administer it as we find it, according to its true intent and meaning when it was adopted.

In the opinion of the court, the legislation and histories of the times, and the language used in the Declaration of Independence, show, that neither the class of persons who had been imported as slaves, nor their descendants, whether they had become free or not, were then acknowledged as a part of the people, nor intended to be included in the general words used in that memorable instrument.

... [I]t is too clear for dispute, that the enslaved African race were not intended to be included, and formed no part of the people who framed and adopted this declaration; for if the language, as understood in that day, would embrace them, the conduct of the distinguished men who framed the Declaration of Independence would have been utterly and flagrantly inconsistent with the principles they asserted; and instead of the sympathy of mankind, to which they so confidently appealed, they would have deserved and received universal rebuke and reprobation. . . .

But there are two clauses in the Constitution which point directly and specifically to the negro race as a separate class of persons, and show clearly that they were not regarded as a portion of the people or citizens of the government then formed.

One of these clauses reserves to each of the thirteen States the right to import slaves until the year 1808, if it thinks proper ... And by the other provision the States pledge themselves to each other to maintain the right of property of the master, by delivering up to him any slave who may have escaped from his service, and be found within their respective territories. . . .

The only two provisions which point to them and include them, treat them as property, and make it the duty of the government to protect it; no other power, in relation to this race, is to be found in the Constitution; and as it is a Government of special, delegated powers, no authority beyond these two provisions can be constitutionally exercised. The Government of the United States had no right to interfere for any other purpose but that of protecting the rights of the owner, leaving it altogether with the several States to deal with this race, whether emancipated or not, as each State may think justice, humanity, and the interests and safety of society, require. The States evidently intended to reserve this power exclusively to themselves. . . .

Upon a full and careful consideration of the subject, the court is of opinion, that, upon the facts stated ... Dred Scott was not a citizen of Missouri within the meaning of the Constitution of the United States, and not entitled as such to sue in its courts; and, consequently, that the Circuit Court had no jurisdiction of the case, and that the judgment on the plea in abatement is erroneous. . . .

We proceed, therefore, to inquire whether the facts relied on by the plaintiff entitled him to his freedom. . . .

The act of Congress, upon which the plaintiff relies, declares that slavery and involuntary servitude, except as a punishment for crime, shall be forever prohibited in all that part of the territory ceded by France, under the name of Louisiana, which lies north of thirty-six degrees thirty minutes north latitude and not included within the limits of Missouri. And the difficulty which meets us at the threshold of this part of the inquiry is whether Congress was authorized to pass this law under any of the powers granted to it by the Constitution; for, if the authority is not given by that instrument, it is the duty of this court to declare it void and inoperative and incapable of conferring freedom upon anyone who is held as a slave under the laws of any one of the states.

The counsel for the plaintiff has laid much stress upon that article in the Constitution which confers on Congress the power "to dispose of and make all needful rules and regulations respecting the territory or other property belonging to the United States"; but, in the judgment of the court, that provision has no bearing on the present controversy, and the power there given, whatever it may be, is confined, and was intended to be confined, to the territory which at that time belonged to, or was claimed by, the United States and was within their boundaries as settled by the treaty with Great Britain, and can have no influence upon a territory afterward acquired from a foreign Government. It was a special provision for a known and particular territory, and to meet a present emergency, and nothing more. . . .

We do not mean, however, to question the power of Congress in this respect. The power to expand the territory of the United States by the admission of new States is plainly given; and in the construction of this power by all the departments of the Government, it has been held to authorize the acquisition of territory, not fit for admission at the time, but to be admitted as soon as its population and situation would entitle it to admission.

... [I]t may be safely assumed that citizens of the United States who migrate to a Territory belonging to the people of the United States cannot be ruled as mere colonists, dependent upon the will of the General Government, and to be governed by any laws it may think proper to impose. The principle upon which our Governments rest, and upon which alone they continue to exist, is the union of

States, sovereign and independent within their own limits in their internal and domestic concerns, and bound together as one people by a general government, possessing certain enumerated and restricted powers, delegated to it by the people of the several States, and exercising supreme authority within the scope of the powers granted to it, throughout the dominion of the United States. A power, therefore, in the General Government to obtain and hold colonies and dependent territories, over which they might legislate without restriction, would be inconsistent with its own existence in its present form. Whatever it acquires, it acquires for the benefit of the people of the several States who created it. It is their trustee acting for them and charged with the duty of promoting the interests of the whole people of the Union in the exercise of the powers specifically granted. . . .

But the power of Congress over the person or property of a citizen can never be a mere discretionary power under our Constitution and form of Government. The powers of the Government and the rights and privileges of the citizen are regulated and plainly defined by the Constitution itself. And, when the Territory becomes a part of the United States, the Federal Government enters into possession in the character impressed upon it by those who created it. It enters upon it with its powers over the citizen strictly defined and limited by the Constitution, from which it derives its own existence, and by virtue of which alone it continues to exist and act as a Government and sovereignty. It has no power of any kind beyond it; and it cannot, when it enters a territory of the United States, put off its character and assume discretionary or despotic powers which the Constitution has denied to it. It cannot create for itself a new character separated from the citizens of the United States and the duties it owes them under the provisions of the Constitution. The Territory, being a part of the United States, the government and the citizen both enter it under the authority of the Constitution, with their respective rights defined and marked out; and the Federal Government can exercise no power over his person or property, beyond what that instrument confers, nor lawfully deny any right which it has reserved. . . .

These powers, and others, in relation to rights of person, which it is not necessary here to enumerate, are, in express and positive terms, denied to the General Government; and the rights of private property have been guarded with equal care. Thus the rights of property are united with the rights of person and placed on the same ground by the Fifth Amendment to the Constitution, which provides that no person shall be deprived of life, liberty, and property without due process of law. And an act of Congress which deprives a citizen of the United States of his liberty or property, without due process of law, merely

because he came himself or brought his property into a particular Territory of the United States, and who had committed no offense against the laws, could hardly be dignified with the name of due process of law. . . .

It seems, however, to be supposed that there is a difference between property in a slave and other property and that different rules may be applied to it in expounding the Constitution of the United States. And the laws and usages of nations, and the writings of eminent jurists upon the relation of master and slave and their mutual rights and duties, and the powers which Governments may exercise over it, have been dwelt upon in the argument.

But, in considering the question before us, it must be borne in mind that there is no law of nations standing between the people of the United States and their Government and interfering with their relation to each other. The powers of the Government and the rights of the citizen under it are positive and practical regulations plainly written down. The people of the United States have delegated to it certain enumerated powers and forbidden it to exercise others. It has no power over the person or property of a citizen but what the citizens of the United States have granted. And no laws or usages of other nations, or reasoning of statesmen or jurists upon the relations of master and slave, can enlarge the powers of the Government or take from the citizens the rights they have reserved. And if the Constitution recognizes the right of property of the master in a slave, and makes no distinction between that description of property and other property owned by a citizen, no tribunal, acting under the authority of the United States, whether it be legislative, executive, or judicial, has a right to draw such a distinction or deny to it the benefit of the provisions and guaranties which have been provided for the protection of private property against the encroachments of the Government.

Now, as we have already said in an earlier part of this opinion, upon a different point, the right of property in a slave is distinctly and expressly affirmed in the Constitution. The right to traffic in it, like an ordinary article of merchandise and property, was guaranteed to the citizens of the United States, in every state that might desire it, for twenty years. And the Government in express terms is pledged to protect it in all future time if the slave escapes from his owner. That is done in plain words—too plain to be misunderstood. And no word can be found in the Constitution which gives Congress a greater power over slave property or which entitles property of that kind to less protection than property of any other description. The only power conferred is the power coupled with the duty of guarding and protecting the owner in his rights.

Upon these considerations it is the opinion of the Court that the act of Congress which prohibited a citizen from holding and owning property of this kind in the territory of the United States north of the line therein mentioned is not warranted by the Constitution and is therefore void; and that neither Dred Scott himself, nor any of his family, were made free by being carried into this territory; even if they had been carried there by the owner with the intention of becoming a permanent resident.

SIGNIFICANCE

Chief Justice Roger B. Taney wrote the majority decision for the Court; he had owned slaves but had also emancipated them. Accused of working for the "pro-slavery" interests by abolitionists and future president Abraham Lincoln, Taney's decision helped increase the divisions between North and South.

According to the Constitution, Taney wrote, Dred Scott, as a person of African descent, was not a citizen and therefore had no right to use the court system to address the question of his freedom. The Constitution included the "three-fifths rule," and other provisions that clearly treated slaves as noncitizens; the Court's interpretation of such laws held that because Dred Scott was not a citizen, his lawsuit was not valid.

Taney's decision tried to skirt the moral issue of slavery by noting that "It is not the province of the court to decide upon the justice or injustice, the policy or impolicy, of these laws.... The duty of the court is, to interpret the instrument they have framed, with the best lights we can obtain on the subject, and to administer it as we find it, according to its true intent and meaning when it was adopted."

The Court's second major argument was that Dr. and Mrs. Emerson owned slaves as property and had the right to move them wherever they wished. Moving a piece of property such as a table or a horse, from one state to another did not change the legalities of ownership, the Court ruled: As noncitizens and property, slaves such as Dred Scott could go from free state to slave state at their owner's will without any change in their legal status. Taney wrote that "no word can be found in the Constitution which gives Congress a greater power over slave property or which entitles property of that kind to less protection than property of any other description."

The Missouri Compromise of 1820, which had established some territories as slave-holding and others as free, was therefore unconstitutional under this ruling. A free state deprived slave owners of their property rights and freedom to move about the country as desired; Taney's decision reached into politics as free vs. slave state tensions peaked. Abolitionists

decried the Court's decision, claiming judicial overreach, while other critics, including Abraham Lincoln, accused then-president James Buchanan of influencing the Court, a charge later proven correct.

Dred Scott v. Sanford was a breaking point in the years before the Civil War. By nullifying the tenuous balance between free and slave state admittance into the Union, and by stripping freed slaves and freeborn descendants of slaves of citizenship, the Court's interpretation fed southern hopes for slavery's legal justification and northern fury that a slave-leaning court would make such a Constitutional determination. Within three years the country was plunged into the U.S. Civil War (1861–65). After the war, the Thirteenth, Fourteenth, and Fifteenth Amendments to the Constitution outlawed slavery and, among other things, declared that "All persons born or naturalized in the United States, and subject to the jurisdiction thereof, are citizens of the United States and of the State wherein they reside,"—regardless of their race.

FURTHER RESOURCES

Books

Colfax, Richard H. *Evidence Against the Views of the Abolitionists, Consisting of Physical and Moral Proofs, of the Natural Inferiority of the Negroes.* New York: James T. M. Bleakley Publishers, 1833.

Fehrenbacher, Don E. *The Dred Scott Case: Its Significance in American Law and Politics.* Oxford University Press, 2001.

Horton, James Oliver, and Lois E. Horton. *Slavery and the Making of America.* Oxford University Press, 2004.

Klarman, Michael J. *From Jim Crow to Civil Rights: The Supreme Court and the Struggle for Racial Equality.* Oxford University Press, USA, 2004.

Women's Disabilities Removal Bill

Speech

By: John Bright

Date: 1889

Source: Bright, John. "Women's Disabilities Removal Bill." London: C. Blackett Robinson, 1889.

About the Author: John Bright (1811–1889) was a British radical who took pride in nonconformity. He was part of the Anti-Corn League, which was a group of

An illustration from *Harper's Weekly* shows disabled women being taught crafts in a class in England, circa 1871. © CORBIS.

politicians who rallied the public into getting the Corn Laws repealed in 1846. The Corn Laws were aimed to protect British farmers from foreign competition. Bright was also noted for his oratory skills, and in 1882 he was elected lord rector of the University of Glasgow.

INTRODUCTION

Conceptions of womanhood in Victorian England (circa 1837 to 1901) called for women to be pious, patient, frugal, and industrious. A woman's sphere was within the home because motherhood and domesticity should have fulfilled her. These conceptions of the dutiful women were reinforced through literature in women's magazines, in popular fiction, and through social orders. Some of these social customs manifested through women's clubs and organizations, for which they developed a sense of community and dignity from work and communication with other females. Other manifestations of social order came from laws.

Victorian England did not permit women to vote, and while they were allowed to be in public without an escort, women did not have a strong legal standing within civil society. Women needed a man to own property, they were expected to get married and have children, and were not expected to work outside the home. Popular romantic fiction often portrayed these

women as weak, but this was generally not the case. Even though social orders told them to be passive members of society who did not interact with political debates, middle- and upper-class women expanded their sphere outside the home. In England and the United States, as well as other countries, a rising women's movement emerged. These women, who labored within their homes because rarely could a middle-class woman afford more than one servant, balanced their time between their homes and social networks. Their social clubs brought forth urban reforms for city sewage and street clean-up and other local causes. Their reforms also brought a heightened awareness of women's lives outside the home.

Newspapers, whose circulation grew steadily in the late nineteenth century, reported on the crimes of women being accosted in the street. In late 1888, these stories—written to incite fear—reflected the social mood of the day. London, particularly the Whitechapel area, buzzed about the serial killer Jack the Ripper. He was never caught, but his slayings of numerous prostitutes caused fears to escalate. These fears of social mayhem reflected tensions about declining morals in society—particularly in cities. Mirroring social reform movements in the United States, middle- and upper-class women in England fought for the reduction and removal of prostitutes, reduced working hours, and a cleaner environment. The working classes also fought for these rights, and middle-class men even joined the crusade for higher wages. The laborer wanted fair wages for his work, and the middle-class businessman wanted higher wages to afford the luxuries of middle-class living. Women wanted reforms to improve the quality of life. One of the ways that Victorian women sought reform was by pushing pieces of legislation like the Women's Disabilities Removal Bill to Parliament.

The Women's Disabilities Removal Bill called for men and women to be treated equally within society. It meandered through Parliament for over thirty years before it was laid aside for more pressing matters. The framework of the bill was similar to the U.S. Equal Rights Amendment (ERA). The ERA, passed by Congress in 1972, called for legal protection against discrimination of anyone. It failed ratification in 1982, but its story is similar to the English Women's Disabilities Removal Bill in the late 1800s. Ardent opponents to the bill declared that a woman needed protection in society because of her gentle and weak status, and events like Jack the Ripper and news stories highlighting the crime helped reinforce beliefs that women had to be protected. The opponents used Victorian ideals on gender to reinforce their point, and they used prescriptive literature that reinforced the notion of a woman's role being in the home. Political leaders like John Bright said that women should not be held equal to men because differences between the sexes called for different rules for each.

■ PRIMARY SOURCE

The bill seems to be based on a proposition which is untenable, and which I think is contradicted by universal experience. In fact it is a Bill based on an assumed hostility between the sexes. Now, I do not believe that any honourable member in this House who is going to support this Bill entertains that view; but if hon. Members have been accustomed to read the speeches of the principal promoters of this Bill out of doors, and if they have had an opportunity, as I have had on many occasions of entering into friendly and familiar conversation on this question with those who support it, I think they will be forced to the admission that the Bill, as it is offered to us, and by those by whom and for whom it is offered to us, is a Bill based upon assumed constant and irreconcilable hostility between the sexes. The men are represented as seeking to rule, even to the length of tyranny; and the women are represented as suffering injustice, even to the length of depth of slavery. These are words which are constantly made use of both in the speeches and in the conversation

of the women who are the chief promoters of this Bill. And this is not said of savage nations or of savages—and there are some in civilized nations—but it is said of men in general, of men in this civilized and Christian country in which we live.

What, if we look over this country and its population, would strike us more than anything else? It is this, that at this moment there are millions of men at work sacrificing their leisure and their health, sustaining hardship, confronting it in every shape, for the sake of the sustenance, the comfort, and the happiness of women and children. Yet it is of these men, of these millions, that language such as I have described is constantly made use, and made use of eminently by the chief promoters of this Bill. The object of the Bill is not the mere extension of the suffrage to 300,000 or 400,000 persons, its avowed object is to enable women in this country to defend themselves against the tyranny of a Parliament of men, and the facts that are brought forward are of the flimsiest character.

There is the question of the property of married women. There may be injustice with regard to the laws that affect the property of married women, but is there no injustice in the laws that affect the property of men? Have younger sons no right to complain just as much as married women? If a man dies in the street worth £100,000 in land, and he leaves no will, what does the fiat of this House say? It says that the £100,000 in land shall all go to the eldest boy, because he happened to come first into the world, and that the rest of the family of the man shall be left to seek their fortunes as they like. Is there any greater injustice than that? But that is an injustice which Parliament inflicts upon men as well as women, and the fact of there being some special or particular injustice of which women may have a right to complain—I am not asserting or denying it—is no argument, no sufficient argument, for the proposition which is now before the House. I have observed when the question of the property of married women has been before Parliament—I think it was brought forward by the right hon. And learned Gentlemen the Member for Southampton (Mr. Russell Gurney)—that he was supported by several hon. And learned gentlemen, lawyers of eminence, in the House, and, so far as my recollection goes, the matter was discussed with great fairness, great good temper, and great liberality; and changes were made which to some extent meet the view of those who had proposed them. There can be no doubt then—I think no member on either side of the House will doubt it—that this House is as fairly disposed to judge of all questions of that kind which affect women as it is qualified and willing to judge all questions of a similar or analogous character which affect men. If married women are wronged in any matter of this kind, surely we all know that many of our customs and laws in regard to property come down from ancient times when power was law, and when women had little power, and the possession and the defence of property was vested, and necessarily vested, almost altogether in men. But there is another side to this question.

It seems almost unnecessary to quote it, but I would recommend some of those very people who blame Parliament in this matter to look at how much there is in favour of women in other directions. Take the question of punishment. There can be no doubt whatever that as regards that question there is much greater moderation, and, I might say, mercy, held out to women than there is to men. Take the greatest of all punishments for the greatest of all crimes. Since I have been in Parliament I think I could specify more than a score of instances in which the lives of women have been spared in cases where the lives of men would have been taken. It is a horror to me to have to speak in a civilized and Christian assembly of the possibility of the lives of women being taken by the law, but the law orders it, and it is sometimes done, but whether it be from mercy in the judge or from mercy in the jury, or mercy in the Home Secretary, there can be no doubt whatsoever that the highest punishment known to the law is much more rarely inflicted upon women, and has been so for the last thirty or forty years, than upon men. Also in all cases of punishment, I say that judges and juries are always more lenient in disposition to women than they are to men. I might also point out to some of those ladies who are very excited in this matter that in cases of breach of promise of marriage the advantage on their side seems to be enormous. As far as I can judge from the reports of the cases in the papers they almost always get a verdict, and very often, I am satisfied, where they ought not to get it; and beyond that, the penalty inflicted is very often, so far as I can judge, greatly in excess of what the case demands.

Take the small case now of taxation. We know that the advocates of this measure deal with very little questions, showing for instance how badly women are treated by Parliament. Take the case of domestic woman-servants, who are numerous; they are not taxed, men are. That is an advantage to the women as against the men. I do not say that it is any reason why you should not pass this Bill, but I am only saying that these little differences do exist, and will exist; they exist in every country, and under every form of government, and, in point of fact, have nothing whatever to do with the real and great question before us.

The argument which tells with many persons who sign the petitions to this House is the argument of equal rights. They say, if a man lives in a house and votes, and a woman lives in another house, why should not she vote also? That is a very fair and a very plain question, and one not always quite easy to answer. It is said that there can be

no harm to the country that women should vote, and I believe that is a thing which many of us, even those who oppose this Bill, may admit; but it is not a question which depends upon a proposition of that kind. As to the actual right, I would say nothing about it; I suppose, however, the country has a right to determine how it will be governed—whether by one man, whether by few, or whether by many. Many men in Britain are, by their official or professional position, deprived by law of the privilege of voting, notwithstanding their property qualifications. Many men, on the other hand, are entitled to vote although possessed of no property qualification of any kind. The intelligence and the experience and the opinion of the country must decide where the power must rest, and upon whom the suffrage shall be conferred.

SIGNIFICANCE

Women continued to push for their right to vote, and they pushed social notions about them to the edge. In the twentieth century, working-class women continued to work outside the home, and during World War I women entered the workforce in unprecedented numbers. Middle-class women left their domestic roles to temporarily help their country in a time of need. Accordingly, Parliament recognized this action in 1918 by affording women the vote, and twelve other countries passed suffrage bills that year. In the United Kingdom, the suffrage bill merely gave women the vote, and prescriptive literature continued to educate women on the social need for them to stay within the home. Throughout their campaign for suffrage, women had been saying that their service to the nation came in a variety of forms, and they reiterated that they could balance their personal and political lives.

FURTHER RESOURCES
Books
Frost, Ginger S. *Promises Broken: Courtship, Class, and Gender in Victorian England*. Charlottesville: University of Virginia Press, 1995.

International Perspectives on Gender and Democratization, edited by Shirin Rai. London: Palgrave MacMillan, 2000.

Web sites
Equal Opportunity Commission. "The Gender Equality Duty." <http://www.eoc.org.uk/Default.aspx?page=15016> (accessed May 12, 2006).

Women and Equality Unit. "What Has the Government Achieved for Women?" <http:// www.womenandequalityunit.gov.uk/about/ government_women.htm> (accessed May 12, 2006).

Plessy v. Ferguson

Legal decision

By: U.S. Supreme Court

Date: May 18, 1896

Source: *Homer A. Plessy v. John H. Ferguson.* 163 US 537 (1896).

About the Author: The U.S. Supreme Court, the highest judicial body in the United States, is composed of the chief justice and eight associate justices. All the justices are nominated by the U.S. President and confirmed by the U.S. Senate. In the case of *Plessy v. Ferguson*, Associate Justice Henry Billings Brown (1836–1913) delivered the majority opinion of the Court.

INTRODUCTION

In the post-Civil War era, southern reconstruction, which included federal military control over portions of the southern United States, the reintegration of former states that made up the Confederate States of America, and the absorption of four million slaves into the American economy and civil society, led to the legal and social enforcement of segregation of the races. While the Thirteenth Amendment to the U.S. Constitution outlawed slavery, the Fourteenth Amendment was required to make former slaves citizens and to provide legal grounds for equal protection rights. Although the Fifteenth Amendment granted all men the right to vote in the United States, a carefully constructed system of legal and social segregation crafted in the southern United States after the Civil War effectively kept many former slaves from voting and enjoying the full benefits and protections of U.S. citizenship.

Andrew Johnson, a former Tennessee Senator, a Democrat, and the Vice-President of Republican President Abraham Lincoln, assumed the presidency after Lincoln's assassination. Though Johnson had been selected as Lincoln's running mate in 1864 because of his anti-secession views, he was in no way a supporter of equal rights for African Americans. A strong supporter of the U.S. Constitution over states' rights, Johnson angered fellow southern legislators; in essence, his views alienated both Republicans and Democrats, northerners and southerners alike. Reconstruction placed certain requirements on Confederate states before their re-admittance to the Union—acceptance of the Fourteenth Amendment, acceptance of African American suffrage, an oath of allegiance, and the

A train conductor signaling from the "Jim Crow" coach, reserved for African Americans. St. Augustine, Florida, January 1943. © CORBIS.

establishment of civil governments. Many states balked at the provisions and passed "black codes" which restricted African American labor rights, created forced apprenticeships for black children, and established stringent vagrancy laws that could result in forced labor for African Americans without identification.

In response, the U.S. Congress passed the Reconstruction Act of March 1867, which divided the South into districts, which the U.S. military would occupy. Only those states that accepted the reconstruction provisions would escape military occupation. Southern states complied, in part because of vetoes from President Johnson on such issues as further black rights and restrictions on Confederate leaders holding political office. The battle between Johnson and the U.S. Congress led to his impeachment in 1868, although the Senate did not convict him. Republicans charged that Johnson's role in weakening African American rights in the antebellum South helped to foster racial separation and increased violence aimed at former slaves. In the meantime, southern states continued to pass segregation laws, cementing the system of the racial separation in the South.

In 1890, Louisiana passed a law separating train coaches by color. Homer Plessy, who was one-eighth black, purchased a railway ticket on the East Louisiana Railway on June 7, 1892, with the intent of challenging that law. Plessy belonged to a group called the Citizens' Committee of African Americans and Creoles. The group had hired a lawyer to represent Plessy should charges be brought against him. When Plessy made his racial status known to the conductor and sat in the "whites only" section, he was asked to leave. He refused and was arrested. The case was appealed to the U.S. Supreme Court in 1896.

PRIMARY SOURCE

Mr. Justice BROWN . . .delivered the opinion of the court.

This case turns upon the constitutionality of an act of the general assembly of the state of Louisiana, passed in 1890, providing for separate railway carriages for the white and colored races. Acts 1890, No. 111, p. 152.

The first section of the statute enacts 'that all railway companies carrying passengers in their coaches in this state, shall provide equal but separate accommodations for the white, and colored races, by providing two or more passenger coaches for each passenger train, or by dividing the passenger coaches by a partition so as to secure separate accommodations: provided, that this section shall not be construed to apply to street railroads. No person or persons shall be permitted to occupy seats in coaches, other than the ones assigned to them, on account of the race they belong to.'

By the second section it was enacted 'that the officers of such passenger trains shall have power and are hereby required to assign each passenger to the coach or compartment used for the race to which such passenger belongs; any passenger insisting on going into a coach or compartment to which by race he does not belong, shall be liable to a fine of twenty-five dollars, or in lieu thereof to imprisonment for a period of not more than twenty days in the parish prison, and any officer of any railroad insisting on assigning a passenger to a coach or compartment other than the one set aside for the race to which said passenger belongs, shall be liable to a fine of twenty-five dollars, or in lieu thereof to imprisonment for a period of not more than twenty days in the parish prison; and should any passenger refuse to occupy the coach or compartment to which he or she is assigned by the officer of such railway, said officer shall have power to refuse to carry such passenger on his train, and for such refusal neither he nor the railway company which he represents shall be liable for damages in any of the courts of this state.'

The third section provides penalties for the refusal or neglect of the officers, directors, conductors, and employees of railway companies to comply with the act, with a proviso that 'nothing in this act shall be construed as applying to nurses attending children of the other race.'

The information filed in the criminal district court charged, in substance, that Plessy, being a passenger between two stations within the state of Louisiana, was assigned by officers of the company to the coach used for the race to which he belonged, but he insisted upon going into a coach used by the race to which he did not belong. Neither in the information nor plea was his particular race or color averred.

The petition for the writ of prohibition averred that petitioner was seven-eighths Caucasian and one-eighth African blood; that the mixture of colored blood was not discernible in him; and that he was entitled to every right, privilege, and immunity secured to citizens of the United States of the white race; and that, upon such theory, he took possession of a vacant seat in a coach where passengers of the white race were accommodated, and was ordered by the conductor to vacate said coach, and take a seat in another, assigned to persons of the colored race, and, having refused to comply with such demand, he was forcibly ejected, with the aid of a police officer, and imprisoned in the parish jail to answer a charge of having violated the above act.

The constitutionality of this act is attacked upon the ground that it conflicts both with the thirteenth amendment of the constitution, abolishing slavery, and the fourteenth amendment, which prohibits certain restrictive legislation on the part of the states.

While we think the enforced separation of the races, as applied to the internal commerce of the state, neither abridges the privileges or immunities of the colored man, deprives him of his property without due process of law, nor denies him the equal protection of the laws, within the meaning of the fourteenth amendment, we are not prepared to say that the conductor, in assigning passengers to the coaches according to their race, does not act at his peril, or that the provision of the second section of the act that denies to the passenger compensation in damages for a refusal to receive him into the coach in which he properly belongs is a valid exercise of the legislative power. Indeed, we understand it to be conceded by the state's attorney that such part of the act as exempts from liability the railway company and its officers is unconstitutional.

It is claimed by the plaintiff in error that, in a mixed community, the reputation of belonging to the dominant race, in this instance the white race, is 'property,' in the same sense that a right of action or of inheritance is property. Conceding this to be so, for the purposes of this case, we are unable to see how this statute deprives him of, or in any way affects his right to, such property. If he be a white man, and assigned to a colored coach, he may have his action for damages against the company for being deprived of his so-called 'property.' Upon the other hand, if he be a colored man, and be so assigned, he has been deprived of no property, since he is not lawfully entitled to the reputation of being a white man.

In this connection, it is also suggested by the learned counsel for the plaintiff in error that the same argument that will justify the state legislature in requiring railways to provide separate accommodations for the two races will also authorize them to require separate cars to be provided for people whose hair is of a certain color, or who are aliens, or who belong to certain nationalities, or to enact laws requiring colored people to walk upon one side of the street, and white people upon the other, or requiring white men's houses to be painted white, and colored men's black, or their vehicles or business signs to be of different colors, upon the theory that one side of the street is as good as the other, or that a house or vehicle of one color is as good as one of another color. The reply to all this is that every exercise of the police power must be reasonable, and extend only to such laws as are enacted in good faith for the promotion of the public good, and not for the annoyance or oppression of a particular class.

So far, then, as a conflict with the fourteenth amendment is concerned, the case reduces itself to the question whether the statute of Louisiana is a reasonable regulation, and with respect to this there must necessarily be a large discretion on the part of the legislature. In determining the question of reasonableness, it is at liberty to act with reference to the established usages, customs, and traditions of the people, and with a view to the promotion of their comfort, and the preservation of the public peace and good order. Gauged by this standard, we cannot say that a law which authorizes or even requires the separation of the two races in public conveyances is unreasonable, or more obnoxious to the fourteenth amendment than the acts of congress requiring separate schools for colored children in the District of Columbia, the constitutionality of which does not seem to have been questioned, or the corresponding acts of state legislatures.

We consider the underlying fallacy of the plaintiff's argument to consist in the assumption that the enforced separation of the two races stamps the colored race with a badge of inferiority. If this be so, it is not by reason of anything found in the act, but solely because the colored race chooses to put that construction upon it. The argument necessarily assumes that if, as has been more than once the case, and is not unlikely to be so again, the colored race should become the dominant power in the state legislature, and should enact a law in precisely similar terms, it would thereby relegate the white race to an inferior position. We imagine that the white race, at least, would not acquiesce in this assumption. The argument also assumes that social prejudices may be overcome by

legislation, and that equal rights cannot be secured to the negro except by an enforced commingling of the two races. We cannot accept this proposition. If the two races are to meet upon terms of social equality, it must be the result of natural affinities, a mutual appreciation of each other's merits, and a voluntary consent of individuals....Legislation is powerless to eradicate racial instincts, or to abolish distinctions based upon physical differences, and the attempt to do so can only result in accentuating the difficulties of the present situation. If the civil and political rights of both races be equal, one cannot be inferior to the other civilly or politically. If one race be inferior to the other socially, the constitution of the United States cannot put them upon the same plane.

The judgment of the court below is therefore affirmed.

Mr. Justice HARLAN dissenting.

In my opinion, the judgment this day rendered will, in time, prove to be quite as pernicious as the decision made by this tribunal in the Dred Scott Case.

The destinies of the two races, in this country, are indissolubly linked together, and the interests of both require that the common government of all shall not permit the seeds of race hate to be planted under the sanction of law. What can more certainly arouse race hate, what more certainly create and perpetuate a feeling of distrust between these races, than state enactments which, in fact, proceed on the ground that colored citizens are so inferior and degraded that they cannot be allowed to sit in public coaches occupied by white citizens? That, as all will admit, is the real meaning of such legislation as was enacted in Louisiana.

The sure guaranty of the peace and security of each race is the clear, distinct, unconditional recognition by our governments, national and state, of every right that inheres in civil freedom, and of the equality before the law of all citizens of the United States, without regard to race. State enactments regulating the enjoyment of civil rights upon the basis of race, and cunningly devised to defeat legitimate results of the war, under the pretense of recognizing equality of rights, can have no other result than to render permanent peace impossible, and to keep alive a conflict of races, the continuance of which must do harm to all concerned. This question is not met by the suggestion that social equality cannot exist between the white and black races in this country. That argument, if it can be properly regarded as one, is scarcely worthy of consideration; for social equality no more exists between two races when traveling in a passenger coach or a public highway than when members of the same races sit by each other in a street car or in the jury box, or stand or sit with each other in a political assembly, or when they use in common the streets of a city or town, or when they are in the same room for the purpose of having their names placed on the registry of voters, or when they approach the ballot box in order to exercise the high privilege of voting.

There is a race so different from our own that we do not permit those belonging to it to become citizens of the United States. Persons belonging to it are, with few exceptions, absolutely excluded from our country.

I allude to the Chinese race. But, by the statute in question, a Chinaman can ride in the same passenger coach with white citizens of the United States, while citizens of the black race in Louisiana, many of whom, perhaps, risked their lives for the preservation of the Union, who are entitled, by law, to participate in the political control of the state and nation, who are not excluded, by law or by reason of their race, from public stations of any kind, and who have all the legal rights that belong to white citizens, are yet declared to be criminals, liable to imprisonment, if they ride in a public coach occupied by citizens of the white race. It is scarcely just to say that a colored citizen should not object to occupying a public coach assigned to his own race. He does not object, nor, perhaps, would he object to separate coaches for his race if his rights under the law were recognized. But he does object, and he ought never to cease objecting, that citizens of the white and black races can be adjudged criminals because they sit, or claim the right to sit, in the same public coach on a public highway. The arbitrary separation of citizens, on the basis of race, while they are on a public highway, is a badge of servitude wholly inconsistent with the civil freedom and the equality before the law established by the constitution. It cannot be justified upon any legal grounds.

I am of opinion that the state of Louisiana is inconsistent with the personal liberty of citizens, white and black, in that state, and hostile to both the spirit and letter of the constitution of the United States. If laws of like character should be enacted in the several states of the Union, the effect would be in the highest degree mischievous. Slavery, as an institution tolerated by law, would, it is true, have disappeared from our country; but there would remain a power in the states, by sinister legislation, to interfere with the full enjoyment of the blessings of freedom, to regulate civil rights, common to all citizens, upon the basis of race, and to place in a condition of legal inferiority a large body of American citizens, now constituting a part of the political community, called the 'People of the United States,' for whom, and by whom through representatives, our government is administered. Such a system is inconsistent with the guaranty given by the constitution to each state of a republican form of government, and may be stricken down by congressional action, or by the courts in the discharge of their solemn duty to maintain the supreme law of the land, anything in the constitution or laws of any state to the contrary notwithstanding.

For the reason stated, I am constrained to withhold my assent from the opinion and judgment of the majority.

[Edited from original language, taken from Westlaw, by project editor.]

SIGNIFICANCE

Plessy's lawyer, white New York attorney Albion Tourgée, had successfully represented black clients in rights cases, and the Citizens' Committee of African Americans and Creoles hired him based on his experience. The Citizens' Committee had been successful in another court case in which a Louisiana district court ruled that segregated railcar laws for interstate transportation were unconstitutional. The group hoped to duplicate that success for intrastate travel as well.

In representing Plessy, Tourgée argued that Louisiana violated both the Thirteenth and the Fourteenth Amendments to the U.S. Constitution when crafting and implementing the 1890 Separate Car Law. Plessy's right to "equal protection" under the law was violated by prohibiting him from using "whites only" railcars, according to Tourgée, while segregation itself implied the inferiority of African Americans, which Tourgée argued violated the Thirteenth Amendment.

The U.S. Supreme Court rejected outright the notion that Homer Plessy's rights had been violated regarding the Thirteenth Amendment, for the railcar law in no way enslaved blacks or returned them to forced servitude; creating an atmosphere of inferiority for one race was not the same as slavery. On the issue of the Fourteenth Amendment, Justice Henry Billings Brown makes the distinction that legal rights are quite different from social policy. According to the court's decision, separate is not inherently unequal. As Justice Brown states in the excerpt above, "If the civil and political rights of both races be equal, one cannot be inferior to the other civilly or politically. If one race be inferior to the other socially, the constitution of the United States cannot put them upon the same plane." The U.S. Supreme Court ruling affirmed the Louisiana's 1890 Separate Car Law.

Justice John Marshall Harlan, a former slave owner and the only voice of dissent in the seven to one ruling, vehemently disagreed with his fellow justices on the grounds that the law's intent is clear. "What can more certainly arouse race hate, what more certainly create and perpetuate a feeling of distrust between these races, than state enactments which, in fact, proceed on the ground that colored citizens are so inferior and degraded that they cannot be allowed to sit in public coaches occupied by white citizens? That, as all will admit, is the real meaning of such legislation as was enacted in Louisiana."

Homer Plessy paid a twenty-five dollar fine under the terms of the Louisiana law. The 1896 decision set the tone for racial segregation in the United States until the 1954 U.S. Supreme Court decision *Brown v. Board of Education*, which rejected the "separate but equal" concept. In the intervening fifty-eight years, segregated schools, neighborhoods, restaurants, private clubs, public restrooms, transportation, and other kinds of race-based separations were completely legal in states that enacted such legislation.

FURTHER RESOURCES
Books

Fireside, Harvey. *Separate and Unequal: Homer Plessy and the Supreme Court Decision that Legalized Racism*. New York: Carroll & Graf, 2004.

Klarman, Michael J. *From Jim Crow to Civil Rights: The Supreme Court and the Struggle for Racial Equality*. New York: Oxford University Press, 2004.

Medley, Keith Weldon. *We as Freemen: Plessy v. Ferguson*. Gretna, La.: Pelican Publishing, 2003.

Lynch Law in America

Magazine article

By: Ida B. Wells-Barnett

Date: 1900

Source: Wells-Barnett, Ida B. "Lynch Law in America." *The Arena* 23, 1 (1900): 15–24.

About the Author: Ida B. Wells-Barnett (1862–1931) was a teacher, journalist, and social activist, renowned for her campaigns against the lynching of African Americans. She was born a slave in Holly Springs, Mississippi. After Emancipation, her parents were associated with Rust College in Holly Springs, where Wells was educated until the death of her parents and youngest brother in a yellow fever epidemic in 1878. After working as a schoolteacher to support her siblings, Wells moved to Memphis around 1880, where she continued to teach. During this period, Wells also began writing for local black publications, using the pseudonym Iola. She became a co-owner and frequent contributor to the Memphis newspaper the *Free Speech and Headlight* in 1889. In 1892, her editorials on the

lynching of three respected Memphis businessmen resulted in the mob destruction of the *Free Speech* building, and Wells's life was repeatedly threatened. She went to New York, where she wrote for the *New York Age*, and published an analysis of lynching in the South entitled *Southern Horrors*.

The following year, Wells moved to Chicago, where she worked for the *Conservator*, a black newspaper founded and edited by Ferdinand Barnett. With Barnett and Frederick Douglass, Wells also co-authored a booklet called *The Reason Why the Colored American Is Not Represented in the World's Columbian Exposition*. In 1895, Wells married Barnett and published *A Red Record*. Wells-Barnett was active in the Niagara Movement in 1906, and was one of the founders of the NAACP (National Association for the Advancement of Colored People) in 1909, although she left the organization in 1912. She remained active in many political groups in Chicago, both for African-Americans and women's suffrage, and ran for the Illinois State Senate in 1930.

INTRODUCTION

Ida B. Wells-Barnett's *Arena* article was groundbreaking in many ways. Although the black press had covered mob violence for many years, *Lynch Law in America* was one of the first uncompromising, graphically descriptive portrayals of lynching to be aimed at an audience that was largely white. *The Arena* was a monthly literary magazine published in Boston from 1889–1909 that was dedicated to "The Betterment of Conditions" with a penchant for muck-raking, so Wells-Barnett's urgent plea for social justice fit the magazine's agenda well, even if the topic was uncomfortable for many of its readers.

Wells-Barnett's claim that lynching was not mindless mob action, but brutality with a hidden motivation, was equally innovative. Her analysis of the unwritten laws used to justify illegal and otherwise unconscionable activities foreshadows modern historical analyses. Dray (2002) and Tolnay and Beck (1995), for instance, expand on Wells-Barnett's ideas to explain lynching as a method of social control, disenfranchisement, and terror, a manner of controlling economic and political competition, and as a way to punish those who challenged the rigid ideology of sexual segregation.

Wells-Barnett's use of statistics to describe the magnitude of the lynching problem was also a first. By using figures collected from white sources, such as the *Chicago Tribune* in Lynch Law in America, Wells-Barnett was able to forestall her critics' dismissal of lynching as an infrequent or usually warranted practice. She also pointed out that fewer than a third of the victims of lynchings were even accused of rape, which was its most common justification.

PRIMARY SOURCE

Our country's national crime is *lynching*. It is not the creature of an hour, the sudden outburst of uncontrolled fury, or the unspeakable brutality of an insane mob. It represents the cool, calculating deliberation of intelligent people who openly avow that there is an "unwritten law" that justifies them in putting human beings to death without complaint under oath, without trial by jury, without opportunity to make defense, and without right of appeal . . .

The alleged menace of universal suffrage having been avoided by the absolute suppression of the negro vote, the spirit of mob murder should have been satisfied and the butchery of negroes should have ceased. But men, women, and children were the victims of murder by individuals and murder by mobs, just as they had been when killed at the demands of the "unwritten law" to prevent "negro domination." Negroes were killed for disputing over terms of contracts with their employers. If a few barns were burned some colored man was killed to stop it. If a colored man resented the imposition of a white man and the two came to blows, the colored man had to die, either at the hands of the white man then and there or later at the hands of a mob that speedily gathered. If he showed a spirit of courageous manhood he was hanged for his pains, and the killing was justified by the declaration that he was a "saucy nigger." Colored women have been murdered because they refused to tell the mobs where relatives could be found for "lynching bees." Boys of fourteen years have been lynched by white representatives of American civilization. In fact, for all kinds of offenses— and for no offenses—from murders to misdemeanors, men and women are put to death without judge or jury; so that, although the political excuse was no longer necessary, the wholesale murder of human beings went on just the same. A new name was given to the killings and a new excuse was invented for so doing.

Again the aid of the "unwritten law" is invoked, and again it comes to the rescue. During the last ten years a new statute has been added to the "unwritten law." This statute proclaims that for certain crimes or alleged crimes no negro shall be allowed a trial; that no white woman shall be compelled to charge an assault under oath or to submit any such charge to the investigation of a court of law. The result is that many men have been put to death whose innocence was afterward established; and to-day, under this reign of the "unwritten law," no colored man, no matter what his reputation, is safe from lynching if a white woman, no matter what her standing or motive, cares to charge him with insult or assault.

It is considered a sufficient excuse and reasonable justification to put a prisoner to death under this "unwritten law" for the frequently repeated charge that these lynching horrors are necessary to prevent crimes against women. The sentiment of the country has been appealed to, in describing the isolated condition of white families in thickly populated negro districts; and the charge is made that these homes are in as great danger as if they were surrounded by wild beasts. And the world has accepted this theory without let or hindrance. In many cases there has been open expression that the fate meted out to the victim was only what he deserved. In many other instances there has been a silence that says more forcibly than words can proclaim it that it is right and proper that a human being should be seized by a mob and burned to death upon the unsworn and the uncorroborated charge of his accuser. No matter that our laws presume every man innocent until he is proved guilty; no matter that it leaves a certain class of individuals completely at the mercy of another class; no matter that it encourages those criminally disposed to blacken their faces and commit any crime in the calendar so long as they can throw suspicion on some negro, as is frequently done, and then lead a mob to take his life; no matter that mobs make a farce of the law and a mockery of justice; no matter that hundreds of boys are being hardened in crime and schooled in vice by the repetition of such scenes before their eyes—if a white woman declares herself insulted or assaulted, some life must pay the penalty, with all the horrors of the Spanish Inquisition and all the barbarism of the Middle Ages. The world looks on and says it is well.

Not only are two hundred men and women put to death annually, on the average, in this country by mobs, but these lives are taken with the greatest publicity. In many instances the leading citizens aid and abet by their presence when they do not participate, and the leading journals inflame the public mind to the lynching point with scare-head articles and offers of rewards. Whenever a burning is advertised to take place, the railroads run excursions, photographs are taken, and the same jubilee is indulged in that characterized the public hangings of one hundred years ago. There is, however, this difference: in those old days the multitude that stood by was permitted only to guy or jeer. The nineteenth century lynching mob cuts off ears, toes, and fingers, strips off flesh, and distributes portions of the body as souvenirs among the crowd. If the leaders of the mob are so minded, coal-oil is poured over the body and the victim is then roasted to death. This has been done in Texarkana and Paris, Tex., in Bardswell, Ky., and in Newman, Ga. In Paris the officers of the law delivered the prisoner to the mob. The mayor gave the school children a holiday and the railroads ran excursion trains so that the people might see a human being burned to death. In Texarkana, the year before, men and boys amused themselves by cutting off strips of flesh and thrusting knives into their helpless victim. At Newman, Ga., of the present year, the mob tried every conceivable torture to compel the victim to cry out and confess, before they set fire to the faggots that burned him. But their trouble was all in vain—he never uttered a cry, and they could not make him confess...

Quite a number of the one-third alleged cases of assault that have been personally investigated by the writer have shown that there was no foundation in fact for the charges; yet the claim is not made that there were no real culprits among them. The negro has been too long associated with the white man not to have copied his vices as well as his virtues. But the negro resents and utterly repudiates the effort to blacken his good name by asserting that assaults upon women are peculiar to his race. The negro has suffered far more from the commission of this crime against the women of his race by white men than the white race has ever suffered through his crimes. Very scant notice is taken of the matter when this is the condition of affairs. What becomes a crime deserving capital punishment when the tables are turned is a matter of small moment when the negro woman is the accusing party...

No scoffer at our boasted American civilization could say anything more harsh of it than does the American white man himself who says he is unable to protect the honor of his women without resort to such brutal, inhuman, and degrading exhibitions as characterize "lynching bees." The cannibals of the South Sea Islands roast human beings alive to satisfy hunger. The red Indian of the Western plains tied his prisoner to the stake, tortured him, and danced in fiendish glee while his victim writhed in the flames. His savage, untutored mind suggested no better way than that of wreaking vengeance upon those who had wronged him. These people knew nothing about Christianity and did not profess to follow its teachings; but such primary laws as they had they lived up to. No nation, savage or civilized, save only the United States of America, has confessed its inability to protect its women save by hanging, shooting, and burning alleged offenders.

SIGNIFICANCE

Wells-Barnett's campaign to eradicate lynching was based on personal experience as well as a desire for social justice. In March 1892, three of Wells-Barnett's friends—Thomas Moss, Calvin McDowell, and Henry Stewart, the owners of a Memphis grocery store—were arrested on suspicion of inciting a riot following altercations over competition with a neighboring white grocery. A lynch mob took the three men from jail and murdered them in a field outside the city. Wells-Barnett's exposé of this tragedy was the beginning of her impassioned pieces on lynching, which included several searing editorials in her Memphis paper, the *Free Speech*. The newspaper offices were subsequently burned by an angry mob, and violent personal threats led Wells-Barnett to leave the South, taking her battle to larger and more receptive audiences in Northern cities and in Europe.

Wells-Barnett was the most active journalist and lecturer to record lynching while it was at its peak in the 1890s. Tolnay and Beck documented over 2,800 people murdered by lynch mobs in the South in the years between 1882 and 1930. Almost 2,500 of these victims were African Americans. These historians also point out that "The scale of this carnage means that, on the average, a black man, woman, or child was murdered nearly once a week, every week, between 1882 and 1930 by a hate-driven white mob." The number of people killed increased sharply in the 1890s, which accounts for some of the urgency and despair voiced by Wells-Barnett in *Lynch Law in America*.

Although the frequency of lynchings decreased in the twentieth century, there was at least one killing by lynch mobs each year until 1952. More than two hundred pieces of anti-lynching legislation were introduced to the U.S. Congress in this time period, in no small part inspired by the work of Ida B. Wells-Barnett and the movement she started. The House of Representatives succeeded in passing laws against lynching three times, but senators from southern states repeatedly refused to endorse the proposed laws. In June 2005, the U.S. Senate passed a resolution apologizing for its failure to enact anti-lynching legislation.

FURTHER RESOURCES
Books

Brown, Mary Jane. *Eradicating This Evil: Women in the Anti-Lynching Movement 1892–1940*. New York: Garland, 2000.

Dray, Philip. *At the Hands of Persons Unknown: The Lynching of Black America*. New York: Random House, 2002.

Schechter, Patricia A. *Ida B. Wells-Barnett & American Reform 1880–1930*. Chapel Hill, N.C.: University of North Carolina Press, 2001.

Tolnay, Stewart E. and E.M. Beck. *A Festival of Violence: An Analysis of Southern Lynchings, 1882–1930*. Urbana, Ill.: University of Illinois Press, 1995.

The Birth of a Nation

Film still

By: D.W. Griffith

Date: March 4, 1915

Source: *The Birth of a Nation.* Reliant-Majestic Studios, 1915. Still courtesy of AP/Wide World Photos. Reproduced by permission.

About the Author: David Wark Griffith (1875–1945) was the son of a former Confederate officer. His family fell on hard times after the Civil War and he was raised in genteel poverty. He struggled for many years as an actor and writer before finding his true calling in the new medium of film. Griffith mastered the art of writing and directing movies. While some of his later films are well-regarded by critics and historians, none were as successful, or controversial, as his first major film, *The Birth of a Nation.*

INTRODUCTION

The film *The Birth of a Nation* has remained controversial in the decades since its 1915 debut for its interpretation of race relations in American history. It was directed by D.W. Griffith, one of the men who helped create the film industry. Griffith demonstrated that huge sums of money could be made in the new medium of films but he made these profits by portraying the Ku Klux Klan as heroic for its vigilante actions against African Americans.

Griffith developed *The Birth of a Nation* script from a popular play and novel about the Civil War, *The Clansman* by Thomas Dixon, Jr. The story centers on two families, the southern Camerons and the northern Stonemans. Their friendship as the film begins symbolizes a united nation. The politics of the film becomes apparent as soon as the arrival of African slaves on American shores is introduced as the event that brought strife to the United States. In the film, Griffith blames the Civil War and its aftermath on African Americans and politicians. During the post-war period known as Reconstruction, Griffith shows a South that is victimized by Northern politicians. The newly freed slaves in the South are portrayed as evil, racially embittered, slovenly, and lustful toward white women. A Cameron son, angered by the death of his sister to escape an attempted rape at the hands of an African American, forms the Ku Klux Klan to protect whites.

Griffith, the son of a Confederate officer, told the history of the Civil War and Reconstruction as southern whites understood it. However, his story had little to do with reality. African Americans held majorities in only two state legislatures during Reconstruction and never had much genuine power. The myth of the African American rapist was exploded by journalist Ida B. Wells (1862–1931) in the 1890s as a means of justifying white violence against blacks. But Griffith's version of history, in which everything was fine until the North decided to meddle and the slaves got uppity endured for decades. Subsequent movies on the subject followed the same line, although with less offensive racism. Not until the civil rights movement of the 1960s would American historians seriously challenge the view that Reconstruction's attempt to create a better world for former slaves was a misguided disaster.

▇ PRIMARY SOURCE

THE BIRTH OF A NATION
See primary source image.

▇▇▇

SIGNIFICANCE

The Birth of a Nation is generally regarded by film historians as the most important film of the early silent era, both artistically and politically. At over three hours, the film was the longest ever made in the United States up to that time. It was also the most technically dazzling with creative camera movement and angles, close-ups, panning and tracking, cross-cutting to simultaneously occurring events, montage editing, iris shots, split screen, fade-ins and fade-outs, and long shots. These techniques had been used before, but never to such great effect and never in such a way as to involve the audience so deeply. The film was a blockbuster, earning $18 million. So many people saw the movie that the film is credited with widening the film audience beyond the working class to include the middle and upper classes. Schoolchildren were taken to the movie to learn history.

The Birth of a Nation was a vivid and dramatic rewriting of history at a time when many white people were frightened by the great migration of African Americans into northern cities. Whether or not Griffith intended to do so, his film helped revive the Ku Klux Klan. The movie also met with protests. Many reviewers noted with dismay that every African American character was evil or stupid at the

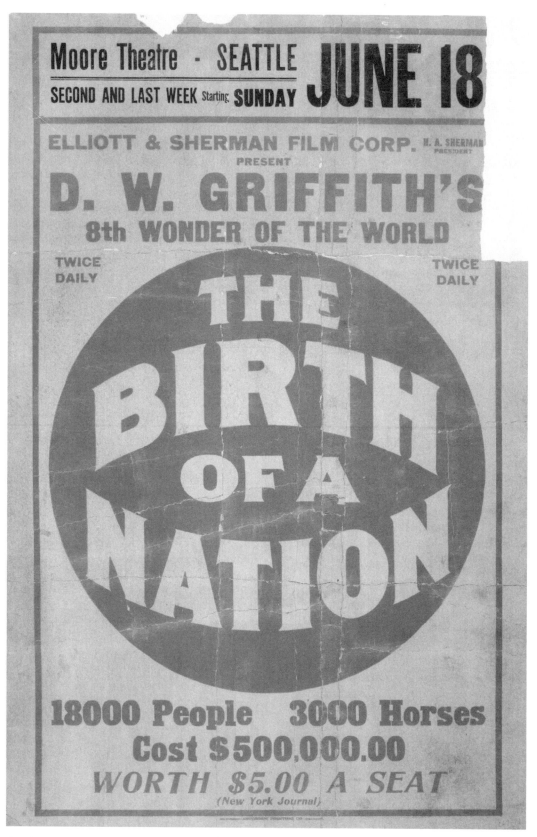

A poster advertising *The Birth of a Nation*. THE LIBRARY OF CONGRESS.

PRIMARY SOURCE

The Birth of a Nation: In this scene from *The Birth of a Nation,* the Ku Klux Klan is shown rescuing a southern town from the rampaging African American soldiers of the Union army. AP/WIDE WORLD PHOTOS. REPRODUCED BY PERMISSION.

same time that they praised Griffith's technical accomplishments. The National Association for the Advancement of Colored People (NAACP) organized a precedent-setting national boycott of the film, probably the first such effort and one of the most successful. The film was banned in three states and several cities. However, the turmoil made other filmmakers wary of using African American characters. As a result, African Americans largely disappeared from mainstream movies until the 1940s.

The Birth of a Nation was the first important American political film. It helped to popularize the image of the South under Reconstruction and influenced the way that Americans thought about

politics. Politicians were portrayed as evil and corrupt, motivated only by self-interest, while the people who became Ku Klux Klan vigilantes were portrayed as good citizens. Within ten years of the film's premier, the Ku Klux Klan rose to the height of its power.

FURTHER RESOURCES
Books
Chadwick, Bruce. *The Reel Civil War: Mythmaking in American Film.* New York: Alfred A. Knopf, 2001.

Christensen, Terry. *Reel Politics: American Political Movies from Birth of a Nation to Platoon.* New York: Basil Blackwell, 1987.

A protest against the race discrimination featured in the movie "The Birth of a Nation" organized by the National Association for the Advancement of Colored People. © CORBIS.

Cuniberti, John. *The Birth of a Nation: A Formal Shot-by-Shot Analysis Together with Microfiches*. New York: Research Publications, 1979.

Snead, James. *White Screens, Black Images: Hollywood from the Dark Side*. New York: Routledge, 1994.

The Causes of the Chicago Race Riot

Magazine article

By: Walter F. White

Date: October 1919

Source: White, Walter. "Chicago and Its Eight Reasons." *The Crisis* XVIII (October 1919): 293–297.

About the Author: Walter F. White was a prolific African-American author and civil rights activist. He was born in Georgia in 1893, and soon after his graduation from Atlanta University in 1916, went to work for the NAACP. He became an assistant executive secretary for the organization's national offices in 1918, and served as its executive secretary (or official spokesman) from 1931 until his death in 1955. Because of his light skin and blue eyes, White was able to pass as white, and undertook several investigations of lynchings, segregation, and race riots between 1918 and 1930. He described his work and thoughts about current affairs and race in numerous articles in *The Crisis*, *The Saturday Evening Post*, *Harper's*, *The New Republic*, and *The Nation*, and in regular columns in The *Chicago Defender* and the *New York Herald Tribune*. His books include the novels *The Fire in the Flint* (1924) and *Flight* (1926), and non-fiction *Rope and Faggot: A Biography of Judge Lynch* (1929), *A Rising Wind: A Report on the Negro Soldier in the European Theatre of War* (1945), and *A Man Called White: The Autobiography of Walter White* (1948).

INTRODUCTION

Walter White's analysis of the reasons underlying the racial violence that engulfed Chicago at the end of July in 1919 is an example of the literature on race and racism written for increasing numbers of African-American readers in the years following World War I. *The Crisis* was a widely read and influential magazine published monthly by the NAACP (The National Association for the Advancement of Colored People). When White's article was written, the NAACP was well on its way to becoming one of the most important educational and political organizations advocating for civil rights in the early twentieth century.

White's article on the riots was published soon after his return from a month in Chicago, where he had gone while some rioting was still happening at the beginning of August. As described by William Tuttle, Jr., in his book on the riots, White's investigations included undercover work at the Chicago stockyards, which were the economic and geographic focus of much of the rioting. White's thoughtful article provided a counterpoint to the impassioned and often inaccurate stories on the riots that had been published by many newspapers. His examination of the reasons behind the riots have been validated by later generations of historians and social scientists, and many use his work as a starting point for more detailed research.

◼ PRIMARY SOURCE

Many causes have been assigned for the three days of race rioting, from July 27 to 30 in Chicago, each touching some particular phase of the general condition that led up to the outbreak. Labor union officials attribute it to the action of the packers, while the packers are equally sure that the unions themselves are directly responsible. The city administration feels that the riots were brought on to discredit the Thompson forces, while leaders of the anti-Thompson forces, prominent among them being State's Attorney Maclay Hoyne, are sure that the administration is directly responsible. In this manner charges and counter-charges are made, but, as is usually the case, the Negro is made to bear the brunt of it all—to be "the scapegoat." A background of strained race relations brought to a head more rapidly through political corruption, economic competition and clashes due to the overflow of the greatly increased colored population into sections outside of the so-called "Black Belt," embracing the Second and Third Wards, all of these contributed, aided by magnifying of Negro crime by newspapers, to the formation of a situation where only a spark was needed to ignite the flames of racial antagonism. That spark was contributed by a white youth when he knocked a colored lad off a raft at the 29th Street bathing beach and the colored boy was drowned.

Four weeks spent in studying the situation in Chicago, immediately following the outbreaks, seem to show at least eight general causes for the riots, and the same conditions, to a greater or less degree, can be found in almost every large city with an appreciable Negro population. These causes, taken after a careful study in order of their prominence, are:

Race Prejudice.
Economic Competition.
Political Corruption and Exploitation of Negro Voters.
Police Inefficiency.
Newspaper Lies about Negro Crime.
Unpunished Crimes Against Negroes.
Housing.
Reaction of Whites and Negroes from War.

Some of these can be grouped under the same headings, but due to the prominence of each they are listed as separate causes.

Prior to 1915, Chicago had been famous for its remarkably fair attitude toward colored citizens. Since that time, when the migratory movement from the South assumed large proportions, the situation has steadily grown more and more tense. This was due in part to the introduction of many Negroes who were unfamiliar with city ways and could not, naturally, adapt themselves immediately to their new environment. Outside of a few sporadic attempts, little was done to teach them the rudimentary principles of sanitation, of conduct or of their new status as citizens under a system different from that in the South. During their period of absorption into the new life, their care-free, at times irresponsible and sometimes even boisterous, conduct caused complications difficult to

adjust. But equally important, though seldom considered, is the fact that many Southern whites have also come into the North, many of them to Chicago, drawn by the same economic advantages that attracted the colored workman. The exact figure is unknown, but it is estimated by men who should know that fully 20,000 of them are in Chicago. These have spread the virus of race hatred and evidences of it can be seen in Chicago on every hand. This same cause underlies each of the other seven causes.

With regard to economic competition, the age-long dispute between capital and labor enters. Large numbers of Negroes were brought from the South by the packers and there is little doubt that this was done in part so that the Negro might be used as a club over the heads of the unions. John Fitzpatrick and Ed Nockels, president and secretary, respectively, of the Chicago Federation of Labor, and William Buck, editor of the *New Majority*, a labor organ, openly charge that the packers subsidized colored ministers, politicians and Y. M. C. A. secretaries to prevent the colored workmen at the stockyards from entering the unions. On the other hand, the Negro workman is not at all sure as to the sincerity of the unions themselves. The Negro in Chicago yet remembers the waiters' strike some years ago, when colored union workers walked out at the command of the unions and when the strike was settled, the unions did not insist that Negro waiters be given their jobs back along with whites, and, as a result, colored men have never been able to get back into some of the hotels even to the present day. The Negro is between "the devil and the deep blue sea." He feels that if he goes into the unions, he will lose the friendship of the employers. He knows that if he does not, he is going to be met with the bitter antagonism of the unions. With the exception of statements made by organizers, who cannot be held to accountability because of their minor official connection, no statements have been made by the local union leaders, outside of high sounding, but meaningless, protestations of friendship for the Negro worker. He feels that he has been given promises too long already. In fact, he is "fed up" on them. What he wants are binding statements and guarantees that cannot be broken at will.

With the possible exception of Philadelphia, there is probably no city in America with more of political trickery, chicanery and exploitation than Chicago. Against the united and bitter opposition of every daily newspaper in Chicago, William Hale Thompson was elected again as mayor, due, as was claimed, to the Negro and German vote. While it is not possible to state that the anti-Thompson element deliberately brought on the riots, yet it is safe to say that they were not averse to its coming. The possibility of such a clash was seen many months before it actually occurred, yet no steps were taken to prevent it. The purpose of this was to secure a twofold result. First, it would alienate the Negro set from Thompson through a belief that was expected to grow among the colored vote when it was seen that the police force under the direction of the mayor was unable or unwilling to protect the colored people from assault by mobs. Secondly, it would discourage the Negroes from registering and voting and thus eliminate the powerful Negro vote in Chicago. Whether or not this results remains to be seen. In talking with a prominent colored citizen of Chicago, asking why the Negroes supported Thompson so unitedly, his very significant reply was:

> The Negro in Chicago, as in every other part of America, is fighting for the fundamental rights of citizenship. If a candidate for office is wrong on every other public question except this, the Negroes are going to vote for that man, for that is their only way of securing the things they want and that are denied them.

The value of the Negro vote to Thompson can be seen in a glance at the recent election figures. His plurality was 28,000 votes. In the second ward it was 14,000 and in the third, 10,000. The second and third wards constitute most of what is known as the "Black Belt."

The fourth contributing cause was the woeful inefficiency and criminal negligence of the police authorities of Chicago, both prior to and during the riots. Prostitution, gambling and the illicit sale of whisky flourish openly and apparently without any fear whatever of police interference. In a most dangerous statement, State's Attorney Maclay Hoyne, on August 25, declared that the riots were due solely to vice in the second ward. He seemed either to forget or to ignore the flagrant disregard of law and order and even of the common principles of decency in city management existing in many other sections of the city.

All of this tended to contribute to open disregard for law and almost contempt for it. Due either to political "pull" or to reciprocal arrangements, many notorious dives run and policemen are afraid to arrest the proprietors.

During the riots the conduct of the police force as a whole was equally open to criticism. State's Attorney Hoyne openly charged the police with arresting colored rioters and with an unwillingness to arrest white rioters. Those who were arrested were at once released. In one case a colored man who was fair enough to appear to be white was arrested for carrying concealed weapons, together with five white men and a number of colored men. All were taken to a police station; the light colored man and the five whites being put into one cell and the other colored men in another. In a few minutes the light colored man and the five whites were released and their ammunition given back to them with the remark, "You'll probably need this before the night is over."

Fifth on the list is the effect of newspaper publicity concerning Negro crime. With the exception of the *Daily* *News*, all of the papers of Chicago have played up in prominent style with glaring, prejudice-breeding headlines every crime or suspected crime committed by Negroes. Headlines such as "NEGRO BRUTALLY MURDERS PROMINENT CITIZEN," "NEGRO ROBS HOUSE" and the like have appeared with alarming frequency and the news articles beneath such headlines have been of the same sort. During the rioting such headlines as "NEGRO BANDITS TERRORIZE TOWN," "RIOTERS BURN 100 HOMES—NEGROES SUSPECTED OF HAVING PLOTTED BLAZE" appeared. In the latter case a story was told of witnesses seeing Negroes in automobiles applying torches and fleeing. This was the story given to the press by Fire Attorney John R. McCabe after a casual and hasty survey. Later the office of State Fire Marshal Gamber proved conclusively that the fires were *not* caused by Negroes, but by whites. As can easily be seen such newspaper accounts did not tend to lessen the bitterness of feeling between the conflicting groups. Further, many wild and unfounded rumors were published in the press—incendiary and inflammatory to the highest degree, a few of them being given below in order to show their nature. Some are:

> Over 1,000 Negroes had been slain and their bodies thrown in "Bubbly Creek" and the Chicago River.
>
> A Negro had been lynched and hanged from a "Loop" building overlooking Madison Street.
>
> A white woman had been attacked and mutilated by a Negro on State Street.
>
> A Negro woman had been slain, her breasts cut off and her infant had been killed by having its brains dashed out against a wall.
>
> A white child had been outraged by a colored man.
>
> A white child had been kidnapped by a band of colored men and its body later found, badly mutilated and dismembered.

Immediately following the riots, a white woman was murdered in Evanston, Ill. Immediately the crime was laid at the door of a colored man with whom the woman had been intimate a number of years. Pitiful stories were told of the woman waiting for hours on street corners for "just one look at her Billiken-like, mulatto lover," played up under headlines such as "CONFESSION EXPECTED TODAY FROM NEGRO SUSPECT," "NEGRO SUSPECT RAPIDLY WEAKENING" and the like which clearly led one to believe that the colored man was guilty. A few days later, in an obscure item on an inside page, a short account was given of the release of the colored suspect "because insufficient evidence to hold him" existed. A long period of such publicity had inflamed the minds of many people against Negroes who otherwise would have been unprejudiced. Much of the blame for the riots can be laid to such sources.

For a long period prior to the riots, organized gangs of white hoodlums had been perpetrating crimes against Negroes for which no arrests had been made. These gangs in many instances masqueraded under the name of "Athletic and Social Clubs" and later direct connection was shown between them and incendiary fires started during the riots. Colored men, women and children had been beaten in the parks, most of them in Jackson and Lincoln Parks. In one case a young colored girl was beaten and thrown into a lagoon. In other cases Negroes were beaten so severely that they had to be taken to hospitals. All of these cases had caused many colored people to wonder if they could expect any protection whatever from the authorities. Particularly vicious in their attacks was an organization known locally as "Regan's Colts."

Much has been written and said concerning the housing situation in Chicago and its effect on the racial situation. The problem is a simple one. Since 1915 the colored population of Chicago has more than doubled, increasing in four years from a little over 50,000 to what is now estimated to be between 125,000 and 150,000. Most of them lived in the area bounded by the railroad on the west, 30th Street on the north, 40th Street on the south and Ellis Avenue on east. Already overcrowded, this so-called "Black Belt" could not possibly hold the doubled colored population. One cannot put ten gallons of water in a five-gallon pail. Although many Negroes had been living in "white" neighborhoods, the increased exodus from the old areas created an hysterical group of persons who formed "Property Owners' Associations" for the purpose of keeping intact white neighborhoods. Prominent among these was the Kenwood-Hyde Park Property Owners' Improvement Association, as well as the Park Manor Improvement Association. Early in June the writer, while in Chicago, attended a private meeting of the first named at the Kenwood Club House, at Lake Park Avenue and 47th Street. Various plans were discussed for keeping the Negroes in "their part of the town," such as securing the discharge of colored persons from positions they held when they attempted to move into "white" neighborhoods, purchasing mortgages of Negroes buying homes and ejecting them when mortgage notes fell due and were unpaid, and many more of the same calibre. The language of many speakers was vicious and strongly prejudicial and had the distinct effect of creating race bitterness.

In a number of cases during the period from January, 1918, to August, 1919, there were bombings of colored homes and houses occupied by Negroes outside of the "Black Belt." During this period no less than twenty bombings took place, yet only two persons have been arrested and neither of the two has been convicted, both cases being continued.

Finally, the new spirit aroused in Negroes by their war experiences enters into the problem. From Local Board No. 4, embracing the neighborhood in the vicinity of State and 35th Streets, containing over 30,000 inhabitants of which fully ninety per cent are colored, over 9,000 men registered and 1,850 went to camp. These men, with their new outlook on life, injected the same spirit of independence into their companions, a thing that is true of many other sections in America. One of the greatest surprises to many of those who came down to "clean out the niggers" is that these same "niggers" fought back. Colored men saw their own kind being killed, heard of many more and believed that their lives and liberty were at stake. In such a spirit most of the fighting was done.

SIGNIFICANCE

The Chicago riot of 1919 began on July 27, when an African-American teenager was killed while swimming near a traditionally white beach on Lake Michigan. The riot—which killed thirty-eight people, left over five hundred wounded, and burned the homes of hundreds more—was not an isolated event. According to historian William Tuttle, Jr., riots that killed well over a hundred people took place in at least twenty-five different cities from April to October, 1919, in the period that James Weldon Johnson called "the Red Summer." At least seventy-eight more people were hung or burned by lynch mobs in the United States in 1919.

As White points out, the beginning of the "Great Migration" of southern African-Americans to northern industrial cities from 1915–1919 created much more intense competition for jobs, housing, and political power. In Chicago, there had already been more than a dozen bombings at Black houses in formerly white neighborhoods in 1919. Property owners' associations had formed to enforce residential segregation, and White was undercover at a June meeting where the residents were urged to arm themselves and take action against "niggers" and "undesirables."

Black stockyard workers, foundry workers, and others were pressured to join trade unions even as many union members discriminated against them on the job. Chicago's meat packing companies had a history of using Black workers as strikebreakers, and strikes or lockouts were already under way or threatened for nearly a quarter of the city's labor force in the summer of 1919. Unemployment rose sharply following World War I.

Several "athletic clubs" like Ragen's Colts, the Irish-American group that White described, were backed by local politicians that opposed Mayor

During the July 1919 race riots in Chicago, the National Guardsmen stand on a city street corner. PHOTO BY JUN FUJITA/GETTY IMAGES.

William Hale Thompson, whose recent and acrimonious election was aided by Black votes. These gangs played a bloody role in the riots, as thousands of young men drove through the neighborhood known as the "Black Belt," shooting, stoning, and burning houses.

A city commission investigating the riot in years directly afterwards, like White, found that the police did little to protect the city's Black residents. Despite the presence of several witnesses, a Chicago policeman at the 29th Street Beach did not arrest the man that threw the rock that caused the death of Eugene William, the teenager whose drowning set off the riot.

FURTHER RESOURCES

Books

The Chicago Commission on Race Relations. *The Negro in Chicago: A Study of Race Relations and a Race Riot.* Chicago: University of Chicago Press, 1922.

Tuttle, William M., Jr. *Race Riot: Chicago in the Red Summer of 1919.* Urbana, Ill.: University of Illinois Press, 1996.

Web sites

Cook County Coroner's Office. *Chicago Public Library.* "The Race Riots: Biennial Report 1918–1919 and Official Record on Inquests on the Victims of the Race Riots of July and August, 1919." <http://www.chipublib.org/004chicago/disasters/text/coroner/intro.html> (accessed April 30, 2006).

Sandburg, Carl. The *Chicago Daily News.* "Says Lax Conditions Caused Race Riots." <http://historymatters.gmu.edu/d/4974> (accessed April 30, 2006).

University of Illinois at Chicago. "Gangs and the 1919 Chicago Race Riot." <http://www.uic.edu/orgs/kbc/ganghistory/Industrial%20Era/Riotbegins.html> (accessed April 30, 2006).

The Social Equality of Whites and Blacks

Magazine article

By: W.E.B. Du Bois

Date: November, 1920

Source: Du Bois, W.E.B. "The Social Equality of Whites and Blacks." *The Crisis.* 21(1920):16.

About the Author: William Edward Burghardt Du Bois was one of the most controversial and influential African-American intellectuals of the early twentieth century. Born in 1868 and raised in a small town in western Massachusetts, Du Bois graduated from Fisk University in Nashville, Tennessee, in 1888. He earned another B.A. from Harvard in 1890, studied at the University of Berlin from 1892–1894, and received his M.A. and Ph.D. from Harvard in 1891 and 1895. In addition to teaching and research jobs at Wilberforce University, the University of Pennsylvania, and Atlanta University, Du Bois was a prolific speaker, activist, author, and editor. He published over twenty books and many hundreds of articles, both fiction and non-fiction. His work is acclaimed as seminal work in sociology, anthropology, and history. A few of his better-known books include *Suppression of the African Slave-Trade* (1896), *The Philadelphia Negro* (1899), *The Souls of Black Folk* (1903), *Darkwater* (1920), *Black Reconstruction in America* (1935), and *Dusk of Dawn* (1940). Du Bois was one of the co-founders of the NAACP (National Association for the Advancement of Colored People) in 1909 and served as the editor of its magazine, *The Crisis*, from 1910 to 1934, when he left following political and personal conflict in the organization. He returned to the NAACP for four years in the mid 1940s, but again left in a whirl of political controversy. At the age of eighty-three, Du Bois was indicted as a foreign agent by a federal grand jury displeased by his leftist political views. After charges were dropped and he regained his passport, in 1958 Du Bois emigrated to Ghana, where he joined the Communist Party and continued to write until his death in 1963.

INTRODUCTION

W.E.B. Du Bois was undoubtedly the "premier architect of the civil rights movement in the United States," as Lewis describes him in his 1993 biography. Du Bois founded *The Crisis* in 1910, and by 1920 it was the most influential African-American publication in the United States. Du Bois personally controlled the magazine's content for twenty-four years, and used it to showcase his passionate, often controversial editorials, highlight current events affecting African Americans, and document the NAACP's legal battles for civil rights. *The Crisis* also promoted the work of many of the artists of the Harlem Renaissance.

Du Bois's essay in the November 1920 issue of *The Crisis* may not seem particularly contentious to modern readers, but in 1920 the concept of social equality was a radical one. It challenged Jim Crow laws in numerous states and defied legal conventions of racial segregation. For the fifty years after Reconstruction, the term "social equality" had been used negatively. White audiences in this period were assured that social equality led to miscegenation (the mixing of races) and the eventual downfall of the social order. In his essay, Du Bois addressed the meaning of social equality, the underlying fear of intermarriage, and the violence done to Black Americans perceived as attempting or advocating any form of social equality.

▌ PRIMARY SOURCE

When The National Association for the Advancement of Colored People was organized it seemed to us that the subject of "social equality" between races was not one that we need touch officially whatever our private opinions might be. We announced clearly our object as being the political and civil rights of Negroes and this seemed to us a sufficiently clear explanation of our work.

We soon found, however, certain difficulties: Was the right to attend a theatre a civil or a social right? Is a hotel a private or a public institution? What should be our stand as to public travel or public celebrations or public dinners to discuss social uplift? And above all, should we be silent when laws were proposed taking away from a white father all legal responsibility for his colored child?

Moreover, no matter what our attitude, acts and clear statements have been, we were continually being "accused" of advocating "social equality" and back of the accusations were implied the most astonishing assumptions: our secretary was assaulted in Texas for "advocating social equality" when in fact he was present to prove that we were a legal organization under Texas law. Attempts were made in North Carolina to forbid a state school from advertising in our organ *The Crisis* on the ground that "now and then it injects a note of social equality" and in general we have seen theft, injustice, lynchings, riot and murder based on "accusations" or attempts at "social equality."

The time has, therefore, evidently come for *The Crisis* to take a public stand on this question in the interest of Justice and clear thinking. Let us openly define our terms and beliefs and let there be no further unjustifiable reticence on our part or underground skulking by enemies of the Negro race. This statement does not imply any change of attitude on our part; it simply means a clear and formal expression on matters which hitherto we have mistakenly assumed were unimportant in their relation to our main work.

We make this statement, too, the more willingly because recent events lead us to realize that there lurks in the use and the misuse of the phrase "social equality" much of the same virus that for thousands of years has separated and insulted and injured men of many races and groups and social classes.

We believe that social equality, by a reasonable interpretation of the words, mean moral, mental and physical fitness to associate with one's fellowmen. In this sense *The Crisis* believes absolutely in the Social Equality of the Black and White and Yellow races and it believes too that any attempt to deny this equality by law or custom is a blow at Humanity, Religion and Democracy.

No sooner is this incontestable statement made, however, than many minds immediately adduce further implications: they say that such a statement and belief implies the right of black folk to force themselves into the private social life of whites and to intermarry with them.

This is a forced and illogical definition of social equality. Social equals, even in the narrowest sense of the term, do not have the right to be invited to, or attend private receptions, or to marry persons who do not wish to marry them. Such a right would imply not mere equality—it would mean superiority. Such rights inhere in reigning monarchs in certain times and countries, but no man, black or white, ever dreamed of claiming a right to invade the private social life of any man.

On the other hand, every self-respecting person does claim the right to mingle with his fellows *if he is invited* and to be free from insult or hindrance because of his presence. When, therefore, the public is invited, or when he is privately invited to social gatherings, the Negro has a right to accept and no other guest has a right to complain; they have only the right to absent themselves. The late Booker T. Washington could hardly be called an advocate of "social equality" in any sense and yet he repeatedly accepted invitations to private and public functions and certainly had the right to.

To the question of intermarriage there are three aspects:.

1. The individual right
2. The social expediency
3. The physical result

As to the individual right of any two sane grown individuals of any race to marry there can be no denial in any civilized land. The moral results of any attempt to deny this right are too terrible and of this the southern United States is an awful and abiding example. Either white people and black people want to mingle sexually or they do not. If they do, no law will stop them and attempted laws are cruel, inhuman and immoral. If they do not, no laws are necessary.

But above the individual problem lies the question of the social expediency of the intermarriage of whites and blacks today in America. The answer to this is perfectly clear: it is not socially expedient today for such marriages to take place; the reasons are evident: where there are great differences of ideal, culture, taste and public esteem, the intermarriage of groups is unwise because it involves too great a strain to evolve a compatible, agreeable family life and to train up proper children. On this point there is almost complete agreement among colored and white people and the strong opinion here is not only that of the whites—it is the growing determination of the blacks to accept no alliances so long as there is any shadow of condescension; and to build a great black race tradition of which the Negro and the world will be as proud in the future as it has been in the ancient world.

The Crisis, therefore, most emphatically advises against race intermarriage in America but it does so while maintaining the moral and legal right of individuals who may think otherwise and it most emphatically refuses to base its opposition on other than social grounds.

The Crisis does not believe, for instance, that the intermarriage of races is physically criminal or deleterious. The overwhelming weight of scientific opinion and human experience is against this assumption and it is a cruel insult to seek to transmute a perfectly permissible social taste or thoughtful social advice into a confession or accusation of physical inferiority and contamination.

To sum up then: *The Crisis* advises strongly against interracial marriage in the United States today because of social conditions and prejudice and not for physical reasons; at the same time it maintains absolute legal right of such marriage for such as will, for the simple reason that any other solution is immoral and dangerous.

The Crisis does not for a moment believe that any man has a right to force his company on others in their private lives but it maintains Just as strongly that the right of any man to associate privately with those who wish to associate with him and publicly with anybody so long as he conducts himself gently, is the most fundamental right of a Human Being.

SIGNIFICANCE

Du Bois's uncompromising essay on social equality—one of a series on this topic in *The Crisis* from 1911–1925—was controversial, even amongst members of the NAACP. The essay itself defied a 1920 Mississippi code, stating:

> [a]ny person . . . presenting for public acceptance or general information, arguments or suggestions in favor of social equality or of intermarriage between whites and negroes, shall be guilty of a misdemeanor and subject to a fine not exceeding five hundred dollars or imprisonment not exceeding six months or both fine and imprisonment in the discretion of the court.

Du Bois's insistence on "the right to mingle with his fellows" also ran counter to goals of some other leaders. In 1920, the charismatic Jamaican Marcus Garvey was the leader of the recently formed UNIA (Universal Negro Improvement Association), which shared many objectives with the NAACP. Although Garvey and Du Bois were both dedicated to an international Pan-African ideology, Du Bois's emphasis on social equality and integration differed sharply from Garvey's call for Black separatism. Garvey's response to Du Bois's essay took the form of a resolution submitted to the League of Nations in August 1921, followed a month later by an editorial in the *New York World* denouncing Du Bois and stating that any amalgamation of races was a "crime against nature."

Almost twenty years previously, in *The Souls of Black Folk*, Du Bois had argued that Booker T. Washington and his Tuskegee Institute emphasized economic gains at the expense of civil rights. In his 1920 essay, Du Bois reiterated that equality was the only moral and just choice, and again repudiated (the now deceased) Washington's more politically expedient, less socially threatening plans as "unjustifiable reticence."

Some white Americans, including President Warren G. Harding, did advocate some degree of legal and political equality for Black Americans. Harding emphasized this in an October 1921 speech in Birmingham, Alabama, which Lewis suggests was an "explicit rebuttal of Du Bois's *Crisis* editorial". Although the Republican Harding called for "an end to prejudice" and voting rights for Black men, he also proclaimed himself against racial amalgamation, and affirmed his belief that "men of both races may well stand uncompromisingly against every suggestion of Social Equality."

W.E.B. Du Bois. FISK UNIVERSITY LIBRARY. REPRODUCED BY PERMISSION.

Historian Nell Painter examines the symbolic (largely psychological and sexual) implications of social equality as well as the material consequences, which provides further insight into why Du Bois's essays were so inflammatory. Although many of the Jim Crow laws supported by *Plessy vs. Ferguson* were overturned in the 1950s, it is worth noting that anti-miscegenation laws (laws against racial intermarriage) in sixteen states were not overturned by the Supreme Court until 1967.

FURTHER RESOURCES
Books
Lewis, David L. *W.E.B. Du Bois–Biography of a Race, 1868–1919*. New York: Henry Holt, 1993.

———. *W.E.B. Du Bois–The Fight for Equality and the American Century, 1919–1963*. New York: Henry Holt, 2000.

Painter, Nell I. *Social Equality, Miscegenation and the Maintenance of Power In The Evolution of Southern Culture*, ed. by Numan V. Bartley. Athens, Ga.: University of Georgia Press, 1988. pp. 47–67.

———. *Southern History Across the Color Line*. Chapel Hill, N.C.: University of North Carolina Press, 2002.

American Women Enfranchised

Newspaper article

By: International Woman Suffrage Alliance

Date: 1920

Source: International Woman Suffrage Alliance. "American Women Enfranchised." *Jus Suffragii: The International Woman Suffrage News* 14, 11 (September 1920).

About the Author: The Internationl Woman Suffrage Alliance (IWSA) was founded in 1902 as an alliance of national organizations fighting for woman suffrage that were interested in working together to further the cause of woman suffrage around the world. *Jus Sufragii* ("The Right of Suffrage") was the organization's monthly newsletter and was published in London during the 1920s. The famed American woman suffrage activist Carrie Chapman Catt played a key role in founding IWSA and was serving as its president when this edition was published. In 1946 IWSA changed its name to the International Alliance of Women.

INTRODUCTION

The history of female voting rights in the United States did not begin with the struggles in the nineteenth century for the vote. In 1776, New Jersey, New York, Massachusetts, and New Hampshire granted women

Alice Paul unfurls a banner from the balcony of the National Women's Party headquarters. The banner shows a star for each state which has ratified the Nineteenth Amendment, which gave women the right to vote. She and other women are celebrating the ratification of the amendment. © BETTMANN/CORBIS.

the vote, though that right was withdrawn throughout the 1780s for New York, Massachusetts, and New Hampshire, and in New Jersey in 1807. Voting became a state matter, and from 1807 to 1869 women could not vote in any state in the United States.

In 1869, Wyoming became the first territory in the United States to permit women the right to vote. By 1919, Utah, Colorado, Washington, California, Oregon, Arizona, Kansas, New York, South Dakota, Oklahoma, and Idaho permitted full suffrage, with Illinois, North Dakota, Indiana, Nebraska, and Michigan giving women partial voting rights. Female enfranchisement in the United States, first introduced to the national Congress in 1878, finally passed the Congress and became part of the Constitution with the ratification of the Nineteenth Amendment by the state of Tennessee, the thirty-sixth state to ratify, on August 18, 1920.

While female suffrage took over fifty years to pass in the United States, other countries worldwide dealt with the issue of the women's vote as well. In 1838, the tiny British colony of the Pitcairn Islands granted women the vote, and in 1862 Sweden granted unmarried women the right to vote in local elections. In 1893, New Zealand became the first country to pass a universal suffrage law. In the twenty-seven years between New Zealand's universal suffrage law and the Nineteenth Amendment ratification in the United States, much of Australia and western Europe granted women equal voting rights or partial voting rights. The United Kingdom granted women over the age of thirty the right to vote in 1918; the legal age for men was twenty-one.

This excerpt from *Jus Suffragii: The International Woman Suffrage News* quotes U.S. Secretary of State Bainbridge Colby's certification of the Nineteenth Amendment, as it was announced and circulated in western Europe. The accompanying article reflect's European suffragettes' support for American women's successful struggle for the vote.

▪ PRIMARY SOURCE

AMERICAN WOMEN ENFRANCHISED

Secretary of State Proclaims Ratification.

The Fight in Tennessee.

Text of the Proclamation Certifying Ratification of 19th Amendment.

Bainbridge Colby, Secretary of State of the United States of America.

To all to whom these presents shall come, greeting:

Know ye, That the Congress of the United States at the first session, sixty-sixth Congress begun at Washington on the nineteenth day of May in the year one thousand nine hundred and nineteen, passed a resolution as follows:

To wit:

Joint resolution.

Proposing an amendment to the Constitution extending the right of suffrage to women.

Resolved by the Senate and House of Representatives of the United States of America in Congress assembled (two thirds of each House concurring therein), that the following article is proposed as an amendment to the Constitution, which shall be valid to all intents and purposes as part of the Constitution when ratified by the Legislatures of three-fourths of the several States.

ARTICLE.

" The right of citizens of the United States to vote shall not be denied or abridged by the United States or by any State on account of sex.

" Congress shall have power to enforce this article by appropriate legislation."

And, further, that it appears from official documents on file in the Department of Sate that the amendment to the Constitution of the United States proposed as aforesaid has been ratified by the Legislatures of the States of Arizona, Arkansas, California, Colorado, Idaho, Illinois, Indiana, Iowa, Kansas, Kentucky, Maine, Massachusetts, Michigan, Minnesota, Missouri, Montana, Nebraska, Nevada, New Hampshire, New Jersey, New Mexico, North Dakota, New York, Ohio, Oklahoma, Oregon, Pennsylvania, Rhode Island, South Dakota, Tennessee, Texas, Utah, Washington, West Virginia, Wisconsin and Wyoming.

And, further, that the States whose Legislatures have so ratified the said proposed amendment, constitute three-fourths of the whole number of States in the United States.

Now, therefore, be it known that I, Bainbridge Colby, Secretary of State of the United States, by virtue and in pursuance of Section 205 of the Revised Statutes of the United States, do hereby certify that the amendment aforesaid has become valid to all intents and purposes as a part of the Constitution of the United States.

In testimony whereof, I have hereunto set my hand and caused the seal of the Department of State to be affixed.

Done at the City of Washington, this 26th day of August, in the year of our Lord one thousand nine hundred, and twenty.

BAINBRIDGE COLBY.

■ ■ ■

Late News. U.S.A. Victory Complete.

Both Houses of Connecticut Legislature ratified the Woman Suffrage Amendment September, 14, 1920.

We print above the text of the Proclamation signed at 8 a.m. on August 26, by the Secretary of State of the United States of America, whereby is ratified the Nineteenth Amendment to the United States of America constitution. The Nineteenth Amendment reads plainly and simply: "The rights of the citizens of the Untied States to vote shall not be denied or abridged by the United States or by any State on account of sex." But the ratification of that Nineteenth Amendment has been no plain and simple task for American women.

On August 25—one day before the Proclamation was signed—the Anti-Suffrage party made a last stand against the amendment. They appeared before Justice Frederick L. Siddons in the District of Columbia Supreme Court, and asked for an injunction to restrain the Secretary of State from issuing a proclamation declaring the amendment ratified by the required thirty-six States. Justice Siddons dismissed the appeal. In the early hours of the following morning the thirty-sixth ratification—that of Tennessee— arrived in Washington. The package was taken to Secretary Colby at 3:45 a.m. by Mr. Cooke of the State Department. In an interview with the Press on August 26, Secretary Colby says:—

> "There were some legal matters connected with the ratification that I wished to have examined by the chief law officer of the State Department, so I sent the papers to F.K. Nielson, the Solicitor of the State Department, with instructions to bring the papers to me at my home at 8 o'clock this morning. I have received a large number of messages asking me to act on the amendment with insistent promptitude. Fears were strong in some minds that the 'Antis' would effect some sort of injunction from the Courts to interfere with my Proclamation. While it was not my opinion that it would be becoming for me to resort to undue eagerness to avoid an opportunity for the judicial interference, I saw no reason whatever why I should conspicuously loiter."

In the meanwhile Tennessee—the eleventh-hour State to ratify—has proceeded to "rat," and has now definitely gone back on its ratification. According to telegrams in London papers it has actually expunged from its State Records all reference to its ratification of the Woman Suffrage Amendment. Depressing cables to this effect, prophesying the indefinite delay of Woman Suffrage in the United States as a result of Tennessee's action, have been appearing in the British Press, and your Editor, who has just returned to Headquarters after a long absence,

has been plunged in the deepest gloom. For this September Victory Number, prepared by Miss Henen Ward, was already in the printer's hands. A printers' strike in Manchester, however, had prevented the setting-up of the paper; and perhaps for once such an happening has been a blessing in disguise, since it permits the addition of these late notes on the American position.

Headquarters has therefore spent a hectic morning (September 9) telephoning every available source of knowledge in London for the latest American news. We were aghast to learn from the American Embassy here that they had *no authentic information later than June 21*—the days of the flood as far as the Nineteenth Amendment is concerned. But the kindly London Editors of the *New York Tribune* and *New York Herald* had received Press cuttings up to August 28—one day later than the dates of the invaluable Press cuttings on this topic just received from Mrs Husted Harper—and told me that according to the latest reports American public opinion was in no doubt that the result of any Supreme Court action would be favourable to the ratification of the Nineteenth Amendment and that Tennessee's treachery was a "back number"!

So we print our Victory Copy—and we greet our fellow Suffragists of America with a cheer as triumphant as any that must have sounded in the ears of Mrs. Catt when she returned to New York on August 27 to make a victorious procession through the City.

I end this note with a quotation from the *New York World* of August 27, which sums up the situation, and says a little of what we feel about the Anti-Suffragists of Tennessee:—

> "To the last, Anti-Suffragists and obscure influences sympathizing with them delude themselves with false hopes. Forced to admit that the amendment was certain to be ultimately adopted, they conspired to deal the event to prevent women in many States from voting in the November elections. In the devices that they employed in Tennessee, the final fighting-ground, they showed the unscrupulousness of desperate tricksters.

> "If they plan further efforts to nullify the action of the thirty-six States that ratified the amendment to the Federal Constitution, the opponents of Suffrage have but one choice. They must appeal to the United States Courts. There they may challenge in orderly manner the decision that has gone against them, on the chance of barring from the pools this year women in a number of States, but the prospects of success are not brilliant.

> "In the meantime, in every State, regardless of the restrictions of local Constitutions and laws, preparations must be made by election officials for the recognition of women as qualified voters on the same terms as men. All obstacles to equal Suffrage have been

swept aside at one stroke. Nowhere does any discretion remain or room or difference of opinion exist in the immediate application of the new provision of the Constitution of the United States."

E. A.

September 9, 1920.

SIGNIFICANCE

Alice Paul, the founder of the National Women's Party in the United States and a strong activist for female suffrage, had begun her career as a suffragette in England, working side by side with Women's Political and Social Union founder Emmaline Pankhurst. Paul had participated in hunger strikes in England while protesting for female suffrage; prison authorities force-fed Paul and fellow hunger strikers Lucy Burns and Pankhurst, among others, creating a media storm that shocked British citizens concerning the women's treatment. When Paul returned to the United States in 1912 after earning her doctorate at the London School of Economics, she was already well-known in England and brought her experience to American women's rights groups in the fight for female suffrage.

Such relationships and connections stimulated British and European support for the women's vote in the United States but also helped further an international coalition of women fighting for broader women's rights. Women in the United Kingdom had the vote in 1918, but not until age thirty; in 1928, British women successfully lobbied to have their voting age lowered to twenty-one, on par with male voter qualifications.

Sweden followed with universal suffrage in 1921, Spain in 1931, and other European countries such as Portugal, Turkey, France, and Italy granted full or nearly full suffrage to women by the end of World War II.

The parliamentary procedures that anti-suffrage groups tried to use to block Tennessee's ratification, as noted above, were quickly negated, but the description of Europe's reaction to the last-minute challenge shows a deep appreciation for and interest in governmental and policy workings behind the achievement of women's suffrage. Activists in the United Kingdom were still working on changing the voting age, French activists fought for another twenty-five years for female voting rights, and western European women involved in efforts for the vote followed legislative efforts as part of their planning and organization. As the article notes, "And now that by the ratification of the States, Woman Suffrage, is, after long years of hope deferred, at last part of the U.S.A. Constitution, we only begin dimly to comprehend what this means for the world. It is the token of certain success to those, all the world over, who still struggle that women may be free. It brings home to them the full significance, the absolute worth-whileness of every bit of endeavour they make."

FURTHER RESOURCES

Books

Becker, Susan D. *The Origins of the Equal Rights Amendment: American Feminism Between the Wars.* Westport, Conn.: Greenwood Press, 1981.

The Concise History of Woman Suffrage: Selections from History of Woman Suffrage, edited by Mary Jo and Paul Buhle. Urbana, Ill.: University of Illinois Press, 2005.

Felder, Deborah G. *A Century of Women: The Most Influential Events in Twentieth-Century Women's History.* New York: Kensington Publishing Corp., 1999.

Man Buying Tickets at Black Entrance to Theater

Photograph

By: Eudora Welty

Date: 1935

Source: © Eudora Welty/Corbis.

About the Photographer: Eudora Welty (1909–2001) worked as a photographer for the Works Progress Administration in 1935. She is best known as one of the greatest American writers of the twentieth century. The Jackson, Mississippi-born author won nearly every major writing prize, including the Pulitzer Prize in 1972 for *The Optimist's Daughter.*

INTRODUCTION

In the immediate aftermath of the Civil War, Republicans introduced several amendments to the Constitution. The Fourteenth Amendment, introduced in 1866 and ratified in 1868, made all native-born persons into American citizens and prohibited the states from denying any citizen equal protection under the law. Southerners strongly opposed the Fourteenth Amendment and attempted to maintain second-class status for African Americans.

By the 1880s, Republicans concerned about civil rights no longer controlled Congress. At the same time, the Supreme Court was becoming increasingly

■ **PRIMARY SOURCE**

Man Buying Tickets at Black Entrance to Theater: An African American buys theater tickets at a segregated ticket counter in Mississippi, circa 1935. © EUDORA WELTY/CORBIS.

On November 25, 1962, two white employees of a downtown cafe in Nashville, Tennessee, form a human barricade to keep African American sit-in demonstrators from entering. AP IMAGES.

hostile to federal civil rights legislation based on the Fourteenth Amendment. This hostility led the Court to invalidate the Civil Rights Act of 1875 in 1883. The act, the last piece of Reconstruction civil rights law, proclaimed the equality of all persons before the law and promised equal justice to people of every race, color, or persuasion in public or private accommodations. It was an attempt to prohibit racial segregation of trains, trolleys, theaters, hotels, restaurants, and other places open to the public. The Court ruled that the Fourteenth Amendment only addressed official, state-sponsored discrimination.

The court decision meant that racial segregation could be imposed by private businesses. The South moved quickly to ensure that African Americans would be unequal before the law. The Black Codes, passed to segregate and control newly freed African Americans, were reinstated. The Court then gave further support to the erosion of black civil rights. In 1896, the Court ruled in *Plessy v. Ferguson* that the Fourteenth Amendment did not intend to require mixing of the races in social situations. The amendment mandated legal equality, not social equality. Accordingly, "separate but equal" facilities for blacks and whites were permitted.

PRIMARY SOURCE

MAN BUYING TICKETS AT BLACK ENTRANCE TO THEATER
See primary source image.

SIGNIFICANCE

In reality, the concept of separate but equal was used to allow legal discrimination against African Americans in all walks of life. Especially in the South, many businesses would refuse to serve African Americans altogether. Those that did, such as the movie theatre in this photo, would almost always separate them from whites and give them access to only the least desirable seats, accommodations, or other services. Public services provided to African Americans, such as schools and public transportation, tended to be of low quality.

Segregation began to come under renewed scrutiny from the Supreme Court in 1938. *Missouri ex rel. Gaines v. Canada* involved a black applicant who was denied admission to the University of Missouri Law School. The state of Missouri, which had no law schools for blacks, attempted to fulfill its separate-but-equal obligations by offering to pay for the black applicant's tuition at a comparable out-of-state school. The Court held that this arrangement violated the applicant's rights guaranteed by the Equal Protection Clause of the Fourteenth Amendment.

Since this decision, the Fourteenth Amendment has proved to be one of the most effective tools for social and legal change in the United States. The efforts of civil rights activists to end the state-mandated segregation of public facilities and racial discrimination in all areas of American life were aided immeasurably by the Court's determination the Equal Protection Clause could be read liberally. This change in the Court's thinking led to the development of standards of judicial review which put certain types of legislation under strict scrutiny and spelled out suspect classifications. Ultimately, the concept of equal protection led to the overturning of the "separate but equal" concept in the 1954 *Brown v. Board of Education* decision.

FURTHER RESOURCES

Books

Adams, Francis D., and Barry Sanders. *Alienable Rights: The Exclusion of African Americans in a White Man's Land.* New York: HarperCollins, 2003.

Freedom and Equality: Discrimination and the Supreme Court, edited by Kermit L. Hall. New York: Garland, 2000.

Wormser, Richard. *The Rise and Fall of Jim Crow.* New York: St. Martin's Press, 2003.

Executive Order 9981

Desegregation of the Armed Forces

Executive order

By: President Harry S. Truman

Date: July 26, 1948

Source: Truman, Harry. Executive Order 9981. July 26, 1948. Available from the *Truman Library* <http://www.trumanlibrary.org/photos/9981a.jpg> (accessed April 30, 2006).

About the Author: Harry S. Truman (1884–1972), served as the 33rd president of the United States from 1945 to 1953. The Missouri-born Truman became the first president to introduce a civil rights bill to Congress. He is best known for making the decision to drop two atomic bombs on Japan to end World War II and for sending U.S. troops to Korea to fight against communism.

INTRODUCTION

World War II (1939–45) and the subsequent Cold War between the United States and the Soviet Union transformed the battle for African American civil rights. The vicious racism of the German Nazis, Italian fascists, and Japanese imperialists focused attention on the need for the United States to improve its own race relations and to provide for equal rights under the law. The increasing conflict with the communist Soviet Union also gave Americans a powerful incentive for improving race relations. The Soviets often compared segregation in the American South to the Nazis's treatment of the Jews. In this context, Harry S. Truman acted more boldly than any president before him in advancing civil rights.

Truman's activism was unexpected. For most of his political career, he had shown little interest in the plight of African Americans. He had grown up in western Missouri assuming that both blacks and whites preferred to be segregated from one another. As president, he had the courage to reassess these convictions.

In the fall of 1946, Truman hosted a delegation of civil rights activists from the National Emergency Committee Against Mob Violence. The activists, urging the president to issue a public condemnation of lynching, graphically described incidents of torture and intimidation against blacks in the South. Truman was stunned at the extent of the abuse and immediately appointed a Committee on Civil Rights to recommend preventive measures. The committee recommended the creation of a civil rights commission to investigate abuses and the denial of federal aid to any state that mandated segregated schools and public facilities. Truman went a step further on July 26, 1948 with Executive Order 9981.

PRIMARY SOURCE

Establishing the President's Committee on Equality of Treatment and Opportunity In the Armed Forces.

WHEREAS it is essential that there be maintained in the armed services of the United States the highest standards of democracy, with equality of treatment and opportunity for all those who serve in our country's defense:

NOW THEREFORE, by virtue of the authority vested in me as President of the United States, by the Constitution and the statutes of the United States, and as Commander in Chief of the armed services, it is hereby ordered as follows:

1. It is hereby declared to be the policy of the President that there shall be equality of treatment and opportunity for all persons in the armed services without

Cadets in training to join the "Tuskegee Airmen," the Army Air Force's segregated unit for African Americans during World War II. Their excellent performance in combat helped justify the ending of segregation in the military. From left to right: Lieutenant John Daniels, Cadet Clayborne Lockett, Cadet Lawrence O'Clark, Cadet William Melton, and civilian instructor Milton Crenshaw.

regard to race, color, religion or national origin. This policy shall be put into effect as rapidly as possible, having due regard to the time required to effectuate any necessary changes without impairing efficiency or morale.

2. There shall be created in the National Military Establishment an advisory committee to be known as the President's Committee on Equality of Treatment and Opportunity in the Armed Services, which shall be composed of seven members to be designated by the President.

3. The Committee is authorized on behalf of the President to examine into the rules, procedures and practices of the Armed Services in order to determine in what respect such rules, procedures and practices may be altered or improved with a view to carrying out the policy of this order. The Committee shall confer and advise the Secretary of Defense, the Secretary of the Army, the Secretary of the Navy, and the Secretary of the Air Force, and shall make such recommendations to the President and to said Secretaries as in the judgment of the Committee will effectuate the policy hereof.

4. All executive departments and agencies of the Federal Government are authorized and directed to cooperate with the Committee in its work, and to furnish the Committee such information or the services of such persons as the Committee may require in the performance of its duties.

5. When requested by the Committee to do so, persons in the armed services or in any of the executive departments and agencies of the Federal Government shall testify before the Committee and shall make available

for use of the Committee such documents and other information as the Committee may require.

6. The Committee shall continue to exist until such time as the President shall terminate its existence by Executive order.

Harry Truman
The White House
July 26, 1948

SIGNIFICANCE

The order to desegregate the armed forces sat unimplemented until the Korean War. In January 1950, Army regulations were issued that directed efficient employment of manpower without regard to race. In March 1950, the Army abolished quotas that restricted the recruiting of black soldiers. As a result, enlistment of black men increased well beyond the requirement of the still-segregated units. Commanders then began assigning black soldiers wherever they were needed and expressed satisfaction with the results. Fears of hostility and tension between blacks and whites proved unfounded. In May 1951, General Matthew B. Ridgway, the Far Eastern commander, recommended assigning black troops to all units in Japan and Korea. In July 1951, the Deparment of the Army approved Ridgway's request and directed the integration of army units over a six-month period. Service units integrated after the combat battalions.

As Ridgway and the Department of the Army realized, a segregated army made no sense militarily. Given the tensions of the Cold War and the need for economical use of manpower in the modern armed forces, it was foolish to make policy decisions based on the social standards of some white Americans. For national security reasons, segregated units had to be phased out.

A large gap loomed between what Truman spoke about civil rights and what his government actually accomplished. Yet desegregation of the military led to far-reaching changes. Truman used his office to set a moral agenda for the nation's long-unfulfilled promise to African Americans. Before Truman, no one in a responsible position had the will to overcome personal prejudice or to strongly confront political opposition to integration. His decision created a military where advancement was based only on merit. The military then served as a model of desegregation for the civilian community.

FURTHER RESOURCES
Books

Dalfiume, Richard M. *Desegregation of the U.S. Armed Forces: Fighting on Two Fronts, 1939–1953*. Columbia: University of Missouri Press, 1969.

MacGregor, Morris J., Jr. *The Integration of the Armed Forces, 1940–1965*. Washington, D.C.: U.S. Army Center of Military History, Government Printing Office, 1989.

McCullough, David. *Truman*. New York: Simon & Schuster, 1992.

Rosa Parks is Fingerprinted by Police

Photograph

By: Gene Herrick

Date: 1956

Source: AP/Wide World Photos. Reproduced by permission.

About the Photographer: Gene Herrick was a staff photographer for the Associated Press, a worldwide news agency based in New York.

INTRODUCTION

Racial segregation was the rule during the 1950s in the southern states, where the great majority of African Americans lived. In Montgomery, Alabama on December 1, 1955, Rosa Parks refused to give up her seat on a bus to a white man. Her action set off a full-scale, nationwide assault on Jim Crow segregation laws.

No segregation law angered African Americans in Montgomery more than bus segregation. There were about 50,000 African Americans in the city, and they made up sixty-six percent of bus riders. More African Americans rode the bus than whites because fewer African Americans could afford a car. An African American entering the bus would step through the first door, pay, exit back out the door, and enter the bus from the second door. On numerous occasions, the white bus drivers would amuse themselves by stepping on the gas as African Americans exited the first door, leaving them to stand on the sidewalk in a cloud of dust. Once through the second door, African Americans were expected to take a seat at the back of the bus, then gradually fill up the seats until meeting the white section. If a white person entered a full bus, an African American was expected to surrender his or her seat since Montgomery

Rosa Parks riding on a public bus in Montgomery, Alabama, in 1956. The bus has been desegregated thanks to her actions and those she inspired. © CORBIS. REPRODUCED BY PERMISSION.

had a local ordinance that required them to give up their seat on public transportation to a white when asked.

African Americans were repeatedly told by the bus company, the city council, and local community activists that the rudeness of the bus drivers was a fact of life in Montgomery. Nothing could be done to stop it. Parks, the secretary of the local National Association for the Advancement of Colored People (NAACP), had already inquired about a possible bus boycott and had been told by others in the African American community that they would not participate because the

walk to work would be too long. Meanwhile, the Montgomery NAACP had begun to contemplate filing suit against the city over bus segregation but they needed the right plaintiff and a winnable case.

Parks was the right plaintiff. Unlike other women who had been arrested on the buses, she did not have a police record and was not pregnant outside of wedlock. Parks was a quiet, church-going, married woman who had gainful employment as a seamstress in a downtown department store. She got on a bus on December 1, 1955. She did not intend to get arrested and, contrary to

■ **PRIMARY SOURCE**

Rosa Parks is Fingerprinted by Police: Rosa Parks is fingerprinted by police Lt. D.H. Lackey, in Montgomery, Ala., on February 22, 1956. AP/WIDE WORLD PHOTOS. REPRODUCED BY PERMISSION.

popular belief, she was also not physically tired. At the next stop, some whites entered and filled up every seat. One white man remained standing and the bus driver, James Blake, asked Parks to give up her seat. Believing that African American compliance with segregation had only led to worse treatment, Parks was tired of giving in. She refused to move and was arrested.

■ **PRIMARY SOURCE**

ROSA PARKS IS FINGERPRINTED BY POLICE
See primary source image.

■

SIGNIFICANCE

In the early morning hours after Parks' arrest, African American community leaders blanketed sections of Montgomery with leaflets urging support of a

one-day bus boycott as a protest. The boycott proved so successful that the leaders decided to continue the protest in an attempt to obtain substantial change. On December 5, leaders of local organizations founded the Montgomery Improvement Association (MIA) to organize and maintain the boycott. Martin Luther King, Jr. came to national prominence as the spokesperson for the MIA.

For months, African Americans formed carpools, hitchhiked, or simply walked. The boycott was almost completely effective. It put economic pressure not only on the bus company but on many Montgomery merchants because the boycotters found it difficult to get to downtown stores and shopped instead in their own neighborhoods. Still, the white town fathers held out against the boycott. In a case initiated by the MIA, a federal district court overturned the "separate but equal" doctrine established by the Supreme Court in the 1896 *Plessy v. Ferguson* decision. In November

1956, the Supreme Court let the lower court decision stand without review. The next day, King and other African Americans boarded the buses in Montgomery. In an attempt to keep the spirit of the bus boycott alive, King and a group of associates founded the Southern Christian Leadership Conference in 1957. It would become one of the leading organizations of the non-violent civil rights movement.

FURTHER RESOURCES

Books

Brinkley, Douglas. *Rosa Parks*. New York: Viking, 2000.

Kohl, Herbert R. *She Would Not Be Moved: How We Tell the Story of Rosa Parks and the Montgomery Bus Boycott*. New York: New Press, 2005.

Parks, Rosa and Jim Haskins. *Rosa Parks: My Story*. New York: Dial Books, 1992.

Williams, Donnie. *The Thunder of Angels: The Montgomery Bus Boycott and the People Who Broke the Back of Jim Crow*. Chicago: Lawrence Hill Books, 2006.

Newton Girl Jailed in Mississippi with Eight Freedom Fighters

Newspaper article

By: Anonymous

Date: June 22, 1961

Source: Anonymous. "Newton Girl Jailed in Mississippi with Eight Freedom Fighters." *Boston Globe*. June 22, 1961.

About the Author: This article was written by an unnamed staff writer for the *Boston Globe*, a Boston-based daily newspaper with a daily circulation of 474,845. The *Boston Globe* is the largest circulating paper in the six New England states.

INTRODUCTION

The path to meaningful civil rights legislation in the United States proved to be complex and arduous. The majority of history books mark the beginning of the movement with the May 17, 1954 *Brown v. Board of Education of Topeka, Kansas* decision. The Court, in its unanimous decision, declared that segregated schools violated the U.S. Constitution. In doing so, the decision overruled the Court's 1896 ruling in *Plessy v. Ferguson* that called state segregated education

constitutional if each party received equal facilities. These cases laid the framework for the 1955–56 Montgomery Bus Boycott—stemming from the staged protest and arrest of Rosa Parks on December 1, 1955—and the 1957 Little Rock Crisis. In Little Rock, Arkansas Governor Orville Faubus refused to uphold the Supreme Court's decision for school de-segregation, and he sent Alabama National Guard troops to prevent black students from entering the school. President Dwight D. Eisenhower (1890–1969) countered Faubus by sending in U.S. Army troops escort the nine black students to and from school.

The fight for civil rights escalated in the following years. The next waves, and manifestations, of the movement came in many forms, and on February 1, 1960, four black college students staged a sit-in at a Woolworth's lunch counter in Greensboro, North Carolina. The North Carolina sit-in was not the first one for the civil rights movement, but it was the first to gain national attention. It occurred in the American South, and the racial complexities of the region sparked more controversy and conflict than protests in other areas. The first sit-in occurred on May 14, 1943, in Chicago, Illinois at Jack Spratt's Coffee Shop. Following the Greensboro sit-in, San Antonio, Texas became the first southern city to desegregate its lunch counters in March 1960. Shortly after the desegregation of San Antonio lunch counters, Eisenhower signed the Civil Rights Act of 1960. The 1960 act prohibited preventing individuals from voting or registering to vote, and the 1961 Freedom Rides continued these social notions of equality and equal accessibility to life and the nation.

These rides took protestors on buses in an attempt to de-segregate interstate travel in the south. Their agenda stemmed from an earlier one in 1947. The April 1947 Journey of Reconciliation took riders through the border states of Virginia, North Carolina, Tennessee, Kentucky, and West Virginia. The states bordered the original dividing lines of the Union and the Confederacy, with Kentucky and West Virginia as border states. West Virginia and Kentucky never succeeded from the Union during the U.S. Civil War (1861–1865), but in the war's aftermath, assumed some of the same policies as the southern states. This ride derived from the 1946 *Morgan v. Commonwealth* case that forbade segregated travel on interstates. In 1947, riders faced danger, but the hostilities they encountered in southern border states only shadowed what occurred fourteen years later.

The Freedom Riders, mainly under the auspices of the Congress of Racial Equality (formed in 1942), set

A bus load of Freedom Riders arrives at the Montgomery, Alabama, bus station under the protection of police and National Guardsmen, May 24, 1961. PHOTOGRAPH BY PETER AYCOCK. AP/WIDE WORLD PHOTOS. REPRODUCED BY PERMISSION.

out from Washington D.C. to reach New Orleans, Louisiana on May 17 (the seventh anniversary of the *Brown* decision). Near Anniston, Alabama, one bus was stopped. An angry mob of about two hundred people stoned the bus, beat its riders, and firebombed it on May 4, 1961. In spite of the violence, the riders pressed forward. The second bus encountered a similar situation at the Birmingham bus depot. While the riders wanted to continue their journey by bus, they were unable to do so because the bus company and its drivers feared being targeted with more violence. The original Freedom Riders, fearing for their lives, ended up flying to New Orleans, but students from Nashville, Tennessee traveled to Birmingham to continue the ride. With pressure from Attorney General Robert Kennedy (1925–1968) the bus company and the Birmingham police agreed to cooperate with the Freedom Riders. On May 20, the riders set out, again, from Birmingham to Montgomery, Alabama. The plan dictated that police would escort the bus and riders into Montgomery, but when they reached the city, police protection dissipated. Riders noted that

everything seemed quiet at the bus terminal, until they exited the bus. Then, a mob of angry whites erupted. The ensuing violence forced Robert Kennedy to call in federal marshals to the city, shortly thereafter. Martin Luther King Jr. was escorted by marshals when he flew to Montgomery to meet with the Freedom Riders, but when he attracted a mob of thousands of angry whites Kennedy was forced to ask Governor John Patterson to send in National Guard troops to restore order.

Again, in spite of the violence and harassment, the riders insisted on continuing their Freedom Ride. Against the wishes of Kennedy, they continued their ride to Jackson, Mississippi. Kennedy requested a cooling off period, but civil rights leaders refused to put their fight on hold. When the riders arrived in Jackson, without incident, local police ushered them through the terminal, through entrances reserved for white people, and into police vans. Before the riders left Alabama, Kennedy and Mississippi Senator James O. Eastland had reached a compromise that federal troops would not be used in Mississippi if mob violence did not occur. So when the protestors were arrested, they fell to the mercy of the local courts. The judge sentenced them to sixty days in the state penitentiary. After the Mississippi case, many Freedom Riders tried to continue the journey, but many spent time in jail. Some nearly died or endured severe injuries from the beatings they received for demanding and supporting desegregation. While the majority of the riders, and civil rights activists were black, many participants were white. Newspapers, and other media outlets, sometimes gave a civil rights incident more coverage if a white person was involved.

PRIMARY SOURCE

A 22-year old Newton girl was among nine new "Freedom Riders" who were arrested in Jackson, Miss., yesterday after trying unsuccessfully to desegregate the white waiting room at the Trailways bus terminal.

Judith Ann Frieze of 31 Tamworth Rd., Waban, who was graduated this month from Smith College was one of several whites in the racially-mixed group arrested on a breach of peace charge.

Miss Frieze, who plans to do graduate work in education at Boston University this Fall, is the daughter of Mr. and Mrs. Philip Frieze.

Her father said early this morning that Judith had phoned him yesterday from Alabama, telling him of her plans to join the Freedom Ride. He told the Globe that he was not aware she had been arrested until notified by newspapermen.

Jackson police reported this morning that Miss Frieze was being held in the county jail and would face arraignment at a later date.

A police spokesman said he was unable to let Miss Frieze talk with the Globe this morning.

The arrest of Miss Frieze and her eight companions brought to 140 the number of arrests during the 29-day siege of Jackson. The nine new riders were ordered arrested by Capt. J. L. Ray after they entered the all-white waiting room and then failed to obey officers' orders to move on.

The only white man in the group, Henry Schwarzchild of Chicago, asked for permission to get a cup of coffee in the lunchroom and Ray told him to move on.

"I believe I have a right to get a cup of coffee," Schwarzchild replied, and Ray told him that he was under arrest. Less than 10 minutes later, the terminal was cleared of the nine riders.

Included among the nine were Rev. Wyatt Tee Walker of Atlanta, executive director of the Southern Christian Leadership Conference; his wife, Theresa Ann Walker, and Dr. Milton Reid of Petersburg, Va., president of the Virginia Christian Leadership Conference.

In other developments, more Freedom Riders were reported on the way to Jackson today from Berkeley, Calif., via Los Angeles and New Orleans. By taking the route of their predecessors they could reach Jackson no sooner than Saturday.

And in the legal division, two separate court cases are still pending.

U.S. District Court Judge Sidney Mize is expected to rule by Tuesday on a writ of habeas corpus filed by Elizabeth Porter Wyckoff, 45-year-old white rider from New York.

Chief Judge Elbert P. Tuttle of the 5th Circuit Court of Appeals in New Orleans told Federal Court there a request from the National Association for the Advancement of Colored People for an order to keep police from arresting riders would go before a three-judge Federal Court July 10. Atty. William Kuntsler of New York, who is representing Miss Wyckoff in her court case, told Judge Mize her arrest was in "open defiance of Federal authority."

An attorney representing the state, Tom Watkins of Jackson, argued that Kuntsler did not want to go through state courts and Miss Wyckoff was "in jail solely because she wants to be." Kuntsler replied that Miss Wyckoff was serving a short term sentence and would be out of jail before the petitions could go through state courts.

Other riders are expected to ask similar orders if Miss Wyckoff is freed.

Florida Trial Opens The N.A.A.C.P. suit is a class action which asks the court to keep the state from enforcing segregation on all Negroes. It asks that officers be ordered not to molest or arrest Negroes seeking to use white facilities at public transportation terminals and white seats on local and inter-city buses.

Meanwhile, in Tallahassee, Fla., 10 Freedom Riders whose attempts to integrate the city airport's white restaurant landed them in jail go on trial today on charges of unlawful assembly.

Also scheduled for trial are three others who joined the segregations-busting group of Northern clergymen in their sit-in demonstration at the airport.

The eight white persons and five Negroes all pleaded innocent before City Judge John Rudd and have been free since last weekend under bonds of $500 each.

The arrests last Friday ended a sit-in demonstration at the airport which had lasted about 15 hours. The Freedom Riders started the sit-in when they arrived at the airport to return home after a bus ride into the South to challenge segregation practices and found the white restaurant closed. City officials refused to order it opened so they could be served.

SIGNIFICANCE

The Freedom Riders did not make their trip in vain. The months and years succeeding the Freedom Riders brought forth a variety of changes and protests for civil rights. Robert Kennedy encouraged the Interstate Commerce Commission to outlaw segregation in interstate bus travel, and its ruling took effect in September 1961. The Civil Rights Act of 1964 banned all acts of discrimination in public places. The Voting Rights Act of 1965 made voting easier for southern blacks because it prohibited such requirements as literacy tests and poll taxes. Then, on September 24, 1965, President Lyndon Johnson issued Executive Order 11246, enforcing affirmative action and requiring government contractors to practice fair hiring procedures toward minorities.

The fight for civil rights has continued into the modern era. Even though the Civil Rights Act of 1968 prohibited discrimination in the sale and rental of housing, further steps were needed to ensure fair and equal treatment of individuals. In 1988, the U.S. Congress overrode a presidential veto to pass the Civil Rights Restoration Act, which forced private institutions that received federal funds to practice fair hiring practices. In 1991, President George H. W. Bush signed another version of the Civil Rights Act. One year later in 1992, Los Angeles fell prey to rioting when an amateur cameraman caught police beating black resident Rodney King. These acts, and a plethora of others, have continued to shape the civil rights movement and the social structure of the United States.

FURTHER RESOURCES
Books

Arsenault, Raymond. *Freedom Riders: 1961 and the Struggle for Racial Justice*. New York: Oxford University Press, 2006.

Dudziak, Mary L. *Cold War Civil Rights: Race and the Image of American Democracy*. Princeton: Princeton University Press, 2000.

Hale, Grace Elizabeth. *Making Whiteness: The Culture of Segregation in the South, 1890–1940*. New York: Vintage Books, 1998.

Moody, Anne. *Coming of Age in Mississippi*. New York: Dell Publishing Group, Inc., 1968.

Periodicals

Morris, Aldon D. "A Retrospective of the Civil Rights Movement: Political and Intellectual Landmarks." *Annual Review of Sociology*. 25(1999): 517–539.

Web sites

The Library of Congress. "African American Odyssey, The Civil Rights Era, Part 2: Sit-Ins, Freedom Rides, and Demonstrations." <http://memory.loc.gov/ammem/aaohtml/exhibit/aopart9b.html> (accessed April 22, 2006).

"I Have a Dream"

Speech

By: Martin Luther King, Jr

Date: August 28, 1963

Source: King, Jr. Martin Luther. "I Have a Dream." Speech delivered in Washington, D.C. Available from: *Avalon Project of Yale Law School*. <http://www.yale.edu/lawweb/avalon/treatise/king/mlk01.htm> (accessed April 30, 2006).

About the Author: Martin Luther King, Jr. (1929–1968) was a Baptist minister and civil rights leader who, as president of the Southern Christian Leadership Council, spearheaded the struggle for racial equality throughout the late 1950s and 1960s.

INTRODUCTION

Martin Luther King, Jr. helped revolutionize race relations in the United States. He was an eloquent and popular voice of the African American civil rights movement from the time of the Montgomery Bus Boycott in 1956 to his murder in 1968. No one else had King's ability to arouse his listeners to indignation against injustice, to persuade them to march and demonstrate at the risk of beatings, and to inspire faith in the triumph of love over hate.

King expressed a philosophy that suited the civil rights movement of the late fifties and early 1960s. He rejected the idea that progress could come through negotiations or favors or the use of courts. He urged direct action by masses of people. Although he recognized that marches and demonstrations would likely result in white-directed violence, King insisted that the protesters be nonviolent. He had been heavily influenced by Henry David Thoreau's willingness to disobey the law to support a moral principle and Mohandas Gandhi's idea that the force of truth, acted out in massive disobedience, could win against the force of arms.

On June 11, 1963, President John F. Kennedy announced his intention to present Congress with a comprehensive civil rights bill. The legislation was intended to ban segregation in all public facilities, to promote black employment, and to end the disfranchisement of black would-be voters. In a dramatic expression of public support for the bill, King led the March on Washington for Jobs and Freedom. On August 28, King addressed an audience of more than 250,000 from the steps of the Lincoln Memorial. His "I Have a Dream" speech has been called the most powerful and important address delivered by a civil rights leader in the twentieth century. In it, he referenced the traditional symbols of American identity: patriotism, religious conviction, the Declaration of Independence, and the Constitution.

The Civil Rights Act passed in 1964, after Kennedy's assassination. In 1967, King went to Memphis, Tennessee to aid striking sanitation workers, most of whom were black, in their struggle for better wages and working conditions. While there, on April 4, 1968, King was assassinated on the balcony of the Lorraine Motel by James Earl Ray.

■ PRIMARY SOURCE

Five score years ago, a great American, in whose symbolic shadow we stand signed the Emancipation Proclamation. This momentous decree came as a great beacon light of hope to millions of Negro slaves who had been seared in the flames of withering injustice. It came as a joyous daybreak to end the long night of captivity.

But one hundred years later, we must face the tragic fact that the Negro is still not free. One hundred years later, the life of the Negro is still sadly crippled by the manacles of segregation and the chains of discrimination. One hundred years later, the Negro lives on a lonely island of poverty in the midst of a vast ocean of material prosperity. One hundred years later, the Negro is still languishing in the corners of American society and finds himself an exile in his own land. So we have come here today to dramatize an appalling condition.

In a sense we have come to our nation's capital to cash a check. When the architects of our republic wrote the magnificent words of the Constitution and the declaration of Independence, they were signing a promissory note to which every American was to fall heir. This note was a promise that all men would be guaranteed the inalienable rights of life, liberty, and the pursuit of happiness.

It is obvious today that America has defaulted on this promissory note insofar as her citizens of color are concerned. Instead of honoring this sacred obligation, America has given the Negro people a bad check which has come back marked "insufficient funds." But we refuse to believe that the bank of justice is bankrupt. We refuse to believe

that there are insufficient funds in the great vaults of opportunity of this nation. So we have come to cash this check—a check that will give us upon demand the riches of freedom and the security of justice. We have also come to this hallowed spot to remind America of the fierce urgency of now. This is no time to engage in the luxury of cooling off or to take the tranquilizing drug of gradualism. Now is the time to rise from the dark and desolate valley of segregation to the sunlit path of racial justice. Now is the time to open the doors of opportunity to all of God's children. Now is the time to lift our nation from the quicksands of racial injustice to the solid rock of brotherhood.

It would be fatal for the nation to overlook the urgency of the moment and to underestimate the determination of the Negro. This sweltering summer of the Negro's legitimate discontent will not pass until there is an invigorating autumn of freedom and equality. Nineteen sixty-three is not an end, but a beginning. Those who hope that the Negro needed to blow off steam and will now be content will have a rude awakening if the nation returns to business as usual. There will be neither rest nor tranquility in America until the Negro is granted his citizenship rights. The whirlwinds of revolt will continue to shake the foundations of our nation until the bright day of justice emerges.

But there is something that I must say to my people who stand on the warm threshold which leads into the palace of justice. In the process of gaining our rightful place we must not be guilty of wrongful deeds. Let us not seek to satisfy our thirst for freedom by drinking from the cup of bitterness and hatred.

We must forever conduct our struggle on the high plane of dignity and discipline. We must not allow our creative protest to degenerate into physical violence. Again and again we must rise to the majestic heights of meeting physical force with soul force. The marvelous new militancy which has engulfed the Negro community must not lead us to distrust of all white people, for many of our white brothers, as evidenced by their presence here today, have come to realize that their destiny is tied up with our destiny and their freedom is inextricably bound to our freedom. We cannot walk alone.

And as we walk, we must make the pledge that we shall march ahead. We cannot turn back. There are those who are asking the devotees of civil rights, "When will you be satisfied?" We can never be satisfied as long as our bodies, heavy with the fatigue of travel, cannot gain lodging in the motels of the highways and the hotels of the cities. We cannot be satisfied as long as the Negro's basic mobility is from a smaller ghetto to a larger one. We can never be satisfied as long as a Negro in Mississippi cannot vote and a Negro in New York believes he has nothing for which to vote. No, no, we are not satisfied, and we will not

Martin Luther King Jr., gives his "I Have a Dream" speech to a crowd before the Lincoln Memorial during the Freedom March in Washington, D.C., on August 28, 1963. UPI/CORBIS BETTMANN. REPRODUCED BY PERMISSION.

be satisfied until justice rolls down like waters and righteousness like a mighty stream.

I am not unmindful that some of you have come here out of great trials and tribulations. Some of you have come fresh from narrow cells. Some of you have come from areas where your quest for freedom left you battered by the storms of persecution and staggered by the winds of police brutality. You have been the veterans of creative suffering. Continue to work with the faith that unearned suffering is redemptive.

Go back to Mississippi, go back to Alabama, go back to Georgia, go back to Louisiana, go back to the slums and ghettos of our northern cities, knowing that somehow this situation can and will be changed. Let us not wallow in the valley of despair.

I say to you today, my friends, that in spite of the difficulties and frustrations of the moment, I still have a dream. It is a dream deeply rooted in the American dream.

I have a dream that one day this nation will rise up and live out the meaning of its creed: "We hold these truths to be self-evident: that all men are created equal." I have a dream that one day on the red hills of Georgia the sons of former slaves and the sons of former slaveowners will be able to sit down together at a table of brotherhood.

I have a dream that one day even the state of Mississippi, a desert state, sweltering with the heat of injustice and oppression, will be transformed into an oasis of freedom and justice.

I have a dream that my four children will one day live in a nation where they will not be judged by the color of their skin but by the content of their character.

I have a dream today.

I have a dream that one day the state of Alabama, whose governor's lips are presently dripping with the words of interposition and nullification, will be transformed into a situation where little black boys and black girls will be able to join hands with little white boys and white girls and walk together as sisters and brothers.

I have a dream today.

I have a dream that one day every valley shall be exalted, every hill and mountain shall be made low, the rough places will be made plain, and the crooked places will be made straight, and the glory of the Lord shall be revealed, and all flesh shall see it together.

This is our hope. This is the faith with which I return to the South. With this faith we will be able to hew out of the mountain of despair a stone of hope. With this faith we will be able to transform the jangling discords of our nation into a beautiful symphony of brotherhood. With this faith we will be able to work together, to pray together, to struggle together, to go to jail together, to stand up for freedom together, knowing that we will be free one day.

This will be the day when all of God's children will be able to sing with a new meaning, "My country, 'tis of thee, sweet land of liberty, of thee I sing. Land where my fathers died, land of the pilgrim's pride, from every mountainside, let freedom ring."

And if America is to be a great nation this must become. So let freedom ring from the prodigious hilltops of New Hampshire. Let freedom ring from the mighty mountains of New York. Let freedom ring from the heightening Alleghenies of Pennsylvania!

Let freedom ring from the snowcapped Rockies of Colorado!

Let freedom ring from the curvaceous peaks of California!

But not only that; let freedom ring from Stone Mountain of Georgia!

Let freedom ring from Lookout Mountain of Tennessee!

Let freedom ring from every hill and every molehill of Mississippi. From every mountainside, let freedom ring.

When we let freedom ring, when we let it ring from every village and every hamlet, from every state and every city, we will be able to speed up that day when all of God's children, black men and white men, Jews and Gentiles, Protestants and Catholics, will be able to join hands and sing in the words of the old Negro spiritual, "Free at last! free at last! thank God Almighty, we are free at last!".

SIGNIFICANCE

Civil rights change was easy to legislate but very difficult to effect. Even after the March on Washington and the passage of the Civil Rights and Voting Rights Acts, racism and inequality remained. In a memorial to King, a Civil Rights Bill passed in 1968 to outlaw housing discrimination but it lacked adequate enforcement mechanisms and could accomplish little. Frustration built up within the African American community at the glacial pace of change.

By the mid–1960s, many African Americans within the civil rights movement had grown tired of turning the other cheek to abuse. The nonviolent phase of the movement gradually began to collapse as Black Power rose. This radical strain of protest represented an explicit challenge to the nonviolent tactics and integrationist objectives of King. While King embraced Black Power's emphasis on racial pride, he dismissed it as a philosophy intent on destruction. His anger was directed particularly at Black Power's celebration of violence. He argued that by promoting urban race riots as legitimate acts of protest, Black Power leaders created political ammunition for white conservatives and a self-destructive mentality among African Americans. The self-destruction identified by King continues at the millennium to cause problems for some African Americans, especially those in the inner cities.

Despite the setbacks that he faced in his later years, King's greatness as a civil rights leader is incontestable. He won the Nobel Peace Prize in 1964, the youngest person to date to do so. Crucially, King gave the civil rights movement a sense of historical urgency. He led by example in public acts of confrontation against the forces of white racism and forced an often reluctant federal government to accelerate the process of civil rights reform.

FURTHER RESOURCES
Books

Taylor Branch. *Parting the Waters: America in the King Years, 1954–63*. New York: Simon & Schuster, 1988.

Drew D. Hansen. *The Dream: Martin Luther King, Jr. and the Speech that Inspired a Nation*. New York: Ecco, 2003.

Stephen Oates. *Let the Trumpet Sound: The Life of Martin Luther King, Jr*. New York: New American Library, 1985.

Civil Rights Act of 1964

Legislation

By: Everett Dirksen

Date: July 2, 1964

Source: "Civil Rights Act of 1964." *Pub. L.* No. 88–352, 78. 2 July 1964. Stat.

Three African Americans hold together to try and withstand the force of firehoses turned against them by police. They are participating in a May 4, 1963 protest march in Birmingham, Alabama. Broadcast on national news, this and other brutal measures used against the peaceful protestors shocked many Americans and helped spur passage of the Civil Rights Act of 1964. © BETTMANN/CORBIS. REPRODUCED BY PERMISSION.

About the Author: Republican Senator Everett Dirksen represented the state of Illinois from 1950 until his death in 1969. Elected Senate Minority Leader in 1959, he worked with Lyndon Johnson in the Senate and later with President Johnson in crafting the Civil Rights Act of 1964.

INTRODUCTION

The 1954 United States Supreme Court decision *Brown v. Board of Education* began the slow but steady path toward desegregated public schools nationwide. Segregation in public settings in the United States—especially the southern states that comprised the former Confederacy—was still a fact of life for black Americans into the 1960s. "Jim Crow" laws, enacted in the late nineteenth century, dictated a strict "color line"—a division of the use of physical facilities and access to services for black and white people in the United States.

Black people living or traveling in the South faced "whites only" sections in restaurants—if they could enter the restaurant at all, segregated drinking fountains, prohibitions on sleeping in hotels, and were often banned from restrooms—even if no other option existed. Medical facilities and ambulances were segregated as well. Real estate agents could—by law—refuse to show homes in "white" neighborhoods to prospective black buyers, and landlords could reject applicants based on race.

Although John F. Kennedy' election to the presidency in1960 initially filled civil rights leaders with hope, by 1963 they expressed concern that he was not doing enough to advance race relations. On June 11, 1963, the president announced his commitment to enforcing the 1954 *Brown v. Board of Education* decision, and his determination to advance civil rights despite protests that included threats, violence, and at times even murder.

Following Kennedy's assassination on November 22, 1963, Vice-President Lyndon Johnson assumed the presidency and declared that he would continue Kennedy's push for sweeping civil rights legislation. The 1964 Civil Rights Act passed the House by a 290–130 vote. In spite of serious political problems with southern senators such as South Carolina's Strom Thurmond, the act passed the Senate by a 73–27 vote. The House then approved the Senate version 289–126.

■ PRIMARY SOURCE

TITLE II—INJUNCTIVE RELIEF AGAINST DISCRIMINATION IN PLACES OF PUBLIC ACCOMMODATION

(a) All persons shall be entitled to the full and equal enjoyment of the goods, services, facilities, and privileges, advantages, and accommodations of any place of public accommodation, as defined in this section, without discrimination or segregation on the ground of race, color, religion, or national origin.

(b) Each of the following establishments which serves the public is a place of public accommodation within the meaning of this title if its operations affect commerce, or if discrimination or segregation by it is supported by State action:

(1) any inn, hotel, motel, or other establishment which provides lodging to transient guests, other than an establishment located within a building which contains not more than five rooms for rent or hire and which is actually occupied by the proprietor of such establishment as his residence;

(2) any restaurant, cafeteria, lunchroom, lunch counter, soda fountain, or other facility principally engaged in selling food for consumption on the premises, including, but not limited to, any such facility located on the premises of any retail establishment; or any gasoline station;

(3) any motion picture house, theater, concert hall, sports arena, stadium or other place of exhibition or entertainment; and

(4) any establishment (A)(i) which is physically located within the premises of any establishment otherwise covered by this subsection, or (ii) within the premises of which is physically located any such covered establishment, and (B) which holds itself out as serving patrons of such covered establishment.

(c) The operations of an establishment affect commerce within the meaning of this title if (1) it is one of the establishments described in paragraph (1) of subsection (b); (2) in the case of an establishment described in paragraph (2) of subsection (b), it serves or offers to serve interstate travelers or a substantial portion of the food which it serves, or gasoline or other products which it sells, has moved in commerce; (3) in the case of an establishment described in paragraph (3) of subsection (b), it customarily presents films, performances, athletic teams, exhibitions, or other sources of entertainment which move in commerce; and (4) in the case of an establishment described in paragraph (4) of subsection (b), it is physically located within the premises of, or there is physically located within its premises, an establishment the operations of which affect commerce within the meaning of this subsection. For purposes of this section, "commerce" means travel, trade, traffic, commerce, transportation, or communication among the several States, or between the District of Columbia and any State, or between any foreign country or any territory or possession and any State or the District of Columbia, or between points in the same State but through any other State or the District of Columbia or a foreign country.

(d) Discrimination or segregation by an establishment is supported by State action within the meaning of this title if such discrimination or segregation (1) is carried on under color of any law, statute, ordinance, or regulation; or (2) is carried on under color of any custom or usage required or enforced by officials of the State or political subdivision thereof; or (3) is required by action of the State or political subdivision thereof.

(e) The provisions of this title shall not apply to a private club or other establishment not in fact open to the public, except to the extent that the facilities of such establishment are made available to the customers or patrons of an establishment within the scope of subsection (b).

SEC. 202. All persons shall be entitled to be free, at any establishment or place, from discrimination or segregation of any kind on the ground of race, color, religion, or national origin, if such discrimination or segregation is or purports to be required by any law, statute, ordinance, regulation, rule, or order of a State or any agency or political subdivision thereof . . . .

TITLE III—DESEGREGATION OF PUBLIC FACILITIES

(a) Whenever the Attorney General receives a complaint in writing signed by an individual to the effect that he is being deprived of or threatened with the loss of his right to the equal protection of the laws, on account of his race, color, religion, or national origin, by being denied equal utilization of any public facility which is owned, operated, or managed by or on behalf of any State or subdivision thereof, other than a public school or public college as defined in section 401 of title IV hereof, and the Attorney General believes the complaint is meritorious and certifies that the signer or signers of such complaint are unable, in his judgment, to initiate and maintain appropriate legal proceedings for relief and that the institution of an action will materially further the orderly progress of desegregation in public facilities, the Attorney General is authorized to institute for or in the name of the United States a civil action in any appropriate district court of the United States against such parties and for such relief as may be appropriate, and such court shall have and shall exercise jurisdiction of proceedings instituted pursuant to this section. The Attorney General may implead as defendants such additional parties as are or become necessary to the grant of effective relief hereunder.

(b) The Attorney General may deem a person or persons unable to initiate and maintain appropriate legal proceedings within the meaning of subsection (a) of this section when such person or persons are unable, either directly or through other interested persons or organizations, to bear the expense of the litigation or to obtain effective legal representation; or whenever he is satisfied that the institution of such litigation would jeopardize the personal safety, employment, or economic standing of such person or persons, their families, or their property.

SEC. 302. In any action or proceeding under this title the United States shall be liable for costs, including a reasonable attorney's fee, the same as a private person.

SEC. 303. Nothing in this title shall affect adversely the right of any person to sue for or obtain relief in any court against discrimination in any facility covered by this title.

TITLE IV—DESEGREGATION OF PUBLIC EDUCATION

DEFINITIONS

As used in this title—

(a) "Commissioner" means the Commissioner of Education.

(b) "Desegregation" means the assignment of students to public schools and within such schools without regard to their race, color, religion, or national origin, but "desegregation" shall not mean the assignment of students to public schools in order to overcome racial imbalance.

(c) "Public school" means any elementary or secondary educational institution, and "public college" means any institution of higher education or any technical or vocational school above the secondary school level, provided that such public school or public college is operated by a State, subdivision of a State, or governmental agency within a State, or operated wholly or predominantly from or through the use of governmental funds or property, or funds or property derived from a governmental source.

(d) "School board" means any agency or agencies which administer a system of one or more public schools and any other agency which is responsible for the assignment of students to or within such system.

SIGNIFICANCE

Southern Democrats spent eighty-three days filibustering the 1964 Civil Rights Act. In the end it passed with overwhelming majorities in both houses of Congress. The act protects Americans from race- and gender-based discrimination; Representative Howard W. Smith added this prohibition in spite of his opposition to civil rights for blacks. This act divided parties along geographic lines; Johnson knew going into the battle that he could cause damage to his own party, the Democrats, which had been opposed to broader rights for African Americans since the post-Civil War period, when Democrats often backed Ku Klux Klan activities and suppressed the black vote.

The 1964 Civil Rights act mandated desegregation in all public schools and approved federal power to enforce it; desegregation of all public venues such as restaurants, theaters, public transportation, restrooms, drinking fountains, gas stations, hotels, and sporting arenas. In addition, the act prohibited discrimination on the basis of "race, color, religion, or national origin" as well as sex. The act strengthened voter rights, but did not abolish such roadblocks as literacy tests for African Americans. Congress went on to remove such obstacles with the Voting Rights Act of 1965.

Worker protection, backed by the Equal Employment Opportunity Commission, was a central part of the 1964 legislation as well. By granting the ability to file grievances and lawsuits against companies that violated the new law, African Americans and women legally gained standing in the courts when faced with labor discrimination.

The act invalidated a wide range of Jim Crow laws overnight and passed the Supreme Court test of constitutionality. Discrimination in government, education, employment, public accommodations, and housing became a federal crime. But society did not change so quickly, and enforcement often involved federal authority to gain compliance, part of a slow shift toward greater freedoms for African Americans and women.

FURTHER RESOURCES

Books

Dudziak, Mary L. *Cold War Civil Rights: Race and the Image of American Democracy*. Princeton, N.J.: Princeton University Press, 2002.

Klarman, Michael J. *From Jim Crow to Civil Rights: The Supreme Court and the Struggle for Racial Equality*. Oxford University Press, USA, 2004.

Rosenberg, Jonathan, and Zachary Karabell. *Kennedy, Johnson, and the Quest for Justice: The Civil Rights Tapes*. New York: W.W. Norton & Company, 2003.

Web sites

John F. Kennedy Library and Museum. "Radio and Television Report to the American People on Civil Rights." <http://www.jfklibrary.org/Historical+Resources/ Archives/Reference+Desk/Speeches/JFK/003POF03 CivilRights06111963.htm> (accessed April 9, 2006).

Voting Rights Act of 1965

Legislation

By: Lyndon B. Johnson

Date: August 6, 1965

Source: *Voting Rights Act of 1965*, Public Law 89–110, 79 Stat. 437.

About the Author: Lyndon Baines Johnson served as a Democratic representative and senator from the state of Texas before being chosen by John F. Kennedy to run as vice president in 1960. Following Kennedy's assassination on November 22, 1963, Johnson became

the thirty-sixth president of the United States. A champion of civil rights, Johnson helped to push the 1964 Civil Rights Act through Congress, in addition to proposing the 1965 Voting Rights Act.

INTRODUCTION

In June 1963, five months before he was assassinated, President John F. Kennedy addressed the nation with a call for powerful civil rights legislation to help give minorities greater legal protection, personal freedoms, and economic opportunity. Civil rights leaders in the black community, upset with what they considered to be slow progress on civil rights at the federal level, expressed ambivalence about such legislation. Civil rights legislation in 1957 and 1960 had raised hopes among African Americans, but the legislation—stripped of power by compromises with southern Democrats—had not altered the status quo, and race-based segregation in daily and political life remained the reality for African Americans in the southern United States.

In the wake of Kennedy's assassination, his vice president, Lyndon B. Johnson, assumed the presidency. Committed to continuing Kennedy's civil rights work, Johnson used his political connections and networking skills to appeal to the House of Representatives and Senate to pass a strong civil rights bill, one that provided blacks with protections in education, housing, law, and employment. Southern Democrats balked, but ultimately the house, and then the senate, passed the Civil Rights Act of 1964. However, the act did not adequately protect voting rights, a key issue Johnson prepared to tackle in future legislation.

On March 15, 1965, President Johnson addressed Congress one week after violence broke out during peaceful protests by African Americans in Selma, Alabama. In Selma, the police attacked protestors led by the Reverend Dr. Martin Luther King, Jr. as they prepared to march to Montgomery, Alabama. The news channels showed images of well-dressed, peaceful protestors being beaten and sprayed with water from fire hoses. A white Unitarian minister from Boston, James J. Reeb, died during the violence.

Johnson's speech was direct and to the point on the issue of voting rights for African Americans. He said, "The harsh fact is that in many places in this country men and women are kept from voting simply because they are Negroes.... The Negro citizen may go to register only to be told that the day is wrong, or the hour is late, or the official in charge is absent. And if he persists, and if he manages to present himself to the registrar, he may be disqualified because he did not spell out his middle name or because he abbreviated a

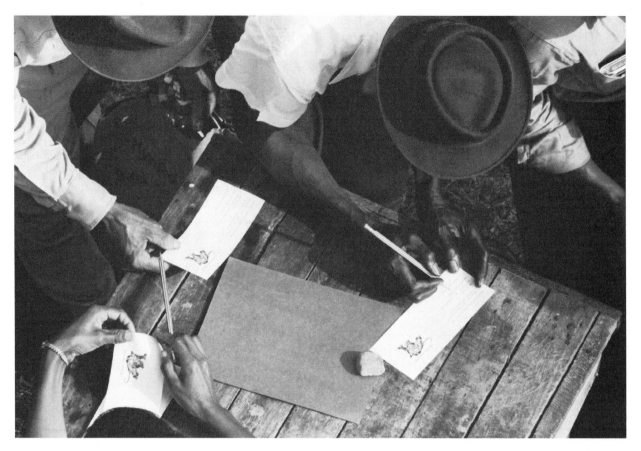

African Americans vote for the first time in Alabama after enactment of the Voting Rights Act of 1966. © FLIP SCHULKE/CORBIS.

word on the application. And if he manages to fill out an application he is given a test. The registrar is the sole judge of whether he passes this test. He may be asked to recite the entire Constitution, or explain the most complex provisions of State law. And even a college degree cannot be used to prove that he can read and write. For the fact is that the only way to pass these barriers is to show a white skin."

The Voting Rights Act passed both houses of Congress, and President Johnson signed the bill into law on August 6, 1965. Selected excerpts from this act follow.

■ PRIMARY SOURCE

An Act To enforce the fifteenth amendment to the Constitution of the United States, and for other purposes.

Be it enacted by the Senate and House of Representatives of the United States of America in Congress assembled, That this Act shall be known as the "Voting Rights Act of 1965."

SEC. 2. No voting qualification or prerequisite to voting, or standard, practice, or procedure shall be imposed or applied by any State or political subdivision to deny or abridge the right of any citizen of the United States to vote on account of race or color.

SEC. 4. (a) To assure that the right of citizens of the United States to vote is not denied or abridged on account of race or color, no citizen shall be denied the right to vote in any Federal, State, or local election because of his failure to comply with any test or device in any State . . . .

SEC. 10. (a) The Congress finds that the requirement of the payment of a poll tax as a precondition to voting: (i) precludes persons of limited means from voting or imposes unreasonable financial hardship upon such persons as a precondition to their exercise of the franchise, (ii) does not bear a reasonable relationship to any legitimate State interest in the conduct of elections, and (iii) in some areas has the purpose or effect of denying persons the right to vote because of race or color. Upon the basis of these findings, Congress declares that the constitutional right of citizens to vote is denied or abridged in some areas by the requirement of the payment of a poll tax as a precondition to voting.

SEC. 11. (a) No person acting under color of law shall fail or refuse to permit any person to vote who is entitled to vote under any provision of this Act or is otherwise qualified to vote, or willfully fail or refuse to tabulate, count, and report such person's vote.

(b) No person, whether acting under color of law or otherwise, shall intimidate, threaten, or coerce, or attempt to intimidate, threaten, or coerce any person for voting or attempting to vote, or intimidate, threaten, or coerce, or attempt to intimidate, threaten, or coerce any person for urging or aiding any person to vote or attempt to vote, or intimidate, threaten, or coerce any person for exercising any powers or duties under section 3(a), 6, 8, 9, 10, or 12(e).

(c) Whoever knowingly or willfully gives false information as to his name, address, or period of residence in the voting district for the purpose of establishing his eligibility to register or vote, or conspires with another individual for the purpose of encouraging his false registration to vote or illegal voting, or pays or offers to pay or accepts payment either for registration to vote or for voting shall be fined not more than $10,000 or imprisoned not more than five years, or both.

SEC. 12. (a) Whoever shall deprive or attempt to deprive any person of any right secured by section 2, 3, 4, 5, 7, or 10 or shall violate section 11(a) or (b), shall be fined not more than $5,000, or imprisoned not more than five years, or both.

Approved August 6, 1965.

SIGNIFICANCE

The effect of the Voting Rights Act of 1965 was immediate in the South; in Mississippi, the percentage of registered African American voters skyrocketed from six percent to forty-four percent. Because the law required that all counties register more than fifty percent of its citizens of voting age or face federal intervention, even intractable southern states that disagreed with civil rights legislation permitted black voter registration rather than face further erosion of states' rights and greater federal intervention.

By removing literacy tests and any qualifier for registering to vote, the Voting Rights Act of 1965 not only gave African Americans the right to vote, but also afforded them the opportunity to elect more African Americans to public office at every level of government. Black voter turnouts shortly after the act passed were as high as ninety-two percent in Tennessee and seventy-four percent in Mississippi. This marked a turning point in southern politics; African American participation in the electoral process was swift, intense, and powerful.

However, the transition was not smooth. Federal examiners were sent to many counties that did not comply with the new law, and more than one-third of all new African American voters were registered by a federal examiner. Federal observers monitored the polls to verify that African American voters were permitted to cast their ballots and to ensure that African American votes were actually counted in tallies.

The Voting Rights Act of 1965 was upheld and strengthened in 1970, 1975, 1982, and 1992. In 1965, fewer than 100 black citizens held elected office in the United States; twenty-five years later more than 7,200 held office. Combined with the Civil Rights Act of 1964, the Voting Rights Act of 1965 set in motion a dramatic change in the political landscape of the United States by ensuring that all eligible Americans, regardless of race or color, could cast their votes and have those votes counted.

FURTHER RESOURCES

Books

Dudziak, Mary L. *Cold War Civil Rights: Race and the Image of American Democracy*. Princeton, N.J.: Princeton University Press, 2002.

Karabell, Jonathan, and Zachary Karabell. *Kennedy, Johnson, and the Quest for Justice: The Civil Rights Tapes*. New York: W.W. Norton, 2003.

Klarman, Michael J. *From Jim Crow to Civil Rights: The Supreme Court and the Struggle for Racial Equality*. New York: Oxford University Press, 2004.

Web sites

John F. Kennedy Library and Museum. "Radio and Television Report to the American People on Civil Rights." <http://www.jfklibrary.net/j061163.htm> (accessed April 9, 2006).

Lyndon Baines Johnson Library and Museum. "Special Message to Congress: The American Promise." <http://www.lbjlib.utexas.edu/johnson/archives.hom/speeches.hom/650315.asp> (accessed April 9, 2006).

City of Memphis v. Martin Luther King, Jr

Statement

By: City of Memphis

Date: April 1968

Source: *City of Memphis v. Martin Luther King, Jr*. National Archives: Records of the United States District Court, 1968.

About the Author: City officials in Memphis clashed with Martin Luther King, Jr. and the other members of the Southern Christian Leadership Council (SCLC) in 1968. SCLC, headed by King, began in 1957 to employ nonviolent direct action in the struggle against segregation. Members of SCLC typically used marches as a protest technique.

INTRODUCTION

By 1968, Martin Luther King, Jr. (1929–1968) had spent over a decade as the chief spokesperson for the African American civil rights movement. In Memphis in the spring of 1968, King and the other ministers who formed the leadership of the premier nonviolent civil rights organization, the Southern Christian Leadership Council (SCLC), prepared to expand the movement to include economic justice for poor, working-class blacks.

As SCLC promoted a Poor People's Campaign, King decided to go to Memphis to support a strike of predominantly black sanitation workers. On February 3, 1968, a group of marching strikers had been attacked by police officers wielding nightsticks and spraying mace. The strikers and their supporters then began a boycott of all stores in the downtown area, the stores owned by city leaders, and the two Memphis newspapers. King went to Memphis to emphasize that most African Americans were part of the working poor who stayed poor because they were unorganized. Union recognition would help reduce black poverty. On March 28, King joined a march through Memphis for black rights. The march turned violent when thieves among the protesters began breaking store windows and grabbing stock along three city blocks. The police then attacked the marchers with tear gas. By day's end, sixty-two people had been injured and a black teenager lay dead.

SCLC debated holding another march. They feared that if they did not demonstrate that they could stage a peaceful march in Memphis, then a scheduled march through Washington, DC for poor people's rights would collapse. King agreed to return to Memphis. On April 4, 1968, King stood with fellow civil rights leaders on a balcony outside of a motel room. He was shot dead by James Earl Ray, an escapee from the Missouri state penitentiary. Although King had been an apostle of nonviolence, his assassination set off a new wave of rioting across the country.

◼ PRIMARY SOURCE

CITY OF MEMPHIS V. MARTIN LUTHER KING, JR.
Complainant vs Martin Luther King, Jr.

No. C-68-80

Hosea Williams, Reverend James Bevel, Reverend James Orange, Ralph D. Abernathy and Bernard Lee, all non-residents of the State of Tennessee, Defendants

Answer *The defendants deny each and every allegation of the complainant except as follows:*

The defendant Martin Luther King, Jr. and members of his staff were invited by local ministers to participate in a march held on March 8, 1967. Said march was held under the supervision of local ministers and the responsibility for planning and supervision to maintain order did not rest with those defendants.

The defendant King at the urgent request of local march leaders did leave the scene of disorder. At the same time, local leaders made immediate and successful efforts to turn the march back.

The defendants have organized and conducted in many communities utilizing the principals of non-violence numerous marches, none of which have resulted in civil disturbance. The defendants are not presently and have never been engaged in any conspiracies as alleged in the complaint. Defendants have in no way in their private or public statements sponsored, fermented, encouraged and incited riots, mobs or breaches of the peace as alleged in the complaint.

Defendants further state that they have never refused to furnish information concerning marches or plans as such information became available; that in fact said information has been furnished on a continuing basis to local law enforcement officers; that there is no statute or ordinance requiring the issuance of a parade or march permit by police authorities. However, to the extent that there is any custom or practice of submitting plans for parades or marches to police officials for discussion and review, the defendants have and will continue to do so as soon as practical after said plans have been made.

The defendants utilizing their experience have undertaken the following general steps to insure that the march will be non-violent and under control at all times. Limitations will be placed on the number of marchers in each line; parade marshals will be carefully selected and give training in their duties; liaison will be maintained with local law enforcement officers and the necessary protection and assistance will be requested; all groups in the community have been contacted to insure the parties in the march will participate on a non-violent basis; a route has been tentatively selected, together with tentative starting and ending times for the march and other necessary organizational steps have been and are continuing to be taken to insure a peaceful march. Steps have further been taken to prohibit the use of signs affixed to sticks or any other object which might be utilized in an improper manner.

Together during a civil rights march in Memphis, Tennessee on March 28, 1968 are the Reverend Ralph Abernathy (right), Bishop Julian Smith (left), and Dr. Martin Luther King Jr (center). AP IMAGES.

Defendant, Martin Luther King, Jr., further states that he has on numerous other occasions received threats or been informed of threats received by others concerning his personal safety; that while all due precautions have been taken, there have been no difficulties encountered as a result of such threats.

Defendants respectfully request that the application for an injunction should be denied or in the alternative that the Court permit the march to be held under such reasonable restrictions as may be necessary giving due regard to the defendants and their First Amendment rights.

SIGNIFICANCE

The Civil Rights Act of 1964 and the Voting Rights Act of 1965 did much to end racial segregation and give formal political power to blacks. Yet these improvements did not fully fix deep problems that kept blacks at the bottom of the economic ladder. As King himself noted in a 1967 speech in Chicago, blacks

had expected sudden, dramatic improvements and when these did not materialize, they became frustrated. This frustration exploded between 1965 and 1967 as more than a hundred riots tore across the United States.

While King reaffirmed his faith in nonviolence and integration, others within the civil rights movement suggested that peaceful tactics be abandoned. The persistence of white hostility and the betrayal of black expectations encouraged new movements, strategies, and ideologies. The most popular new idea was that of black power, by which black people would assume control of their own communities, lives, and destinies. Politically, black power meant electing blacks and forcing them to address black needs. Economically, black power demanded that the money spent by black people remain in the black community.

As subsequent race riots, notably the Los Angeles riots of 1992, have demonstrated, many blacks continue to feel the same frustration that the 1960s generation experienced. The civil rights legislation had limited significance in the day-to-day lives of most

African Americans. Economic differences continue to loom large. In 1970, 33.5 percent of African Americans lived below the poverty line, while only 9.9 percent of whites did so. By 2000, 26.1 percent of blacks qualified as poor compared to 10.5 percent of whites. In the decades since King died trying to help poor blacks, more than a quarter of the African-American population remains mired in poverty.

FURTHER RESOURCES
Books

Branch, Taylor. *Parting the Waters: America in the King Years, 1954–63*. New York: Simon & Schuster, 1988.

Fairclough, Adam. *To Redeem the Soul of America: The Southern Christian Leadership Conference and Martin Luther King, Jr.* Athens, Ga.: University of Georgia Press, 1987.

Garrow, David. *Bearing the Cross: Martin Luther King, Jr. and the Southern Christian Leadership Conference*. New York: Harper Perennial Modern Classics, 2004.

Oates, Stephen. *Let the Trumpet Sound: The Life of Martin Luther King, Jr.* New York: New American Library, 1985.

International Convention on the Suppression and Punishment of the Crime of Apartheid

Convention

By: United Nations General Assembly

Date: November 30, 1973

Source: United Nations General Assembly. *International Convention on the Suppression and Punishment of the Crime of Apartheid*. General Assembly Resolution 3068 (XXVIII). New York: United Nations, November 30, 1973.

About the Author: The phrase "United Nations" was used during World War II (1939–1945) to describe the dozens of nations allied together to fight Germany and Japan, most notably including China, France, Great Britain, the Soviet Union, and the United States of America. These allies decided to develop a new organization to facilitate international cooperation and help prevent future wars. It would replace the League of Nations, which had failed to prevent World War II. They called it the United Nations (UN). The UN Charter was ratified on October 24, 1945. In the years since, the UN has served as a forum for international negotiation and cooperation on many issues,

including international security, human rights, trade and economics, and the environment. The General Assembly is the primary bosy for deliberation within the United Nations, in which all member nations have a seat.

INTRODUCTION

South Africa, a nation with a long history of colonization by western countries, gained its independence from Great Britain in 1934. Until the 1940s, when the Afrikaner National Party gained political control, South Africa remained a country divided politically and socially. When the ANP gained political control, it initiated apartheid to solidify and extend racial separation and maintain ANP (i.e. white domination) control. The unifying control that the ANP brought to South Africa was exclusively one-sided—its programs favored whites.

In 1948, racial discrimination and separation laws took effect throughout South Africa. These laws encompassed almost every facet of daily life. Among other things, the new laws prohibited marriage between blacks and whites, and they classified individuals into one of three racial categories. These categories of white, black (African), and colored (mixed heritage) stemmed from the 1950 Population Registration Act, aimed at solidifying job, housing, financial, and political restrictions. In 1951, these racial divisions were further codified by the Bantu Authorities Act, which established African "homelands" and assigned each African in South Africa to one of these homeland states. These homeland states acted with nominal independence within the larger nation of South Africa, but once a person resided within a homeland he or she lost citizenship rights within South Africa. Furthermore, all voting and political functions were connected to these homelands. Between 1976 and 1981, the ANP established four homeland states that denationalized nine million Africans. Yet, these restricted homeland zones within South Africa only showcase a small percentage of the civil rights that apartheid systematically violated.

ANP legislation was designed to repress blacks in South Africa, and these legal measures continued to strengthen racial divisions. In 1953, the Public Safety Act and the Criminal Law Amendment were passed. These pieces of legislation allowed the government to declare states of emergency (as it deemed fit), imposed increased penalties for protesting, and made it a crime to support the repeal of a law. In 1960, several blacks from Sharpeville tested these laws by refusing to carry their passes. A state of emergency was declared for 156 days; sixty-nine individuals died and 187 were

Police drag away an anti-apartheid protester at a demonstration in Soweto, South Africa, in 1980. © WILLIAM CAMPBELL/SYGMA/CORBIS.

wounded. The Sharpeville incident was not the only black resistance action or the only time that a state of emergency was declared in response to the apartheid policy. The South African government intermittently declared states of emergency until 1989. To make these acts of governmental repression more objectionable, individuals could be detained without hearings or trials for up to six months, and the condition of the detention centers was reported to be horrendous. Detainees who survived their experiences often reported the lack of food, water, clean areas for rest, and fresh air in jails and detention centers. They also testified that some detainees died from various forms of torture, and some detainees received life sentences for minimal crimes or actions of governmental dissent.

One of the most noted resisters against the apartheid system is Nelson Mandela. Mandela was born in July 1918 and was educated at the University College of Fort Hare. Throughout his college years, he participated in and led student organizations, and his rapid progression to national politics in the 1940s

and 1950s stemmed from his collegiate activities. Mandela was an active member of the African National Congress, a group that denounced apartheid and promoted equality throughout Africa, and he eventually held key positions within the organization. As a result of his fight for racial equality, he faced several criminal trials, and, in 1952, he was sentenced to a suspended prison sentence and confined to Johannesburg for six months. He received a light sentence because he and his co-accused advocated non-violent opposition to white rule. Mandela then joined the legal profession, and he continued his political work. His continual public addresses and advocacy for racial equality made him a target of governmental suppression throughout the 1950s. To avoid detection and imprisonment, he adopted many disguises and his followers named him the "Black Pimpernel" for his many successful and creative evasions of the police. After illegally leaving the country in 1961 to give several international addresses on the state of South African politics and social life, he returned to South

Africa. He was arrested and received a five-year prison sentence for his political actions. While serving this sentence, he was charged with sabotage in the Rivonia Trial. Mandela was found guilty of sabotage and sentenced to life imprisonment.

The plight of Mandela, and other South Africans, became a growing point of contention with world leaders. More importantly, spies within the country and South African defectors forced the world to hear about (and see) the crimes apartheid committed against individuals. In 1973, the United Nations brought apartheid to the forefront of the political arena again. Since arms and financial embargos do not convince the regime of the need to change, the UN created the International Convention on the Supression and Punishment of the Crime of Apartheid.

◼ PRIMARY SOURCE

THE STATES PARTIES TO THE PRESENT CONVENTION,

Recalling the provisions of the Charter of the United Nations, in which all Members pledged themselves to take joint and separate action in co-operation with the Organization for the achievement of universal respect for, and observance of, human rights and fundamental freedoms for all without distinction as to race, sex, language or religion.

Considering the Universal Declaration of Human Rights, which states that all human beings are born free and equal in dignity and rights and that everyone is entitled to all the rights and freedoms set forth in the Declaration, without distinction of any kind, such as race, colour or national origin,

Considering the Declaration on the Granting of Independence to Colonial Countries and Peoples, in which the General Assembly stated that the process of liberation is irresistible and irreversible and that, in the interests of human dignity, progress and justice, an end must be put to colonialism and all practices of segregation and discrimination associated therewith,

Observing that, in accordance with the International Convention on the Elimination of All Forms of Racial Discrimination, States particularly condemn racial segregation and *apartheid* and undertake to prevent, prohibit and eradicate all practices of this nature in territories under their jurisdiction,

Observing that, in the convention on the Non-Applicability of Statutory Limitations to War Crimes and Crimes Against Humanity, "inhuman acts resulting from the policy of *apartheid*" are qualified as crimes against humanity,

Observing that the General Assembly of the United Nations has adopted a number of resolutions in which the policies and practices of *apartheid* are condemned as a crime against humanity,

Observing that the Security Council has emphasized that *apartheid* and its continued intensification and expansion seriously disturb and threaten international peace and security,

Convinced that an International Convention on the Suppression and Punishment of the Crime of *Apartheid* would make it possible to take more effective measures at the international and national levels with a view to the suppression and punishment of the crime of *apartheid*, *Have agreed* as follows:

ARTICLE I

1. The States Parties to the present Convention declare that *apartheid* and similar policies and practices of racial segregation and discrimination, as defined in article II of the Convention, are crimes violating the principles of international law, in particular the purposes and principles of the Charter of the United Nations, and constituting a serious threat to international peace and security.

2. The State Parties to the present Convention declare criminal those organizations, institutions and individuals committing the crime of *apartheid*

ARTICLE II

For the purpose of the present Convention, the term "the crime of *apartheid*", which shall include similar policies and practices of racial segregation and discrimination as practiced in southern Africa, shall apply to the following inhuman acts committed for the purpose of establishing and maintaining domination by one racial group of persons over any other racial group of persons and systematically oppressing them:

(a) Denial to a member or members of a racial group or groups of the right to life and liberty of person:

(i) By murder of members of a racial group or groups;

(ii) By the infliction upon the members of a racial group or groups of serious bodily or mental harm, by the infringement of their freedom or dignity, or by subjecting them to torture or to cruel, inhuman or degrading treatment or punishment;

(iii) By arbitrary arrest and illegal imprisonment of the members of a racial group or groups;

(b) Deliberate imposition on a racial group or groups of living conditions calculated to cause its or their physical destruction in whole or in part;

(c) Any legislative measures and other measures calculated to prevent a racial group or groups from participation in the political, social, economic and cultural life of the country and the deliberate creation of conditions preventing the full development of such a group or groups, in particular by denying to members of a racial group or groups basic human rights and freedoms, including the right to work, the right to form recognized trade unions, the right to education, the right to leave and to return to their country, the right to a nationality, the right to freedom of movement and residence, the right to freedom of opinion and expression, and the right to freedom of peaceful assembly and association;

(d) Any measures, including legislative measures, designed to divide the population along racial lines by the creation of separate reserves and ghettos for the members of a racial group or groups, the prohibition of mixed marriages among members of various racial groups, the expropriation of landed property belonging to a racial group or groups or to members thereof;

(e) Exploitation of the labour of the members of a racial group or groups, in particular by submitting them to forced labour;

(f) Persecution of organizations and persons, by depriving them of fundamental rights and freedoms, because they oppose *apartheid*

ARTICLE III

International criminal responsibility shall apply, irrespective of the motive involved, to individuals, members of organizations and institutions and representatives of the State, whether residing in the territory of the State in which the acts are perpetrated or in some other State, whenever they:

(a) Commit, participate in, directly incite or conspire in the commission of the acts mentioned in article II of the present Convention;

(b) Directly abet, encourage or co-operate in the commission of the crime of *apartheid*

ARTICLE IV

The States Parties to the present Convention undertake:

(a) To adopt any legislative or other measures necessary to suppress as well as to prevent any encouragement of the crime of *apartheid* and similar segregationist policies or their manifestations and to punish persons guilty of that crime;

(b) To adopt legislative, judicial and administrative measures to prosecute, bring to trial and punish in accordance with their jurisdiction persons responsible for, or accused of, the acts defined in article II of the present Convention, whether or not such persons reside in the territory of the State in which the acts are committed or are nationals of that State or of some other State or are stateless persons.

ARTICLE V

Persons charged with the acts enumerated in article II of the present Convention may be tried by a competent tribunal of any State Party to the Convention which may acquire jurisdiction over the person of the accused or by an international penal tribunal having jurisdiction with respect to those States Parties which shall have accepted its jurisdiction.

ARTICLE VI

The States Parties to the present Convention undertake to accept and carry out in accordance with the Charter of the United Nations the decisions taken by the Security Council aimed at the prevention, suppression and punishment of the crime of *apartheid*, and to co-operate in the implementation of decisions adopted by other competent organs of the United Nations with a view to achieving the purposes of the Convention.

ARTICLE VII

1. The States Parties to the present Convention undertake to submit periodic reports to the group established under article IX on the legislative, judicial, administrative or other measures that they have adopted and that give effect to the provisions of the Convention.

2. Copies of the reports shall be transmitted through the Secretary-General of the United Nations to the Special Committee on *Apartheid*.

ARTICLE VIII

Any Sate Party to the present Convention may call upon any competent organ of the United Nations to take such action under the Charter of the United Nations as it considers appropriate for the prevention and suppression of the crime of *apartheid*.

ARTICLE IX

1. The Chairman of the Commission on Human Rights shall appoint a group consisting of three members of the Commission on Human Rights, who are also representatives of States Parties to the present Convention, to consider reports submitted by States Parties in accordance with article VII.

2. If, among the members of the Commission on Human Rights, there are no representatives of States Parties to the present Convention or if there are fewer than three such representatives, the Secretary-General of the United Nations shall, after consulting all States Parties to the Convention, designate a representative of the State Party or representatives of the States Parties which are not members of the Commission on Human Rights to take part in the work of the group established in accordance with paragraph 1 of this article, until such time as

representatives of the States Parties to the Convention are elected to the Commission on Human Rights.

3. The group may meet for a period of not more than five days, either before the opening or after the closing of the session of the Commission on Human Rights, to consider the reports submitted in accordance with article VII.

ARTICLE X

1. The States Parties to the present Convention empower the commission on Human Rights:

(a) To request United Nations organs, when transmitting copies of petitions under article 15 of the International Convention on the Elimination of All Forms of Racial Discrimination, to draw its attention to complaints concerning acts which are enumerated in article II of the present Convention;

(b) To prepare, on the basis of reports from competent organs of the United Nations and periodic reports from States Parties to the present Convention, a list of individuals, organizations, institutions and representatives of States which are alleged to be responsible for the crimes enumerated in article II of the Convention as well as those against whom legal proceedings have been undertaken by States Parties to the Convention;

(c) To request information from the competent United Nations organs concerning measures taken by the authorities responsible for the administration of Trust and Non-Self-Governing Territories, and all other Territories to which General Assembly resolution 1514 (XV) of 14 December 1960 applies, with regard to such individuals alleged to be responsible for crimes under article II of the Convention who are believed to be under their territorial and administrative jurisdiction.

2. Pending the achievement of the objectives of the Declaration on the Granting of Independence to Colonial Countries, and Peoples, contained in General Assembly resolution 1514 (XV), the provisions of the present Convention shall in no way limit the right of petition granted to those peoples by other international instruments or by the United Nations and its specialized agencies.

ARTICLE XI

1. Acts enumerated in article II of the present Convention shall not be considered political crimes for the purpose of extradition.

2. The States Parties to the present Convention undertake in such cases to grant extradition in accordance with their legislation and with the treaties in force.

ARTICLE XII

Disputes between States Parties arising out of the interpretation, application or implementation of the present Convention which have not been settled by negotiation shall, at the request of the States Parties to the dispute, be brought before the International Court of Justice, save where the parties to the dispute have agreed on some other form of settlement.

ARTICLE XIII

The present Convention is open for signature by all States. Any State which does not sign the Convention before its entry into force may accede to it.

ARTICLE XIV

1. The present Convention is subject to ratification. Instruments of ratification shall be deposited with the Secretary-General of the United Nations.

2. Accession shall be effected by the deposit of an instrument of accession with the Secretary-General of the United Nations.

ARTICLE XV

1. The present Convention shall enter into force on the thirtieth day after the date of the deposit with the Secretary-General of the United Nations of the twentieth instrument of ratification or accession.

2. For each State ratifying the present Convention or acceding to it after the deposit of the twentieth instrument of ratification or instrument of accession, the Convention shall enter into force on the thirtieth day after the date of the deposit of its own instrument of ratification or instrument of accession.

ARTICLE XVI

A State Party may denounce the present Convention by written notification to the Secretary-General of the United Nations. Denunciation shall take effect one year after the date of receipt of the notification by the Secretary-General.

ARTICLE XVII

1. A request for the revision of the present Convention may be made at any time by any State Party by means of a notification in writing addressed to the Secretary-General of the United Nations.

2. The General Assembly of the United Nations shall decide upon the steps, if any, to be taken in respect of such request.

ARTICLE XVIII

A Secretary-General of the United Nations shall inform all States of the following particulars:

(a) Signatures, ratifications and accessions under articles XIII and XIV;

(b) The date of entry into force of the present Convention under article XV;

(c) Denunciations under article XVI;

(d) Notifications under article XCVII.

ARTICLE XIX

1. The present Convention, of which the Chinese, English, French, Russian and Spanish texts are equally authentic, shall be deposited in the archives of the United Nations.

2. The Secretary-General of the United Nations shall transmit certified copies of the present Convention to all States.

SIGNIFICANCE

Apartheid officially ended in February 1990, when President F. W. de Klerk released Mandela from prison and began dismantling apartheid. Mandela left prison on February 11, 1990, and a temporary truce was called on fighting against apartheid. The ANC and other African groups agreed to the truce in a good faith effort toward the government. Since Mandela and other political prisoners had been released, they felt it appropriate to give the newly emerging democratic government time to reform political and social orders.

Governmental reforms took hold fairly quickly throughout South Africa. The nine million Africans who had been denationalized regained their South African citizenship. Housing zones (for blacks and whites) were abolished and job segregation slowly began to end. Non-whites no longer had to carry pass books, and publicly segregated areas like beaches became areas where everyone could gather. Finally, racial divisions and stereotypes began to ease within African society, and the initial days of protests by whites demanding a re-instatement of apartheid and by blacks demanding an end to the racial system subsided.

Key political leaders also saw the need to step down and let a new generation of leaders take control of the government, and, in 1999, Nelson Mandela retired from public life. His retirement, along with many of his allies, demonstrated faith in South Africa's new democratic leadership.

FURTHER RESOURCES

Books

Clark, Nancy L., and William H. Worger. *South Africa: The Rise and Fall of Apartheid*. New York: Longman, 2004.

Wilson, Richard A. *The Politics of Truth and Reconciliation in South Africa: Legitimizing the Post-Apartheid State*. New York: Cambridge University Press, 2001.

Periodicals

Stultz, Newell M. "Evolution of the United Nations Apartheid Strategy." *Human Rights Quarterly* 13 (February 1991): 1–23.

Web sites

United Nations. "Human Rights: Historical Images of Apartheid in South Africa." <http://www.un.org/av/photo/subjects/apartheid.htm> (accessed May 1, 2006).

Mourners Surround the Coffin of Black Leader Steve Biko

Photograph

By: The Associated Press

Date: September 25, 1977

Source: AP Images.

About the Photographer: The Associated Press is a worldwide news agency based in New York.

INTRODUCTION

Apartheid is an Afrikaans word meaning "apartness" and it refers to a system of racial segregation practiced by a white minority against a black majority in South Africa from 1948 to 1991. Many white and black South Africans opposed the system, including a Bantu man, Steve Biko.

Biko, a charismatic speaker and tireless activist, traveled around South Africa in the 1970s promoting a message known as black consciousness. The philosophy holds that blacks could only be free if they did not feel inferior to whites. Biko's activism is credited with contributing to the 1976 Soweto riots, a turning point in the struggle against apartheid. He encouraged black pride and self-reliance in an era when South African authorities feared that a black uprising would destroy white control. Biko's activism made him a marked man.

The police arrested Biko on August 18, 1977 in Grahamtown. He had broken a court order restricting him to his home in nearby East London and allegedly possessed inflammatory pamphlets. He was fatally injured within thirty minutes of being arrested. Five police officers stated that Biko had tried to attack one of his interrogators while in custody in Port Elizabeth. They tackled Biko and claimed to have accidentally slammed his head against the wall. The unresponsive prisoner remained chained to a metal gate in a standing position for two days while police waited to see if

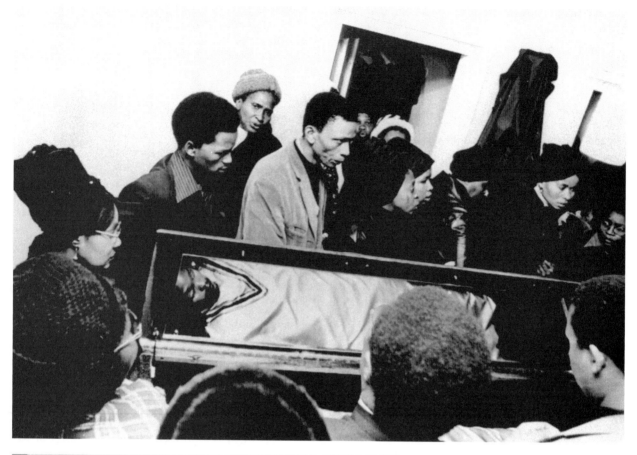

PRIMARY SOURCE

Mourners Surround the Coffin of Black Leader Steve Biko: On September 25, 1977, mourners surround the coffin of black leader Steve Biko, in his hometown of Ginsberg, South Africa. Biko—a prominent anti-aparthied leader—died under suspicious circumstances while in the custory of South African police. AP IMAGES.

they could continue the interrogation. Eventually, Biko was taken in a police van, naked and bleeding, on a 1,200-kilometer (745.6-mile) trip to a prison in Pretoria where he died of brain injuries on September 12, 1977. In 1999, the Truth and Reconciliation Committee of the South African government declared that Biko had probably been murdered because the police wanted to teach him a lesson about his defiance of white authority.

PRIMARY SOURCE

MOURNERS SURROUND THE COFFIN OF BLACK LEADER STEVE BIKO

See primary source image.

SIGNIFICANCE

Steve Biko's death did not lead to any immediate policy change. It did, however, further inflame opinion against the system of apartheid. The image of the young law student, nude, shackled hand and foot to a gate, and incoherent due to head injuries, became part of the legend of black nationalism. By 1981, South Africa and Namibia were the only remaining white-ruled countries in Africa. International and domestic pressures pushed these countries to change. South Africa faced increasingly strict international economic sanctions, which included U.S. corporations' divestiture of their South African holdings. Internally, the need for more skilled labor led to the lifting of limits on black wages and the legalization of black labor unions with the right to strike.

In 1989, F.W. de Klerk became South African prime minister and immediately announced the

Commission, with Nobel Peace Prize winner Archbishop Desmond Tutu as its chair. In 1999, the commission denied amnesty to the four surviving policemen accused of killing Biko. In 2003, the Justice Ministry declined to prosecute the officers due to insufficient evidence remaining to support a murder charge. In that same year, new President Thabo Mbeki announced that the South African government would pay 660 million Rand (about 109 million U.S. dollars) to 22,000 people who had been detained or tortured, or who were surviving family members of those murdered during the apartheid era.

FURTHER RESOURCES

Books

Millard Arnold, ed. *Steve Biko: Black Consciousness in South Africa*. New York: Random House, 1978.

Tim J. Juckes. *Opposition in South Africa: The Leadership of Z.K. Matthews, Nelson Mandela, and Stephen Biko*. Westport, CT: Praeger, 1995.

Robin Malan, ed. *The Essential Steve Biko*. Cape Town: David Philip, 1997.

Donald Woods. *Biko*. New York: Henry Holt, 1987.

In 1977, demonstrators in Trafalger Sqaure, London, England, protest against police brutality in South Africa. They are demanding a neutral inquiry into the death of Steve Biko, the Black Consciousness leader, who died in South African police custody. © HULTON-DEUTSCH COLLECTION/CORBIS.

Nelson Mandela's Second Court Statement

Book excerpt

By: Nelson Mandela

Date: 1964

Source: Mandela, Nelson R. *Nelson Mandela: The Struggle Is My Life*. London: International Defense and Aid Fund for South Africa, 1978.

About the Author: Nelson Mandela achieved global recognition for his struggles against apartheid in South Africa, for his several-decades-long incarceration as a result, and for his election to the presidency in South Africa's first all-race democractic election in 1994. He has been a political activist for nearly all of his adult life and was a central figure in the black South African fight against apartheid. In 1993, along with F. Willem De Klerk, Mandela was awarded the Nobel Prize for Peace in recognition of his long-standing efforts to put an end to the oppression of the black South African people by helping to abolish apartheid.

release of many black political prisoners. In February 1990, he declared in Parliament that apartheid had failed, that bans on all political parties would be lifted, and that African National Congress leader Nelson Mandela would be released after twenty-seven years of imprisonment. In 1991, all the remaining apartheid laws were repealed. After three years of intense negotiation, all sides agreed in 1993 to a framework for a multiracial, multiparty transitional government. Elections were held in April 1994, and Mandela became the first freely elected, black president in South African history.

To help heal South Africa's emotional and psychological wounds from the system of apartheid, Mandela created the Truth and Reconciliation

INTRODUCTION

Nelson Mandela became involved with the African National Congress (ANC) as a young man and was instrumental in the development of the ANC's Youth League (ANCYL). With Oliver Tambo, he co-founded the first law office run by black South Africans in 1952. He began resisting apartheid immediately after it was instituted and had long been in support of ending what he called racialism (analogous to racism) in South Africa.

In the early 1950s, Mandela became deeply involved in the Defiance Campaign, dedicated to eradicating legal discrimination against black South Africans. He was arrested and criminally charged for his role in this movement, given a suspended prison sentence, and confined to remain in Johannesburg for six months. Near the end of the 1950s, Mandela was a defendant in the Treason Trials, which came about as a result of the adoption of the Freedom Charter by the African National Congress, the Congress of Democrats, the South African Indian Congress, the South African Congress of Trade Unions, and the Colored People's Congress. These were primarily black South African groups, and the Freedom Charter was concerned with ending apartheid and abolishing racial segregation and separatism. It advocated freedom and equality for all people in South Africa, regardless of racial or cultural origin. The police arrested more than 150 people during the first two weeks of December in 1956, most of whom were black and the majority of whom were executives in the above-named groups.

Those arrested were charged with the capital crime (able to receive the death sentence) of high treason. Of the 156 people arrested, ninety-five were made to stand trial. Ultimately, all charges were dropped. After the Sharpeville Massacre in 1960, the African National Congress was banned from South Africa, and Mandela was detained by the legal authorities until 1961 for his participation in the group. After his release, Mandela went underground and adopted a series of different disguises in order to avoid capture as he worked to try to gather support for governmental changes. He left the country illegally to gather international support for his movement and was arrested when he re-entered South Africa. He was convicted in 1962 and sentenced to five years in prison. While he was serving his sentence, he was charged with sabotage in the Rivonia case, along with the other leaders of the African National Congress. During the Rivonia Trial in 1963–1964, seven of the defendants, including Mandela, were found guilty of treason for allegedly plotting to overthrow the apartheid government, and were sentenced to life imprisonment.

■ PRIMARY SOURCE

Our fight is against real, and not imaginary, hardships or, to use the language of the State Prosecutor 'so-called hardships.' Basically, we fight against two features which are the hallmarks of African life in South Africa and which are entrenched by legislation which we seek to have repealed. These features are poverty and lack of human dignity, and we do not need communists or so-called 'agitators' to teach us about these things.

South Africa is the richest country in Africa, and could be one of the richest countries in the world. But it is a land of extremes and remarkable contrasts. The whites enjoy what may well be the highest standard of living in the world, whilst Africans live in poverty and misery. Forty per cent of Africans live in hopelessly overcrowded and, in some cases, drought-stricken Reserves, where soil erosion and the overworking of the soil makes it impossible for them to live properly off the land. Thirty per cent are labourers, labour tenants, and squatters on white farms and work and live under conditions similar to those of the serfs of the Middle Ages. The other 30 per cent live in towns where they have developed economic and social habits which bring them closer in may respects to white standards. Yet most Africans, even in this group, are impoverished by low incomes and high cost of living.

The highest-paid and the most prosperous section of urban African life is in Johannesburg. Yet their actual position is desperate. The latest figures were given on 25 March 1964 by Mr. Car, manager of the Johannesburg Non-European Affairs Department. The poverty datum line for the average African family in Johannesburg (according to Mr. Carr's department) is R42.84 per month. He showed that the average monthly wage is R32.84 and that 46 per cent of all African families in Johannesburg do not earn enough to keep them going.

Poverty goes hand in hand with malnutrition and disease. The incidence of malnutrition and deficiency diseases is very high amongst Africans. Tuberculosis, pellagra, kwashiorkor, gastroenteritis, and scurvy bring death and destruction of health. The incidence of infant mortality is one of the highest in the world. According to the Medical Officer of Health for Pretoria, tuberculosis kills forty people a day (almost all Africans), and in 1961 there were 58,491 new cases reported. These diseases not only destroy the vital organs of the body, but they result in retarded mental conditions and lack of initiative, and reduce powers of concentration. The secondary results of such conditions affect the whole community and the standard of work performed by African labourers.

The complaint of Africans, however, is not only that they are poor and the whites are rich, but that the laws which are made by the whites are designed to preserve this situation. There are two ways to break out of poverty. The first is by formal education, and the second is by the worker acquiring a greater skill at his work and thus higher wages. As far as Africans are concerned, both these avenues of advancement are deliberately curtailed by legislation.

The present Government has always sought to hamper Africans in their search for education. One of their early acts, after coming into power, was to stop subsidies for African school feeding. Many African children who attended schools depended on this supplement to their diet. This was a cruel act.

There is compulsory education for all white children at virtually no cost to their parents, be they rich or poor. Similar facilities are not provided for the African children, though there are some who receive such assistance. African children, however, generally have to pay more for their schooling than whites. According to figures quoted by the South African Institute of Race Relations in its 1963 journal, approximately 40 per cent of African children in the age group between seven to fourteen do not attend school. For those who do attend school, the standards are vastly different from those afforded to white children. In 1960-61 the *per capita* Government spending on African students at State-aided schools was estimated at R12.46. In the same years, the *per capita* spending on white children in the Cape Province (which are the only figures available to me) was R144.57. Although there are no figures available to me, it can be stated, without doubt, that the white children on whom R144.57 per head was being spent all came from wealthier homes than African children on whom R12.46 per head was being spent.

The quality of education is also different. According to the Bantu Educational Journal, only 5,660 African children in the whole of South Africa passed their Junior Certificate in 1962, and in that year only 362 passed matric.* This is presumably consistent with the policy of Bantu education about which the present Prime Minister said, during the debate on the Bantu Education Bill in 1953:

> "When I have control of Native education I will reform it so that Natives will be taught from childhood to realize that equality with Europeans is not for them . . .People who believe in equality are not desirable teachers for Natives. When my Department controls Native education it will know for what class of higher education a Native is fitted, and whether he will have a chance in life to use his knowledge."

The other main obstacle to the economic advancement of the African is the industrial colour-bar under which all the better jobs of industry are reserved for Whites only. Moreover, Africans who do obtain employment in the unskilled and semi-skilled occupations which are open to them are not allowed to form trade unions which have recognition under the Industrial Conciliation Act. This means that strikes of African workers are illegal, and that they are denied the right of collective bargaining which is permitted to the better-paid White workers. The discrimination in the policy of successive South African Governments towards African workers is demonstrated by the so-called 'civilized labour policy' under which sheltered, unskilled Government jobs are found for those White workers who cannot make the grade in industry, at wages which far exceed the earnings of the average African employee in industry.

The Government often answers its critics by saying that Africans in South Africa are economically better off than the inhabitants of the other countries in Africa. I do not know whether this statement is true and doubt whether any comparison can be made without having regard to the cost-of-living index in such countries. But even if it is true, as far as the African people are concerned it is irrelevant. Our complaining is not that we are poor by comparison with people in other countries, but that we are poor by comparison with the white people in our own country, and that we are prevented by legislation from altering this imbalance.

The lack of human dignity experienced by Africans is the direct result of the policy of white supremacy. White supremacy implies black inferiority. Legislation designed to preserve white supremacy entrenches this notion. Menial tasks in South Africa are invariably performed by Africans. When anything has to be carried or cleaned the white man will look around for an African to do it for him, whether the African is employed by him or not. Because of this sort of attitude, whites tend to regard Africans as a separate breed. They do not look upon them as people with families of their own; they do not realize that they have emotions—that they fall in love like white people do; that they want to be with their wives and children like white people want to be with theirs; that they want to earn enough money to support their families properly, to feed and clothe them and send them to school. And what 'house-boy' or 'garden-boy' or labourer can ever hope to do this?

Pass laws, which to the Africans are among the most hated bits of legislation in South Africa, render any African liable to police surveillance at any time. I doubt whether there is a single African male in South Africa who has not at some stage had a rush with the police over his pass. Hundreds and thousands of Africans are thrown into jail each year under pass laws. Even worse than this is the fact that pass laws keep husband and wife apart and lead to the breakdown of family life.

Poverty and the breakdown of family life have secondary effects. Children wander about the streets of the townships because they have no schools to go to, or no money to enable them to go to school, or no parents at home to see that they go to school, because both parents (if there be two) have to work to keep the family alive. This leads to a breakdown in moral standards, to an alarming rise in illegitimacy, and to growing violence which erupts not only politically, but everywhere. Life in the townships is dangerous. There is not a day that goes by without somebody being stabbed or assaulted. And violence is carried out of the townships in the white living areas. People are afraid to walk alone in the streets after dark. Housebreakings and robberies are increasing, despite the fact that the death sentence can now be imposed for such offences. Death sentences cannot cure the festering sore.

Africans want to be paid a living wage. Africans want to perform work which they are capable of doing, and not work which the Government declares them to be capable of. Africans want to be allowed to live where they obtain work, and not be endorsed out of an area because they were not born there. Africans want to be allowed to own land in places where they work, and not be obliged to live in rented houses which they can never call their own. Africans want to be part of the general population, and not confined to living in their own ghettoes. African men want to have their wives and children to live with them where they work, and not be forced into an unnatural existence in men's hostels. African women want to be with their menfolk and not be left permanently widowed in the Reserves. Africans want to be allowed out after eleven o'clock at night and not to be confined to their rooms like little children. Africans want to be allowed to travel in their own country and to seek work where they want to and not where the Labour Bureau tells them to. Africans want a just share in the whole of South Africa; they want security and a stake in society.

Above all, we want equal political rights, because without them our disabilities will be permanent. I know this sounds revolutionary to the whites in this country, because the majority of voters will be Africans. This makes the white man fear democracy.

But this fear cannot be allowed to stand in the way of the only solution which will guarantee racial harmony and freedom for all. It is not true that the enfranchisement of all will result in racial domination. Political division, based on colour, is entirely artificial, and, when it disappears, so will the domination of one colour group by another. The ANC has spent half a century fighting against racialism. When it triumphs it will not change that policy.

This then is what the ANC is fighting. Their struggle is a truly national one. It is a struggle of the African people, inspired by their own suffering and their own experience. It is a struggle for the right to live.

During my lifetime I have dedicated myself to this struggle of the African people. I have fought against white domination, and I have fought against black domination. I have cherished the ideal of a democratic and free society in which all persons live together in harmony and with equal opportunities. It is an ideal which I hope to live for and to achieve. But if needs be, it is an ideal for which I am prepared to die.

(*) The Junior Certificate examination was generally taken by white children at the age of 15, and they cannot normally leave school before this. Matriculation is taken two years later and qualifies students for higher education. The educational system, however, ensures that very few Africans reach Junior Certificate level, so that what represents a basic standard for whites is one of achievement for Africans. Even fewer attain matriculation level.

SIGNIFICANCE

Nelson Mandela served twenty-eight years in prison. During that time, he remained a role model for other prisoners and was deeply committed to the struggle to end apartheid in South Africa. He worked to create educational programs, teaching basic skills as well as politics in every prison in which he was placed. Mandela never ceased his political activism, despite his adverse and oppressive circumstances. He remained a very powerful political figure throughout the decades he spent in prison. Several times during the course of his incarceration, he was offered the opportunity to be released in exchange for renunciation of his political beliefs. He never compromised his ethics or his beliefs, and he refused to be released on those grounds. With the ending of apartheid, Nelson Mandela was released from prison on Sunday, February 11, 1990.

In 1991, Nelson Mandela presided at the first sanctioned meeting of the African National Congress held in South Africa since it was banned in 1960. He was elected President of the ANC that year as well. In 1993, Nelson Mandela and F. Willem De Klerk shared the Nobel Peace Prize, following in the distinguished tradition of fellow South African opponents of apartheid Chief Albert Lutuli (Nobel Prize for Peace, 1967) and Archbishop Desmond Tutu (Nobel Prize for Peace, 1984). The Nelson Mandela who won the Nobel Prize for Peace in 1993 was a far different man than the young radical who had studied (and mastered) guerilla warfare, and who had advocated violent uprisings as a means of opposing apartheid and attempting to overthrow the white South African apartheid government. The older Nelson Mandela referred to himself as a person who was accepting the Nobel Laureate as "a representative of the millions of people across the globe, the anti-apartheid movement, the governments and organisations that joined with us, not to fight against

Anti-aparthied leader Nelson Mandela in prison. © DAVID TURNLEY/CORBIS.

South Africa as a country or any of its peoples, but to oppose an inhuman system and sue for a speedy end to the apartheid crime against humanity.

These countless human beings, both inside and outside our country, had the nobility of spirit to stand in the path of tyranny and injustice, without seeking selfish gain. They recognised that an injury to one is an injury to all and therefore acted together in defense of justice and a common human decency."

On May 10, 1994, Nelson Mandela was elected State President of South Africa in the first democratic all-race elections held after the ending of apartheid, and served in that capacity from May of 1994 until June of 1999, when he officially retired. He was the first black President in South African History.

FURTHER RESOURCES
Books

Apartheid Unravels, edited by R. Hunt Davis, Jr. Gainesville, Fla.: University of Florida Press, 1991.

Culverson, Donald R. *Contesting Apartheid: U.S. Activism, 1960–1987*. Boulder, Colo.: Westview Press, 1999.

Eades, Lindsey Michie. *The End of Apartheid in South Africa*. Westport, Conn.: Greenwood Press, 1999.

Klotz, Audie. *Norms in International Relations: The Struggle Against Apartheid*. Ithaca, N.Y.: Cornell University Press, 1995.

Mandela, Nelson. *Nelson Mandela Speaks: Forging a Democratic, Nonracial South Africa*. New York: Little Brown, 1994.

Mandela, Tambo, and the African National Congress: The Struggle Against Apartheid, 1948–1990, edited by Sheridan Johns and R. Hunt Davis, Jr. New York: Oxford University Press, 1991.

Pomeroy, William J. *Apartheid, Imperialism, and African Freedom*. New York: International Publishers, 1986.

Web sites

NobelPrize.org. "Nelson Mandela—Nobel Acceptance and Lecture." <http://nobelprize.org/peace/laureates/1993/mandela-lecture.html> (accessed May 6, 2006).

Tiananmen Square Protest

Photograph

By: Jeff Widener

Date: May 30, 1989

Source: © Peter Turnley/Corbis. Reproduced by permission.

About the Photographer: Peter Turnley is a freelancer photographer who has covered wars, disasters, protests, and many other events for a variety of news organizations.

INTRODUCTION

On June 3, 1989, six weeks of predominantly peaceful student and worker protests in the Chinese capital of Beijing (also known as Peking) came to a violent conclusion. These protesters demanded more democratic freedoms in China, and the protest reflected the growing working class movement. About 40,000 soldiers from the Peoples Liberation Army descended upon the thousands of protesters, and their use of tanks, other weapons of warfare, and tear gas brought the protest movement to a moment of chaos. Witness accounts remarked that Army tanks came in and knocked people off barricades, buses, and buildings. Some of these obstacles caught fire, but the mood of the protesters stayed indignant and did not immediately turn to fear. As the crowd of protesters yelled and chanted sayings like "You pig" and "Go on strike," the military fired rounds of ammunition at them. Previously, rubber bullets had been used to quell the protesters, but the events of June 3 reflected the agitated mood of the protesters and the Chinese government. The Chinese Red Cross estimated that about 2,600 people died from the protest's violent conclusion, and not all of these causalities were protesters. Many by-standers and local residents were caught in the crossfire of bullets and the burning buildings and buses. Numerous scholars, media reports, and critics have agreed the 1989 protests proved the most difficult social uprising in Chinese history since its 1949 revolution.

Tiananmen Square is the largest square in the world; it could hold the entire Summer Olympics with all the events occurring simultaneously. The size of the square made it the perfect location for the protest, though the square has no trees, no benches, no public water fountains, and no venders for food or beverage. It is also one of the most heavily monitored public squares. The light posts are equipped with speakers and swiveling video cameras. These cameras work rather well, as the protester who threw paint on the painting of Mao Tse-tung in Tiananmen Square received a life sentence for his action. The video cameras captured his act of dissent. The lack of facilities heightened the hardships of the protesters, and the video surveillance enabled the Chinese government to convict and suppress many protesters once the hostilities ended.

Before the violent conclusion of the Tiananmen Square protest, a series of events and calculated moves (by the protesters and Chinese government) paved the way for social unrest. Students marched to Tiananmen Square in late December 1986 and early January 1987, but the police arrested and forcefully removed them before a serious protest could get underway. Hu Yaobang stepped in and prevented the student protesters from being jailed, and his opponents saw this action as weak and sympathetic to the students. These protesters demanded larger democratic freedoms in China, and they wanted economic and governmental reforms that would encourage fair hiring and selling practices. Hu was forced to resign his governmental post after the 1987 protest, and his death in 1989 is often marked as a catalyst for the Tiananmen Square uprising. Hu served as general secretary of the Communist Party in 1980 and as party chairman in 1981.

In 1988, the Chinese economy was improving, but many citizens were still disenchanted that government corruption was enabling some members of society to obtain wealth while other individuals could not or could barely pay their bills. Then in April 1989, Hu died from a heart attack, prompting students throughout Beijing to display posters of him from campus buildings. The students rallied on three key demands: more democratic representation, authority to organize student unions, and the end of government corruption. On April 21, students began gathering in Tiananmen Square in anticipation of Hu's funeral. The students camped in the square to prevent the police from barring them from Hu's funeral, and on April 22, some students maneuvered past the police line. They waited for over an hour to give their position to the country's leaders, but official leaders refused to see them. Then, on April 26, a line of protesters—exceeding four miles (6.4 kilometers) long—marched to Tiananmen Square. Workers and civilians joined the movement.

The protesters refused to leave, and on May 13 they viewed the opening of the Sino-Soviet Summit as an opportunity to gain international attention for their cause. Mikhail Gorbachev, leader of the Soviet Union, convened with Chinese leader Deng Xiaoping. The

PRIMARY SOURCE

Tiananmen Square protest: Thousands of protestors surround a statue they errected as a symbol of their protest, called the "Goddess of Democracy," in Tiananmen Square in Beijing, China, on May 30, 1989. © PETER TURNLEY/CORBIS. REPRODUCED BY PERMISSION.

summit, an attempt to ease Soviet and Chinese relations, took a second seat to the scene of protesters in Tiananmen Square. The students, wearing white headbands, declared a hunger strike that would end when the government met their demands. International media coverage focused on protesters fainting and being removed from the square via stretcher. Amid the chaos, the protesters remained unorganized. The lack of facilities and access to water exasperated the situation with the hunger strikers, and the open arena of the square left various student and worker organizations to set up makeshift tent headquarters throughout the area. These ad hoc constructions added to the perception of disarray. The scene tended to reflect a lively party with music and drinking. As the protest continued, students and workers eagerly traveled to Beijing to unite with the movement, and housewives, journalists, doctors, and many others also joined the cause.

As the protest progressed, the Chinese government struggled over how to handle the uprising.

Deng argued for military force, but Zhao Ziyang urged for reconciliation and mediation between the protesters and the government. Zhao, the secretary-general for the Chinese Communist party, went to the square to talk with the masses. His attempts failed, and Deng later removed him of his position and banned him from future public life. On May 19, the day after Zhao attempted to negotiate with the Tiananmen Square group, martial law was declared in Beijing and the students called off their hunger strike, which had lasted for five to six days. Yet, they did not leave the square.

In late May, students brought a large "Goddess of Liberty" statue into the square. Several students from the Central Academy for Fine Arts had made the statue, and they framed it on the Statue of Liberty in the United States. As students and workers continued to gather in Tiananmen Square, western journalists frequently captured pictures of the student's statue with Chinese leader Mao Tse-tung overlooking the events. His portrait hung near Tiananmen Square, and the juxtaposition of Mao overlooking the protests brought more international attention to the events. Mao was the leader of the Chinese Communist party that brought widespread economic reforms throughout China with its 1949 revolution. Aside from the images of the student statue, numerous media outlets broadcasted images of Chinese military tanks approaching the square and of the violent conflict between the military and the protesters.

PRIMARY SOURCE

TIANANMEN SQUARE PROTEST
See primary source image.

SIGNIFICANCE

In response to the use of military force and media coverage showing death and violence at Tiananmen Square, world leaders spoke out against the Chinese government's actions. United States President George Bush and British Prime Minister Margaret Thatcher both made international statements condemning the use of force against the protesters. Chinese politicians who had been assured that excessive force would not be used to end the protest were shocked and shamed at the use of violence. Unsubstantiated reports state that Communist leader Deng Xiaoping ordered the deployment of troops on the protesters.

The first tanks to approach Tiananmen Square toppled the tent headquarters of the Workers Autonomous Federation, and the military presence and takeover of the capital only signaled the beginning of governmental retaliation upon dissidents. Demonstrations continued to speckle the Chinese landscape, in Beijing and in outlying providences, and these were handled in brutal and harsh fashions. Following the protests, nearly 40,000 people were arrested, with a large majority of them being contacts of worker organizations and unions. Hundreds of workers and student protesters remain in jail, and some of them received death sentences shortly after the incident. For the most part, students received light punishments, with most returning to their campuses. Beijing University decreased its enrollment immediately following the 1989 uprising, but within a few years its campus population exceeded pre-1989 enrollment figures.

The reforms that the students and workers sought have not been completely addressed, but throughout the 1990s China continued its economic reforms. These reforms, started in 1979, opened businesses up to private ownership and competition, and state-owned firms have shifted to privately owned corporations. Adding to the complexity of the situation, western presses quickly changed their coverage of the Tiananmen Square protests from the students and workers to the international business community. One such example of ties and concerns for the Chinese market came from Bob Hawke. Hawke was the Australian Prime Minister in 1989, but in 1991 he left public office to emerge as a consultant for corporate investment in China. Critics have used Hawke as an example of why the 1989 protests failed. Many of the student and worker leaders left the country or spent years in exile or in jail, and the lack of international intervention on their behalf left them feeling jaded.

FURTHER RESOURCES

Books
Hung, Wu. *Remaking Beijing: Tiananmen Square and the Creation of a Political Space.* Chicago: University of Chicago Press, 2005.

Miles, James. *The Legacy of Tiananmen.* Ann Arbor, Mich.: University of Michigan Press, 1996.

Periodicals
Pfaff, Steven and Guobin Yang. "Double-Edged Rituals and the Symbolic Resources of Collective Action: Political Commemorations and the Mobilization of Protest in 1989." *Theory and Society* 30, 4 (August 2001): 539–589.

Web sites
PBS.org. "Frontline: The Gate of Heavenly Peace." <http://www.pbs.org/wgbh/pages/frontline/gate> (accessed May 2, 2006).

U.S. House of Representatives: Congressman Chris Smith. "Remembering Tiananmen Square." June 3, 2004. <http://www.house.gov/apps/list/press/nj04_smith/Tiananmen.html> (accessed May 2, 2006).

Secretary of State's Morning Summary for June 5 and 6, 1989

Government record

By: James A. Baker III

Date: June 5–6, 1989

Source: Baker, James. "Secretary of State's Morning Summary for June, 1989" and "Secretary of State's Morning Summary for June 6, 1989." Department of State. Washington, D.C., 1989.

The bodies of dead civilians lie near Beijing's Tiananmen Square on June 4, 1989, the result of the violent suppression of demonstrations for democratic reform in China. AP IMAGES.

About the Author: Texan-born James A. Baker III served as Secretary of State from January 1989 to August 1992 under President George H.W. Bush. Baker now serves as Chair of the James A. Baker III Institute of Public Policy at Rice University in Houston, Texas.

INTRODUCTION

In June 1989, the world watched as the China's People's Liberation Army (PLA) forcibly removed thousands of demonstrators from Tiananmen Square in Beijing. An estimated 1,000–2,600 people were killed at the hands of the military in the events that unfolded beginning in April of that year. By 1991, the Chinese government confirmed that 2,578 demonstrators from the events in Tiananmen Square in 1989 had been arrested. The circumstances which led to the unprecedented suppression of the protests in June of 1989 actually began in 1985 and 1986. During this time, students and workers began to demonstrate in support of broad democratic reforms in China. These protests originated on university campuses as students opposed the presence of the PLA in

the schools. In addition, protesters demonstrated against nuclear testing that occurred in the Xinjiang province. The movement became a pro-democracy demonstration and adopted slogans of "Law, not authoritarianism" and "Long live democracy." As these demonstrations escalated to nation-wide protests, members of the Chinese Communist Party (CCP) supported a harsh government response. However, party chairman Hu Yaobang was sympathetic to the reformers and refused to respond with military force. As a result, in 1987 he lost his position as party chairman.

On April 15, 1989, Hu Yaobang died. People began to gather in Tiananmen Square in his remembrance and in support for his political stand. On April 26, however, an editorial appeared in the *People's Daily* newspaper discrediting the gathering of Hu Yaobang's supporters. As a result, the mood shifted from an expression of grief to a political stand for democratic reforms. According to Chinese government figures, the demonstrations that began in Tiananmen Square began to spread to twenty-nine provinces and eighty-four cities. On May 13, students began a hunger strike and by May 17, approximately one million demonstrators had converged on Tiananmen Square. Many of these protesters were students. However, unlike demonstrations in the past, this gathering became a cross-class protest that included students, urban workers, party and government employees, and others. In all, over seven hundred organizations participated.

On May 20, the party leadership, under the control of Deng Xiaoping (1904–1997), declared martial law. Initial attempts on the part of the PLA to dispel the demonstrators failed. By May 30, the protesters erected a ten-meter-high (about 33.5-feet-tall) plaster statue called the "Goddess of Democracy." The statue, inspired partly by the Statue of Liberty, was raised to face the portrait of China's historical Communist Party leader Mao Zedong (1893–1976) hanging in Tiananmen Square. As a result, the Chinese government began to implement a policy of forceful removal and disbursement of the protesters. This policy began on June 1, 1989, by removing the access of foreign journalists to the events. The next day, convoys of tanks and soldiers began to move into central Beijing. By June 3, the military began to use tear gas and rubber bullets to force the demonstrators' eviction of the square. The PLA's tanks entered Tiananmen Square by midnight on June 3, at which time many demonstrators agreed to leave the square. However, the army began to open fire on the protesters in the early morning of June 4.

In a cable written to the U.S. State Department from the American Embassy in Beijing, approximately 10,000 troops surrounded the 3,000 remaining protesters resulting in violent clashes along Changan Boulevard, the main thoroughfare in Tiananmen Square. The military used automatic weapons, tanks, and armored personnel carriers to suppress the demonstration, which until this point had been peaceful. According to reports, the military opened fire on unarmed civilians, to include members of the press. The U.S. Embassy reported that journalists for CBS had been beaten by the PLA, and their equipment, especially cameras, had been smashed.

As is customary with all pressing situations overseas, the U.S. Secretary of State, then James A. Baker III, kept the president, then George H. W. Bush, aware of developments through frequent updates. The following reports, initially labeled "top secret" were excised of still-sensitive material and made available to the American public in 1993.

■ PRIMARY SOURCE

Secretary of State's Morning Summary for June 5, 1989, China: After the Bloodbath 1. China

A. After the bloodbath

Yesterday and this morning troops continued to fire indiscriminately at citizens in the area near Tianamen [*sic*] Square. Citizens tried to block streets and burned armored vehicles and army trucks. Hundreds of military vehicles including at least 34 tanks and numerous armored personnel carriers have been destroyed over the last two days, according to [unidentified source] and press reports.

Secured a university campus where students had captured an armored personnel carrier, and issued a warning that executions of students will begin tonight, according to [unidentified source] units are poised outside several other colleges, and the military said troops will move against the campuses if resistance does not cease. Some students have seized weapons and are vowing to resist. Non-violent protests have occurred in half a dozen other cities....

Press have reported that more than 1,000 soldiers and police were killed or wounded and that some civilians were killed. Foreign estimates range from hundreds to as many as 2,600 civilians killed and thousands injured. But the severity of the assault on Tianamen Square is clear. Troops shot indiscriminately into crowds of unarmed civilians, including women and children, often with automatic weapons. In one case, students attempting to parlay with troops were gunned down. Foreign journalists report seeing fleeting protesters shot in the back. Enraged protesters burned personnel carriers and killed some security personnel.

Secretary of State's Morning Summary for June 6, 1989, China: Descent into Chaos In the western edge of the city, according to press reports, elements of the 28th army clashed with the 27th army, which is being blamed for the worst atrocities against civilians during Saturday night's attack on Tiananmen Square. Told [unidentified source] that Chinese troops are out of control.

That at least some of the troops still entering Beijing are arriving without authorization and are intent upon attacking the 27the army. An unconfirmed Hong Kong television broadcast today reported fighting at Nanyuan military airport, where several thousand fresh troops may have arrived today from the Nanjing military region.

The Nanijng commander is believed to be personally loyal to Deng. A security guard in the great hall of the people shot Premier Li Peng in the thigh yesterday, according to press reports. The would-be assassin was immediately killed by security forces. The report, from a reliable Hong Kong newspaper, will gain wide dissemination.

Sporadic gunfire continued in the center of Beijing yesterday, with some civilian casualties, according to press reports. Troops, supported by tanks, have taken up defensive positions near the US embassy.

Strikes and protests are spreading to other cities; martial law has been declared in Chengdu where violent clashes between troops and demonstrators have left at least 300 dead. According to the consulate general, on Monday night an angry mob tried to break into the hotel where the consulate is housed, although looting, rather than attacks on foreigners, was believed to be the purpose.

Unconfirmed accounts suggest that troops are poised outside Shanghai to intervene if ordered, and the city is paralyzed by strikes and roadblocks erected by protesters. Demonstrations have also occurred in Guanghzhou and other cities.

Leaders and army commanders who have ordered or conducted atrocities now feel they are fighting for their lives. They have ringed the Zhongnanhai leadership compound with armored vehicles and troops.

Convoy of limousines like mini-buses, escorted by tanks, left Zhongnanhai Sunday night for a wartime command center in the suburbs, according to unconfirmed press reports.

SIGNIFICANCE

The U.S. Embassy in Beijing reported that relative calm had been restored to the region by June 8, 1989. Human rights organizations assert that approximately 1,000–2,600 people were killed during the events. By 1991, the Chinese government had confirmed 2,578 arrests of those involved in participating and organizing the protests. Unlike the gentle handling of the 1985–1986 pro-democracy protests, the CCP leadership enacted sweeping responses to prevent future demonstrations from occurring. In addition to jailing protesters, many of the demonstration's leadership were exiled. Policy changes also occurred. The CCP intensified the political education of students through programs such as an eight-week university program that teaches party principles. Many schools adopted state written curriculum that focuses on China's achievements and the excesses of the West.

FURTHER RESOURCES

Books

Casserly, Jack. *The Triumph at Tiananmen Square*. Lincoln, Neb.: ASJA Press, 2005.

Periodicals

Mason, T. David., Clements, Jonathan. "Tiananmen Square 13 Years After: The Prospects for Civil Unrest in China." *Asian Affairs: An American Review*. 29 (2002): 159.

Web sites

The Guardian Unlimited. "Tiananmen: Ten Years On." 1999. <http://www.guardian.co.uk/Tiananmen/0,2759,193066,00.html> (accessed April 30, 2006).

National Security Archive Electronic Briefing Book No.16. "Tiananmen Square, 1989." <http://www.gwu.edu/~nsarchiv/NSAEBB/NSAEBB16/> (accessed April 30, 2006).

Tiananmen Square Declaration of Human Rights

Declaration

By: Anonymous

Date: Spring, 1989

Source: Angle, Stephen and Marina Svensson. *The Chinese Human Rights Reader*. Birmingham, Ala.: M.E. Sharpe, 2001.

About the Author: The unknown authors of the primary source included here were Chinese pro-democracy protestors involved in the Tiananmen Square protests in Beijing, 1989.

INTRODUCTION

In the late 1980s, inspired partly by political liberalization in the Soviet Union under the leadership of Mikhail Gorbachev (1931–), many intellectuals, students, and industrial workers in China believed that the time had come for democratic reforms. (China has been governed since the 1940s by a non-elected authoritarian oligarchy, nominally Communist, that punishes criticism of the government.) Pro-democracy protests occurred in 1986 and 1987, but the most important—and violently repressed—was that which took place in Tiananmen Square in 1989. Tiananmen Square is a large plaza in Beijing, the capital city of China. It is directly south of the Forbidden City, the ancient palace of the emperors of China.

Starting in early May 1989, at least a hundred thousand students and workers occupied the square for one month. They erected a large statue representing the "Goddess of Democracy" and issued several documents defining their movement's principles, including a constitution and the declaration of human rights given here. The influence of such documents as the U.S. Constitution and Bill of Rights is clear in the language and content of this document.

The Chinese government was for several weeks uncertain how to respond to the nonviolent protesters. Thanks to documents later smuggled out of China, it is now known that the five-man Standing Committee of the Politburo, the top decision-making body in the Chinese government, was deadlocked over whether to use force to end the protest: two were for, two were against, one member abstained. The head of the Chinese Communist Party, Deng Xiaoping, decided the stalemate in favor of force. On June 3 and 4, 1989, tanks and foot soldiers drove the protestors from Tiananmen Square. Armored personnel carriers ran over protestors and troops indiscriminately fired into the crowd, killing hundreds or perhaps thousands and injuring thousands more. Several leaders managed to escape the country, but many participants (accurate numbers are not known) were executed or imprisoned. Many who were imprisoned were tortured.

■ PRIMARY SOURCE

In view of the widespread ignorance and neglect of, or even apathy toward, human rights in Chinese society; in view of several thousand years of cruel interference in and infringement of human rights by our rulers; and in view of the need to create a new society, a new order, and a new morality, we hereby solemnly declare the following to be the inviolable and inalienable natural rights of human beings:.

1. Everyone is born free and equal, regardless of origin, status, age, sex, professional level of schooling, religion, party affiliation, and ethnicity.
2. The rights to life and security, and to oppose oppression, are humankind's inalienable natural rights.
3. ...Everyone has the freedom to believe or not believe in a religion or in various theories [such as Marxism].
4. ...Everyone has the right to travel and to reside inside or outside the country.
5. Personal dignity shall not be infringed on because of criminal conviction.
6. The individual has the right to privacy. One's family, domicile, and correspondence are protected by law.
7. Everyone has the right to education. Higher education should be open to everyone based on achievement scores.
8. Private property acquired through one's [own] labor is sacred and inviolable.
9. Freedom of marriage between adult men and women shall not be interfered with by any outside force. Marriage must be voluntarily agreed upon by both parties.
10. Everyone has the right to assembly and association, whether openly or secretly.
11. The power of the government comes from the people. In the absence of free elections..., the people may rescind any power usurped either by force or under the guise of the will of the people by any individual or group (including any of the political parties).
12. Everyone has the right to either direct or indirect participation in government (through free elections of representatives).
13. The law is the embodiment of the popular will and cannot be changed arbitrarily by one individual or any one political party. Everyone is equal before the law.
14. The army is the defender of the interests of the people and of the state. It must strictly observe neutrality in political affairs and not [be subordinate to] an individual or a political party.
15. Democracy and freedom are the basic guarantees of social stability, people's well-being, and national prosperity. Therefore, each person has the right and the duty to establish and safeguard such a system and to oppose autocracy and tyranny.

SIGNIFICANCE

After the Tiananmen Square protests, the government executed and jailed many protestors, especially leaders. Students, who tended to come from more affluent families than industrial workers, generally received less harsh treatment, but some spent years in jail. Three men were arrested for throwing paint at a large outdoors portrait of Mao Zedong (1893–1976), founder of Communist China; all three were sentenced to twenty years in prison. One, Yu Dongyue, was freed in February 2006, after being driven into mental breakdown by years of torture and solitary confinement. The United Nations Special Rapporteur on Torture, who visited China in 2005, confirmed that prisoner torture is widespread in China, although it was officially outlawed there in 1996.

The political aspirations expressed in Tiananmen Square have not disappeared from China. In 1998 and 1999, dissidents sought to establish a legal opposition party, the China Democracy Party. Its goals were similar to those of the Tiananmen Square protestors, including a call for human rights. The China Democracy Party was immediately outlawed. Its members were arrested and some received prison sentences of up to thirteen years.

Over 25 years later, discussion of the Tiananmen Square incident in China remains illegal. The government's filtering of Internet traffic, for instance, blocks all sites that discuss the protests. In 2004, the Chinese journalist Shi Tao was sentenced to ten years in prison for revealing to foreign Web sites a message from the Chinese government warning newspapers not to report on the twenty-fifth anniversary of the Tiananmen Square protests. (Computer records enabling the Chinese authorities to track Shi Tao down were provided by the Internet company Yahoo! Inc.) Also in 2004, Dr. Jiang Yanyong, a seventy-two year-old dissident, sent a letter to Chinese leaders asking for official reassessment of the government's response to the Tiananmen protests. Dr. Jiang was arrested and imprisoned for over a month. After his release, he remained under orders to not discuss political matters or travel without Government approval.

In 2006, Google Inc. aroused controversy when it inaugurated an in-China version of its famous search engine. The new search engine, google.cn, blocks searches for references to the Tiananmen Square protests as well as other forbidden topics such as Tibet (occupied by China since 1950 and subjected to a variety of genocidal measures) or the Falun Gong religious movement.

In 2000, a group called the Tiananmen Mother's Campaign was founded by several women whose children were killed during the crackdown on the Tiananmen Square protest. The group demanded an end to persecution of protestors and the release from jail of all protestors still in jail. Members of the group were arrested and imprisoned. After their release, their telephone calls were monitored and they were forbidden to have any contact with each other.

Although China is moving steadily toward a capitalist-style market economy, its government continues to restrict free speech and is alleged to practice torture and otherwise deny the human rights called for by the Tiananmen Square protestors of 1989.

FURTHER RESOURCES
Books

Suettinger, Roberts. *Beyond Tiananmen: The Politics of U.S.-China Relations, 1989–2000.* Washington, D.C.: Brookings Institutuion Press, 2003.

Liang, Zhen, et al., eds. *The Tiananmen Papers.* New York: PublicAffairs, 2001.

Web sites

BBC News. "Tiananmen Activist 'Mentally Ill.'" February 23, 2006. <http://news.bbc.co.uk./2/hi/asia-pacific/4742478.stm> (accessed April 28, 2006).

The National Security Archive, George Washington University. "The U.S. Tiananmen Papers." June 4, 2001. <http://www.gwu.edu/~nsarchiv/NSAEBB/NSAEBB47/> (accessed April 28, 2006).

Appeal for Action to Stop Repression and Trials in South Africa

Speech

By: Oliver Reginald Tambo

Date: October 8, 1963

Source: *Apartheid and the International Community, Addresses to United Nations Committees and Conferences,* edited by E. S. Reddy. New Delhi, India: Sterling Publishers Private Limited, 1991.

About the Author: Oliver Reginald Tambo was the Acting President of the African National Congress between 1967 and 1978. In 1952, in partnership with Nelson Mandela, Tambo opened the first legal partnership run by black Africans in South Africa. A lifelong political activist, he worked both within his homeland and by traveling to other countries to meet with world leaders to gather global support to end apartheid. He played a pivotal role in making the voice of black South Africans heard and in gathering the momentum necessary to end apartheid and to free South African political prisoners.

INTRODUCTION

Colonialists from the United Kingdom and Holland settled in South Africa during the seventeenth century, with the British exerting political domination over the Dutch settlers. Colonial rule was in effect until the end of the Boer War (1899–1902), when South Africa achieved independence from British colonialism. There was a strife-laden relationship between the white and black populations for centuries, finally culminating in the imposition of apartheid against black South Africans in 1948 by the ruling white South African Afrikaner National Party. In effect, the most extreme forms of racism and racial segregation were given credence and institutionalized through the imposition of apartheid. Socialization between the races was prohibited; inter-racial marriage was strictly outlawed. Whites were given preferential jobs, with blacks being prohibited from many occupations.

In Cape Town, South Africa, a group of Black protesters raise their fists in the air during funerals for victims of police repression in South African townships, September 21, 1985. © BERNARD BISSON/CORBIS SYGMA.

All South Africans were required by the Population Registration Act of 1950 to be classified into one of three racial/ethnic groups: white, black African, or colored. Categorization was based upon physical appearance as well as some demographic (educational and socioeconomic, primarily) characteristics. People who were deemed colored were neither black nor white; they were either of mixed race or were of Indian or Asian heritage. Each person's classification was recorded at the Department of Home Affairs, and all blacks were required to keep with them at all times a pass book containing a photograph, fingerprints, and personal information, which must be shown upon request by a government official, or whenever the individual needed to gain entrance to a geographic or business area prohibited to blacks.

By the early 1950s, South Africa had been divided into four geographic regions referred to as homelands.

Every black African living in South Africa was assigned a specific homeland based upon data contained in government records. The homelands became their designated place of citizenship, effectively stripping black Africans of any civil rights previously accorded them as citizens of the country of South Africa.

Apartheid rule became progressively more stringent and punitive toward the black Africans. The government used enactment of harsh legislation as a means of limiting the ability of black citizens to protest the conditions under which they were forced to exist. Penalties for civil disobedience or for any form of protest were meted out under the umbrella of the Public Safety Act and the Criminal Law Amendment, and could consist of incarceration, financial penalties, or public beating or whipping. Many former political activists were arrested and held in police custody for many months without any criminal charges or adjudication. Others were tortured, sentenced to death, exiled from the country, or sentenced to life in prison. Nelson Mandela was among the latter group.

PRIMARY SOURCE

APPEAL FOR ACTION TO STOP REPRESSION AND TRIALS IN SOUTH AFRICA

Statement at the meeting of the Special Political Committee of the General Assembly, New York, October 8, 1963 I wish to express my deep gratitude for the privilege accorded to me to address this important body. It was with considerable reluctance that I applied for leave to appear before this Committee, recognising, as I did, the supreme effort which the United Nations is making to induce the South African Government to abolish and abandon policies which are a cruel scourge on the conscience of every civilised being and an unequalled example of man's inhumanity to man. But we feel we cannot too frequently appeal to the nations of the world to call South Africa to sanity, nor do we feel we can be too emphatic in pointing out what a great deal of the damage which the Government of South Africa and its White supporters are doing daily, consistently and with arrogance may prove impossible to repair and thus remain an enduring source of anguish for future generations.

The readiness with which my request was granted by your Committee, Mr. Chairman, confirms and is consistent with the declared desire of the nations and peoples of the world to see the end of apartheid and white domination, and the emergence of a South Africa loyal to the United Nations and to the high principles set forth in the Charter— a South Africa governed by its people as fellow citizens of equal worth whatever the colour, race or creed of any one of them. This kind of South Africa is the precise goal of our political struggle.

In thanking you and your Committee, therefore, Mr. Chairman, I wish to emphasise that I do so not on my own behalf, but also on behalf of my organisation, the African National Congress, and its sister organisations in South Africa, on behalf of the African people and all the other victims of racial discrimination, together with that courageous handful of white South Africans who have fully identified themselves with the struggle for the liberation of the oppressed people of South Africa.

I should also like to take this opportunity to place on record the deep appreciation of my people for the steps which have been taken by various governments against South Africa, which alone can give any meaning to condemnation of the policies practised by the Government of South Africa. On the other hand, I cannot exaggerate the sense of grievance—to put it mildly—which we feel towards those countries which have done and are even now doing so much to make apartheid the monstrous and ghastly reality which it is, and which have thereby created in our country the conditions which, if nothing else happens, will ensure an unparalleled bloodbath. Assured of the support of these countries the South African rulers, who boast openly of this support, are not only showing open defiance for the United Nations and treating its resolutions with calculated contempt, they are liquidating the opponents of their policies, confident that the big Powers will not act against them.

This brings me to the special matter which, with your permission, Mr. Chairman, I beg leave to submit to the distinguished members of this Committee for their urgent consideration. It arises out of news of the latest developments in the South African situation.

Trials of Mandela and Other Leaders By a significant coincidence, this, the first day of this Committee's discussion of the policy of apartheid happens also to be the first day of a trial in South Africa which constitutes yet another challenge to the authority of the United Nations and which has as its primary aim the punishment by death of people who are among South Africa's most outstanding opponents of the very policies which the General Assembly and the Security Council have in numerous resolutions called upon the South African Government to abandon.

Today some thirty persons are appearing before a Supreme Court Judge in South Africa in a trial which will be conducted in circumstances that have no parallel in South African history, and which, if the Government has its way, will seal the doom of that country and entrench the feelings of bitterness which years of sustained persecution have already engendered among the African people.

The persons standing trial include Nelson Mandela and Walter Sisulu, which are household names throughout South Africa, Nelson Mandela being known personally to a

number of African Heads of State; Govan Mbeki, a top-ranking African political leader and an accomplished economist who has borne the burdens of his oppressed fellow men ever since he left the university; Ahmed Kathrada, a South African of Indian extraction who started politics as a passive resister in 1946 at the age of seventeen, since when he has been consistently a leading participant in the struggle of the Indian and other Asian South Africans against the Group Areas Act and other forms of racial discrimination, and has, with other Indian leaders, joined the Africans in the liberation struggle; Dennis Goldberg, a white South African, whose home in the Western Cape was the scene of a bomb explosion in 1962, when Government supporters sought to demonstrate their disapproval of his identifying himself with the African cause; Ruth Slovo (alias Ruth First), a South African white mother of three minor children, author of a recently published book on South West Africa, and one of South Africa's leading journalists. I could enumerate several others, and as I have shown, they consist of outstanding African nationalist leaders as well as others who have for long been associated with every conceivable form of protest against injustices perpetrated in the name of Christian civilisation and white supremacy. Trials against well over a hundred others are due to start at other centres in different parts of the country.

The charge against the accused is said to be "sabotage." This means in fact that they have contravened a law, or a group of laws which have been enacted for the express purpose of forcibly suppressing the aspirations of the victims of apartheid laws which no active opponent of the policies of the South African Government can evade. A study of the statutory definition of "sabotage," which distinguished delegates will find in official documents which I believe have been circulated to members, will show that a person accused of sabotage can be sentenced to death for one of the least effective and most peaceful forms of protest against apartheid.

Genocide Masquerading under Guise of Justice The relations between the government and those it rules by force in South Africa have never been worse. The law of the country has since the 1956 Treason Trial been altered so as to make it practically impossible for an accused person to escape a conviction. Lawyers who accepted briefs in political trials have been subjected to increasing intimidation and it has now become difficult to find counsel to appear in such trials. This has been particularly true in the case of the accused who are now facing trial. The law of procedure has also been altered with the result that whereas the State allows itself any amount of time to prepare its case against accused persons, the accused, held in solitary confinement, are kept ignorant of the charge against them until they appear in court. The time allowed them to prepare their defence is subject to the discretion of the court, and in the majority of cases the State insists on proceeding with the trial with as little delay as possible. Preparing a defence from a prison cell hardly enables an accused person to make any proper preparation.

An atmosphere of crisis has been whipped up and its effects have been reflected in the severity of sentences passed by the judges and, not infrequently, in the statements they make in the course of pronouncing sentence. Of special significance in this regard is the judgement passed last week by a Pretoria judge on seven Africans whom he found guilty of allegedly receiving training in the use of firearms in a country outside South Africa. In sentencing each of the accused to twenty years' imprisonment, the judge stated that he had seriously considered passing the death sentence, but had decided not to do so because he felt the accused had been misled. This judgement and these remarks are a sufficient—and deliberate—hint as to what sentences the South African public and the world are to expect in the new trials where leaders of the political struggle against the apartheid policies of the South African Government are the accused. It is known that the State will demand the death sentence.

Already more than 5,000 political prisoners are languishing in South Africa's jails. Even as recently as the month of September of this year and after the Security Council, in its resolution of 7 August, had called for the release of "all persons imprisoned, interned, or subjected to other restrictions for having opposed the policy of apartheid," three detainees have died in jail in circumstances strongly suggesting deliberate killing. All these are the direct victims of a situation which would never have arisen had the South African Government taken heed of the many appeals which have been addressed to it by the world public and expressed in resolutions of the General Assembly and the Security Council.

Call for Immediate Action | I cannot believe that this world body, the United Nations, could stand by, calmly watching what I submit is genocide masquerading under the guise of a civilised dispensation of justice. The African and other South Africans who are being dragged to the slaughter house face death, or life imprisonment, because they fearlessly resisted South Africa's violations of the United Nations Charter and the Universal Declaration of Human Rights, because they fought against a Government armed to the teeth and relying on armed force, to end inhumanity, to secure the liberation of the African people, to end racial discrimination, and to replace racial intolerance and tyranny with democracy and equality, irrespective of colour, race or creed.

If you, Mr. Chairman, and the distinguished delegates here assembled, consider, as I urge you to accept, that the developments I have referred to are of a nature which calls for immediate action by the United Nations, then I am content to leave it to you and your distinguished Committee, Sir, to decide on the action which it deems appropriate.

For our part, I wish to observe that every single day spent in jail by any of our people, every drop of blood drawn from any of them, and every life taken—each of these represents a unit of human worth lost to us. This loss we can no longer afford. It is surely not in the interests of South Africa or even of the South African Government that this loss should be increased any further.

Thank you, Sir.

SIGNIFICANCE

It is important to note that apartheid rule was imposed by a minority racial and ethnic group upon the majority of South African citizens. In general, whites made up about one fourth of the population, yet they controlled nearly ninety percent of the land and made three quarters of the total national income.

Apartheid codified and institutionalized segregation and racism, depriving black South Africans not only of virtually all of their civil rights, but also of the power to protest the conditions under which they were required to live and work. In 1961, a group of black South Africans living in an area called Sharpeville staged a peaceful protest by refusing to carry their passbooks. In response, the government declared a state of emergency, allowing them to invoke martial law and take aggressive action in response. By the end of what has become known as the Sharpeville Massacre, sixty-nine black South Africans were killed and nearly two hundred more injured by law enforcement authorities.

The passbooks were a very effective means of maintaining control of the population. In addition to the photograph, fingerprints, and extensive personal data contained in them, they were linked to a rather sophisticated computerized database system that detailed information about whether an individual had a history of anti-government expression or protest. All black South Africans were issued passbooks when they turned sixteen years of age. The passbooks and computerized database were part of what was called an influx control system, monitoring the movements of black South Africans throughout the country. It was also used as a means of funneling black workers into menial jobs at remote locations on an as-needed basis. Virtually every aspect of the black South Africans' lives were controlled by the government under apartheid, including how and where they were allowed to live. The workers were separated from their families and made to live in hostel-type housing. Rents and taxes were much higher for blacks than for whites, so most black individuals lived in poverty. It was difficult to maintain social ties and family structure because of the forced housing restrictions, and there was little communication between family members who lived under those conditions. Often, individuals viewed as political dissidents or threats to the apartheid government were apprehended by the police and held in legal custody for months, with no charges filed or hearings held. Rarely were employers or family members notified of those circumstances—in fact, they almost never knew what had happened to the individual until he was released from custody—if and when that occurred.

By the last quarter of the twentieth century, global anti-apartheid reached a point where other nations began to impose sanctions and take action directed at ending apartheid. In 1974, South Africa was barred from involvement with the United Nations until apartheid was abolished. In 1976, there were student uprisings staged in the townships of Soweto and Sharpeville, in which schoolchildren and youth attempted a peaceful protest of a Ministry of Education mandate requiring them to be taught half of their school curriculum in Afrikaans—the dominant language of the white government. In both places, the police opened fire on the students, using live ammunition rather than crowd control blanks or rubber bullets. By the end of the protests, the police had killed more than six hundred black South African children and youth. The Soweto Uprising, in particular, attracted attention from the rest of the world, which began to actively mobilize to put an end to apartheid.

During the 1980s, the anti-apartheid protests within black South Africa, as well as the response from the white government, grew progressively more violent. In an effort to maintain control, the government began to have armed police officers cruise through townships, shooting dissidents and quelling riots by using force. The dissidents were led primarily by the African National Congress and the Pan Africanist Congress. In 1984, many of the apartheid laws were repealed, including the use of passbooks. Because of the enormous amount of civil unrest and internal violence and destabilization, the economy of South Africa grew progressively more unstable as well. The government declared a state of emergency in 1985, which remained in force until 1990. Between 1990 and 1991, the apartheid government was completely dismantled. In 1993, a new anti-discriminatory constitution was drafted, and democratic all-race elections were held in South Africa in 1994.

FURTHER RESOURCES

Books

Culverson, Donald R. *Contesting Apartheid: U.S. Activism, 1960–1987*. Boulder, Colo.: Westview Press, 1999.

Eades, Lindsey Michie. *The End of Apartheid in South Africa*. Westport, Conn.: Greenwood Press, 1999.

Kunnie, Julian. *Is Apartheid Really Dead? Pan-Africanist Working-Class Cultural Critical Perspectives*. Boulder, Colo.: Westview Press, 2000.

Mandela, Tambo, and the African National Congress: The Struggle Against Apartheid, 1948–1990, edited by Sheridan Johns and R Hunt Davis, Jr. New York: Oxford University Press, 1991.

Pomeroy, William J. *Apartheid, Imperialism, and African Freedom*. New York: International Publishers, 1986.

Price, Robert M. *The Apartheid State in Crisis. Political Transformation in South Africa: 1975–1990*. New York: Oxford University Press, 1991.

Afghan Women Approach a Voting Station

Photograph

By: Teru Kuwayama

Date: 2004

Source: "Afghan Women Approach a Voting Station." © Teru Kuwayama/Corbis. 2004.

About the Photographer: Teru Kuwayama is a Brooklyn-based photographer best known for his work in Asia and the Middle East. He is a contributor to such publications as *Time*, *National Geographic*, *Life*, *Newsweek*, *Outside*, and *Fortune*.

INTRODUCTION

In October 2001, the United States invaded Afghanistan and overthrew its government, which had since 1996 been run by an ultra-conservative Islamist political party called the Taliban. The Taliban had refused to extradite members of the terrorist organization Al Qaeda after the Sep. 11, 2001 attacks on the United States. The U.S. installed a "transitional government" which held Afghanistan's first multi-party elections in twenty years in October 2004, as required by the Afghan Bonn Agreement (December 5, 2001).

Women's rights had been severely curtailed under the Taliban; news coverage worldwide emphasized that women would participate, both as voters

PRIMARY SOURCE

Afghan Women Approach a Voting Station: A group of Afghan women approach a voting station at the Idgah Mosque in Kabul, Afghanistan, on October 9, 2004. © TERU KUWAYAMA/CORBIS.

and as one out of the fifteen presidential candidates. This picture shows women wearing burkas, the head-to-toe body covering that conservative Muslims consider mandatory for women and which was legally required under the Taliban, approaching voting stations in the large Idgah mosque complex in Afghanistan's capital city, Kabul. Idgah mosque, with ten polling stations, was one of Kabul's largest voting centers. Afghan soldiers stood by, reflecting the U.S. State Department's view that "Special steps must be taken to assist women seeking to vote, as cultural custom and security concerns may inhibit many women from leaving their homes to go to the polling places." Separate voting stations were set aside for women.

The 2004 election faced many obstacles. First, the hold of the official government of Afghanistan was (and, as of 2006, remained) tenuous or nonexistent over most of the country's area: various private warlords and the Taliban (fighting as a guerilla force)

were competing for control of the countryside. Further, Afghanistan is a poor country where no national census has ever been taken. Women had never been entitled to vote in Afghanistan, and none were registered to vote. In preparation for the 2004 vote, the United Nations fielded 305 voter registration teams of six men and six women each (all Afghans). About 10.5 million Afghans registered to vote before the 2004 elections, forty-one percent of them women. In the southern provinces of the country, where the Taliban remained strong, figures for registration of women were much lower: in Uruzgan only nine percent, in Zabul ten percent, in Helmand sixteen percent. Turnout for registered voters was seventy-five percent—significantly higher than the 55.3 percent turnout seen in the 2004 U.S. presidential election.

The voter registration process was probably riddled with fraud. Voter registration significantly exceeded pre-election U.N. estimates of the entire population of eligible Afghan voters. As the BBC noted at the time, "the 10m-plus figure for registered voters can be accurate if every single male in the country has registered—at least once"—which, in a country as poor and disorganized as Afghanistan, was essentially impossible. Because of voter registration inflation, the percentage of women voting was probably even less than the official figure of forty-one percent.

PRIMARY SOURCE

AFGHAN WOMEN APPROACH A VOTING STATION
See primary source image.

SIGNIFICANCE

Hamid Karzai (1957–) appeared to have won the election. However, his victory was immediately challenged by almost all of his rivals, who claimed that massive fraud had invalidated the election. In particular, a supposedly indelible ink used to mark voters' hands to prevent multiple voting proved to be washable. A U.N-Afghan Joint Electoral Commission investigated the charges and announced on Nov. 1, 2004 that despite some voting irregularities, Karzai was the winner with 55.4 percent of the vote.

A round of national-parliamentary and provincial-government elections was held in 2005. However, severe problems continued to plague the process. Forty-five candidates were barred by the U.N.-Afghan Joint Electoral Management body on the grounds that they maintained links to armed militias or held local government jobs (against election rules). However, numerous powerful warlords with well-established records of human rights abuses were not disqualified. To add to the confusion, all barred candidates still appeared on the ballots, which had already been printed, causing many voters to waste their votes. The Taliban threatened attacks and killed sixteen Afghans for having voter registration cards in Uruzgan province. Voter participation declined by over twenty percent from the 2004 elections. One polling station supervisor said that voters may have "lost all faith in politicians and leaders" due to the slow pace of reconstruction.

Also, electoral fraud remained a problem. The chief of the UN-Afghan Joint Election Management

Board said that ballot boxes from four percent of the 26,000 polling stations had been set aside for investigation of fraud.

The status of women has been a particular issue in post-Taliban Afghanistan. Under the Taliban, the situation of women was harsh. Religious police beat women in the streets for failing to dress properly and for other violations. Women were virtually excluded from all education and employment. According to the nongovernmental organization Human Rights Watch, although conditions for women in Afghanistan are better today than under the Taliban, "Afghan women continue to suffer some of the worst levels of poor health, illiteracy, and poverty in the world." One in six Afghan women dies in childbirth; eighty-six percent of women over age fifteen are illiterate. Again, according to Human Rights Watch, "Violence against women, forced marriage, and early marriage remain endemic problems in Afghanistan." Curiously, because the Afghan constitution guarantees a minimum of twenty-five percent of the seats National Assembly, women have more representation at the national level in Afghanistan than in the United States, where in 2006, only fourteen percent of U.S. Senators and fifteen percent of U.S. Representatives were women. However, female candidates in Afghanistan face routine threats of violence and harassment from warlords, the Taliban, government officials, and relatives.

FURTHER RESOURCES

Periodicals

Gall, Carlotta. "Monitors Find Significant Fraud in Afghan Elections." The *New York Times*. (October 3, 2005).

Web sites

Huckerby, Martin. *BBC News*. "Afghan Voting Number Puzzle." <http://news.bbc.co.uk/2/hi/south_asia/3600742.stm> (accessed April 30, 2006).

Human Rights Watch. "Campaigning Against Fear: Women's Participation in Afghanistan's 2005." <http://hrw.org/backgrounder/wrd/afghanistan0805/index.htm> (accessed April 30, 2006).

Soutik, Biswas. *BBC News*. "Puzzle of the Stay-Away Voters." <http://news.bbc.co.uk/1/hi/world/south_asia/4258514.stm> (accessed April 30, 2006).

United States State Department. "Afghanistan Elections 2004: Women's Participation." <http://www.state.gov/g/wi/rls/24792.htm> (accessed April 30, 2006).

Borders, Sovereignty and Culture

Conflicts often arise over national borders or issues of sovereignty. "To Every Englishman in India" highlights India's struggle for political sovereignty. Another article features the on-going struggle between Israel and its neighbors over borders and sovereignty, an issue complicated by endemic violence. Far from simple territorial wars, these brutal disputes fueled by ethnic and religious tension can devlove into warfare on civilians, mass killings, and genocidal "ethnic cleansing." After the fall of Yugoslavia, the Balkans descended into prolonged war as rival groups fought to establish fledgling nations. "A Pictorial Guide to Hell" describes the experiences of a photojournalist during the Balkan Wars.

Conflict also arises within national borders. There is a long-standing struggle between many national governments and indigenous populations. Sometimes, indigenous populations exist within one nation's borders, but wish for greater freedom to practice and protect indigenous ways of life. In other instances, such as Mayan populations in Central America, national borders transect traditional indigenous lands, possibly fragmenting indigenous populations and jeopardizing uniform preservation of indigenous culture. The article on the Framework Convention for the Protection of National Minorities discusses the ongoing effort of the international community to balance the interests of national governments and minority populations while addressing these issues.

Minority populations, whether indigenous or immigrant, are too often victims of human rights abuses. Australia's Aborigine (Indigenous Australian) population endured a two-century brutal campaign of cultural genocide. The Australian government has taken great strides in the past four decades to protect Aboriginal culture and atone for former anti-indigenous policies. "Millicent," part of an oral history project for Indigenous Australians, recounts a personal story of forced removal of Aborigine children. The American Indian and early Chinese immigrant experience in the United States is similarly discussed in this chapter.

Human rights issues rooted in religion are included in this chapter. The United Nations Declaration on Human rights advocates freedom of religion and promotes religious tolerance. One article profiles significant barriers to religious freedom. Others discuss state limitations on religious expression (see, "Chriac Calls for Ban on Headscarves). The editors recognize that religion is a significant aspect of many national, ethnic, and cultural identities. However, this chapter also profiles instances where a significant portion of the international community condemned a practice rooted in ethnic tradition or religious law. Caste systems, honor killings, child marriage, and forced rape are some of the examples of such human rights abuses; all are profiled in this chapter.

Finally, this chapter includes two entries on the impact of the Internet; the Internet is reshaping cultures and redefining borders. Information can travel the world in seconds, a threatening prospect to some regimes. The medium raises new questions about censorship and the free exchange of information.

Chinese Exclusion Act (1882)

Legislation

By: United States Congress

Date: May 6, 1882

Source: "Chinese Exclusion Act." United States Congress, May 6, 1882.

About the Author: The Forty-seventh United States Congress passed the Chinese Exclusion Act in 1882; ten years later the Fifty-second Congress renewed the act's provisions and strengthened Chinese immigration laws with the Geary Act.

INTRODUCTION

The California Gold Rush in the late 1840s sparked the first major wave of Chinese immigration to the United States. U.S.-Chinese trade relations had been in place since 1784, and Chinese immigrants had been a part of American immigration for decades, though their numbers had been very small. News of California gold reached China just as China's empire experienced economic hardship; by 1851, more than 25,000 Chinese had emigrated to the west coast of the United States.

Chinese immigrants initially came as gold prospectors but many settled into mine work, laundry services, and as peddlers of household or mining goods. Discrimination and outright resentment of the Chinese ran high among native prospectors; mine owners often exploited Chinese workers by paying low wages, fellow prospectors forced Chinese prospectors to work depleted mines, and violence against Chinese immigrants was common.

In the 1850s, many Chinese immigrants began to work on railroad construction; in the 1860s, the Central Pacific Railroad specifically recruited Chinese workers for jobs on the Transcontinental Railroad. Anti-Chinese sentiment ran high after the Civil War, when former slaves, poor southerners, and migrating eastern immigrants from countries such as Ireland and Russia moved west in search of opportunity. Viewing the Chinese immigrants as competition for jobs, nativist sentiment led to scapegoating and increased discrimination against the Chinese. In 1871, an anti-Chinese riot led by white men in Los Angeles led to the killings of more than twenty Chinese immigrants.

An 1876 report on Chinese immigration from the California State Senate, titled "An Address to the People of the United States upon the Evils of Chinese Immigration," increased federal interest in Chinese immigration. An 1877 report from the Joint Special Committee to Investigate Chinese Immigration claimed that Chinese immigrants took jobs away from white immigrants, were unable to understand democracy as they came from "despotic" government systems, refused to learn English, and would harm the republican ideals of the United States by their presence in large numbers on the west coast.

In 1882, the forty-seventh Congress passed the Chinese Exclusion Act, and President Chester A. Arthur signed the act, with strong public, labor union, and government support.

PRIMARY SOURCE

CHINESE EXCLUSION ACT

An Act to execute certain treaty stipulations relating to Chinese

Whereas in the opinion of the Government of the United States the coming of Chinese laborers to this country endangers the good order of certain localities within the territory thereof: Therefore,

Be it enacted by the Senate and House of Representatives of the United States of America in Congress assembled, That from and after the expiration of ninety days next after the passage of this act, and until the expiration of ten years next after the passage of this act, the coming of Chinese laborers to the United States be, and the same is hereby, suspended; and during such suspension it shall not be lawful for any Chinese laborer to come, or having so come after the expiration of said ninety days to remain within the United States.

SEC. 2. That the master of any vessel who shall knowingly bring within the United States on such vessel, and land or permit to be landed, any Chinese laborer, from any foreign port or place, shall be deemed guilty of a misdemeanor, and on conviction thereof shall be punished by a fine of not more than five hundred dollars for each and every such Chinese laborer so brought, and may be also imprisoned for a term not exceeding one year.

SEC. 3. That the two foregoing sections shall not apply to Chinese laborers who were in the United States on the seventeenth day of November, eighteen hundred and eighty, or who shall have come into the same before the expiration of ninety days next after the passage of this act, and who shall produce to such master before going on board such vessel, and shall produce to the collector of the port in the United States at which such vessel shall arrive, the evidence hereinafter

An editorial cartoon about the Chinese Exclusion Act of 1882. Supporters of the bill are shown in stylized form trying to pull a stereotyped Chinese man off of a branch labelled "Freedom to All." The tiger represents the Democrat's Tammany "Tigers" political machine. The elephant is a traditional symbol of the Republican Party. © HULTON GETTY/LIAISON AGENCY. REPRODUCED BY PERMISSION.

in this act required of his being one of the laborers in this section mentioned; nor shall the two foregoing sections apply to the case of any master whose vessel, being bound to a port not within the United States, shall come within the jurisdiction of the United States by reason of being in distress or in stress of weather, or touching at any port of the United States on its voyage to any foreign port or place: Provided, That all Chinese laborers brought on such vessel shall depart with the vessel on leaving port.

SEC. 4. That for the purpose of properly identifying Chinese laborers who were in the United States on the seventeenth day of November eighteen hundred and eighty, or who shall have come into the same before the expiration of ninety days next after the passage of this act, and in order to furnish them with the proper evidence of their right to go from and come to the United States of their free will and accord, as provided by the treaty between the United States and China dated November seventeenth, eighteen hundred and eighty, the collector of customs of the district from which any such Chinese laborer shall depart from the United States shall, in person or by deputy, go on board each vessel having on board any such Chinese laborers and cleared or about to sail from his district for a foreign port, and on such vessel make a list of all such Chinese laborers, which shall be entered in registry-books to be kept for that purpose, in which shall be stated the name, age, occupation, last place of residence, physical marks of peculiarities, and all facts necessary for the identification of each of such Chinese laborers, which books shall be safely kept in the custom-house; and every such Chinese laborer so departing from the United States shall be entitled to, and shall receive, free of any charge or cost upon application therefor, from the collector or his deputy, at the time such list is taken, a certificate, signed by the collector or his deputy and attested by his seal of office, in such form as the Secretary of the Treasury shall prescribe, which certificate shall contain a statement of the name, age, occupation, last place of residence, personal description, and facts of identification of the Chinese laborer to whom the certificate is issued, corresponding with the said list and registry in all particulars. In case any Chinese laborer after having received such certificate shall leave such vessel before her departure he shall deliver his certificate to the master of the vessel, and if such Chinese laborer shall fail to return to such vessel before her

departure from port the certificate shall be delivered by the master to the collector of customs for cancellation. The certificate herein provided for shall entitle the Chinese laborer to whom the same is issued to return to and re-enter the United States upon producing and delivering the same to the collector of customs of the district at which such Chinese laborer shall seek to re-enter; and upon delivery of such certificate by such Chinese laborer to the collector of customs at the time of re-entry in the United States said collector shall cause the same to be filed in the custom-house anti duly canceled.

SEC. 5. That any Chinese laborer mentioned in section four of this act being in the United States, and desiring to depart from the United States by land, shall have the right to demand and receive, free of charge or cost, a certificate of identification similar to that provided for in section four of this act to be issued to such Chinese laborers as may desire to leave the United States by water; and it is hereby made the duty of the collector of customs of the district next adjoining the foreign country to which said Chinese laborer desires to go to issue such certificate, free of charge or cost, upon application by such Chinese laborer, and to enter the same upon registry-books to be kept by him for the purpose, as provided for in section four of this act.

SEC. 6. That in order to the faithful execution of articles one and two of the treaty in this act before mentioned, every Chinese person other than a laborer who may be entitled by said treaty and this act to come within the United States, and who shall be about to come to the United States, shall be identified as so entitled by the Chinese Government in each case, such identity to be evidenced by a certificate issued under the authority of said government, which certificate shall be in the English language or (if not in the English language) accompanied by a translation into English, stating such right to come, and which certificate shall state the name, title or official rank, if any, the age, height, and all physical peculiarities, former and present occupation or profession, and place of residence in China of the person to whom the certificate is issued and that such person is entitled, conformably to the treaty in this act mentioned to come within the United States. Such certificate shall be prima-facie evidence of the fact set forth therein, and shall be produced to the collector of customs, or his deputy, of the port in the district in the United States at which the person named therein shall arrive.

SEC. 7. That any person who shall knowingly and falsely alter or substitute any name for the name written in such certificate or forge any such certificate, or knowingly utter any forged or fraudulent certificate, or falsely personate any person named in any such certificate, shall be deemed guilty of a misdemeanor; and upon conviction thereof shall be fined in a sum not exceeding one thousand dollars, and imprisoned in a penitentiary for a term of not more than five years.

SEC. 8. That the master of any vessel arriving in the United States from any foreign port or place shall, at the same time he delivers a manifest of the cargo, and if there be no cargo, then at the time of making a report of the entry of the vessel pursuant to law, in addition to the other matter required to be reported, and before landing, or permitting to land, any Chinese passengers, deliver and report to the collector of customs of the district in which such vessels shall have arrived a separate list of all Chinese passengers taken on board his vessel at any foreign port or place, and all such passengers on board the vessel at that time. Such list shall show the names of such passengers (and if accredited officers of the Chinese Government traveling on the business of that government, or their servants, with a note of such facts), and the names and other particulars, as shown by their respective certificates; and such list shall be sworn to by the master in the manner required by law in relation to the manifest of the cargo. Any willful refusal or neglect of any such master to comply with the provisions of this section shall incur the same penalties and forfeiture as are provided for a refusal or neglect to report and deliver a manifest of the cargo.

SEC. 9. That before any Chinese passengers are landed from any such line vessel, the collector, or his deputy, shall proceed to examine such passenger, comparing the certificate with the list and with the passengers; and no passenger shall be allowed to land in the United States from such vessel in violation of law.

SEC. 10. That every vessel whose master shall knowingly violate any of the provisions of this act shall be deemed forfeited to the United States, and shall be liable to seizure and condemnation in any district of the United States into which such vessel may enter or in which she may be found.

SEC. 11. That any person who shall knowingly bring into or cause to be brought into the United States by land, or who shall knowingly aid or abet the same, or aid or abet the landing in the United States from any vessel of any Chinese person not lawfully entitled to enter the United States, shall be deemed guilty of a misdemeanor, and shall, on conviction thereof, be fined in a sum not exceeding one thousand dollars, and imprisoned for a term not exceeding one year.

SEC. 12. That no Chinese person shall be permitted to enter the United States by land without producing to the proper officer of customs the certificate in this act required of Chinese persons seeking to land from a vessel. And any Chinese person found unlawfully within the United States shall be caused to be removed therefrom to the country from whence he came, by direction of the President of the United States, and at the cost of the United States, after being brought before some justice, judge, or commissioner of a court of the United States and found to be one not lawfully entitled to be or remain in the United States.

SEC. 13. That this act shall not apply to diplomatic and other officers of the Chinese Government traveling upon the business of that government, whose credentials shall be taken as equivalent to the certificate in this act mentioned, and shall exempt them and their body and household servants from the provisions of this act as to other Chinese persons.

SEC. 14. That hereafter no State court or court of the United States shall admit Chinese to citizenship; and all laws in conflict with this act are hereby repealed.

SEC. 15. That the words "Chinese laborers," wherever used in this act shall be construed to mean both skilled and unskilled laborers and Chinese employed in mining.

Approved, May 6, 1882.

SIGNIFICANCE

The Chinese Exclusion Act stopped all Chinese immigration into the United States for ten years, with exceptions for teachers, students, merchants, and travelers. The Act prevented Chinese immigrants from becoming naturalized citizens. This was the first piece of immigration legislation in the United States that targeted one specific ethnic group or nationality.

Ten years later, Congress renewed the act and passed the Act to Prohibit the Coming of Chinese Persons into the United States in May 1892. Commonly known as the Geary Act, named after Congressman Thomas J. Geary of California, the 1892 act increased restrictions on Chinese immigrants. All Chinese immigrants were required under the Geary Act to carry a certificate proving residence and legal status in the United States; no other immigrants were required to carry such documentation. Failure to produce such documentation on demand from law enforcement officers could lead to deportation or forced hard labor sentences.

In addition, the Geary Act denied Chinese immigrants the right to post bail and to appear as witnesses in court. The Geary Act extended the Chinese Exclusion Act for ten years; by 1902 it was renewed once more with no expiration date.

Anti-Chinese sentiment decreased over time as development, urbanization, and expansion on the west coast lessened economic competition. By the end of World War I, immigration was a powerful force in shaping the United States demographically and culturally, though the Chinese Exclusion Act remained in place with Chinese immigrants as the sole object of such targeted legislation. The 1943 Magnuson Act repealed the Chinese Exclusion Act, though a quota of 105 Chinese immigrants per year was set. In 1945, more than six thousand Chinese women were permitted to enter the United States as part of the War Brides Act. Chinese immigrants did not receive equal legal treatment until the Immigration Act of 1965, which set a limit of 170,000 immigrants per year, with no more than 20,000 immigrants from any one country.

FURTHER RESOURCES

Books

Claiming America: Constructing Chinese Identities During the Exclusion Era, edited by K. Scott Wong and Sucheng Chan. Philadelphia: Temple University Press, 1998.

Gyory, Andrew. *Closing the Gate: Race, Politics, and the Chinese Exclusion Act*. Chapel Hill, N.C.: University of North Carolina Press, 1998.

Lee, Erika. *At America's Gates: Chinese Immigration During the Exclusion Era, 1882–1943*. Chapel Hill, N.C.: University of North Carolina Press, 2003.

Web sites

National Archives and Records Administration. "Chinese Immigration and the Chinese in the United States." <http://www.archives.gov/locations/finding-aids/chinese-immigration.html> (accessed April 30, 2006).

Dawes Severalty Act 1887

Legislation

By: Henry Dawes

Date: February 8, 1887

Source: United States Congress. "Dawes Severalty Act of 1887." *United States Statutes at Large* 24 (1887): 388–391.

About the Author: As a Congressman from Massachusetts, Henry Dawes sponsored the General Allotment Act, also named the Dawes Severalty Act. Dawes was a proponent of property ownership as a means toward the assimilation of Native Americans into U.S. society.

INTRODUCTION

Prior to 1870, the United States government negotiated treaties with the Native American tribes as sovereign nations. Many of these treaties resulted in a reservation system managed by the Bureau of Indian Affairs. However, as the century came to a close, the handling of Indian affairs began to change. In 1881, Helen Hunt Jackson's book, "A Century of Dishonor" alleged the unfair treatment of Native Americans by the American government. As a result, groups supporting the rights of Native Americans emerged and a movement to help make Native Americans become U.S. citizens began to gain momentum. Other factors created the political climate needed to pass the Dawes Severalty Act. Many tribes, including the Choctaw and Chickasaw, allied with the Confederacy during the American Civil War. As a result, many politicians sought retribution against these tribes. In addition, westward expansion brought on by railroad development, timber companies, and homesteaders pressured the government to reassess its relationship with Native Americans.

The Dawes Severalty Act passed on February 8, 1887 and was billed as a humanitarian reform with the intent to help Native Americans achieve U.S. citizenship. The Act divided tribal property into 160-acre (65-hectare) and 180-acre (73-hectare) land grants that were distributed to members of the tribe. After twenty-five years of cultivating the land as responsible farmers and a certification of competence, the Native Americans would receive full ownership of the land.

PRIMARY SOURCE

An Act to Provide for the Allotment of Lands in Severalty to Indians on the Various Reservations, and to Extend the Protection of the Laws of the United States and the Territories over the Indians, and for Other Purposes.

Be it enacted by the Senate and House of Representatives of the United States of America in Congress assembled, That in all cases where any tribe or band of Indians has been, or shall hereafter be, located upon any reservation created for their use, either by treaty stipulation or by virtue of an act of Congress or executive order setting apart the same for their use, the President of the United States be, and he hereby is, authorized, whenever in his opinion any reservation or any part thereof of such Indians is advantageous for agricultural and grazing purposes, to cause said reservation, or any part thereof, to be surveyed, or resurveyed if necessary, and to allot the lands in said reservation in severalty to any Indian located thereon in quantities as follows:

To each head of a family, one-quarter of a section;
To each single person over eighteen years of age, one-eighth of a section;
To each orphan child under eighteen years of age, one-eighth of a section; and
To each other single person under eighteen years now living, or who may be born prior to the date of the order of the President directing an allotment of the lands embraced in any reservation, one-sixteenth of a section:

Provided, That in case there is not sufficient land in any of said reservations to allot lands to each individual of the classes above named in quantities as above provided, the lands embraced in such reservation or reservations shall be allotted to each individual of each of said classes pro rata in accordance with the provisions of this act: And provided further, That where the treaty or act of Congress setting apart such reservation provides the allotment of lands in severalty in quantities in excess of those herein provided, the President, in making allotments upon such reservation, shall allot the lands to each individual Indian belonging thereon in quantity as specified in such treaty or act: And provided further, That when the lands allotted are only valuable for grazing purposes, an additional allotment of such grazng lands, in quantities as above provided, shall be made to each individual.

SEC. 2. That all allotments set apart under the provisions of this act shall be selected by the Indians, heads of families selecting for their minor children, and the agents shall select for each orphan child, and in such manner as to embrace the improvements of the Indians making the selection. Where the improvements of two or more Indians have been made on the same legal subdivision of land, unless they shall otherwise agree, a provisional line may be run dividing said lands between them, and the amount to which each is entitled shall be equalized in the assignment of the remainder of the land to which they are entitled under his act: Provided, That if any one entitled to an allotment shall fail to make a selection within four years after the President shall direct that allotments may be made on a particular reservation, the Secretary of the

Interior may direct the agent of such tribe or band, if such there be, and if there be no agent, then a special agent appointed for that purpose, to make a selection for such Indian, which selection shall be allotted as in cases where selections are made by the Indians, and patents shall issue in like manner.

SEC. 3. That the allotments provided for in this act shall be made by special agents appointed by the President for such purpose, and the agents in charge of the respective reservations on which the allotments are directed to be made, under such rules and regulations as the Secretary of the Interior may from time to time prescribe, and shall be certified by such agents to the Commissioner of Indian Affairs, in duplicate, one copy to be retained in the Indian Office and the other to be transmitted to the Secretary of the Interior for his action, and to be deposited in the General Land Office.

SEC. 4. That where any Indian not residing upon a reservation, or for whose tribe no reservation has been provided by treaty, act of Congress, or executive order, shall make settlement upon any surveyed or unsurveyed lands of the United States not otherwise appropriated, he or she shall be entitled, upon application to the local land-office for the district in which the lands are located, to have the same allotted to him or her, and to his or her children, in quantities and manner as provided in this act for Indians residing upon reservations; and when such settlement is made upon unsurveyed lands, the grant to such Indians shall be adjusted upon the survey of the lands so as to conform thereto; and patents shall be issued to them for such lands in the manner and with the restrictions as herein provided. And the fees to which the officers of such local land-office would have been entitled had such lands been entered under the general laws for the disposition of the public lands shall be paid to them, from any moneys in the Treasury of the United States not otherwise appropriated, upon a statement of an account in their behalf for such fees by the Commissioner of the General Land Office, and a certification of such account to the Secretary of the Treasury by the Secretary of the Interior.

SEC. 5. That upon the approval of the allotments provided for in this act by the Secretary of the Interior, he shall cause patents to issue therefore in the name of the allottees, which patents shall be of the legal effect, and declare that the United States does and will hold the land thus allotted, for the period of twenty-five years, in trust for the sole use and benefit of the Indian to whom such allotment shall have been made, or, in case of his decease, of his heirs according to the laws of the State or Territory where such land is located, and that at the expiration of said period the United States will convey the same by patent to said Indian, or his heirs as aforesaid, in fee, discharged of said trust and free of all charge or incumbrance whatsoever: Provided, That the President of the United States may in any case in his discretion extend the period. And if any conveyance shall be made of the lands set apart and allotted as herein provided, or any contract made touching the same, before the expiration of the time above mentioned, such conveyance or contract shall be absolutely null and void: Provided, That the law of descent and partition in force in the State or Territory where such lands are situate shall apply thereto after patents therefore have been executed and delivered, except as herein otherwise provided; and the laws of the State of Kansas regulating the descent and partition of real estate shall, so far as practicable, apply to all lands in the Indian Territory which may be allotted in severalty under the provisions of this act: And provided further, That at any time after lands have been allotted to all the Indians of any tribe as herein provided, or sooner if in the opinion of the President it shall be for the best interests of said tribe, it shall be lawful for the Secretary of the Interior to negotiate with such Indian tribe for the purchase and release by said tribe, in conformity with the treaty or statute under which such reservation is held, of such portions of its reservation not allotted as such tribe shall, from time to time, consent to sell, on such terms and conditions as shall be considered just and equitable between the United States and said tribe of Indians, which purchase shall not be complete until ratified by Congress, and the form and manner of executing such release prescribed by Congress: Provided however, That all lands adapted to agriculture, with or without irrigation so sold or released to the United States by any Indian tribe shall be held by the United States for the sole purpose of securing homes to actual settlers and shall be disposed of by the United States to actual and bona fide settlers only tracts not exceeding one hundred and sixty acres to any one person, on such terms as Congress shall prescribe, subject to grants which Congress may make in aid of education: And provided further, That no patents shall issue therefor except to the person so taking the same as and homestead, or his heirs, and

after the expiration of five years occupancy thereof as such homestead; and any conveyance of said lands taken as a homestead, or any contract touching the same, or lieu thereon, created prior to the date of such patent, shall be null and void. And the sums agreed to be paid by the United States as purchase money for any portion of any such reservation shall be held in the Treasury of the United States for the sole use of the tribe or tribes Indians; to whom such reservations belonged; and the same, with interest thereon at three per cent per annum, shall be at all times subject to appropriation by Congress for the education and civilization of such tribe or tribes of Indians or the members thereof. The patents aforesaid shall be recorded in the General Land Office, and afterward delivered, free of charge, to the allottee entitled thereto. And if any religious society or other organization is now occupying any of the public lands to which this act is applicable, for religious or educational work among the Indians, the Secretary of the Interior is hereby authorized to confirm such occupation to such society or organization, in quantity not exceeding one hundred and sixty acres in any one tract, so long as the same shall be so occupied, on such terms as he shall deem just; but nothing herein contained shall change or alter any claim of such society for religious or educational purposes heretofore granted by law. And hereafter in the employment of Indian police, or any other employees in the public service among any of the Indian tribes or bands affected by this act, and where Indians can perform the duties required, those Indians who have availed themselves of the provisions of this act and become citizens of the United States shall be preferred.

SEC. 6. That upon the completion of said allotments and the patenting of the lands to said allottees, each and every number of the respective bands or tribes of Indians to whom allotments have been made shall have the benefit of and be subject to the laws, both civil and criminal, of the State or Territory in which they may reside; and no Territory shall pass or enforce any law denying any such Indian within its jurisdiction the equal protection of the law. And every Indian born within the territorial limits of the United States to whom allotments shall have been made under the provisions of this act, or under any law or treaty, and every Indian born within the territorial limits of the United States who has voluntarily taken up, within said limits, his residence separate and apart from any tribe of

Indians therein, and has adopted the habits of civilized life, is hereby declared to be a citizen of the United States, and is entitled to all the rights, privileges, and immunities of such citizens, whether said Indian has been or not, by birth or otherwise, a member of any tribe of Indians within the territorial limits of the United States without in any manner affecting the right of any such Indian to tribal or other property.

SEC. 7. That in cases where the use of water for irrigation is necessary to render the lands within any Indian reservation available for agricultural purposes, the Secretary of the Interior be, and he is hereby, authorized to prescribe such rules and regulations as he may deem necessary to secure a just and equal distribution thereof among the Indians residing upon any such reservation; and no other appropriation or grant of water by any riparian proprietor shall permitted to the damage of any other riparian proprietor.

SEC. 8. That the provisions of this act shall not extend to the territory occupied by the Cherokees, Creeks, Choctaws, Chickasaws, Seminoles, and Osage, Miamies and Peorias, and Sacs and Foxes, in the Indian Territory, nor to any of the reservations of the Seneca Nation of New York Indians in the State of New York, nor to that strip of territory in the State of Nebraska adjoining the Sioux Nation on the south added by executive order.

SEC. 9. That for the purpose of making the surveys and resurveys mentioned in section two of this act, there be, and hereby is, appropriated, out of any moneys in the Treasury not otherwise appropriated, the sum of one hundred thousand dollars, to be repaid proportionately out of the proceeds of the sales of such land as may be acquired from the Indians under the provisions of this act.

SEC. 10. That nothing in this act contained shall be so construed to affect the right and power of Congress to grant the right of way through any lands granted to an Indian, or a tribe of Indians, for railroads or other highways, or telegraph lines, for the public use, or condemn such lands to public uses, upon making just compensation.

SEC. 11. That nothing in this act shall be so construed as to prevent the removal of the Southern Ute Indians from their present reservation in Southwestern Colorado to a new reservation by and with consent of a majority of the adult male members of said tribe.

SIGNIFICANCE

Proponents of the Dawes Severalty Act asserted that property ownership was the first step in assimilating Native Americans into U.S. society. The Act, however, failed to provide such assimilation, took land out of tribal control, and marked the shift in policy of treating Native Americans as sovereign peoples to wards of the government. Prior to the Act, lands within reservations were owned by tribes as set out in treaties or executive orders. These reservations continued the cultural view of collective ownership of the land. Reformers asserted that in order to integrate tribe members into society, the collectivism should be replaced with private land ownership. As a result, the Act provided for the loss of legal standings of tribes in exchange for the land being divided among its members. Native Americans were taught English and discouraged from speaking their tribal languages. They were expected to cut their hair and also adopt Christianity. This treatment of Native Americans as wards of the states failed to bring about the desired assimilation into U.S. society.

The Dawes Severalty Act also removed land from control of Native Americans. By 1934, when the Act was superseded by the Indian Reorganization Act, two-thirds of reservation lands had been removed from tribal control. In 1887, tribes owned 138 million acres (56 million hectares) of land. By 1900 that amount had been reduced to 78 million acres (31.5 million hectares). Lands not allocated to tribe members were sold to homesteaders and other western expansionists. This resulted in a "checkerboard" of land ownership, meaning that the title to land is held by an assortment of entities, such as an individual Native American, the tribe, the state, the county, the federal government, or even a non-native group.

The Act disregarded previous treaties established between the U.S. government and the various tribes. This marked a shift in handling relations with Native Americans as sovereign people to ward of the U.S. government. The Act was intended to help assimilate the tribes into U.S. society through a renunciation of traditional nomadic culture and the adoption of private land ownership and successful farming. These provisions were intended to "civilize" Native Americans, making them more likely candidates for citizenship.

The Act was terminated on June 18, 1934, when congress passed the Indian Reorganization Act. This act restored ownership to tribes of any land not allocated or sold under the Dawes Severalty Act. The Indian Reorganization Act was intended to conserve and develop tribal lands, create private enterprise and credit systems, and to grant home rule to tribes.

Native American leader Sitting Bull sits outside his tepee with his wife, children, and a visitor, while being held as a prisoner of war at Fort Randall in present day South Dakota, 1883. THE LIBRARY OF CONGRESS.

The Dawes Severalty Act continues to affect the Native American community. In 1996, Eloise Cobell filed a class action lawsuit on behalf of 280,000 Native Americans. The suit, against the Bureau of Indian Affairs, claims that billions of dollars that were held in trust were either lost due to inaccurate or missing records or were pilfered by the U.S. government. In addition, the Act has created generational fractionation of the allotments, particularly in cases of deaths without a will.

FURTHER RESOURCES

Periodicals

Kilpinen, Jon T. "The Supreme Court's Role in Choctaw and Chickasaw Dispossession." *The Geographical Review* (October 1, 2004).

Web sites

Indian Land Working Group. "Taking a Stand on Indian Land." <http://www.ilwg.net/impact.htm> (accessed May 14, 2006).

To Every Englishman in India

Speech

By: Mohandas Karamchand Gandhi

Date: October 20, 1920

Source: Mahatma Gandhi. *Speeches and Writings of Mahatma Gandhi.* Madras: G. A. Natesan & Co., 1933.

About the Author: Mohandas Karamchand Gandhi was born on October 2, 1869, in the commercial town of Porbander in Gujarat, India. He is also popularly known as *Mahatma,* meaning "Great Soul" Gandhi and *Bapu,* or "Father." A mediocre student during his primary school days, Gandhi later studied law in England and qualified to be a barrister. He spent most of his early years as a professional barrister in South Africa. On his return to India, Mahatma Gandhi commenced his non-violent struggle against British rule with the Non-Cooperation movement in 1920. This was followed by numerous non-violent movements that were instrumental in obtaining independence for India from British rule. On January 30, 1948, Mahatma Gandhi was on his way to a prayer meeting in New Delhi when he was assassinated by Hindu extremist Nathuram Godse.

INTRODUCTION

The East India Company, established in 1600 primarily as a trading enterprise, gradually transformed itself into a ruling enterprise and colonized the Indian subcontinent. By 1756, the company had attained colonial rule in most parts of India. More than a century later, in 1864, India became a formal colony under the British rule.

The British pursued various policies exploiting the subcontinent's natural resources such as cotton, indigo, spices, and tea to sustain Britain's economy. Many commercial policies favored England, creating a trade imbalance with India.

Formed in 1885, the Indian National Congress (INC) proposed economic reforms and wanted a larger role in the making of British policy for India. Though initially not opposed to the idea of British Governance of India, it soon actively became the forefront of the non-violent freedom struggle. Under the leadership and guidance of Mahatma Gandhi, Jawaharlal Nehru (1889–1964), Vallabhbhai Patel (1875–1950), and others, the INC organized various movements based on the principles of non-violence to oppose British policies that were deemed discriminatory.

Gandhi, during his early years, practiced law in South Africa—a country then ruled by the United Kingdom—for over twenty years. After being treated unequally on several occasions, Gandhi started playing an active role in the civil rights movement in South Africa. Soon, he began to perfect a policy of passive disobedience and non-violent resistance against the British Government in South Africa. He called his pursuit of political reform and non-violent resistance, *Satyagraha,* a Sanskrit word that means "the quest for truth".

On his return to India, the unequal status of Indians and policies encouraging Hindu-Muslim divide prompted Gandhi to initiate a nationwide non-cooperation movement against the British Empire. Launched in 1920, the non-cooperation movement demonstrated to Britain that it was futile to rule a society where a collective unwillingness to be ruled existed.

The primary source is the transcript of an open letter "To Every English Man in India" published on October 20, 1920, in *Young India,* a weekly magazine started by Mahatma Gandhi. A year later, Gandhi wrote another open letter in *Young India.* Marking the commencement of the non-cooperation movement, through these letters, Gandhi sought to reach out to the English people themselves. The purpose of the letter was to establish a common bonding between the English and the Indians by addressing key problems and unfair policies imposed by the British rule. The letter is excerpted here.

Mahatma Ghandi enjoys a laugh with his two granddaughters Ava and Manu at Birla House in New Delhi in 1947. © BETTMANN/CORBIS.

■ **PRIMARY SOURCE**

Dear Friend,—I wish that every Englishman will see this appeal and give thoughtful attention to it.

Let me introduce myself to you. In my humble opinion no Indian has co-operated with the British Government more than I have for an unbroken period of twenty-nine years of public life in the face of circumstances that might well have turned any other man into a rebel. I ask you to believe me when I tell you that my co-operation was not based on the fear of the punishments provided by your laws or any other selfish motives. It is free and voluntary co-operation based on the belief that the sum-total of the British government was for the benefit of India. I put my life in peril four times for the sake of the Empire—at the time of the Boer War when I was in charge of the Ambulance corps whose work was mentioned in General Buller's dispatches, at the time of the Zulu revolt in Natal when I was in charge of a similar corps, at the time of the commencement of the late War when I raised an Ambulance Corps and as a result of the strenuous training had a severe attack of pleurisy and, lastly, in fulfillment of

my promise to Lord Chelmsford at the War Conference in Delhi, I threw myself in such an active recruiting campaign in Kaira District involving long and trying marches that I had an attack of dysentery which proved almost fatal. I did all this in the full belief that acts such as mine must gain my country an equal status in the Empire. So last December I pleaded hard for the trustful co-operation. I fully believed that Mr. Lloyd George would redeem his promise to the Mussulmans and that the revelations of the official atrocities in the Punjab would secure full reparation for the Punjabis. But the treachery of Mr. Lloyd George and its appreciation by you, and the condonation of the Punjab atrocities, have completely shattered my faith in the good intentions of the Government and the nation which is supporting it.

But though my faith in your good intentions is gone, I recognise your bravery and I know that what you will not yield to justice and reason, you will gladly yield to bravery.

See what this Empire means to India:

Exploitations of India's resources for the benefit of Great Britain.

An ever-increasing military expenditure and a civil service the most expensive in the world.

Extravagant working of every department in utter disregard of India's poverty.

Disarmament and consequent emasculation of a whole nation, lest an armed nation might imperil the lives of a handful of you in our midst.

Traffic in intoxicating liquors and drugs for the purpose of sustaining a top heavy administration.

Progressively representative legislation in order to suppress an ever-growing agitation, seeking to give expression to a nation's agony.

Degrading treatment of Indians residing in your dominions, and,

You have shown total disregard of our feelings by glorifying the Punjab administration and flouting the Mussulman sentiment.

I know you would not mind if we could fight and wrest the scepter form your hands. You know that we are powerless to do that, for you have ensured our incapacity to fight in open and honourable battle. Bravery on the battlefield is thus impossible for us. Bravery of the soul still remains open to us. I know you will respond to that also. I am engaged in evoking that bravery. Non-co-operation means nothing less than training in self-sacrifice. Why should we co-operate with you when we know that, by your administration of this great country, we are being daily enslaved in an increasing degree. This response of the people to my appeal is not due to my personality. I would like you to dismiss me, and for that matter the Ali Brothers too, from your consideration. My personality will fail to evoke any response to anti-Muslim cry if I were foolish enough to raise it, as the magic name of the Ali Brothers would fail to inspire the Mussulmans with enthusiasm if they were madly to raise an anti-Hindu cry. People flock in their thousands to listen to us, because we to-day represent voice of a nation groaning under iron heels. The Ali Brothers were your friends as I was, and still am. My religion forbids me to bear any ill-will towards you. I would not raise my hand against you even if I had the power. I expect to conquer you only by my suffering. The Ali Brothers will certainly draw the sword if they could, in defence of their religion and their country. But they and I have made common cause with the people of India in their attempt to voice their feelings and to find a remedy for their distress.

You are in search of a remedy to suppress this rising ebullition of national feeling. I venture to suggest to you that the only way to suppress it is to remove the causes. You have yet the power. You can repent of the wrongs done to Indians. You can compel Mr. Lloyd George to redeem his promises. I assure you he has kept many escape doors. You can compel the viceroy to retire in favour of a better one, you can revise your ideas about Sir Michael O'Dwyer and General Dyer. You can compel the government to summon a conference of the recognized leaders of the people duly elected by them and representing all shades of opinion so as to devise mans for granting *Swaraj* in accordance with the wishes of the people of India.

But this you cannot do unless you consider every Indian to be in reality your equal and brother. I ask for no patronage. I merely point out to you, as a friend, an honourable solution of a grave problem. The other solution, namely, repression is open to you. I prophesy that it will fail. It has begun already. The Government has already imprisoned two brave men of Panipat for holding and expressing their opinions freely. Another is on his trail in Lahore for having expressed similar opinions. One in the Oudh District is already imprisoned. Another awaits judgment. You should know what is going on in your midst. Our propaganda is being carried on in anticipation of repression. I invite you respectfully to choose the better way and make common cause with the people of India whose salt you are eating. To seek to thwart their aspirations is disloyalty to the country.

I am,.

Your faithful friend,.

M.K. Gandhi.

SIGNIFICANCE

According to Mahatma Gandhi, the open letter excerpted in the primary source was written with the purpose of apprising the common Englishman about the unjust policies and initiatives of the British Empire in India. In his letter, Gandhi mentions that the only way for India to seek independence from British rule is through non-cooperation.

The widely reproduced letter attracted favorable responses from many Englishmen. One of the replies—reprinted in 2003 as part of an E-book titled *Freedom's Battle, by Mahatma Gandhi* stated, "May we say at once that in so far as the British Empire stands for the domination and exploitation of other races for Britain's benefit, for degrading treatment of any, for traffic in intoxicating liquors, for repressive legislation, for administration such as that which to the Amritsar incidents, we desire the end of it as much as you do? We quite understand that in the excitement of the present crisis, owing to certain acts of the British Administration, which we join with you in condemning …" Similarly, there were others who exhibited resonance and camaraderie with the Indian people on this issue.

Gandhi's letter marked the beginning of the non-cooperation movement. This movement attains great significance because it shattered the economic might of the British Empire in India. During the non-cooperation movement, the Indian society did not cooperate in any economic or social activity associated with the British Empire.

There was no movement of goods, telegraph lines did not work, and foreign produce such as clothes manufactured in English mills were boycotted. Many Indians gave up their titles and posts across national and local bodies. Eventually, many daily services that were dependent on Indians for smooth operation were disrupted.

Ensuing an episode of violence, the non-cooperation movement came to a premature end on February 12, 1922. A group of policemen assaulted a few nationalist demonstrators in the town of Chauri Chaura in the north east state of Uttar Pradesh. Enraged by such actions, the demonstrators killed more than twenty policemen. Disturbed by these acts of violence, Mahatma Gandhi suspended the non-cooperation movement.

Though the movement did not last long, it is considered by many to be instrumental in the Indian independence struggle. The non-cooperative movement laid the foundation for several other initiatives such as the Salt March of Dandi, and the Quit India movement. The British rule could not withstand an opponent that did not indulge in violence or break any laws. Eventually, India attained independence on August 15, 1947.

Other British colonies are also known to have followed Gandhi's philosophies. Besides, eminent personalities, such as Martin Luther King, —who successfully campaigned for Black rights in North America in the 1960s, and Nelson Mandela, who waged a relentless struggle against apartheid in South Africa, were deeply inspired by his principles of non-cooperation and non-violence.

Gandhian principles of non-cooperation and non-violence have seen resurgence with political developments in the twenty-first century, especially among human rights advocates.

FURTHER RESOURCES
Books

Bakshi, S. R. *Gandhi and Non-Cooperation Movement, 1920–22.* South Asia Books, December 1983.

Nicholson, Michael. *Mahatma Gandhi: Leader of Indian Independence.* Blackbirch Press, November 2003.

Web sites

GandhiServe Foundation. "Brief Outline of Gandhi's Philosophy." <http://www.gandhiserve.org/information/brief_philosophy/brief_philosophy.htm> (accessed April 27, 2006).

Ministry of Home Affairs, Government of India. "Milestones in Indian History." <http://mha.nic.in/his3.htm> (accessed April 27, 2006).

Nobelprize.org. "Nelson Mandela and the Rainbow of Culture." <http://nobelprize.org/peace/articles/mandela/index.html> (accessed April 27, 2006).

Nobelprize.org. "The Nobel Peace Prize 1964." <http://nobelprize.org/peace/laureates/1964/press.html> (accessed April 27, 2006).

Project Gutenberg. "Freedom's Battle by Mahatma Gandhi." December 2, 2003. <http://www.gutenberg.org/catalog/world/readfile?fk_files=41935> (accessed April 27, 2006).

Tata Institute of Fundamental Research. "Mohandas Karamchand Gandhi." <http://theory.tifr.res.in/bombay/persons/mk-gandhi.html> (accessed April 27, 2006).

Dalai Lama, Holy Ruler of the Land of Tibet

Photograph

By: Anonymous

Date: September 28, 1939

Source: © Bettmann/Corbis.

About the Photographer: Otto Bettmann, a librarian and curator in Berlin in the 1930s, began collecting photographs to preserve as a historical archive. After fleeing Germany with several trunks of photographs in his possession, he settled in the United States. By 1995 his collection included over 11 million items; the picture of the Dalai Lama is part of the collection. The Bettmann Archive is owned by the Corbis Corporation.

INTRODUCTION

According to Tibetan Buddhism, the Dalai Lama is the embodiment of the bodhisattva of compassion, a Buddha figure who chooses not to reach nirvana after death but instead to be reincarnated and remain on earth until all human beings have been freed from suffering. According to this belief, the Dalai Lama never dies; when his body reaches the end of its natural life his spirit passes into another human who is being born, continuing his lineage and presence on earth. Tibetans consider the Dalai Lama their spiritual leader and head of state.

The current Dalai Lama is the fourteenth since 1391. He was born Lhamo Dhondrub on July 6, 1935, to parents who were peasants in the northeastern section of Tibet. At the age of three he was recognized as the reincarnation of the thirteenth Dalai Lama by a search committee appointed by the government of Tibet. When, following a series of visions, the party came to Lhamo Dhondrub's house, the little boy demanded to be given a rosary that he recognized, worn by one of the religious leaders. He correctly identified persons in the party by name, and after successfully passing other tests was declared the fourteenth Dalai Lama.

Because of his young age, the government was led by a regent after the thirteenth Dalai Lama's death. When Lhamo Dhondrub, renamed Tenzin Gyatso, reached the age of eighteen, he was expected to assume his role as head of state. In 1949, however, China came under Communist leadership, and the Chinese government announced its intention to "liberate" Tibet, which it considered a province, not a separate, sovereign nation. Calling the Tibetan government a "feudal regime," China declared the country in need of a return to Chinese—and Communist—leadership.

China invaded Tibet's eastern provinces on October 7, 1950. Forty thousand Chinese soldiers easily defeated a Tibetan force one-fifth its size. Half of those soldiers were killed, and at an emergency meeting of the Tibetan National, the sixteen-year-old Dalai Lama was given full powers as head of state.

International reaction to the Chinese invasion was ineffectual; India had attempted to act as an intermediary between the two nations; the United States and Great Britain had advised the Tibetans to use diplomacy as a way to mitigate Chinese aggression. Tibet appealed to the United Nations in November 1950, but repeated requests for intervention went unheeded.

In April 1951, a five-member delegation from Tibet met with Chinese leaders; under pressure and alleged coercion, the delegates signed the "Agreement of the Central People's Government and the Local Government of Tibet on Measures for the Peaceful Liberation of Tibet," a seventeen-point plan acknowledging China's control over Tibet. The Dalai Lama repudiated the plan, which gave China the power to occupy Tibet and control all foreign relations, although it preserved his powers and the existing government structure in Tibet.

PRIMARY SOURCE

Dalai Lama, Holy Ruler of the land of Tibet: The fourteenth Dalai Lama as a young boy, September 28, 1939. After a three year search determined that he is the reincarnation of the previous Dalai Lama, he is being transported to Lhasa, Tibet, for the first time. © BETTMANN/CORBIS.

For the next eight years tensions between Tibetans and the Chinese occupiers escalated; Tibet experienced famine conditions in some areas, with no assistance from the Chinese government and no recourse through international relations. Tibetans protested and used nonviolent means to resist; some guerillas clashed directly with Chinese troops. In December 1958 the Chinese government threatened to bomb the Tibetan capital city of Lhasa and the Dalai Lama's residence if guerillas refused to stop their attacks.

By March 1959 Lhasa was engulfed in fighting. The Chinese bombed parts of the city, and within a few weeks as many as 86,000 Tibetans—many monks living in religious communities—died. On March 31, 1959 the Dalai Lama and his family were smuggled out of Tibet and into northern India.

■ PRIMARY SOURCE

DALAI LAMA, HOLY RULER OF THE LAND OF TIBET
See primary source image.

■

SIGNIFICANCE

After a fifteen-day trek from Tibet to India, the Dalai Lama's first official act was to repudiate the seventeen-point plan. Creating a government in exile in Dharamsala, India, he advocated for a free Tibet, provided spiritual and political guidance for more than 120,000 fellow Tibetans in exile, published books and gave public lectures on matters of faith as well as political issues.

In 1961, the United Nations General Assembly declared Tibet's right to self-determination; the Chinese government ignored the statement and answered with the claim that the Tibetan people prospered under Chinese control. A 1997 International Commission of Jurist's report echoed the UN and called for freedom for Tibet.

In the intervening years, China has completely cut off Tibet from the rest of the world and poured immigrants into the country. Refugees report that in some areas Chinese immigrants outnumber Tibetans two or three to one, with some conflict reported between the two. Six million Tibetans remain in Tibet under tight Chinese control. The Tibet government in exile estimates that since 1949, approximately 1.2 million Tibetans have been killed by Chinese authorities through fighting, famine, or imprisonment.

During the 1980s, the Chinese government tried unsuccessfully to convince the Dalai Lama to return to Tibet. He has supported a "Middle Way" in dealing with the Chinese government, asking not for full independence, but for autonomy in all affairs except self-defense and foreign relations. Other officials in the Tibetan government in exile disagree with this stance, and China has repudiated it, willing only to discuss the Dalai Lama's return to Tibet. In 1989, the Dalai Lama was awarded the Nobel Peace Prize for his efforts to free the Tibetan people. In his acceptance speech, the Dalai Lama criticized the Chinese government for their harsh repression of Tibetan nationalists, and their use of violence in the Tiananmen Square massacre.

In 2005 the Dalai Lama turned seventy years of age and asked the Chinese government for permission to return to Tibet with no conditions placed on him. The Chinese government refused. Unless negotiations between the Dalai Lama and the Chinese government

The fourteenth Dalai Lama, Tibet's spiritual leader and ruler in exile, meditates while listening to a speech in the eastern Indian city of Calcutta, on November 24, 2003. © JAYANTA SHAW/REUTERS/CORBIS.

change, the fourteenth Dalai Lama may never return to his homeland. Questions concerning his reincarnation have prompted the Dalai Lama to declare that his successor will most likely not be found in Tibet. Historical conditions forced him to leave the country, and therefore, in his opinion, his reincarnation may be the first Dalai Lama reborn outside of Tibet.

FURTHER RESOURCES
Books

Avedon, John. *In Exile from the Land of Snows*. New York: Harper Perennial, 1997.

Shakya, Tsering. *The Dragon in the Land of Snows: A History of Modern Tibet Since 1947*. New York: Penguin, 2000.

Tenzin Gyatso, Dalai Lama XIV. *My Land and My People: The Original Autobiography of His Holiness the Dalai Lama of Tibet*. New York: Warner Books, 1997.

Web sites

The Office of Tibet. "Invasion and Illegal Annexation of Tibet: 1949–1951." February 2, 1996. <http://www.tibet.com/WhitePaper/white2.html> (accessed April 29, 2006).

UN Resolution 242

Resolution

By: United Nations Security Council

Date: November 22, 1967

Source: United Nations Security Council. Resolution 242. November 22, 1967.

About the Author: The United Nations Security Council is a sub-committee of the United Nations whose mandate is the maintenance of international peace and security. The committee is made up of representatives from UN member nations and is invested with the power to arbitrate international conflicts, make recommendations (binding or non-binding) in the form of resolutions, issue cease-fire orders and provide military presence in the form of UN peace keeping forces. In November of 1967, the Security Council President was Mr. Mamadou Boubacar Kanté of Mali. Resolution 242 was drafted and put forward by the British ambassador, Lord Hugh Caradon, and received unanimous assent from the representatives of Argentina, Brazil, Bulgaria, Canada, China, Denmark, Ethiopia, France, India, Japan, Mali, Nigeria, Union of Soviet Socialist Republics, United Kingdom of Great Britain for Northern Ireland and the United States of America.

INTRODUCTION

United Nations Security Council Resolution 242 was adopted on November 22, 1967 and was directed at finding a peaceful settlement to the conflict between the state of Israel and its Arab neighbors, Egypt, Syria and Jordan. The resolution was the direct response to the Six Day War, fought between June 5 and 10, 1967, and the Israeli occupation of Syria's Golan Heights, the West Bank of the Jordan River (including East Jerusalem), the Sinai Peninsula and Gaza Strip in Egypt. Although the Security Council's resolution intended the return of annexed territory to its rightful occupants, the ambiguous language of the recommendations and a lack of enforcement resulted in Israel's non-compliance with the Security Council's proposal. Resolution 242 has become one of the most cited and referenced documents in the controversy over land rights in the Middle East because it is believed that the failure of the resolution contributed in

large part to the perpetuation of the Arab-Israeli conflict. Israel eventually withdrew from the Sinai Peninsula in 1979, and from the Gaza Strip and part of the West Bank in September of 2005, but the Middle East remains a site of much tension and conflict.

◼ PRIMARY SOURCE

Resolution 242 (1967)

The Security Council of 22 November 1967

Expressing its continuing concern with the grave situation in the Middle East.

Emphasizing the inadmissibility of the acquisition of territory by war and the need to work for a just and lasting peace in which every State in the area can live in security.

Emphasizing further that all Member States in their acceptance of the Charter of the United Nations have undertaken a commitment to act in accordance with Article 2 of the Charter.

1. *Affirms* that the fulfillment of Charter principles requires the establishment of a just and lasting peace in the middle East which should include the application of both the following principles:

  (i) Withdrawal of Israel armed forces from territories occupied in the recent conflict;
  (ii) Termination of all claims or states of belligerency and respect for and acknowledgement of the sovereignty, territorial integrity and political independence of every State in the area and their right to live in peace within secure and recognized boundaries free from threats or acts of force;

2. *Affirms further* the necessity

  (a) For guaranteeing freedom of navigation through international waterways in the area:
  (b) For achieving a just settlement of the refugee problem;
  (c) For guaranteeing the territorial inviolability and political independence of every State in the area through measures including the establishment of demilitarized zones;

3. *Requests* the Secretary-General to designate a Special Representative to proceed to the Middle East to establish and maintain contacts with the States concerned in order to promote agreement and assist efforts to achieve a peaceful and accepted settlement in accordance with the provision and principles in this resolution;

4. *Requests* the Secretary-General to report to the Security Council on the progress of the efforts of the Special Representative as soon as possible.

Adopted unanimously at the 1382nd meeting.

SIGNIFICANCE

The notion of "land for peace" is the most important concept coming out of resolution 242. The Security Council suggested that Israel be willing to return conquered lands in exchange for peace with Egypt, Jordan and Syria. However, due to problems of ambiguous language and Israel's preoccupation with the resolution's second point—"the termination of all claims or states of belligerency"—Israel refused to end the occupation of Arab territories until their demands for the cessation of hostilities and terrorism had been met, while the Arab states interpreted the resolution to mean that it was incumbent upon Israel to first return the occupied territories.

The wording of the resolution was deliberately non-specific in its recommendations, requiring the involved parties to negotiate a mutually acceptable solution. An earlier draft put forward by the USSR with support from the Arab states that required Israel to fully withdraw from all territories occupied after June 4, 1967 was vetoed by the United States of America, who were in favor of a less binding resolution. As a compromise, the British representative, Lord Caradon, put forward a draft that referred to the "withdrawal of Israel armed forces from territories occupied in the recent conflict." The main innovation in this draft was the removal of the words "all the" from the previous draft, thereby refusing to make a definitive statement about exactly which territories should be returned. The British draft, however, added the statement "emphasizing the inadmissibility of the acquisition of territory by war," thereby codifying the United Nation's position on the occupation and annexation of land through armed conflict, and pointing to the need for Israel's complete return of the conquered territory. The British draft was adopted as resolution 242 and the statement on the inadmissibility of the acquisition of territory by war has since been referenced repeatedly as protecting the land rights and integrity of nations and their citizenry in the event of an armed conflict.

According to analysts, the major mistake made by the Security Council in resolution 242 was its failure to specifically mention the situation and interests of the Palestinians as a part of the peace settlement. Following the Holocaust and the Second World War, the 2.3 million Jewish people who had survived in Europe had no place to go and no homes to return to. The United Nations, agreeing that the Jewish people needed an independent state, decided to partition Palestine into a Jewish state, an Arab state and a Neutral UN territory containing the city of Jerusalem, which is sacred to Christianity, Islam, and Judaism. The state of Israel was proclaimed on May 14, 1948 and immediately thrown into conflict. Palestinians fled or were forcibly exiled from Israel and the rest of the Arab world immediately attacked Israel in an attempt to destroy the new country. By 1949, when the dust settled, Israel had twice as much land as the UN had originally given them, Egypt had taken the Gaza Strip, Jordan had claimed the West Bank and the Palestinians had nothing. They became a people without a place—their country had effectively been taken from them.

Those Palestinians who remained in the West Bank and Gaza Strip were poorly treated, the subjects of religious hatred and violence, living in refugee camps with no citizenship rights. Many fled to neighboring Arab nations. In the late 1950s, Yasser Arafat founded the militant group al-Fatah to fight for the destruction of Israel and the liberation of Palestine, causing a surge in violence and acts of terrorism by Palestinians against Israelis. The Palestine Liberation Organization (PLO) was founded in 1964 to organize the wide variety of fractured Palestinian groups fighting against Israel. Israeli soldiers returned aggression, resulting in continuous violence and acts of terrorism in Israel, the West Bank and the Gaza Strip that persist to this day.

The aftermath of the Six Days War and the creation of resolution 242 provided an opportunity for the United Nations, through the Security Council, to redress the harm done by the division of Palestine and the displacement of the Palestinians. Following the Israeli occupation of the West Bank and Gaza strip in 1967, Palestinians in refugee camps were even more poorly treated by the Israelis who began to settle the land that the Palestinians hoped to reclaim for their own. Instead of directly addressing the state of the Palestinian people as a nation without land, the Security Council referred to them as the "refugee problem" and offered no concrete solutions for reparation and repatriation of their homeland. Rather, the resolution offers the vague suggestion of a "just settlement of the refugee problem," refusing to acknowledge the Palestinian people as a nation with a right to an equal say in the Middle East peace settlement.

Since their exile in 1948, Palestinians have been adamant about their right to return to the lands that were taken from them by the United Nations' division of their country, although the Jewish people argue that they have a historic claim to the land that predates the nation of Palestine. The Palestinians maintain that according to the stipulations of resolution 242, Israel must return their land and only then will the Palestinians cease hostilities and aggression. They wish to be recognized as a nation and to reclaim the rights of citizens and the land rights that accompany sovereignty. The ambiguity and non-binding nature of resolution 242 has prolonged the dispute over the occupied territories and indirectly contributed to the

Israeli soldiers round up Egyptian prisoners in the area of the Gaza-El Arish crossroad in the Sinai penninsula, which Israel captured during the June 1967 conflict known as the Six-Day War. AP IMAGES.

continued violence between Palestinians and Israelis. Although Israel withdrew from the Gaza Strip on September 12, 2005, they continue to maintain their occupation of the West Bank territory, which contains the sacred city of Jerusalem. Palestinian interpretation of resolution 242 still requires the complete withdrawal of Israel from the territories taken in the 1967 Six Days War to cease hostilities and recognize Israel, while Israel maintains that an end to the state of war and Palestinian recognition of Israeli sovereignty are necessary before they will withdraw from the West Bank. The specter of resolution 242 continues to haunt the Middle East peace process.

FURTHER RESOURCES

Books

Jones, Bruce D. "The Middle East Peace Process" in Malone, David M., ed. *The UN Security Council: From the Cold War to the 21st Century.* Boulder, Colo.: Lynne Reinner Publishers, 2004.

Lall, Arthur. *The UN and the Middle East Crisis, 1967.* New York: Columbia University Press, 1968.

Periodicals

Goldberg, Arthur J. "United Nations Security Council Resolution 242 and the Prospects for Peace in the Middle East." *Columbia Journal of Transnational Law.* 12 (1973): 187–195.

Khalidi, Rashid I. "Observations on the Right of Return." *Journal of Palestine Studies.* 21(2) (1992): 29–40.

Radovanovic, Ljubomir. "Reflections on the November 22, 1967 Security Resolution." *Journal of Palestine Studies.* 1(2) (1972): 61–69.

Cast Out Caste

Photograph

By: Indranil Mukherjee

Date: January 19, 2004

Source: Indranil Mukherjee/AFP/Getty Images.

About the Photographer: Indranil Mukherjee is a photographer with AFP (Agence France-Presse). The world's oldest established news agency, the AFP was founded by Charles-Louis Havas in 1835. The agency, headquartered in Paris, has branches in Washington, Hong Kong, Nicosia, and Montevideo. It provides news and photographs to other news agencies and individuals across the world.

INTRODUCTION

Since ancient times, the caste system is considered to be one of the pillars of the Hindu social order in India. A hierarchically interlinked system, it includes numerous castes and sub-castes. One such caste, *Dalit*, occupies the lowest position in the Hindu social hierarchy.

The etymology of the term *Dalit* is traced to the ancient Indian language Sanskrit. *Dal* in Sanskrit means to split or crack. In Hebrew, Dal refers to something low, weak, and poor. In modern times, the term *Dalit* is usually referred to those people of a community among Hindus and Christians in India who are split, scattered or crushed, and seen as inferior by people of high castes.

Although *Dalits* have always been considered an inferior caste, it was mainly during the nineteenth century that they were referred to as Untouchables. Considered outcasts, members of the *Dalit* community were denied basic civil rights and were often subjected to atrocities. The *Dalits* were not allowed to touch or enter places and even temples frequented by higher caste members. In the nineteenth century, the British who ruled India at the time coined the terms depressed classes and scheduled castes for *Dalits*.

Mahatma Gandhi (1869–1948) used the more polite term *Harijan* (son of God) for this community. In recent times, apart from scheduled castes, the *Dalits* also form a part of the scheduled tribes, and all these communities are, in varying degrees, considered Untouchables. Reports in the past have highlighted various instances of discrimination and brutality against the *Dalit* community, especially in the rural regions.

According to a 1999 Human Rights Watch report, more than 160 million *Dalits* in India face severe discrimination—many of these are denied basic civil rights such as access to drinking water, education, and jobs. Although untouchability was abolished by the Indian Constitution in 1950 and subsequent anti-discrimination acts such as the Anti-Untouchability

Act have been implemented, the report maintains that there has been a rise in violence against *Dalits* in the past decades.

A report by the Commission for Scheduled Caste and Schedule Tribe found the average number of cases of crimes against Untouchables registered under the Anti-Untouchability Act were 480 in the 1950s, 1,903 in the 1960s, 3,240 in the 1970s, 3,875 in the 1980s and 1,672 during the early 1990s. The report also states that between the periods of 1981 and 1986 as well as 1995 and 1997, two hundred thousand cases of criminal offenses against Untouchables were registered. These include cases of murder, arson, rape, and other criminal offences.

The United Nations has on numerous occasions censured the Indian government for being unable to prevent brutality against the *Dalits*. In one of its reports in the mid–1990s, the United Nations condemned the Indian Government for "failing to prevent acts of discrimination towards Untouchables and failing to punish those found responsible and provide just and adequate reparation to the victims."

Since the 1990s, there has also been an increase in the number of *Dalit* rights movements. Several rallies with the purpose of educating people about the plight of *Dalits* have been organized. The primary source, a photograph by AFP photographer Indranil Mukherjee, shows a *Dalit* woman who took part in a protest rally organized by anti-globalization activists at the 2004 World Social Forum. The Forum was held in Mumbai, India.

■ PRIMARY SOURCE

CAST OUT CASTE

See primary source image.

■

SIGNIFICANCE

The issue of *Dalits* in India is perceived as a socioeconomic problem. Despite a clear mention in India's Constitution and the Directive Principles that there would be no discrimination against any citizen on grounds of religion, race, caste, place, and birth, there continues widespread discrimination against members of lower communities. Although it is the largest democracy in the world, India has been plagued with social inequalities and a great divide between the rich and the poor.

According to People's Union for Civil Liberties (PUCL) report, there are more *Dalits* in India than make up the population of Pakistan. The scheduled

PRIMARY SOURCE

Cast Out Caste: An Indian woman who is a member of Hinduism's lowest caste, the Dalits or "Untouchables" marches during a demonstration in Bombay, India, during the World Social Forum, January 19, 2004. INDRANIL MUKHERJEE/AFP/GETTY IMAGES.

castes are about sixteen percent of India's population and they contribute mainly in manual labor, art, and culture. However, oppression of *Dalits*, especially in the rural regions, adversely impacts the country socially and economically.

Experts indicate that the cause of *Dalit's* social status is two-fold. The main factor is poverty; sometimes people of the *Dalit* community literally starve because they are unable to participate in the economy. Lack of formal education also contributes to their poverty and social status.

A PUCL report estimated that over seventy-seven percent of lower caste people live in the rural regions of India and do menial jobs, especially in the unorganized agriculture sector. Most of them live in poverty,

earning less than thirty rupees a day (about seventy-five cents). Parents send their children not to schools, but to earn daily wages. Consequently, the children supplement their parents' meager income and are deprived of education at an early age. The situation in urban areas fares a little better. Although only twenty percent of *Dalits* live in cities, many do have jobs. There are fewer reported cases of discrimination. However, owing to lack of competency in technical fields, *Dalits* cannot match the lifestyles and incomes of those belonging to the upper castes.

The Indian government has taken several steps to improve the condition of *Dalits* and other lower castes. However, reports from human rights organizations indicate that more plans appear on paper than are actually implemented. The northeastern state of Bihar that has the highest population of *Dalits* in the country is reportedly affected the most. Although, *Dalits* have been elected to political parties in the state, the condition of *Dalits* being treated as untouchables remains a pervasive concern.

On a national level, several panels set by the Indian government have recommended reservation, a program similar to affirmative action in the United States, for the lower caste communities in education, and employment. Soon after independence from British rule, the Indian Constitution advocated a quota system for *Dalits* and other backward communities in government organizations and educational institutions.

The controversial Mandal Commission, set up in 1979, recommended a quota hike from twenty-seven percent to 49.5 percent for Scheduled Castes and Scheduled Tribes in government jobs and universities. However, the move to implement these recommendations in 1990 caused widespread discord and brought about the downfall of the incumbent government. Critics argue that a quota system in jobs, especially specialized posts, would give rise to "brain drain," where highly skilled and educated professionals would seek employment outside India. Opponents of such policies state that jobs and admissions should be rendered solely on merit.

As of 2006, the Government of India has proposed a quota system for the private sector and educational institutions. This initiative, deemed by critics as a means to garner votes from oppressed castes, has been marked with protests around the country. Economists have also questioned the intention behind such policies. Infzal Ali, chief economist of the Asian Development Bank, stated in April 2006 that "reservation in private sector would prove counterproductive."

Villagers grieve over the bodies of family members massacred at Vermachak village in Bihar, India on December 18, 2000. The slain were Dalits, or untouchables, the lowest in the heap in India's millenia-old caste system. AP IMAGES.

Discrimination against some communities is widespread in most developing countries. Moreover, experts state that the condition of *Dalits* is similar to that of the African American community in the early and mid-twentieth century United States. Although discrimination against *Dalits* continues in India, there have been notable contributions from members of this community. These include B.R. Ambedkar (1891–1956), the chief architect of India's Constitution, and K.R. Narayanan (1920–2005), President of India from 1997–2002.

FURTHER RESOURCES
Books

Hiltebeitel, Alf. *Rethinking India's Oral and Classical Epics: Draupadi among Rajputs, Muslims, and Dalits.* Chicago: University Of Chicago Press, May 1, 1999.

Rajeshekar, V.T. and Y. N. Kly. *Dalit: The Black Untouchables of India.* Clarity Press, June 1997.

Web sites

BBC News. "Dalits' political awakening." September 28, 1999. <http://news.bbc.co.uk/1/hi/world/south_asia/459591.stm> (accessed May 11, 2006).

Human Rights Watch. "Broken People: Caste Violence Against India's "Untouchables." April 14, 1999. <http://www.hrw.org/reports/1999/india> (accessed May 11, 2006).

IndiaInfo.com. "Job quota in private sector to trigger brain drain." April 27, 2006. <http://news.indiainfo.com/2006/04/27/2704job-quota-adb.html> (accessed May 11, 2006).

India Together. "Hindu social order and the human rights of dalits." November 2002. <http://www.indiatogether.org/combatlaw/issue4/hinduorder.htm> (accessed May 11, 2006).

PUCL Bulletin. "Dalits & Human Rights: The Battles Ahead—I." June 1999. <http://www.pucl.org/from-archives/Dalit-tribal/battles1.htm> (accessed May 11, 2006).

Rigoberta Menchú Tum's Nobel Lecture

Speech

By: Rigoberta Menchú Tum

Date: December 10, 1992

Source: *Nobelprize.org.* "Rigoberta Menchú Tum—Nobel Lecture." December 10, 1992. <http://nobelprize.org/peace/laureates/1992/tum-lecture.html> (accessed April 29, 2006).

About the Author: Rigoberta Menchú Tum, a native of Guatemala, was awarded the Nobel Peace Prize in 1992. Menchú fought for greater rights for women and peasants in Guatemala through such organizations as the Committee for Peasant Unity and the 31st of January Popular Front. She helped to create the United Representation of the Guatemalan Opposition and received the Nobel Prize for her efforts to aid indigenous peoples in Guatemala in their struggle against military oppression.

Nobel Peace Prize winner Rigoberta Menchú, in Washington, D.C., on April 24, 1993. © REUTERS/CORBIS.

INTRODUCTION

In 1992, the Nobel committee awarded the Nobel Peace Prize to Rigoberta Menchú, a thirty-three-year-old Guatemalan-Mayan woman who fought for indigenous rights. A few days after the 500th anniversary of the landing of Christopher Columbus and his crew in the New World, the Nobel committee's choice of Menchú, the first indigenous person to win a Nobel prize, was timely.

Menchú published her autobiography in English in 1983; *I, Rigoberta Menchú: An Indian Woman in Guatemala* was a publishing success. It told the story of Menchú's struggle against the Guatemalan government as she fought for greater rights for indigenous peoples. In her book, Menchú chronicles her early life as a poor peasant's daughter, moving to the coast each year for the harvest, during which time children and adults worked on plantations seasonally. Menchú describes her inability to receive a formal education and her efforts to teach herself to read with the help of several nuns while working as a maid in a convent school. Her decision to learn Spanish, at the age of seventeen, facilitated her work as an organizer and revolutionary in fighting against the Guatemalan military government in the 1980s.

From the early 1960s until 1996, the Guatemalan government was engaged in an ongoing conflict with a revolutionary group, the Guatemalan National Revolutionary Unity (URNG). During the conflict, more than 200,000 people were killed and indigenous people of Mayan descent were targeted specifically between 1978 and 1983 during a period of increased violence and repression on the part of the Guatemalan military.

According to Menchú, her father, Victor, helped to form the Committee for Peasant Unity, an organization she later joined in 1979. Menchú describes intense conflicts between her father and wealthy European and government interests, and details the killings of her mother, father, brother, and other family members. Her brother, Petrocinio, was burned alive in public, and her family was forced by authorities to watch.

By the early 1980s, Menchú had joined the 31st of January Popular Front, a radical anti-government group, to fight for indigenous rights, freedom from violence, and to help protect Mayan villages from military attacks as the government fought to destroy perceived leftist strongholds. During the early 1980s, more than 400 villages were completely destroyed by the Guatemalan government during the most violent period of the thirty-six-year war. This increase in violent activity coincided with Menchú's popularity worldwide as her book gained a wide audience.

Menchú was forced into exile in Mexico in 1981; she worked from Mexico as an organizer, and, in 1991, assisted the United Nations in crafting a declaration of rights for indigenous peoples. In 1992, she received the Nobel Peace Prize.

■ PRIMARY SOURCE

...Ladies and gentlemen, allow me to say some candid words about my country.

The attention that this Nobel Peace Prize has focused on Guatemala, should imply that the violation of the human rights is no longer ignored internationally. It will also honor all those who died in the struggle for social equality and justice in my country.

It is known throughout the world that the Guatemalan people, as a result of their struggle, succeeded in achieving, in October 1944, a period of democracy where institutionality and human rights were the main philosophies. At that time, Guatemala was an exception in the American Continent, because of its struggle for complete national sovereignty. However, in 1954, a conspiracy that associated the traditional national power centers, inheritors of colonialism, with powerful foreign interests, overthrew the democratic regime as a result of an armed invasion, thereby re-imposing the old system of oppression which has characterized the history of my country.

The economic, social and political subjection that derived from the Cold War, was what initiated the internal armed conflict. The repression against the organizations of the people, the democratic parties and the intellectuals, started in Guatemala long before the war started. Let us not forget that.

In the attempt to crush rebellion, dictatorships have committed the greatest atrocities. They have leveled villages, and murdered thousands of peasants particularly Indians, hundreds of trade union workers and students, outstanding intellectuals and politicians, priests and nuns. Through this systematic persecution in the name of the safety of the nation, one million peasants were removed by force from their lands; 100,000 had to seek refuge in the neighboring countries. In Guatemala, there are today almost 100,000 orphans and more than 40,000 widows. The practice of "disappeared" politicians was invented in Guatemala, as a government policy.

As you know, I am myself a survivor of a massacred family.

The country collapsed into a crisis never seen before and the changes in the world forced and encouraged the military forces to permit a political opening that consisted in the preparation of a new Constitution, in an expansion of the political field, and in the transfer of the government to civil sectors. We have had this new regime for eight years and in certain fields there have been some openings of importance.

However, in spite of these openings, repression and violation of human rights persists in the middle of an economic crisis, that is becoming more and more acute, to the extent that 84% of the population is today considered as poor, and some 60% are considered as very poor. Impunity and terror continue to prevent people from freely expressing their needs and vital demands. The internal armed conflict still exists.

The political life in my country has lately centered around the search for a political solution to the global crisis and the armed conflict that has existed in Guatemala since 1962. This process was initiated by the Agreement signed in this City of Oslo, between the Comisión Nacional de Reconciliación with government mandate, and the Unidad Revolucionaria Nacional Guatemalteca (URNG) as a necessary step to introduce to Guatemala the spirit of the Agreement of Esquipulas.

As a result of this Agreement and conversations between the URNG and different sectors of Guatemalan society, direct negotiations were initiated under the government of President Serrano, between the government and the guerrillas, as a result of which three agreements have already been signed. However, the subject of Human Rights has taken a long time, because this subject constitutes the core of the Guatemalan problems, and around this core important differences have arisen. Nevertheless, there has been considerable progress.

The process of negotiations aims at reaching agreements in order to establish the basis for a real democracy in Guatemala and for an end to the war. As far as I understand, with the goodwill of the parties concerned and the active participation of the civil sectors, adapting to a great national unity, the phase of purposes and intentions could be left behind so that Guatemala could be pulled out of the crossroads that seem to have become eternal.

Dialogues and political negotiations are, no doubt, adequate means to solve these problems, in order to respond in a specific way to the vital and urgent needs for life and for the implementation of democracy for the Guatemalan people. However, I am convinced that if the diverse social sectors which integrate Guatemalan society find bases of unity, respecting their natural differences, they would together find a solution to those problems and therefore resolve the causes which initiated the war which prevails in Guatemala.

Other civil sectors as well as the international community must demand that the negotiations between the Government and the URNG surpass the period in which they are finding themselves in discussing Human Rights and move ahead as soon as possible to a verifiable agreement with the United Nations. It is necessary to point out, here in Oslo, that the issue of Human Rights in Guatemala constitutes, at present, the most urgent problem that has to be solved. My statement is neither incidental nor unjustified.

As has been ascertained by international institutions, such as The United Nations Commission on Human Rights, The Interamerican Commission of Human Rights and many other humanitarian organizations, Guatemala is one of the countries in America with the largest number of violations of these rights, and the largest number of cases of impunity where security forces are generally involved. It is imperative that the repression and persecution of the people and the Indians be stopped. The compulsory mobilization and integration of young people into the Patrols of Civil Self Defense, which principally affects the Indian people, must also be stopped.

Democracy in Guatemala must be built-up as soon as possible. It is necessary that Human Rights agreements be fully complied with, i.e. an end to racism; guaranteed freedom to organize and to move within all sectors of the country. In short, it is imperative to open all fields to the multi-ethnic civil society with all its rights, to demilitarize the country and establish the basis for its development, so that it can be pulled out of today's underdevelopment and poverty.

Among the most bitter dramas that a great percentage of the population has to endure, is the forced exodus. Which means, to be forced by military units and persecution to abandon their villages, their Mother Earth, where their ancestors rest, their environment, the nature that gave them life and the growth of their communities, all of which constituted a coherent system of social organization and functional democracy.

The case of the displaced and of refugees in Guatemala is heartbreaking; some of them are condemned to live in exile in other countries, but the great majority live in exile in their own country. They are forced to wander from place to place, to live in ravines and inhospitable places, some not recognized as Guatemalan citizens, but all of them are condemned to poverty and hunger. There cannot be a true democracy as long as this problem is not satisfactorily solved and these people are reinstated on their lands and in their villages.

In the new Guatemalan society, there must be a fundamental reorganization in the matter of land ownership, to allow for the development of the agricultural potential, as well as for the return of the land to the legitimate owners. This process of reorganization must be carried out with the greatest respect for nature, in order to protect her and return to her, her strength and capability to generate life.

No less characteristic of a democracy is social justice. This demands a solution to the frightening statistics on infant mortality, of malnutrition, lack of education, analphabetism, wages insufficient to sustain life. These problems have a growing and painful impact on the Guatemalan population and imply no prospects and no hope.

Among the features that characterize society today, is that of the role of women, although female emancipation has not, in fact, been fully achieved so far by any country in the world.

The historical development in Guatemala reflects now the need and the irreversibility of the active contribution of women to the configuration of the new Guatemalan social order, of which, I humbly believe, the Indian women already are a clear testimony. This Nobel Peace Prize is a recognition to those who have been, and still are in most parts of the world, the most exploited of the exploited; the most discriminated of the discriminated, the most marginalized of the marginalized, but still those who produce life and riches.

Democracy, development and modernization of a country are impossible and incongruous without the solution of these problems . . . .

SIGNIFICANCE

Menchú drew worldwide attention to human rights abuses and the needs of the indigenous people in Guatemala. In 1996, after the end of the war, a truth commission was formed to study the Guatemalan conflict. The commission found widespread abuse of indigenous peoples had occurred, ranging from forced displacement and exile to rape, torture, and summary executions in violation of international human rights conventions. In 2000, Menchú filed suit in a Spanish court against Guatemalan military commanders for human rights abuses against Spaniards during the war, while a separate group of Mayans filed a suit against two military officers for the crime of genocide.

In the years after Menchú's received the Nobel Peace Prize, anthropology professor David Stoll investigated her life, interviewing family members and villagers to compare her autobiography against his scholarly research. Stoll's book, *Rigoberta Menchú and the Story of All Poor Guatemalans*, describes several inconsistencies between his research and Menchú's account of her family life and early years. According to Stoll's research, Menchú's father was prosperous enough that the family did not have to work on coastal plantations. In addition, school records indicate that Rigoberta Menchú attended Catholic and public schools through the eighth grade. Menchú's brother Petrocinio was shot, not burned, and the family was not present at his death. Stoll was careful in his 1999 book to point out that none of the inconsistencies affected Menchú's actual work for indigenous rights. In setting the record straight, Stoll wished to portray a more accurate picture of Mayan life, Menchú's background, and her family's financial condition. According to Stoll's portrait, Menchú was more literate and more able to organize resistance to the government than the average Guatemalan peasant.

Stoll's book received a great deal of attention and publicity, taking attention away from Menchú's work for indigenous rights and focusing it instead on the alleged factual discrepancies in her story. Menchú initially stood behind her account, but later admitted to having blended her experience with that of other Guatemalan villagers to bring attention to the violence in Guatemala and to gain sympathy for the revolutionary cause.

In the aftermath of Stoll's revelations, questions about Menchú's receipt of the Nobel Peace Prize led to calls for the Nobel Committee to withdraw the prize. The Nobel Committee later stated that giving the prize to Menchú "was not based exclusively or primarily on the autobiography." Menchú was allowed to keep her prize.

In 2001, a Guatemalan court declared that two former Guatemalan presidents—Romeo Lucas Garcia and Efrain Rios Montt—would be investigated on genocide charges. This court decision along with the court cases brought by Menchú and other Mayan Guatemalans have been part of a slow but steady campaign to hold the Guatemalan government accountable for the deaths and torture of hundreds of thousands of indigenous people. Rigoberta Menchú's autobiography, work for justice, and even the controversy surrounding her book helped draw attention to the plight of the indigenous Mayan people of Guatemala and their efforts to recover from thirty-six years of conflict.

FURTHER RESOURCES
Books

Grandin, Greg. *The Blood of Guatemala: A History of Race and Nation*. Durham, N.C.: Duke University Press, 2000.

Menchú, Rigoberta. *I, Rigoberta Menchú: An Indian Woman in Guatemala*. New York: Verso, 1987.

Stoll, David. *Rigoberta Menchú and the Story of All Poor Guatemalans*. New York: HarperCollins, 2000.

Websites

BBC News. "Spain May Judge Guatemala Abuses." October 5, 2005. <http://news.bbc.co.uk/2/hi/europe/4313664.stm> (accessed April 29, 2006).

Human Rights Abuses of Jews in Arab Countries After the Six-Day War

Book excerpt

By: Netanel Lorch

Date: June 21, 1967

Source: Lorch, Netanel, ed. *Major Knesset Debates: 1948–1981*. Lanham, MD, University Press of America, 1993.

About the Author: Netanel Lorch is an author and former Secretary-General of the Knesset. The Knesset [trans. 'Assembly'] is the Israeli Parliament. First convened in February 1949 it consists of 120 elected members. The principle speakers in the below source are Asher Hassin (1918–1995), a Moroccan born Knesset member of the Ma'arach, and Shlomo Cohen-Tsiddon (1923–), an Egyptian born Knesset member of the Herut-Liberal bloc.

INTRODUCTION

On June 5 1967, after months of border skirmishes and diplomatic arguments and fearing an attack by a united Arab force, Israel launched pre-emptive air strikes against Egypt. In so doing it wiped out almost the entire Egyptian air force and precipitated a major regional conflict that also embroiled Jordan, Syria and Iraq. Over the following week the Israeli army waged an effective war before a ceasefire was agreed on June 11. By this time, Israel's territory had trebled in size, then occupying the Sinai Desert, the Golan Heights, the West Bank, and Gaza.

What became known as the Six-Day War would have enormous consequences for Middle Eastern politics for years to come. The speed and relative ease of military victory was a surprise to Israeli military planners second only to the size of the territorial gains war had brought. To neighboring Arab nations, this was as much a disaster.

In 1948, the establishment of Israel was closely followed by a mass immigration of Jewish communities to Israel that had lived in Arab countries for centuries. In 1948, the Jewish population of Arab

On June 8, 1967 a group of Israeli soldiers reverently take their first look at the Jewish religion's holiest place, the Wailing Wall in the old city of Jerusalem, after it was captured from Jordan during the Six-Day War. AP IMAGES.

countries numbered around 850,000. Within twenty years this stood at between 150,000–200,000, although not all who had left had moved to Israel.

Israel's Law of Return gave the right to settlement of any Jewish born person within its borders, but the reasons for population shifts were many. Though some emigrated for religious reasons, many others moved because of economic imperatives. A better standard of life was promised in Israel, or generous incentives to emigrate made the move appealing. A third group were impelled to emigrate to Israel because of expulsion from their homelands, or because of the human rights violations that followed Israel's war of independence.

Both during and after Israel's War of Independence anti-Jewish riots and violence broke out across the Middle East. Forty-four Jews were killed during rioting in Morocco; in Cairo, a campaign of bomb attacks on Jewish property and businesses killed

seventy. In Aden, which had a substantial Jewish community, a number of pogroms took place, while Libya witnessed both rioting and the destruction of synagogues. The situation worsened when post-colonial independence came to many of these countries in the 1950s. Anti-Jewish legislation and restriction on movement were frequently features of the statute books of these newly independent states.

The Six-Day War sparked intense Arab frustration. Anger at Israel's victory and its growing power in the region soon spilled over into violence on streets across the Middle East.

PRIMARY SOURCE

21 June 1967 (13 Sivan 5727).

A. Hassin (Ma'arach): Mr. Speaker, distinguished Knesset, almost 150,000 Jews still live in Moslem countries such as Morocco, Tunisia, Libya, Egypt, Syria, Lebanon and Iraq. When some of those countries became independent certain Jews left for other countries, while those who remained demonstrated their loyalty and expected to be given the same rights as everyone else....This, however, was not borne out by circumstances. The Jews were treated as second-class citizens... subjected to officially-sanctioned harassment and attack...and made a general scapegoat.....

In the last few days two Jews were murdered in Morocco, others were tortured and a great deal of property was stolen. In Tunisia many Jews were beaten, including old people and pregnant women, stores were looted and the great and beautiful synagogue was desecrated and destroyed. In Egypt a large number of Jews were imprisoned. They were tortured in ways invented by the Nazis and no one paid any heed to the cries of the young and the old....In Libya Jews were beaten and slaughtered by mobs....We have heard disturbing rumors about the fate of our brethren in Lebanon, Syria and Iraq, where they cower in fear and trembling behind the locked doors of their homes....We have heard that the Jewish community of Aden has been wiped out brutally....Meanwhile the world sits idly by, no country protesting or intervening or even displaying any pity or concern.....

All the powers have representatives in the countries I have mentioned, and they undoubtedly saw what was being done to the Jews there...but they said and did nothing...yet at the same time we are attacked in international forums by those countries, in words and deeds, we, who protect our citizens, who constantly extend our hand in peace, who respect others and do not interfere in the sovereign affairs of other countries....The riots and killings have never been placed on the agenda of the U.N.

Assembly....We, the bearers of the vision: "and the wolf shall lie down with the lamb," "nation shall not lift up the sword against nation," and "they shall beat their swords into plowshares," are persecuted in the Moslem countries....The representatives of some of the Powers dare to place us in the dock. Blood has flowed like water, peace-loving youngsters and defenders of the Holy Land have been killed...but the U.N. has said nothing.... It is blind and deaf when we are affected.....

I know that the government is concerned about this and is doing what it can at this fateful hour...but the rioters act faster and there is no one to put out the fire in the Jewish quarters in the Moslem countries. That is why the government and the nation should take more vigorous action to place this subject on the agenda of the world and put an end to the suffering of our brethren.... I must add a word of praise for King Hassan of Morocco and President Bourguiba of Tunisia, who condemned the rioters, arrested some of them and issued orders to guard the Jewish quarters. This had very little effect, for in the final event it is the voice of the people which decides.... In view of the importance of the issue...I would like the Knesset to discuss it.....

S. Cohen-Sidon (sic) **(Gahal):** Mr. Speaker, distinguished Knesset, from the moment the Arab leaders regarded the Jewish people's liberation movement, namely, Zionism, whereby the return of the Jewish people to its ancient homeland and its redemption from the oppression of the diaspora is fulfilled, as a rival to the movement to liberate the Arab peoples from the yoke of foreigners, mobs have been incited from above and have vented their anger on the Jewish minority living in Arab countries. Our brethren there have suffered persecution, murder, rape and the burning of synagogues. Whenever the Arab leaders have been unsuccessful in implementing their threats against our state, and whenever they realize that there is an immense gap between their speeches and the results of their machinations against us, mobs are inflamed and sent to conduct pogroms against defenseless Jews.....

At the beginning of the week several Knesset Members, myself included, submitted a memorandum to the Prime Minister which said inter alia: "The State of Israel has absorbed some 750,000 Jews who resided formerly in Arab countries. These Jews, who...are full and equal citizens of Israel today and an integral part of the country's economic, political and social life, can easily be regarded as former residents of the Arab countries who have made room for the Arabs who lived in the territory of Israel prior to the establishment of the state and who live in Arab countries today, although still designated 'refugees.'.

Information has reached us of murders and damage to the persons and property of the Jews of Morocco, Algeria, Tunisia, Libya, Egypt and Syria. We appeal to the Prime Minister and voice our protest at these riots, demanding that the International Red Cross and the U.N. intervene immediately to rescue these Jews.

Just as the international organizations came to the aid of the Arabs known as refugees and who live among their people today, the same international organizations should extend their protection to the Jews in Arab countries and transfer them to Europe, where they will be able to choose where to go next....

Since the establishment of the State of Israel...the vast majority of the Jewish communities in the Arab countries has left...most of them being absorbed by Israel...and the great part of their property having been left behind and confiscated by the governments of the countries concerned....In effect, there has been a population exchange between the Arab countries and Israel, counterbalancing the demands made on behalf of the Arab refugees by the Arab governments....The Arab countries did not stand the test of minimal tolerance where a small Jewish minority was concerned....I note this with deep disappointment, because the Arabs, and the Moslems in particular, were noted for their tolerance and have played a distinguished role in the annals of Jewish-Moslem cooperation. I would like to use this opportunity to appeal to the Arab peoples to cease to be influenced by European Nazi theories of race, which fit neither the Arab character nor the principles of Islam.....

By agreeing to the transfer of 750,000 Jews from the Arab countries to their ancient homeland of Israel, the Arab rulers recognized that Israel was the homeland of the Jews, yet they nonetheless continue to clamor that the Arabs must return to Palestine, and since no one takes any notice of them they incite the masses to attack defenseless Jews.....

I ask the Knesset to transmit our protest against the aforementioned riots to all the parliaments of the world, the International Red Cross and the U.N. institutions. I would like our representatives to take this opportunity of stressing that for the last twenty years there has been a population exchange between the Arabs who lived formerly in Israel and the Jews who lived in Arab countries, and that the Arab countries must return the private and communal property of the Jews who lived there to their representatives in Israel or pay appropriate compensation for it.....

The Prime Minister, L. Eshkol: Mr. Speaker, distinguished Knesset, the two previous speakers did well to bring the plight of the Jews in certain Arab countries before the Knesset....There are approximately 100,000 Jews still in Arab countries, most of them concentrated in two or three countries....The attitude of the various Arab countries to the Jews residing there varies, and we should be careful not to make sweeping generalizations.....

During the last few days several governments have begun to persecute the Jews and the Jewish communities....In Egypt Jews are arrested and deported. In other countries official broadcasts incited the public against Israel and the Jews. In others, including Libya, Iraq and Aden, there were attacks and pogroms. In some places the authorities acted to put a stop to these attacks and protect the Jews....We know from our long and bitter history that if a government wishes to stop attacks on Jews it can, and if it does nothing or encourages them, the attacks will continue.....

Israel's ability to protect Jews in Arab countries is, regrettably, limited....Our activities in this sphere are usually conducted via outside agencies of various kinds, including those bodies which have been mentioned here....Needless to say, the nation, the Knesset and the Government are as shocked and distressed by the news as the distinguished Members of the Knesset who spoke on the subject....We are doing everything we can to prevent riots and the shedding of Jewish blood. For obvious reasons, I will not go into detail as to the situation and our activities in the various countries. I am prepared to discuss it and submit additional information in the Foreign Affairs and Defense Committee if the subject is transferred to it....I propose that the speakers agree that the subject be transferred to the appropriate committee for further debate.

(The proposal to transfer the subject to the Foreign Affairs and Defense Committee is adopted.).

SIGNIFICANCE

The concerns expressed in the Knesset were not without basis, either in history or contemporary fact. After the Six-Day War, riots against Jews in Libya, Morocco, Syria, Tunisia and Yemen broke out. In Libya, violence was so severe that the country's remaining Jewish population of around 4,000 was evacuated en masse to Italy.

While some governments, notably that of Morocco, moved to protect their Jewish populations, others used the aftermath of the Six-Day War to persecute their Jewish communities. In Egypt, the government of Gamal Abdul Nasser ordered the round up of around 500 prominent Jews and incarcerated them without charge or trial for months, before releasing them on the condition that they relinquished all their property and citizenship rights. A number of Syria's Jews met a similar fate.

The plight of Jews following the Six-Day War hastened efforts to extricate them from Arab countries. Zionist organizations helped organize their emigration to Israel, western Europe or the United States. There are today less than 10,000 Jews living in Arab countries and most of the remainder of Jewish immigration from the Arab world took place in the years following the Six-Day War. In the 1970s, concern for Jewish minorities suffering human rights abuses turned to Iran and the USSR and large scale immigration took place from these nations during that period.

Human rights abuses against Jews living in the Arab World were not, however, universal nor always systemically carried out with state backing. In Morocco, King Hassan II (1929–1999), retained an invitation for Moroccan Jews to return and provided funds to maintain the synagogues and some of the homes of exiled Jews. It is noticeable that in many Moroccan villages the best kept building is often an abandoned synagogue. Today, only around 5,000 Moroccan Jews remain out of a pre–1948 population of more than 250,000. Critics of Jewish emigration from largely benevolent countries such as Morocco say that the mass emigration of historically ancient Jewish populations have helped feed the polarization of the current Arab-Israeli conflict.

FURTHER RESOURCES
Books
Gilbert, Martin. *Israel: A History*. London: Doubleday, 1998.

Schulze, Kirsten E. *The Arab Israeli Conflict*. New York: Longman, 1999.

Shlaim, Avi. *The Iron Wall: Israel and the Arab World*. London: Penguin, 2001.

Framework Convention for the Protection of National Minorities

Treaty

By: Council of Europe

Date: 1995

Source: "Framework Convention for the Protection of National Minorities." Council of Europe, 1995.

About the Author: The Council of Europe is an association of forty-six European states, founded in 1949 and distinct from the European Union.

INTRODUCTION

The Framework Convention for the Protection of National Minorities (FCPNM) is a treaty signed by most of the member states of the Council of Europe that seeks to protect the rights of national minorities. A "national minority" is a minority population that has a linguistic, religious, or ethnic identity distinct from that of the surrounding majority, such as German-speaking residents of Russia. Historically, such minorities have often been targets of persecution.

The Council of Europe, the body under whose auspices the FCPNM was created and is enforced, is an association of forty-six European states (as of 2006) that was founded by ten original member states in 1949. The Council of Europe is distinct from the European Union, which was founded in 1992; however, the two groups use the same flag, are both headquartered in the French city of Strasbourg, and have many member states in common. The Council's primary interest is the protection of democratic principles, including human rights, language rights, freedom of speech, and the rights of national minorities.

Radical changes swept the European political scene in the late 1980s and early 1990s as the former Soviet Union disintegrated and democratic or at least quasi-democratic governments appeared in a number of former Soviet states. These events motivated the Council of Europe to design a treaty to guard the rights of national minorities, which became more mobile and more vulnerable to nationalistic animosity in their countries of residence. In 1991, the Steering Committee for Human Rights of the Council of Europe was tasked with exploring the means by which the Council might protect national minorities. The Steering Committee appointed a group of experts who in 1993 recommended the drafting of the FCPNM, which was duly written and adopted by the Committee of Ministers of the Council of Europe in November 1994. The treaty was opened for signature in early 1995 and entered into force in 1998 after being ratified by twelve states. As of 2005, thirty-eight states were party to the treaty.

■ PRIMARY SOURCE

FRAMEWORK CONVENTION FOR THE PROTECTION OF NATIONAL MINORITIES
SECTION I

Article 1 The protection of national minorities and of the rights and freedoms of persons belonging to those minorities forms an integral part of the international protection of human rights, and as such falls within the scope of international co-operation.

Article 2 The provisions of this framework Convention shall be applied in good faith, in a spirit of understanding and tolerance and in conformity with the principles of good neighbourliness, friendly relations and co-operation between States.

Article 3

1. Every person belonging to a national minority shall have the right freely to choose to be treated or not to be treated as such and no disadvantage shall result from this choice or from the exercise of the rights which are connected to that choice.
2. Persons belonging to national minorities may exercise the rights and enjoy the freedoms flowing from the principles enshrined in the present framework Convention individually as well as in community with others.

SECTION II
Article 4

1. The Parties undertake to guarantee to persons belonging to national minorities the right of equality before the law and of equal protection of the law. In this respect, any discrimination based on belonging to a national minority shall be prohibited.
2. The Parties undertake to adopt, where necessary, adequate measures in order to promote, in all areas of economic, social, political and cultural life, full and effective equality between persons belonging to a national minority and those belonging to the majority. In this respect, they shall take due account of the specific conditions of the persons belonging to national minorities.
3. The measures adopted in accordance with paragraph 2 shall not be considered to be an act of discrimination.

Article 5

1. The Parties undertake to promote the conditions necessary for persons belonging to national minorities to maintain and develop their culture, and to preserve the essential elements of their identity, namely their religion, language, traditions and cultural heritage.
2. Without prejudice to measures taken in pursuance of their general integration policy, the Parties shall refrain from policies or practices aimed at assimilation of persons belonging to national minorities against their will and shall protect these persons from any action aimed at such assimilation.

Article 6

1. The Parties shall encourage a spirit of tolerance and intercultural dialogue and take effective measures to promote mutual respect and understanding and

co-operation among all persons living on their territory, irrespective of those persons' ethnic, cultural, linguistic or religious identity, in particular in the fields of education, culture and the media.

2. The Parties undertake to take appropriate measures to protect persons who may be subject to threats or acts of discrimination, hostility or violence as a result of their ethnic, cultural, linguistic or religious identity.

Article 7 The Parties shall ensure respect for the right of every person belonging to a national minority to freedom of peaceful assembly, freedom of association, freedom of expression, and freedom of thought, conscience and religion.

Article 8 The Parties undertake to recognise that every person belonging to a national minority has the right to manifest his or her religion or belief and to establish religious institutions, organisations and associations.

Article 9

1. The Parties undertake to recognise that the right to freedom of expression of every person belonging to a national minority includes freedom to hold opinions and to receive and impart information and ideas in the minority language, without interference by public authorities and regardless of frontiers. The Parties shall ensure, within the framework of their legal systems, that persons belonging to a national minority are not discriminated against in their access to the media.

2. Paragraph 1 shall not prevent Parties from requiring the licensing, without discrimination and based on objective criteria, of sound radio and television broadcasting, or cinema enterprises.

3. The Parties shall not hinder the creation and the use of printed media by persons belonging to national minorities. In the legal framework of sound radio and television broadcasting, they shall ensure, as far as possible, and taking into account the provisions of paragraph 1, that persons belonging to national minorities are granted the possibility of creating and using their own media.

4. In the framework of their legal systems, the Parties shall adopt adequate measures in order to facilitate access to the media for persons belonging to national minorities and in order to promote tolerance and permit cultural pluralism.

Article 10

1. The Parties undertake to recognise that every person belonging to a national minority has the right to use freely and without interference his or her minority language, in private and in public, orally and in writing.

2. In areas inhabited by persons belonging to national minorities traditionally or in substantial numbers, if those persons so request and where such a request corresponds to a real need, the Parties shall endeavour to ensure, as far as possible, the conditions which would make it possible to use the minority language in relations between those persons and the administrative authorities.

3. The Parties undertake to guarantee the right of every person belonging to a national minority to be informed promptly, in a language which he or she understands, of the reasons for his or her arrest, and of the nature and cause of any accusation against him or her, and to defend himself or herself in this language, if necessarily with the free assistance of an interpreter.

Article 11

1. The Parties undertake to recognise that every person belonging to a national minority has the right to use his or her surname (patronym) and first names in the minority language and the right to official recognition of them, according to modalities provided for in their legal system.

2. The Parties undertake to recognise that every person belonging to a national minority has the right to display in his or her minority language signs, inscriptions and other information of a private nature visible to the public.

3. In areas traditionally inhabited by substantial numbers of persons belonging to a national minority, the Parties shall endeavour, in the framework of their legal system, including, where appropriate, agreements with other States, and taking into account their specific conditions, to display traditional local names, street names and other topographical indications intended for the public also in the minority language when there is a sufficient demand for such indications.

Article 12

1. The Parties shall, where appropriate, take measures in the fields of education and research to foster knowledge of the culture, history, language and religion of their national minorities and of the majority.

2. In this context the Parties shall inter alia provide adequate opportunities for teacher training and access to textbooks, and facilitate contacts among students and teachers of different communities.

3. The Parties undertake to promote equal opportunities for access to education at all levels for persons belonging to national minorities.

Article 13

1. Within the framework of their education systems, the Parties shall recognise that persons belonging to a

national minority have the right to set up and to manage their own private educational and training establishments.

2. The exercise of this right shall not entail any financial obligation for the Parties.

Article 14

1. The Parties undertake to recognise that every person belonging to a national minority has the right to learn his or her minority language.

2. In areas inhabited by persons belonging to national minorities traditionally or in substantial numbers, if there is sufficient demand, the Parties shall endeavour to ensure, as far as possible and within the framework of their education systems, that persons belonging to those minorities have adequate opportunities for being taught the minority language or for receiving instruction in this language.

3. Paragraph 2 of this article shall be implemented without prejudice to the learning of the official language or the teaching in this language.

Article 15 The Parties shall create the conditions necessary for the effective participation of persons belonging to national minorities in cultural, social and economic life and in public affairs, in particular those affecting them.

Article 16 The Parties shall refrain from measures which alter the proportions of the population in areas inhabited by persons belonging to national minorities and are aimed at restricting the rights and freedoms flowing from the principles enshrined in the present framework Convention.

Article 17

1. The Parties undertake not to interfere with the right of persons belonging to national minorities to establish and maintain free and peaceful contacts across frontiers with persons lawfully staying in other States, in particular those with whom they share an ethnic, cultural, linguistic or religious identity, or a common cultural heritage.

2. The Parties undertake not to interfere with the right of persons belonging to national minorities to participate in the activities of non-governmental organisations, both at the national and international levels.

Article 18

1. The Parties shall endeavour to conclude, where necessary, bilateral and multilateral agreements with other States, in particular neighbouring States, in order to ensure the protection of persons belonging to the national minorities concerned.

2. Where relevant, the Parties shall take measures to encourage transfrontier co-operation.

Article 19 The Parties undertake to respect and implement the principles enshrined in the present framework Convention making, where necessary, only those limitations, restrictions or derogations which are provided for in international legal instruments, in particular the Convention for the Protection of Human Rights and Fundamental Freedoms, in so far as they are relevant to the rights and freedoms flowing from the said principles.

SECTION III

Article 20 In the exercise of the rights and freedoms flowing from the principles enshrined in the present framework Convention, any person belonging to a national minority shall respect the national legislation and the rights of others, in particular those of persons belonging to the majority or to other national minorities.

Article 21 Nothing in the present framework Convention shall be interpreted as implying any right to engage in any activity or perform any act contrary to the fundamental principles of international law and in particular of the sovereign equality, territorial integrity and political independence of States.

Article 22 Nothing in the present framework Convention shall be construed as limiting or derogating from any of the human rights and fundamental freedoms which may be ensured under the laws of any Contracting Party or under any other agreement to which it is a Party.

Article 23 The rights and freedoms flowing from the principles enshrined in the present framework Convention, in so far as they are the subject of a corresponding provision in the Convention for the Protection of Human Rights and Fundamental Freedoms or in the Protocols thereto, shall be understood so as to conform to the latter provisions.

SIGNIFICANCE

In Europe, national boundaries have not always been drawn so as to neatly outline areas of cultural purity, and indeed they could not have been, given that many areas of mixed nationality or cultural dominance have developed over the centuries. From the perspective of the Council of Europe, promoting the acceptance of national minorities is therefore not only a human rights issue but a security and stability issue. An example of the kind of instability that can result when coexistence of national groups is not peaceful is the conflict between Serbs, Croats, and Bosniaks co-inhabiting parts of the former Yugoslavia in the 1990s. Military intervention by the North Atlantic Treaty

Organization (NATO) resulted. Approximately one hundred thousand people died in the war and two million were driven from their homes.

The FCPNM's provisions are intended as a starting point for national legislation and government policies, including bilateral and multilateral treaties, rather than as a complete solution to the many-sided question of national minorities in Europe. The FCPNM itself provides for monitoring, not enforcement. As with several United Nations human rights bodies, the goal is to encourage good practices at the national level by credibly exposing abuses, praising progress, and making suggestions for specific improvements. To monitor treaty compliance, the Committee of Ministers of the Council of Europe appoints eighteen experts, ideally "independent and impartial," to form an Advisory Committee. The treaty requires each signatory state to submit a report to the Advisory Committee describing what measures it has taken to put the FCPNM's provisions into effect. As of 2005, the Advisory Committee had reviewed thirty-five state reports and issued thirty-four Opinions or official reactions to the state reports. Working groups of the Advisory Committee also make international visits as part of the monitoring process.

It is notable that the FCPNM contains no definition of the term "national minority." This has created differences of opinion between the international bodies and certain member states: for example, France has declared that it contains no national minorities. The Human Rights Committee of the United Nations has stated that it "is unable to agree that France is a country in which no ethnic, religious or linguistic minorities exist." There is no set method for deciding which party is correct in a legally binding sense in such cases.

A uniquely trans-European national minority issue is that of the Roma, or gypsies. (The word "gypsy" is considered derogatory by some but not all Roma.) This ethnic group originated as migrants from northern India about a thousand years ago and is now found across Europe, in the United Kingdom, and even in the United States. The Roma have for centuries faced discrimination in almost every country where they reside as a national minority. The Advisory Committee has devoted special attention to monitoring the condition of the Roma and to helping states design measures for accommodating their presence in ways that fulfill the terms of the FCPNM and other human rights treaties.

FURTHER RESOURCES

Books

Cházár, Edward. *The International Problem of National Minorities*. Toronto: Matthias Corvinus, 1999.

Klebes, Heinrich. *The Quest for Democratic Security: The Role of the Council of Europe and U.S. Foreign Policy*. Washington, DC: U.S. Institute of Peace, 1999.

Web sites

Council of Europe. <http://www.coe.int> (accessed May 6, 2006).

European Centre for Minority Issues. "Implementing the Framework Convention for the Protection of National Minorities." August 1999. <http://www.ecmi.de/download/report_3.pdf> (accessed May 6, 2006).

Millicent

Government report

By: Australian Human Rights and Equal Opportunity Commission

Date: April 1997

Source: "Millicent." In *Bringing Them Home: Report of the National Inquiry into the Separation of Aboriginal and Torres Strait Islander Children from Their Families*. Australian Human Rights and Equal Opportunity Commission, April 1997.

About the Author: The Australian Human Rights and Equal Opportunity Commission formed in 1985 by order of the Federal Parliament. It is an independent, five-person, statutory organization that reports to Parliament through the Attorney General. In 1995, the commission inquired into the past laws, practices and policies which resulted in the separation of Aboriginal and Torres Strait Islander children from their families by compulsion, duress or undue influence, and the effects of those laws, practices and policies.

INTRODUCTION

Aboriginal children were removed from their families from 1883 to 1969 in the largest human rights violation in Australian history. The Australian government argued that it attempted to protect the moral and physical welfare of the children. However, the only crime committed by the parents was that of being Aborigine. No court hearings were necessary. A government official simply ordered the children removed. Often, they never saw their parents again.

The removal had its roots in prejudices held by whites about Aborigines. The first inhabitants of Australia, the Aborigines established more than 250 separate and distinct indigenous groups. They varied greatly in lifestyle and habits, a result of the dramatic differences in the Australian climate. In general, Aborigines maintained a rich ceremonial and spiritual culture. They developed superb adaptive behaviors, learning to find food and water in the deserts. They also developed musical instruments and sophisticated forms of artistic expression.

White Australians did not value the culture of the Aborigines. The government typically viewed the indigenous people in harshly negative terms and saw little worth in saving their cultures and traditions. Many officials worried that children were not being looked after properly within Aboriginal communities and were quick to remove them to either orphanages or foster homes. Thousands of children were removed over generations. The government believed that they were automatically better off within non-Aborigine society.

Only in the 1980s and 1990s did the practice of Aborigine removal become the focus of national debate in Australia. The resulting national inquiry led to the release of a major report, *Bringing Them Home*, which documents the great pain and hardship suffered by the Aborigine children and their families.

■ PRIMARY SOURCE

MILLICENT

At the age of four, I was taken away from my family and placed in Sister Kate's Home—Western Australia where I was kept as a ward of the state until I was eighteen years old. I was forbidden to see any of my family or know of their whereabouts. Five of us D. children were all taken and placed in different institutions in WA. The Protector of Aborigines and the Child Welfare Department in their "Almighty Wisdom" said we would have a better life and future brought up as whitefellas away from our parents in a good religious environment. All they contributed to our upbringing and future was an unrepairable scar of loneliness, mistrust, hatred and bitterness. Fears that have been with me all of my life. The empty dark and lonely existence was so full of many hurtful and unforgivable events, that I cannot escape from no matter how hard I try. Being deprived of the most cherished and valuable thing in life as an Aboriginal Child—love and family bonds. I would like to tell my story of my life in Sister Kate's home—WA.

My name is Millicent D. I was born at Wonthella WA in 1945. My parents were CD and MP, both "half-caste" Aborigines. I was one of seven children, our family lived in the sandhills at the back of the Geraldton Hospital. There was a lot of families living there happy and harmonious. It was like we were all part of one big happy family.

In 1949 the Protector of Aborigines with the Native Welfare Department visited the sandhill camps. All the families living there were to be moved to other campsites or to the Moore River Aboriginal Settlement. Because my parents were fair in complexion, the authorities decided us kids could pass as whitefellas. I was four years old and that was the last time I was to see my parents again. Because my sisters were older than me they were taken to the Government receiving home at Mount Lawley. My brother Kevin was taken to the boys home in Kenwick. Colin and I were taken to the Sister Kate's Home. We were put in separate accommodations and hardly ever saw each other. I was so afraid and unhappy and didn't understand what was happening.

We were told Sundays was visiting day when parents and relatives came and spent the day. For Colin and I that was a patch of lies because our family were not allowed to visit. We spent each Sunday crying and comforting each other as we waited for our family. Each time it was the same—no one came. That night we would cry ourselves to sleep and wonder why. We were too young to understand we were not allowed family visits.

A couple of years passed and I started primary school.

It had been such a long time since I had seen my brother Colin. I was so helpless and alone. My brother had been taken away to the boys' home in Kenwick and now I was by myself. I became more withdrawn and shy and lived in a little world of my own hoping one day Mum would come and take me out of that dreadful place. As the years passed I realised that I would never see my family again.

They told me that my family didn't care ... They told me that my family didn't care or want me and I had to forget them. They said it was very degrading to belong to an Aboriginal family and that I should be ashamed of myself, I was inferior to whitefellas. They tried to make us act like white kids but at the same time we had to give up our seat for a whitefella because an Aboriginal never sits down when a white person is present.

Then the religion began. We had church three times a day, before breakfast, lunchtime and after school. If we were naughty or got home from school late we had to kneel at the altar for hours and polish all the floors and brass in the church. We had religion rammed down our throats from hypocrites who didn't know the meaning of the word. We used to get whipped with a wet ironing cord and sometimes had to hold other children (naked) while they were whipped, and if we didn't hold them we got another whipping. To wake us up in the morning we were sprayed up the backside with an old fashioned pump fly spray. If we complained we got more. Hurt and humiliation was a part of our every day life and we had to learn to live with it. Several more years passed and I still had no contact with my family, I didn't know what they looked like or how I could ever find them. By this time I was old enough to go to High School. This meant I didn't have to look after several of the younger kids as I had previously done, bathing, feeding and putting them on the potty and then off to bed, chopping wood before school and housework which all of us kids done and the housemothers sat back and collected wages—for doing nothing. My life was miserable, and I felt I was a nobody and things couldn't get any worse. But I was wrong.

The worst was yet to come.

While I was in first year high school I was sent out to work on a farm as a domestic. I thought it would be great to get away from the home for a while. At first it was. I was made welcome and treated with kindness. The four shillings I was payed went to the home. I wasn't allowed to keep it, I didn't care. I was never payed for the work I did at Sister Kate's so you don't miss what you didn't get, pocket money etc.

The first time I was sent to the farm for only a few weeks and then back to school. In the next holidays I had to go back. This time it was a terrifying experience, the man of the house used to come into my room at night and force me to have sex. I tried to fight him off but he was too strong.

When I returned to the home I was feeling so used and unwanted. I went to the Matron and told her what happened. She washed my mouth out with soap and boxed my ears and told me that awful things would happen to me if I told any of the other kids. I was so scared and wanted to die. When the next school holidays came I begged not to be sent to that farm again. But they would not listen and said I had to.

I ran away from the home, I was going to try to find my family. It was impossible, I didn't even know where to go. The only thing was to go back. I got a good belting and had to kneel at the altar everyday after school for two weeks. Then I had to go back to that farm to work. The anguish and humiliation of being sent back was bad enough but the worse was yet to come.

This time I was raped, bashed and slashed with a razor blade on both of my arms and legs because I would not stop struggling and screaming. The farmer and one of his workers raped me several times. I wanted to die, I wanted my mother to take me home where I would be safe and wanted. Because I was bruised and in a state of shock I

didn't have to do any work but wasn't allowed to leave the property.

When they returned me to the home I once again went to the Matron. I got a belting with a wet ironing cord, my mouth washed out with soap and put in a cottage by myself away from everyone so I couldn't talk to the other girls. They constantly told me that I was bad and a disgrace and if anyone knew it would bring shame to Sister Kate's Home. They showed me no comfort which I desperately needed. I became more and more distant from everyone and tried to block everything out of my mind but couldn't. I ate rat poison to try and kill myself but became very sick and vomited. This meant another belting.

After several weeks of being kept away from everyone I was examined by a doctor who told the Matron I was pregnant. Another belting, they blamed me for everything that had happened. I didn't care what happened to me anymore and kept to myself. All I wanted now was to have my baby and get away as far as I could and try and find my family.

My daughter was born [in 1962] at King Edward Memorial Hospital. I was so happy, I had a beautiful baby girl of my own who I could love and cherish and have with me always.

But my dreams were soon crushed: the bastards took her from me and said she would be fostered out until I was old enough to look after her. They said when I left Sister Kate's I could have my baby back. I couldn't believe what was happening. My baby was taken away from me just as I was from my mother.

My baby was taken away from me just as I was from my mother. Once again I approached the Matron asking for the Address of my family and address of the foster family who had my daughter. She said that it was Government Policy not to give information about family and she could not help me. I then asked again about my baby girl and was told she did not know her whereabouts. In desperation I rang the King Edward Memorial Hospital. They said there was no record of me ever giving birth or of my daughter Toni. Then I wrote to the Native Welfare Department only to be told the same thing and that there were no records of the D. family because all records were destroyed by fire.

I now had no other options but to find a job and somewhere to live. After working for a while I left Western Australia and moved to Adelaide to try and get my life together and put the past behind me. I was very alone, shy and not many friends and would break down over the simplest thing. Every time I saw a baby I used to wonder, could that by my little girl. I loved her and so desperately wanted her back. So in 1972 I returned to Western Australia and again searched for my family and child. I returned to see the Matron from Sister Kate's. This time she told me that my daughter was dead and it would be in my best interest to go back to South Australia and forget about my past and my family. I so wanted to find them, heartbroken I wandered the streets hoping for the impossible. I soon realized that I could come face to face with a family member and wouldn't even know.

Defeated I finally returned to Adelaide. In my heart I believed that one day everything would be alright and I would be reunited with my family. My baby was dead. (That's what I was told.) I didn't even get to hold her, kiss her and had no photographs, but her image would always be with me, and I would always love her. They couldn't take that away from me.

SIGNIFICANCE

On October 24, 2001, the Northern Territory became the last Australian state or territory to apologize for the taking of Aboriginal children from their parents. Apologies are the only form of compensation that the members of the stolen generation will receive. In a case brought in 2000 by Lorna Cubillo, the Federal Court ruled that the commonwealth is not liable for the removal of Aboriginal children. Despite the court ruling, it is documented by such reports as *Bringing Them Home* that the victims of removal carry psychological scars which have significantly affected their abilities to achieve happy, prosperous, and stable lives.

The issue of stolen children remains very much a hot-button topic in Australia, partly because of continuing racial strife in the country. Some white Australians continue to argue at the turn of the millennium that the children were not stolen, but instead removed from their families purely for their own good. They make references to the higher rates of alcohol abuse, illiteracy, and joblessness among Aborigines. This claim of beneficial removal is hotly disputed by Aboriginal activists and more liberal Australians. As the various state and territorial governments have all acknowledged, the way in which Aboriginal children were treated is a matter of great national shame. With Aboriginal children taken from their parents through 1969, it will be many decades before the last of the stolen generations disappears from the Australian landscape. Removal is therefore likely to remain an issue in Australian life.

FURTHER RESOURCES
Books

Briskman, Linda. *The Black Grapevine: Aboriginal Activism and the Stolen Generations*. Annandale, NSW, Australia: Federation Press, 2003.

Fraser, Rosalie. *Shadow Child: A Memoir of the Stolen Generation*. Alexandria, NSW, Australia: Hale & Iremonger, 1999.

Web sites

The Human Rights and Equal Opportunity Commission. <http://www.hreoc.gov.au/info_sheet.html> (accessed May 5, 2006).

A Pictorial Guide to Hell

Newspaper article

By: John Kifner

Date: January 24, 2001

Source: Kifner, John. "A Pictorial Guide to Hell." The *New York Times* (January 24, 2001).

About the Author: John Kifner is an award-winning journalist and foreign correspondent at the *New York Times*, where he has worked since his graduation from Williams College in 1963. Kifner's stories focus on national politics, war, and current events, and he has worked in Chicago, Boston, Egypt, Lebanon, Poland, Bosnia, Iran, Afghanistan, and Iraq.

INTRODUCTION

John Kifner's poignant review of *Blood and Honey: A Balkan War Journal* brought a photograph that was widely published in 1992 back into the limelight. The photograph was taken by Ron Haviv, a photojournalist who documented the Bosnian Serb takeover of the town of Bijeljina in Bosnia and Herzegovina in April 1992. As Kifner describes, for many, Haviv's photograph—a young soldier with sunglasses and a cigarette, casually kicking the body of a woman in the street next to her house—personifies the horror of ten years of war in the former Yugoslavia.

Haviv's book serves as a searing testament to the violence that killed over 300,000 Europeans in the 1990s. The wars in the Balkans included the greatest occurrence of genocide since World War II and introduced the term "ethnic cleansing" to the world. Exhibits of Haviv's photographs based on *Blood and Honey* have been displayed in several museums since Kifner's review. In addition to shows in New York and Sarajevo, exhibits have also taken place in Dubrovnik, Croatia, where tourists from Adriatic cruise ships encounter the shocking images from the previous decade, and in several towns in Serbia, where violent protest caused the exhibit to close in two cities in 2002.

The image is stark, one of the most enduring of the Balkan wars: a Serb militiaman casually kicking a dying Muslim woman in the head. It tells you everything you need to know.

Ron Haviv was 27 when he took that photograph in the early spring of 1992, and even today the words come tumbling out, every detail etched in his memory, when he talks about it. The picture is one of the most gripping in his new book, "Blood and Honey: A Balkan War Journal" (TV Books/Umbrage Editions), a collection of searing photographs. Some of the photos are on view through Feb. 8 at the Saba Gallery (116 East 16th Street, Manhattan) and will go on permanent exhibition at the war museum in Sarajevo.

The previous year in Vukovar, Serbs had killed a Croatian woman in front of Mr. Haviv and prevented him from taking the picture. He had vowed it would not happen again.

This time it was the town of Bijeljina, at the very beginning of the Bosnian phase of a war that tore the former Yugoslavia apart. Tensions were high as reports and rumors spread of Serbian plans for what would eventually be termed "ethnic cleansing." Zeljko Raznatovic, the gangster turned paramilitary leader known as Arkan, stormed into the largely Muslim town with his Tigers militia, and the carnage began.

"They were going house to house, looking for fighters and things to take," Mr. Haviv remembered. "Inside a mosque, they had taken down the Islamic flag and were holding it like a trophy. They had a guy, they said he was a fundamentalist from Kosovo. He was begging for his life.

"There was shouting outside. They had taken the town butcher and his wife, and they were screaming. They shot him, and he was lying there.

"The soldiers were shouting in Serbian, 'No pictures, no pictures.'

"I felt like I had to photograph it. There was a truck that had crashed nearby. I got between the cab and the body and turned my back so the soldiers couldn't see me. They shot the woman, then they brought out her sister and shot her.

"I was trying to think as clearly as possible. It was incredibly important for evidence to try to get the soldiers with the bodies in the same picture. I framed it, I was probably about 30 feet away.

"There were the two soldiers. Another came from my left, he had a cigarette in one hand and sunglasses on top of his head. When he kicked her, it was like the ultimate disrespect for everything."

He had the pictures, but he still needed clearance from Arkan to leave. As Mr. Haviv waited for the warlord, he frantically stripped his cameras, hid the rolls of film and reloaded.

"I heard this crash," he said. "The Kosovar came flying out of a third-floor window and landed at my feet. I started photographing him."

A few minutes later, Arkan arrived. "I need your film," he said.

At first Arkan said he would have the film processed and give back the pictures he approved of, Mr. Haviv said. But he immediately began a long, complicated argument about the poor quality of film processing in Belgrade, which so distracted Arkan that he wound up taking the two rolls of film in the cameras and not bothering to search for more. When the pictures were published abroad, Mr. Haviv was put on a Serbian death list and was once held and beaten for three days.

Mr. Haviv had been, at this point, a major international photographer for about three years. He had studied journalism at New York University, graduating in 1987, but only took up photography as a hobby in his senior year.

He started out as an assistant to a fashion photographer, then broke in as a street photographer—working free at first—for the New York City Tribune, the defunct Unification Church newspaper, then Agence France-Presse.

Chris Morris, a swashbuckling war photographer, took the young man under his wing, helping him get to Panama for his first big glimpse of history in 1989. He scored a rare trifecta—the covers of *Time, Newsweek* and *U.S. News & World Report*—with his shot of a vice presidential candidate being beaten by paramilitary thugs.

He knew little about the Balkans when he set out for Slovenia, where a brief war was brewing in 1991. A decade later, he is wiser and sadder.

"I was very happy when the pictures were published," he said. "It was a week before the first shots were fired in Sarajevo. There were lots of reports from journalists, diplomats, spies, everybody, that Bosnia was going to be very bad. I thought these pictures would provide a final push, so the world would stop this. But obviously nothing happened. It was really incredibly disappointing.

"I went from this very idealistic view of the power of photography to feeling it was just really frustrating. We all wound up feeling that way all through Bosnia—photographers, journalists, television people. Nobody was really listening. There were just halfhearted efforts to solve the situation. Then Kosovo, and once again the waffling that led to so many deaths. And the victims become

Supporters of NATO military operations in the Balkans demonstrate in front the Federal Building on April 3, 1999 in Los Angeles, California. HECTOR MATA/AFP/GETTY IMAGES.

aggressors, and the aggressors become victims, and it goes around and around."

SIGNIFICANCE

Ron Haviv's photographs from April 1992 were among the first that the international media saw of the ethnic violence that accompanied the dissolution of Yugoslavia. Bijeljina, the scene of his most famous photograph, was the first town in Bosnia and Herzegovina attacked in what came to be known as the Bosnian War. As *Human Rights Watch* notes, the attack on the Bijeljina Bosniaks (one of the minority ethnic groups of Bosnia and Herzegovina, predominantly Muslim) foreshadowed methods of ethnic cleansing that were used by several different factions in Croatia, Kosovo, Macedonia, and Serbia and Montenegro in the following ten years and documented in *Blood and Honey*. In the four days following Arkan's invasion, many more civilians were killed and houses and stores were looted and burned. Over the next few years, most of the surviving Bosniaks in

Bijeljina were forced into the army, sent to detention camps, or sentenced to forced labor. By the time the Dayton Agreement was signed in December 1995, fewer than a tenth of Bijeljina's 30,000 Bosniaks remained in the city.

Blood and Honey and Haviv's more recent work, *Afghanistan: The Road to Kabul*, bring war photography and its role in influencing international policy into the news and onto coffee tables. A Serbian documentary film entitled *Vivisect* explores Serbian reactions to Haviv's work, and *National Geographic* featured Haviv in a film examining the risks taken by freelance photographers in combat. Susan Sontag uses Haviv and his Bijeljina photograph as an illustration of the war photography genre in her essay on the meanings and social impact of photographs of human-led violence.

Journalist John Flinn summed up his experience of the *Blood and Honey* exhibit in the new War Photo Limited gallery in Dubrovnik in 2005:

...there were no captions on the photos. You had to go over to the far wall to learn which of the subjects were Croat victims of Serbian attacks, which were Serbs suffering at the hands of Croats, which were Bosnians ducking Croat bullets and which were Albanians being attacked by Montenegrins. Maybe someone from the Balkans could tell the victims apart, but they all looked the same to me. It made clear that every side in the war had blood on its hands, that innocent people suffered everywhere.

FURTHER RESOURCES

Books

Haviv, Ron, et al. *Blood and Honey: A Balkan War Journal*. New York: TV Books/Umbrage Editions, 2000.

Haviv, Ron, and Ilana Ozernoy. *Afghanistan: The Road to Kabul*. Millbrook, N.Y.: de.MO, 2002.

Periodicals

Flinn, John. "Life After War: An 'Adriatic Camelot,' Dubrovnik Packs in Tourists While Patching Scars." *San Francisco Chronicle* (December 4, 2005).

Lommen, Andre. "Bosnia and Hercegovina Unfinished Business: The Return of Refugees and Displaced Persons to Bijeljina." *Human Rights Watch* 12, 7 (May 2000).

Sontag, Susan. "Looking at War: Photography's View of Devastation and Death." The *New Yorker* (December 9, 2002): 82–98.

Honor Killings

Photograph

By: Lynsey Addario

Date: 2001

Source: © Lynsey Addario/Corbis.

About the Photographer: Lynsey Addario is a freelance photojournalist with a passion for human rights issues. She is best known for her coverage of women's issues in the developing world, including the treatment of women in Afghanistan under the Taliban. Her work has appeared in the *New York Times*, *Boston Globe*, *Time*, *Newsweek*, *National Geographic*, and the Associated Press, among other publications. In 2002, Addario was named Young Photographer of the Year by the International Center of Photography and one of the Thirty Best Emerging Photographers by Photo District News. She was also awarded the Fujifilm Young Photographer Prize in 2005 for her coverage of life in Iraq before and during the American invasion. Originally from Westport, Connecticut, Addario

holds a degree in International Relations from the University of Wisconsin at Madison and currently resides in Istabul, Turkey.

INTRODUCTION

The photograph below portrays the tragic aftermath of an attempted honor killing in Pakistan. The term "honor killing" refers to the premeditated murder of a female by members (generally male) of her own family in response to a perceived threat to family honor or esteem. Under the laws of Islam, women in Pakistan and many other predominantly Islamic countries are considered to be the property and responsibility of their male relatives, first of their father and brothers and then of their husbands when they marry. A woman's conduct is seen as reflective of the honor and reputation of her family. Any behavior that is deemed to bring shame or dishonor to the family may be punished with physical abuse or death. This abuse of women is sanctioned under *Shar'iah*, the traditional Islamic law that governs family matters and the everyday lives of Muslim followers. Honor killings and the abuse of women in the name of family honor have been known to occur in many Middle Eastern countries and among immigrants to western nations, but are particularly prevalent in the country of Pakistan.

■ PRIMARY SOURCE

HONOR KILLINGS

See primary source image.

SIGNIFICANCE

The perceived link between female sexuality and family honor is a strong one in fundamentally religious and patriarchal cultures. Women's sexuality, courtship, whom they may marry, their virginity and the loss of virginity in wedlock, and even separation and divorce are strongly regulated by the family. Any suggestion of impropriety is seen to cast a shadow on the reputation and esteem of the family, particularly its male members, and must be harshly punished in order to restore the family honor.

Honor killing takes many forms and is exacted in a variety of circumstances, all primarily related to sexual conduct or perceptions of impropriety on the part of the woman. Allegations of infidelity or pre-marital intercourse, disobedience to a male relative, refusal to participate in an arranged marriage, separation and divorce (even from an abusive husband), bearing a child out of wedlock, venturing into public without a

PRIMARY SOURCE

Honor Killings: Nayyar Shahzaidi, a victim of an attempted honor killing, at her parent's home in Pakistan, February 2003. © LYNSEY ADDARIO/CORBIS.

chaperone, becoming the victim of a rape—all of these have been cited as reasons for the abuse or murder of women. Women have been raped, beaten, stoned to death, shot, strangled, burned alive, dismembered, disfigured, stabbed, and had their throats slashed. These atrocities are committed in the name of honor.

The United Nations' 1948 Universal Declaration of Human Rights states that "all human beings are born free and equal in dignity and rights . . . everyone has the right to life, liberty and security of the person and . . . no one shall be subject to torture or to cruel, inhuman or degrading treatment or punishment" (Articles 3, 1 and 5). The declaration also codifies the right to equal treatment and protection under the law and the right to marry a person of one's choosing and not to be forced into an unwanted marriage (Articles 7 and 16). Clearly, the practice of honor killing constitutes the violation of women's fundamental human rights as they are set out by the United Nations, yet the authorities of many Islamic countries have overlooked and condoned the abuse of women as the ritual practice of *Shar'iah* law.

Although Pakistan, like many other predominantly Islamic states, has a secular system of criminal law and prohibits murder and abuse, police and courts have regularly turned a blind eye to honor killings, failing to prevent or prosecute them. The state has generally allowed family disputes to be resolved under *Shar'iah* rather than through the secular legal system. This system affords no justice for women who lose their dignity and their lives at the hands of their family members. The principles of *Qisas* and *Diyat* in *Shar'iah* law allow the family of a murder victim to forgive the killer, or demand retribution or blood money. Since the perpetrators of honor killings are nearly always family members of the victim, they go unpunished when other relatives choose to forgive them.

Despite attempts to legitimize honor killing through its basis in cultural and religious beliefs,

A Pakistani woman holds a placard carrying names of honor killing victims at a rally on October 8, 2004, in Islamabad, Pakistan. About 300 human right activists and lawmakers held a protest march to condemn violence against women and honor killings that claim hundreds of lives each year. AP IMAGES.

scholars such as Sev'er and Yurdakul (2001) argue that honor killings need to be considered as separate from the religious practice of Islam and considered as part of a larger continuum of patriarchy and misogyny that allows the abuse of women to take place. They point out that honor killings have been occurring since before the inception of Islam and *Shar'iah* and are not supported by the Qur'an. In fact, the justifications used for honor killings in Turkey are based in cultural notions of honor and not in religion. Feminists and human rights organizations have made efforts to increase international awareness of the systemic abuses of women in the Middle East, bringing media and public attention to the practice of honor killing and the role of patriarchy. While this problem is still rampant, progress is being made toward condemning and eradicating the abuse of women in the name of honor.

In January of 2005, President of Pakistan Pervez Musharraf passed a law making honor killings illegal and punishable by death. Although murder has always been illegal in Pakistan, the "grave and sudden

provocation" defense clause in Pakistan's legal system (inherited from the British common law) was used to justify and avoid conviction in cases of premeditated honor killings. In essence, the accused would argue that he was justified in committing the murder because he was provoked by the actions of the victim. Using this defense, the acquittal ratio was more than eighty percent in cases of honor killings. The new legislation precludes the use of the provocation defense, aiming to provide justice for the victims of these honor-based murders.

Honor killings occur most often in rural, socio-economically depressed areas. Like any other human phenomenon, there are two sides to every story—honor killings are not always undertaken lightly, and the cultural importance placed on honor and respect leaves some men with little choice. Take for example the words of a Turkish farmer, cited by Sev'er and Yurdakal, who killed his own daughter: "I would not have want [sic] to harm my own child, but I had no choice. Nobody would buy my produce. I had to make a living for my other children." While remorse does not excuse the crime committed, this quote illustrates the complexity of the human emotions and cultural/religious beliefs involved in taking the life of a daughter, wife, or sister for the sake of honor. Many social, cultural, and legal changes are required to eliminate the practice of honor killing and protect the intrinsic human rights of Muslim women.

FURTHER RESOURCES

Periodicals

Hajjar, Lisa. "Religion, State Power, and Domestic Violence in Muslim Societies: A Framework for Comparative Analysis." *Law & Social Inquiry* 29, 1 (2004): 1–38.

Jamal, Amina. "Gender, Citizenship and the Nation-State in Pakistan: Willful Daughters or Free Citizens?" *Signs* 31, 2 (2006): 283–305.

Maris, Cees and Sawtiri Saharso. "Honour Killing: A Reflection on Gender, Culture and Violence." *Netherlands Journal of Social Sciences* 37, 1 (2001): 52–73.

Mullally, Siobhán. "'As Nearly as May Be': Debating Women's Human Rights in Pakistan." *Social and Legal Studies* 14, 3 (2005): 341–358.

Web sites

Amnesty International. "Pakistan: Honour Killings of Girls and Women." September 1, 1999. <http://web.amnesty.org/library/Index/engASA330181999> (accessed May 6, 2006).

Human Rights Commission of Pakistan. "The State of Human Rights in 2005." <http://www.hrcp-web.org/ar_home_05.cfm> (accessed May 6, 2006).

United Nations. "Universal Declaration of Human Rights." December 10, 1948. <http://www.un.org/Overview/rights.html> (accessed May 6, 2006).

Refugees and Asylum: Global Figures for 2002

Book excerpt

By: Anonymous

Date: 2002

Source: "Refugees and Asylum: Global Figures for 2002," *Pocket World in Figures 2005.* London: The Economist Group, 2005.

About the Author: These tables are reproduced from *Pocket World in Figures 2005*, a book produced by *The Economist*, a London-based weekly news magazine devoted to economics and politics.

INTRODUCTION

Refugees and other displaced persons are created by wars, repressive governments, natural disasters, poverty, and other factors. In the late twentieth and early twenty-first centuries, refugees of one sort or another numbered in the millions worldwide; the tables from this primary source give an idea of the scope of the problem as of 2002.

The figures in this table are derived from figures compiled by the United Nations High Commissioner on Refugees (UNHCR). The office of the UNHCR was created by the General Assembly of the United Nations (UN) in 1950 and tasked with resettling the 1.2 million European refugees displaced by World War II. The mission of the UNHCR was renewed by the UN every five years for over half a century, as refugees continued to be created in many parts of the world. In 2003, the traditional five-year limit was removed and the UNHCR's mission was extended indefinitely. As of 2006, the UNHCR employed over 6,500 personnel who worked in 116 countries attempting to help 19.2 million displaced people. The agency won the Nobel Peace Prize in 1954 and 1981.

PRIMARY SOURCE

REFUGEES AND ASYLUM

[Below, units are thousands; e.g., "574.4" means 574,400.]

Largest refugee nationalities

1.	Afghanistan	2480.9
2.	Burundi	574.4
3.	Sudan	505.2
4.	Angola	432.8
5.	Somalia	429.5
6.	West Bank and Gaza	428.7
7.	Congo	415.5
8.	Iraq	400.6
9.	Bosnia	371.6
10.	Vietnam	348.3
11.	Eritrea	315.6
12.	Liberia	274.5
13.	Croatia	269.7
14.	Azerbaijan	254.7
15.	Serbia & Montenegro	161.3
16.	Myanmar	148.5
17.	Sierra Leone	139.2
18.	Sri Lanka	126.5
19.	China	126.3
20.	Bhutan	112.4

Countries with largest refugee populations

1.	Iran	1306.3
2.	Pakistan	1227.4
3.	Germany	903.0
4.	Tanzania	689.4
5.	United States	485.2
6.	Serbia and Montenegro	354.4
7.	Congo	333.0
8.	Sudan	328.2
9.	China	297.3
10.	Armenia	247.6
11.	Zambia	246.8
12.	Saudi Arabia	245.3
13.	Kenya	233.7
14.	Uganda	217.3
15.	Guinea	182.2
16.	Algeria	169.2
17.	India	168.9
18.	United Kingdom	159.2
19.	Netherlands	148.4
20.	Sweden	142.2

Nationality of asylum applications in industrialized countries

1.	Iraq	51.0
2.	Serbia & Montenegro	33.1
3.	Turkey	29.6
4.	China	26.3
5.	Afghanistan	25.7
6.	Russia	20.0
7.	India	14.0
8.	Nigeria	13.6

9.	Congo	13.2
10.	Somalia	12.9
11.	Colombia	12.4
12.	Iran	11.6
13.	Mexico	10.4
14.	Pakistan	10.4
15.	Sri Lanka	10.2
16.	Algeria	9.8
17.	Zimbabwe	8.6
18.	Georgia	8.3
19.	Armenia	8.2
20.	Bosnia	8.0

Asylum applications in industrialized countries

1.	United Kingdom	110.7
2.	United States	81.1
3.	Germany	71.1
4.	France	50.8
5.	Austria	37.1
6.	Canada	33.4
7.	Sweden	33.0
8.	Switzerland	26.2
9.	Belgium	18.8
10.	Netherlands	18.7
11.	Norway	17.5
12.	Ireland	11.6
13.	Slovakia	9.7
14.	Czech Republic	8.5
15.	Italy	7.2
16.	Hungary	6.4
17.	Spain	6.2
18.	Australia	6.0

SIGNIFICANCE

Displaced persons are generally categorized as refugees, internally displaced persons, or stateless persons. Collectively, people in these groups are referred to by the UNHCR as "persons of concern." The number of persons of concern rose by thirteen percent from early 2004 to early 2005, that is, from seventeen million to 19.2 million.

Refugees are defined as persons who have fled persecution or war in their home countries to seek refuge in other states. There were about 9.2 million refugees worldwide in 2004. In that year, according to the UNHCR, about 1.5 million refugees returned to their homelands voluntarily, including 940,500 who returned to Afghanistan and 194,000 to Iraq. About 232,100 new refugees were created in the same period, however, mostly in Sudan, where the government-sponsored militias are (according to the U.S.

government and other observers) committing genocide against the inhabits of the Darfur region.

Some refugees apply formally for sanctuary in some state other than their home country, in which case they are asylum seekers. Asylum seekers usually apply for asylum in nearby, relatively peaceful, prosperous countries where human rights are usually respected; two thirds of asylum applications are made to European countries.

Internally displaced persons are people who have been driven from their homes by violence or other disasters but who remain inside their home country. The Sudan genocide in the Darfur region has created about 1.8 internally displaced persons in that country. In Colombia, conflict between government and rebel forces, in what the United Nations called in 2006 "the worst humanitarian crisis in the Western Hemisphere," has produced over two million internally displaced persons plus many refugees to neighboring states, including 26,000 to Ecuador since 2000.

Stateless persons are refugees or asylum seekers who do not have citizenship in any state and have no home state to which they can return.

The UNHCR notes that many factors drive people to move from their homes, whether they stay in-country or flee to a neighboring state. Some suffer extreme poverty and wish to move elsewhere in order to survive; some are displaced by environmental destruction, development projects, persecution because of religion, race, or ethnicity, or human trafficking (e.g., sexual slavery). The UNHCR stated in 2006 that "the world has witnessed a decline in armed conflict from a peak in the early 1990s," with correspondingly fewer refugees caused by armed conflict. However, it also noted that the global 'war on terror' has complicated many refugee crises, as the war on terror has been cited by various states to "justify new or intensified military offensives" in Aceh (in Indonesia), Afghanistan, Chechnya (in the Russian Federation), Georgia, Iraq, Pakistan, and Palestine, with the United States and European states being less likely to grant asylum due to anti-terror measures.

The UNHCR also states that economic globalization is causing many regions to undergo massive social upheavals, which in turn cause mass international migration. The system of international agreements and corporate freedoms often termed free trade allows for the rapid movement of goods, money, and corporations across national boundaries, but there is no corresponding freedom of movement for workers who are displaced by globalization's disruption of traditional markets in their home areas. Many persons therefore become illegal migrants, like the twelve million undocumented migrants in the United States. A migrant is anyone who lives outside their birth country for a year or more. Migrants are not necessarily synonymous with refugees; there are about 175 million migrants worldwide, about 3% of the world's population, but only about nineteen million refugees (still a tremendous number—about a third larger than the entire population of New England).

Many refugees end up living for long periods of time in camps or other confined zones, usually located in unstable border areas. Only voluntary repatriation (return to the home country), acceptance by the country of refuge, or resettlement to some other country offers a permanent solution to the refugee dilemma. An example of a largely successful repatriation program is Liberia, where after the end of a fourteen-year civil war in 2003, repatriation of over 300,000 refugees from neighboring countries began under UNHCR auspices in 2004 and was expected to run through 2007. To support the returning population, the UN oversaw scores of development projects focusing on water, sanitation, schools, and infrastructure.

FURTHER RESOURCES

Books

Newman, Edward and Joanna van Selm, eds. *Refugees and Forced Displacement: International Security, Human Vulnerability, and the State.* New York: United Nations University Press, 2003.

Periodicals

Wilson, Scott. "Iraqi Refugees Overwhelm Syria." *The Washington Post.* February 3, 2005.

Web sites

United Nations High Commissioner for Refugees. "The State of the World's Refugees 2006." 2006. <http://www.unhcr.org/cgi-bin/texis/vtx/> (accessed May 5, 2006).

Global Internet Freedom Act

Legislation

By: Christopher Cox and Thomas Lantos

Date: October 2, 2002

Source: U.S. Congress. House. *Global Internet Freedom Act of 2002.* HR 5524. 107th Congress, 2nd session. Available online at <http://thomas.loc.gov/cgi-bin/query/z?c107:H.R.5524:%20This%20act,%20proposed %20in%202002,%20predates%20Yahoo%20and%20 Google's%20willingness%20to%20incluse%20censorship %20technology%20in%20its%20products%20for% 20the%20Chinese%20market> (accessed April 30, 2006).

About the Author: Representative Christopher Cox (R, CA) served in the U.S. House of Representatives from 1989 to 2005. Representative Tom Lantos (D, CA) has served in the House since 1981 and, as of 2006, was still serving.

INTRODUCTION

House Resolution 5524, the Global Internet Freedom Act, was introduced in the U.S. House of Representatives in October 2002 by Representatives Christopher Cox (R, CA) and Tom Lantos (D, CA). It was a bipartisan effort to counter censorship of the Internet by various non-U.S. countries. The act would have established an Office of Global Internet Freedom inside the International Broadcasting Bureau, which is the federal agency that oversees all U.S. government propaganda broadcasts abroad. The act would also have provided $50 million per year for 2004 and 2005 to fund implementation of a global Internet freedom policy.

The bill stalled in committee and was not voted on by the House during the 108th Congress. Its provisions were subsumed into Title V, subtitle B of H.R. 1950 during the 109th Congress (Foreign Relations Authorization Act of 2004–05). This bill was passed by the House in July 2003. However, the Internet-freedom provisions did not take effect because the corresponding Senate bill, S. 925, did not contain them.

The Global Internet Freedom Act was re-introduced by Representative Cox during the 109th Congress on May 10, 2005 as H.R. 2216. The bill was referred to the House Committee on International Relations, and, as of May 2006, it had not come to the House for a vote.

■ PRIMARY SOURCE

Mr. COX (for himself and Mr. LANTOS) introduced the following bill; which was referred to the Committee on International Relations.

A BILL.

To develop and deploy technologies to defeat Internet jamming and censorship.

Be it enacted by the Senate and House of Representatives of the United States of America in Congress assembled.

Yi Li, a graduate student from Taiwan, using a computer at the New York Public Library. He supports the federal court decision issued in Philadelphia that bans government censorship of the Internet, stating "We can use the (free flow of) information to unite the world." AP IMAGES.

SECTION 1. SHORT TITLE.

This Act may be cited as the 'Global Internet Freedom Act'.

SEC. 2. FINDINGS.

The Congress makes the following findings:.

(1) Freedom of speech, freedom of the press, and freedom of association are fundamental characteristics of a free society. The first amendment to the Constitution of the United States guarantees that 'Congress shall make no law ... abridging the freedom of speech, or of the press; or the right of the people peaceably to assemble.' These constitutional provisions guarantee the rights of Americans to communicate and associate with one another without restriction, including unfettered communication and association via the Internet. Article 19 of the United Nation's Universal Declaration of Human Rights explicitly guarantees the freedom to 'receive and impart

information and ideas through any media and regardless of frontiers'.

(2) All people have the right to communicate freely with others, and to have unrestricted access to news and information, on the Internet.

(3) With nearly 10 percent of the world's population now online, and more gaining access each day, the Internet stands to become the most powerful engine for democratization and the free exchange of ideas ever invented.

(4) Unrestricted access to news and information on the Internet is a check on repressive rule by authoritarian regimes around the world.

(5) The governments of Burma, Cuba, Laos, North Korea, the People's Republic of China, Saudi Arabia, Syria, and Vietnam, among others, are taking active measures to keep their citizens from freely accessing the Internet and

obtaining international political, religious, and economic news and information.

(6) Intergovernmental, nongovernmental, and media organizations have reported the widespread and increasing pattern by authoritarian governments to block, jam, and monitor Internet access and content, using technologies such as firewalls, filters, and 'black boxes'. Such jamming and monitoring of individual activity on the Internet includes surveillance of e-mail messages, message boards, and the use of particular words; 'stealth blocking' individuals from visiting websites; the development of 'black lists' of users that seek to visit these websites; and the denial of access to the Internet.

(7) The Voice of America and Radio Free Asia, as well as hundreds of news sources with an Internet presence, are routinely being jammed by repressive governments.

(8) Since the 1940s, the United States has deployed anti-jamming technologies to make Voice of America and other United States Government sponsored broadcasting available to people in nations with governments that seek to block news and information.

(9) The United States Government has thus far commenced only modest steps to fund and deploy technologies to defeat Internet censorship. To date, the Voice of America and Radio Free Asia have committed a total of $1,000,000 for technology to counter Internet jamming by the People's Republic of China. This technology, which has been successful in attracting 100,000 electronic hits per day from the People's Republic of China, has been relied upon by Voice of America and Radio Free Asia to ensure access to their programming by citizens of the People's Republic of China, but United States Government financial support for the technology has lapsed. In most other countries there is no meaningful United States support for Internet freedom.

(10) The success of United States policy in support of freedom of speech, press, and association requires new initiatives to defeat totalitarian and authoritarian controls on news and information over the Internet.

SEC. 3. PURPOSES.

The purposes of this Act are—.

(1) to adopt an effective and robust global Internet freedom policy;.

(2) to establish an office within the International Broadcasting Bureau with the sole mission of countering Internet jamming and blocking by repressive regimes;.

(3) to expedite the development and deployment of technology to protect Internet freedom around the world;.

(4) to authorize the commitment of a substantial portion of United States international broadcasting resources to the

continued development and implementation of technologies to counter the jamming of the Internet;.

(5) to utilize the expertise of the private sector in the development and implementation of such technologies, so that the many current technologies used commercially for securing business transactions and providing virtual meeting space can be used to promote democracy and freedom; and

(6) to bring to bear the pressure of the free world on repressive governments guilty of Internet censorship and the intimidation and persecution of their citizens who use the Internet.

SEC. 4. DEVELOPMENT AND DEPLOYMENT OF TECHNOLOGIES TO DEFEAT INTERNET JAMMING AND CENSORSHIP.

(a) ESTABLISHMENT OF OFFICE OF GLOBAL INTERNET FREEDOM—There is established in the International Broadcasting Bureau the Office of Global Internet Freedom (hereinafter in this Act referred to as the 'Office'). The Office shall be headed by a Director who shall develop and implement a comprehensive global strategy to combat state-sponsored and state-directed Internet jamming, and persecution of those who use the Internet.

(b) AUTHORIZATION OF APPROPRIATIONS—There are authorized to be appropriated to the Office $50,000,000 for each of the fiscal years 2003 and 2004.

(c) COOPERATION OF OTHER FEDERAL DEPARTMENTS AND AGENCIES—Each department and agency of the United States Government shall cooperate fully with, and assist in the implementation of, the strategy developed by the Office and shall make such resources and information available to the Office as is necessary to the achievement of the purposes of this Act.

(d) REPORT TO CONGRESS—On March 1 following the date of the enactment of this Act and annually thereafter, the Director of the Office shall submit to the Congress a report on the status of state interference with Internet use and of efforts by the United States to counter such interference. Each report shall list the countries that pursue policies of Internet censorship, blocking, and other abuses; provide information concerning the government agencies or quasi-governmental organizations that implement Internet censorship; and describe with the greatest particularity practicable the technological means by which such blocking and other abuses are accomplished. In the discretion of the Director, such report may be submitted in both a classified and nonclassified version.

(e) LIMITATION ON AUTHORITY—Nothing in this Act shall be interpreted to authorize any action by the United States to interfere with foreign national censorship for the purpose of protecting minors from harm, preserving public morality, or assisting with legitimate law enforcement aims.

SEC. 5. SENSE OF CONGRESS.

It is the sense of the Congress that the United States should—.

(1) publicly, prominently, and consistently denounce governments that restrict, censor, ban, and block access to information on the Internet;.

(2) direct the United States Representative to the United Nations to submit a resolution at the next annual meeting of the United Nations Human Rights Commission condemning all governments that practice Internet censorship and deny freedom to access and share information; and.

(3) deploy, at the earliest practicable date, technologies aimed at defeating state-directed Internet censorship and the persecution of those who use the Internet.

SIGNIFICANCE

The anti-blocking activities proposed by the Global Internet Freedom Act would not be entirely new. The Broadcasting Board of Governors, which oversees the U.S. International Broadcasting Bureau, already conducts federally funded anti-Internet-blocking activities. However, as noted in the Global Internet Freedom Act, only $1 million was appropriated for the Broadcasting Board of Governors' Internet anti-censorship program in fiscal year 2004. Another million dollars was appropriated in 2005. Most of this money was spent on the creation of Chinese-language e-mail programs that would enable Internet users inside China to exchange forbidden information—especially political information—using frequently-changing proxy servers. A proxy server is a computer that an Internet user employs to access the Internet indirectly; a proxy server can accelerate access to Web pages by compressing and archiving them, it can censor or filter content, and it can strip identifying information from a user's messages, rendering the user anonymous. The latter ability makes proxy servers particularly useful for Internet users in China who wish to evade that country's strict and comprehensive controls on Web access. However, proxy servers must be changed frequently lest they be tracked down by government agents.

China is, as the Act notes, not the only country to censor or filter Internet content. Even some countries not generally thought of as anti-democratic, such as Germany, block Internet access to certain sites (in Germany's case, Nazi websites). However, China has

by far the greatest number of blocked Internet users of any country—about 103 million as of June 2005. It employs approximately 30,000 full-time Internet police censors to monitor e-mail, Web usage, chat rooms, and the like. It also uses powerful computers located at points where international data lines leave and enter China to search for key terms and block objectionable material. Through threats of punishment it motivates Internet service companies inside China to self-censor, so that the government censorship apparatus need only catch whatever material evades private network censorship. Banned subject matter includes pro-democracy websites, any reference to the Tiananmen Square protests in Beijing in 1989, and any reference to the forbidden Falun Gong religious movement, which the government in China has outlawed.

It is difficult to evaluate the success of the U.S. Board of Broadcast Governors' efforts to improve Web and e-mail access to persons in countries such as Iran and China. This would require detailed in-country surveys that are not feasible, given the level of political repression in those countries. However, the U.S.-China Economic and Security Review Commission noted in its 2005 annual report to Congress that efforts to provide uncensored Web access to computer users in Iran and China had been partly defeated by U.S. efforts to block sexual content from those users. By attempting to censor the Web for Iranian and Chinese users in a way that it is not censored for U.S. users, the United States ended up blocking, the Commission reported, "thousands of useful and non-controversial sites such as sites for the U.S. Embassy, a presidential election campaign, and a popular email service." The United States, the Commission concluded, "was over-blocking in its own effort to control what Iranian and Chinese users could view." Blockage of sexual content inside the United States, with the exception of child pornography, would be a violation of the First Amendment to the U.S. Constitution.

Independent computer experts have also sought to develop software to bypass Internet censorship by governments. Such private efforts are not hampered by a desire to censor sexual material, but their effectiveness is as difficult to evaluate as that of U.S. government efforts.

Attempts to view forbidden material remain personally risky in China. Scores of individuals (possibly many more) have been sentenced to long prison terms for accessing forbidden websites. In Iran, similar numbers of Web users have received, and continue to receive, similar punishments.

FURTHER RESOURCES

Books

Chase, Michael, and James Mulvenon. *You've Got Dissent! Chinese Dissident Use of the Internet and Beijing's Counter-Strategies.* Santa Monica, Calif.: Rand, 2002.

Periodicals

MacLeod, Calum. "Web Users Walk Great Firewall of China." *USA Today* (April 3, 2006).

Web sites

Congressional Research Service. "Internet Development and Information Control in the People's Republic of China." February 10, 2006. <fpc.state.gov/documents/organization/64789.pdf> (accessed May 2, 2006).

Chirac Calls for Ban on Headscarves

News article

By: News Service

Date: December 17, 2003

Source: *CBC News.* "Chirac Calls for Ban on Headscarves." December 17, 2003. <http://www.cbc.ca/story/news/national/2003/12/17/france_scarves031217.html> (accessed April 20, 2006).

About the Author: The Canadian Broadcasting Company, Canada's premier news source, was created by an Act of Parliament in 1936. CBC operations include radio, television, and Internet news services.

INTRODUCTION

France is home to Europe's largest Muslim population; at least five million people—approximately 8–9 percent of the country's 60 million inhabitants. As an openly secular country, France's 1789 Constitution established freedom of religion. In 1905, France added a law that strictly separates church and state. This policy of *laïcité* requires neutrality from the government in all religious affairs; this extends to public schools, all government institutions, and even to political statements made by politicians. Religion, in French culture, is treated as a private matter.

For nearly two decades, the issue of headscarves worn by female Muslims has been debated in French society. Religious symbols such as the cross and yarmulke had been tolerated in public schools and by government institutions, as long as the display of faith was modest and did not overtly violate separation of church and state. As the Muslim population increased in France and more young women entered schools wearing headscarves, this highly visible mode of religious expression became a subject of contention. Throughout the 1990s, the Ministry of Education turned to the Council of State to rule on numerous individual cases involving Muslim girls and headscarves. France had no federal law to deal with such cases.

Muslims claim that forbidding the headscarves violates freedom of religion for schoolgirls, makes them the target of ridicule and anger by fellow Muslims who accuse them of shirking their religion, and that the scarves are not inherently a tool for proselytizing or religious militancy. On the other side of the debate, President Jacques Chirac has argued that "Wearing a veil, whether we want it or not, is a sort of aggression that is difficult for us to accept." In addition, some public school teachers claim that the scarves are prominent and interfere with educational religious neutrality in the classroom, while some feminists argue that the head covering, with roots in the idea that women must cover themselves to thwart male advances, stands out as a symbol of female oppression.

In 2003, French President Jacques Chirac called for an investigation into the issue.

■ PRIMARY SOURCE

PARIS—French President Jacques Chirac wants to shore up the country's secular tradition by banning religious symbols from public schools, a move that some believe will stigmatize Muslims by forcing girls to take off their headscarves.

Chirac asked the French parliament to introduce a law, following the recommendations issued by a presidential panel last week.

The 20-person panel, struck to look into the issue of secularism, said all ostentatious displays of religion or political affiliation should be banned from public buildings.

Warning that "fanaticism is gaining ground" in the country, Chirac said he also wanted to clear the way for businesses to impose similar bans.

"Secularism is one of the great successes of the Republic," Chirac said in an address to the nation. "It is a crucial element of social peace and national cohesion. We cannot let it weaken."

France has the largest Muslim population in Europe – five million people.

Many in France see the headscarf as a symbol of Muslim militancy.

Muslim women demonstrate against a French government proposal to bar them from wearing headscarves in state schools, on January 17, 2004, in Paris, France. PHOTO BY PASCAL LE SEGRETAIN/GETTY IMAGES.

Many Muslims see the headscarf as a mark of modesty and a symbol of their Islamic identity. They oppose a ban, calling it a discriminatory violation of their rights.

The ban, which Chirac wants in place for the start of the next school year in the fall of 2004, would also ban Jewish yarmulkes and large crucifixes.

The law is expected to have enough support from both sides of the political spectrum to pass the French parliament.

Chirac also asked for a law that would prevent patients in public hospitals from refusing treatment because of the gender of the treating physician or medical personnel. The panel's report included accounts of Muslim men refusing to let male doctors treat their wives.

The commission recommended that the Jewish holiday of Yom Kippur and the Muslim Eid el-Kabir feast be made school holidays. Chirac rejected that.

SIGNIFICANCE

According to 2004 surveys, more than sixty-nine percent of the French population (including more than forty percent of Muslims) support the prohibition of headscarves and other conspicuous religious symbols from classrooms. There were no Muslim members of Parliament at the time of the law's passage; Muslim critics note that this lack of representation meant that religious voices and perspectives were not taken into account in the creation of such legislation.

As Chirac notes above, "Secularism is one of the great successes of the Republic": proponents of the legislation state that Muslim political representation in Parliament is a private matter; a legislator's religion should not affect state policy or law. In addition to the argument that church and state should remain separate, the ban on overt religious symbols, according to proponents, also protects minors from pressure to follow a particular religion, be it endorsed by a teacher or a fellow classmate.

The debate over the law sparked protests in France, with thousands taking to the streets on February 14, 2004. Chirac signed the law on March 15, 2004, to take effect on September 2, 2004, the beginning of the French school year. In August 2004, two French citizens, Christian Chesnot and George Malbrunot, were taken hostage in Iraq and held by Muslim kidnappers. The hostage-takers demanded the repeal of the new law; Chirac refused to comply, and the hostages were later released alive.

The law went into effect on September 2, 2004, as planned. While a few hundred reports of violations of the law involving Muslim girls wearing headscarves were logged in the first few weeks, the overwhelming support of the French public, including forty-nine percent of French Muslim women, led to a fairly quiet acceptance of the new law.

FURTHER RESOURCES

Books

Cesari, Jocelyne. *When Islam and Democracy Meet: Muslims in Europe and in the United States.* New York: Palgrave Macmillan, 2004.

Klausen, Jytte. *The Islamic Challenge: Politics and Religion in Western Europe.* New York: Oxford University Press, USA, 2005.

Lumbard, Joseph. *Islam, Fundamentalism, and the Betrayal of Tradition: Essays by Western Muslim Scholars (Perennial Philosophy Series).* Bloomington, Ind.: World Wisdom, 2004.

Web sites

BBC News. "Islam Tests French Secularism." December 8, 2005. <http://news.bbc.co.uk/1/hi/world/europe/4507528.stm> (accessed April 20, 2006).

How Has 9/11 Changed America's Approach To Human Rights?

Magazine article

By: Harold Hongju Koh

Date: October 30, 2003

Source: Koh, Harold Hongju. "How Has 9/11 Changed America's Approach To Human Rights?" *The Economist* (October 30, 2003).

About the Author: Harold Hongju Koh was Assistant Secretary of State for Democracy, Human Rights and Labor under President Bill Clinton, starting on November 13, 1998. At the time this article was written, he was a professor of international law at Yale. In 2004, he became dean of the Yale Law School.

INTRODUCTION

The events of September 11, 2001, have often been compared to those of December 7, 1941, when Japanese aircraft attacked the U.S. Naval base at Pearl Harbor, Hawaii. In both cases, the U.S. public was shocked by sudden proof of unsuspected national vulnerability. In both cases, the nation responded by going to war.

During World War II (1939–1945), however, the enemy was a definite group of nation-states with traditional military forces. To fight the war primarily meant pitting armies, navies, and air forces against other armies, navies, and air forces, all easily identified. In what the U.S. government has termed "the war on terror," however, there is no national enemy. The declared foe is a methodology—the use of violence, terror, and intimidation to achieve a desired end—rather than any particular state or group. The United States has instituted a number of policies with possible effects on human rights since 9/11, citing as justification for these policies the peculiar secretiveness and elusiveness of terrorism. Most of these policies have been controversial. Critics have accused the United States of systematically violating human rights in its pursuit of the war on terror.

This primary source is written by American law professor Harold Hongju Koh, a critic of many of post-9/11 policies. Similar views have been expressed by many writers and speakers, but as a Yale University law professor, Koh backs his claims with professional credentials not held by most citizens.

PRIMARY SOURCE

I would argue that September 11th ended the euphoria brought on by the fall of the Berlin Wall, the belief that American-led global co-operation could solve global problems. The American administration responded to the twin-towers tragedy with a sweeping new global strategy: an emerging "Bush doctrine," if you will.

One element of this doctrine is what I call "Achilles and his heel." September 11th brought upon America, as once upon Achilles, a schizophrenic sense of both exceptional power and exceptional vulnerability. Never has a superpower seemed so powerful and so vulnerable at the same time. The Bush doctrine asked: "How can we use our superpower resources to protect our vulnerability?"

The administration's answer has been "homeland security." To preserve American power and prevent future attack, the government has asserted a novel right under international law to disarm through "pre-emptive self-defence" any country that poses a threat. At home it has instituted sweeping strategies of immigration control,

Travelers wait in line to be screened by security personnel at Hartsfield-Jackson Atlanta International Airport on June 1, 2004. AP IMAGES.

security detention, governmental secrecy and information awareness.

The administration has also radically shifted its emphasis on human rights. In 1941, Franklin Delano Roosevelt called the allies to arms by painting a vision of the world we were trying to make: a post-war world of four fundamental freedoms: freedom of speech, freedom of religion, freedom from want, freedom from fear.

This framework foreshadowed the post-war human-rights construct—embedded in the Universal Declaration of Human Rights and subsequent international covenants—that emphasised comprehensive protection of civil and political rights (freedom of speech and religion), economic, social and cultural rights (freedom from want), and freedom from gross violations and persecution (the Refugee Convention, the Genocide Convention and the Torture Convention). But Bush administration officials have now reprioritised "freedom from fear" as the

number-one freedom we need to preserve. Freedom from fear has become the obsessive watchword of America's human-rights policy.

Witness five faces of a human-rights policy fixated on freedom from fear. First, closed government and invasions of privacy. Second, scapegoating immigrants and refugees. Third, creating extra-legal zones, most prominently at the naval base at Guantanamo Bay in Cuba. Fourth, creating extra-legal persons, particularly the detainees of American citizenship labelled "enemy combatants." Fifth, a reduced American human-rights presence through the rest of the globe.

The following vignettes illustrate this transformation of human rights.

Closed government and invasion of privacy. Two core tenets of a post-Watergate world had been that our government does not spy on its citizens, and that American citizens should see what our government is doing. But since September 11th, classification of government documents has risen to new heights.

The Patriot Act, passed almost without dissent after September 11th, authorises the Defence Department to develop a project to promote something called "total information awareness." Under this programme, the government may gather huge amounts of information about citizens without proving they have done anything wrong. They can access a citizen's records—whether telephone, financial, rental, internet, medical, educational or library—without showing any involvement with terrorism. Internet service providers may be forced to produce records based solely on FBI declarations that the information is for an anti-terrorism investigation.

Many absurdities follow: the Lawyers Committee for Human Rights, in a study published in September, reports that 20 American peace activists, including nuns and high-school students, were recently flagged as security threats and detained for saying that they were travelling to a rally to protest against military aid to Colombia. The entire high-school wrestling team of Juneau, Alaska, was held up at airports seven times just because one member was the son of a retired Coast Guard officer on the FBI watch-list.

Scapegoating immigrants. After September 11th, 1,200 immigrants were detained, more than 750 on charges based solely on civil immigration violations. The Justice Department's own inspector-general called the attorney-general's enforcement of immigration laws "indiscriminate and haphazard." The Immigration and Naturalisation Service, which formerly had a mandate for humanitarian relief as well as for border protection, has been converted into an arm of the Department of Homeland Security.

The impact on particular groups has been devastating. The number of refugees resettled in America declined from 90,000 a year before September 11th to less than a third that number, 27,000, this year. The Pakistani population of Atlantic County, New Jersey has fallen by half.

The creation of extra-legal zones. Some 660 prisoners from 42 countries are being held in Guantanamo Bay, some for nearly two years. Three children are apparently being detained, including a 13-year-old, several of the detainees are aged over 70, and one claims to be over 100. Courtrooms are being built to try six detainees, including two British subjects who have been declared eligible for trial by military commission. There have been 32 reported suicide attempts. Yet the administration is literally pouring concrete around its detention policy, spending another $25m on buildings in Guantanamo that will increase the detention capacity to 1,100.

The creation of extra-legal persons. In two cases that are quickly working their way to the Supreme Court, Yasser Hamdi and José Padilla are two American citizens on American soil who have been designated as "enemy combatants," and who have been accorded no legal channels to assert their rights.

The racial disparities in the use of the "enemy combatant" label are glaring. Contrast, for example, the treatment of Mr. Hamdi, from Louisiana but of Saudi Arabian ancestry, with that of John Walker Lindh, the famous "American Taliban," who is a white American from a comfortable family in the San Francisco Bay area. Both are American citizens; both were captured in Afghanistan in late 2001 by the Northern Alliance; both were handed over to American forces, who eventually brought them to the United States. But federal prosecutors brought criminal charges against Mr. Lindh, who got an expensive lawyer and eventually plea-bargained to a prison term. Meanwhile, Mr. Hamdi has remained in incommunicado detention, without a lawyer, in a South Carolina military brig for the past 16 months.

The effect on the rest of the world. America's anti-terrorist activities have given cover to many foreign governments who want to use "anti-terrorism" to justify their own crackdowns on human rights. Examples abound. In Indonesia, the army has cited America's use of Guantanamo to propose building an offshore prison camp on Nasi Island to hold suspected terrorists from Aceh. In Australia, Parliament passed laws mandating the forcible transfer of refugees seeking entry to detention facilities in Nauru, where children as young as three years old are being held, so that Australia does not (in the words of its defence minister) become a "pipeline for terrorists."

In China, Wang Bingzhang, the founder of the pro-democracy magazine *China Spring,* was recently sentenced to life imprisonment for "organising and leading a terrorist group," the first time, apparently, that the Chinese government has charged a democracy activist with terrorism. In Russia, Vladimir Putin on September 12th 2001 declared that America and Russia "have a common foe" because Osama bin Laden's people are connected to events in Chechnya. Within months the American government had added three Chechen groups to its list of foreign terrorist organisations.

In Egypt, the government extended for another three years its emergency law, which allows it to detain suspected national-security threats almost indefinitely without charge, to ban public demonstrations, and to try citizens before military tribunals. President Hosni Mubarak announced that America's parallel policies proved that "we were right from the beginning in using all means, including military tribunals, to combat terrorism."

What's wrong with this picture? Each prong of the Bush doctrine places America in the position of promoting double standards, one for itself, and another for the rest of the world. The emerging doctrine has placed startling pressure upon the structure of human-rights and international law that the United States itself designed and supported since 1948. In a remarkably short time, the United States has moved from being the principal supporter of that system to its most visible outlier.

Around the globe, America's human-rights policy has visibly softened, subsumed under the all-encompassing banner of the "war against terrorism." And at home, the Patriot Act, military commissions, Guantanamo and the indefinite detention of American citizens have placed America in the odd position of condoning deep intrusions by law, even while creating zones and persons outside the law.

At this point, you are surely asking: "Why did this happen?" and "What can we do about it?" People living outside America sometimes suggest that the reason is rooted in the American national culture of unilateralism, parochialism, and an obsession with power. With respect, let me urge you to see it differently. The Bush doctrine, I believe, is less a broad manifestation of American national character than of short-sighted decisions made by a particularly extreme American administration.

Many, if not most, Americans would have supported dealing with September 11th in a different way. Imagine, for example, the Bush administration dealing with the atrocity through the then prevailing multilateralist strategy of using global co-operation to solve global problems. On the day after the attack, George Bush could have flown to New York to stand in solidarity with the world's ambassadors in front of the United Nations.

He could have supported the International Criminal Court as a way of bringing the Osama bin Ladens and Saddam Husseins of the world to justice. He could have refrained from invading Iraq without a second UN resolution and he could have maintained a host of human-rights treaties to signal the need for even greater global solidarity in a time of terror. I am convinced that the American people would have supported him in all those efforts.

So to those who would blame American culture for America's unilateralism, let me remind you that not every American is equally well-placed to promote American uni-lateralism. In recent years, such individuals as Mr. Bush, Donald Rumsfeld, John Bolton, Jesse Helms, and Justice Antonin Scalia have held particularly strategic positions that enabled them to promote this sea-change in human-rights policy.

But if particular politicians and judges are part of the problem, they are also part of the solution. For, in recent months, American human-rights lawyers have launched multiple efforts to counter these trends, par-ticularly through lawsuits seeking to persuade judges to consider American law in light of universal human-rights principles.

What are the signs of this trend? With each passing day, I see growing resistance to these policies among ordinary Americans. Some promising examples:

- Career bureaucrats have started to challenge the administration's policies for undoing years of hard work.
- Military judges and former federal prosecutors have expressed dismay over military commissions.
- A group of former federal judges filed a brief in the Padilla case challenging the president's detention of American citizens without express congressional authorisation. They were joined in those efforts by two conservative libertarian groups: the Cato Institute and the Rutherford Institute.
- Career diplomats have told me of early retirements by those who refuse to implement what they view as discriminatory visa policies.
- A group of former American diplomats and former American prisoners-of-war have challenged the administration's flouting of the Geneva Conventions before the Supreme Court.
- Librarians and booksellers have joined a bipartisan group of 133 congressional representatives to press for a law, called the Freedom to Read Protection Act, that would shield library and bookstore records from government surveillance.

These grassroots efforts are finally reaching the political actors. The public outcry following the leak of a proposed second Patriot Act has put that legislation on hold. Resolutions opposing the first Patriot Act have passed in three states and 162 municipalities. The House of Representatives has refused to provide funding for the part of the Patriot Act that allows so-called "sneak and peek" searches of private property without prompt notice to the resident. A battle is brew-ing in Congress over whether parts of the current act should be eliminated in 2005.

Most important, the key cases are finally starting to make their way to the United States Supreme Court. Now you may ask: what influence can a combination of interna-tional pressure and protest from ordinary Americans have on such a conservative court?

But recent cases may give hope. For instance, last June in *Lawrence v. Texas,* the Supreme Court finally overruled its 17-year-old decision in *Bowers v. Hardwick,* which had permitted states to ban same-sex sodomy among consenting adults. Representing Mary Robinson, the former UN Human Rights High Commissioner, and several other human-rights groups, I had filed an amicus curiae brief urging the court to consider two decades of European human-rights precedent rejecting the criminal-isation of same-sex sodomy as a violation of the European Convention's right to privacy.

In a six-to-three vote, Justice Anthony Kennedy wrote, citing our brief, that the rationale of Bowers had been rejected by "values we [Americans] share with a wider civilisation." The court noted that "the right peti-tioners seek in this case has been accepted as an integral part of human freedom in many other countries" and that "[t]here has been no showing in [the United States] that governmental interest in circumscribing personal choice is somehow more legitimate or urgent."

What this may mean is that when the September 11th cases get to the Supreme Court, American human-rights lawyers can similarly argue that the legality of our policies must be evaluated by "values we [Americans] share with a wider civilisation." Citing Lawrence, human-rights advo-cates can urge the court to decide whether the rights being asserted by detainees like Mr. Hamdi, Mr. Padilla and those on Guantanamo "have been accepted as an integral part of human freedom in many other countries" and can argue that our government has not demonstrated "that the governmental interest in circumscribing [these freedoms] is somehow more legitimate or ugent" in the United States than in other countries that have seen fit to forgo such legal restrictions.

Whether our Supreme Court will accept these arguments remains unclear. But these cases may well determine whether historians will remember these past two years as a fundamental change, or as only a temporary eclipse, in America's human-rights leadership. I, for one, have neither given up hope, nor accepted as inevitable a 21st-century American human-rights policy that is increas-ingly at odds with core American and universal values.

In our "Declaration of Independence," Thomas Jefferson wrote: "When in the course of human events, it becomes necessary for one people ...to assume among the Power of the Earth, the separate and equal Station to which the Laws of Nature...entitle them, a decent respect to the opinions of mankind requires that they should declare the causes..." Most patriotic Americans, I believe, still think that our human-rights policy should pay "decent respect to the opinions of mankind." As a nation conceived in liberty and dedicated to certain inalienable rights, our country has strong primal instincts to address the world not just in the language of power, but through a combination of power and principle.

In 1759, Benjamin Franklin wrote: "They that can give up essential liberty to obtain a little temporary safety deserve neither." In the months ahead, I believe, we can both obtain our security and preserve our essential liberty, but only so long as we have courage from our courts, commitment from our citizens, and pressure from our foreign allies. Even after September 11th, America can still stand for human rights, but we can get there only with a little help from our friends.

SIGNIFICANCE

There is disagreement over whether U.S. government policy toward human rights has changed since 9/11. The U.S. government and those who support its post-9/11 policies maintain that the U.S. commitment to human rights is unchanged and that all official U.S. actions have been both morally and legally justified. Others have argued that many of the new policies are illegal, immoral, or both, and reflect an increased official disregard of human rights since 9/11. Koh represents the latter school of thought.

Some controversial post-9/11 human rights policies include:

(1) The United States has detained hundreds of persons captured in Afghanistan, Iraq, and other countries since 9/11. Almost all of these prisoners are held in detention centers outside U.S. borders, and only a few have been formally charged with any crime. The most famous of these detention centers is that at the U.S. Naval base at Guantanamo Bay, Cuba. The holding of prisoners for years without charge has been criticized as illegal and unjust. Further, the U.S. government does not categorize the prisoners it captures in the war on terror as prisoners of war and has argued that the protections of the Geneva Conventions do not apply to them. It also has argued that since these prisoners are not U.S. citizens and are not held inside U.S. territory, they are not entitled to rights granted by U.S. domestic law. In *Rasul v. Bush* (2004), the U.S. Supreme Court ruled that foreign nationals imprisoned at Guantanamo were entitled to challenge their detentions. In response, the U.S. government began reviewing the status of detainees before military tribunals. In February 2005, a federal judge ruled that the tribunals were illegal and that the detainees must be allowed to challenge their detentions in U.S. civilian courts. The case went before the U.S. Supreme Court again in 2006; a ruling was due by the end of June 2006.

(2) The possibility of torturing persons suspected of being terrorists has been widely discussed in the United States since 9/11. Prominent civil rights attorney Alan Dershowitz argued publicly in 2002 that, since torture will inevitably be practiced by the government, it would be best to provide for legalized torture. Also in 2002, a memorandum from the Justice Department to the White House claimed that torture could be used legally on members of the terrorist organization Al Qaeda. In 2003, a Defense Department memorandum declared that the president is not bound by U.S. federal anti-torture law or by the Torture Convention of 1984, an anti-torture treaty signed by the United States. According to the *New York Times*, an official 2002 memo of the U.S. administration authorized the use of an interrogation technique called "water boarding," in which a suspect is strapped to a board and held under water until they think they are going to be drowned. President George W. Bush has insisted, however, that the United States does not use torture or employ other illegal means of interrogation. "We do not torture," he stated during a 2005 visit to Panama. In 2005, the International Committee of the Red Cross concluded that U.S. interrogation practices at Guantanamo were "tantamount to torture." In February 2006, the United Nations Human Rights Commission demanded that the United States cease the interrogation and force-feeding practices deemed "tantamount to torture" by the Red Cross. In 2005, Craig Murray, the former British Ambassador to Uzbekistan, claimed that U.S. intelligence agencies routinely accept information obtained in Uzbekistan using torture. The U.S. government maintains that it has never approved of the use of torture or other illegal interrogation methods.

(3) In 2005, the *Washington Post* reported that the Central Intelligence Agency (CIA) was running a network of secret prisons outside the United States. The CIA seemed to acknowledge the existence of such a system of prisons by requesting that the Justice Department conduct a criminal investigation of the source of the information given in the article. Secret

imprisonment is illegal in the United States and in most countries allied with it.

(4) The Bush administration has been widely criticized for a secret CIA program to transfer terrorist suspects to foreign countries for interrogation. The practice, called "special rendition," was authorized by a directive signed by President Bush a few days after the 9/11 attacks, according to a March 6, 2005, report in the *New York Times*. Critics of the program have argued that its purpose is to have suspects tortured in countries where torture is routine, such as Egypt and Jordan.

(5) Increased surveillance of U.S. citizens and others has occurred since 9/11. Most controversially, it was reported by the *New York Times* in December 2005 that President Bush had authorized eavesdropping on the telephone calls of U.S. citizens and others in the United States without the issuing of warrants. This action has been described as illegal by a number of members of Congress, including Republican Arlen Specter (PA), chairman of the Senate Judiciary Committee. Its legality has been defended by the Bush Administration.

This list of controversial policies could be extended. Many experts and commentators have argued that all U.S. actions in the war on terror have, in fact, been fully legal and fully justified. Others, both in the United States and abroad, have argued that this is not the case, and that some policies, justified as necessary tactics in the war on terror, violate human rights.

FURTHER RESOURCES

Books

Nacos, Brigitte L. *Terrorism and Counterterrorism: Understanding Threats and Responses in the Post-9/11 World*. New York: Pearson/Longman, 2006.

Schulz, William F. *Tainted Legacy: 9/11 and the Ruin of Human Rights*. New York: Thunder's Mouth Press/Nation Books, 2003.

Periodicals

Leonnig, Carol. "Judge Rules Detainee Tribunals Illegal." *Washington Post* (February 1, 2005).

Lewis, Neil A. "Red Cross Finds Detainee Abuse in Guantanamo." *New York Times* (November 30, 2004).

Priest, Dana. "CIA Holds Terror Suspects in Secret Prisons: Debate Is Growing Within Agency About Legality and Morality of Overseas System Set Up After 9/11." *Washington Post* (November 2, 2005).

Risen, James, and Eric Lichtblau. "Bush Lets U.S. Spy on Callers Without Courts." *New York Times* (December 16, 2005).

National Identity Card

Photograph

By: Dave Caulkin

Date: November 17, 2004

Source: AP Images.

About the Photographer: The Associated Press is a worldwide news agency based in New York. Dave Caulkin is its chief photographer in London. He won a Pulitzer Prize in 1999.

INTRODUCTION

National identity cards are not creations of the twenty-first century. The Nazis used them, and under apartheid, the South African government required blacks and "coloureds" to carry them at all times. In both cases, the cards listed name, residence, and work information; if found in an area to which the bearer was denied access, they were subject to arrest. Accordingly, national ID cards inspire distrust and fear among many. In an age of terrorism and identity fraud, however, some countries are considering them. Identity fraud alone cost countries like the United Kingdom about 1.7 pounds (three million dollars) a year.

Many countries currently use national identity cards, including most European nations. As technology has progressed, their functions have evolved as well. Taiwan, a country that has used national ID cards since 1947, continued their use from the Japanese colonial government. Taiwan's cards also act as a police record, and the law mandates that they be carried at all times. In 2005, the government proposed storing fingerprint data in the cards. This issue is still being debated because many citizens fear that fingerprint data will be used to violate their human rights.

In the summer of 2005, shortly after the terrorists attacks on the London, England subway system, the British Parliament reopened the debate on national identity. During World War II, the United Kingdom implemented a national ID card system, but it ended the program in 1952. Proponents believe that the cards would help thwart terrorism because every person entering, working in, or living in the country would be required to have one. They would increase the possibility of identifying terrorists before an attack could be carried out. Opponents argue that they cannot guarantee to stop terrorism and could facilitate the quarantining of individuals based on family lineage, ethnic background, or country of origin.

IDENTITY CARD
United Kingdom of Great Britain and Northern Ireland

Surname/Nom
BLAIR
Nationality/Nationa...
BRITISH CITIZE...
Place of Birth/Lieu...
UK
Date of Birth/Date...
06 MAY 1953
Date of Issue/Date...
05 NOV 2004
Date of Expiry/Date...
04 NOV 2014
Sex/Sexe   Number/Nombre
M   5795-3957-110944-YFD

Holder's signature/Signature du titulaire

Prénoms

PRIMARY SOURCE

National Identity Card: On November 17, 2004, protestors in central London burn a mock-up of an identity card of Prime Minister Tony Blair in demonstration as Home Secretary David Blunkett was making a keynote speech on his plans to introduce a national identity card. AP IMAGES.

On November 17, 2004, protestors burned a mock identity card of Prime Minister Tony Blair in central London, a throwback to Vietnam-era protests in the United States when protestors burned their draft cards. The message of British protestors is clear: They do not want their personal data compiled into a database that could possibly be seen by a computer hacker, nor do they want the government to have large files of their personal information. Also, individuals fear that the cards could make their movements and financial transactions too easy to track.

PRIMARY SOURCE

NATIONAL IDENTITY CARD

See primary source image.

SIGNIFICANCE

The idea of national identity cards has stirred international debate. The United States has examined the idea of national ID cards, although in 1971 the Social Security Administration rejected using Social Security Numbers as a universal ID, and in 1973 and 1976 the idea was thwarted by two other federal agencies.

Public concern increased in February 2006 when the British Parliament passed the Identity Cards Act. Currently, the British government is streamlining proposals for the card's database, on how to get biometric readers to banks, post offices, police stations, and others places of interest. Registry will be mandatory when applying for documents like a passport, but individuals will not have to carry them at all times. Additionally, the cards will be recognized travel documents in the European Union, and they will contain a microchip holding a set of fingerprints as well as facial and iris scans to increase security and prevent card fraud. The United Kingdom will begin issuing national ID cards in 2008.

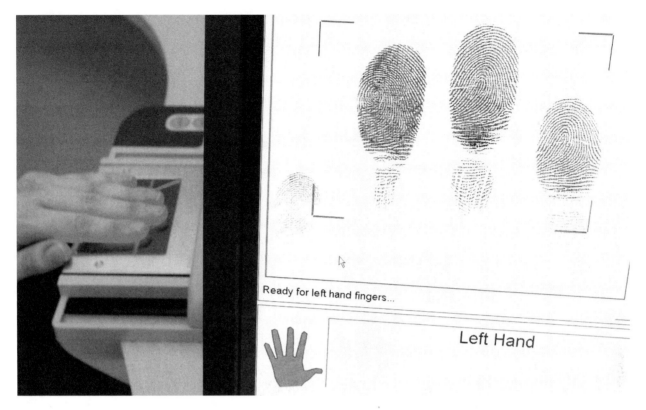

On April 26, 2004, a British Passport Office volunteer has his fingerprints scanned for a biometrics enrollment card in London. © PETER MACDIARMID/REUTERS/CORBIS.

FURTHER RESOURCES

Periodicals

Thomas, Philip A. "Identity Cards." *Modern Law Review.* 58.5 (September 1995): 702–713.

Web sites

Privacy International. "Identity Cards: Frequently Asked Questions." August 24, 1996. <http://www.privacy.org/pi/activities/idcard/idcard_faq.html> (accessed May 1, 2006).

CNN. "Private Eyes." September 25, 2001. <http://archives.cnn.com/2001/TECH/industry/09/25/private.eyes.idg/index.html> (accessed May 1, 2006).

International Religious Freedom Report for 2005

Report

By: U.S. Department of State

Date: November 8, 2005

Source: U.S. Department of State. Bureau of Democracy, Human Rights, and Labor. "International Religious Freedom Report for 2005." November 8, 2005. Available online at: <http://www.state.gov/g/drl/rls/irf/2005/index.htm> (accessed May 3, 2006).

About the Author: The U.S. Department of State seeks to protect and assist U.S. citizens working and living abroad, oversees Constitutional issues concerning U.S. foreign policy, and informs the U.S. public of U.S. foreign policy.

INTRODUCTION

In 1962, the United Nations began discussions concerning ways in which to extend protections for religious freedom, and, in 1982, it finally promulgated the Elimination of Religious Intolerance and Discrimination Declaration. Unfortunately, the United Nations has not imposed substantial sanctions and punishments on nations that violate these rights. In November 2005, the U.S. State Department issued its 2005 annual report on international religious freedom. This report describes numerous countries that have, according to the guidelines of the department, violated basic human and civil rights. The U.S. State

A state visit to France by Chinese President Hu Jintao in January 2004 led to protest against China's occupation of Tibet. © J.L.BULCAO/CORBIS.

Department's annual report on religious freedom is submitted to the U.S. Congress in compliance with Section 102(b) of the International Religious Freedom Act (IRFA) of 1998. That act requires that the Secretary of State with the assistance of the Ambassador at Large for Religious Freedom "shall transmit to Congress...detailed information with respect to matters involving international religious freedom."

While popular media accounts frequently focus on religious groups that hinder a woman's education, social interactions, or freedom of choice in marriage, other forms of governmental religious intolerance and suppression receive less media attention. The governments of many countries place curbs on basic elements of the religious freedom for a number of reasons, including political domination by a single religious group, misunderstanding of smaller religious

groups, and fears that minority religious groups sponsor terrorist acts or contribute to political instability. The U.S. State Department's 2005 report focuses on countries whose governments act in a totalitarian fashion to prevent targeted religious groups from flourishing.

PRIMARY SOURCE

EXECUTIVE SUMMARY
PART I: BARRIERS TO INTERNATIONAL RELIGIOUS FREEDOM

Totalitarian or Authoritarian Actions to Control Religious Belief or Practice

Totalitarian and authoritarian regimes seek to control religious thought and expression. Such regimes regard some or all religious groups as enemies of the state because of their religious beliefs or their independence from central authority. The practice of religion is often seen as a threat to the state's ideology or power. Oftentimes, the state suppresses religious groups based on the dominant ethnicity of groups.

Burma. The Government continued to engage in particularly severe violations of religious freedom. The Government generally infiltrated or monitored the meetings and activities of virtually all organizations, including religious ones. Religious organizations of all faiths also were subject to broad government restrictions on freedom of expression and association. The Government systemically restricted efforts by Buddhist clergy to promote human rights and political freedom, discouraged or prohibited non-Buddhist groups from constructing new places of worship or repairing existing ones, and actively promoted Buddhism over other religions, particularly among members of ethnic minorities. Anti-Muslim violence continued to occur, Muslim activities were monitored, and the Government restricted the ability of Muslims to travel freely. Non-Buddhists experienced employment discrimination at upper levels of the public sector.

China. The Government's respect for freedom of religion and freedom of conscience remained poor. Communist Party officials restated that party membership and religious belief were incompatible. The Government continued to seek to manage religious affairs by restricting religious practice to government-sanctioned organizations and registered places of worship and to control the growth and scope of activities of religious groups to prevent the rise of possible competing sources of authority outside the control of the Government. Unregistered religious groups continued to experience varying degrees of official interference and harassment. Members of some unregistered groups were subjected to restrictions, including intimidation, harassment, and detention. In some localities, "underground" religious leaders reported pressure to register with a government agency or become affiliated with and supervised by an official government-sanctioned religious association. Religious leaders and adherents, including those in official churches, were detained, arrested, or sentenced to prison or reeducation-through-labor camps. Underground Christian groups, Muslim Uighurs, Tibetan Buddhists, and members of groups that the Government considered "cults" were subjected to increased government scrutiny. In some areas, security officials used threats, demolition of unregistered property, extortion, interrogation, detention, and at times beatings and torture to harass leaders of unauthorized groups and their followers. The arrest, detention, and imprisonment of Falun Gong practitioners continued; those who refused to recant their beliefs were sometimes subjected to harsh treatment in prisons and reeducation-through-labor camps, and there were credible reports of deaths due to torture and abuse.

In Tibetan areas, the Government maintained tight controls on religious practices and places of worship. Government authorities forcibly suppressed activities they viewed as vehicles for political dissent or advocacy of Tibetan independence, including such religious activities as venerating the Dalai Lama. The most important figures in Tibetan Buddhism, such as the Dalai Lama and the Karmapa Lama, remained in exile. Dozens of monks and nuns continued to serve prison terms for their resistance to "patriotic education." The Government refused free access to Tibetan areas for most international observers, tightly controlled observers who were granted access, and closely controlled publication of information about conditions in Tibet. These limitations made it impossible to determine accurately the scope of restrictions on religious freedom.

Cuba. The Government continued to control and monitor religious activities and to use surveillance, infiltration, and harassment against religious groups, clergy, and laypersons. The Government ignored unregistered groups' pending applications for legal recognition. The law allows for the construction of new churches once the required permits are obtained; however, the Government has rarely issued construction permits, forcing many churches to meet in private homes, which also requires a permit. Government harassment of private houses of worship continued, with evangelical denominations reporting evictions from houses used for worship. Religious groups must obtain authorization from the Government to reconstruct or repair existing places of worship; however, the process of obtaining permission and purchasing construction materials from government outlets is lengthy and expensive. The authorities restricted the import and distribution of religious literature and materials and monitored church-run publications. The Government maintained its policy of not allowing the Catholic Church to train or transfer from abroad enough priests for its needs; the Government also did not allow the Church to establish social institutions, including schools and universities, hospitals and clinics, and nursing homes.

North Korea. There was no change in the extremely poor level of respect for religious freedom. Religious freedom does not exist. The regime continued to repress unauthorized religious groups, and there were indications that the regime used authorized religious entities for external propaganda and political purposes and that local citizens were barred from entering their places of worship. Religious persons who proselytized or who had ties to overseas evangelical groups operating in the People's Republic of China were subjected to arrest and harsh penalties, according to several unconfirmed reports. Defectors continued to allege that the regime arrested and executed members of underground Christian churches in prior years. Over the years, defectors have claimed that Christians were imprisoned and tortured for reading the Bible and talking about God. Due to the inaccessibility of the country and inability to gain timely information, it was difficult to confirm these reports.

State Hostility Toward Minority or Nonapproved Religions
Some governments, while not implementing full control over minority religions, nevertheless are hostile and repressive towards certain groups or identify them as "security threats." These governments implement policies designed to demand adherents to recant their faith, cause religious group members to flee the country, or intimidate and harass certain religious groups, or have as their principal effect the intimidation and harassment of certain religious groups.

Eritrea. The Government's poor respect for religious freedom for minority religious groups continued to worsen. Following a 2002 decree requiring all religious groups to register or cease religious activities, the Government closed all religious facilities not belonging to the four religions registered by the Government. The closures, the Government's failure to authorize any of the groups that applied for registration, and the arbitrarily enforced restriction on holding religious meetings continued. The Government harassed, arrested, and detained members of Pentecostal and other independent evangelical groups and Jehovah's Witnesses. Some religious detainees were held in harsh conditions that included extreme temperature fluctuations with limited or no access to family. There also were numerous reports of attempts to force recantations.

Iran. The Government engaged in particularly severe violations of religious freedom. Members of religious minorities—including Sunni Muslims, Baha'is, Jews, and Christians—reported imprisonment, harassment, intimidation, and discrimination based on their religious beliefs. All religious minorities continued to suffer varying degrees of officially sanctioned discrimination, particularly in the areas of employment, education, and housing. The Government continued to imprison and detain Baha'is based on their religious beliefs, and state-controlled media conducted a campaign of defamation against the group. Baha'is could not teach or freely practice their faith, nor could they maintain links with co-religionists abroad. The Government vigilantly enforced its prohibition on proselytizing activities by evangelical Christians by closing evangelical churches and arresting converts. In September 2004, security officials arrested 85 leaders of the Assemblies of God Church. The Government's anti-Israel policies, along with a perception among radical Muslims that all Jewish citizens support Zionism and the state of Israel, continued to create a hostile atmosphere for the Jewish community. Sunni Muslims encountered religious discrimination at the local, provincial, and national levels, and there were reports of discrimination against practitioners of the Sufi tradition.

Laos. The Government continued to interpret the Constitution in a manner that restricted religious practice, and application of the law was arbitrary. Persons arrested for their religious activities were sometimes charged with exaggerated security or other criminal offenses. Persons detained could be held for lengthy periods without trial, and an accused person's defense rights were limited. There were five known religious prisoners, all members of the Lao Evangelical Church, the country's domestic Protestant Christian group. Central authorities continued to withhold permission for the printing of non-Buddhist religious material. Central government control over the behavior of local officials was weak. In some areas, local officials displayed intolerance for minority religions, particularly evangelical Protestants. There were reports that local officials pressured Christians to renounce their faith; in two instances, persons were detained and evicted from their villages for resisting such efforts. Local authorities often refused to grant permission to construct new places of worship or repair existing facilities.

Saudi Arabia. Freedom of religion does not exist. Islam is the official religion, and all citizens must be Muslims. Religious freedom is not recognized or protected under the country's laws, and basic religious freedoms are denied to all but those who adhere to the state-sanctioned version of Sunni Islam. The Government's official policy is to permit non-Muslims to practice their religions freely at home and in private; however, the Government does not always respect this right in practice. Citizens are denied the freedom to choose or change their religion. Members of the Shi'a minority are subject to officially sanctioned political and economic discrimination, including limited employment opportunities, little representation in official institutions, and restrictions on the practice of their faith and the building of mosques and community centers. The Government enforces a strictly conservative version of Sunni Islam and discriminates against other branches of Islam. The Government prohibits the public practice of other religions; non-Muslim worshippers risk arrest, imprisonment, lashing, deportation, and torture for engaging in religious activity that attracts official attention, especially of the Mutawwa'in (religious police). All public school children receive mandatory religious instruction that conforms to the Salafi tradition. While there was an improvement in press freedom, open discussion of religious issues was limited.

Sudan. The Government considers itself an Islamic government, and Islamization is an objective of the governing party. It continued to place many restrictions on and discriminate against non-Muslims, non-Arab Muslims, and Muslims from tribes or groups not affiliated with the ruling party. Applications to build mosques generally were granted; however, the process for applications to build churches continued to be difficult—the last permit was issued around 1975. Many non-Muslims stated that they are treated as second-class citizens and discriminated against in government jobs and contracts. Some Muslims received preferential treatment regarding limited government services, such as access to medical care, and preferential treatment in court cases involving Muslims against non-Muslims.

Uzbekistan. There was a slight decline in the already poor status of religious freedom. The Government continued its campaign against unauthorized Islamic groups suspected of extremist sentiments or activities. Government authorities arrested numerous alleged members of these groups and sentenced them to lengthy jail terms. In thousands of cases, authorities have asserted membership in Hizb ut-Tahrir (HT), a banned political organization that encourages terrorism, based solely on outward expressions of devout belief, or have made false assertions of HT membership as a pretext for repressing the innocent expression of religious belief. The Government pressured the banned Islamic group Akromiylar (Akromiya), especially in Tashkent and Andijon, and those actions resulted in violence and deaths in Andijon in May 2005. Following three terrorist bombings in Tashkent in July 2004, the Government took into custody several hundred persons; the overwhelming majority of detainees were identified as having belonged to HT or other so-called "Wahhabi" groups. Most of these were released after questioning, but approximately 115 were convicted on terrorism-related charges. A number of minority religious groups, including congregations of various Christian confessions, had difficulty satisfying the strict registration requirements set out by law. As in previous years, Protestant groups with ethnic Uzbek members reported operating in a climate of harassment and fear. Some registered groups experienced raids and harassment, including de-registration and closing of several groups. A small but growing number of "underground" mosques, such as those that were tolerated during the Soviet period, operated under the close scrutiny of religious authorities and security services. After the May 2005 violence in Andijon, the number of congregants at these mosques declined significantly.

Vietnam. Although there was some improvement in respect for religious freedom, the Government continued to restrict organized activities of religious groups that it declared to be at variance with state laws and policies. Despite the introduction of less restrictive legislation governing religion, the legal framework continued to require that the organization and activities of all religious denominations be officially sanctioned by the Government. Restrictions on the hierarchies and clergy of religious groups remained in place. Oversight of recognized religions and harassment of followers of nonrecognized religions varied with the locality, often as a result of diverse local interpretations of national policy. There were reports that on several occasions, local officials pressured ethnic minority Protestants to recant their faith. According to reports, police arbitrarily detained and sometimes beat religious believers, particularly in the mountainous ethnic minority areas. At least 6 persons were in prison or detention for religious reasons, and at least 15 other persons were under various levels of restrictions on their activities.

SIGNIFICANCE

The United Nations Universal Declaration of Human Rights states in Article 18 that "[e]veryone has the right to freedom of thought, conscience and religion... [and] to manifest his religion or belief in teaching, practice, worship and observance." There is a strong correlation among nations that restrict religious freedom and nations that commit other human rights abuses. Regime restriction of private religious liberties often accompanies restrictions of speech, press, and political dissent.

The U.S. State Department's 2005 report is just one of many studies dealing with religious freedoms. It documents governmental violations of religious freedom and also points to countries where improvements in religious tolerance have occurred and are continuing to occur. Although the U.S. government advocates

for and supports religious freedom around the globe, its record at home is not perfect. In February 2005, the bi-partisan U.S. Commission on International Religious Freedom issued a report that spotlighted the hardships refugees may face in the United States. The report documented inconsistencies in the implementation of established procedures for processing refugees and asylum seekers by U.S. Immigration officials. These shortcomings put legitimate asylum seekers at risk of being returned to countries where they may face persecution, including religious persecution. The report also made recommendations for improvements in the system.

FURTHER RESOURCES

Books

Evans, Malcolm D. *The Religious Liberty and International Law in Europe*. New York: Cambridge University Press, 1997.

Sullivan, Winnifred Fallers. *The Impossibility of Religious Freedom*. Princeton, N.J.: Princeton University Press, 2005.

Periodicals

Slaughter, Anne-Marie. "Security, Solidarity, and Sovereignty: The Grand Themes of UN Reform." *American Journal of International Law* 99 (July 2005): 610–631.

Sullivan, Donna J. "Advancing the Freedom of Religion or Belief Through the UN Declaration on the Elimination of Religious Intolerance and Discrimination." *American Journal of International Law* 82 (July 1988): 487–520.

Web sites

U.S. Commission on International Religious Freedom. "United States Commission on International Religious Freedom." <http://www.uscirf.gov/> (accessed May 3, 2006).

U.S. Department of State. "International Religious Freedom." <http://www.state.gov/g/drl/irf/> (accessed May 3, 2006).

Googling the Great Firewall

Google Kowtowed to Communist Censorship

Newspaper editorial

By: Erping Zhang

Date: January 31, 2006

Source: Zhang, Erping. "Googling the Great Firewall: Google Kowtowed to Communist Censorship." The *New York Sun*. (January 31, 2006).

About the Author: In 2005, Erping Zhang, a graduate of the Kennedy School of Government at Harvard University, was the executive director of the Association for Asian Research, a private group that seeks to increase U.S. public awareness of Asian issues.

INTRODUCTION

This essay was published a few days after the Internet search-engine company Google opened a search service inside China, google.cn, on January 27, 2006. The new service blocked access of Internet users in China to content that the government of China considers objectionable, including pornography, pro-democracy material, the free online encyclopedia Wikipedia, and material favorable to the religious movement Falun Gong, which the Chinese government considers subversive and has repressed. The author, Erping Zhang, was one of many persons who have criticized Google and other Internet companies, such as Yahoo and Microsoft, for collaborating with the Chinese government's censorship.

Most Internet traffic leaves and enters China through three major fiber-optic bundles. Each of these large underground data pipelines encounters a large computer or "router" before interfacing with China's internal communications network. The router scans content before allowing it to enter or leave the country and blocks content that the government deems objectionable. This system is sometimes referred to as the Great Firewall of China.

Prior to January 2006, Google searches performed inside China produced a message that left the country, caused Google-owned computers in countries such as the United States to perform a search, and imported the results back through the Great Firewall—if the Firewall would let them through. If results were blocked by the Firewall, the user would receive an error message and might be denied Google access for several minutes as a penalty. Because of these inconveniences, a Chinese search company called Baidu had captured almost fifty percent of the Chinese Internet search market by 2005, while Google had only twenty-seven percent. Globally, Google has over fifty percent of the Internet search market. Google had also been directly penalized for returning results for forbidden sites: in 2002, the Chinese Government blocked Google entirely for two weeks.

Google decided to compromise. Since the Chinese government would not supply a list of officially banned sites, Google set up a computer that systematically attempted to access millions of Web sites and noted which ones were censored by the Chinese government. These sites are now pre-censored by the google.cn search engine inside China. When a Chinese user's Google search produces hits to forbidden sites, the user will receive a notice saying that this has occurred. In Germany and France, attempts to access pro-Nazi websites produce a similar notice of blocked content.

▌ PRIMARY SOURCE

"Focus on the user and all else will follow." This is principle number one listed on Google's Web site of "Ten Things Google Has Found to be True."

This principle holds great irony upon release of announcements that Google has agreed to comply with Chinese government censors in launching its new site www.google.cn, catering to Internet users inside China. With this in mind, it would seem more appropriate for the principle to read: "Focus on the user, unless the user happens to be Chinese, in which case the government is more important than the user."

If the user is Chinese, allowing listings of Web sites regarding human rights, religious freedom, and Chinese government abuses of religious freedom may perhaps expose the user to information the government considers "threatening."

Google's acceptance of Chinese government censorship comes as an even greater disappointment in light of its recent vigor in resisting subpoenas from the United States Department of Justice. The Department of Justice subpoenas came as a part of U.S. efforts to enforce the Child Online Protection Act, which Congress passed in attempts to combat Internet child pornography.

Google's efforts to defend the right to privacy of United States citizens might seem more genuine were the company not so ready and willing to facilitate the Chinese government's denial to its own citizens of freedom of the press, freedom of religion and rights to free expression. In this instance, it appears that Google lawyers will go to bat to defend the right to privacy of Americans doing searches for child pornography, but they deem it less important to defend the rights of Chinese citizens to learn more about religious freedom and democracy.

Recent studies from the OpenNet Initiative show that while Chinese Internet filters block about 7% of the top 100 search results for pornography, more than 70% of the top 100 results were blocked in searches on the Falun Gong movement, outlawed in China in 1999. More than 80% were blocked in searches for the China Democracy Party. Now searches on www.google.cn will yield similar results.

An ongoing experiment, the first of its kind, initiated by Reebok, demonstrates that companies can push local

Protesters gather in front of Google Inc. on January 25, 2006 to fight the company's agreement to censor Internet search results in China. AP IMAGES.

limits in China and still make money. In 2002, despite regulations that outlaw free trade unions, executives at Reebok decided to make association rights a priority at their factories in China by instituting a process for factory-wide elections at sites of their largest contracting plants.

Reebok executives claim they undertook tense negotiations to ensure that rank-and-file workers would have their say and that the elections would offer workers representation. Of course, the Reebok union, like every other union in China, still falls under the umbrella of the All China Federation of Trade Unions, however, impartial observers report that conditions have improved since its installation.

The experiment is far from perfect, but it never would have started had Reebok not taken a stand. Likewise, Google could have countered Beijing's censorship with tenacity equal to its ongoing efforts to resist compliance with subpoenas from the Department of Justice.

Google has said that it complies with regulations in China in the same way that it complies with regulations

elsewhere. Has its board of ethics considered that laws and regulations and rule of law operate on a different plane in China than in most other countries?

In America, a lengthy process exists. It includes checks and balances on government agencies, which must seek thorough approval to demonstrate their lawful right to demand companies turn over any sort of corporate records. Additional processes guarantee the rights of defendants to fight such subpoenas in court.

In China, the process is quite different. It relies not upon legitimate rule of law, but upon a priority to preserve the power of the Communist Party. The top leadership of the Chinese Communist Party writes a list of the topics it deems threatening to its complete control over political and social capital within the country. It hands that list to Google executives, who proceed to build their China search engines with filters installed. Chinese Internet users log on and search for information on Falun Gong and they receive results of sites for Chinese propaganda of an "evil cult." They receive no information regarding the imprisonment of thousands of Falun Gong practitioners in Chinese reeducation through labor camps.

Perhaps Google may argue, at least they logged on, at least there is a search engine, and some Chinese users may learn ways to evade the censors. Those who evade the censors may then contribute to the ongoing efforts of the Chinese people to push for greater governmental accountability and for greater individual rights. It is unfortunate, though, that they will be forced to fight the technology of a giant like Google in order to get around the limitations that the search engines have succumbed to.

It is unfortunate that through their compliance, companies like Yahoo, MSN, and now Google have implied that the Chinese Communist Party has legitimate rights to enforce such limitations.

SIGNIFICANCE

Several Internet companies have helped implement Chinese censorship policies. In December 2004, Microsoft corporation agreed to delete from its servers political blogs by a writer named Zhao Jing. Remarkably, the postings were stored on computers in the United States, not in China. U.S. computer maker Cisco has been criticized for manufacturing the computers that implement the Great Firewall. E-mail and Internet search provider Yahoo, which has been doing business inside China since 1999, has been widely criticized for its behavior. In 2004, it was revealed that Yahoo had handed over e-mail account information for a dissident named Shi Tao who had sent to foreign Web sites copies of a government order that Chinese reporters not discuss the anniversary of the Tiananmen Square pro-democracy uprising. Shi Tao was tracked down with the help of the digital evidence supplied by Yahoo, convicted, and sentenced to ten years in jail.

The co-founder of Yahoo, Jerry Yang, defended his company's actions by saying that "To be doing business in China, or anywhere else in the world, we have to comply with local law." Critics argued that Yahoo was not obliged to do business in China at all, except by its desire to compete for market share and increased profits. In 2006, it was reported that in 2003 Yahoo had also supplied evidence crucial to jailing Chinese dissident Li Zhi, who had criticized government corruption online and tried to join the outlawed China Democracy Party. The nongovernmental organization Reporters Without Borders has argued dozens of such cases have probably gone unreported.

The Committee on International Relations of the U.S. House of Representatives held hearings entitled "The Internet in China: A Tool for Freedom or Repression?" on February 15, 2006. Representatives from Google, whose informal corporate slogan is "Don't Be Evil," were accused of hypocrisy. Rep. Jim Leach (R-IA) told a Google representative that the built-in censorship of google.cn "makes you a functionary of the Chinese government... So if this Congress wanted to learn how to censor, we'd go to you."

In the 1990s, the Internet was widely hailed as a powerful force for democratization, one that governments would not be able to control. This turned out to be incorrect; a number of countries, including China, censor Internet traffic. China employs 30,000 full-time Internet police who use software tools to monitor Internet users.

Google's relationship to the U.S. government was also headline news in 2005, with the difference that it was Google non-cooperativenes, rather than its cooperativeness, that was newsworthy. Google refused a request from the Justice Department to hand over lists of one million search queries submitted during a one-week period and a random sample of one million Web addresses reachable through Google. The Justice Department said it wanted the information in order to determine how often U.S. Internet users search for child pornography and did not ask for identifying information on which individual users had made the searches. Google denied that it was refusing the request on privacy-protection grounds, but refused to explain what its grounds actually were; some industry observers speculated that Google was afraid trade secrets would be revealed. Google does reportedly record personal identifying information on all Google Internet searches.

Groups such as the American Civil Libertarian Union criticized the Justice Department's request for information without specific need as a precedent that might eventually lead to the use of Google (and similar databases) for the improper surveillance of Internet users. In March 2006, a Federal judge ruled that Google would have to give the Justice Department 50,000 randomly selected Web addresses and 5,000 search queries. Google said it would comply with the order.

FURTHER RESOURCES
Books

Chase, Michael and James Mulvenon. *You've Got Dissent!: Chinese Dissident Use of the Internet and Beijing's Counterstrategies*. Santa Monica, Calif.: Rand, 2002.

China and the Internet: The Politics of the Digital Leap Forward, edited by Christopher Hughes and Gudrun Wacker. London and New York: RoutledgeCurzon, 2003.

Periodicals

Arshad, Mohammad. "Google Refuses Demand for Search Information." The *Washington Post* (January 20, 2006).

Goodman, Peter S. "Yahoo Says It Gave China Internet Data." The *Washington Post* (September 11, 2005).

MacLeod, Calum. "Web Users Walk Great Firewall of China." *USA Today* (April 3, 2006).

Thompson, Clive. "Google in China: The Big Disconnect." The *New York Times* (April 23, 2006).

Education and Childhood

The United Nations Declaration of Human Rights proclaims that every individual has a right to an education. It advocates free and compulsory elementary education, but does not specify what such an education should entail—other that it should promote peace and tolerance—nor does it specify for how many years children should attend school.

While the goal of universal elementary education is realized throughout most of the developed world, children in developing nations are less likely to have access to education. Some nations in Africa, Southern Asia, and the Middle East have the illiteracy rates of forty to fifty percent. In some nations schools are not provided, or rural children do not have schools near where they live. In other areas, children are kept from school and sent to work, either to earn income for struggling families or to participate in farm work.

Women are especially affected by educational inequalities. In some regimes, they are wholly denied a meaningful education. During the rule of the Taliban in Afghanistan, girls were barred from schools, and women risked their lives to establish underground schools in homes. After the Taliban was removed from power in 2001, Afghan schools were once again opened to women. However, as the article "Attacks Beset Afghan Girls' Schools" notes, educating girls remains controversial to religious fundamentalists and Islamist factions. Girls' schools were routinely attacked and vandalized, and teachers harassed.

This chapter also briefly surveys some of the events that made the United States education system increasingly more inclusive. "*Brown v. Board of Education*" discusses the racial desegregation of schools. Other articles profile legislation that demands equity for women's sports or created special education programs for handicapped students. Finally, "*Plyler v. Doe*" profiles the landmark case that guaranteed foreign-nationals and undocumented alien students the right to attend U.S. public schools.

The United Nations Declaration of Human Rights also proclaims that childhood should be valued and protected. The UN Convention on Rights of the Child (included in this chapter) further enumerates these goals. However, for many of the world's children, childhood remains a period of substantial burden and peril. A lack of adequate housing, food, and potable water challenges the health of most of the world's endangered children. These issues are covered in depth in the chapter *Health and Housing*. Children are also often victims of human rights crimes, some by the actions of their own family. This chapter highlights child soldiers, laborers, and sex workers, as well as the practice of child marriage.

No Church Need Apply

Editorial cartoon

By: Thomas Nast

Date: May 8, 1875

Source: Nast, Thomas. "No Church Need Apply." *Harper's Weekly* (May 8, 1875). Provided courtesy of HarpWeek.

About the Illustrator: Thomas Nast (1840–1902) was the most famous American political cartoonist of the nineteenth century. The bulk of Nast's work appeared in *Harper's Weekly* between 1859 and 1896—his best-known inventions include the goateed Uncle Sam, the Republican Elephant, the Democratic donkey, and the jolly appearance of the modern American Santa Claus.

INTRODUCTION

This cartoon by Nast was published in 1875 in the journal *Harper's Weekly*. Nast published cartoons through the time of the American Civil War and the period immediately following it. Nast had become extremely popular by the end of the 1860s and was the only contributor of whom *Harper's* boasted repeatedly in its editorial columns.

This cartoon, which originally occupied an entire page of the magazine, shows a caricature of Pope Pius IX (1792–1878) carrying a hatbox full of "Hats Caps and Gowns From Rome" and bundles of documents bearing legends like "The Ecclesiastical Power is Superior to the Civil" and "I Am Infallible, Therefore Must Rule." The figure's mitre combines "School," "State," and "Church" in a single structure—an implicit threat to American liberties. A figure dubbed Little Jonathan, standing at the door of a "Common Public School," says that "Miss Columbia"—Columbia being a female figure symbolizing the United States, almost entirely replaced today by the Uncle Sam image that was first popularized by Nast himself—"will not try your teaching, as it has proved to be so injurious in Dame Europa's school, that our adopted children who left her don't care to learn under that system again." "Oh, you Godless, infidel vipers," replies the Pope, "I'll be revenged on you, for I keep the keys of Heaven!"

The gist of the cartoon is that the American public school system is under threat by a sectarian attack from Roman Catholics, who supposedly owe, according to one of the documents in the cartoon, "First Allegiance to the Pope of Rome."

Anti-Catholic sentiment ran high in late nineteenth-century America in the majority Protestant population. Because of immigration from Catholic-majority European countries such as Ireland, the number of Catholics in the U.S. had increased greatly by the 1870s, when this cartoon was published. In 1789, less than one percent of Americans were Catholics; by 1891, approximately sixteen percent of Americans were Catholics. In some urban areas they were a majority. Catholics established Catholic schools in these areas and sought public funding for them, efforts met by nativist, Protestant backlash as typified by this Nast cartoon.

▌ PRIMARY SOURCE

NO CHURCH NEED APPLY
See primary source image.

▌

SIGNIFICANCE

The U.S. Constitution's First Amendment (1791) states that "Congress shall make no law respecting an establishment of religion." However, until the early twentieth century, when the Supreme Court first ruled that the Fourteenth Amendment (1868) extends the First Amendment to individual states, it was commonplace for public schools—funded by states, not by the federal government—to offer religious instruction in the classroom. Bible reading, hymn singing, and instruction in generic Protestant doctrine were the rule rather than the exception in the 1870s. The objection of Nast and others to "sectarian" religious observances in public schools therefore referred only to Roman Catholic observances, not to the presence of Christianity as such in the classroom; Protestant religious observances were considered normal, not "sectarian."

The uproar over the alleged Catholic threat to American liberty was intense, nationwide, and had legal repercussions that are felt to this day. In late 1875, some months after this cartoon was published, a Republican congressman named James G. Blaine (1830–1893) proposed an amendment to the U.S. Constitution, generally known as the Blaine Amendment, stipulating that "no money raised by taxation in any state for the support of public schools... shall ever be under the control of any religious sect..." In 1876, the Blaine Amendment was passed overwhelmingly in the House of Representatives (180–7) but fell just four votes short of ratification in the Senate. Supporters of the Amendment then took their fight to the states, and

MAY 8, 1875.]　　　　　　　　HARPER'S WEEKLY.　　　　　　　　　585

NO CHURCH NEED APPLY.

PRIMARY SOURCE

No Church Need Apply: An editorial cartoon from *Harper's Weekly,* May 8, 1875 supporting the separation of church and state.

PROVIDED COURTESY OF HARPWEEK.

A Roman Catholic mission school in Puerto Asis, Columbia, in 1965. PHOTO BY ART RICKERBY//TIME LIFE PICTURES/GETTY IMAGES.

succeeded in attaching "Blaine Amendments" to the constitutions of thirty-seven U.S. states, where they still remain.

For about a century, in a majority of U.S. states, the Blaine Amendments settled the question of whether public money could be used to fund religious school. In the late twentieth century, however, the concept of school voucher programs became prominent. School vouchers are certificates with a fixed cash value that parents or guardians of children are issued by the states and which they can use toward paying tuition at any school of their choice—including a religious school. Blaine Amendments stand directly in the way of using public funds in this way. A number of legal challenges to voucher programs and to Blaine Amendments have been mounted in recent years. In 2002, the U.S. Supreme Court upheld a Colorado vouchers program in *Zelman v. Simmons-Harris*. However, in 2006 the Florida Supreme Court overturned Florida's vouchers program.

Today, numerous court cases have established that any form of religious observance in the public-

school classroom, including prayer, moments of silence, Bible reading, posting of religious texts, or the introduction of anti-evolutionary, pro-Creationism, or pro-Intelligent Design materials, is forbidden by the establishment clause of the First Amendment ("Congress shall make no law respecting an establishment of religion"). However, the question of whether public money can be used to fund religious schools, as through voucher systems or busing programs, remains legally unstable, with some court decisions upholding vouchers and others denying them. Laws dating directly to the period of this Thomas Nast cartoon are being vigorously challenged and defended in U.S. courts today. The larger issue of religion's role in public and political life also remains contentious.

FURTHER RESOURCES
Books

Perry, Michael J. *Under God?: Religious Faith and Liberal Democracy*. New York: Cambridge University Press, 2003.

Periodicals

Justice, Benjamin. "Thomas Nast and the Public School of the 1870s." *History of Education Quarterly* 45, 2 (Summer 2005): 171–206.

McAfee, Ward M. "The Historical Context of the Failed Federal Blaine Amendment of 1876." *First Amendment Law Review* 2 (2003): 1–22.

Web sites

CNN.com. "Supreme Court Affirms School Voucher Program." June 27, 2002. <http://archives.cnn.com/2002/LAW/06/27/scotus.school.vouchers/index.html> (accessed May 4, 2006).

National Public Radio. "Court Throws Out Florida School Voucher Program." January 16, 2006. <http://www.npr.org/templates/story/story.php?storyId=5159138> (accessed May 4, 2006).

The Pew Forum on Religion and Public Life. "School Voucher Supporters Go After 'Blaine Amendments.'" February 5, 2003. <http://pewforum.org/news/display.php?NewsID=1976> (accessed May 4, 2006).

Girl in a Bean Field

Migrant Farm Worker Children

Photograph

By: Anonymous

Date: 1949

Source: © Bettmann/Corbis.

About the Photographer: This photograph is part of the collection at Corbis Images, a worldwide provider of visual content materials to advertisers, broadcasters, designers, magazines, new media organizations, newspapers, and producers. The photographer is not known.

INTRODUCTION

For most of history, children have worked. The notion of a childhood in which children play and go to school instead of supplementing family income is a relatively recent one. In the nineteenth century, rising wealth allowed middle-class parents the luxury of keeping their children out of the workplace. Poor parents did not have this option.

With few adult industrial and agricultural workers able to earn enough to support and educate a family in the nineteenth century, children were compelled by necessity to enter the work force. By 1900, about 1.7 million children labored in American industries, more than double the number in 1870. In the 10- to 15-year-old age

group, 18.2 percent were employed, with more than half working in agricultural trades.

Because they were cheap to employ and had small, nimble fingers, children were well suited to the small repetitive tasks that American industry demanded— but their labor came at a high price. Breaker boys in coal mines sorted coal from slate and developed hunched-over backs along with pallor. Snapping-up boys in glass factories suffered eye damage from the bright, glaring light of molten glass and lung damage from inhaled glass dust. Children of both sexes cracked open sharp oyster shells and shelled shrimp in canneries then soaked their bleeding hands in a strong alum solution to toughen the skin and help heal the wounds. Mill children lost fingers or limbs to machinery, while boys and girls who peeled apples or shelled peas often injured themselves with slipped knives.

In the early twentieth century, new ideas about child development emerged. Americans began to see childhood as a series of stages, each with specific physical and psychological demands that had to be satisfied for the child to progress into a healthy adult able to fulfill his or her potential. Children who spent crucial years at labor would progress into "human junk," as one poster in the 1920s proclaimed—adults doomed to become burdens upon society because of weakened bodies and uncultivated minds. Halting child labor, it was believed, would help end the cycle of poverty, reduce crime, and ensure the preservation of democracy.

A number of states instituted reforms designed to influence the supply of child labor, including compulsory education and minimum ages for employment. However, the laws proved relatively easy to evade. The names of underage workers typically did not appear in company books because their pay went to an older brother or sister. Some states required only a signed statement by a parent or guardian that a child was of the legal employment age. Agricultural and domestic workers were typically exempt from such laws.

PRIMARY SOURCE

GIRL IN BEAN FIELD
See primary source image.

SIGNIFICANCE

The number of undocumented workers in the U.S. is estimated at 11–15 million. The rising debate over the effects of such immigration is focusing more attention on migrant children, especially the sons and

PRIMARY SOURCE

Girl in Bean Field: A young migrant worker picks beans on a Wisconsin farm in 1949. © BETTMANN/CORBIS.

daughters of undocumented workers, who continue to be part of the modern American workforce. The exact numbers of child workers is unknown because of the difficulty in measuring illegal labor, but the effects of migrant labor on children are well documented.

In 2005, the national poverty rate for immigrants and their American-born children was 18.4 percent. One-third of immigrants lacked health insurance. In California, which had the highest number of immigrant arrivals from January 2000 to March 2005 with 1.8 million, nearly half the immigrants and their children lived in or near poverty. Almost half the California households using a welfare program such as food stamps or supplemental social security income were headed by immigrants.

Migrant children, often on the move and worried about being identified by authorities, rarely attend school on a regular basis. In 2005, 31 percent of adult

immigrants lacked a high school degree, condemning them to low-wage jobs. To combat this problem, in 2001 the Texas legislature permitted some undocumented immigrants to qualify for in-state tuition at public colleges. An undocumented student pays $616 a semester for a 12-hour course load at Alamo Community College while a non-Texas resident pays $2,056. In 2005, 3,700 undocumented workers took advantage of this program.

The legislation has since come under attack by opponents who argue that it violates the Illegal Immigration Reform and Immigrant Responsibility Act of 1996, which prohibits states from providing access to colleges and universities at rates not available to citizens. Critics also cite concerns about terrorists being given potential access to American schools, while others claim that reduced tuition payments strain public budgets and deny educational opportunities to Americans. A similar law was struck down in Kansas, but immigrant tuition laws remain in place in California, New York, Utah, Illinois, Washington, and Oklahoma.

FURTHER RESOURCES

Books

Coles, Robert. *Migrants, Sharecroppers, Mountaineers: Children of Crisis*. Boston: Little, Brown, 1971.

Hayes, Curtis W., Robert Bahruth, and Carolyn Kessler. *Literacy con Carino: A Story of Migrant Children's Success*. Portsmouth, NH: Heinemann, 1998.

Martinez, Ruben. *Crossing Over: A Mexican Family on the Migrant Trail*. New York: Metropolitan Books, 2001.

Brown v. Board of Education

Opinion of the Supreme Court of the United States

Legal decision

By: U.S. Supreme Court

Date: May 17, 1954

Source: *Brown vs. Board of Education of Topeka*. 347 US 483 (1954).

About the Author: The Supreme Court of the United States is comprised of eight justices and one chief justice. In 1954, the associate justices were Felix Frankfurter, Tom C. Clark, Hugo L. Black, Robert H. Jackson, Harold Burton, Stanley Reed, Sherman Minton, and William O. Douglas. Earl Warren was the chief justice. Thurgood Marshall, who represented Brown before the court, later became the U.S. Solicitor General and a Supreme Court justice, serving on the court from 1967 to 1991.

INTRODUCTION

In the 1896 U.S. Supreme Court case *Plessy v. Ferguson*, the Supreme Court determined that "separate but equal" facilities for black and white persons was an acceptable legal standard for such public venues as movie houses, restaurants, trains, hotels, and restrooms. This "separate but equal" standard applied to education as well; segregating black and white children into separate schools was legal as long as the "separate but equal" standard was met.

Court cases dealing with desegregated schools stretch back to 1850, when Robert Morris, an African-American attorney, and Charles Sumner

argued in *Roberts v. The City of Boston* that segregated schools violated the Massachusetts constitution and created psychological conditions of inferiority in black students. Although Morris and Sumner lost the case, it became part of the court precedent in future desegregation cases. In 1885, a California case, *Tape v. Hurley*, held that a child of Chinese ancestry must be permitted to enroll in any public school. In response, the San Francisco school superintendent succeeded in lobbying the state assembly to pass a law that created "separate schools for children of Mongolian or Chinese descent. When such separate schools are established, Chinese or Mongolian children must not be admitted into any other schools." This law remained in effect in California until 1947.

The first court case ending segregation on the district level occurred in California; the 1931 case *Roberto Alvarez vs. the Board of Trustees of the Lemon Grove School District* held that the school district could not segregate Hispanics into a separate school. In 1947, California schools across the state were desegregated with the *Mendez v. Westminster* decision; the governor of California at the time was Earl Warren, who later wrote the *Brown v. Board of Education* decision as chief justice of the U.S. Supreme Court.

Before 1954, seventeen states required segregation in public schools, while sixteen prohibited it. All states requiring segregation were in the southern United States, stretching from Texas to Maryland. Between 1896 and 1954, the "separate" aspect of *Plessy v. Ferguson* was often part of educational systems, but the "equal" was not.

In 1951, Oliver Brown and Charles Scott attempted to enroll their African-American children in a neighborhood school in Topeka, Kansas. Their requests were denied, and Brown contacted a local attorney to pursue legal action. The attorney referred Brown to the National Association for the Advancement of Colored People (NAACP), and Thurgood Marshall, an attorney with the organization, stepped in as counsel.

Kansas law allowed for segregation at the elementary level; junior high and high schools were integrated. The District Court that heard the *Oliver Brown et al v. The Board of Education of Topeka, Kansas* case found for the board of education, citing the *Plessy v. Ferguson* case as precedent. The Topeka schools, however, quietly began to integrate all schools as the *Brown v. Board of Education* case made its way through the courts; the entire district was integrated by 1956.

Brown v. Board of Education was argued before the U.S. Supreme Court on December 8, 1952, reargued on December 7, 1953, and decided on May 17, 1954. This case was decided with three other cases—*Briggs v.*

A classroom in Fort Myer Elementary School on September 8, 1954, the day it was desegregated. © BETTMANN/CORBIS.

Elliott, Davis v. County School Board of Prince Edward County, and *Gebhart v. Belton.*

PRIMARY SOURCE

BROWN ET AL. V. BOARD OF EDUCATION OF TOPEKA ET AL. APPEAL FROM THE UNITED STATES DISTRICT COURT FOR THE DISTRICT OF KANSAS.*

Segregation of white and Negro children in the public schools of a State solely on the basis of race, pursuant to state laws permitting or requiring such segregation, denies to Negro children the equal protection of the laws guaranteed by the Fourteenth Amendment—even though the physical facilities and other "tangible" factors of white and Negro schools may be equal.

(a) The history of the Fourteenth Amendment is inconclusive as to its intended effect on public education.

(b) The question presented in these cases must be determined not on the basis of conditions existing when the Fourteenth Amendment was adopted, but in the light of the full development of public education and its present place in American life throughout the Nation.

(c) Where a State has undertaken to provide an opportunity for an education in its public schools, such an opportunity is a right which must be made available to all on equal terms.

(d) Segregation of children in public schools solely on the basis of race deprives children of the minority group of equal educational opportunities, even though the physical facilities and other "tangible" factors may be equal.

(e) The "separate but equal" doctrine adopted in *Plessy v. Ferguson*, 163 U.S. 537, has no place in the field of public education.

(f) The cases are restored to the docket for further argument on specified questions relating to the forms of the decrees.

MR. CHIEF JUSTICE WARREN delivered the opinion of the Court.

These cases come to us from the States of Kansas, South Carolina, Virginia, and Delaware. They are premised on different facts and different local conditions, but a common legal question justifies their consideration together in this consolidated opinion.

In each of the cases, minors of the Negro race, through their legal representatives, seek the aid of the courts in obtaining admission to the public schools of their community on a nonsegregated basis. In each instance, they had been denied admission to schools attended by white children under laws requiring or permitting segregation according to race. This segregation was alleged to deprive the plaintiffs of the equal protection of the laws under the Fourteenth Amendment. In each of the cases other than the Delaware case, a three-judge federal district court denied relief to the plaintiffs on the so-called "separate but equal" doctrine announced by this Court in *Plessy v. Ferguson*, 163 U.S. 537. Under that doctrine, equality of treatment is accorded when the races are provided substantially equal facilities, even though these facilities be separate. In the Delaware case, the Supreme Court of Delaware adhered to that doctrine, but ordered that the plaintiffs be admitted to the white schools because of their superiority to the Negro schools.

The plaintiffs contend that segregated public schools are not "equal" and cannot be made "equal," and that hence they are deprived of the equal protection of the laws. Because of the obvious importance of the question presented, the Court took jurisdiction. Argument was heard in the 1952 Term, and reargument was heard this Term on certain questions propounded by the Court.

Reargument was largely devoted to the circumstances surrounding the adoption of the Fourteenth Amendment in 1868. It covered exhaustively consideration of the Amendment in Congress, ratification by the states, then-existing practices in racial segregation, and the views of proponents and opponents of the Amendment. This discussion and our own investigation convince us that, although these sources cast some light, it is not enough to resolve the problem with which we are faced. At best,

they are inconclusive. The most avid proponents of the post-War Amendments undoubtedly intended them to remove all legal distinctions among "all persons born or naturalized in the United States." Their opponents, just as certainly, were antagonistic to both the letter and the spirit of the Amendments and wished them to have the most limited effect. What others in Congress and the state legislatures had in mind cannot be determined with any degree of certainty.

An additional reason for the inconclusive nature of the Amendment's history with respect to segregated schools is the status of public education at that time. In the South, the movement toward free common schools, supported by general taxation, had not yet taken hold. Education of white children was largely in the hands of private groups. Education of Negroes was almost nonexistent, and practically all of the race were illiterate. In fact, any education of Negroes was forbidden by law in some states. Today, in contrast, many Negroes have achieved outstanding success in the arts and sciences, as well as in the business and professional world. It is that public school education at the time of the Amendment had advanced further in the North, but the effect of the Amendment on Northern States was generally ignored in the congressional debates. Even in the North, the conditions of public education did not approximate those existing today. The curriculum was usually rudimentary; ungraded schools were common in rural areas; the school term was but three months a year in many states, and compulsory school attendance was virtually unknown. As a consequence, it is not surprising that there should be so little in the history of the Fourteenth Amendment relating to its intended effect on public education.

In the first cases in this Court construing the Fourteenth Amendment, decided shortly after its adoption, the Court interpreted it as proscribing all state-imposed discriminations against the Negro race. The doctrine of "separate but equal" did not make its appearance in this Court until 1896 in the case of *Plessy v. Ferguson*, supra, involving not education but transportation. American courts have since labored with the doctrine for over half a century. In this Court, there have been six cases involving the "separate but equal" doctrine in the field of public education. In Cumming v. County Board of Education, 175 U.S. 528, and Gong Lum v. Rice, 275 U.S. 78, the validity of the doctrine itself was not challenged. In more recent cases, all on the graduate school level, inequality was found in that specific benefits enjoyed by white students were denied to Negro students of the same educational qualifications. Missouri ex rel. Gaines v. Canada, 305 U.S. 337; Sipuel v. Oklahoma, 332 U.S. 631; Sweatt v. Painter, 339 U.S. 629; McLaurin v. Oklahoma State Regents, 339 U.S. 637. In none of these cases was it necessary to reexamine the doctrine to grant relief to the Negro plaintiff. And in Sweatt v. Painter, supra, the Court expressly reserved decision on the question whether *Plessy v. Ferguson* should be held inapplicable to public education.

In the instant cases, that question is directly presented. Here, unlike Sweatt v. Painter, there are findings below that the Negro and white schools involved have been equalized, or are being equalized, with respect to buildings, curricula, qualifications and salaries of teachers, and other "tangible" factors. Our decision, therefore, cannot turn on merely a comparison of these tangible factors in the Negro and white schools involved in each of the cases. We must look instead to the effect of segregation itself on public education.

In approaching this problem, we cannot turn the clock back to 1868, when the Amendment was adopted, or even to 1896, when *Plessy v. Ferguson* was written. We must consider public education in the light of its full development and its present place in American life throughout the Nation. Only in this way can it be determined if segregation in public schools deprives these plaintiffs of the equal protection of the laws.

Today, education is perhaps the most important function of state and local governments. Compulsory school attendance laws and the great expenditures for education both demonstrate our recognition of the importance of education to our democratic society. It is required in the performance of our most basic public responsibilities, even service in the armed forces. It is the very foundation of good citizenship. Today it is a principal instrument in awakening the child to cultural values, in preparing him for later professional training, and in helping him to adjust normally to his environment. In these days, it is doubtful that any child may reasonably be expected to succeed in life if he is denied the opportunity of an education. Such an opportunity, where the state has undertaken to provide it, is a right which must be made available to all on equal terms.

We come then to the question presented: Does segregation of children in public schools solely on the basis of race, even though the physical facilities and other "tangible" factors may be equal, deprive the children of the minority group of equal educational opportunities? We believe that it does.

In Sweatt v. Painter, supra, in finding that a segregated law school for Negroes could not provide them equal educational opportunities, this Court relied in large part on "those qualities which are incapable of objective measurement but which make for greatness in a law school." In McLaurin v. Oklahoma State Regents, supra, the Court, in requiring that a Negro admitted to a white graduate school be treated like all other students, again resorted to intangible considerations: "...his ability to study, to

engage in discussions and exchange views with other students, and, in general, to learn his profession." Such considerations apply with added force to children in grade and high schools. To separate them from others of similar age and qualifications solely because of their race generates a feeling of inferiority as to their status in the community that may affect their hearts and minds in a way unlikely ever to be undone. The effect of this separation on their educational opportunities was well stated by a finding in the Kansas case by a court which nevertheless felt compelled to rule against the Negro plaintiffs:.

> "Segregation of white and colored children in public schools has a detrimental effect upon the colored children. The impact is greater when it has the sanction of the law, for the policy of separating the races is usually interpreted as denoting the inferiority of the negro group. A sense of inferiority affects the motivation of a child to learn. Segregation with the sanction of law, therefore, has a tendency to [retard] the educational and mental development of negro children and to deprive them of some of the benefits they would receive in a racial[ly] integrated school system."

Whatever may have been the extent of psychological knowledge at the time of *Plessy v. Ferguson*, this finding is amply supported by modern authority. Any language in *Plessy v. Ferguson* contrary to this finding is rejected. We conclude that, in the field of public education, the doctrine of "separate but equal" has no place. Separate educational facilities are inherently unequal. Therefore, we hold that the plaintiffs and others similarly situated for whom the actions have been brought are, by reason of the segregation complained of, deprived of the equal protection of the laws guaranteed by the Fourteenth Amendment. This disposition makes unnecessary any discussion whether such segregation also violates the Due Process Clause of the Fourteenth Amendment.

Because these are class actions, because of the wide applicability of this decision, and because of the great variety of local conditions, the formulation of decrees in these cases presents problems of considerable complexity. On reargument, the consideration of appropriate relief was necessarily subordinated to the primary question—the constitutionality of segregation in public education. We have now announced that such segregation is a denial of the equal protection of the laws. In order that we may have the full assistance of the parties in formulating decrees, the cases will be restored to the docket, and the parties are requested to present further argument on Questions 4 and 5 previously propounded by the Court for the reargument this Term. The Attorney General of the United States is again invited to participate. The Attorneys General of the states requiring or permitting segregation in public education will also be permitted to appear as amici curiae upon request to do so by September 15, 1954, and submission of briefs by October 1, 1954.

It is so ordered.

* Together with No. 2, *Briggs et al. v. Elliott et al.,* on appeal from the United States District Court for the Eastern District of South Carolina, argued December 9–10, 1952, reargued December 7-8, 1953; No. 4, Davis et al. v. County School Board of Prince Edward County, Virginia, et al., on appeal from the United States District Court for the Eastern District of Virginia, argued December 10, 1952, reargued December 7-8, 1953, and No. 10, *Gebhart et al. v. Belton et al.,* on certiorari to the Supreme Court of Delaware, argued December 11, 1952, reargued December 9, 1953.

SIGNIFICANCE

In the Kansas district court case, one of the primary arguments advanced was that of social inferiority. As witness Dr. Hugh W. Speer testified, "...if the colored children are denied the experience in school of associating with white children, who represent 90 percent of our national society in which these colored children must live, then the colored child's curriculum is being greatly curtailed. The Topeka curriculum or any school curriculum cannot be equal under segregation." In the U.S. Supreme Court case, Thurgood Marshall argued this concept, while the justices also examined the fourteenth amendment, questioning whether "separate but equal" violated the "equal protection" aspect of the amendment.

The U.S. Supreme Court focused on the question of "separate." While some of the four cases that combined to become *Brown v. Board of Education* dealt with unequal facilities, the Kansas case did not. Investigators found the facilities involved in the Kansas case to be roughly equal. The issue of "separate" and the social stigma or exclusion from white society it created, was the central theme of the decision: "Segregation of white and colored children in public schools has a detrimental effect upon the colored children. The impact is greater when it has the sanction of the law, for the policy of separating the races is usually interpreted as denoting the inferiority of the negro group. A sense of inferiority affects the motivation of a child to learn. Segregation with the sanction of law, therefore, has a tendency to [retard] the educational and mental development of negro children and to deprive them of some of the benefits they would receive in a racial[ly] integrated school system."

In the aftermath of the Brown decision, a 1955 U.S. Supreme Court decision, nicknamed "Brown II," required states to use "all deliberate speed" to implement desegregation. Violence and refusal to comply with the law erupted in many southern states. In 1956, the presence of a black student at the University of Alabama led to rioting; in Clinton, Tennessee, a high school was bombed in 1958; in 1962, James Meredith enrolled at the University of Mississippi with federal troops present to control rioting. From 1959 to 1964, Price Edward County, Virginia, closed all its schools rather than comply with desegregation requirements.

The 1964 Civil Rights Act, ten years after the Brown decision, helped to strengthen desegregation in public venues and to tighten laws against racial discrimination. By reversing *Plessy v. Ferguson,* the *Brown v. Board of Education* decision added fuel to the growing civil rights movement in the United States and changed the landscape of public education for minority children.

FURTHER RESOURCES
Books

Clotfelter, Charles T. *After "Brown": The Rise and Retreat of School Desegregation.* Princeton: Princeton University Press, 2004.

Klarman, Michael J. *From Jim Crow to Civil Rights: The Supreme Court and the Struggle for Racial Equality.* New York: Oxford University Press,2004.

Patterson, James T. *Brown v. Board of Education: A Civil Rights Milestone and Its Troubled Legacy.* New York: Oxford University Press, 2001.

Title IX, Educational Amendments of 1972

Legislation

By: United States Code

Date: June 23, 1972

Source: U.S. Code. "Title IX Educational Amendments of 1972." Title 20, Chapter 38, Sections 1681–1688. June 23, 1972.

About the Author: The United States Code is the set of general and permanent laws that govern the United States. The House of Representatives prepares the Code and revisions are published every six years. The Code is arranged into fifty Titles. Title 20 deals with education. Chapter 38 describes the laws pertaining to "Discrimination Based on Sex or Blindness."

INTRODUCTION

In the landmark Civil Rights Act of 1964, Representative Martha Griffiths, a Democrat from the state of Michigan, worked to insert "gender" into the language of the act, thereby offering women in the United States the legal protections granted to minorities. While the act included the desegregation of all public schools and the federal power to enforce it, as well as the desegregation of restaurants, movie houses, public transportation, restrooms, fountains, gas stations, hotels, and sporting arenas, it also prohibited discrimination on the basis of gender.

President Lyndon Johnson's 1965 Executive Order 11246, which prohibited discrimination by federal contractors, was amended in 1968 to include gender as a protected class. Representative Martha Griffiths, aided by a University of Maryland professor, Bernice Sandler, worked on the issue of discrimination against women in education. The two began their work in 1970, and Griffiths was joined by Representative Edith Green, a Democrat from Ohio, in drafting legislation that would expressly forbid discrimination against women in education. In the early 1970s, women earned eighteen percent of all bachelor's degrees, nine percent of all medical degrees, seven percent of all law degrees, and twenty-five percent of all doctoral degrees, in spite of the fact that women were just over fifty percent of the overall population of the United States.

Initial efforts included the revision of previous civil rights legislation, such as Title VI and Title VII of the Civil Rights Act, and the extension of the Equal Pay Act of 1963 to executives, administrators, and professionals. With the support of Democratic Senator Birch Bayh of Indiana and Democratic Senator George McGovern of South Dakota, by 1972 the bill drafted by Representative Green had acquired a separate title: Title IX.

As the preamble to Title IX states, "No person in the United States shall, on the basis of sex, be excluded from participation in, be denied the benefits of, or be subject to discrimination under any educational programs or activity receiving federal financial assistance." When President Richard Nixon signed the act into law on June 23, 1972, few realized the impact this law would have on gender relations, education, and sports in the United States.

On November 10, 1972, Holy Cross's first two women Air Force ROTC students, Lesley Darling (second row, left) and Cindi Norris (first row, left), stand attention with fellow cadets during morning drill. © BETTMANN/CORBIS.

the benefits of, or be subjected to discrimination under any education program or activity receiving Federal financial assistance, except that:

(1) Classes of educational institutions subject to prohibition in regard to admissions to educational institutions, this section shall apply only to institutions of vocational education, professional education, and graduate higher education, and to public institutions of undergraduate higher education;

(2) Educational institutions commencing planned change in admissions in regard to admissions to educational institutions, this section shall not apply (A) for one year from June 23, 1972, nor for six years after June 23, 1972, in the case of an educational institution which has begun the process of changing from being an institution which admits only students of one sex to being an institution which admits students of both sexes, but only if it is carrying out a plan for such a change which is approved by the Secretary of Education or (B) for seven years from the date an educational institution begins the process of changing from

PRIMARY SOURCE

TITLE IX, EDUCATIONAL AMENDMENTS OF 1972

Section 1681. Sex (a) Prohibition against discrimination; exceptions. No person in the United States shall, on the basis of sex, be excluded from participation in, be denied

being an institution which admits only students of one sex to being an institution which admits students of both sexes, but only if it is carrying out a plan for such a change which is approved by the Secretary of Education, whichever is the later;

(3) Educational institutions of religious organizations with contrary religious tenets this section shall not apply to any educational institution which is controlled by a religious organization if the application of this subsection would not be consistent with the religious tenets of such organization;

(4) Educational institutions training individuals for military services or merchant marine this section shall not apply to an educational institution whose primary purpose is the training of individuals for the military services of the United States, or the merchant marine;

(5) Public educational institutions with traditional and continuing admissions policy in regard to admissions this section shall not apply to any public institution of undergraduate higher education which is an institution that traditionally and continually from its establishment has had a policy of admitting only students of one sex;

(6) Social fraternities or sororities; voluntary youth service organizations this section shall not apply to membership practices—

(A) of a social fraternity or social sorority which is exempt from taxation under section 501(a) of Title 26, the active membership of which consists primarily of students in attendance at an institution of higher education, or

(B) of the Young Men's Christian Association, Young Women's Christian Association; Girl Scouts, Boy Scouts, Camp Fire Girls, and voluntary youth service organizations which are so exempt, the membership of which has traditionally been limited to persons of one sex and principally to persons of less than nineteen years of age;

(7) Boy or Girl conferences this section shall not apply to—

(A) any program or activity of the American Legion undertaken in connection with the organization or operation of any Boys State conference, Boys Nation conference, Girls State conference, or Girls Nation conference; or

(B) any program or activity of any secondary school or educational institution specifically for—

(i) the promotion of any Boys State conference, Boys Nation conference, Girls State conference, or Girls Nation conference; or

(ii) the selection of students to attend any such conference;

(8) Father-son or mother-daughter activities at educational institutions this section shall not preclude father-son or mother-daughter activities at an educational institution, but if such activities are provided for students of one sex, opportunities for reasonably comparable activities shall be provided for students of the other sex; and

(9) Institutions of higher education scholarship wards in "beauty" pageants this section shall not apply with respect to any scholarship or other financial assistance awarded by an institution of higher education to any individual because such individual has received such award in any pageant in which the attainment of such award is based upon a combination of factors related to the personal appearance, poise, and talent of such individual and in which participation is limited to individuals of one sex only, so long as such pageant is in compliance with other nondiscrimination provisions of Federal law.

(b) Preferential or disparate treatment because of imbalance in participation or receipt of Federal benefits; statistical evidence of imbalance. Nothing contained in subsection (a) of this section shall be interpreted to require any educational institution to grant preferential or disparate treatment to the members of one sex on account of an imbalance which may exist with respect to the total number or percentage of persons of that sex participating in or receiving the benefits of any federally supported program or activity, in comparison with the total number or percentage of persons of that sex in any community, State, section, or other area: Provided, that this subsection shall not be construed to prevent the consideration in any hearing or proceeding under this chapter of statistical evidence tending to show that such an imbalance exists with respect to the participation in, or receipt of the benefits of, any such program or activity by the members of one sex.

(c) Educational institution defined. For the purposes of this chapter an educational institution means any public or private preschool, elementary, or secondary school, or any institution of vocational, professional, or higher education, except that in the case of an educational institution composed of more than one school, college, or department which are administratively separate units, such term means each such school, college or department.

Section 1682. Federal administrative enforcement; report to Congressional committees Each Federal department and agency which is empowered to extend Federal financial assistance to any education program or activity, by way of grant, loan, or contract other than a contract of insurance or guaranty, is authorized and directed to effectuate the provisions of section 1681 of this title with respect to such program or activity by issuing rules, regulations, or orders of general applicability which shall be consistent with achievement of the objectives of the statute authorizing the financial assistance in connection with which the action is taken. No such rule, regulation, or order shall become effective unless and until approved by the

President. Compliance with any requirement adopted pursuant to this section may be effected (l) by the termination of or refusal to grant or to continue assistance under such program or activity to any recipient as to whom there has been an express finding on the record, after opportunity for hearing, of a failure to comply with such requirement, but such termination or refusal shall be limited to the particular political entity, or part thereof, or other recipient as to whom such a finding has been made, and shall be limited in its effect to the particular program, or part thereof, in which such noncompliance has been so found, or (2) by any other means authorized by law: Provided, however, that no such action shall be taken until the department or agency concerned has advised the appropriate person or persons of the failure to comply with the requirement and has determined that compliance cannot be secured by voluntary means. In the case of any action terminating, or refusing to grant or continue, assistance because of failure to comply with a requirement imposed pursuant to this section, the head of the Federal department or agency shall file with the committees of the House and Senate having legislative jurisdiction over the program or activity involved a full written report of the circumstances and the grounds for such action. No such action shall become effective until thirty days have elapsed after the filing of such report.

Section 1683. Judicial Review Any department or agency action taken pursuant to section 1682 of this title shall be subject to such judicial review as may otherwise be provided by law for similar action taken by such department or agency on other grounds. In the case of action, not otherwise subject to judicial review, terminating or refusing to grant or to continue financial assistance upon a finding of failure to comply with any requirement imposed pursuant to section 1682 of this title, any person aggrieved (including any State or political subdivision thereof and any agency of either) may obtain judicial review of such action in accordance with chapter 7 of title 5, United States Code, and such action shall not be deemed committed to unreviewable agency discretion within the meaning of section 701 of that title.

Section 1684. Blindness or visual impairment; prohibition against discrimination No person in the United States shall, on the ground of blindness or severely impaired vision, be denied admission in any course of study by a recipient of Federal financial assistance for any education program or activity; but nothing herein shall be construed to require any such institution to provide any special services to such person because of his blindness or visual impairment.

Section 1685. Authority under other laws unaffected Nothing in this chaper shall add to or detract from any existing authority with respect to any program or activity under which

Federal financial assistance is extended by way of a contract of insurance or guaranty.

Section 1686. Interpretation with respect to living facilities Notwithstanding anything to the contrary contained in this chapter, nothing contained herein shall be construed to prohibit any educational institution receiving funds under this Act, from maintaining separate living facilities for the different sexes.

Section 1687. Interpretation of "program or activity" For the purposes of this title, the term "program or activity" and "program" mean all of the operations of—

(l)(A) a department, agency, special purpose district, or other instrumentality of a State or of a local government; or

(B) the entity of such State or local government that distributed such assistance and each such department or agency (and each other State or local government entity) to which the assistance is extended, in the case of assistance to a State or local government;

(2)(A) a college, university, or other postsecondary institution, or a public system of higher education; or

(B) a local educational agency (as defined in section 2854(a)(10) of this title), system of vocational education, or other school system;

(3)(A) an entire corporation, partnership, or other private organization, or an entire sole proprietorship—

(i) if assistance is extended to such corporation, partnership, private organization, or sole proprietorship as a whole; or

(ii) which is principally engaged in the business of providing education, health care, housing, social services, or parks and recreation; or

(B) the entire plant or other comparable, geographically separate facility to which Federal financial assistance is extended, in the case of any other corporation, partnership, private organization, or sole proprietorship; or

(4) any other entity which is established by two or more of the entities described in paragraph (l), (2) or (3);

any part of which is extended Federal financial assistance, except that such term does not include any operation of an entity which is controlled by a religious organization if the application of section 1681 if this title to such operation would not be consistent with the religious tenets of such organization.

Section 1688. Neutrality with respect to abortion Nothing in this chapter shall be construed to require or prohibit any person, or public or private entity, to provide or pay for any benefit or service, including the use of facilities, related to an abortion. Nothing in this section shall be construed to permit a penalty to be imposed on any person or individual because such person or individual is seeking or has received any benefit or service related to a legal abortion.

SIGNIFICANCE

The role that Title IX would play in sports equality was not a major impetus for its passage in 1972. Over time, however, Title IX became a powerful legal tool in the courts for women, girls, their parents, and coaches to fight for equal access, equipment, and facilities in sporting events and teams.

Lawsuits such as the 1984 *Grove City v. Bell* decision, which reaffirmed that Title IX applied only to sports in which federal funds were used, or the 1992 *Franklin v. Gwinnett County Public Schools*, which held that punitive damages could be applied if intentional violation of Title IX was at the heart of court cases, helped to clarify Title IX's role in regulating gender equality in education and sports.

According to a National Collegiate Athletic Association (NCAA) report on gender equity in college sports, while women represent fifty-four percent of all enrolled college students, their participation rate in college sports is only at forty-one percent. Other inequities in collegiate athletics, some thirty years after Title IX's passage, include the fact that on the whole, women received a percentage of athletic scholarship dollars greater than their participation percentage, leading critics to point to perceived unfairness with Title IX application. Critics of the legislation have long argued that Title IX punishes male athletes, turning the legislation into a quota system.

In terms of educational opportunities in federally funded institutions, surveys show that compared to 1972 rates, in 1994 twenty-seven percent of women earned bachelor's degrees, thirty-eight percent of medical degrees, forty-three percent of law degrees, and forty-four percent of doctoral degrees. Title IX's role in providing protection against discrimination for women in federally funded educational institutions—both on the playing field and in the classroom—combined with such legislation as the Equal Pay Act of 1963 and the Civil Rights Act of 1964, led to a marked increase in female participation in educational opportunity and sports, and continues to be a topic of debate in U.S. society.

Critics of Title IX claim that in order to achieve equal participation rates in sports, many schools must drop male-only athletic teams, such as wrestling or football. Others charge that Title IX is in effect a quota system, and inherently discriminatory.

In 2005, the Supreme Court upheld the right of a basketball coach to sue his school district for retaliating against him when he reported Title IX violations; Roderick Jackson, a Birmingham Alabama girls' basketball coach, complained that boys were receiving better equipment than his team. After being fired by his school district, Jackson sued. The case went to the Supreme Court, where his right to sue was upheld in part by the court's determination that Title IX' impact would be diluted if those who report infractions are met with retaliation and no legal recourse. In its decision the court stressed the importance of such reports to enforce Title IX in full.

FURTHER RESOURCES
Books

Wushanley, Wang. *Playing Nice and Losing: The Struggle for Control of Women's Intercollegiate Athletics, 1960–2000*. Syracuse, N.Y.: Syracuse University Press, 2004.

Web sites

The Chronicle of Higher Education. "Title IX at 30." June 21, 2002. <http://chronicle.com/free/v48/i41/41a03801.htm> (accessed May 14, 2006).

NCAA. "1999–2000 Gender-Equity Report." <http://www.ncaa.org/library/research/gender_equity_study/1999-00/1999-00_gender_equity_report.pdf> (accessed May 14, 2006).

Washington Post. "High Court Supports Title IX Protection." March 30, 2005. <http://www.washingtonpost.com/wp-dyn/articles/A9404-2005Mar29.html> (accessed May 14, 2006).

Education for all Handicapped Children Act

Speech

By: Gerald R. Ford

Date: December 2, 1975

Source: Ford, Gerald R. *Education for all Handicapped Children Act, Signing Statement*. December 2, 1975. Ford Library and Museum, Ann Arbor, Michigan.

About the Author: Gerald R. Ford was the 38th president of the United States, serving from 1974–1978. A member of congress for more than twenty-five years, Ford assumed the presidency after President Richard M. Nixon resigned.

A teacher instructs a special education class for disabled students at the Kennedy-Krieger Institute for Handicapped Children in Baltimore, Maryland, 1990. © RICHARD NOWITZ/CORBIS. REPRODUCED BY PERMISSION.

INTRODUCTION

Education of physically, mentally, and emotionally handicapped children in the United States, until the 1960s, was provided through a mixture of institutionalization, private tutoring, private schooling, or state-run schools for the handicapped. The Perkins School for the Blind, founded in 1829, was the first school for the blind in the United States, and similar schools for the blind and deaf opened throughout the United States in the latter part of the 19th century.

Students with other disabilities, such as those with conditions that prevented or hampered walking, developmental disabilities, or genetic conditions such as Down Syndrome were often ignored, institutionalized, or kept at home without schooling. In 1907, Maria Montessori, an Italian doctor, founded the *Casa dei Bambini*, a school for children with developmental disabilities in which she used experimental education approaches, with hands-on learning and self-correcting materials to teach "unteachable" mentally retarded children. Her ability to train children labeled mentally retarded to read and do arithmetic stunned educators

and gained admiration from Alexander Graham Bell, who helped found the Montessori Education Association in 1913 in Washington, D.C.

Other methods and schools for the handicapped included the 1864 founding of Gallaudet University in Washington D.C., which specialized in education for deaf people, and the New York Institute for the Blind, which changed its name after 135 years to the New York Institute for Special Education in 1986, reflecting the broad change in society as the concept of "handicapped" shifted to the more inclusive term "special needs."

In 1966 Congress established the Bureau for Education of the Handicapped as part of Title VI of the Elementary and Secondary Schools Act (ESEA). Through this government bureau advocates for special education students began to pursue Free Appropriate Public Education, or FAPE, for students with physical and mental issues that required special assistance. Many states passed laws requiring local school districts to remove barriers to education for children in wheelchairs, or to provide aides and speech therapy to students with emotional or processing disabilities.

At the same time, the concept of a disability or a "special need" changed as well. Understanding of learning disabilities such as dyslexia, attention deficit disorder, auditory processing disorder, speech and language disorders, and other behavioral and neurological disorders improved; giving students access to FAPE included diagnosing and treating these students as part of their educational experience as well as those students with classic physical and mental disabilities. As government agencies, smaller appropriations, and local and state governments passed a mixture of disparate measures, the push for a cohesive federal plan for special education led to the Education for All Handicapped Children Act in 1975, which mandated FAPE and required that all children, regardless of severity of disability, must receive FAPE from their local public school district. The ensuing costs would, according to the act, be federally supported.

President Ford's signing statement reflects many of the concerns expressed by advocates and critics alike when he signed the act into law on December 2, 1975.

PRIMARY SOURCE

President Gerald R. Ford's Statement on Signing the Education for All Handicapped Children Act of 1975
December 2, 1975
I have approved S. 6, the Education for All Handicapped Children Act of 1975.

Unfortunately, this bill promises more than the Federal Government can deliver, and its good intentions could be thwarted by the many unwise provisions it contains. Everyone can agree with the objective stated in the title of this bill—educating all handicapped children in our Nation. The key question is whether the bill will really accomplish that objective.

Even the strongest supporters of this measure know as well as I that they are falsely raising the expectations of the groups affected by claiming authorization levels which are excessive and unrealistic.

Despite my strong support for full educational opportunities for our handicapped children, the funding levels proposed in this bill will simply not be possible if Federal expenditures are to be brought under control and a balanced budget achieved over the next few years.

There are other features in the bill which I believe to be objectionable and which should be changed. It contains a vast array of detailed, complex, and costly administrative requirements which would unnecessarily assert Federal control over traditional State and local government functions. It establishes complex requirements under which tax dollars would be used to support administrative

paperwork and not educational programs. Unfortunately, these requirements will remain in effect even though the Congress appropriates far less than the amounts contemplated in S. 6.

Fortunately, since the provisions of this bill will not become fully effective until fiscal year 1978, there is time to revise the legislation and come up with a program that is effective and realistic. I will work with the Congress to use this time to design a program which will recognize the proper Federal role in helping States and localities fulfill their responsibilities in educating handicapped children. The Administration will send amendments to the Congress that will accomplish this purpose.

SIGNIFICANCE

In 1975 fewer than half of all children with known physical, developmental, and emotional disabilities were receiving a public or private school education. Part of the act's purpose was to increase opportunity for this underserved population; another purpose was to provide better education for those already in the system. A student in a wheelchair could not be deprived of physical education classes under this act; the classes must be modified to meet his need and to be "appropriate" and "fair." Students with emotional or neurobiological disabilities must be placed in a setting that is least restrictive; in many instances this means a classroom of four students and one teacher, or the assignment of a one-to-one aide for the student.

By the 1980s and 1990s the costs to school districts for providing FAPE to students with disabilities rose dramatically. The law required all students with any form of disability to be accommodated; the student with dyslexia or food allergies has the same rights to accommodation as a student in a wheelchair with cerebral palsy, or a blind or hearing impaired student. Ford's concerns about funding and federal administrative control have both been issues as this act has been implemented over time.

In the early 1990s, autism diagnoses began to rise in the United States; from a rate of one in two thousand in the late 1980s to one in 166 in 2005, diagnoses of autism spectrum disorders have overwhelmed many school districts. Because each student's needs must be fully accommodated, in some instances one student may need a one-to-one aide, hours of time with an occupational therapist, a speech therapist, and extra time from the regular classroom teacher. In addition, while special education students were placed in separate classes in past decades, by the 1990s "mainstreaming," or integrating special education students into regular classes, became the goal for many special education advocates and parents who argued that socialization and academic success depending on mainstreaming when appropriate.

Each child with a diagnosed special need represents budget dollars, and the Education for All Handicapped Children Act—renamed the Individuals with Disabilities Education Act during later revisions—requires that school districts must meet these needs, or send students to facilities that can provide the services the students need, at the local school district's cost. The student's right to a Fair Appropriate Public Education includes sending the child to a private school at public school district expense if needed; these cases generally result in the child being sent to a facility that costs between four and ten times the public school expenditure per pupil, causing strains on public school budgets.

Critics of such policies argue that all children are harmed by the exercise of this right for special needs children; in 2004 eleven school districts in the state of Washington sued the state, the governor, the Superintendent of Public Instruction, the President of the Senate, and the Speaker of the House to force the state to pay for special education services after the costs of administering such programs became onerous.

The Education for All Handicapped Children Act pledged that the federal government would pay for forty percent of a special education student's costs. According to the National Education Association, in 2004, the federal government provided slightly less than twenty percent, a difference of more than $10.6 billion that states and local school districts do not receive.

FURTHER RESOURCES

Books

Montessori, Maria. *The Discovery of the Child*. Ballantine Books, 1986.

Richardson, J. *Common, Delinquent, and Special: The institutional Shape of Special Education (Studies in the History of Education)*. Routledge Falmer, 1999.

Winzer, Margaret. *The History of Special Education*. Gallaudet University Press, 1993.

Web sites

U.S. Department of Education. "Special Education & Rehabilitative Services." <http://www.ed.gov/policy/speced/guid/idea/idea2004.html> (accessed April 14, 2006).

Plyler v. Doe

Legal decision

By: U.S. Supreme Court

Date: June 5, 1982

Source: *Plyler v. Doe*. 457 US 202 (1982).

About the Author: The Supreme Court of the United States is the nation's highest court, currently with eight associate justices and one chief justice. In 1982, the associate justices were Thurgood Marshall, John Paul Stevens, William J. Brennan, Lewis F. Powell, William H. Rehnquist, Byron R. White, Sandra Day O'Connor, and Harry A. Blackmun; the chief justice was Warren E. Burger. The majority opinion in the *Plyler v. Doe* case was delivered by Justice William J. Brennan.

INTRODUCTION

In 1975, Texas passed a law that cut funds for the education of the children of illegal immigrants and authorized school districts to not enroll these children. Lawyers filed a class-action suit in 1975 in a Federal District Court on behalf of Mexican children denied education in the Tyler, Texas school district. The suit claimed that the new Texas law violated the Equal Protection Clause of the Fourteenth Amendment of the U.S. Constitution, which states that "No State ... shall deny to any person within its jurisdiction the equal protection of the law." (All cases brought on appeal to the U.S. Constitution are handled in Federal courts.).

In 1980, the U.S. District Court found against Texas. Texas appealed to the Fifth Circuit Court of Appeals (also a Federal court), which again decided in favor of the plaintiffs (the Mexican children). Texas appealed a second time, its last recourse being the U.S. Supreme Court. In 1982, the Supreme Court upheld the judgment of the two lower courts by a 5–4 vote. Blackmun, Brennan, Marshall, Powell, and Stephens were in the majority, with Burger, White, Rehnquist, and O'Connor in the minority.

◼ PRIMARY SOURCE

PLYLER, SUPERINTENDENT, TYLER INDEPENDENT SCHOOL DISTRICT, ET AL. V. DOE, GUARDIAN, ET AL. APPEAL FROM THE UNITED STATES COURT OF APPEALS FOR THE FIFTH CIRCUIT
Held: .

A Texas statute which withholds from local school districts any state funds for the education of children who were not "legally admitted" into the United States, and which authorizes local school districts to deny enrollment to such children, violates the Equal Protection Clause of the Fourteenth Amendment. Pp. 210-230.

(a) The illegal aliens who are plaintiffs in these cases challenging the statute may claim the benefit of the Equal Protection Clause, which provides that no State shall "deny to any person within its jurisdiction the equal protection of the laws." Whatever his status under the immigration laws, an alien is a "person" in any ordinary sense of that term. This Court's prior cases recognizing that illegal aliens are "persons" protected by the Due Process Clauses of the Fifth and Fourteenth Amendments, which Clauses do not include the phrase "within its jurisdiction," cannot be distinguished on the asserted ground that persons who have entered the country illegally are not "within the jurisdiction" of a State even if they are present within its boundaries and subject to its laws. Nor do the logic and history of the Fourteenth Amendment support such a construction. Instead, use of the phrase "within its jurisdiction" confirms the understanding that the Fourteenth Amendment's protection extends to anyone, citizen or stranger, who is subject to the laws of a State, and reaches into every corner of a State's territory. Pp. 210-216.

(b) The discrimination contained in the Texas statute cannot be considered rational unless it furthers some substantial goal of the State. Although undocumented resident aliens cannot be treated as a "suspect class," and although education is not a "fundamental right," so as to require the State to justify the statutory classification by showing that it serves a compelling governmental interest, nevertheless the Texas statute imposes a lifetime hardship on a discrete class of children not accountable for their disabling status. These children can neither affect their parents' conduct nor their own undocumented status. [457 U.S. 202, 203] The deprivation of public education is not like the deprivation of some other governmental benefit. Public education has a pivotal role in maintaining the fabric of our society and in sustaining our political and cultural heritage; the deprivation of education takes an inestimable toll on the social, economic, intellectual, and psychological well-being of the individual, and poses an obstacle to individual achievement. In determining the rationality of the Texas statute, its costs to the Nation and to the innocent children may properly be considered. Pp. 216-224.

(c) The undocumented status of these children vel non does not establish a sufficient rational basis for denying them benefits that the State affords other residents. It is true that when faced with an equal protection challenge respecting a State's differential treatment of aliens, the courts must be attentive to congressional policy concerning aliens. But in the area of special constitutional sensitivity presented by these cases, and in the absence of any

contrary indication fairly discernible in the legislative record, no national policy is perceived that might justify the State in denying these children an elementary education. Pp. 224-226.

(d) Texas' statutory classification cannot be sustained as furthering its interest in the "preservation of the state's limited resources for the education of its lawful residents." While the State might have an interest in mitigating potentially harsh economic effects from an influx of illegal immigrants, the Texas statute does not offer an effective method of dealing with the problem. Even assuming that the net impact of illegal aliens on the economy is negative, charging tuition to undocumented children constitutes an ineffectual attempt to stem the tide of illegal immigration, at least when compared with the alternative of prohibiting employment of illegal aliens. Nor is there any merit to the suggestion that undocumented children are appropriately singled out for exclusion because of the special burdens they impose on the State's ability to provide high-quality public education. The record does not show that exclusion of undocumented children is likely to improve the overall quality of education in the State. Neither is there any merit to the claim that undocumented children are appropriately singled out because their unlawful presence within the United States renders them less likely than other children to remain within the State's boundaries and to put their education to productive social or political use within the State.

JUSTICE BRENNAN delivered the opinion of the Court.

The question presented by these cases is whether, consistent with the Equal Protection Clause of the Fourteenth Amendment, Texas may deny to undocumented school-age children the free public education that it provides to children who are citizens of the United States or legally admitted aliens.

A

Sheer incapability or lax enforcement of the laws barring entry into this country, coupled with the failure to establish an effective bar to the employment of undocumented aliens, has resulted in the creation of a substantial "shadow population" of illegal migrants—numbering in the millions—within our borders. This situation raises the specter of a permanent caste of undocumented resident aliens, encouraged by some to remain here as a source of cheap labor, but nevertheless denied the benefits that our society makes available to citizens and lawful residents. The existence of such an underclass presents most difficult problems for a Nation that prides itself on adherence to principles of equality under law.

The children who are plaintiffs in these cases are special members of this underclass. Persuasive arguments support the view that a State may withhold its beneficence from those whose very presence within the United States is the product of their own unlawful conduct. These arguments do not apply with the same force to classifications imposing disabilities on the minor children of such illegal entrants. At the least, those who elect to enter our territory by stealth and in violation of our law should be prepared to bear the consequences, including, but not limited to, deportation. But the children of those illegal entrants are not comparably situated. Their "parents have the ability to conform their conduct to societal norms," and presumably the ability to remove themselves from the State's jurisdiction; but the children who are plaintiffs in these cases "can affect neither their parents' conduct nor their own status." Even if the State found it expedient to control the conduct of adults by acting against their children, legislation directing the onus of a parent's misconduct against his children does not comport with fundamental conceptions of justice.

> "[V]isiting . . . condemnation on the head of an infant is illogical and unjust. Moreover, imposing disabilities on the . . . child is contrary to the basic concept of our system that legal burdens should bear some relationship to individual responsibility or wrongdoing. Obviously, no child is responsible for his birth and penalizing the . . . child is an ineffectual—as well as unjust—way of deterring the parent."

Of course, undocumented status is not irrelevant to any proper legislative goal. Nor is undocumented status an absolutely immutable characteristic since it is the product of conscious, indeed unlawful, action. But 21.031 is directed against children, and imposes its discriminatory burden on the basis of a legal characteristic over which children can have little control. It is thus difficult to conceive of a rational justification for penalizing these children for their presence within the United States. Yet that appears to be precisely the effect of 21.031.

Public education is not a "right" granted to individuals by the Constitution. But neither is it merely some governmental "benefit" indistinguishable from other forms of social welfare legislation. Both the importance of education in maintaining our basic institutions, and the lasting impact of its deprivation on the life of the child, mark the distinction. The "American people have always regarded education and [the] acquisition of knowledge as matters of supreme importance." We have recognized "the public schools as a most vital civic institution for the preservation of a democratic system of government," and as the primary vehicle for transmitting "the values on which our society rests." "[A]s . . . pointed out early in our history, . . . some degree of education is necessary to prepare citizens to participate effectively and intelligently in our open political system if we are to preserve freedom and independence." And these historic "perceptions of the public schools as inculcating fundamental values necessary to the maintenance

of a democratic political system have been confirmed by the observations of social scientists." In addition, education provides the basic tools by which individuals might lead economically productive lives to the benefit of us all. In sum, education has a fundamental role in maintaining the fabric of our society. We cannot ignore the significant social costs borne by our Nation when select groups are denied the means to absorb the values and skills upon which our social order rests.

In addition to the pivotal role of education in sustaining our political and cultural heritage, denial of education to some isolated group of children poses an affront to one of the goals of the Equal Protection Clause: the abolition of governmental barriers presenting unreasonable obstacles to advancement on the basis of individual merit. Paradoxically, by depriving the children of any disfavored group of an education, we foreclose the means by which that group might raise the level of esteem in which it is held by the majority. But more directly, "education prepares individuals to be self-reliant and self-sufficient participants in society." Illiteracy is an enduring disability. The inability to read and write will handicap the individual deprived of a basic education each and every day of his life. The inestimable toll of that deprivation on the social, economic, intellectual, and psychological well-being of the individual, and the obstacle it poses to individual achievement, make it most difficult to reconcile the cost or the principle of a status-based denial of basic education with the framework of equality embodied in the Equal Protection Clause. What we said 28 years ago in Brown v. Board of Education, still holds true:.

> "Today, education is perhaps the most important function of state and local governments. Compulsory school attendance laws and the great expenditures for education both demonstrate our recognition of the importance of education to our democratic society. It is required in the performance of our most basic public responsibilities, even service in the armed forces. It is the very foundation of good citizenship. Today it is a principal instrument in awakening the child to cultural values, in preparing him for later professional training, and in helping him to adjust normally to his environment. In these days, it is doubtful that any child may reasonably be expected to succeed in life if he is denied the opportunity of an education. Such an opportunity, where the state has undertaken to provide it, is a right which must be made available to all on equal terms."

B

These well-settled principles allow us to determine the proper level of deference to be afforded 21.031. Undocumented aliens cannot be treated as a suspect class because their presence in this country in violation of federal law is not a "constitutional irrelevancy." Nor is education a fundamental right; a State need not justify by compelling necessity every variation in the manner in which education is provided to its population. But more is involved in these cases than the abstract question whether 21.031 discriminates against a suspect class, or whether education is a fundamental right. Section 21.031 imposes a lifetime hardship on a discrete class of children not accountable for their disabling status. The stigma of illiteracy will mark them for the rest of their lives. By denying these children a basic education, we deny them the ability to live within the structure of our civic institutions, and foreclose any realistic possibility that they will contribute in even the smallest way to the progress of our Nation. In determining the rationality of 21.031, we may appropriately take into account its costs to the Nation and to the innocent children who are its victims. In light of these countervailing costs, the discrimination contained in 21.031 can hardly be considered rational unless it furthers some substantial goal of the State.

IV

It is the State's principal argument, and apparently the view of the dissenting Justices, that the undocumented status of these children vel non establishes a sufficient rational basis for denying them benefits that a State might choose to afford other residents. The State notes that while other aliens are admitted "on an equality of legal privileges with all citizens under non-discriminatory laws," the asserted right of these children to an education can claim no implicit congressional imprimatur. Indeed, in the State's view, Congress' apparent disapproval of the presence of these children within the United States, and the evasion of the federal regulatory program that is the mark of undocumented status, provides authority for its decision to impose upon them special disabilities. Faced with an equal protection challenge respecting the treatment of aliens, we agree that the courts must be attentive to congressional policy; the exercise of congressional power might well affect the State's prerogatives to afford differential treatment to a particular class of aliens. But we are unable to find in the congressional immigration scheme any statement of policy that might weigh significantly in arriving at an equal protection balance concerning the State's authority to deprive these children of an education.

To be sure, like all persons who have entered the United States unlawfully, these children are subject to deportation. But there is no assurance that a child subject to deportation will ever be deported. An illegal entrant might be granted federal permission to continue to reside in this country, or even to become a citizen. In light of the discretionary federal power to grant relief from deportation, a State cannot realistically determine that any particular undocumented child will in fact be deported until after

deportation proceedings have been completed. It would of course be most difficult for the State to justify a denial of education to a child enjoying an inchoate federal permission to remain.

We are reluctant to impute to Congress the intention to withhold from these children, for so long as they are present in this country through no fault of their own, access to a basic education. In other contexts, undocumented status, coupled with some articulable federal policy, might enhance state authority with respect to the treatment of undocumented aliens. But in the area of special constitutional sensitivity presented by these cases, and in the absence of any contrary indication fairly discernible in the present legislative record, we perceive no national policy that supports the State in denying these children an elementary education.

VI

If the State is to deny a discrete group of innocent children the free public education that it offers to other children residing within its borders, that denial must be justified by a showing that it furthers some substantial state interest. No such showing was made here. Accordingly, the judgment of the Court of Appeals in each of these cases is.

Affirmed.

SIGNIFICANCE

Illegal immigration has been a contentious issue in the U.S. since the early twentieth century. Although both legal and illegal immigrants have been a necessary component of the U.S. economy, the latter have engendered much resentment on the part of some citizens, who believe that their jobs are threatened by unfair, low-wage competition and that immigrants enjoy services and benefits funded by citizen taxpayers. (Many illegal immigrants pay income tax because it is deducted from their paycheck.) In recent decades, politicians have responded to this sentiment at the state and federal levels with measures designed to restrict government-supplied services to immigrants. The 1975 Texas Alien Children Education Act—overturned by *Plyler v. Doe*—was one such measure.

Children who are born in the United States are, according to the Fourteenth Amendment, citizens, and there is little controversy about whether they must receive all benefits provided by government: children born outside the U.S. to non-citizens are non-citizens.

Plyler v. Doe is one leg of a tripod of federal cases that govern the schooling in the U.S. of children who do not speak English fluently or at all. In *Lau v. Nichols* (1973), the U.S. Supreme Court ruled that non-English speaking students must be taught English in order to have equal access to education. In *Castenada v. Pickard* (1981), a Fifth Circuit Court of Appeals set standards for judging whether a school's program to teach non-English-speaking students is adequate. *Plyler v. Doe*, by ruling that undocumented children have a right to the same education as citizen children, effectively required schools to apply *Lau v. Nichols* and *Castenada v. Pickard* to undocumented children.

Plyler v. Doe defines the only major service to illegal immigrant children that is constitutionally protected: public-school education through high school. In fact, children of illegal immigrants are not only allowed but required to attend school while they are in the U.S. Other services can be and are denied by various laws, but not education. A number of laws seeking to restrict benefits to immigrants were passed by state legislatures in the 1990s and early 2000s. For example, in 1994, California voters enacted Proposition 187, which was described on its ballot argument as "the first giant stride in ultimately ending the ILLEGAL ALIEN invasion." This proposition sought to cut off all medical and public services for undocumented non-citizens and to deny their children public education. The law was overturned in U.S. Federal District Court that same year, partly because *Plyler v. Doe* indicated that the denial-of-education provision in Proposition 187 was unconstitutional.

In 2004, Proposition 200 passed in Arizona. It requires employees of all state and federal agencies to verify the immigration status of those receiving benefits—including maternity health clinic services for pregnant women—and criminalizes failure to do so. Because of *Plyler v. Doe* and the fate of California's Proposition 187, the Arizona law does not attempt to block the education of undocumented children.

In 2006, there were approximately twelve million undocumented aliens in the U.S.—about one worker in twenty—and the U.S. Congress was considering highly controversial immigration-related legislation that would enact more severe penalties for undocumented immigrants. Possible measures include building a large wall along the U.S.-Mexican border, legalizing the status of long-term residents of the United States despite originally illegal status, and criminalizing the provision of aid to illegal immigrants by priests, social workers, or anyone else. Consideration of the bill by Congress in early 2006 elicited record-setting mass protest marches in some U.S. cities.

FURTHER RESOURCES

Books

Gordan F. Ewell, ed. *Mexico: Migration, U.S. Economic Issues and Counter Narcotic Efforts*. New York: Novinka, 2005.

Periodicals

Glanton, Dahleen. "Illegal Immigrants Brace for State Laws." *Chicago Tribune* (April 10, 2006).

Mailman, Stlaney. "California's Proposition 187 and Its Lessons." *New York Law Journal* (January 3, 1995).

Web sites

National Immigration Law Center. "Most State Proposals to Restrict Benefits for Immigrants Failed in 2005." November 21, 2005. <http://www.nilc.org/immspbs/sf_benefits/2005_anti-imm_proposals_article_112105.pdf> (accessed May 12, 2006).

Young Children Weave Carpets at a Kathmandu Factory

Photograph

By: Alison Wright

Date: 1989

Source: © Alison Wright/Corbis.

About the Photographer: Alison Wright is an award-winning freelance photographer and journalist based in San Francisco. In the late 1980s, Wright worked for the United Nations Children's Fund (UNICEF) in Nepal for about four years, where she focused on children engaged in child labor. In 1993, she received the Dorothea Lange Award in Documentary Photography for her portrayal of child labor in Asia.

INTRODUCTION

The carpet industry in Nepal, over the years, has accounted for a significant proportion of foreign exchange for the country. Carpets have been one of the major exports of Nepal, especially in the late 1980s and early 1990s. At its peak in 1994, revenue generated from carpet exports was nearly $180 million, with Germany and the United States being the biggest export markets. According to Nepal's Commerce Ministry, carpet exports accounted for half of the total exports in the same year.

However, the labor-intensive carpet industry employs a significant number of underage children. According to Child Workers in Nepal, a child rights organization, out of 200,000 people employed in the Nepalese carpet industry in the early 1990s, thirty-eight percent were children below the age of fourteen.

Reports indicate that most industries in Nepal employ child laborers. A fact sheet prepared by the International Labor Organization as part of its International Program on the Elimination of Child Labor (ILO-IPEC) mentioned that nearly 2.6 million children worked in Nepal in the 1990s. These children, generally between five and fourteen years of age, comprised more than forty percent of the total child population in Nepal during the above-mentioned period.

The carpet industry in Nepal gained prominence as a result of the Chinese occupation of Tibet in 1959, when many Tibetans were forced out of the region. A majority of them took refuge in Nepal, bringing with them their traditional carpet-weaving skills. The circumstances in Nepal at the time, such as low cost of child labor, proved favorable for the expansion of the country's carpet industry.

Human Rights organizations, such as ILO, have often highlighted in their reports the lowly conditions of child laborers in the carpet weaving industry. Carpet makers defend such recruitment practices claiming that children are better at weaving intricate designs— a key requirement in the carpet industry.

Children are often forced to work for extremely long hours in cramped and dimly lit conditions for little or no compensation. These organizations state that the children, often ill-fed and beaten, are made to work in hazardous conditions. For instance, the air inside carpet factories is filled with woolen fluff, making breathing extremely difficult.

According to ILO-IPEC, some child laborers are enslaved in accordance with local custom that involves setting off the wages earned by them for the debts their parents have incurred from carpet factory owners. There have also been reports of sexual abuse and child trafficking to neighboring countries.

PRIMARY SOURCE

YOUNG CHILDREN WEAVE CARPETS AT A KATHMANDU FACTORY

See primary source image.

SIGNIFICANCE

Child labor is widespread in various countries, especially the least developed nations. According to UNICEF, as of 2005 there were an estimated 246 million child laborers in the world. Nearly seventy percent of these children work in hazardous conditions. Nepal, one of the least developed countries in the world, has faced this scourge for many years.

Experts maintain that child labor, apart from being illegal, affects a country in many ways. Education plays an important role in the progress of any country. High prevalence of child labor implies fewer educated children. This would affect the economy in the long run.

According to the ILO there are various reasons that force children in Nepal to work. These include extreme poverty, lack of education, large-scale transition of labor from the agricultural sector to other areas, traditionalist societal values and customs, and absence of effective implementation of existing legislation. There are laws that prohibit child labor in any industry in Nepal. The Nepal Children's Act of 1992 terms child labor as illegal. Article 20 of the Constitution of Nepal, formulated in 1990, guarantees the right against exploitation to children. Child labor in hazardous occupations has been banned since 1956. Under the Labor Act of 1992, it is a criminal offense to employ children less than fourteen years of age. Moreover, the country is also a signatory of the United Nations Convention on the Rights of the Child. However, due to the above-mentioned factors and weak implementation of such laws, child labor has been rampant.

Neighboring countries such as India and Bangladesh show similar trends. Both India and Bangladesh reportedly have a high percentage of child laborers. Like Nepal, some of the main reasons for child labor in these countries are poverty, lack of education, and poor implementation of laws. Nevertheless, owing to the magnitude of child labor in Nepal, several anti-child-labor campaigns have been organized since the early 1990s. For instance, there was an aggressive consumer awareness campaign in Europe in 1990 that highlighted employment of children in carpet manufacturing. According to a Ford Foundation report, Senator Tom Harkin of Iowa co-sponsored the Pease-Harkin bill in the mid-1990s, proposing a ban on import of all goods that involved child labor. However, this bill was not passed.

Such initiatives did lead to numerous other developments for the prevention of child labor in Nepal. The Government of Nepal set up the Child Labor Free Certification Coordination Committee in 1994. The committee, as a means of discouraging child labor, issues child-labor-free certification to carpet manufactures that do not employ child workers. In 1995, the ILO also commenced its IPEC program to create awareness, education, and rehabilitation schemes for children.

Another organization—RUGMARK International— has been successful in diminishing child labor in Nepal to a considerable extent. RUGMARK Nepal,

PRIMARY SOURCE

Young Children Weave Carpets at a Kathmandu Factory: Child labor is often used in the traditional carpet-weaving industry in Nepal. These children are weaving carpets at a factory in Kathmandu, Nepal, in 1989. © ALISON WRIGHT/CORBIS.

launched in the 1990s, has a team of independent inspectors that regularly inspect carpet manufacturers participating in their program. According to the organization, between 1996 and 2004 it has been responsible for rehabilitating 1,760 children. As of 2004, 517 manufacturers representing seventy percent of Nepal's carpet exports are inspected by RUGMARK. According to a 1999 UNICEF report titled "Situation Analysis of Child Labor in Carpet Industry of Nepal," in 1996 an estimated fifty percent of Nepal's carpet weavers were children. Four years after RUGMARK launched in Nepal this figure dropped to less than five percent.

Such initiatives are thought to have significantly reduced the number of child workers in Nepal's carpet industry. According to the Ford Foundation, as of the mid-2000s the number of children working in this industry has dropped to two percent. Moreover, trade figures from the Carpet Industry of Nepal indicate that

two-thirds of the nearly three thousand carpet manufacturers in 1993 went out of business as a result of the anti-child-labor awareness. However, trade figures also indicate a substantial slowdown in carpet manufacturing in the country. Also, with the reduction in employment of children in the carpet industry, there have been simultaneous reports indicating a rise in child trafficking to neighboring countries.

FURTHER RESOURCES

Books

Roberts-Davis, Tanya. *We Need to Go to School: Voices from the Rugmark Children*. Toronto: Groundwood Books, 2003.

Web sites

Center for Contemporary Studies. "Child Labour in South Asia." <http://www.cuts-international.org/Brf-3–2003.pdf> (accessed May 4, 2006).

Ford Foundation. "Children of the Looms." <http://www.fordfound.org/publications/ff_report/

view_ff_report_detail.cfm?report_index=287>
(accessed May 4, 2006).

International Labour Organization. "IPEC at a Glance."
<http://www.ilo.org/public/english/region/asro/
kathmandu/projects/child_l.htm> (accessed May 4,
2006).

Nepal RUGMARK Foundation. <http://
www.nepalrugmark.org/index1.html> (accessed May 4,
2006).

South-North Development Monitor. "Nepal: Carpet Industry
Under Scrutiny for Flouting Laws." <http://
www.sunsonline.org/trade/process/followup/1999/
01190699.htm> (accessed May 4, 2006).

World Tibet Network News. "Duty Relief to Boost Nepal
Carpet Exports to EU." <http://www.tibet.ca/en/
wtnarchive/1995/1/28_3.html> (accessed May 4, 2006).

United Nations Convention on the Rights of the Child

Declaration

By: United Nations General Assembly

Date: November 20, 1989

Source: United Nations General Assembly. *United Nations Convention on the Rights of the Child.* United Nations, November 20, 1989.

About the Author: The phrase "United Nations" was used during World War II (1939–1945) to describe the dozens of nations allied together to fight Germany and Japan, most notably including China, France, Great Britain, the Soviet Union, and the United States of America. These allies decided to develop a new organization to facilitate international cooperation and help prevent future wars. It would replace the League of Nations, which had failed to prevent World War II. They called it the United Nations (UN). The UN Charter was ratified on October 24, 1945. In the years since the UN has served as a forum for international negotiation and cooperation on many issues, including international security, human rights, trade and economics, and the environment. The General Assembly is the primary body for deliberation within the United Nations, in which all member nations have a seat.

INTRODUCTION

In response to growing international concerns governing the treatment, handling, and rights of children, the United Nations proposed the Committee on the Rights of the Child (CRC). In 1999, the CRC—ratified on November 20, 1989—ranked as the single most endorsed human rights treaty, and as of 2006 the United States and Somalia are the only two countries who have not signed it. The treaty, seeking to provide safe harbor for children, shows a continuation in twentieth-century history to expand and solidify the rights of minors.

The question of children's rights precedes the twentieth century. Though the United States did not have a concise program for children's rights as of 2006, it has taken action throughout its history. In 1852, Massachusetts mandated that children attend school. Also in the mid-1800s, Orphan Trains began transporting parentless children westward across the United States in an effort to keep them off the streets and out of factories. The Orphan Trains subsided in the early twentieth century, but their principles extended to other realms of society. Civic organizations such as the Masons and other groups established homes for orphan children. These group homes also existed in Europe and other areas outside the United States.

Other reforms for child labor concerned restricting the working hours of women and children. The state of Oregon enacted such a law in 1903 that was upheld in the 1908 *Muller v. Oregon* ruling. But, issues with child labor were not the only prevailing issues concerning the rights of children.

In World War II (1938–1945) and other wars, children fought in the battle zones, acting as couriers, intelligence collectors, and in underground resistance groups. One example of child resisters during World War II can be seen from Poland. Here, children often traveled in large groups, committing acts of violence to denounce Nazi control. A more memorable account of Polish children's wartime activities involved presenting Nazi personnel with flowers containing crushed glass. Pope John Paul II was a child resister in World-War-II-era Poland. In Nazi Germany, children worked to resist the regime, in some instances, but the government also recruited them to work in factories and do courier tasks throughout the country.

These wartime actions are just one realm of the abuses of children. Street children, those deemed homeless or without adequate parental control and guidance, are a large segment of the child population who continually fall outside of mainstream society and civil rights. In countries like Guatemala, Egypt, Brazil, and Columbia, these children are randomly gathered up and confined in jail cells for several days or weeks. Frequently, police or adult prisoners beat them, sexually abuse them, and deny them food and water. Guatemala has established a system to help street children report

Four Indonesian children play on a jungle gym in a park in Jakarta on April 12, 2005. © BAGUS INDAHONO/EPA/CORBIS.

instances of abuse by police and law enforcement officials, but of three hundred cases, less than half have been brought to prosecution. A variety of other countries have problems with street children, and they are often thought of as anti-social and dangerous.

In an effort to eradicate these crimes against children and to protect children within the global environment, the United Nations Committee on the Rights of the Child (CRC) consists of independent experts who review reports, examine issues, and propose protocols for change. The first report must be submitted within two years of ascending to the Committee, and then afterward a study must be delivered every five years. It meets in Geneva three times per year.

PRIMARY SOURCE

UNITED NATIONS CONVENTION ON THE RIGHTS OF THE CHILD

Article 1 For the purposes of the present Convention, a child means every human being below the age of eighteen years unless, under the law applicable to the child, majority is attained earlier.

Article 2

1. States Parties shall respect and ensure the rights set forth in the present Convention to each child within their jurisdiction without discrimination of any kind, irrespective of the child's or his or her parent's or legal guardian's race, colour, sex, language, religion, political or other opinion, national, ethnic or social origin, property, disability, birth or other status.

2. States Parties shall take all appropriate measures to ensure that the child is protected against all forms of discrimination or punishment on the basis of the status, activities, expressed opinions, or beliefs of the child's parents, legal guardians, or family members.

Article 3

1. In all actions concerning children, whether undertaken by public or private social welfare institutions, courts of law, administrative authorities or legislative bodies, the best interests of the child shall be a primary consideration.

2. States Parties undertake to ensure the child such protection and care as is necessary for his or her well-being, taking into account the rights and duties of his or her parents, legal guardians, or other individuals legally responsible for him or her, and, to this end, shall take all appropriate legislative and administrative measures.

3. States Parties shall ensure that the institutions, services and facilities responsible for the care or protection of children shall conform with the standards established by competent authorities, particularly in the areas of safety, health, in the number and suitability of their staff, as well as competent supervision.

Article 4 States Parties shall undertake all appropriate legislative, administrative, and other measures for the implementation of the rights recognized in the present Convention. With regard to economic, social and cultural rights, States Parties shall undertake such measures to the maximum extent of their available resources and, where needed, within the framework of international co-operation.

Article 5 States Parties shall respect the responsibilities, rights and duties of parents or, where applicable, the members of the extended family or community as provided for by local custom, legal guardians or other persons legally responsible for the child, to provide, in a manner consistent with the evolving capacities of the child, appropriate direction and guidance in the exercise by the child of the rights recognized in the present Convention.

Article 6

1. States Parties recognize that every child has the inherent right to life.
2. States Parties shall ensure to the maximum extent possible the survival and development of the child.

Article 7

1. The child shall be registered immediately after birth and shall have the right from birth to a name, the right to acquire a nationality and, as far as possible, the right to know and be cared for by his or her parents.
2. States Parties shall ensure the implementation of these rights in accordance with their national law and their obligations under the relevant international instruments in this field, in particular where the child would otherwise be stateless.

Article 8

1. States Parties undertake to respect the right of the child to preserve his or her identity, including nationality, name and family relations as recognized by law without unlawful interference.
2. Where a child is illegally deprived of some or all of the elements of his or her identity, States Parties shall

provide appropriate assistance and protection, with a view to speedily re-establishing his or her identity.

Article 9

1. States Parties shall ensure that a child shall not be separated from his or her parents against their will, except when competent authorities subject to judicial review determine, in accordance with applicable law and procedures, that such separation is necessary for the best interests of the child. Such determination may be necessary in a particular case such as one involving abuse or neglect of the child by the parents, or one where the parents are living separately and a decision must be made as to the child's place of residence.
2. In any proceedings pursuant to paragraph 1 of the present article, all interested parties shall be given an opportunity to participate in the proceedings and make their views known.
3. States Parties shall respect the right of the child who is separated from one or both parents to maintain personal relations and direct contact with both parents on a regular basis, except if it is contrary to the child's best interests.
4. Where such separation results from any action initiated by a State Party, such as the detention, imprisonment, exile, deportation or death (including death arising from any cause while the person is in the custody of the State) of one or both parents or of the child, that State Party shall, upon request, provide the parents, the child or, if appropriate, another member of the family with the essential information concerning the whereabouts of the absent member(s) of the family unless the provision of the information would be detrimental to the well-being of the child. States Parties shall further ensure that the submission of such a request shall of itself entail no adverse consequences for the person(s) concerned.

Article 10

1. In accordance with the obligation of States Parties under article 9, paragraph 1, applications by a child or his or her parents to enter or leave a State Party for the purpose of family reunification shall be dealt with by States Parties in a positive, humane and expeditious manner. States Parties shall further ensure that the submission of such a request shall entail no adverse consequences for the applicants and for the members of their family.
2. A child whose parents reside in different States shall have the right to maintain on a regular basis, save in exceptional circumstances personal relations and direct contacts with both parents. Towards that end and in accordance with the obligation of States Parties under article 9, paragraph 2, States Parties shall

respect the right of the child and his or her parents to leave any country, including their own, and to enter their own country. The right to leave any country shall be subject only to such restrictions as are prescribed by law and which are necessary to protect the national security, public order (ordre public), public health or morals or the rights and freedoms of others and are consistent with the other rights recognized in the present Convention.

Article 11

1. States Parties shall take measures to combat the illicit transfer and non-return of children abroad.
2. To this end, States Parties shall promote the conclusion of bilateral or multilateral agreements or accession to existing agreements....

Article 18

1. States Parties shall use their best efforts to ensure recognition of the principle that both parents have common responsibilities for the upbringing and development of the child. Parents or, as the case may be, legal guardians, have the primary responsibility for the upbringing and development of the child. The best interests of the child will be their basic concern.
2. For the purpose of guaranteeing and promoting the rights set forth in the present Convention, States Parties shall render appropriate assistance to parents and legal guardians in the performance of their child-rearing responsibilities and shall ensure the development of institutions, facilities and services for the care of children.
3. States Parties shall take all appropriate measures to ensure that children of working parents have the right to benefit from child-care services and facilities for which they are eligible.

Article 19

1. States Parties shall take all appropriate legislative, administrative, social and educational measures to protect the child from all forms of physical or mental violence, injury or abuse, neglect or negligent treatment, maltreatment or exploitation, including sexual abuse, while in the care of parent(s), legal guardian(s) or any other person who has the care of the child.
2. Such protective measures should, as appropriate, include effective procedures for the establishment of social programmes to provide necessary support for the child and for those who have the care of the child, as well as for other forms of prevention and for identification, reporting, referral, investigation, treatment and follow-up of instances of child maltreatment described heretofore, and, as appropriate, for judicial involvement.

Article 20

1. A child temporarily or permanently deprived of his or her family environment, or in whose own best interests cannot be allowed to remain in that environment, shall be entitled to special protection and assistance provided by the State.
2. States Parties shall in accordance with their national laws ensure alternative care for such a child.
3. Such care could include, inter alia, foster placement, kafalah of Islamic law, adoption or if necessary placement in suitable institutions for the care of children. When considering solutions, due regard shall be paid to the desirability of continuity in a child's upbringing and to the child's ethnic, religious, cultural and linguistic background.

Article 21 States Parties that recognize and/or permit the system of adoption shall ensure that the best interests of the child shall be the paramount consideration and they shall:

(a) Ensure that the adoption of a child is authorized only by competent authorities who determine, in accordance with applicable law and procedures and on the basis of all pertinent and reliable information, that the adoption is permissible in view of the child's status concerning parents, relatives and legal guardians and that, if required, the persons concerned have given their informed consent to the adoption on the basis of such counselling as may be necessary;

(b) Recognize that inter-country adoption may be considered as an alternative means of child's care, if the child cannot be placed in a foster or an adoptive family or cannot in any suitable manner be cared for in the child's country of origin;

(c) Ensure that the child concerned by inter-country adoption enjoys safeguards and standards equivalent to those existing in the case of national adoption;

(d) Take all appropriate measures to ensure that, in inter-country adoption, the placement does not result in improper financial gain for those involved in it;

(e) Promote, where appropriate, the objectives of the present article by concluding bilateral or multilateral arrangements or agreements, and endeavour, within this framework, to ensure that the placement of the child in another country is carried out by competent authorities or organs.

Article 22

1. States Parties shall take appropriate measures to ensure that a child who is seeking refugee status or who is considered a refugee in accordance with

applicable international or domestic law and procedures shall, whether unaccompanied or accompanied
by his or her parents or by any other person, receive
appropriate protection and humanitarian assistance in
the enjoyment of applicable rights set forth in the
present Convention and in other international human
rights or humanitarian instruments to which the said
States are Parties.

2. For this purpose, States Parties shall provide, as they
    consider appropriate, co-operation in any efforts by
    the United Nations and other competent intergovern-
    mental organizations or non-governmental organiza-
    tions co-operating with the United Nations to protect
    and assist such a child and to trace the parents or
    other members of the family of any refugee child in
    order to obtain information necessary for reunification
    with his or her family In cases where no parents or
    other members of the family can be found, the child
    shall be accorded the same protection as any other
    child permanently or temporarily deprived of his or her
    family environment for any reason, as set forth in the
    present Convention.

Article 23

1. States Parties recognize that a mentally or physically
    disabled child should enjoy a full and decent life, in
    conditions which ensure dignity, promote self-reli-
    ance and facilitate the child's active participation in
    the community.
2. States Parties recognize the right of the disabled
    child to special care and shall encourage and ensure
    the extension, subject to available resources, to the
    eligible child and those responsible for his or her
    care, of assistance for which application is made
    and which is appropriate to the child's condition and
    to the circumstances of the parents or others caring
    for the child.

SIGNIFICANCE

In addition to the 1989 treaty, the CRC has
enacted two optional protocols. One is for the removal
of children in armed conflict; the other is to prevent
the sale of children and use of children in prostitution
or pornography. All states are required to submit a
report on children's rights. These additional sections
of the treaty came about in 1996 in response to a
special UN report about children in war zones and
the recruitment of children under fifteen to serve in
militaries. Additionally, the International Criminal
Court (ICC) adopted the war statute, and in 1997 the

Mine Ban Treaty was ratified. The Mine Ban Treaty
also stems from studies of children in war zones, and it
directly addresses the issues of children (and adults)
encountering land mines left over from previous battles or recently placed ones. The treaty argues that land
mines can be more detrimental after a battle has completed because unknowing individuals stumble upon
these devices, losing life or limb.

Even though the CRC treaty has been overwhelmingly signed, many violations of children's rights continue to occur. In 2004, a group of children aged two,
three, seven, and eight were sentenced to three years in
a Waziristan prison. Waziristan is a mountainous
region in Northwest Pakistan. The children received
jail time because under tribal law immediate family
members of criminals can be jailed in their place. In
the United States, polygamous unions occur with child
brides as young as twelve or thirteen, and in India
reports have noted that parents were willing to marry
their twelve-year-old daughter to a fifty-year-old man
to pay off a debt.

These instances of child mistreatment, and many
others, are still prevalent worldwide. The CRC continually looks to expand its scope of power, but
although many nations have signed the treaty, not all
have fully complied with its statements.

FURTHER RESOURCES

Books

*Children's Human Rights: Progress and Challenges for Children
    Worldwide*, edited by Mark Ensalaco and Linda C.
    Majka. Lanham, Md.: Rowman and Littlefield
    Publishers, 2005.

Guggenheim, Martin. *What's Wrong With Children's Rights*.
    Cambridge, Mass.: Harvard University Press, 2005.

Periodicals

Cohen, Cynthia Price, Stuart N. Hart, and Susan M.
    Kosloske. "Monitoring the United Nations Convention
    on the Rights of the Child: The Challenge of
    Information Management." *Human Rights Quarterly* 18,
    2 (1996): 439–471.

Mason, Mary Ann. "The U.S. and the International
    Children's Rights Crusade: Leader or Laggard?"
    Journal of Social History 38, 4 (Summer 2005): 955–963.

Pitts, Lewis. "Fighting for Children's Rights: Lessons from
    the Civil Rights Movement." *University of Florida
    Journal of Law and Public Policy* 16, 2 (August 2005): 337–
    360.

Web sites

Cornell Law School. "Children's Rights." <http://
    www.law.cornell.edu/wex/index.php/
    Children's_Rights> (accessed May 4, 2006).

United Nations Rules for the Protection of Juveniles Deprived of their Liberty

Resolution

By: United Nations General Assembly

Date: December 14, 1990

Source: United Nations General Assembly. Resolution 45/113. *United Nations Rules for the Protection of Juveniles Deprived of their Liberty.* December 14, 1990.

About the Author: The phrase "United Nations" was used during World War II (1939–1945) to describe the dozens of nations allied together to fight Germany and Japan, most notably including China, France, Great Britain, the Soviet Union, and the United States of America. These allies decided to develop a new organization to facilitate international cooperation and help prevent future wars. It would replace the League of Nations, which had failed to prevent World War II. They called it the United Nations (UN). The UN Charter was ratified on October 24, 1945. In the years since the UN has served as a forum for international negotiation and cooperation on many issues, including international security, human rights, trade and economics, and the environment. The General Assembly is the primary bosy for deliberation within the United Nations, in which all member nations have a seat.

INTRODUCTION

In 1989 the United Nations set forth recommendations and guidelines for the international rights of children. The UN Convention on the Rights of the Child (CRC) went into force on November 20, 1989, and it acts as an umbrella for three other UN initiatives concerning children. These are the UN Guidelines for the Administration of Juvenile Delinquency (Riyadh Guidelines), the UN Standard Minimum Rules for the Protection of Juvenile Justice (Beijing Rules), and the UN Rules for the Protection of Juveniles Deprived of their Liberty. These platforms seek to monitor and improve the conditions of juvenile welfare and health, and they are elaborations of the CRC.

The UN Rules for the Protection of Juveniles Deprived of their Liberty operates to ensure that juvenile detainees, and offenders, are given fair treatment and receive consideration for their age. This UN agenda reflects the perceptual rise in juvenile criminal behavior in the late twentieth century, and it shows consciousness of a growing trend (in many nations) to

remove juvenile justice laws. The removal of juvenile justice laws pertains to the decrease in age that offenders are tried as adults. Many countries, including the United States, convict juveniles as adults. Since 1978, in the United States, forty-one states have established laws that make transferring juveniles to adult court easier. Sometimes these transfers occur because the crime is exceptionally heinous, and in other instances these reassignments take place because local and national politics incite emotions. For instance, courts in Paducah, Kentucky decided that Michael Carneal should be tried as an adult for his killings at West Paducah High School in December 1997. Before the Grand Jury voted to try Carneal as an adult, the shock of the public and the media frenzy played heavily into public opinion about the case. None-the-less, critics continually argue for the continuation and reinstatement of juvenile laws.

In Pakistan the Penal Code states that a twelve year old is fully responsible for his or her crimes, and children between seven and twelve can be tried and convicted as those older than twelve if a judge believes they are mature enough to understand the consequences of their actions. These stringent rules are harnessed by the large number of juveniles in Pakistani prisons for murder, causing harm with a weapon, theft, having sexual relations outside of marriage, and a variety of other charges. Pakistan, like several other countries, has executed and placed children on death row. Pakistan has not, as of 2006, executed a child as young as thirteen, but it has executed offenders that were sentenced at thirteen. In contrast, in 1993, a thirteen year old was publicly executed in Yemen. Since 1990 Iran, Pakistan, Saudi Arabia, Yemen, and the United States are the only countries who have formally executed a juvenile offender.

The issue of executing juveniles, or individuals who committed capital punishment crimes as juveniles, is just one aspect of the UN's Rules for the Protection of Juveniles Deprived of their Liberty. These points also set forth agendas for sentencing lengths for children, the conditions in which children should or should not be imprisoned, and how children should be treated in detention, jail, or prison.

■ PRIMARY SOURCE

I. FUNDAMENTAL PERSPECTIVES

1. The juvenile justice system should uphold the rights and safety and promote the physical and mental well-being of juveniles. Imprisonment should be used as a last resort.

2. Juveniles should only be deprived of their liberty in accordance with the principles and procedures set forth in these Rules and in the United Nations Standard Minimum Rules for the Administration of Juvenile Justice (The Beijing Rules). Deprivation of the liberty of a juvenile should be a disposition of last resort and for the minimum necessary period and should be limited to exceptional cases. The length of the sanction should be determined by the judicial authority, without precluding the possibility of his or her early release.

3. The Rules are intended to establish minimum standards accepted by the United Nations for the protection of juveniles deprived of their liberty in all forms, consistent with human rights and fundamental freedoms, and with a view to counteracting the detrimental effects of all types of detention and to fostering integration in society.

4. The Rules should be applied impartially, without discrimination of any kind as to race, colour, sex, age, language, religion, nationality, political or other opinion, cultural beliefs or practices, property, birth or family status, ethnic or social origin, and disability. The religious and cultural beliefs, practices and moral concepts of the juvenile should be respected.

5. The Rules are designed to serve as convenient standards of reference and to provide encouragement and guidance to professionals involved in the management of the juvenile justice system.

6. The Rules should be made readily available to juvenile justice personnel in their national languages. Juveniles who are not fluent in the language spoken by the personnel of the detention facility should have the right to the services of an interpreter free of charge whenever necessary, in particular during medical examinations and disciplinary proceedings.

7. Where appropriate, States should incorporate the Rules into their legislation or amend it accordingly and provide effective remedies for their breach, including compensation when injuries are inflicted on juveniles. States should also monitor the application of the Rules.

8. The competent authorities should constantly seek to increase the awareness of the public that the care of detained juveniles and preparation for their return to society is a social service of great importance, and to this end active steps should be taken to foster open contacts between the juveniles and the local community.

9. Nothing in the Rules should be interpreted as precluding the application of the relevant United Nations and human rights instruments and standards, recognized by the international community, that are more conducive to ensuring the rights, care and protection of juveniles, children and all young persons.

10. In the event that the practical application of particular Rules contained in sections II to V, inclusive, presents any conflict with the Rules contained in the present section, compliance with the latter shall be regarded as the predominant requirement.

II. SCOPE AND APPLICATION OF THE RULES

For the purposes of the Rules, the following definitions should apply:

(a) A juvenile is every person under the age of eighteen. The age limit below which it should not be permitted to deprive a child of his or her liberty should be determined by law;.

(b) The deprivation of liberty means any form of detention or imprisonment or the placement of a person in a public or private custodial setting, from which this person is not permitted to leave at will, by order of any judicial, administrative or other public authority.

The deprivation of liberty should be effected in conditions and circumstances which ensure respect for the human rights of juveniles. Juveniles detained in facilities should be guaranteed the benefit of meaningful activities and programmes which would serve to promote and sustain their health and self-respect, to foster their sense of responsibility and encourage those attitudes and skills that will assist them in developing their potential as members of society.

Juveniles deprived of their liberty shall not for any reason related to their status be denied the civil, economic, political, social or cultural rights to which they are entitled under national or international law, and which are compatible with the deprivation of liberty.

The protection of the individual rights of juveniles with special regard to the legality of the execution of the detention measures shall be ensured by the competent authority, while the objectives of social integration should be secured by regular inspections and other means of control carried out, according to international standards, national laws and regulations, by a duly constituted body authorized to visit the juveniles and not belonging to the detention facility.

The Rules apply to all types and forms of detention facilities in which juveniles are deprived of their liberty. Sections I, II, IV and V of the Rules apply to all detention facilities and institutional settings in which juveniles are detained, and section III applies specifically to juveniles under arrest or awaiting trial.

The Rules shall be implemented in the context of the economic, social and cultural conditions prevailing in each Member State. . . .

E. EDUCATION, VOCATIONAL TRAINING AND WORK

Every juvenile of compulsory school age has the right to education suited to his or her needs and abilities and designed to prepare him or her for return to society. Such education should be provided outside the detention facility in community schools wherever possible and, in any case, by qualified teachers through programmes integrated with the education system of the country so that, after release, juveniles may continue their education without difficulty. Special attention should be given by the administration of the detention facilities to the education of juveniles of foreign origin or with particular cultural or ethnic needs. Juveniles who are illiterate or have cognitive or learning difficulties should have the right to special education.

Juveniles above compulsory school age who wish to continue their education should be permitted and encouraged to do so, and every effort should be made to provide them with access to appropriate educational programs.

Diplomas or educational certificates awarded to juveniles while in detention should not indicate in any way that the juvenile has been institutionalized.

Every detention facility should provide access to a library that is adequately stocked with both instructional and recreational books and periodicals suitable for the juveniles, who should be encouraged and enabled to make full use of it.

Every juvenile should have the right to receive vocational training in occupations likely to prepare him or her for future employment.

With due regard to proper vocational selection and to the requirements of institutional administration, juveniles should be able to choose the type of work they wish to perform.

All protective national and international standards applicable to child labour and young workers should apply to juveniles deprived of their liberty.

Wherever possible, juveniles should be provided with the opportunity to perform remunerated labour, if possible within the local community, as a complement to the vocational training provided in order to enhance the possibility of finding suitable employment when they return to their communities. The type of work should be such as to provide appropriate training that will be of benefit to the juveniles following release. The organization and methods of work offered in detention facilities should resemble as closely as possible those of similar work in the community, so as to prepare juveniles for the conditions of normal occupational life.

Every juvenile who performs work should have the right to an equitable remuneration. The interests of the juveniles and of their vocational training should not be subordinated to the purpose of making a profit for the detention facility or a third party. Part of the earnings of a juvenile should normally be set aside to constitute a savings fund to be handed over to the juvenile on release. The juvenile should have the right to use the remainder of those earnings to purchase articles for his or her own use or to indemnify the victim injured by his or her offence or to send it to his or her family or other persons outside the detention facility.

SIGNIFICANCE

Since this UN treaty numerous cases of juvenile mistreatment still occur. In October 2001 a sixteen-year-old Egyptian boy received a five year prison sentence for homosexual acts. His lawyers and international human rights investigators claimed that he was held in detention for several days, without the right to see his family or legal council, and that his confessions were made under duress. Other instances of juveniles receiving extended prison sentences can be seen with children connected with resistance groups. Children fighting with Middle Eastern groups, like the Hamas and Islamic Jihad organizations, are routinely held in adult prisons without recourse for release or relocation.

As the international court of public opinion continues to scrutinize countries that treat juveniles as adults, more critics are emerging with discussion concerning the cognitive development of children. These studies range in diversity, with some focusing on early childhood trauma that juveniles may endure and others sighting that full cognitive development and understanding of consequences does not fully set in until the teens and early twenties. Proponents of reducing age limits for crimes note that technology and an increase of violence in media and society enables children to develop criminal behaviors earlier than previous generations. When most modern juvenile justice systems took hold they did not fathom hundreds and thousands of delinquent children. Rather, the systems sought to house a few hundred children annually. Modern discourse and social expectations have expanded laws, legitimized new crimes, and eradicated others.

A young bonded laborer working in a slate mine in Mandsaur, India, in 1990. Child labor is common in the region despite laws prohibiting the employment of children under 14. © SOPHIE ELBAZ/SYGMA/CORBIS.

In March 2006 the US Supreme Court made a nod toward the international community on the treatment of juveniles. In its five to four decision in *Roper v Simmons* the Court set aside seventy-two juvenile death-row sentences. This decision also banned the future placement of minors on death row. In justifying its decision, members of the Court remarked that the United States is the only country that still routinely sentences minors to death sentences, and that even though the United States has not signed the CRC treaty it should pay note to international public opinion.

FURTHER RESOURCES

Periodicals

Ainsworth, Janet E. "The Court's Effectiveness in Protecting the Rights of Juveniles in Delinquency Cases." *The Future of Children*. 6.3 (Winter 1996): 64-74.

Farber, Hillary B. "Constitutionality, competence, and conflicts: what is wrong with the state of the law when it comes to juveniles and Miranda? (Symposium: Constitutionality, Competence, and Culpability: Emerging Issues in Criminal Juvenile Law." *New*

England Journal of Criminal and Civil Confinement. 32.1 (Winter 2006): 29-42.

Web sites

Amnesty International. "Death Penalty and Children: New Report Shows USA is Chief Culprit." July 18, 2003. <http://www.amnesty.org.uk/news/press/14732.shtml> (accessed May 5, 2006).

UNICEF. "Factsheet: Children Deprived of Their Liberty and Juvenile Justice." <http://www.unicef.org/protection/justice.pdf> (accessed May 5, 2006).

Protocol to Prevent, Suppress, and Punish Trafficking in Persons, Especially Women and Children

Protocol

By: United Nations

Date: 2000

Source: United Nations General Assembly. *Protocol to Prevent, Suppress and Punish Trafficking in Persons, Especially Women and Children, Supplementing the United Nations Convention Against Transnational Organized Crime.* 2000.

About the Author: The phrase "United Nations" was used during World War II (1939–1945) to describe the dozens of nations allied together to fight Germany and Japan, most notably including China, France, Great Britain, the Soviet Union, and the United States of America. These allies decided to develop a new organization to facilitate international cooperation and help prevent future wars. It would replace the League of Nations, which had failed to prevent World War II. They called it the United Nations (UN). The UN Charter was ratified on October 24, 1945. In the years since the UN has served as a forum for international negotiation and cooperation on many issues, including international security, human rights, trade and economics, and the environment.

INTRODUCTION

Human trafficking for the purposes of labor and/or commercial sex has a long history, but it gained particular attention of policymakers worldwide in the twentieth century. International conventions on human trafficking include the 1910 International Convention for the Suppression of the White Slave Traffic, the 1921 International Convention for the Suppression of the Traffic in Women and Children, and the International Convention for the Suppression of the Traffic in Women of Full Age in 1933. While these conventions focused on women and children, future conventions, such as the 1949 United Nations Convention for the Suppression of the Traffic in Persons and of the Exploitation of the Prostitution of Others, used more gender-neutral language and focused more on the elimination of human trafficking for the sex trade.

The United Nations defines trafficking as "the recruitment, transportation, transfer, harboring or receipt of persons, by means of the threat or use of force or other forms of coercion, of abduction, of fraud, of deception, of the abuse of power or of a position of vulnerability or of the giving or receiving of payments or benefits to achieve the consent of a person having control over another person, for the purpose of exploitation. Exploitation shall include, at a minimum, the exploitation of the prostitution of others or other forms of sexual exploitation, forced labor or services, slavery or practices similar to slavery, servitude or the removal of organs."

Child prostitutes in the Brazilian mining town of Curionopolis, 1985. © STEPHANIE MAZE/CORBIS.

Women who are used as workers in the sex industries in regions such as southeast Asia find themselves sold into brothels and turned into virtual slaves due to lack of education, debt, or drug addiction. According to an International Labor Organization 1998 estimate, the sex trade and sex tourism represents between two percent and fourteen percent of the economic activities of the countries of Thailand, Indonesia, Malaysia, and the Philippines.

Labor trafficking of men, women and children for work in sweatshop clothing factories, agricultural settings, construction, domestic settings, and in restaurants involves the exploitation of human beings and either the flagrant refusal to obey labor laws or the use of legal, but not always ethical, practices. Reports of women in India offered high-paying jobs in Saudi Arabia and forced to work for low wages for over seventy hours per week, or Chinese immigrants to the United States placed in virtual indentured servitude, working eighty or more hours in restaurants to pay back the person who smuggled them into the country are examples of illegal and dangerous aspects of forced labor. Not only does labor trafficking represent a significant percentage of the 1.4 million people trafficked within countries and across international borders, the practice often involves minors as well.

In 2000, the United Nations developed the following Protocol to control human trafficking.

■ PRIMARY SOURCE

Article 3 Use of terms For the purposes of this Protocol: (a) "Trafficking in persons" shall mean the recruitment, transportation, transfer, harbouring or receipt of persons, by means of the threat or use of force or other forms of coercion, of abduction, of fraud, of deception, of the abuse of power or of a position of vulnerability or of the giving or receiving of payments or benefits to achieve the consent of a person having control over another person, for the purpose of exploitation. Exploitation shall include, at a minimum, the exploitation of the prostitution of others or other forms of sexual exploitation, forced labour or services, slavery or practices similar to slavery, servitude or the removal of organs;

(b) The consent of a victim of trafficking in persons to the intended exploitation set forth in subparagraph (a) of this article shall be irrelevant where any of the means set forth in subparagraph (a) have been used;

(c) The recruitment, transportation, transfer, harbouring or receipt of a child for the purpose of exploitation shall be considered "trafficking in persons" even if this does not involve any of the means set forth in subparagraph (a) of this article;

(d) "Child" shall mean any person under eighteen years of age.

Article 4 Scope of application This Protocol shall apply, except as otherwise stated herein, to the prevention, investigation and prosecution of the offences established in accordance with article 5 of this Protocol, where those offences are transnational in nature and involve an organized criminal group, as well as to the protection of victims of such offences.

Article 5 Criminalization 1. Each State Party shall adopt such legislative and other measures as may be necessary to establish as criminal offences the conduct set forth in article 3 of this Protocol, when committed intentionally.

2. Each State Party shall also adopt such legislative and other measures as may be necessary to establish as criminal offences:

(a) Subject to the basic concepts of its legal system, attempting to commit an offence established in accordance with paragraph 1 of this article;

(b) Participating as an accomplice in an offence established in accordance with paragraph 1 of this article; and

(c) Organizing or directing other persons to commit an offence established in accordance with paragraph 1 of this article.

II. Protection of victims of trafficking in persons

Article 6 Assistance to and protection of victims of trafficking in persons 1. In appropriate cases and to the extent possible under its domestic law, each State Party shall protect the privacy and identity of victims of trafficking in persons, including, inter alia, by making legal proceedings relating to such trafficking confidential.

2. Each State Party shall ensure that its domestic legal or administrative system contains measures that provide to victims of trafficking in persons, in appropriate cases:

(a) Information on relevant court and administrative proceedings;

(b) Assistance to enable their views and concerns to be presented and considered at appropriate stages of criminal proceedings against offenders, in a manner not prejudicial to the rights of the defense.

3. Each State Party shall consider implementing measures to provide for the physical, psychological and social recovery of victims of trafficking in persons, including, in appropriate cases, in cooperation with non-governmental organizations, other relevant organizations and other elements of civil society, and, in particular, the provision of:

(a) Appropriate housing;

(b) Counselling and information, in particular as regards their legal rights, in a language that the victims of trafficking in persons can understand;

(c) Medical, psychological and material assistance; and

(d) Employment, educational and training opportunities.

4. Each State Party shall take into account, in applying the provisions of this article, the age, gender and special needs of victims of trafficking in persons, in particular the special needs of children, including appropriate housing, education and care.

5. Each State Party shall endeavour to provide for the physical safety of victims of trafficking in persons while they are within its territory.

6. Each State Party shall ensure that its domestic legal system contains measures that offer victims of trafficking in persons the possibility of obtaining compensation for damage suffered.

Article 7 Status of victims of trafficking in persons in receiving States

1. In addition to taking measures pursuant to article 6 of this Protocol, each State Party shall consider adopting legislative or other appropriate measures that permit victims of trafficking in persons to remain in its territory, temporarily or permanently, in appropriate cases.

2. In implementing the provision contained in paragraph 1 of this article, each State Party shall give appropriate consideration to humanitarian and compassionate factors.

SIGNIFICANCE

The Protocol compels UN member states to create legislation with severe penalties for those persons directly involved in human trafficking. In 2003, the United States updated the U.S. Code to make illegal the importation of minors for use in the commercial sex trade or in the creation of pornographic materials. Human trafficking, according to the International Labor Organization, is the third most profitable criminal activity in the world, after the sale of illegal drugs and weaponry.

The Council of Europe, with forty-six member nations, crafted the 2005 "Council of Europe Convention on action against trafficking in human beings," which would require nations who sign the convention to adopt policies that reduce human trafficking, increase penalties for human smugglers, provide basic housing, food, and medical assistance to trafficked persons seeking safe harbor, and to permit trafficked persons to remain in the country for thirty or more days.

International recognition of the scope of human trafficking was highlighted by recent stories of humans perishing in ship containers, in the backs of vans, or in semi trucks. The 2000 story of sixty Chinese immigrants found in a truck container in Dover, England—fifty-eight of whom had suffocated to death—triggered international outcry and fed international and national policy directives and conventions to control human trafficking. As the Protocol to Prevent, Suppress and Punish Trafficking in Persons illustrates, effective measures against human trafficking—a $13 billion per year industry—challenge human rights policy on a global scale.

FURTHER RESOURCES

Books

Barnitz, Laura A. *Commercial Sexual Exploitation of Children: Youth Involved in Prostitution, Pornography & Sex Trafficking.* Washington, D.C.: Youth Advocate Program International, 1998.

Oxfam International. *Gender, Trafficking, and Slavery.* Oxford: Oxfam, 2002.

Periodicals

Estes, Richard J. and Neil Alan Weiner. "The Commercial Sexual Exploitation of Children in the U.S., Canada, and Mexico." *Center for the Study of Youth Policy, Full Report.* February 2002.

Web sites

Council of Europe. "Council of Europe Convention on Action against Trafficking in Human Beings." <https://wcd.coe.int/> (accessed April 15, 2006).

UNICEF. "Child Trafficking Research Hub." <http://www.childtrafficking.org> (accessed April 11, 2006).

United Nations Office on Drugs and Crime. "Trafficking in Human Beings." <http://www.unodc.org/unodc/en/trafficking_human_beings.html> (accessed April 11, 2006).

Attacks Beset Afghan Girls' Schools

Newspaper article

By: Pamela Constable

Date: September 8, 2003

Source: Constable, Pamela. "Attacks Beset Afghan Girls' Schools." *Washington Post* (September 8, 2003).

About the Author: Pamela Constable is the deputy foreign editor for the *Washington Post* and the author of the book *Fragments of Grace: My Search for Meaning in the Strife of South Asia.*

INTRODUCTION

In December 2001, the Islamic fundamentalist government in Afghanistan, the Taliban, was removed from power by U.S. forces in the wake of the September 11, 2001, attacks on U.S. soil by Al-Qaeda members. The Taliban—a word that means "seeker" or "student of Islam"—had gained control of Afghanistan in September 1996 and initiated a strict fundamentalist government based on *sharia,* or Islamic religious law.

For more than five years, the Taliban implemented a series of restrictions on women and girls, including the removal of such rights as voting, access to education and healthcare, and the right to work. In addition, the Taliban required all women to wear a full-length *burqa,* a garment that covers a woman from

Two female students preparing to attend the girl's school in Kandahar, Afghanistan on August 12, 2002. Schools for women were banned under the Taliban regime. AP IMAGES.

head to toe and allows for a small mesh section for the eyes. Women were forbidden to wear white, the official color of the Taliban, or to wear shoes that made noise. Any woman who appeared in public without a male relative as an escort could be beaten and in homes where women lived, windows had to be painted. In 1997, the Taliban segregated hospitals by sex, forcing hundreds of thousands of women and children to lose access to health care, which in turn drove the infant and maternal mortality rates to new highs.

The Taliban made female education illegal; in late 2001, when President Hamid Karzai gained power, he pledged to reverse the Taliban's policy on female education, noting that "We are fully committed to the education of our girls, as all the international experience has demonstrated the return of investing in girls' education. We will ensure active participation of Afghan women in all spheres of reconstruction." Under the new president's administration, schools reopened, welcoming girls, and, by 2002, more than three million boys and girls were enrolled in schools, with reconstruction and new construction of schools a stated priority for the new government.

As the schools opened and welcomed girls, however, the reaction to such change was not unanimously favorable. Taliban loyalists and other fundamentalists targeted girl's schools for attacks. As this source notes, the resumption of female education was not simple.

PRIMARY SOURCE

Zahidabad, Afghanistan— It was little more than a shed, with no chairs or desks. But for the 50 girls who had

studied there since April, the two-room school in this pastoral pocket of Logar province was all that stood between a lifetime of ignorance and a glimmer of knowledge.

Now, the doors have been padlocked, the teacher says he is too scared to return, and the former students are back to their customary chores—pumping water at the village well, weeding onion fields and carrying loads of animal fodder on their heads.

That may be exactly what the unknown assailants had in mind when they broke into the shed late at night 10 days ago, doused the classrooms with fuel and set them afire, leaving behind leaflets in the Dari language warning that girls should not go to school and that teachers should not teach them.

"When I was walking home today, the little girls followed me and asked when they could go back to school, but I am not ready to teach them again because I am afraid for my own safety," confided Fazel Ahmed, 39, the school's only teacher. "I'm very upset. These students will make the future of our community and our country."

The attack was followed two days later by the midnight burning of three tents used as classrooms outside another school in Logar province. According to officials of UNICEF, which is helping to revive the country's long-neglected education system, there have been 18 incidents of school sabotage nationwide in the past 18 months, often accompanied by similar warnings.

The assailants could be from the Taliban, the former Islamic government that opposed girls' education as morally corrupting, and whose armed supporters recently have been regrouping. Or they could be from another of the conservative Islamic groups that once fought the Taliban but are now plotting a political comeback as guardians of religious purity.

Whoever they are, said school officials in Logar and education experts in Kabul, the capital, their goal is clearly to undermine Afghanistan's emergence into the modern world after 25 years of military conflict and religious repression that paralyzed its development in every sphere—particularly the emancipation of women.

And yet everyone involved in Afghan education—from village elders to foreign charities—insists that such tactics cannot slow the extraordinarily swift and widespread revival of girls' education that has taken place since the Taliban were defeated and replaced by a U.S.-backed government under President Hamid Karzai in December 2001.

"We have 4.2 million children in 7,000 schools now, and a 37 percent increase in the number of girls in school since last year," said Sharad Sapra, the UNICEF director for Afghanistan.

The increase amounts to 400,000 more girls in school this year. "There is concern that these sporadic incidents should not become a wave, but almost everyone wants their daughters to go to school, and overall, people do not seem to be intimidated," said Sapra.

The second Logar province school to be attacked, a primary school in the village of Mogul Khel where girls and boys study in separate shifts and separate areas, has already achieved national fame because of its resistance to the threat. Karzai, speaking at a news conference in Kabul on Sunday with Defense Secretary Donald Rumsfeld, noted proudly that almost all students and teachers there had returned to class the day after the attack.

On Saturday, classes were in full, noisy swing, if in hastily improvised settings. Groups of boys recited their multiplication tables in unison, sitting on the playground next to the burned tents. Groups of girls huddled on straw mats in the front lobby, reading their Pashto language lessons from a portable blackboard.

"We do not know who these saboteurs are, but our school is the cradle of education in Logar, and we will defend it," said Mahmoud Ayub Saber, 50, the principal, who returned home last year after waiting out the Taliban era in Pakistan. "If some girls were occasionally absent before this happened, their parents are saying from now on none of their daughters will miss a single day."

Education Ministry officials in Kabul said they were determined to ensure the success of girls' education, but they acknowledged that they had limited resources to physically protect schools, and they noted with alarm that a rising tide of Islamic fundamentalism was challenging the modernizing policies of the Karzai government.

"Our society is going through many changes, and there are fundamentalists who want to resist this change," said Ashrak Hossaini, deputy minister of education. "We are trying to move to a modern and civilized stage, and girls' schools are attacked because they represent this movement. We must not only provide physical protection, but also prepare the people mentally for these changes."

While there seems to be near-universal public support for girls' elementary school education, the idea of female study beyond sixth grade is far more controversial, particularly in traditional, rural areas steeped in social and gender taboos that existed long before the Taliban took power in 1996.

In the relatively prosperous Logar province, there are hundreds of schools that teach boys and girls up to sixth grade, but very few higher-level schools for girls. Co-education is out of the question in conservative Afghan society, and most parents do not want their adolescent daughters attending even an all-female high school if it is not in or close to their village.

"In our district, there is no opportunity for girls to go beyond the fifth class," said Saber, the Mogul Khel principal. "After that, most of them get married and have no need to continue their educations." He said education officials in Kabul had ordered a girls' high school to be built in Logar, but community elders opposed it because students would be required to travel some distance from their homes.

By turning schools into social service centers where people receive vaccinations, register births and even pump well water, Sapra said, the idea of education can become an integral part of village life. But in villages such as Zahidabad, where the two-room girls' school was built last spring, the most serious obstacle to education today is fear.

"We are all afraid of these bad people. We are Muslims, and we fear for the honor of our daughters," said Shah Agha, 50, a water and power department worker in Zahidabad whose 12-year-old daughter attended the village school until last week.

"We were very happy when this school opened, but one morning we went to pray, and we found it was all burned," he said. "Unless the government brings us more security, we cannot let our daughters go back there."

SIGNIFICANCE

As attacks on girls and girls' schools increased, female enrollment dropped. While many attacks involve vandalism and damage to the school buildings, other attacks include direct threats and intimidation to known female enrollees, physical attacks on girls and their families, and direct violence against teachers. In many instances, girls' schools are set on fire and destroyed while boys' schools next door are left untouched.

By 2005, more than five million children were enrolled in Afghan schools and more than forty percent were girls. UNICEF estimates that in spite of this change in female enrollment, nearly sixty percent of all girls under the age of eleven in Afghanistan are not enrolled in school, unable to access education due to parental choice, physical threats and intimidation from outside sources, the distance of schools from homes, or the need to work to bring in income.

U.S. President George W. Bush and Afghanistan President Hamid Karzai, in a joint press conference held on May 23, 2005, discussed the issue of female education in Afghanistan as part of a diplomatic meeting. President Bush noted that "Over 40 percent of the voters on that October day [the first elections in Afghanistan after the end of Taliban rule] were women voters. Girls are now going to school. Women entrepreneurs are opening businesses. The president was telling me that there's quite a number of candidates who filed for the upcoming legislative elections who are women." At the same time, according to UNICEF's Deputy Executive Director Rima Salah, "One in five children in this country do not survive long enough even to reach school age. Others will drop out of school, to support their families. This is a tragedy that threatens progress made in recent years."

In January 2006, Malim Abdul Habib, the headmaster of the Shaikh Mathi Baba high school in Zabul, Afghanistan, was stabbed and beheaded by Taliban sympathizers. Prominent Afghan Muslim clerics have publicly stated that there is no justification in the Koran or in other Islamic writing for banning female education, and support in Afghanistan for basic female education is overwhelming. Some surveys show that ninety percent of Afghan adults agree that girls should be permitted to attend school. According to UNICEF, literacy rates for women are as low as three to four percent in rural areas, and only approximately thirty percent of men in Afghanistan as a whole are literate.

FURTHER RESOURCES
Books

Brodsky, Anne. *With All Our Strength: The Revolutionary Association of Women in Afghanistan*. New York: Routledge, 2003.

Skaine, Rosemarie. *The Women of Afghanistan Under the Taliban*. Jefferson, N.C.: McFarland & Company, 2001.

Web sites

FoxNews.com. "Transcript: Bush and Karzai." May 23, 2005. <http://www.foxnews.com/story/0,2933,157375,00.html> (accessed April 23, 2006).

National Geographic News. "Change Slow for Afghan Women." March 12, 2002. <http://news.nationalgeographic.com/news/2002/03/0312_020312_afghanwomen.html> (accessed April 20, 2006).

Physicians for Human Rights. "1999 Report: The Taliban's War on Women—A Health and Human Rights Crisis in Afghanistan." <http://www.phrusa.org/research/health_effects/exec.html> (accessed April 20, 2006).

UNICEF. "On Eve of New Afghan School Year, UNICEF Warns of Continued Threat Facing Women and Children." March 23, 2006. <http://www.unicef.org/media/media_31773.html> (accessed April 23, 2006).

U.S. Department of State. "Report on the Taliban's War Against Women." November 17, 2001. <http://www.state.gov/g/drl/rls/c4804.htm> (accessed April 20, 2006).

Sources Consulted

BOOKS AND WEBSITES

Acuna, Rodolfo. *Occupied America: A History of Chicanos*. New York: Pearson Longman, 2004.

Adams, Francis D., and Barry Sanders. *Alienable Rights: The Exclusion of African Americans in a White Man's Land*. New York: HarperCollins, 2003.

Adams, John Quincy. *Argument of John Quincy Adams, before the Supreme Court of the United States, in the Case of the United States, Appellants, vs. Cinque, and others, Africans, Captured in the Schooner Amistad...* New York: S. W. Benedict, 1841.

Alfredson, Gudmundur and Asbjorn Eide. *The Universal Declaration of Human Rights: A Common Standard of Achievement*. The Hague: Martinus Nijhoff, 1999.

Amar, Akhil Reed. *The Bill of Rights: Creation and Reconstruction*. New Haven, CT: Yale University Press, 2000.

American Memory. "Library of Congress." <http://memory.loc.gov/ammem/index.html> (accessed on June 24, 2006).

American Rhetoric. "American Rhetoric." <http://www.americanrhetoric.com/> (accessed on June 24, 2006).

Amnesty International. "Amnesty International." <http://www.amnesty.org/> (accessed on June 24, 2006).

Amnesty International. "An International Crime: Even One Torture Victim Is One Too Many." <http://web.amnesty.org/library/index/engamr220101999> (accessed on April 30, 2006).

Amnesty International. "Pakistan: Honour Killings of Girls and Women." September 1, 1999. <http://web.amnesty.org/library/Index/engASA330181999> (accessed on May 6, 2006).

Amnesty International. "The Death Penalty." <http://web.amnesty.org/pages/deathpenalty-index-eng> (accessed on May 07, 2006).

Ancker, Carsten. *Determinants of the Death Penalty: A Comparative Study of the World*. New York, New York: Routledge, 2004.

Angle, Stephen and Marina Svensson. *The Chinese Human Rights Reader*. Birmingham, Ala.: M.E. Sharpe, 2001.

Anti-Slavery International. "The History of Anti-Slavery International." April 20, 2006. <http://www.antislavery.org/homepage/antislavery/history.htm> (accessed on May 1, 2006).

Applebaum, Anne. *Gulag, A History*. New York: Doubleday, 2003.

Arsenault, Raymond. *Freedom Riders: 1961 and the Struggle for Racial Justice*. New York: Oxford University Press, 2006.

Bakshi, S. R. *Gandhi and Non-Cooperation Movement, 1920–22*. South Asia Books, December 1983.

Barnett, Michael. *Eyewitness to a Genocide: The United Nations and Rwanda*. Ithaca, New York; Cornell University Press, 2002.

Barnitz, Laura A. *Commercial Sexual Exploitation of Children: Youth Involved in Prostitution, Pornography & Sex Trafficking*. Washington, D.C.: Youth Advocate Program International, 1998.

Becker, Susan D. *The Origins of the Equal Rights Amendment: American Feminism Between the Wars*. Westport, CT: Greenwood Press, 1981.

Bedau, Hugo Adam, and Paul G. Cassell, eds. *Debating the Death Penalty: Should America Have Capital Punishment? The Experts on Both Sides Make Their Best Case*. New York, New York: Oxford University Press, 2004.

Bender, Thomas. *The Antislavery Debate: Capitalism and Abolitionism as a Problem in Historical Interpretation*. Berkeley: University of California Press, 1992.

Bennett, C.L. *Africa in America: Slave Acculturation and Resistance in the American South and the British Caribbean.* Chicago, Illinois: University of Illinois Press, 1995.

Bennett, Scott H. *Radical Pacifism: the War Resisters League and Gandian Nonviolence in America, 1915–1963.* Syracuse, New York; Syracuse University Press, 2003.

Berkowitz, Peter, ed. *Terrorism, the Laws of War, and the Constitution: Debating the Enemy Combatant Cases.* Palo Alto: Hoover Institution Press, Stanford University, 2005.

Black, Edwin. *War Against the Weak: Eugenics and America's Campaign to Create a Master Race.* New York: Four Walls Eight Windows, 2004.

Bliss, Charles Henry. *Labor Strikes and Their Effects on Society: A Common Sense Discussion of the Rights and Relations of Labor and Capital.* Pensacola, Fla.: C. H. Bliss, 1902.

Bortolotti, Dan. *Hope in Hell: Inside the World of Doctors Without Borders.* Buffalo, N.Y. and Richmond Hill, Ontario: Firefly Books Ltd., 2004.

Branch, Taylor. *Parting the Waters: America in the King Years, 1954–63.* New York: Simon & Schuster, 1988.

Braude, Ann. *Radical Spirits: Spiritualism and Women's Rights in Nineteenth-Century America.* Bloomington: Indiana University Press, 2001.

Brinkley, Douglas. *Rosa Parks.* New York: Viking, 2000.

Briskman, Linda. *The Black Grapevine: Aboriginal Activism and the Stolen Generations.* Annandale, NSW, Australia: Federation Press, 2003.

British and Foreign Anti-Slavery Society. *Fourteenth Annual Report of the British and Foreign Anti-Slavery Society.* London: British and Foreign Anti-Slavery Society, 1853.

British Broadcasting Corporation. "The League of Nations and the United Nations." May 29, 2006. <http://www.bbc.co.uk/history/state/nations/league_nations_01.shtml> (accessed on May 29, 2006).

British Library. "British Library Images Online." <http://www.imagesonline.bl.uk/britishlibrary/> (accessed on June 24, 2006).

Brodsky, Anne E. *With All Our Strength: The Revolutionary Association of Women in Afghanistan.* Routledge, 2003.

Browning, Christopher R. *The Path to Genocide: Essays On Launching the Final Solution.* Cambridge, U.K. and New York: Cambridge University Press, 1992.

Bruinius, Harry. *Better for All the World: The Secret History of Forced Sterilization and America's Quest for Racial Purity.* New York: Knopf, 2006.

Brysk, Allison. *Globalization and Human Rights.* Los Angeles: University of California Press, 2002.

BUBL LINK Social Sciences. "Centre for Digital Library Research." <http://bubl.ac.uk/link/linkbrowse.cfm?menuid=2822> (accessed on June 24, 2006).

Byers, Michael. *War Law: Understanding International Law and Armed Conflict.* New York: Grove Press, 2006.

Cable, Mary. *Black Odyssey: The Case of the Slave Ship* Amistad. New York: Viking Press, 1971.

Cambridge University. "Cambridge University, Institute of Public Health." <http://www.iph.cam.ac.uk> (accessed on June 24, 2006).

Caplan, Arthur C., James J. McCartney, and Dominic A. Sisti. *The Case of Terri Schiavo: Ethics at the End of Life.* Amherst, New York: Prometheus Books, 2006.

Cashman, Sean Dennis. *America in the Gilded Age: From the Death of Lincoln to the Rise of Theodore Roosevelt.* New York: New York University Press, 1993.

Casserly, Jack. *The Triumph at Tiananmen Square.* Lincoln, Neb.: ASJA Press, 2005.

CDC (Centers for Disease Control and Prevention). "CDCSite Index A-Z." <http://www.cdc.gov/az.do> (accessed on June 24, 2006).

Census Bureau. "United States Census Bureau." <http://www.census.gov/> (accessed on June 24, 2006).

Center for Contemporary Studies. "Child Labour in South Asia." <http://www.cuts-international.org/Brf-3–2003.pdf> (accessed on May 4, 2006).

Center for Disease Control and Prevention. "Tuskegee Syphilis Study." <http://www.cdc.gov/nchstp/od/tuskegee/> (accessed on April 26, 2006).

Cesari, Jocelyne. *When Islam and Democracy Meet: Muslims in Europe and in the United States.* New York: Palgrave Macmillan, 2004.

Cháaszár, Edward. *The International Problem of National Minorities.* Toronto: Matthias Corvinus, 1999.

Chadwick, Bruce. *The Reel Civil War: Mythmaking in American Film.* New York: Alfred A. Knopf, 2001.

Chase, Michael, and James Mulvenon. *You've Got Dissent! Chinese Dissident Use of the Internet and Beijing's Counter-Strategies.* Santa Monica, Calif.: Rand, 2002.

Cholewinski, Ryszard. *Migrant Workers in the International Human Rights Law: Their Protection in Countries of Employment.* New York: Oxford University Press, 1997.

Chomsky, Noam, and Edward Herman. *After the Cataclysm.* South End Press, 1979.

Christensen, Terry. *Reel Politics: American Political Movies from* Birth of a Nation *to* Platoon. New York: Basil Blackwell, 1987.

Clark, Nancy L., and William H. Worger. *South Africa: The Rise and Fall of Apartheid.* New York: Longman, 2004.

Cobble, Dorothy Sue. *The Other Women's Movement: Workplace Justice and Social Rights in Modern America.* Princeton, NJ: Princeton University Press, 2004.

Coles, Robert. *Migrants, Sharecroppers, Mountaineers: Children of Crisis.* Boston: Little, Brown, 1971.

Cornell Law School. "Children's Rights." <http://www.law.cornell.edu/wex/index.php/Children's_Rights> (accessed on May 4, 2006).

Council of Europe. "Council of Europe Convention on Action against Trafficking in Human Beings." <https://wcd.coe.int/> (accessed on April 15, 2006).

Country Studies US. "Somalia." <http://countrystudies.us/somalia> (accessed on April 28, 2006).

Cowling, Mark, ed. *The Communist Manifesto: New Interpretations*. Washington Square, N.Y.: New York University Press, 1998.

Crampton, R J. *Return to Diversity: A Political History of East Central Europe Since World War II*. London: Routledge, 1997.

Crimes of War. "Kashmir and International Law: How War Crimes Fuel the Conflict." July 17, 2002. <http://www.crimesofwar.org/onnews/news-kashmir.html> (accessed on April 29, 2006).

Culverson, Donald R. *Contesting Apartheid: U.S. Activism, 1960–1987*. Boulder, Colo.: Westview Press, 1999.

Dalfiume, Richard M. *Desegregation of the U.S. Armed Forces: Fighting on Two Fronts, 1939–1953*. Columbia: University of Missouri Press, 1969.

Dallek, Robert. *Franklin D. Roosevelt and American Foreign Policy, 1932–1945: With a New Afterword*. Oxford University Press, 1995.

Daniels, Roger, Sandra C. Taylor and Harry H.L. Kitano. *Japanese Americans: From Relocation to Redress*. Seattle: University of Washington Press, 1991.

Daniels, Roger. *Coming to America: A History of Immigration and Ethnicity in American Life*. New York: Harper Perennial, 2002.

Daniels, Roger. *Prisoners Without Trial: Japanese Americans in World War II*. New York: Hill and Wang, 1993.

Davis, David Brion. *Inhuman Bondage: The Rise and Fall of Slavery in the New World*. New York: Oxford University Press, 2006.

Doctors Without Borders. "Doctors Without Borders." <http://www.doctorswithoutborders.org/> (accessed on June 24, 2006).

Dolgopol, Ustinia. *Comfort Women: An Unfinished Ordeal*. International Commission of Jurists, 1994.

Donald Bloxham. *The Great Game of Genocide: Imperialism, Nationalism, and the Destruction of the Ottoman Armenians*. New York: Oxford University Press, 2005.

Donald Woods. *Biko*. New York: Henry Holt, 1987.

Donnelly, Jack. *Universal Human Rights in Theory and Practice*. Ithaca, New York: Cornell University Press, 2002.

Douglass, Frederick. *Narrative of the Life of Frederick Douglass, An American Slave*. 1845.

Dray, Philip. *At the Hands of Persons Unknown: The Lynching of Black America*. New York: Random House, 2002.

Drew D. Hansen. *The Dream: Martin Luther King, Jr. and the Speech that Inspired a Nation*. New York: Ecco, 2003.

Dubofsky, Melvin. *Hard Work: The Making of Labor History*. Champaign, Illinois: University of Illinois Press, 2000.

Dubois, Ellen Carol. *Feminism and Suffrage: The Emergence of an Independent Women's Movement in America, 1848–1869*. Ithaca, New York: Cornell University Press, 1999.

Dudziak, Mary L. *Cold War Civil Rights: Race and the Image of American Democracy*. Princeton, N.J.: Princeton University Press, 2002.

Dwork, Deborah, ed. *Voices & Views: A History of the Holocaust*. The Jewish Foundation for the Righteous, 2002.

Eades, Lindsey Michie. *The End of Apartheid in South Africa*. Westport, Conn.: Greenwood Press, 1999.

Economic Reconstruction and Development in South East Europe. "The Helsinki Final Act." <http://www.seerecon.org/region/sp/helsinki.htm> (accessed on April 30, 2006).

Edwards, Susan S. M. *Women on Trial: A Study of the Female Suspect, Defendant and Offender in the Criminal Law and Criminal Justice System*. Dover, NH: Manchester University Press, 1984.

El-Saadawi, Nawal. *The Hidden Face of Eve: Women in the Arab World*. London: Zed Books, 1980.

Embassy of India (Washington, D.C.). "Frequently Asked Questions on Jammu and Kashmir." <http://www.indianembassy.org/policy/Kashmir/FAQ-Kashmir.htm> (accessed on April 29, 2006).

Equal Opportunity Commission. "The Gender Equality Duty." <http://www.eoc.org.uk/Default.aspx?page=15016> (accessed on May 12, 2006).

Esbenshade, Jill Louise. *Monitoring Sweatshops: Workers, Consumers, and the Global Apparel Industry*. Philadelphia: Temple University Press, 2004.

Eugenics Archive. "The Image Archive on the American Eugenics Movement." <http://www.eugenicsarchive.org/eugenics/> (accessed on April 29, 2006).

Eurasianet.org. "The 25th Anniversary of the Helsinki Final Act: Evaluating Human Rights." July 31, 2000. <http://www.eurasianet.org/departments/rights/articles/eav073100.shtml> (accessed on April 30, 2006).

Evans, Malcolm D. *The Religious Liberty and International Law in Europe*. New York: Cambridge University Press, 1997.

Fairclough, Adam. *To Redeem the Soul of America: The Southern Christian Leadership Conference and Martin Luther King, Jr*. Athens, Ga.: University of Georgia Press, 1987.

Fang Lizhi. *Bringing Down the Great Wall: Writings on Science, Culture, and Democracy in China.* New York; Norton, 1992.

Fantasia, Rick and Kim Voss. *Hard Work: Remaking the American Labor Movement.* University of California Press, 2004.

Federal Government Agencies Directory. "Louisiana State University." <http://www.lib.lsu.edu/gov/fedgov.html> (accessed on June 24, 2006).

Federation of American Scientists. "Federation of American Scientists, ProMED Initiative." <http://www.fas.org/promed> (accessed on June 24, 2006).

FedStats. "FedStats." <http://www.fedstats.gov> (accessed on June 24, 2006).

Fehrenbacher, Don E. *The Dred Scott Case: Its Significance in American Law and Politics.* Oxford University Press, 2001.

Felder, Deborah G. *A Century of Women: The Most Influential Events in Twentieth-Century Women's History.* Kensington Publishing Corp., 1999.

Feldman, David. *Civil Liberties and Human Rights in England and Wales.* New York: Oxford University Press, 1993.

Figes, Orlando. *A People's Tragedy: The Russian Revolution 1891–1924.* London: Jonathan Cape, 1996.

Findlaw. "Findlaw/West." <http://public.findlaw.com/library/> (accessed on June 24, 2006).

Fireside, Harvey. *Separate and Unequal: Homer Plessy and the Supreme Court Decision that Legalized Racism.* New York: Carroll & Graf, 2004.

Fong, Vanessa. *Only Hope: Coming of Age Under China's One-Child Policy.* Palo Alto: Stanford University Press, 2004.

Foote, Shelby. *The Civil War: A Narrative.* New York: Vintage Books USA, 1986.

Ford, Gerald R. *Education for all Handicapped Children Act, Signing Statement.* December 2, 1975. Ford Library and Museum, Ann Arbor, Michigan.

Francis, Leslie, and Anita Silvers, eds. *Americans with Disabilities: Exploring Implications of the Law for Institutions and Individuals.* New York: Routledge, 2000.

Friedan, Betty. *The Feminine Mystique.* New York: W.W. Norton, 1963.

GAO (Government Account Office). "Site Map." <http://www.gao.gov/sitemap.html> (accessed on June 24, 2006).

Gilbert, Martin. *Israel: A History.* London: Doubleday, 1998.

Grandin, Greg. *The Blood of Guatemala: A History of Race and Nation.* Durham, N.C.: Duke University Press, 2000.

Guggenheim, Martin. *What's Wrong With Children's Rights.* Cambridge, Mass.: Harvard University Press, 2005.

Gyory, Andrew. *Closing the Gate: Race, Politics, and the Chinese Exclusion Act.* Chapel Hill, N.C.: University of North Carolina Press, 1998.

Hale, Grace Elizabeth. *Making Whiteness: The Culture of Segregation in the South, 1890–1940.* New York: Vintage Books, 1998.

Hayes, Curtis W., Robert Bahruth, and Carolyn Kessler. *Literacy con Carino: A Story of Migrant Children's Success.* Portsmouth, NH: Heinemann, 1998.

Headland, Ronald. *So Others Will Remember: Holocaust History and Survivor Testimony.* Véhicule Press, 1999.

Health Resources and Services Administration (HRSA). "Health Resources and Services Administration (HRSA)." <http://www.hrsa.gov> (accessed on June 24, 2006).

Heinzen, Karl. *The Rights of Women and the Sexual Relations.* Chicago: Charles H. Kerr & Co., 1898.

Hicks, George L. *The Comfort Women: Japan's Brutal Regime of Enforced Prostitution in the Second World War.* London: W. W. Norton, 1997.

Hiltebeitel, Alf. *Rethinking India's Oral and Classical Epics: Draupadi among Rajputs, Muslims, and Dalits.* Chicago: University Of Chicago Press, May 1, 1999.

Hindman, Hugh D. *Child Labor: An American History.* M.E. Sharpe, 2002.

Hodges, Donald Clark. *The Literate Communist: 150 Years of the Communist Manifesto.* New York: P. Lang, 1999.

Hood, Roger. *The Death Penalty: A World-Wide Perspective.* Oxford, United Kingdom: Clarendon Press, 2002.

Horton, James Oliver, and Lois E. Horton. *Slavery and the Making of America.* Oxford, New York: Oxford University Press, 2004.

Horton, James, and Lois E. Horton. *Slavery and the Making of America.* New York: Oxford University Press, 2004.

Hosmer, William. *Slavery and the Church.* New York: W. J. Moses, 1853.

Howland, Courtney W. *Religious Fundamentalism and the Rights of Women.* New York: St. Martin's Press, 1999.

Hull, N. E. H., and Peter Charles Hoffer. *Roe V. Wade: The Abortion Rights Controversy in American History.* Lawrence: University Press of Kansas, 2001.

Human Rights Commission of Pakistan. "The State of Human Rights in 2005." <http://www.hrcp-web.org/ar_home_05.cfm> (accessed on May 6, 2006).

Human Rights in China. "Background to the 1989 Democracy Movement." May 1, 2006. <http://www,hrichina.org/fr/downloadables/pdf/downloadable-resources/June-Fourth.pdf?revision-id=14517> (accessed on May 29, 2006).

Human Rights Watch. *Human Rights in Iraq.* New Haven, Conn.: Yale University Press, 1990.

Human Rights Watch. "Human Rights Watch." <http://www.hrw.org/> (accessed on June 24, 2006).

Human Rights Watch. "Child Labor." <http://www.hrw.org/children/labor.htm> (accessed on April 29, 2006).

Human Rights Watch. "China and Tibet." <http://hrw.org/> (accessed on May 5, 2006).

Human Rights Watch. "Israel and the Palestinian Authority Reports." 2006. <http://www.hrw.org/campaigns/israel/> (accessed on April 27, 2006).

Human Rights Watch. "The Small Hands of Slavery." September 1996. <http://www.hrw.org/reports/1996/India3.htm> (accessed on April 27, 2006).

Hung, Wu. *Remaking Beijing: Tiananmen Square and the Creation of a Political Space*. Chicago: University of Chicago Press, 2005.

Independent International Commission on Kosovo. *Kosovo Report: Conflict * International Response * Lessons Learned*. Oxford and New York: Oxford University Press, 2001.

International Committee of the Red Cross. "What Is International Humanitarian Law?" July 31, 2004. <http://www.icrc.org/web/eng/siteeng0.nsf/html/humanitarian-law-factsheet> (accessed on April 29, 2006).

International Labor Organization. "General Activities: Social Protection." May 5, 2005. <http://www.ilo.org/public/english/dialogue/actrav/genact/socprot/migrant/> (accessed on April 28, 2006).

Internet Modern History Sourcebook. "Fordham University." <http://www.fordham.edu/halsall/mod/modsbook.html> (accessed on June 24, 2006).

Irons, Peter. *Justice at War: The Story of the Japanese American Internment Cases*. New York: Oxford University Press, 1983.

Ishay, Micheline. *The History of Human Rights: From Ancient Times to the Globalization Era*. University of California Press, 2004.

Jeffrey, Julie Roy. *The Great Silent Army of Abolitionism: Ordinary Women in the Antislavery Movement*. Chapel Hill, N.C.: University of North Carolina Press 1998.

Jinks, Derek. *The Rules of War: The Geneva Convention in the Age of Terror*. New York: Oxford University Press, 2005.

Johnson, Robert. *Death Work: A Study of the Modern Execution Process*. Pacific Grove, California: Brooks Cole Publishing Company, 1990.

Judah, Tim. *Kosovo: War and Revenge*. New Haven, CT: Yale University Press, 2002.

Karen, Greenberg J., ed. *The Torture Debate in America*. New York: Cambridge University Press, 2006.

King, Jr. Martin Luther. *"I Have a Dream." Speech delivered in Washington, D.C. Available from: Avalon Project of Yale Law School*. <http://www.yale.edu/lawweb/avalon/treatise/king/mlk01.htm> (accessed on April 30, 2006).

Klausen, Jytte. *The Islamic Challenge: Politics and Religion in Western Europe*. New York: Oxford University Press, USA, 2005.

Klotz, Audie. *Norms in International Relations: The Struggle Against Apartheid*. Ithaca, N.Y.: Cornell University Press, 1995.

Kolchin, Peter. *American Slavery: 1619–1877*. New York: Hill & Wang, 2003.

Kornbluh, Peter. *The Pinochet File: A Declassified Dossier on Atrocity and Accountability*. New York: New Press, 2004.

Kuperman, Allan J. *The Limits of Humanitarian Intervention: Genocide in Rwanda*. Washington; Brookings Institute Press, 2001.

Labor and Labor Movements. "American Sociological Association." <http://www.bgsu.edu/departments/soc/prof/mason/ASA/> (accessed on June 24, 2006).

Lakshmidhar Mishra. *Child Labor in India*. New York: Oxford University Press, 2000.

Lall, Arthur. *The UN and the Middle East Crisis, 1967*. New York: Columbia University Press, 1968.

Lane, Harlan, and Francois Grosjean, eds. *Recent Perspectives on American Sign Language*. Hillsdale, N.J.: Lawrence Erlbaum Associates, 1980.

Lee, Erika. *At America's Gates: Chinese Immigration During the Exclusion Era, 1882–1943*. Chapel Hill, N.C.: University of North Carolina Press, 2003.

Legal Information Institute, Cornell University. "Code of Federal Regulations." <http://www4.law.cornell.edu/cfr/> (accessed on June 24, 2006).

Lerner, Gerda. *The Grimke Sisters from South Carolina: Pioneers for Women's Rights and Abolition*. Chapel Hill, N.C.: University of North Carolina Press, 2004.

Levy, Leonard. *Origins of the Bill of the Rights*. Yale Contemporary Law Series. New Haven, CT: Yale University Press, 2001.

Lewis, David L. *W.E.B. Du Bois—Biography of a Race, 1868–1919*. New York: Henry Holt, 1993.

Liang, Zhen, et al., eds. *The Tiananmen Papers*. New York: PublicAffairs, 2001.

Library of Congress. "Library of Congress Online Catalog." <http://catalog.loc.gov/cgi-bin/Pwebrecon.cgi?DB=local&PAGE=First> (accessed on June 24, 2006).

Link, William A. *Roots of Secession: Slavery and Politics in Antebellum Virginia (Civil War America)*. Chapel Hill, NC: University of North Carolina Press, 2005.

Little, Peter D. *Somalia: Economy Without State*. Indianapolis: Indiana University Press, 2003.

Lyndon Baines Johnson Library and Museum. "Special Message to Congress: The American Promise." <http://www.lbjlib.utexas.edu/johnson/archives.hom/speeches.hom/650315.asp> (accessed on April 9, 2006).

Mahatma Gandhi. *Speeches and Writings of Mahatma Gandhi*. Madras: G. A. Natesan & Co., 1933.

Making of America. "Cornell University." <http://cdl.library.cornell.edu/moa/> (accessed on June 24, 2006).

Maly, Michael T. *Beyond Segregation: Multiracial and Multiethnic Neighborhoods in the United States*. Philadelphia: Temple University Press, 2005.

Mandela, Nelson R. *Nelson Mandela: The Struggle Is My Life*. London: International Defense and Aid Fund for South Africa, 1978.

Marschark, Mark, and Patricia Elizabeth Spencer, eds. *Oxford Handbook of Deaf Studies, Language, and Education*. New York: Oxford University Press, 2003.

Martinez, Ruben. *Crossing Over: A Mexican Family on the Migrant Trail*. New York: Metropolitan Books, 2001.

Marx, Karl, and Friedrich Engels. *The Communist Manifesto*. 1848.

Mayer, Henry. *All on Fire: William Lloyd Garrison and the Abolition of Slavery*. New York: St. Martin's Griffin, 2000.

Medical News Today. "Beliefs May Hinder HIV Prevention Among Africn-Americans." January 26, 2005. <http://www.medicalnewstoday.com/medicalnews.php?newsid=19276> (accessed on April 26, 2006).

Meier, Richard P., Kearsey Cormier, and David Quinto-Pozos, eds. *Modality and Structure in Signed and Spoken Languages*. Cambridge, U.K.: Cambridge University Press, 2002.

Mcrtus, Julie. *United Nations and Human Rights A Guide for a New Era*. New York: Routledge, 2005.

Miers, Susan. *Slavery in the Twentieth Century: The Evolution of a Global Problem*. Walnut Creek, California; Altamira Press, 2003.

Miers, Suzanne. *Britain and the Ending of the Slave Trade*. London: Longman, 1975.

Miles, James. *The Legacy of Tiananmen*. Ann Arbor, Mich.: University of Michigan Press, 1996.

Miller, H. Lynn. *The Limits of Authority: Science and Dissent in Post-Mao China*. Seattle: University of Washington Press, 1996.

Millet, Kate. *Sexual Politics*. Champlaign, IL: University of Illinois Press, 2000.

Nacos, Brigitte L. *Terrorism and Counterterrorism: Understanding Threats and Responses in the Post-9/11 World*. New York: Pearson/Longman, 2006.

National Geographic News. "Change Slow for Afghan Women." March 12, 2002. <http://news.nationalgeographic.com/news/2002/03/0312_020312_afghanwomen.html> (accessed on April 20, 2006).

National Labor Committee. "Sean John's Sweatshops." October 2003. <http://www.nlcnet.org/campaigns/setisa/> (accessed on April 18, 2006).

National Security Archive Electronic Briefing Book No.16. "Tiananmen Square, 1989." <http://www.gwu.edu/~nsarchiv/NSAEBB/NSAEBB16/> (accessed on April 30, 2006).

National Women's Political Caucus. <http://www.nwpc.org> (accessed on April 17, 2006).

NCAA. "1999–2000 Gender-Equity Report." <http://www.ncaa.org/library/research/gender_equity_study/1999-00/1999-00_gender_equity_report.pdf> (accessed on May 14, 2006).

Newman, Edward and Joanna van Selm, eds. *Refugees and Forced Displacement: International Security, Human Vulnerability, and the State*. New York: United Nations University Press, 2003.

Ngai, Mae M. *Impossible Subjects: Illegal Aliens and the Making of Modern America*. Princeton, N.J.: Princeton University Press, 2005.

NICHD — National Institute of Child Health and Human Development. "NICHD — National Institute of Child Health and Human Development." <http://www.nichd.nih.gov> (accessed on June 24, 2006).

Nicholson, Michael. *Mahatma Gandhi: Leader of Indian Independence*. Blackbirch Press, November 2003.

Nobelprize.org. "Nelson Mandela and the Rainbow of Culture." <http://nobelprize.org/peace/articles/mandela/index.html> (accessed on April 27, 2006).

NobelPrize.org. "Nelson Mandela—Nobel Acceptance and Lecture." <http://nobelprize.org/peace/laureates/1993/mandela-lecture.html> (accessed on May 6, 2006).

Nobelprize.org. "The Nobel Peace Prize 1964." <http://nobelprize.org/peace/laureates/1964/press.html> (accessed on April 27, 2006).

O'Leary, Cecilia Elizabeth. *To Die For: The Paradox of American Patriotism*. Princeton, N.J.: Princeton University Press, 1999.

Oates, Stephen. *Let the Trumpet Sound: The Life of Martin Luther King, Jr*. New York: New American Library, 1985.

Ofer, Dalia and Lenore J. Weitzman, eds. *Women in the Holocaust*. Yale University Press, 1998.

Office of Global Health Affairs. "Office of Global Health Affairs." <http://www.globalhealth.gov> (accessed on June 24, 2006).

Office of the High Commissioner for Human Rights, United Nations. "Convention against Torture and Other Cruel, Inhuman or Degrading Treatment or Punishment." 1984. <http://www.unhchr.ch/html/menu3/b/h_cat39.htm> (accessed on April 20, 2006).

Oxfam International. *Gender, Trafficking, and Slavery*. Oxford: Oxfam, 2002.

Oxford Blueprint. "Stalin's Gulags Still Used as Prisons." January 31, 2002. <http://www.ox.ac.uk/blueprint/2001-02/3101/05.shtml> (accessed on May 31, 2006).

Patterson, James T. Brown v. Board of Education: *A Civil Rights Milestone and Its Troubled Legacy*. New York: Oxford University Press, 2001.

Pearse, Richard L., Jr. *In Re: The Guardianship of Theresa Schiavo, An Incapacitated Person. Report of Guardian Ad Litem. Case No. 90-2908GD-003.* The Circuit Court for Pinellas County, Florida: Probate Division, December 29, 1998.

Perry, Elizabeth J., and Mark Selden. *Chinese Society: Change, Conflict, and Resistance (Asia's Transformations).* New York; Routledge, 2000.

Perry, Greg M. *Disabling America: The Unintended Consequences of Government Protection of the Handicapped.* Nashville, Tenn.: WND Books, 2003.

Physicians for Human Rights. *No Mercy in Mogadishu: The Human Cost of the Conflict and the Struggle for Relief.* Boston: Physicians for Human Rights; New York: Africa Watch, 1992.

Physicians for Human Rights. "1999 Report: The Taliban's War on Women—A Health and Human Rights Crisis in Afghanistan." <http://www.phrusa.org/research/health_effects/exec.html> (accessed on April 20, 2006).

Pipes, Richard. *Russia under the Old Regime.* London: Penguin, 1995.

Pollock, Frederick. *The League of Nations.* Clark, New Jersey; Lawbook Exchange, 2003.

Pomeroy, William J. *Apartheid, Imperialism, and African Freedom.* New York: International Publishers, 1986.

Price, Robert M. *The Apartheid State in Crisis. Political Transformation in South Africa: 1975–1990.* New York: Oxford University Press, 1991.

Privacy International. "Identity Cards: Frequently Asked Questions." August 24, 1996. <http://www.privacy.org/pi/activities/idcard/idcard_faq.html> (accessed on May 1, 2006).

Rajeshekar, V.T. and Y. N. Kly. *Dalit: The Black Untouchables of India.* Clarity Press, June 1997.

Ramcharan, B. G. *Human Rights: Thirty Years After the Universal Declaration.* The Hague: Martinus Nijhoff, 1979.

ReliefWeb. "Darfur: Humanitarian Emergency Fact Sheet # 3 (FY 2004)." April 30, 2004. <http://www.reliefweb.int/rw/rwb.nsf/AllDocsByUNID/383daba36e89935185256e86006c1f21> (accessed on May 12, 2006).

Reverby, Susan M. *Tuskegee's Truths: Rethinking the Tuskegee Syphilis Study.* University of North Carolina Press, 2000.

Richani, Nazih. *Systems of Violence: The Political Economy of War and Peace in Colombia.* Albany, N.Y.: The State University of New York Press, 2002.

Richardson, J. *Common, Delinquent, and Special: The institutional Shape of Special Education (Studies in the History of Education).* Routledge Falmer, 1999.

Ripley, C. Peter, Ed. *The Black Abolitionist Papers, Volume One: The British Isles, 1830–1865.* Chapel Hill, North Carolina: The University of North Carolina Press, 1985.

Roberts-Davis, Tanya. *We Need to Go to School: Voices from the Rugmark Children.* Toronto: Groundwood Books, 2003.

Robin Malan, ed. *The Essential Steve Biko.* Cape Town: David Philip, 1997.

Robinson, Nehemiah. *The Universal Declaration of Human Rights: Its Origin, Significance, Application, and Interpretation.* New York: Institute of Jewish Affairs, 1958.

Rosen, Ellen D. *A Wobblie Life: IWW Organizer E.F. Doree.* Wayne State University Press, 2004.

Rosen, Ellen Doree. *A Wobblie Life: IWW Organizer E.F. Doree.* Detroit: Wayne State University Press, 2004.

Rosenberg, Jonathan, and Zachary Karabell. *Kennedy, Johnson, and the Quest for Justice: The Civil Rights Tapes.* New York: W.W. Norton & Company, 2003.

Ross, Robert J. S. *Slaves to Fashion: Poverty and Abuse in the New Sweatshops.* Ann Arbor: University of Michigan Press, 2004.

Rothschild, Joseph. and Nancy M. Wingfield. *Return to Diversity: A Political History of East Central Europe Since World War II.* Oxford University Press, 2000.

Scheffler, Judith A. (ed). *Wall Tappings.* New York.: Feminist Press, 2002.

Schulz, William F. *Tainted Legacy: 9/11 and the Ruin of Human Rights.* New York: Thunder's Mouth Press/Nation Books, 2003.

Schulze, Kirsten E. *The Arab Israeli Conflict.* Harlow. Longman, 1999.

Shakya, Tsering. *The Dragon in the Land of Snows: A History of Modern Tibet Since 1947.* New York: Penguin, 2000.

Shelley, Mary. *Frankenstein; or, the Modern Prometheus.* London: Lackington, Allen & Co., 1818.

Shlaim, Avi. *The Iron Wall: Israel and the Arab World.* London: Penguin, 2001.

Simon Wiesenthal Center. "Simon Wiesenthal Center." <http://www.wiesenthal.com> (accessed on June 24, 2006).

Skaine, Rosemarie. *The Women of Afghanistan Under the Taliban.* Jefferson, N.C.: McFarland & Company, 2001.

Skowronek, Stephen. *Building A New American State: The Expansion of National Administrative Capacities, 1877–1920.* Cambridge, U.K. and New York: Cambridge University Press, 1984.

Social Science Information Gateway. "SOSIG." <http://www.sosig.ac.uk/> (accessed on June 24, 2006).

Social Sciences Virtual Library. "Digilogical." <http://www.dialogical.net/socialsciences/index.html> (accessed on June 24, 2006).

SocioWeb. "Blairworks." <http://www.socioweb.com/> (accessed on June 24, 2006).

Solzhenitsyn, Alexander. *The Gulag Archipelago*. New York: Harper & Row, 1978.

Southern Poverty Law Center. "Southern Poverty Law Center." <http://www.splcenter.org/> (accessed on June 24, 2006).

Steiner, Henry and Philip Alston. *International Human Rights in Context: Law, Politics, Morals*. Oxford and New York: Oxford University Press, 2000.

Stephen Oates. *Let the Trumpet Sound: The Life of Martin Luther King, Jr*. New York: New American Library, 1985.

Stetson, Dorothy M. *Women's Rights in the U.S.A: Policy Debates and Gender Roles*. New York: Routledge, 2004.

Stoll, David. *Rigoberta Menchú and the Story of All Poor Guatemalans*. New York: HarperCollins, 2000.

Subcommittee on the Middle East and Central Asia of the Committee on International Relations, U.S. House of Representatives. *Human Rights Violations under Saddam Hussein: Victims Speak out*. Washington, D.C.: U.S. Government Printing Office, 2004.

Suettinger, Roberts. *Beyond Tiananmen: The Politics of U.S.-China Relations, 1989–2000*. Washington, D.C.: Brookings Institutuion Press, 2003.

Sullivan, Winnifred Fallers. *The Impossibility of Religious Freedom*. Princeton, N.J.: Princeton University Press, 2005.

Svensson, Marina. *Debating Human Rights in China: A Conceptual and Political History*. Lanham, Md.: Rowman & Littlefield, 2002.

Tamer Akcam. *A Shameful Act: The Armenian Genocide and the Question of Turkish Responsibility*. New York: Metropolitan Books, 2006.

Taylor Branch. *Parting the Waters: America in the King Years, 1954–63*. New York: Simon & Schuster, 1988.

Tec, Nechama. *Resilience and Courage: Women, Men, and the Holocaust*. Yale University Press, 2003.

Temperley, Howard. *British Antislavery, 1833–1870*. London: Longman, 1972.

Terry, Fiona. *Condemned to Repeat?: The Paradox of Humanitarian Action*. Ithaca, N.Y.: Cornell University Press, 2002.

The Human Rights and Equal Opportunity Commission. <http://www.hreoc.gov.au/info_sheet.html> (accessed on May 5, 2006).

The Knesset. "Israel's Basic Laws: An Introduction." 2003. <http://www.knesset.gov.il/description/eng/eng_mimshal_yesod.htm> (accessed on April 27, 2006).

The Organization for Security and Co-operation in Europe. "CSCE/OSCE Timeline." <http://www.osce.org/item/15801.html> (accessed on April 30, 2006).

The United States House of Representatives. "The United States House of Representatives." <http://www.house.gov/> (accessed on June 24, 2006).

The United States Senate. "The United States Senate." <http://www.senate.gov/> (accessed on June 24, 2006).

The White House. "White House Office of Communications." <http://www.whitehouse.gov/news/> (accessed on June 24, 2006).

Thomas. "Library of Congress." <http://thomas.loc.gov/> (accessed on June 24, 2006).

Tolley Jr., Howard. *The U.N. Commission on Human Rights*. Boulder, Colo.: Westview Press, 1987.

Totten, Samuel, William S. Parsons, and Israel W. Charny, eds. *A Century of Genocide: Critical Essays and Eyewitness Accounts*. Second edition. New York: Routledge, 2004.

Truman, Harry. Executive Order 9981. July 26, 1948. Available from the Truman Library <http://www.trumanlibrary.org/photos/9981a.jpg> (accessed on April 30, 2006).

Tsesis, Alexander. *The Thirteenth Amendment and American Freedom: A Legal History*. New York: New York University Press, 2004.

Tuttle, William M., Jr. *Race Riot: Chicago in the Red Summer of 1919*. Urbana, Ill.: University of Illinois Press, 1996.

U.S. Committee for Refugees and Immigrants. "World Refugee Survey 2004 Country Report." <http://www.refugees.org/countryreports/> (accessed on April 28, 2006).

U.S. Department of Education. "Special Education & Rehabilitative Services." <http://www.ed.gov/policy/speced/guid/idea/idea2004.html> (accessed on April 14, 2006).

U.S. Department of State. *Documenting Atrocities in Darfur*. U.S. Department of State Publication Number 11182. Washington, D.C.: U.S. Government Printing Office, 2004.

U.S. Department of State. "India: Country Reports on Human Rights Practices, 2004." February 28, 2005. <http://www.state.gov/g/drl/rls/hrrpt/2004/41740.htm> (accessed on April 29, 2006).

U.S. Department of State. "International Religious Freedom." <http://www.state.gov/g/drl/irf/> (accessed on May 3, 2006).

U.S. Department of State. "Report on the Taliban's War against Women." November 17, 2001. <http://www.state.gov/g/drl/rls/c4804.htm> (accessed on April 20, 2006).

U.S. Department of State. "Report on the Taliban's War Against Women." November 17, 2001. <http://www.state.gov/g/drl/rls/c4804.htm> (accessed on April 20, 2006).

U.S. Department of State. "War Crime Issues." <http://www.state.gov/s/wci> (accessed on May 3, 2006).

U.S. *Library of Congress*. "Library of Congress Country Studies: Iran—Savak." December 1987 <http://lcweb2.loc.gov/cgi-bin/query/r?frd/cstdy:@field (DOCID+ir0187)> (accessed on April 25, 2006).

UNAIDS. "UNAIDS Research." <http://www.unaids.org/en/Issues/Research/default.asp> (accessed on June 24, 2006).

UNICEF. "Child Protection: The Picture in India." <http://www.unicef.org/india/child_protection_152.htm> (accessed on April 27, 2006).

UNICEF. "Child Trafficking Research Hub." <http://www.childtrafficking.org> (accessed on April 11, 2006).

UNICEF. "Factsheet: Children Deprived of Their Liberty and Juvenile Justice." <http://www.unicef.org/protection/justice.pdf> (accessed on May 5, 2006).

United Nations General Assembly. *International Convention on the Suppression and Punishment of the Crime of Apartheid*. General Assembly Resolution 3068 (XXVIII). New York: United Nations, November 30, 1973.

United Nations General Assembly. *Protocol to Prevent, Suppress and Punish Trafficking in Persons, Especially Women and Children, Supplementing the United Nations Convention Against Transnational Organized Crime*. 2000.

United Nations General Assembly. *United Nations Convention on the Rights of the Child*. United Nations, November 20, 1989.

United Nations General Assembly. Resolution 45/113. *United Nations Rules for the Protection of Juveniles Deprived of their Liberty*. December 14, 1990.

United Nations High Commissioner for Human Rights. "Contemporary Forms of Slavery." January 1, 2006. <http://193.194.138.190/html/menu6/2/fs14.htm> (accessed on May 29, 2006).

United Nations High Commissioner for Refugees. "The State of the World's Refugees 2006." 2006. <http://www.unhcr.org/cgi-bin/texis/vtx/> (accessed on May 5, 2006).

United Nations Office for the Coordination of Humanitarian Affairs. "IRIN Web Special on Civilian Protection in Armed Conflict." 2003. <http://www.irinnews.org/webspecials/civilprotect/sec1cp1.asp> (accessed on May 6, 2006).

United Nations Office of the High Commissioner for Human Rights. "United Nations." <http://www.ohchr.org/english/> (accessed on June 24, 2006).

United Nations Office on Drugs and Crime. "Trafficking in Human Beings." <http://www.unodc.org/unodc/en/trafficking_human_beings.html> (accessed on April 11, 2006).

United Nations-Water. "International Decade for Action: Water for Life, 2005–2015." <http://www.un.org/water forlifedecade/index.html gt; (accessed on April 12, 2006).

United Nations. "Convention on the Prevention and Punishment of the Crime of Genocide." August 16, 1994. Last edited on January 27, 1997. <http://www.hrweb.org/legal/genocide.html> (accessed on April 28, 2006).

United Nations. "Human Rights." <http://www.un.org/rights/> (accessed on May 7, 2006).

United Nations. "Human Rights: Historical Images of Apartheid in South Africa." <http://www.un.org/av/photo/subjects/apartheid.htm> (accessed on May 1, 2006).

United Nations. "International Criminal Tribunal for Rwanda." May, 2006. <http://69.94.11.53/default.htm> (accessed on May 29, 2006).

United Nations. "Key Conference Outcomes on Human Rights" <http://www.un.org/esa/devagenda/humanrights.html> (accessed on April 22, 2006).

United Nations. "United Nations Interim Mission in Kosovo." May 5, 2006. <http://www.unmikonline.org/> (accessed on May 5, 2006).

United Nations. "Universal Declaration of Human Rights." December 10, 1948. <http://www.un.org/Overview/rights.html> (accessed on May 5, 2006).

United States Census Bureau. "United States Census Bureau." <http://www.census.gov> (accessed on June 24, 2006).

United States Congress. *China: Human Rights Violations and Coercion in One-Child Policy Enforcement: Hearing Before the Committee on International Relations*. Washington, D.C.: U.S. Government Printing Office, 2005.

United States Department of Labor. "Women's Bureau." <http://www.dol.gov/wb/> (accessed on May 8, 2006).

United States Senate. "Legislation, Laws and Acts: Chapter 1: Bills." <http://www.senate.gov/pagelayout/legislative/d_three_sections_with_teasers/bills.htm> (accessed on April 28, 2006).

University of Virginia Health System. "Final Report of The Tuskegee Syphilis Study Legacy." <http://www.health system.virginia.edu/internet/library/historical/medical_history/bad_blood/report.cfm> (accessed on April 26, 2006).

Van Kley, Dale, ed. *The French Idea of Freedom: The Old Regime and the Declaration of Rights of 1789*. Stanford: Stanford University Press, 1994.

Wailoo, Keith. *Drawing Blood: Technology and Disease Identity in Twentieth-Century America*. The Johns Hopkins University Press, 1999.

Wehrle, Edmund F. *Between a River and a Mountain: The AFL-CIO and the Vietnam War*. Ann Arbor: University of Michigan Press, 2005.

Wellcome Library for the History and Understanding of Medicine. "The Guide to History of Medicine Resources on the Internet." <http://medhist.ac.uk/> (accessed on June 24, 2006).

Wienk, Ronald E., Clifford E. Reid, and John C. Simonson. *Measuring Racial Discrimination in American Housing Markets: The Housing Market Practices Survey.* Washington, D.C.: U.S. Department of Housing and Urban Development, 1979.

Williams, Donnie. *The Thunder of Angels: The Montgomery Bus Boycott and the People Who Broke the Back of Jim Crow.* Chicago: Lawrence Hill Books, 2006.

Wilson, Richard A. *The Politics of Truth and Reconciliation in South Africa: Legitimizing the Post-Apartheid State.* New York: Cambridge University Press, 2001.

Winzer, Margaret. *The History of Special Education.* Gallaudet University Press, 1993.

Women and Equality Unit. "What Has the Government Achieved for Women?" <http://www.womenandequality unit.gov.uk/about/government_women.htm> (accessed on May 12, 2006).

World Bank. *India: Achievements and Challenges in Reducing Poverty.* Geneva: World Bank Publications, June 1997.

World Health Organization. "WHO Bulletin." <http://www.who.int/bulletin/en> (accessed on June 24, 2006).

Wormser, Richard. *The Rise and Fall of Jim Crow.* New York: St. Martin's Press, 2003.

Wushanley, Wang. *Playing Nice and Losing: The Struggle for Control of Women's Intercollegiate Athletics, 1960–2000.* Syracuse, N.Y.: Syracuse University Press, 2004.

Zinn, Howard, Dana Frank, and Robin D. G. Kelley. *Three Strikes: Miners, Musicians, Salesgirls, and the Fighting Spirit of Labor's Last Century.* Boston: Beacon Press, 2001.

Index

Boldface indicates a primary source.
Italics indicates an illustration on the page.